SNA & TCP/IP Enterprise Networking

SNA & TCP/IP
Enterprise Networking

EDITORS
DANIEL LYNCH
JAMES P. GRAY
EDWARD RABINOVITCH

MANNING

Greenwich
(74° w. long.)

For electronic browsing and ordering of this book, see
http://www.browsebooks.com

The publisher offers discounts on this book when ordered in quantity. For more
information, please contact:

    Special Sales Department
    Manning Publications Co.
    3 Lewis Street
    Greenwich, CT 06830

    Fax: (203) 661-9018
    email: orders@manning.com

⊗ Recognizing the importance of preserving what has been written, it is Manning's
policy to have the books they publish printed on acid-free paper, and we exert our
best efforts to that end.

Library of Congress Cataloging-in-Publication Data
SNA and TCP/IP enterprise networking / [edited by] Daniel Lynch,
      James P. Gray, Edward Rabinovitch
       p.   cm.
     Includes bibliographical references and index.
     ISBN 0-13-127168-7
     1. TCP/IP (Computer network protocol).   2. SNA (Computer
network architecture).   I. Lynch, Daniel C.   II. Gray, James P.
III. Rabinovitch, Edward.
    TK5105.585.S596   1997
    004.6'5—dc21   97-25853
                                        CIP

/▌▌ Manning Publications Co.
     3 Lewis Street
     Greenwich, CT 06830

     Copyeditor: Elizabeth Martin
     Typesetter: Heather W. Lyon
     Cover designer: Leslie Haimes

Printed in the United States of America
1 2 3 4 5 6 7 8 9 10 – CR – 00 99 98 97

contents

Part II   SNA interoperability today

9   SNA across the data link 288

10   Transporting SNA across TCP/IP 308

PART I

Tutorials

chapter 1

SNA in the multinetworking era

Eddie Rabinovitch

The jury is still out on which network architecture will survive into the next millennium. One answer is definite: it's not going to be the full-blown *open systems interconnection* (OSI) model as some believed a few years ago.

Transmission control protocol/Internet protocol (TCP/IP) and *systems network architecture* (SNA) were designed from diametrically opposite standpoints: SNA once was a centrally managed architecture with predefined static routing aimed at high bandwidth utilization and optimal response time, whereas TCP/IP is a decentralized network with dynamic routing aimed at easier connectivity.

In many cases, *decision support systems* (DSS) client/server applications, which by nature are not transaction oriented, would not require synchronization points, two-phase commits, or concurrent updates of distributed databases. Since most of the

PART I

Tutorials

 *c h a p t e r   1*

SNA in the multinetworking era

EDDIE RABINOVITCH

The jury is still out on which network architecture will survive into the next millennium. One answer is definite: it's not going to be the full-blown *open systems interconnection* (OSI) model as some believed a few years ago.

Transmission control protocol/Internet protocol (TCP/IP) and *systems network architecture* (SNA) were designed from diametrically opposite standpoints: SNA once was a centrally managed architecture with predefined static routing aimed at high bandwidth utilization and optimal response time, whereas TCP/IP is a decentralized network with dynamic routing aimed at easier connectivity.

In many cases, *decision support systems* (DSS) client/server applications, which by nature are not transaction oriented, would not require synchronization points, two-phase commits, or concurrent updates of distributed databases. Since most of the

SNA/*advanced peer-to-peer networking* (APPN) advantages are not applicable in such environments, many have chosen TCP/IP as the underlying network protocol for better positioning of upcoming client/server applications. However, as for any good rule, there are exceptions: we can probably identify some cases where SNA/APPN (with *high performance routing* [HPR]) would make more sense than TCP/IP.

Only a few years ago many analysts and industry watchers predicted a premature death for SNA. However, based on the recent statistics, these estimates seem to be a bit over-exaggerated. Although the number of TCP/IP installations is growing at an exponential rate (almost any PC-based communications package includes the IP stack), not too many of the 50,000+ SNA installations migrated their mission-critical applications to IP. On the contrary, IDC's survey shows that the number of SNA gateway installations in the mid-1990s continues to grow at a 15–20 percent rate and 68 percent of networking budget is spent by SNA managers. According to Tom Nolle, president of CIMI Corp. (Voorhees, N.J.), in November 1996, 61 percent of all data packets carried SNA data.

So for the next several years, the network infrastructure for most organizations will include a combination of SNA/APPN and TCP/IP.

Since not too many companies have the luxury of turning off their existing network infrastructure and waiting for the emerging new single networking architecture—the real question for network managers today is: what is the most effective way of supporting new applications over the existing infrastructure. Fortunately for the users, there are a handful of good answers.

This book, written by industry luminaries and strategic consultants, takes the reader through these answers, presenting real-time solutions for the short-, medium- and long-term SNA integration.

The book guides the reader through the history and developments in the multiprotocol communications arena. It takes us through the history and developments in local and wide area networks, where, following a successful deployment of new applications on the *local area networks* (LANs), there was a need to connect them over the *wide area networks* (WANs). Shortly after, the developers and users had realized that, unfortunately, the bandwidth of the WAN is not sufficient for LAN-based protocols. Most of the LAN protocols (AppleTalk, *network basic input/output systems* [NetBIOS], *internetwork packet exchange* [IPX]) are too chatty and may cause so-called broadcast storms. The next natural step was to utilize the least expensive and most available protocol for WAN communications. However, there was no magic with TCP/IP either: the overhead was significantly higher than what it was with SNA. While this was not a real problem on LANs, it became a major headache on the WANs. An additional problem is with TCP/IP's use of congestion detection as opposed to congestion avoidance used in SNA;

TCP/IP networks are more susceptible to runaway overloads at high line utilization. Other problems are introduced by the ancient, but still the most popular, *IP routing information protocol* (RIP). As a distance-vector protocol, RIP is inflexible, it introduces additional overhead, and can create loops and black holes in complex IP networks.

The traditional (pre-APPN) SNA, commonly associated with 3270 applications, is connection-oriented protocol with routing only at the fourth—Transport—layer of the OSI model (equivalent to the transmission control layer in SNA). The downside is that this layer lacks dynamic rerouting capabilities, and high intelligence is required in all routing nodes. The APPN today is usually associated with application-to-application (peer-to-peer) networking. It employs a connection-oriented *intermediate session routing* (ISR) link-state protocol. Link-state routers (network nodes) are characterized by a topology database, which contains information about states of all network links included in each network node. Each node is responsible for computing the best routes to any other node in the network. APPN network nodes are responsible for maintaining the topology database, integrity of which is preserved by using sessions between adjacent Network Nodes. This is different from distance-vector based protocols (i.e., RIP), where such information is periodically broadcast (every thirty seconds with RIP), regardless of whether there were any changes. The more advanced TCP/IP link-state based routing protocols (such as *open shortest path first* [OSPF]) also broadcast their routing information when a link state is changed. However, they also periodically broadcast (every thirty minutes) this information regardless of changes in the link states.

When a session is established between two nodes in the APPN network it will live as long as the preferred route, selected during the session setup, is available. The major drawback of this method is that the preferred route, during a long-lived session setup, will not necessarily remain the optimal route for the life of the session. There is also no rerouting around failures (i.e. sessions have to be restarted even due to an intermediary node failure), which may potentially disrupt a client/server application.

To address the major concerns of SNA/APPN, IBM came out with HPR, a connectionless protocol, allowing dropping packets during network congestion and nondisruptive rerouting around failures. *Rapid transport protocol* (RTP) is used at the end-points of an APPN HPR session to guarantee delivery and resequencing of packets. An *adaptive rate based* (ARB) flow control mechanism is used at the end points of an HPR session to prevent network congestion. HPR can be mixed with ISR nodes within an SNA/APPN network. This handbook takes the reader through the insights of the most recent developments in SNA/APPN/HPR.

Since the number of TCP/IP-based client/server applications and LAN-based applications is constantly growing, in most cases one can find a mix of SNA and non-SNA (i.e., TCP/IP, IPX/*sequenced packet exchange* [SPX], NetBIOS, Virtual Network

System [VINES, a LAN architecture developed by BANYAN Corp.], AppleTalk, etc.) networks next to each other. Such network strategy is probably safe but too costly. Rather than maintaining parallel networks for different protocols, networks can now be combined without impacting application support.

Many vendors realized the importance of consolidation of the network infrastructure and the potential savings and developed products allowing utilization of non-SNA networks for SNA traffic. The most popular approaches for multiprotocol network consolidation include SNA transport over IP with *data-link switching* (DLSw), frame relay with Request for Comments (RFC) 1490, and LAN transport over SNA/APPN backbone.

Multiprotocol routers with DLSw are some of the more important examples of the SNA-over-IP approach, which was originally introduced by IBM and in March 1993 adopted by Internet Engineering Task Force (IETF) as RFC 1434. This RFC for DLSw was enhanced and superseded by RFC 1795 in April 1995. Because of the high timing sensitivity of SNA sessions, DLSw is the only dependable technique of transporting SNA over IP networks. Actually, encapsulated SNA data into IP frames is not new to the router vendors, but similar pre-DLSw attempts ran into time-out problems. IBM created DLSw to address this shortcoming, reducing the likelihood of time-outs, by providing a local polling and logical local termination of the data link, often named *spoofing*. By keeping the acknowledgment local, routers also reduce the amount of traffic traversing the wide area link. Additional advantages of DLSw include the ability to route around link failure, support for an extended source route bridging hop count, and NetBIOS name caching which greatly reduces NetBIOS broadcasts.

To address scaleability and improve connection setup time AIW developed DLSw Version 2 (DLSw v2), defined in RFC 2166 (DLSw v2 over IP Multicast). Among some of the major benefits of DLSw v2 are reduced bandwidth requirements for setup and connections, improved memory utilization, reduction in TCP overhead and number of tunnels, and reduced overhead for NetBIOS.

DLSw is certainly not a universal solution for consolidation of SNA and multiprotocol networks, mainly because it does not resolve the shortcomings of TCP/IP networks compared to SNA. For example, when SNA data are encapsulated and sent over IP, there are no provisions for defining SNA *class of services* (COS) necessary to secure prioritization of interactive sessions versus file transfer or printing. There is also a significant overhead of IP framing that adds more than 50 bytes to each encapsulated frame. This is one of the reasons most major vendors of multiprotocol routers licensed APPN technology and include APPN offerings in their solutions.

Increasing popularity of frame relay networks introduced a new alternative for networks consolidation—RFC 1490. It allows transport of multiple protocols over the same access line and even the same virtual circuit—*data-link connection identifier* (DLCI). The overhead associated with RFC 1490 for transporting SNA traffic is about one-fifth of the DLSw overhead. On the other hand, RFC 1490 does not allow assembling separate short messages into a single frame—a function supported by DLSw. Therefore, in a typical SNA environment the aftereffect of a shorter RFC 1490 header on WAN performance would be negligible. Some vendors of frame relay access devices allow separate queues for different protocols and a protocol-level prioritization scheme. However, within the frame relay cloud there are no provisions for protocol prioritization or SNA COS.

Although RFC 1490 supports protocol mixing for a single DLCI, in most cases it may be advantageous to keep the SNA traffic rather than the less critical traffic on a separate DLCI, with a higher committed information rate. Planning for frame relay access lines consolidation is a critical issue that has to be very carefully addressed. One must take all precautions to isolate mission-critical traffic from less critical applications.

Specification of the frame relay flow control standard is quite vague, which obviously caused inconsistencies with implementation of indications for *forward explicit congestion notification* (FECN), *backward explicit congestion notification* (BECN), and *discard eligibility* (DE) bits among different vendors. FECN or BECN is set in the frame address to notify the *frame relay data terminal equipment* (FRTE) users of a congestion condition on this DLCI's queue. At this point, however, frames will not be discarded until severe congestion is reached—setting the DE bit on. Before severe congestion occurs, the FRTE devices have a chance to help relieve congestion by reacting to the FECN/BECN bits with the opening and closing of network window sizes. The FECN bit has meaning to the originating FRTE, who is essentially being asked to slow transmission of the data. BECN bit's meaning, to the destination FRTE, is a request to slow down its frame transmission. But, because of the vague standard formulation, in each specific case of frame relay implementation, the following questions have to be asked:

- How does the selected equipment deal with exceeding of the CIR?
- Are the FECN/BECN/DE bits set?
- Does the FRTE honor the FECN/BECN/DE bits?

Although most frame relay carriers provide FECN, BECN, and DE indications, some frame relay switches do not include the FECN/BECN warnings to attached FRTEs, so that they can react to congestion conditions. They may just wait until the committed information rate is exceeded and discard everything. DE in a frame relay network comes into play when a network is severely congested. Dropping the discard-eligible frames will relieve congestion in the network so that frames not eligible for discard have a better chance of passing successfully through the network. It is the responsibility of the FRTE to set the DE bits on. The FRTE sets the DE bit so that the *frame relay frame handler* (FRFH) knows which frames to discard in order to protect itself in case of severe congestion. However, if the FRFH's DLCI queue is full and the FRTE continues sending frames with no DE set, the FRFH will mark all frames from that FRTE as DE, notifying the FRTE that it has exceeded its committed burst. To be more specific: during a mild congestion, most SNA users of a frame relay WAN will slow down (by reducing the window size) in order to avoid frame loss and the need to retransmit. Most of the known frame relay TCP/IP users ignore the mild congestion and continue to send frames until severe congestion occurs on their DLCI. Then, during severe congestion, FRFH discards TCP/IP frames so that frame loss will cause TCP/IP to slow. Technically speaking, response time for the polite SNA frame relay users will suffer during mild congestion; however, they are less likely to get into severe congestion trouble. Impolite TCP/IP users that cannot throttle down during mild congestion will definitely get into severe congestion trouble causing frame losses, and consequently, retransmissions. The bottom line: capacity planning in a consolidated multiprotocol frame relay network becomes truly challenging.

A vast majority of SNA shops are reluctant to convert their SNA backbones to TCP/IP, protecting performance of mission-critical applications. Both DLSw and RFC 1490 are possible avenues for network integration, but, as mentioned before, neither one can resolve all the shortcomings of the less dependable protocols and fully assure reliability and performance for SNA-based mission-critical applications. This prompted some vendors to take a different approach for network consolidation. Their solutions provide SNA-based gateways and routers to allow utilization of SNA backbone for non-SNA traffic. This approach permits capitalization on investments that many corporations have already made in their SNA backbones. It also grants the users a better utilized and more cost-effective SNA network, supporting many new applications. For example, end-users on IPX LANs can now access and communicate with other IPX LANs worldwide across SNA networks. Any client/server application that runs on a Novell LAN can now run over an SNA network. The new products will not affect the SNA backbone, protecting it by filtering out broadcasts from LAN-based protocols. Users on NetBIOS LANs can now also access and communicate with other NetBIOS LANs worldwide across SNA networks. Once again, any NetBIOS application (i.e., Lotus Notes, cc:Mail, MsMail, etc.) will safely run over an SNA network that is protected by filtering NetBIOS broadcasts. The same applies to TCP/IP applications' connectivity across SNA networks. End-users on TCP/IP networks can now access and communicate with other TCP/IP networks worldwide across SNA networks. And, obviously, any of the important TCP/IP applications (i.e., DCE, FTP, Telnet, etc.) will safely run over an SNA network.

As a handbook for a network practitioner, this book covers not only the more popular concepts, but also some of the more important products in the SNA multiprotocol integration arena. For example, Novell's products were designed to run on the existing NetWare, eliminating the need for a dedicated internetworking device in the branch. NetWare for SAA provides access to 3270, 5250, LU6.2, and LU0 applications on mainframes and AS/400 minicomputers. It supports *synchronous data-link control* (SDLC) and X.25/*qualified logical-link control* (QLLC). NetWare SNA Links provides LAN-to-LAN connectivity over an SNA network, which also allows managers to use Novell's NetWare Management System (NMS) and administrative tools, such as System Configuration (SYSCON), over the SNA network. NetWare SNA Links can also be used for store-and-forward electronic mail traffic. The NetWare Multi-Protocol Router (MPR) Plus is a software-based router for PCs. It routes IPX, IP, AppleTalk, and OSI over a variety of LANs and provides source-route bridging for token-ring LANs. For WAN connectivity, it supports leased lines using Point-to-Point Protocol (PPP), frame relay, Integrated Services Digital Network (ISDN), Switch Multimegabit Data Service (SMDS), and X.25.

Additionally, to the traditional deployment models for SNA gateways, Microsoft introduced a distributed deployment model based on its *SNA open gateway architecture* (SOGA). SOGA is a scaleable framework for SNA enterprise gateways offering different options for integrating branch offices via routed internetworks with IBM mainframe and AS/400 computers. This book describes the different popular deployment methods for SNA gateways in details.

Another software-based solution for routing LAN-based traffic over SNA is built on IBM's networking blueprint *multiprotocol transport network* (MPTN) concept. It is the so-called family of AnyNet products. IBM 2217 Nways Multiprotocol Concentrator (MpC) is one of the representatives of this technology. With AnyNet, non-SNA protocols (i.e., TCP/IP, IPX, etc.) are converted and then routed across the SNA/APPN WAN. At the destination point, another AnyNet node must be used to convert the messages into their native protocol. AnyNet technology allows transparent multiprotocol LAN-to-LAN communications without requiring any modifications to the applications. In addition to the 2217, MpC product AnyNet Sockets over SNA come on different platforms—that is, mainframes, RS/6000 AS/400 and PS/2. This family of products will provide multiprotocol support for TCP/IP, IPX, NetBIOS (and, of course SNA), over SNA/APPN WAN backbones, along with LAN network management support over frame relay, X.25, or SDLC links.

Now is a good time to mention Enterprise Connectivity Node (ECN) by an Israeli vendor ATLan. ECN is based on *concurrent backbone architecture* (CBA) technology, that addresses parallel utilization of SNA and non-SNA backbones to transfer LAN-based traffic.

One of the conventional approaches taken by network managers is maintaining redundant network infrastructures (with excess capacity for non-SNA links): one for deterministic, bandwidth-efficient, mission-critical SNA applications and another one for non-deterministic, bandwidth-hungry LAN and IP networks. Because of their worries about congestion—the main cause of data loss and unpredictable performance—most network managers play it safe. However, with products that efficiently utilize SNA/APPN architecture, SNA-centric networks will not succumb to congestion, and the costly solution of ordering excess capacity for the links can be avoided. Such products are especially attractive for users running a traditional SNA or SNA/APPN WAN backbone. Although many already have a multiprotocol network, it is expected that all of them will still have SNA/APPN as the predominant network architecture for mission-critical applications in the foreseeable future. By providing a multiprotocol solution, based on the advantages of SNA/APPN, the requirements for transporting multiple protocols across a WAN can be satisfied.

Many network managers are reluctant to neglect their SNA/APPN experience and trust transport of mission-critical data over IP-based router solutions. This handbook provides useful insights into the most recent developments in integration of SNA and the multiprotocol network world, such as distributed network management, distributed presentation with Java, and Web integration. It will assist the reader in implementation of the most reliable and cost-effective networking solutions, making use of the SNA/APPN knowledge base and providing a dependable and efficient migration path to future technologies.

chapter 2

The evolution of SNA

JAMES P. GRAY

SNA, in more than two decades since its introduction and in its recent incarnation—APPN/HPR—has gone through many development cycles and evolutions. It has been the single most successful protocol, dominant in several major industries and Fortune 1000 companies throughout the years. To understand a person, it is said, one must look to the home of origin. In the same way, to understand a technical development, one must consider the cradle in which it was developed, including the individual's as well as the company's culture and its preexisting product cousins. In this chapter, James P. Gray, IBM fellow and one of SNA's original developers, presents a narrated family album, taking the reader through the evolution of SNA from its inception to its future and the next steps in SNA's development cycles.

2.1 Introduction

During the early 1970s, presentations on SNA were given to thousands of IBM customers. SNA was three things:

- A strategy
- A set of products
- An architecture

The strategy was simple: IBM products connected into networks tailored to each customer's requirements, and the architecture specified the network protocols.

The first SNA products were unveiled in 1973 with the announcement of the 3600 banking system and matching host support—a full year before SNA itself was announced in September 1974. By then, the products included additional host programs, additional operating system choices, three additional industry systems (retail, supermarket, and insurance), and, most significantly, the general purpose 3270 display system adapted to the SNA environment from its initial *binary synchronous communications* (BISYNC) and channel attached versions. The 3767 keyboard-printer terminal and 3770 family of remote job entry (RJE) stations completed the general purpose terminal offerings. SNA began by integrating products with diverse network protocols, making SNA an internetworking protocol from its inception. SNA grew to become the internetworking protocol of choice for enterprises.

The configurations supported were limited but revolutionary for the time: star configurations rooted in single hosts were able to provide access by *any terminal to any application.* This promise to eliminate duplicate networks was the easiest for many customers to appreciate. Some, however, were drawn to SNA through their desire to purchase one of the industry specific products and others through SNA's cost/performance benefits.[1]

SNA has been the work of thousands of people, all of whom cannot be named here. When individuals are named, the teams they led or represented are included by reference.

2.2 The design process

SNA's public introduction completed an exciting twenty-two months. But it was not initially the corporatewide effort that it became. In the early 1970s, IBM as a whole was concerned with specific industries—such as banking and retailing—and was not interested in advanced network technology. IBM's development at the time was organized into four divisions. Systems Development Division (SDD) was responsible for all hardware and software for the S/370 product line, including peripheral devices such as *direct access storage device* (DASD), printers, tapes, and communications equipment. Small systems were in the General Systems Division (GSD); office products were covered by the Office Products Division (OPD). The Federal Systems Division (FSD) primarily worked on government projects.

In the late 1960s, networks were under active investigation in IBM. Two laboratories in particular were involved: those in Kingston, N.Y. and Raleigh, N.C. The system I/O group in Kingston was led by Gene Thomas.[2] The SDLC group in Raleigh was led by Ray Kersey and Bob Donnan.[3] In 1970, SDD President Bob Evans sent Ed Sussenguth to Raleigh to direct the Raleigh and Kingston advanced technology groups. During this period, Thomas, John Murdoch, and others worked on network routing, or Path Control in SNA parlance. Thomas also led work on session, or end to end, protocols. It was also during this time that VTAM (virtual telecommunications access method) was introduced into S/370 to complement TCAM (telecommunications access method), and both were made to work with NCP (network control program for the 3705 communications front end). While SNA drew upon this prior work, it did not come together until 1972.

In September 1972, Bob Marshall was assigned to review the status of the 3600 banking system. He discovered that *each* of the major system components (the 3600 banking controller, VTAM, and NCP) mistakenly assumed that the other two were

---

1. "A Cost/Performance Analysis of Synchronous Data Link Control and Binary Synchronous Communications," by William T. McClelland and Arthur Schiff, TR 21.478, May 10, 1972, helped to support the arguments for a Single Network Strategy (SNS), in which all products announced after January 1972 would support SDLC.

2. IBM communications products started long before SNA. A good reference is: "IBM Data Communications: A Quarter Century of Evolution and Progress," *IBM Journal Of R&D*, Vol. 25, No. 5, pp. 391–404, by David R. Jarema and Edward H. Sussenguth.

3. SDLC was originally called Advanced Data Communications Control Procedure.

following *its* design lead. Since network protocols were involved, it was natural for Earl Wheeler, the SDD vice president in charge of the 3600 system, to call upon Sussenguth to fix the problem.

The solution was delivered by a task force directed technically by Thomas. Bringing to bear the insights and ideas developed over the previous seven years during his work on I/O subsystem architecture for systems beyond S/360 and S/370, Thomas sold his vision of data networking.[4] Thomas enriched his vision with the ideas of others to create SNA, which was first documented in the task force report: "Standard Network Architecture."[5]

Sussenguth became the champion of SNA within IBM, seizing the opportunity created by Thomas. Sussenguth and Lin Hoberecht, the manager of his team in Kingston, undertook a sales campaign among IBM's executives. During their blitz, the concept of SNA, quickly renamed Single Network Architecture and then Systems Network Architecture, was sold to Bob Evans and other executives. The arguments were compelling since they extended the accepted paradigm of S/360 architecture—a general-purpose system for a variety of applications—to the network domain. With adequate support in place, including product managers such as the banking system's Jim DeRose and retail/supermarket's Jim Bookstaver, the next step was to compress the delivery cycle to seven months.[6] This forced schedule was the price of management buy-in: a commitment to weave SNA into the existing network and application products and industry system development efforts without slipping the September 1973 announcement of the 3600 banking system, code-named Liberty.

It fell to Paul Lindfors, the manager of Sussenguth's team in Raleigh, to lead the fulfillment of this commitment as he ran the Liberty task force. In six weeks they developed detailed definitions of SNA sufficient for development to proceed. Lindfors was an experienced developer of networked applications, fresh from leading the implementation of National Westminster Bank's banking network when he joined Sussenguth. Thomas provided technical leadership of the Liberty task force.

---

4. For example, *System Considerations for Graphic Data Processing*, by Eugene M. Thomas, TR 21.295, reprinted from *Computers and Automation*, Newtonville, MA: Berkeley Enterprises, November 1967, p. 3, discusses load sharing, later called distributed processing. Thomas was aware of Arpanet, but was not heavily influenced by it in his design of SNA.

5. The "Cox Task Force Report," dated October 1972, was named after Jim Cox, the management leader of the task force. Sixty pages were appendices previously written by the Kingston and Raleigh architects, while the report's one-hundred pages were created by the task force members during their work together. Thomas defined SNA's distinctive layer structure in this report. The correctness of this structure has been proven by twenty years of extensions and modifications.

6. Bookstaver's agreement to use the common Universal Controller microprocessor in his products helped pave the way for SNA by establishing the principle that industry products should share components and designs when possible.

The Liberty task force was staffed with key product designers and architects. Gene Thomas brought his comprehensive knowledge of network protocols. Allan Rommelfinger contributed in-depth understanding of the practical constraints of NCP for the 3705 front-end processor. Jeff Knauth of VTAM specialized in *logical unit* (LU)-to-LU session protocols, Dale Reed of VTAM dealt with protocols for control of the network components on *systems services control point* (SSCP)-to-*physical unit* (PU) and SSCP-to-LU sessions, while Larry Brown represented the banking system microcode. Lindfors brought his knowledge of *information management system* (IMS) and *customer information control system* (CICS) to bear on the decisions being made. Product design changes were done in parallel with architecture decisions, which Thomas made quickly. He kept line control separate from device control, rejecting the view derived from BSC products that hardware functions should be defined as direct extensions to a data-link control. Some of the distinctive features of SNA include:

- *Managed layered structure* SNA is defined by layers whose network behavior is overseen by control services. The *systems services control point* maintains central control of a network domain; VTAM implemented the first SSCP. *Physical units* operate at each node as agents of the SSCP to control activation, operation, and deactivation of network resources such as links. *Logical units* at each application or terminal act as agents of the SSCP in the creation of sessions. The orginal layers were: link, path control, session control, data-flow control, and session services. Within a few years the physical layer was split from the data-link protocols and the application layer was split from the presentation layer.

- *Physical and logical units* Channel concepts also influenced terminology: hardware *devices* such as disks, tapes, and printers were attached to device *control units,* which were in turn attached by *original equipment manufacturer* (OEM) channel *cables* to hardware I/O channels and by channel programs to host *programs.* In the SNA generalization, *devices* were attached to programs at *logical units* that shared residency within *physical units* and were connected by *sessions* to partner *logical units* to which were attached host *programs.* By symmetry, hosts became a type of physical unit as well.

- *Distributed processing* The 3600 banking system's requirements and Thomas's experience with display controllers shaped SNA's support for distributing applications between hosts and remote controllers.

- *Record orientation* Channel programming concepts, the ubiquity of record files in IBM operating systems, and SNA's focus on distributed processing moved the architecture to a record orientation rather than towards a character or byte stream orientation. Reduction of host interrupt rates and attendant application processor savings became a significant customer value of SNA.

- *Synchronous data-link control* SDLC promoted SNA's success by receiving traffic from one station while simultaneously sending traffic to another station on the same line.

When the Liberty task force finished its work, not only was there a great amount of product design, coding, and testing ahead, there was a large number of SNA architecture issues to deal with. Drawing upon his experience deploying production networks, Lindfors narrowed the scope of decisions in order to reduce risks. Addressing was limited to 16 bits, in spite of the vision by Thomas and others of much larger networks. After all, 16 bits was not only the integer width of the 3705 communications controller on which NCP ran, it would sustain a banking system with 64,000 tellers—ten times larger than envisioned by the planners. As shown in figure 2.1, Lindfors limited routing to simple networks with a host, one or more local NCPs, optional remote NCPs and multidropped SDLC lines to the industry controllers. Important functions, such as alternate routing, were deferred for later specification.

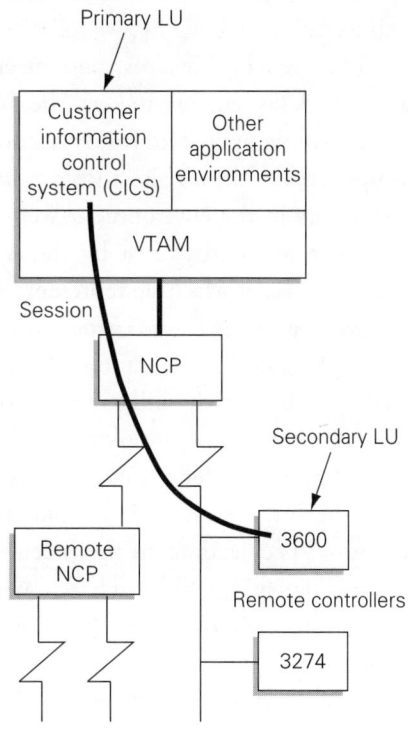

Figure 2.1 SNA 0/1/2:Single host tree

2.3 Crisis crystallizes change

The period after the Liberty task force ended had more than one difficulty. For example, Sussenguth had to defend SNA against the claims of *future system* (FS), which aimed to replace S/370 with a quantum leap in processor architecture. Many FS technologies were eventually shipped in the S/38 and the AS/400. But management decided FS as a whole strayed too far from the incremental, nondisruptive growth required by S/370 customers. SNA, with its emphasis on incremental growth and protection of customer investments, became a beneficiary of the decision to cancel FS.

Another problem was that the architecture processes that SNA needed to thrive did not exist. Once again, it was a crisis that crystallized change. Another status review, this time just before announcement of the banking system, showed that shipment schedules were seriously exposed by product arguments over the details of the architecture. The solution was the creation of the Architecture Maintenance Board (AMB). Hoberecht formed the AMB, modeled after a similar board chaired by Fred Brooks for the S/360. Initially led by Art Schiff and Jon Oseas, the membership consisted of key designers and architects.

Later led by Lindfors, and meeting every two weeks, the AMB made decisions about SNA fast enough to keep the products on schedule. Many of these decisions were made possible only after Tom Piatkowski realized that a state machine definition of the components of the architecture was needed if protocol interactions with each other and with errors in the environment were to be understood. But Piatkowski's contribution was not recognized at first by the AMB representatives. Not, that is, until the 3614 Automatic Teller Machine representative asked the AMB to rule on the proper action to take when a `Release Quiesce` command for a session was received following a `Shutdown` command for the same session. Three different answers, not one, were offered by AMB members, each with support from the architecture specifications.

Lindfors had been looking for just such an opportunity to persuade the AMB to accept finite state definitions. He declared that, henceforth, state machine descriptions would be authoritative. Piatkowski and a supporting team of architects began to recast the prose specifications in the precise form that became one of the hallmarks and distinctive benefits of SNA. That it would take several years to create a state machine description for SNA was not then apparent. Completion of the task required the creation of an executable specification written in *Format and Protocol Language* (FAPL), a dialect of *Programming Language/1* (PL/1). Colin West of IBM's Zurich research laboratory used the executable specifications in a series of protocol validation studies, spanning more than a decade, that significantly improved SNA's quality.

Meanwhile, it was found that important functions had been missed. Distributed processing was good, all agreed. But what about terminals for use with centralized applications, especially the increasingly popular 3270 displays? A second release that featured terminal support was the result. SNA's first public visibility came as part of the announcement of product support for the terminal-oriented extensions to SNA, sometimes called SNA 2.

2.4 Software given a featured role

In the pre-SNA period, terminals and devices were designed by hardware teams with little consideration for the impact their decisions would have on supporting software programs. After all, software was free, so it couldn't be very important. It certainly didn't make any money.

Key executives and designers understood the critical role that *operating systems* software played in turning the latent value of computers into usable value for which customers would gladly pay. However, the role of *application monitors*—as represented by CICS, IMS, and TCAM, was not broadly appreciated in the engineer-dominated development community. But Lindfors was not from a development engineering background. His experience was grounded in enterprise use of networks where application monitors were highly valued. A bridge between the hardware and software views was provided by financial planners: if every device were unique, then unique software would have to be written in each application monitor. Arithmetic showed that the hardware plans could not be supported by the available software development capacity.

The hardware would somehow have to be supported by a single module in each software product. Thus were born canonical models of product behavior, called *logical unit* (LU) types: LU type 0 (LU 0), to incorporate product-specific usage of SNA session protocols; LU 1, to represent keyboard/printer and RJE terminals; and LU 2, to represent the 3270 display family.[7] The mapping of 3270 BISYNC into LU 2 was done by Ed Cobb of IMS, Julian Jones and Colin Powell of CICS, and Bill Kippenhan of the 3270 controller. Their ability to preserve 3270 semantics while still capturing SNA's performance benefits was important to SNA's widespread adoption. In an accommodation of architecture to reality, LU 3 was added when the CICS product team declared that they could not migrate an existing base of applications from the pre-SNA 3270 printer family to SNA unless a class of printers that specifically used 3270 datastreams was included.

The controversy over this decision, as over many others, was heated; SNA's progress through such turbulence depended critically on the strong technical leadership of Lindfors and his successors as AMB chairman such as John Broughton II. This leadership flourished under the support of Sussenguth until he relinquished his position as director of architecture to become an IBM Fellow in 1981.

One of the properties of pre-SNA software support that was crucial to CICS, IMS, and other application monitors was the ability to have complete control over the state of the device. Did the user at the terminal need to input data at the same time that an application program needed to output data? This race condition was managed by integrating line scheduling decisions with the state of the applications and testing the resulting effect on the terminal state. But in SNA, the line scheduling decisions were made in NCP, far away from the application scheduling decisions being made in CICS, IMS,

---

7. The need for LU types was discussed at the AMB and among the SNA community. Bill Bernstein and Lin Hoberecht proposed to Ed Sussenguth that Communications Systems Architecture in Kingston define their protocols, with initial focus on the terminal LU types to support the September 11, 1974, announcement of SNA and related products.

and other host applications. The consequence was a need for session-level protocols sufficient to represent the application scheduling actions that needed to be taken. Some of these functions, such as session creation and termination, were included in SNA from the beginning. But one function—the allocation of the use of the session resource to the next application and the ability for the next application to be started at either the host or terminal end—was not discovered until late in 1973 in a design task force led by Bill Bernstein of Kingston architecture.

The resulting *bracket* protocol—which allowed the host systems to bid for use of the session resource and left to the terminal or controller end of the session the ownership of the resource—had more race and error conditions implicit in its design requirements than the most ardent devotee of finite state protocol methods could wish. But by the time this need was apparent, the finite state machine tools had already been created. As has happened throughout SNA's evolution, providence provided.

2.5 Small but sufficient need envisioned for multisystem SNA

Most were content with SNA as a system for connecting a host and its varied resources, and felt customers would not be interested in larger networks. Some visionaries, though, saw a need for SNA's second release and the official unveiling to the world, on September 11, 1974, was followed by a full networking version capable of connecting multiple host systems. In the face of much skepticism, Etienne Gorog led a worldwide marketing task force to determine if there were sufficient customer demand to undertake the software investment that was required. In what today seems a cosmic understatement, he reported that a few tens or a hundred such networks might be sold, with several hundred hosts in aggregate. At the time, this estimate was considered quite optimistic. But enough of these networks would involve incremental sales of host systems to sustain the software expense that would be involved. Multisystem SNA was born.

Fortunately, the VTAM session services design, led by Reed, had laid a solid foundation for multisystems networking. The characterization of the ports into the network from hosts as primary logical units (PLUs) in contrast to terminals and outboard controllers as secondary LUs (SLUs) brought both power and problems to be overcome during the move to multisystem networking.

The power was derived from assigning VTAM, where host programming power and central site operational skills could be used, responsibility for overseeing the creation of sessions with SLUs. Users at SLUs (e.g., at terminals) invoked the services of VTAM to logon to applications, and applications similarly depended upon the session services provided by VTAM's SSCP to create sessions with terminals.

VTAM's SSCV:

- Provided alias translations of LU names
- Looked up network addresses for LUs
- Activated links (including automatically dialing) to create sessions between LUs
- Queued multiple session requests when necessary
- Queued individual session requests when needed to overcome a temporary network outage condition, or when waiting for a link activation sequence to complete
- Passed a session partner from one application to another upon request
- Provided a number of services and commands used by network operation staffs

Problems to be overcome in moving from a single host orientation included:

- A limitation to a single session between any pair of LUs, a side-effect of the original network addressing structure
- A limitation of a single route between any two nodes
- VTAM code structures that limited PLUs to be VTAM applications
- Inadequate control of network congestion under stress
- Absence of priority for network traffic
- Static routing determined by system definitions input to VTAM and NCP
- Implicit dependency upon VTAM for recovery in failure scenarios that could not occur in single host cases but did in multihost networks

Table 2.1   Major SNA developments

Release	Date	Development
SNA 0	9/74	3600 banking system, VTAM R1, single host
SNA 1	3/75	3650 retail, 3660 supermarket systems
SNA 2	9/75	3270 displays, 3767 and 3770 terminals, VTAM R2
SNA 3	12/77	Multiple host networks, VTAM R3
SNA 4.1	11/80	Parallel sessions, LU 6.0, VTAM V1R3
SNA 4.2	12/81	Fully meshed hosts, priority, etc., VTAM V2R1
SNI	9/84	SNA network interconnect, VTAM V2R2
ENA	5/85	Extended network addressing, 23 bits, VTAM V3R1
APPN	12/86	APPN on S/36
ESA	9/88	Extended subarea addressing, 31 bits, VTAM V3R2
AnyNet	4/93	MPTN architecture, VTAM V3R4.2
APPN/390	5/93	APPN for S/390, VTAM V4R1, V4R2, V4R3
HPR	5/95	APPN/HPR, VTAM V4R4

2.6 SNA generations

These problems were addressed in steps, beginning with the third and fourth main architecture shipments—SNA 3 in 1977 and SNA 4.2 in 1980—and continuing through APPN/HPR in 1995.

Assignment of SNA release numbers was abandoned after SNA 4.2 because product support no longer progressed in simple linear sequences. Major SNA developments are shown in table 2.1. Today, the architectures of the main components of peer SNA—APPN and advanced program-to-program communications (APPC)—are described in terms of a required base level of support and option sets on that base.[8]

SNA 3 provided the essential elements of multisystem networking, as shown in figure 2.2, including the ability for any terminal to access any host in the network and the ability for host applications to access host applications anywhere in the network (but limited to a single session between any two applications). CICS and network job entry (NJE) products used the application connectivity that this provided to supply distributed services. In CICS, this included the architecture of a new LU type, LU 6.0, as the first step towards a full distributed application and distributed operating system capability.[9] SNA 3 was understood to be a stepping-stone on the way to a more coherent and fully satisfactory networking service, which arrived in SNA 4.2.

SNA 4.2 was created by an AMB task force led by Glen Huff and Jim Gray with broad VTAM, TCAM, and NCP support. As shown in figure 2.3, SNA 4.2 supported a fully meshed network. It also attacked most of the deficiencies listed above:

- Improved recovery with session outage notification along the session path so that failure processing ceased to be dependent on VTAMs

- Added takeover logic to allow VTAMs to be started, stopped, and recovered after failures

- Supplied packet priority to support mixed batch and interactive traffic

- Enabled multiple simultaneously active routes with some load spreading and recovery

---

8. SNA was a peer architecture from the beginning, but product subsets taken to control implementation costs had to be reversed in later releases. In order to migrate networks from release to release without disruption it was necessary to introduce peer behavior over several releases.

9. And what about the mysterious LU 5? IMS proposed that an entry LU 6 be defined, to be called LU 5, and proceeded to build their SLU P support. Although given serious consideration, this proposal was eventually rejected. The reserved LU type number remains as a mute reminder of the debate. The mysterious PU 3 was reserved due to an earlier confusion about PU and LU functionality: the 3767 was a PU 1, the 3770 was a PU 2, so the 3790 was thought for a few weeks to be a PU 3 until it was clearly seen to be a PU 2 like the 3770 and many other products, merely differentiated by the LU functions provided.

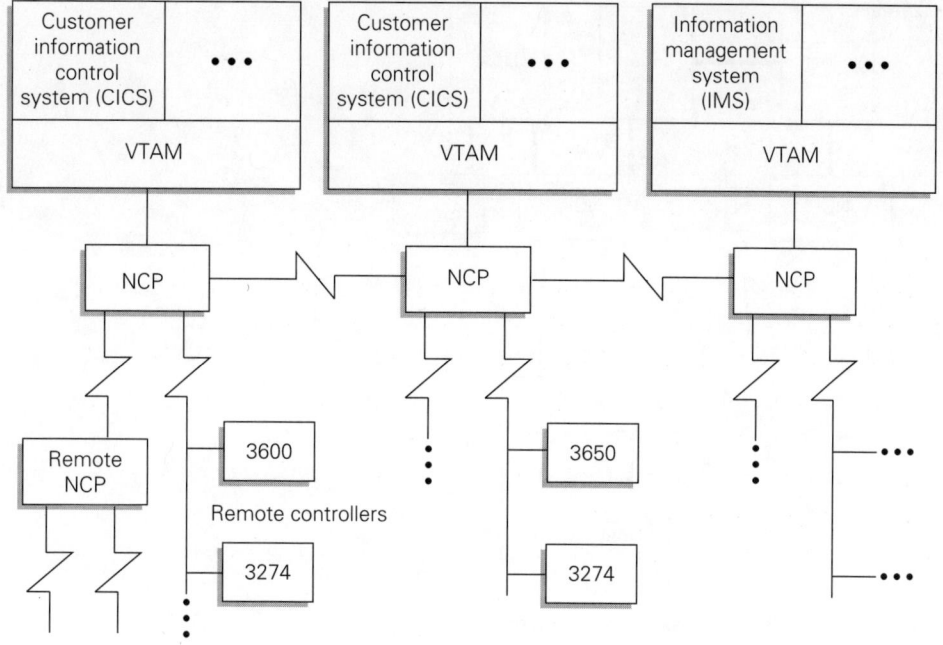

Figure 2.2 SNA 3: Forest of trees

- Delivered the network congestion control essential to stable production use and without which priority is ineffective

One of the key elements of SNA 4.2 was the use of simulation modeling studies to determine effective congestion control strategies. Led by Mike Doss, Jim Markov, and George Deaton, this work established the importance of key design choices such as virtual routes to keep traffic queues at the edges of the network and the use of network priority for virtual route pacing responses. The SNA 4.2 designs and their attendant rationales were published[10] in the late 1970s, but the Internet community failed to notice. Partially as a result, difficulties with congestion are a continuing problem in TCP/IP networks; congestion is not a problem in SNA networks.

During this same period, other AMB task forces were led by Cobb, Jones, Knauth, and Gray with the goal of extending the CICS implementation of LU 6.0 to make it more widely useful. Parallel sessions were added to support multiple simultaneously active network transactions. Distributed synchronization of database updates and a

---

10. J. P. Gray and T. B. McNeill, "SNA Multiple-system Networking," *IBM Systems Journal,* Vol. 18, No. 2 1979, pp. 263-297.

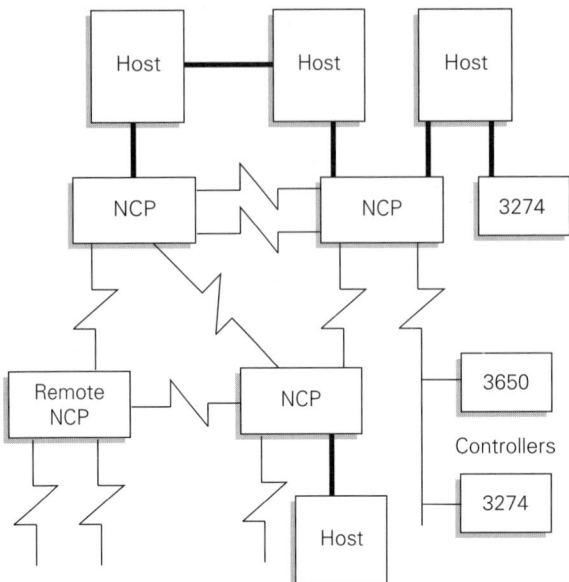

Figure 2.3   SNA 4.2: Fully meshed networking

variety of distributed processing services were defined. The resulting LU 6.1 was implemented by CICS and IMS for communication to themselves and each other. The basic relationships among LU 6.x, transaction programs, and sessions is shown in figure 2.4.

The vision of heterogeneous distributed processing that drove this work proved to be flawed in the actual product shipments because the abstract concepts of the LU 6 architecture were implemented divergently by CICS and IMS. CICS implemented the architecture's *transaction programs* (TPs), which were application or services programs, as CICS tasks. This was a good mapping, as would be expected of SNA, whose prototypical system configuration began as CICS on VTAM/NCP driving network connections.[11] But IMS implemented TPs as IMS mapping programs. While structurally correct, since TPs are in direct control of sessions and IMS's mapping programs do directly control sessions, this failed to match CICS because IMS's user-supplied application logic is only easily supplied in IMS message-processing programs that run above the mapping programs and are decoupled from sessions by message queues.

The mismatch showed up most clearly in recovery situations, where database commitment in CICS could be directly coupled to session events, while database commitment

---

11. The definition of LU 6 was made possible by David Eade of CICS who suggested that the architects adopt the CICS system structure as a model.

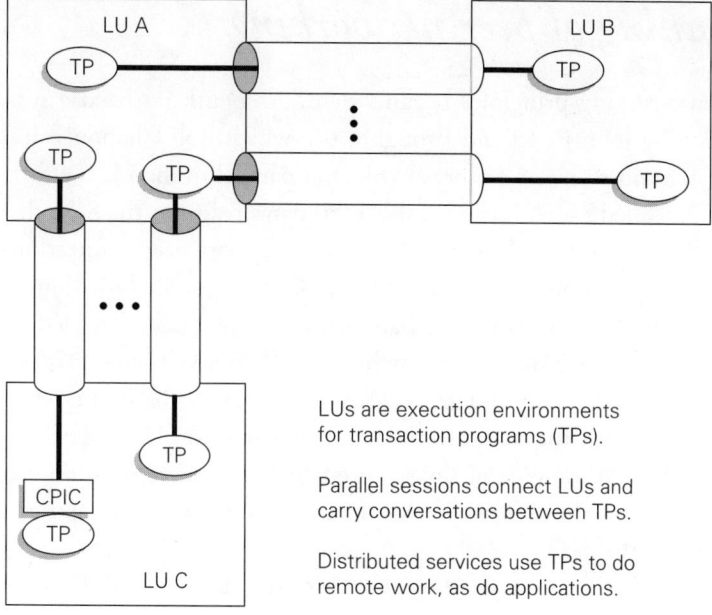

LUs are execution environments for transaction programs (TPs).

Parallel sessions connect LUs and carry conversations between TPs.

Distributed services use TPs to do remote work, as do applications.

Figure 2.4   SNA's network operating system: APPC

in IMS was always indirectly mediated through the message queues. Only with effort could applications be written that integrated CICS and IMS into a seamless application network. On the other hand, the CICS-to-CICS use of LU 6.1 included such truly innovative network services as:

- Distributed commitment of database updates (also referred to as distributed sync point)
- Distributed access to remote DL/1 and relational databases
- Distributed access to remote record and indexed files
- Distributed access to message queues
- Access to remote application programs, either call or schedule
- Access to remote terminals (routing per transaction, not per session)

Putting aside the mismatch between CICS and IMS, the large amount of function in the LU 6.1 protocols was more than smaller products such as the S/34 could afford. The exploration of distributed processing by some of these teams emphasized peer networking principles in SNA.

2.7 The beginning of peer networking

SNA's recovery of peer networking principles began when Sussenguth initiated a sub-group of the AMB guided by John Rood and Broughton in which Bob Chappuis, Jim Crutcher, Larry Tate, Bob Sundstrom, and others worked in parallel to the LU 6 efforts to create a modified LU 2. Called LU 7, it carried the 5250 datastream for the S/36 display terminals, as well as an extended LU 1 called LU 4 to support peer connections among printers, intelligent typewriters, and fax machines. GSD also needed distributed operating system services, but was very concerned about the size of LU 6.1, so, led by Peter Hansen, they developed the GSD Interchange Architecture (GSDIA) based on LU 4.

Sussenguth persuaded IBM to consolidate GSDIA and SNA, with the first step being a detailed requirements study for the converged LU, code named LU_C. The cost concerns of small systems were at the core of the requirements. A creative solution was found: a small base of functions that everyone was required to support and optional functions, or towers, built on the base.

LU_C, which became LU 6.2, was defined by an architecture team of Mike Lerner, Gray, Pete Homan, Hansen, and Mark Pozefsky. It shipped in CICS and S/36 in 1983 and has shipped in many other products since then.

LU 6.2 rigorously defined the semantic model for implementation, correcting the semantic mismatch in LU 6.1. This was done by defining an architected *application programming interface* (API) for the LU. Products at first resisted making this a portable API, but the *common programming interface for communications* (CPI-C) was later defined under the leadership of John Fedvedt and Pozefsky.[12] Initially APPC was used for the various implementations of an API to LU 6.2, but after the emergence of CPI-C as the portable API, APPC became a synonym for LU 6.2.

2.8 The APPN component

In the new generation of SNA, APPC and CPI-C address the upper layers of the networking architecture, while APPN deals with the lower layers above the data links. The APPN step in network evolution attacked the problems of network dynamicity, cost of entry implementations, and operations cost. APPN was not always the designated

---

12. LU 6.2 is the basis for many distributed services, including distributed commit of database updates (a.k.a., syncpt), the Distributed Relational Data Base model, the Distributed Data Model (for file access to record, indexed, and byte stream files), and SNA Distribution Services used for mail exchanges and asynchronous file distribution. A standardized application suite also has been developed that includes 3270 access (A3270), file transfers (AFTP), remote execution (AREXEC), and ping (APING).

evolutionary step for SNA. In fact, it was just one of several alternatives under development to address these issues. Although the first APPN implementation shipped in 1986, it was not formally designated as the successor for subarea SNA until 1990.

Originally started as part of GSDIA and SNA convergence, and substantially encouraged by Paul Green of IBM's Research Division, a detailed requirements study led by Diane Pozefsky and Chuck Wood established the need for a more substantial step than merely agreeing on the PU type to be shared across IBM. The architecture was created by a task force led by Diane Pozefsky, Gray, Knauth, Alan Baratz, and Jean Lorrain. It was initially implemented for the S/36 by a team led by Baratz. The success of the S/36 and its networking established APPN's place within SNA, and it was carried forward to the S/38 and the AS/400. It is now available on all IBM platforms and in many products from other vendors since IBM has licensed the code and published the specifications. Tens of thousands of AS/400 networks are operated with low levels of staff networking skill, thanks to APPN and its careful implementation by the AS/400.

The next major improvement, APPN/HPR shipped in 1995. It added nondisruptive route switching for failure recovery and connectionless intermediate routing of packets (figure 2.5). While connectionless in the sense that intermediate routers (i.e., network nodes) do not keep state for connections, HPR is deterministic. It allows support of policy routing and the superior congestion control of SNA that are so essential to traffic prioritization, stable network performance, and the high line loadings needed to minimize network costs.

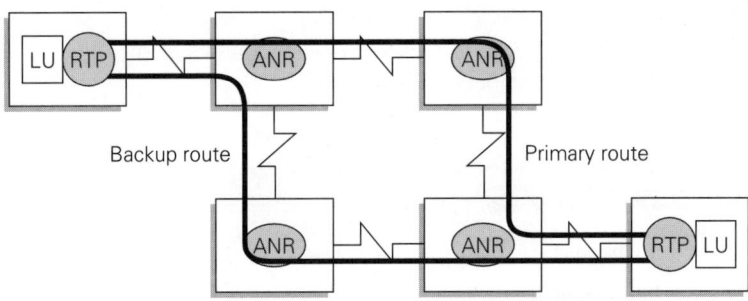

RTP: rapid transport protocol
ANR: automatic network routing

Figure 2.5 APPN/HPR: high performance routing

2.9 Connecting multiple networks and extending addresses

Along the way to the ultimate networking envisioned by those who shaped SNA and APPN, more than one controversy arose. For instance, should extended network addressing ship before or after network interconnection? The architects argued that extending the network address space should come first, while the product planners heard from customers the urgent need to connect separate networks with more flexible naming. The architects thankfully lost the argument so that SNI was delivered before ENA.

The SNI release announced in November 1983 was architected under the leadership of Ellis Miller and Matt Hess. SNI made it possible to interconnect SNA networks around the world into one large internetwork by extending SNA naming from the original single 8-character LU names to fully qualified LU names consisting of an 8-character network identifier (NETID) that scopes the 8-character LU name, as shown in figure 2.6.

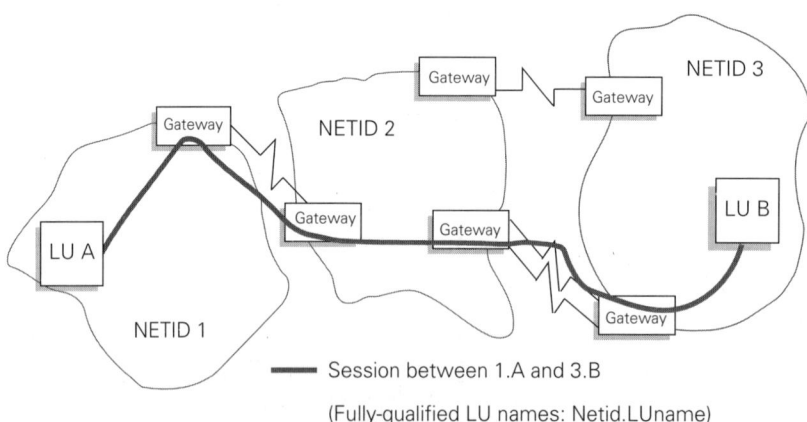

Figure 2.6   SNI: SNA Network Interconnect

This choice of a two-part name was driven by a combination of affordability and the study by Leonard Kleinrock that showed that more than two tokens provided only marginal savings in table space.[13] Later work showed that multiple *levels* of tokens were necessary to allow multiple name-creation authorities, with the result that the network

---

13. Even one extra token was a large cost burden in an already large release.

CHAPTER 2   THE EVOLUTION OF SNA

identifier was divided into several subfields. This division is encouraged by the network identifier registration service operated by IBM as a service for SNA network owners, but nonconforming net IDs can also be used.

SNA addresses were actually extended four times. First, in the SNA 4.2 release, the address field was increased from 16 bits to 48, but only 16 were usable. In September 1984 came 23-bit addressability with 8 bits for subarea number and 15 for element within a subarea. In September 1988 this was further increased to 16 bits for subarea, giving 31 bits of addressability within a single network. In 1990, with the adoption of APPN as the successor to subarea SNA, an SNA network can configure up to 8 characters (42 usable bits) of LUs, with 8 characters (42 bits) of net ID. The total SNA addressing of 84 usable bits is comfortably larger than the 2^{32} people on the planet.

2.10 Protecting customer investment

An important part of SNA's evolution has been incremental migration, not just from SNA release to SNA release, but from non-SNA to SNA configurations. Most products shipped since 1973 continue to work with today's networks, and new releases are typically tested and supported in interoperation with many prior releases of both hardware and software products.[14] This concern for incremental change is typical of successful architectures, and reflects the value of the investments that surround the core architecture and products. Billions of dollars have been invested by enterprises around the world in the deployment of SNA production networks, and this investment must be leveraged and production maintained even as technical innovation is pursued on many fronts. Integration of APPN into VTAM on the mainframe took six years after APPN's initial release on the S/36, in part because of the effort needed to create this seamless integration and migration.

When SNA was begun, the LAN revolution was beginning in research labs, although LANs were not deployed commercially until the early 1980s. Similarly, X.25 arrived on the scene after SNA began. Both technologies, and many others such as S/390 *enterprise systems connection* (ESCON) Channels, ISDN, frame relay, *asynchronous transfer mode* (ATM), and now TCP/IP, have been assimilated into SNA's structure. In each case, the subnetwork technology could be mapped to SNA's data-link layer and further integrated into SNA's automatic dialing provisions whenever switched services were available.

Beyond that, APPN's dynamic route creation services take advantage of switched subnetworks through a construct called a *connection network*. This is an abstraction that

---

14. Network Products Reference, GX28-8002, summarizes the interoperability of VTAM and NCP releases.

represents the switched facility to APPN's optimal route calculation algorithms so that APPN can dynamically create direct links between nodes that share a common subnetwork. In a related service, APPN dynamically detects and exploits multiple simultaneous link connections (called *tail vectors*) from terminals, hosts, and other servers (called *end nodes*). This APPN feature capitalizes on the separation between addressing and routing in SNA. The products support LANs as connection networks today, and the architecture permits other types, including X.25, the public-switched network (including ISDN), emerging switch services such as frame relay and ATM, and dynamic routing services such as IP subnets.

SNA has assimilated application technologies as well as subnetwork technologies. This assimilation began with the inclusion of CICS, IMS, TCAM, and other existing application environments, continued with the incorporation of the 3270 display family, and has continued through the integration of ASCII terminals, BSC devices, and a wide range of personal computer technologies. More recently, the full range of Internet applications, including the World Wide Web, have been assimilated into SNA. The creation of *AnyNet* by a team led by Diane Pozefsky has codified assimilation by defining a uniform method for adding new application layers and new subnetwork layers to SNA. But AnyNet goes beyond assimilating other technologies into SNA: it can equally be viewed as assimilating SNA into other networks, for example, into TCP/IP. This step represents a major achievement in the march towards realizing the grand vision that has fueled SNA since its birth.

2.11 Any-to-any: the grand vision of SNA

Historically, all major industries have developed through incorporation of adjacent technologies. For example, the automobile industry adopted or interacted with hundreds of technologies, including rubber, ball bearings, gasoline refining, road building, and even microprocessors for engine control. Similarly, components of the networking and computing industries adopt and interact with relevant technologies. The process of integration is a symbiotic changing and interweaving as SNA incorporates, adapts, and extends. Where SNA ends and something else, such as TCP/IP, begins, is increasingly difficult to determine as integration and assimilation operate on both sides of every boundary. In the process, even SNA's names are changing, as the very name SNA, which began by standing for three very distinct things, is now used to mean a broad network framework, with more specific terms such as APPN, CPI-C, and APPN/HPR being used where more specific meanings are intended.

But any-to-any, the grand vision that has driven SNA from its inception, the vision of a single internetwork, deployed everywhere, and making everything interoperable even as the public-switched telephone network makes all telephones mutually interoperable, is not merely alive and well, it is nearly achieved. For AnyNet achieves exactly that goal, and achieves it in the only way that is economically possible: by incorporating all relevant components (APPN, TCP/IP, IPX, etc.) into the larger whole.[15] It does this by enabling applications from any network family (e.g., sockets applications from TCP/IP) to operate over any collection of subnetworks. This allows network users to incorporate the best distributed services from diverse sources into an integrated whole.

2.12 The next steps

SNA developers need to add support for isochronous traffic—real-time voice, digital video, and the like that require resource reservation in the network path—in order to operate. The power of assimilation is already at work to borrow *resource reservation protocol* (RSVP) from IP for APPN/HPR to create interoperable resource reservation services for applications. The path to the future is clear for SNA: assimilate, incorporate, and interoperate, for interoperation with investment protection is the fundamental customer value in SNA networking.

2.13 Conclusion

Many important things have been omitted from this brief history of SNA. One area is network management—how Gene Thomas's design for network management grew into the Network Communications Control Facility management platform and then into the SystemView products is a fascinating story. Standards is another area. To describe the interactions between SNA and OSI, including the story of IBM's 1979 submission of SNA as the basis of OSI, would take many pages. The early episodes in SNA's displacement of BSC, or the details of APPN's development would be interesting, as would many other stories.

It is with sincere appreciation that I acknowledge the dedication and accomplishments of the many tens of thousands of people, IBMers, customers, and competitors, who have created the reality of SNA. Gene Thomas deserves special mention for his creation of SNA and for his review of this history.

---

15. The power of universal network interoperability has also motivated the work of the TCP/IP community.

chapter 3

Data-link layer tutorial

Radia Perlman

We begin with a set of tutorials which move up the protocol stack. In this first tutorial on the data-link layer, Radia Perlman provides us with a wealth of technical information as well as her opinions about what is most important to understand about the data-link layer in the context of internetworking. Despite brilliant innovations, the limitations of existing technologies will remain with us for many years to come. On the bright side, the newer data-link protocols are taking into account large-scale internetworking and a healthy relationship with the upper layers. This chapter describes the methods and techniques used in data-link layer to detect and handle garbled information. It also defines local and wide-area network terminology used throughout the book.

3.1 Introduction

The data-link layer is the second layer in the OSI stack. That's about the only definite thing one can say about it. There is enormous variability in protocols deemed to be data-link layer protocols. Partly this is due to lack of industry consensus about what the data-link layer should do. This is also due in part to a general confusion about networks because of the fact that multiaccess *links* (such as token rings or *carrier sense multiple access/collision detection*, CSMA/CD, links) were called local-area *networks*. In this chapter we'll cover the data-link layer as it has evolved. We'll discuss:

- How the data-link layer detects garbled information
- How the data-link layer detects packet boundaries
- Reliable vs. datagram data-link layer protocols
- Connection-oriented vs. connectionless data-link layer protocols
- Multiaccess links
- Multiprotocol operation
- Bridges: source routing and transparent

3.2 Detecting garbled information

Originally the data-link layer was responsible for getting a packet of information from one machine to another directly adjacent. A wire connected the two machines. One couldn't assume that every machine that ever wanted to talk to another had a wire between them. Imagine if the telephone company worked that way, with wires from your house to each of the phones in the world! So the network layer was designed to be responsible for relaying messages between machines.

In the beginning, the technology connecting machines was extremely error-prone (early technology involved tin cans and string, or something not too much better, like modems operating over noisy phone lines). If a packet had to traverse multiple hops to get from the source to the destination machine, the probability of it making it all the way to the end was extremely low, so the data-link layer had to do more than merely transmit the information—it had to check up to make sure that the information arrived intact and retransmit anything that didn't.

How does the data-link protocol know when information has arrived intact? It certainly doesn't peruse your text when you are transferring—for instance, source code for some program—and say to itself, "That code is doing a jump into a table. That can't be right. Maybe the information got garbled somehow." People have the same problem when they talk to one another. If you hear someone say, "Your fish jumps chocolate books," you'd assume you didn't hear correctly, and ask for a retransmission. People have never completely solved the problem of ensuring that a message is received correctly. As any parent knows, the message "Go to sleep now" is often misreceived as "Feel free to jump on your bed." Computers have significantly less CPU power to invest in analyzing the information and the information is far less constrained than messages between human beings. So how can a very simple, efficient program on a computer detect that a message has gotten garbled?

One possible method is to have the transmitter send everything twice, and compare. But this is inefficient (requires sending twice as much information) and, surprisingly, not a very good method of checking for errors, since some kinds of errors could be transmission errors with compensating errors that would not be detected with that checksum.

A more complicated error detection code is known as a *cyclic redundancy check* (CRC). The basic idea behind the CRC is that the message is treated like a giant number. Then there's another number, agreed to beforehand by the receiver and transmitter, known for obscure reasons as the *CRC polynomial*. Basically the message is divided by the CRC polynomial and the remainder is appended to the message. The receiver does the same division and if the math checks out, the receiver assumes the message arrived OK. Of course, it's not really numbers. In the correct and obscure terminology, the message is treated like a polynomial with coefficients in the Galois field of order 2. Think of the message as a really big number, the CRC polynomial as a reasonably sized number (say 32 bits or 64 bits), and the CRC itself as the remainder when the CRC polynomial is divided into the message. This gives the intuition behind CRCs. I assume none of you will ever have to compute a CRC. If you do, you can look up the details in another book.

You can be even fancier than an error *detection* code. There are error *correcting* codes that not only detect that the message was garbled, but can often fix the message (if only a few bits were garbled). Error correcting codes are a lot bigger than CRCs and are more difficult to compute. They are appropriate for high-delay links, such as satellite links, where it is worth the extra CPU and bandwidth overhead to have a more complex code if it prevents the necessity (and cost and delay) of retransmitting some of the garbled packets.

3.3 Packet boundaries

A message is just a sequence of bits. The physical layer allows transmission of a sequence of bits. How can you tell where one packet ends and the next begins? Here are two examples. The first is *byte stuffing* and is used by *binary synchronous communications* (BISYNC, also abbreviated BSC). The second is *bit stuffing* and is used by SDLC and *high-level data-link control* (HDLC).

BISYNC was an early data-link protocol. It assumed the message was a sequence of bytes (not bits), and marked the beginning and end of a message with special characters. Let's say that the beginning of a message was marked by the special character BOM, and the end marked by a special character EOM, which would be some byte values that do not appear in text. It's actually a little more complicated than that with BISYNC, since there's a marker for the beginning of the header, and a different marker for the beginning of the message. But that level of detail is not appropriate for this chapter.

Sometimes the message was printable text, in which case the BISYNC control characters could not appear in the message. But sometimes what was being transmitted was arbitrary data. In those cases, if the same byte as a control character happened to appear inside the data it had to be disguised so as not to trick the receiver into mistaking it for a control character. BISYNC accomplished this with a special character known as *data-link escape* (DLE, 10 hex). When the data was binary data, the control characters became two character sequences. Instead of merely transmitting *start of text* (STX), you'd transmit DLE STX. Instead of transmitting *end of text* (ETX), you'd transmit DLE ETX. If STX or ETX appeared in the data, there was no problem, provided that the previous byte was not the value for DLE. So BISYNC merely had to protect itself from a byte of data that equaled DLE. This was done by having the transmitter add an extra DLE to any DLE that appeared in the data (byte stuffing). The receiver, when it received a DLE, would check the next character. If it was another DLE, the receiver deleted one of the DLEs and treated the sequence as a received data byte whose value happened to equal DLE.

SDLC and HDLC use a different method for delimiting messages. This method assumes a message is a sequence of bits (rather than bytes), and uses the bit sequence 01111110 to mark the beginning and end of a message. It has to ensure that this sequence of bits does not occur inside the data. It does this by having the transmitter insert a 0 bit following any occurrence of five 1 bits in the data. The receiver, when it detects five 1 bits in a row, checks the next bit. If it's a 1, the receiver treats the sequence as a message delimiter. If it's a 0, the receiver treats the 0 as a *stuffed bit* and discards it.

3.4 *Reliable versus datagram protocols*

There are two categories of protocols. One is known as *reliable* and the other is known as *datagram*. A reliable protocol makes sure that every piece of information arrives intact. If one piece of information gets lost, subsequent pieces of information will not be delivered until the protocol recovers the lost information. In contrast, a datagram protocol is a best effort service. If a piece of information is lost, the protocol doesn't worry about it—it just continues on, delivering new stuff. It assumes that, if necessary, some layer above it will notice and handle the problem. There are times when each type of protocol is appropriate, and there are times when it's not obvious which is the best choice.

In the case of an error-prone link, it is usually preferable to have a reliable protocol. There are many applications (such as file transfer) in which missing information is intolerable. However, it is not necessary to have reliable protocols at every layer in order to give the application a reliable method of transferring data. For instance, it is possible to have a datagram data-link layer and a datagram network layer, and a reliable transport layer. There are some applications (for instance, packet voice) which tolerate lost data and prefer giving up on lost information rather than incurring the delay necessary for the transmitter to discover the information lost and retransmit it. In these cases a datagram protocol is more appropriate.

A datagram protocol is very simple: each message is packaged with an error detection code; if the error detection code detects an error, the message is discarded.

A reliable protocol typically involves having the transmitter add extra information to the message, such as a message number or sequence number. The receiver sends back an acknowledgment (ack), indicating which message it received, as shown in figure 3.1.

That's the general idea, but there are problems with this scheme. How big is the message number field? What happens if it maxes out? What happens if a message or an ack is lost? Further, it's inefficient to wait for an ack for every packet.

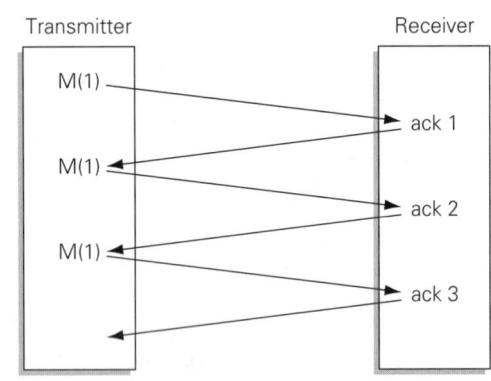

Figure 3.1 Reliable protocol messages and acknowledgments

A typical solution to these problems is to use a *sliding window protocol.* The message number field in such protocols is set to a finite-sized field, say 1 byte (which can represent values up to 255). When it reaches the maximum value it wraps around. That is, the message number would start at 0, increase by 1 each time up to 255, and then the next message would be numbered 0 again.

Further, in a sliding window protocol, the transmitter is allowed a window of unacknowledged packets. For instance, if the window is 10, then the transmitter can start by sending 10 packets in a row. If the transmitter receives an ack for message number n, it can send through message $n + 10$.

What happens if a message or an ack is lost? The transmitter needs to have a timer, and if an ack is not received for message n before the timer goes off, the transmitter will start retransmitting from message n.

Another optimization is having the ack be cumulative. In other words, the receiver does not need to send an ack for every single packet. If the receiver receives a clump of messages, say messages 25, 26, 27, and 28, and the last ack it sent was for message 24, then the receiver can merely send ack(28), and the transmitter will assume messages 25, 26, and 27 also arrived fine.

A further optimization is the ability to send a negative acknowledgment (nak). If the receiver has received message n properly and then it receives a garbled message (one in which the CRC indicates that a transmission error occurred), the receiver can send nak($n + 1$). Then the transmitter does not need to wait for its timer to go off before retransmitting the lost information. The receiver might also send a nak for message n if it receives message $n + 1$ and has not received message n. Most data-link layers do not misorder packets, so receipt of message $n + 1$ without having yet received message n is a good indication that message n was lost.

Usually conversations are *full duplex,* which means that both sides can be transmitting as well as receiving information at the same time. (Conversations in which sending and receiving of information cannot be done simultaneously are called *half duplex flip-flop.*) In such cases there are really two conversations going on, one in which one end is the receiver and the other is the transmitter, and the other in which the ends play the opposite roles.

It is usually more efficient, if one side is sending a message, to *piggyback* acknowledgment information onto the message being sent, rather than sending an extra packet as the acknowledgment. For this reason, most data-link protocols have a field in the header of a data message that indicates the number of the message being acknowledged.

3.5 Connection-oriented versus connectionless protocols

There's another major philosophical difference in the design of protocols. Some are *connection-oriented* and some are not. A connection-oriented protocol is one in which, before data can be transferred, the parties involved in the conversation must set up *state*. This is similar to making a telephone call. Before you can talk, you have to dial the number and wait for the person at the other end to answer. In contrast, a *connectionless* protocol is similar to mailing a letter. Each letter is an independent chunk of communication. You just give it to the post office which will know what to do with it.

The concept of connections is not entirely independent of the concept of reliability in a protocol, since a reliable protocol really has to be connection-oriented, at least to some degree. However, it is possible to build connection-oriented protocols that are not reliable.

It might seem that connection without reliability is the worst of both worlds. You have to go through the overhead of setting up a connection, and you don't get reliability. Why would anyone want to do that? It turns out to be exactly the right thing to do in many cases. For instance, for convenience of address assignment it is useful to have large, complex addresses, but it might be difficult to build packet switches that can parse large addresses at high speeds. So the solution, termed *label swapping*, is to calculate a path by setting up a connection first, to assign the connection a short conversation number, and to have the packet switches merely remember the forwarding direction for the conversation number.

Another example of a nonreliable, connection-oriented data-link protocol is *Point-to-Point Protocol* (PPP, RFC 1661), which reliably establishes communication between neighbors on a point-to-point link so that if one crashes and restarts, the other will know. During connection setup, the neighbors agree on the parameters of the communication. However, data packets are not numbered or acknowledged.

Reliable data-link protocols need to be connection-oriented so that communicating parties can be synchronized about message numbers. The assumption is that a computer can crash and restart without knowledge of what it was doing previously. So if A and B are communicating and B sends message 1 to A and then crashes, restarts, and sends messages 0 and 1 to A, and then receives A's ack (as a result of message 1 that A received before the crash), then B will falsely assume its new messages have arrived intact.

For this reason, reliable data-link protocols start out with a handshake, where one end says "I'd like to start a conversation," and the other side responds, "OK." Actually, this exchange usually consists of three messages ("I want to start a fresh connection," "OK," "I heard your OK"), so it is known as a *three-way handshake*.

3.6 Multiaccess links

Sometimes a single wire can connect multiple stations. But stations cannot be carrying on simultaneous conversations. If A sends a packet to B at exactly the same time C is sending a packet to D, the result will be a jumbled mess and neither B nor D will read the message correctly. For this reason there must be a mechanism for stations to take turns using the wire. Ideally the mechanism will be both efficient and fair.

3.6.1 Multipoint links

Early multiaccess links were known as *multipoint* links, and involved having one station act as a master, with all the remainder being slaves. As shown in figure 3.2, the master gave permission for each station to talk, and packets were either sent from a slave to the master, or vice versa. Packets were not transmitted directly between slaves. In such a case two slave stations are not really neighbors, but each slave is a neighbor with the master.

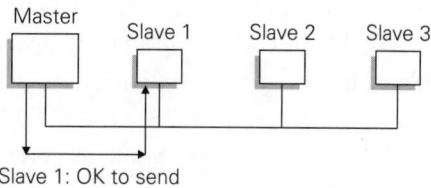

Figure 3.2   Multipoint wiring

Typically link sharing is done by having the master poll the slaves. "OK, Alice, your turn to talk now if you have anything to say." Because information is directed to a specific slave, the packet has to explicitly say which slave is to receive the packet. So, in addition to a message number in the header, there is an address. When the master transmits the packet, the address indicates which slave is to receive the packet. When a slave transmits a packet, the address indicates which slave transmitted it.

Some data-link protocols (e.g., HDLC and SDLC) were designed around multipoint links, and even when it is used on a point-to-point link (a wire between two machines) it retains the complexity that was only necessary to negotiate link sharing. The endpoints are not equals; rather one end must become the master and the other the slave. It doesn't affect the protocol very much—it is possible to do full duplex communication—but the header fields leave room for addresses (which aren't necessary when there are only two stations on a wire), and the initialization sequence is harder to understand than it would have been had the protocol been designed for two-part, peer-to-peer communication.

3.6.2 SDLC

Introduced by IBM in the early 1970s, SDLC was the first data-link protocol designed for IBM's SNA. SNA was one of the first architectures to divide the handling of data communications into multiple protocol layers, of which the data link is found in the lower layers.

Using the terms previously defined, SDLC can be described as a multiaccess, multipoint, reliable connection-oriented protocol. It uses bit-stuffing, CRC error checking, and sliding window acknowledgments. Many of the concepts first introduced in SDLC were later used in other data-link protocols, such as X.25's *link access protocol-balanced* (HDLC/LAPB), ISDN's *link access procedure on D channel* (LAPD) and the *logical link control type 2* (LLC2) protocol used for connection-oriented Institute of Electrical and Electronics Engineers (IEEE) 802 LAN data links.

SDLC is used to communicate between multiple SNA devices or PUs. In SNA, PU once meant only the software representation of a single physical piece of hardware. Today, because of the increased capacity of computers, many SNA PUs can be contained in a single piece of hardware such as a PC or communication controller.

Each PU represents a single SDLC link station. SDLC is a multipoint protocol but is also used in SNA for point-to-point lines. In SDLC, a single link station acts as the primary or master station and all other link stations act as secondaries. The role of primary and secondary stations may be predetermined by device type, configured, or, for some PU types, negotiated at link start-up time.

The initial main purpose of SDLC was to replace BISYNC for host-to-3270 terminal communications. Later additions to SDLC include NCP-to-remote-NCP communication and host-to-remote-NCP communication.

In the late 1980s, IBM added more peer-to-peer capability to SDLC by introducing Type 2.1 nodes communication. In node Type 2.1 communication, either side of a two-way communication negotiates roles (primary or secondary) and miscellaneous data-link layer parameters for the connection. This is accomplished via exchanging XID (eXchange ID) messages containing informational and negotiable data-link parameters. Once the XID exchanges are complete, one side assumes the role of primary and the other side assumes the secondary role. This version of SDLC was first introduced with APPC and is currently used in IBM's APPN architecture.

Other features such as group addressing to reduce polling overhead and full-duplex communications options were eventually added to SDLC for improved host-to-host and host-to-gateway communications.

With all of these extensions and enhancements, most SDLC lines today still carry PU2 3270 half-duplex data on point-to-point or multipoint lines, and probably will for many years.

SDLC has been a very successful protocol. Figure 3.3 shows some of the connectivity options available in SDLC, which is usually represented as a lightning jag line.

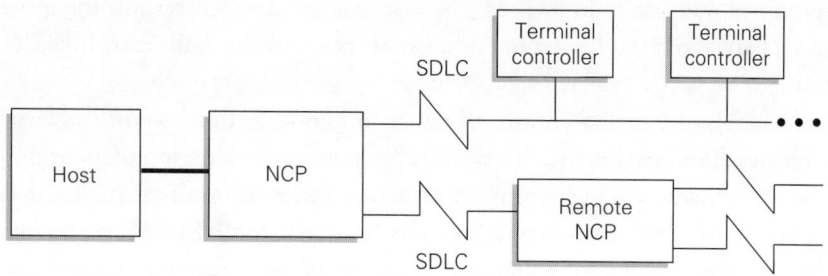

Figure 3.3 Synchronous data-link control

In networking technologies where SDLC was inappropriate, IBM integrated SNA into those architectures by replacing the SDLC data-link layer with a connection-oriented data link, network, or transport protocol. This was necessary since the SNA architecture requires a connection-oriented error-corrected protocol in the underlying link in order to function properly. One example of this integration of new subnetwork technologies is SNA's use of LLC type 2 in IEEE 802 LANs and frame relay networks. Another is its use of TCP/IP to act as a link protocol in DLSw to carry SNA across TCP/IP networks.

3.6.3 LANs

A LAN is a means of interconnecting many stations so that they are all equal and all neighbors. Just as with multipoint technology, it is necessary to have a mechanism to ensure that stations don't clobber each other's packets by transmitting at inopportune times.

Since any station on a LAN can transmit to any other station, there need to be two addresses in the header. One is for the station that transmitted; the other indicates who is supposed to receive the packet.

In LAN technology, every station sees every packet. The interface to the LAN is designed to be smart about not sending every packet on the wire to its station, since most stations have better things to do than look at traffic for some other node. Some stations, like traffic monitors or bridges, do need to listen to every packet on the wire. This is known as *listening promiscuously.*

Unicast and multicast LAN addresses   Because every packet is capable of being received simultaneously by all stations on the wire, LANs offer the capability of addressing a packet so that multiple stations will receive the packet. The destination address can either be an address of a specific station or an address that is listened to by any subset of the stations. A specific station address is known as a *unicast* address. An address intended to include a group of stations is known as a *multicast* address. Each station independently informs its hardware as to the set of addresses (unicast and/or multicast) it wishes to receive.

One specific address set aside to mean *all stations* is known as the *broadcast* address. The idea of such an address makes little sense in today's multiprotocol, internetworking world. There is no protocol that all stations implement, so there is no single packet that makes sense to be received by all stations. Many protocols that run on LANs were written without their designers having the slightest premonition that other protocols might also exist in the world—these protocols use the broadcast address since, for their designers, *all stations implementing IP* must be equivalent to *all stations*. IP isn't the only protocol that has had the arrogance to use the broadcast address. Appletalk, NetBIOS, IPX, and some ill-conceived cooperative game programs also use the broadcast address. Using the broadcast address will impact performance, since the broadcast address is really a multicast address that must be shared by many protocols. Preferably, protocols choose a multicast address to obtain a unique address and all packets transmitted with that address as the destination *are* for that protocol.

Ideally the interface hardware would allow you to specify the set of addresses you'd like to receive. Unfortunately, most LAN chips on the market do not allow you to do that. Some are sufficiently stupid that you must either specify a single address or you have to listen promiscuously. Some allow you to specify a single unicast address, but then you either have to listen to all multicast traffic or none. Some others allow you to listen to only one unicast address plus the broadcast address (which gives some logic to the protocols that use the broadcast address, since there would be no other way to operate with those chips). Others allow you to specify a small number of unicast addresses and have a hashing algorithm for multicast addresses. You can specify which buckets you wish to receive. If some other protocol is using a multicast address that happens to hash into the same bucket as one you are using, then you have to look at those packets, decide they are not for you, and discard them.

The IEEE 802 committee standardizes various aspects of LANs. An IEEE 802 address is 48 bits long. This might seem excessive since none of the LAN technology allows more than perhaps thousands of stations to be on a single link or broadcast domain. The reason they standardized on such a large address was for ease of use. The idea is that a manufacturer obtains a range of addresses from the IEEE and uses a unique address for each station it manufactures. Each station contains a *read-only memory* (ROM) so that it knows its own address. You simply buy a station from your local discount department store, plug it into a LAN, and it works. You don't have to tell it an address to use.

You can also determine the vendor from the address: Addresses come in blocks of 2^{24} (16,777,216). That means that IEEE gives the manufacturer addresses in blocks of 3 bytes of constant (known as the *organizationally unique identifier*, OUI), and the manufacturer assigns the remaining 3 bytes uniquely to each interface card. One bit is reserved to indicate whether the address is a unique address obtained from IEEE, or whether it's obtained by some other means. If you use an address obtained from IEEE, then you can be assured that no other station can (legally) use that address. If you obtain your addresses some other way, you're on your own.

Multicast addresses are generally distinguished from unicast addresses by one of the bits. That is, an address with the multicast bit on is a multicast address. If that bit is off, the address is for an individual station. This allows 2^{46} multicast addresses. The reason it's 46 rather than 48 is that one bit is reserved to indicate whether the address is multicast or unicast, and another bit, as noted above, is reserved to indicate whether the address is obtained from IEEE.

Unfortunately, for some reason, many of the chips for 802.5 (token rings) were not capable of receiving multicast addresses in this way. Instead, they constrained multicast addresses to having a single bit on. For example, you could tell your interface, "Give me everything with bit 5 on." This constrained form of multicast address is a *functional address*. Functional addresses make it difficult to work over 802.5 LANs (with the current chip sets), since so few group addresses are available—46 functional addresses, rather than 2^{46} multicast addresses.

Several types of LAN technology exist. By far, however, the leading LANs are 802.3 (ethernet) and 802.5 (token ring).

Token ring   In a token ring, stations are wired together into a big circuit. Instead of having a master station poll them one by one and giving them permission to transmit, as on multipoint links, a particular bit pattern known as the *token* circulates around the ring, forwarded from station to station. When a station receives an open token, it has permission to transmit a packet and the token is busy. After successfully transmitting the packet, the station regenerates the open token.

One station (monitor) takes on a special role in the ring, for instance to notice if the token gets lost or corrupted and to regenerate it in that case. Often token rings are designed so all stations are equivalent. Even in the case where one station is a master (serves as a monitor), any of the stations can serve as master (standby monitors) if necessary, and one is dynamically chosen among the stations that are alive.

Token rings are usually wired in a star configuration, but the token always moves in a logical ring. Figure 3.4 shows the physical star and logical ring concept. A token ring is usually represented as a circle or oval with workstations attached to it.

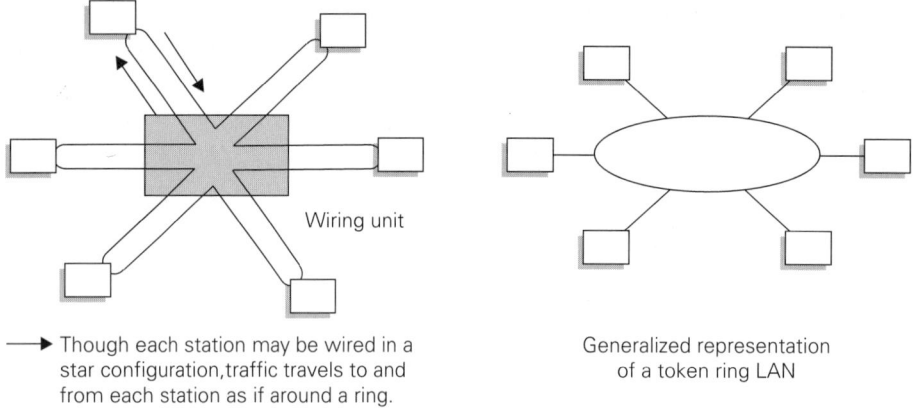

Though each station may be wired in a star configuration,traffic travels to and from each station as if around a ring.

Generalized representation of a token ring LAN

Figure 3.4   Token ring physical star and logical ring

CSMA/CD (ethernet)   IEEE 802.3 is called CSMA/CD. The first commercial CSMA/CD LAN was known as the Ethernet and many people continue to call the technology ethernet, since it's a nicer name than CSMA/CD. The official ethernet, as standardized by Digital, Intel, and Xerox (DIX Ethernet), had a slightly different packet header than the CSMA/CD LAN standardized by the IEEE 802.3 committee. The hardware is compatible, and the two formats can coexist on the LAN. It is even possible for a particular station to choose, on a packet-by-packet basis, which format to use, and be capable of receiving either format.

CSMA/CD technology is based on *contention*, differentiating it from a token-based technology. *Multiple access* means that more than two stations can coexist on the wire. Anyone who wants to transmit does so and hopes for the best. But stations are polite and first listen to hear if someone else is transmitting (*carrier sense*). If so, they do not initiate transmission. A collision happens when two stations, sensing the wire was idle, transmit at almost the same time. Both stations realize a collision has happened (*collision detection)* and back off for a random period of time before retransmitting. Surprisingly, this technology works quite well.

Since 802.3/ethernet LANs operate as a bus, they are usually depicted as a line with workstations attached to it, as shown in figure 3.5. With newer LAN hubs and switches, an Ethernet network may actually be star wired, but the logical topology still acts as a bus.

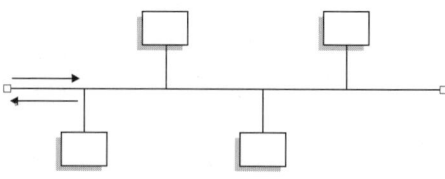

Figure 3.5   802.3/Ethernet topology

To alleviate the bandwidth constraints recently faced by some of the modern client/server applications, new (or rather modified) technologies are gaining popularity. In addition to the ATM switching, quite often the natural migration path for shared token ring/Ethernet LANs is to migrate into a switched token ring/ethernet, where the entire bandwidth is preserved for a single station.

3.7 Multiprotocol operation

People speak many languages. When someone walks up to you and says something, how do you know what language they are speaking? It is possible that the sequence of sounds in one language that means "Can you please tell me what time it is?" might mean "Your house is on fire!" in another. People somehow muddle along. It doesn't take many syllables before it is obvious whether someone is speaking a language you understand or not.

With computers, the situation is not as simple. A packet is just a bunch of bits. Packets are usually encoded reasonably efficiently, so that most bit patterns can be interpreted as a legal packet in most protocols. And computers (unlike most humans) do not possess common sense.

There are many protocol suites that operate over a data-link layer, including SNA, IP, IPX, *Digital Equipment Corp. network* (DECNET—also called *DEC network architecture* or DNA), *connectionless network protocol* (CLNP), and AppleTalk. Suppose a station has implemented multiple protocols or it has implemented a protocol that uses the broadcast address (and therefore it might receive packets for other protocols that use that address). How can the station know how to interpret the packet?

Maybe we're extraordinarily lucky and if we were to lay out the packet formats for all the popular protocols, there would be no sequence of bits that could be interpreted ambiguously. Dream on!

Maybe all protocol designers are very conscientious and aware of their place in the world, that is, that their protocol is only one protocol in a multiprotocol world. Maybe all protocol designers carefully peruse the packet formats of all existing protocols to ensure that the packets they are designing cannot be confused with any other protocols. That's an even more outrageous dream than pure luck!

So we really need help from the data-link layer. A data-link layer protocol ought to provide a field that indicates which protocol the packet is. Ideally the designers of data link protocols would assign values to the protocols, so that each has a unique value.

Unfortunately, many data-link protocols (such as HDLC) do not provide such a field. In those cases, some proprietary mechanism must be devised for adding such a field, usually as a new layer of header between the HDLC header and the data, as shown in figure 3.6.

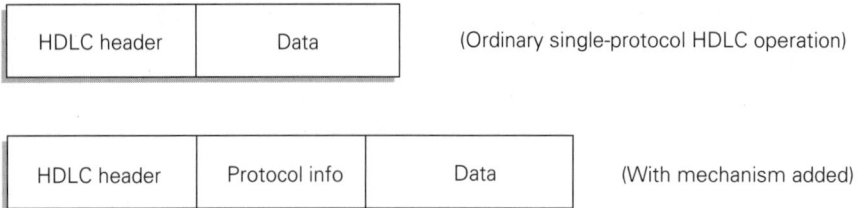

Figure 3.6 Protocol-identifying header

The original ethernet protocol had a 2-byte protocol-type field for which Xerox gave out values. With 2 bytes, there were probably enough values (65,536) so that anyone inventing yet another protocol could get one. When the IEEE committee standardized LANs, however, it decided, instead of a single field for which someone would give out values, there would be a separate 1-byte field for the source and destination, each known as a *service access point* (SAP). Then it would not be necessary to assign values for SAPs. Those in charge of a machine could number the protocols inside their own machine however they liked. This would place a limit of 256 protocols in any one machine, although it does not limit the total number of protocols that might be implemented in other machines.

Unfortunately, there were no good proposed mechanisms for how to make this work. How do you know, before sending protocol X packet to machine M, what to use as the SAP value on M's machine? IEEE couldn't assign the SAP values the same way Ethernet protocol type values were assigned because IEEE only had 1 byte (256 values), which was probably not enough to give unique values to everyone who needed one. If IEEE did that, on a first-come, first-served basis, then it would not be fair (and IEEE might even be sued) if anyone had to be denied a value because the numbers had run out.

To make assigned values of SAP even scarcer, IEEE set aside two of the bits in the same spirit as the 48-bit IEEE address. One bit indicated whether the SAP was assigned by IEEE or assigned by some other mechanism and the other reserved bit indicated whether it was a group or an individual SAP. Apparently, the committee felt that if a group/individual bit was useful in an address it would be useful in an SAP. I disagree. The convention could be that, no matter what the actual value of the SAP, if multiple processes requested receipt of packets for that SAP, the data-link layer would replicate a packet for that SAP and give it to each of the requesting processes.

In any case, this left only 64 SAP values that IEEE could assign—6 bits or 64 values. Clearly, with only 64 values, they could not assign a value to every company's protocol. IEEE did assign a few values, primarily for the most popular protocols such as SNA, and then left the rest to be locally assigned. Ironically, those protocols which received an IEEE-assigned value for the SAP really treated the SAP as a protocol-type field. The *destination SAP* (DSAP) and *source SAP* (SSAP) fields were both set to be the IEEE-assigned value. Protocols that did not receive one of the 64 remaining values were left with an awkward problem. They could choose one of the locally assigned SAP numbers, or even assume that there were 128 locally assigned values up for grabs (if they didn't care about the group bit in the SAP), or they could try an independent approach.

Someone came up with a clever idea: select a single SAP value to mean the header is extended to include a protocol type. This SAP value came to be known as the *subnetwork access protocol* (SNAP) SAP. If the SNAP SAP value (AA hex), appears in the DSAP field (and will presumably also appear in the SSAP field), this means that the header is extended to include a 5-byte protocol-type field, which is big enough for anyone who needs one to get a value. In fact, it might seem ridiculously large. Five bytes was chosen as an odd number (to make the total header length even) and to be large enough to be easily administered. Instead of needing to hand out protocol-type numbers separately, anyone with an OUI (because of having purchased an address block) could use that OUI as the first 3 bytes of any protocol type.

A convention was made for protocols that already had a 2-byte ethernet type to fit into the 802 structure. The OUI consisting of 3 bytes of 0 was set aside to indicate that the final 2 bytes of protocol type consists of an ethernet type.

To summarize, there are several possible conventions for differentiating protocols on various data links:

- For data links that follow the IEEE 802 convention for protocol demultiplexing, there are several possible choices:
  - The protocol might have a globally assigned SAP value.
  - The protocol might use a locally assigned SAP value and hope that nobody else uses that value.
  - The protocol could use the SNAP SAP and obtain a 5-byte protocol type.
  - The protocol could use the SNAP SAP and use a 2-byte ethernet protocol type padded with 3 bytes of 0.
- For data links that do not follow the 802 convention:
  - Some (like PPP) have their own protocol types defined, in which case a protocol would need to obtain one of the values to run on top of that data link.
  - Other data links (like HDLC) do not define any mechanism for protocol demultiplexing. In this case, the usual procedure is to use the 802 conventions (DSAP, SSAP, or SNAP SAP plus protocol type) as the first part of what the data link would consider the data field.

3.8 Overview of data-link protocols

Protocols designed for point-to-point links include:

- *BISYNC* BISYNC is an early reliable connection-oriented protocol still in use today. Its disadvantages include low throughput due to allowing the transmitter to send only one packet before getting an ack and low reliability due to the fact that acknowledgments are not error-controlled packets but merely single-character sequences (an ack for message 1 is only 1 bit different from an ack for message 0).

- *HDLC/SDLC/LAPB* HDLC, SDLC, and LAPB are reliable, connection-oriented protocols. These are all similar in that they do bit-stuffing for transparency and provide for point-to-point or multipoint operation. SDLC is the underlying data link for most of the SNA networks installed today, though an increasing percent include LANs.

- *Digital Data Communication Protocol (DDCMP)* (DDCMP)is a reliable, connection-oriented protocol. The chief difference between DDCMP and the HDLC family is that DDCMP includes in the header the length of the packet, so that bit stuffing is not required.

On LANs, the data-link protocol is known as Logical Link Control (LLC). If datagram data-link protocols had been sufficient to meet all needs, the LLC layer would not have been invented. However, some people wanted a connection-oriented data-link layer also, to support protocols such as SNA that require one. The 802 committee therefore specified an additional layer of protocol on top of what was provided by the LAN. LLC type 1 is simply a datagram service and does not really add anything to the LAN header. LLC type 2 basically adds HDLC header information to the packet to provide a reliable, connection-oriented service.

The distinction between network-layer protocols (layer 3) and data-link protocols (layer 2) is often blurred. Often what seems like an entire network to the provider is used as a method of coordinating components in a larger network. The following are examples of protocols that are usually provided by a cloud that looks like a mesh network inside and are often treated simply as a multiaccess link by attached stations:

- *X.25* A reliable, connection-oriented protocol
- *Frame relay* An unreliable, connection-oriented protocol
- *SMDS* A connectionless, datagram protocol
- *ATM* An unreliable, connection-oriented protocol.

ATM is a lower layer than the data-link layer and provides for sending small packets known as *cells,* which are each 53 bytes long. It was designed so that applications like voice would not incur delay by having to wait while a relatively long packet was transmitted. What stations generally see is not simply ATM but rather a layer built upon ATM, known as an *adaptation layer.*

3.9 Bridges

I believe the best way to understand bridges is as a historical accident. The data-link layer is supposed to carry information between directly connected stations. Routers, which operate in the network layer, are supposed to create a path through a network of interconnected links. A bridge is also designed to create a path through a network of interconnected links. The difference is that a bridge is supposed to operate at the data-link layer rather than at the network layer. Why was there a need for bridges, since the network layer was already defined for creating multihop paths?

It all happened because of LANs. Perhaps because the acronym stands for local area *network*, many implementers designed their protocol as if the LAN were the entire network. In order to cooperate with a router, a station has to implement a network layer protocol. But, perhaps assuming that LANs made the network layer obsolete, implementers designed their stations without a network layer.

In reality, a LAN *is* a limited environment and people do want protocols confined to a single LAN. But stations designed without a network layer could not use routers to forward packets between LANs.

What does it mean for a station to implement a network layer protocol? It means additional control information (a network layer header) is attached to packets with information such as a hop count to detect lost packets and addresses designed to give hints as to location. It also means there is a protocol for the network to inform the station of illegally formed packets, unreachable destinations, and other problems.

What the world wanted was a magic box that would act like a router despite the fact that people did not design their stations to work with routers. Two competing standards emerged, one known as a transparent bridge, the other a source routing bridge.

3.9.1 Transparent bridge

The *transparent bridge* acts like a station on two or more LANs. It listens promiscuously, stores each received packet, and forwards it onto the other LANs when, as a station, it has permission to send. To cut down on unnecessarily forwarded packets (for instance when the transmitter and receiver are on the same LAN), the bridge learns the location

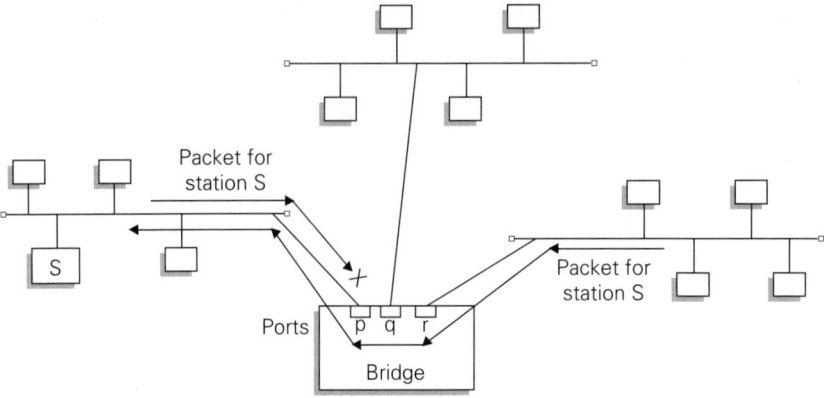

If station S has sent any traffic, bridge knows station S is through port p.
Packets destined for station S will be sent through port p.
However, traffic for station S *from* port p will be ignored by the bridge,
because the packet will reach S directly on the LAN.

Figure 3.7   Transparent bridge

of stations and does not forward packets that it knows it does not need to. For instance, if it has received a packet with *source* address S from port p and later receives a packet with *destination* address S, it then forwards the packet only to port p, as shown in figure 3.7. If the packet was received from port p, the bridge does not forward the packet at all, since the bridge knows that S is also on that network.

This simple idea allows interconnection of LANs with no cooperation from the end stations, but it is disastrous if there are loops in the topology. Therefore, a simple protocol was added to the bridges known as the *spanning tree protocol*. Only bridges participate in the spanning tree protocol, which runs continuously, finding a loop-free subset of the topology. The tree computed by the spanning tree algorithm is the path upon which data packets are forwarded. If the topology changes, the bridges compute a new spanning tree.

3.9.2 Source-routing bridges

Source-routing bridges are not really bridges at all because they require the stations to implement a protocol that is easily as complex as a network-layer protocol, and it involves extra control information in each packet. However, since the IEEE 802 committee that standardized source-routing bridges was chartered to do data-link layer protocols, the standard became known as a bridge rather than a router.

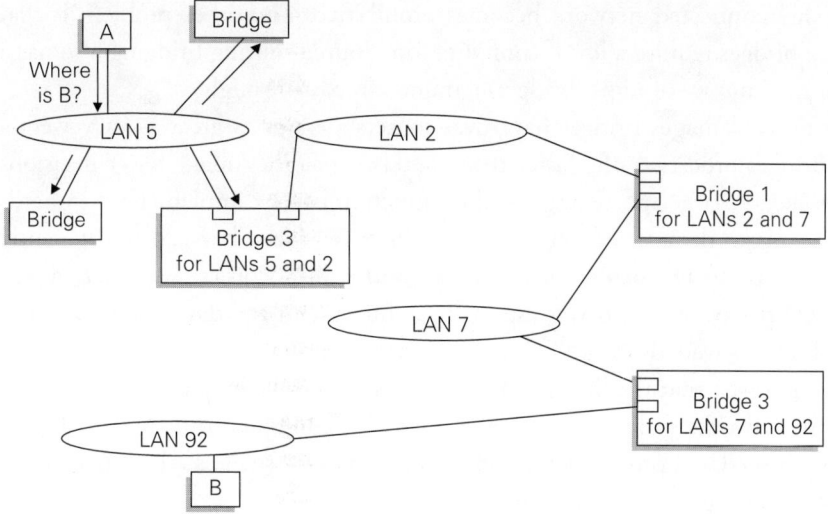

→ All-paths explorer packet is propagated to all bridges. Responses contain path.
Route from A to B: LAN 5, bridge 3, LAN 2, bridge 1, LAN 7, bridge 3, LAN 92

Figure 3.8 Source-routing bridges

A station must add extra control information to each data packet which contains a route. A route consists of an alternating sequence specifying bridges and LANs. A LAN is specified by a 12-bit number. A bridge is specified by a 4-bit number which is of local significance to the pair of LANs specified before and after the bridge number in the route. For instance, as shown in figure 3.8, if the route consists of LAN 5, bridge 3, LAN 2, bridge 1, LAN 7, bridge 3, LAN 92, the first *bridge 3* is not the same as the *bridge 3* specified later in the route.

How does station A know the route to station B? It discovers the route by using a special packet known as an *all-paths explorer* packet, which collects a diary of its travels, and creates copies of itself whenever there is a choice of routes. The recipient of the many copies of an all-paths explorer packet then has a choice of routes from the source to itself.

3.9.3 Problems and advantages of bridges

Bridges are not an ideal solution to the problem of LAN interconnection. Transparent bridges have the problem that routes are constrained to a spanning tree, and tree computation after a topology change can be slow in some circumstances. Source-routing bridges have two problems. The most serious problem is that each all-paths explorer packet spawns an enormous number of copies, so the overhead of route discovery in a reasonably richly connected network becomes prohibitive. The other problem is that source-routing bridges require a lot of configuration. Source-routing bridging also has a limitation for the number of hops (bridges) a frame can pass through.

Most of the advantages bridges have over routers are not as great as they were a decade ago. Bridges process traffic faster than routers, since they make fewer decisions about each packet. A larger percentage of their function can be implemented in hardware, which increases their speed. They can be less expensive. They can transparently carry multiple-transport protocols, whereas most routing protocols are specific to a particular transport protocol, which was especially significant in the days before efficient multiprotocol routers were developed.

I believe, however, that the limitations of bridges outweigh their advantages as networks and internetworks scale into very large, complex configurations. More efficient emerging data-link-related protocols for high-speed networks, such as ATM, may offset some of these limitations.

3.10 Summary

This chapter has covered how the data-link layer can detect and handle garbled information, generally by the use of CRCs. Also noted was how boundaries are recognized, usually with a beginning-of-message and end-of-message character or sequence. Bit stuffing or byte stuffing is used to avoid confusion of the message characters that occur within a message.

For the purposes of this discussion, we defined reliable protocols (with acknowledgments) and datagram protocols (without acknowledgments) and noted there are some applications which tolerate lost data better than the delay of error detection and retransmission. The examination of reliable protocols reveals the general use of an algorithm, such as the sliding window, to send traffic more efficiently, as well as the ack timer, cumulative acks, naks, and piggyback acks.

Connection-oriented and connectionless protocols were defined as well. Connection-orientation is similar in concept to a telephone call, with a set-up and constant connection until termination of the session. By contrast, connectionless protocols can be compared with mailing a letter. Although connection-oriented protocols are usually reliable (through the use of acknowledgments) some connection-oriented protocols use datagrams, like label-swapping protocols (e.g., ATM) and PPP.

More complex applications of data-link protocols were also examined—multiaccess links, including multipoint networks are LANs. Early multipoint data-link protocols such as HDLC and SDLC require a master/slave arrangement (primary and secondaries) to manage the sharing of the link. In LANs, this is managed differently, with a peer orientation (i.e., no master) and special algorithms are used to handle sharing of the link.

LAN addressing was examined with three defined types: unicast, multicast, and broadcast. Several drawbacks were examined for broadcast addressing, particularly in multiprotocol environments because of the limitations inherent in the chip sets used in most LAN adapters.

In the multiprotocol environment, unfortunately, most network protocols do not consistently identify their protocol type. For this reason, most data-link protocols include, or have been adapted in practice to include, a protocol-type identifier. An example of this is the IEEE 802 data-link protocol use of the SAP field to inform the data link of the protocol process for delivery of the received packet. The SNAP SAP extends the number of possible destinations.

It was noted in this chapter that the IEEE 802 committee has defined two logical link control types—LLC1 for datagram service such as Ethernet, and LLC2 for connection-oriented services such as token ring. However, the distinction between the network-layer protocols and data-link layer protocols is often blurred and becoming less clear as many data-link protocols take on network layer functionality.

This blurring is particularly obvious as some bridges take on additional functionality. Source-routing bridges, for example, provide many functional services that extend almost to the same level of routers, but do so in a manner that can lead to inefficient use of network resources.

As networks advance, all that can be said with certainty is that no data-link technology has completely vanished from use. Therefore, despite brilliant innovations, the limitations of existing technologies will remain for years to come. On the bright side, the newer data-link protocols are taking into account large-scale internetworking and a healthy relationship with the upper layers.

chapter 4

SNA and APPN tutorial

Donald H. Czubek

Moving up the protocol stack, Donald H. Czubek's tutorial on the traditional (a.k.a. subarea) SNA and APPN/HPR describes formats and protocols, as well as key concepts, products, terminology and definitions. Originally designed, like most protocols, for an insular environment, it has nonetheless interacted with other protocols since its early days, carrying different transports across itself or being transported across them, incorporating different data links, and coexisting with different protocols.

4.1 Introduction

SNA is IBM's architecture for enterprise networking. SNA was originally introduced in 1974 to define a standard set of networking protocols and services that would be implemented across the IBM networking product line. SNA has since evolved into an industry standard for enterprise networking products.

Prior to the introduction of SNA, IBM's networking products implemented a variety of product-specific networking protocols. The protocols supported were simple synchronous or asynchronous data-link level protocols. Some of these protocols, such as IBM's BSC or BISYNC data-link protocols, were similar to one another, but incompatible. This made it difficult for IBM customers to move from one product line to another as their networks evolved.

Another limitation of the early communications protocols was that they only supported direct connections between devices over a single data link. Early enterprise networks used dedicated data links to connect terminals to mainframe computers. There was no real networking capability to allow network users to share resources such as wide-area data links. The role of SNA was to provide an architecture for building enterprise-wide networks using a single set of protocols and procedures.

4.1.1 The scope of SNA

SNA is a complete specification of all of the protocols and services required in an enterprise network. SNA can be contrasted with industry standards such as X.25 and frame relay which only define interfaces to networks and specify the services to be provided by the network. They do not provide all of the protocols and procedures used within the network.

The scope of SNA is similar to that of protocol suites such as TCP/IP and, to a greater degree, the networking protocols that have been developed within the OSI reference model.

4.1.2 The evolution of SNA

Since its introduction, SNA has evolved to meet the changing requirements of enterprise networking. The original design of SNA is a reflection of the enterprise computing environment that existed in the 1970s and still exists today in many organizations. In this environment, application programs run on mainframes located in the corporate data center and users access these applications through nonprogrammable terminals. While many of the nonprogrammable terminals have been replaced by PCs and workstations, the host-centric computing model is still widely used, particularly in large corporations.

The networks required to support this environment are hierarchical in structure with mainframe computers at the top of the hierarchy and the end user's terminals, personal computers, and workstations at the bottom. The style of SNA networking that is designed to support this environment is called *subarea* SNA networking.

In recent years networking technologies and end-user requirements have changed so radically that a new style of SNA networking—APPN—was developed by IBM. APPN is more than just an evolutionary step in the development of SNA; it is an almost completely new style of SNA networking. APPN is designed to take advantage of new LAN and WAN technologies and to support users of decentralized computing models such as client/server computing.

It should be noted that the two most important technologies shaping networks today—LANs and personal computers—did not exist through most of SNA's evolution. It is not surprising, therefore, that a fundamental redesign of SNA, and not just incremental changes, was appropriate. Of course, subarea SNA had been continuously and significantly enhanced and extended since its introduction in 1974.

Today there are two distinct styles of networking supported by SNA—subarea networking and APPN. Some features and functions are common to both styles of SNA networking while others are unique to either.

4.2 SNA functional layers

The protocols and services defined by SNA are described by a seven-layer functional model. This model is similar in scope to the OSI reference model. Figure 4.1 shows the functional layers defined by SNA.

The three lower layers of the SNA layering model make up the SNA transport network, also called the path-control network. The transport network provides the basic message delivery infrastructure of an SNA network. The upper four layers of SNA provide end-to-end protocols for communications between network users.

Transaction services	Provides basic application-level services such as distributed database and electronic mail.
Presentation services	Handles the mapping of end user data formats.
Data-flow control	Controls the end-to-end interactions between users. Provides end-to-end responses and protocols for logically grouping related data.
Transmission control	Provides a logical connection between a pair of users. Also provides a flow control protocol and, optionally, data encryption.
Path control	Routes messages across the network and segments or blocks messages for link-level transmission.
Data-link control	Provides reliable transmission of data over linksbetween adjacent nodes.
Physical control	Defines physical and electrical interfaces between adjacent nodes.

Figure 4.1   SNA seven-layer model

4.2.1 The physical control layer

The physical layer of SNA defines the mechanical and electrical interfaces between the nodes in the network and the data links that interconnect them.

In general, SNA employs industry-standard interfaces and protocols at the physical and data-link layers. Some examples of the industry-standard physical interfaces supported by SNA are RS-232, V.35, and X.21 for wide area networking. SNA also supports industry-standard LAN interfaces such as Ethernet, token ring, *fiber distributed data interface* (FDDI), and ATM.

4.2.2 The data-link control layer

Data-link control layer protocols control the transmission of data over individual LAN and WAN data links. SNA generally employs industry-standard data-link protocols such as *synchronous data-link control* (SDLC, compatible with HDLC) for wide-area networking and LAN technologies such as token ring and Ethernet. In addition to the standard data links are the local *channel* interfaces that provide connections to and between mainframes. These very high speed local channels are based on IBM technologies, though several other vendors implement channel technology or interface to it, for example, for LAN-to-mainframe communication.

4.2.3 The path control layer

The path control layer is responsible for forwarding messages from hop to hop across SNA networks. SNA subarea and APPN networks each use different routing technologies. Path control routing in both subarea and APPN networks is connection oriented. SNA's path control is similar to, but much more extensive in functionality than, TCP/IP's network layer protocol, IP, and similar to OSI's *connection-oriented network-layer service* (CONS) which are discussed in chapter 5.

4.2.4 The transmission control layer

The transmission control layer provides end-to-end connections, called *sessions*, which support communications between pairs of network users. The transmission control layer provides a flow control protocol called session pacing and it optionally supports the encryption of data to provide security.

4.2.5 The data-flow control layer

The data-flow control layer provides a set of protocols that can be used to manage the interactions between a pair of communicating end users. End-to-end response protocols are provided to indicate normal completion of requests or to inform the sender of exception conditions. A protocol called *chaining* for grouping logically related messages is provided. The *bracket* protocol can be used to delimit a logical conversation between a pair of end users.

4.2.6 The presentation layer

The presentation layer defines and maps the types of application data streams being exchanged by a pair of users. SNA defines several standard types of data streams, the most popular of which is the 3270 data stream. The presentation services layer also supports user-defined data streams.

4.2.7 The transaction services layer

Applications which provide network services reside within this layer, which today is sometimes called the application layer as in the OSI reference model. Software that provides application services such as electronic mail and remote database access reside within the transaction services layer.

4.3 Structure of SNA networks

SNA networks are made up of systems, called *nodes*, that are interconnected by *data links*. Each of the nodes implements a set of SNA protocols and functionality. SNA defines several categories of nodes and each of these node types supports a specific set of SNA functions and protocols.

One of the most fundamental differences between subarea networks and APPN networks is the types of nodes that can be supported in each type of network. They also differ in the ways that nodes can be interconnected. The nodes in subarea networks support hierarchical networking, while the nodes in APPN networks are designed to support decentralized, peer-to-peer networking.

The data links are LAN and WAN communications facilities that nodes use to communicate with one another. As discussed above, SNA generally uses industry-standard data-link technologies in addition to its own high-speed local channel interface.

SNA uses primarily SDLC protocols for communications over dedicated wide area data links. SDLC is compatible with the international standard HDLC protocol. Industry-standard packet switching interfaces including X.25 and frame relay are also supported.

SNA also supports IBM's local channel interfaces for connecting local nodes to mainframes. Both the parallel bus and tag channel and the newer *enterprise systems connection* (ESCON) technologies are supported by SNA.

SNA requires that its data links provide reliable message delivery, which is further discussed in chapter 3 on data-link technologies. While some other types of networking protocols such as TCP/IP can operate over either reliable or unreliable data links, SNA always requires reliable data links.

The data-link protocols used in SNA networks also require that link-level acknowledgments be received within a fixed time interval—usually several seconds. This can present problems when dedicated LAN and WAN data links are replaced by shared-access networks that cannot provide fixed-transit delays for messages. This situation occurs when SNA data is sent over packet switching networks or when SNA data is tunneled through TCP/IP internets.

4.3.1 The transport network

The lower three layers of the SNA functional layering model—physical control, data-link control, and path control—describe the networking services and protocols that provide the basic message forwarding infrastructure of SNA networks. These layers are collectively called the transport network.

The physical control and data-link control layers provide connections between adjacent nodes in an SNA network. These connections can be either LANs or WANs. SNA requires that the data-link services be connection-oriented and reliable.

The path control layer is responsible for routing messages from hop-to-hop across the SNA network. Subarea and APPN network use different addressing and routing techniques, but the level of service they each provide to the upper layers is similar.

4.3.2 Network accessible units

The SNA software components that support end-to-end communications are called *network accessible units* (NAUs), also called network addressable units. The top four layers of SNA are implemented within NAUs. These layers are the transmission control layer, the data-flow control layer, the presentation services layer, and the transaction services layer. The protocols implemented in the four layers are end-to-end protocols that are designed to support communications between a single pair of NAUs.

The NAU is defined as the implementation in software of these upper four layers and not as the physical hardware device itself in which they may be running. Usually more than one NAU is present in a single piece of computing or networking hardware.

The four types of NAUs found in SNA networks are:

- LU
- SCCP
- PU
- CP

These NAU types differ in the types of communications supported—end user or network management—and the types of SNA networks where they are used—subarea, APPN, or both.

Logical unit LUs are used in both subarea and APPN networks. LUs are the NAUs through which end users of the network communicate. That is, LUs are the software representation of the end user in a network. In SNA, an end user may be any item at the end of a network that makes use of the network, such as a human at a terminal, an application on a host, or a printer. In APPN networks, LUs are also used to support network management functions, while in SNA, LUs are used only for end-user communication and other NAUs in the device handle network management flows.

SNA defines several varieties of LUs, called logical unit *types*. Each LU type defines a subset of end-to-end SNA protocols that are used to support communications between different categories of end users. For example, terminals use a different type of communication than printers. Some of the more common types are:

- *LU type 0*   Early SNA program-to-program communications support, used mainly in industry-specific terminal products for the financial and retail industries
- *LU type 1*   Supports communications with character-oriented printers
- *LU type 2*   Supports communications with interactive 3270 display stations
- *LU type 3*   Supports communications with 3270 printers
- *LU type 4*   Supports 5250 printers
- *LU type 7*   Supports 5250 terminals
- *LU type 6.2*   Current SNA program-to-program communications protocols, also called APPC

LU 6.2 is the most recent LU type and is also a new concept in LU types—a converged LU type that can be used for all categories of LUs. Until recently, LU 6.2 was the only LU type supported across APPN networks.

System services control point   The SSCP is the NAU used by management software in subarea networks to communicate with managed systems. In the hierarchical management scheme used by subarea networks, the SSCP is at the top of the management hierarchy.

Physical unit   A PU is the software interface for managed systems in SNA subarea networks. That is, managed systems communicate with network management software through their PUs. Even though its name implies otherwise, a PU is implemented in software within the nodes of SNA subarea networks. The term PU came from the initial SNA concept of each hardware device having a single PU software component and usually one or more LUs. Today a hardware device, such as a communication gateway, may contain several PUs.

Control point   CPs support communications between network management software components in APPN networks. The APPN software that supports functions such as dynamic routing-table updates and distributed directory services communicates through CPs.

4.4 NAU sessions and names

All communications in SNA networks occur between pairs of NAUs.

4.4.1 Sessions between NAUs

A pair of NAUs must establish a logical connection with one another before they can communicate. These logical connections between NAUs are called *sessions*. SNA communication is always connection-oriented at the session level.

The following is a summary of the types of sessions between NAUs that are used in both subarea and APPN networks.

- Subarea network management sessions:
  – *SSCP–SSCP sessions* Supports communications between management control points in subarea network
  – *SSCP–PU sessions* Used by managers in subarea networks to communicate with the systems that they manage
  – *SSCP–LU sessions* Used by LUs in subarea networks to request session services such as logons and logoffs
- APPN network management sessions:
  – *CP–CP sessions* Provide peer-to-peer communications to support network management functions in APPN networks
- Subarea and APPN end-user sessions:
  – *LU–LU sessions* Provide end-user connectivity in both subarea and APPN networks

In addition, LUs are also categorized into those that are dependent on SSCPs for session activation—dependent LUs—and those that can start session independent of SSCPs—independent LUs. LU 6.2s can either be dependent or independent LUs, while all other LU types are always dependent on an SSCP for session activation.

4.4.2 NAU names

Every NAU in an SNA network must be assigned a unique name. The naming conventions used in subarea and APPN networks are similar. SNA uses a two-level naming scheme that includes a network name and an NAU name. Each of these names is an eight-character alphanumeric identifier. The combination of a network name and NAU name is called a network-qualified name.

Network administrators are responsible for ensuring that NAU names are unique across a network. Network names should be unique across all SNA networks worldwide. IBM provides a name registration service to ensure that unique network names are assigned, although SNA users are not required to participate.

The network-qualified names are made up of a network name and an NAU name separated by a period, such as XYZINC.DBHOST1. Unique network-qualified names ensure that ambiguous names do not exist during communications between interconnected SNA networks.

4.5 SNA data formats

The messages that flow between NAUs are called requests and responses. Requests are messages that contain either SNA commands or end-user data. Responses are replies to requests. They indicate whether a request or group of requests has been received and processed successfully or if some exception condition has occurred. Note that these responses are generally end-to-end responses that flow between NAUs and they should not be confused with the data-link level responses used to provide error detection and recovery on individual data links.

Figure 4.2 shows the general format of messages within SNA networks. This format is used for both requests and responses.

4.5.1 The basic information unit

The message format used by NAUs for end-to-end communications is the *basic information unit* (BIU). The BIU is made up of two elements—the request unit and the *request/response header* (RH). The *request unit* (RU) is a variable-length field that

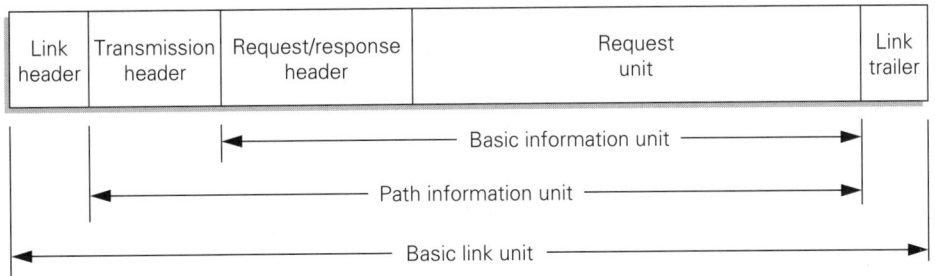

Figure 4.2 SNA message formats

contains the message payload. The RU can contain either end-user data or SNA commands or responses. The maximum RU size is set when a session is established between a pair of NAUs.

The RH is a 3-byte field that contains information used by the communicating NAUs to convey session-level control information. The RH contains a field that indicates whether a message is a request or a response. It also includes indicators that control session level functions such as the direction of data flow and the logical grouping of related messages flowing on a session.

4.5.2 The path information unit

The path control layer is responsible for forwarding BIUs to their destinations. The addresses and other information needed by the path control layer is contained in the *transmission header* (TH) which it adds to each BIU. The combination of a transmission header and a BIU is called a *path information unit* (PIU). In addition to a destination and origin address, the TH contains a sequence number and, in some cases, fields that provide other routing information and flow control protocols.

Several different TH formats are defined by SNA. Each type of TH is assigned a *format identification* (FID) type. The most commonly used FID types are FID1, FID2, and FID4:

- FID1 THs are used in PIUs flowing between subarea nodes. The FID1 headers are used by subarea nodes running older versions of VTAM and NCP that do not support explicit and virtual routes.

- The FID2 TH format is used by peripheral nodes in subarea networks and for *all* PIUs in APPN networks.

- The FID4 format is also used in PIUs flowing between subarea nodes, but it is used by VTAM and NCP for explicit and virtual routes support.

Two additional FIDs are: FID3 for PU1 support: that is, 3270 non-SNA cluster controllers, and FID5 for APPN/HPR frames.

4.5.3 The basic-link unit

When a PIU is forwarded over LAN or WAN data links, the data-link control layer adds headers which are appropriate for the type of data link being used. Data-link technologies such as token ring LANs and SDLC wide area circuits are commonly used in SNA networks. When data-link headers and trailers are added to a PIU, the data structure is called a *basic-link unit* (BLU).

When applications send buffers of data over SNA networks, the data may be segmented into smaller blocks by SNA software. In some cases, the data blocks might also be combined into larger units. At the presentation layer, buffers of application data are packaged into RUs. In situations where the maximum RU size is smaller than the application data buffer, presentation services creates multiple RUs. The RUs that contain data from a single application-level buffer can be logically grouped together through the use of a data-flow control-layer protocol called chaining.

4.5.4 Segmentation and blocking

Maximum RU sizes are determined by the size of buffers used by presentation services software. The maximum RU sizes rarely match the frame sizes used by the data-link layer protocols used in the network. The path control layer is responsible for resolving the differences between maximum RU size and maximum data-link frame sizes.

When RUs are larger than the data-link frame size, the path control layer breaks RUs into segments that match the data-link requirements. This is called RU segmentation. Figure 4.3 shows how an RU is segmented. The first segment contains the TH, the RH, and the portion of the RU that will fit into the first BLU. Each subsequent segment contains a copy of the TH along with information from the RU. A field in the TH is used to indicate that an RU has been segmented. The receiving path control element uses this field to reconstruct the original RU.

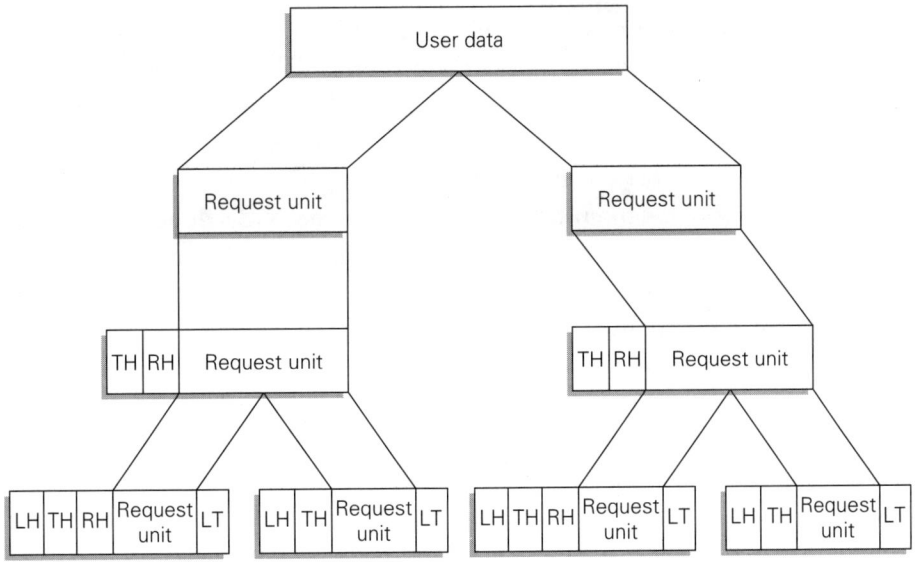

Figure 4.3　SNA message unit segmentation

In situations where a group of small RUs are to be sent over a data link it can be beneficial to pack them into a single data-link level frame. This function, called RU blocking, is also performed by the path control layer. Blocking is only implemented for data flowing between SNA subarea nodes. Peripheral nodes and nodes in APPN networks do not support RU blocking.

4.6 The structure of SNA subarea networks

SNA subarea networks are designed to support hierarchical communications and centralized network control. Subarea networks can be made up of several different types of nodes that are interconnected by data links. The types of nodes found in subarea networks are:

- *Host nodes*   Type 5 nodes
- *Communications controller nodes*   Type 4 nodes
- *Peripheral nodes*   Type 2.0 and type 2.1 nodes

Host nodes provide the centralized control and management services. Therefore, a subarea network must always include at least one host node. Figure 4.4 shows the configuration of a simple SNA subarea network.

4.6.1 Host nodes

Host nodes, also called type 5 nodes, control virtually all of the operations of a subarea network. They can also function as application platforms supporting application programs that can be accessed by all users of the network. Host nodes can further act as intermediate routing nodes to forward messages across a subarea network. Multiple host nodes can be present in a subarea network.

Host nodes always contain an SSCP. The SSCP is the NAU through which the host-based network management applications communicate with managed systems. Hosts can, optionally, support one or more LUs. These LUs are the NAUs that provide access to host-based applications.

Host nodes are generally implemented on hardware platforms that are compatible with IBM System/370 (S/370) and S/390 architectures. These systems are commonly called mainframe computers. Host node functionality has also been implemented on other types of hardware platforms by several computer vendors.

The IBM software product which implements host node functionality is the VTAM. VTAM runs on System/370 (S/370) and S/390 compatible processors. The

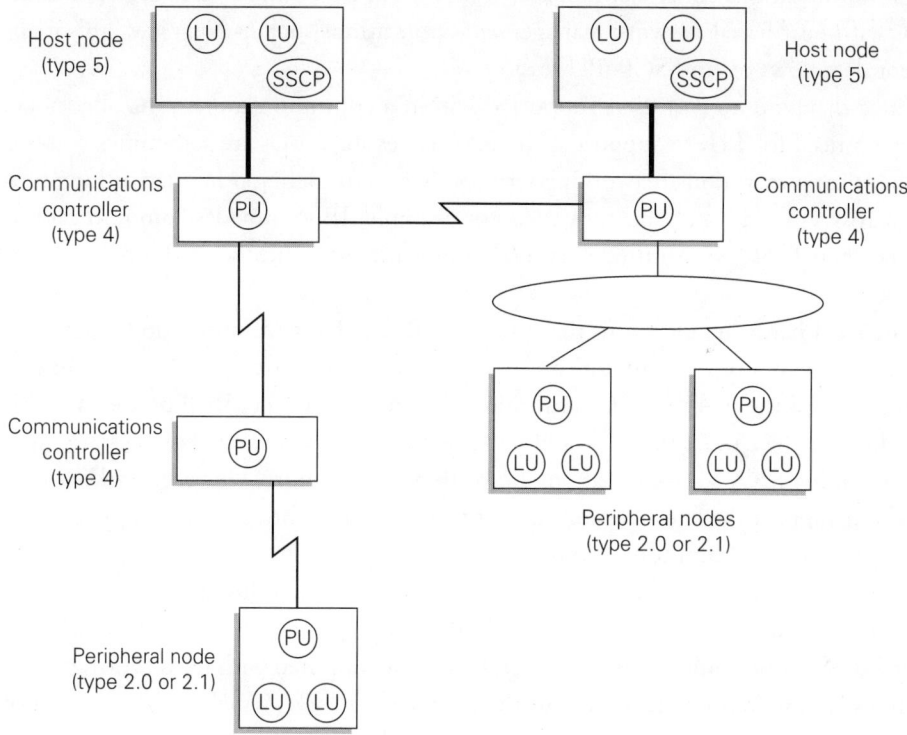

Figure 4.4   Simple SNA network with different node types

SSCP and a basic set of management functions are included in VTAM. Additional management functions are provided by IBM's NetView management product. NetView is a software package that provides additional management functions and can be used as a platform for running other management applications from IBM as well as other vendors. NetView communicates with managed systems through the SSCP within VTAM.

4.6.2 Communications controller nodes

Communications controller nodes, originally called *front-end processors* (FEPs), provide intermediate message routing services for subarea networks. They are also responsible for managing their WAN and LAN data links. Communications controller nodes are also known as type 4 nodes. They are generally dedicated to communications processing and do not support local end users.

Communications controller nodes always contain a PU that is used for communications with host-based network management applications such as NetView. This management data flows on an SSCP–PU session.

Since there are no end users supported within a communications controller node, there is no need for LUs to support such end user sessions. LUs are sometimes present, though, to support various networking services such as tunneling other networking protocols across subarea backbone networks. For example, IBM provides communication-controller-based software to tunnel TCP/IP and some other protocols through subarea networks.

The IBM hardware platforms that can be configured as communications controller nodes are the 37xx line of communications controllers. The current products in this line are designated as the 3745/6 Communications Controllers. Earlier IBM products in this line include the 3725, 3720, 3705, and 3704. All of these hardware platforms are capable of providing SNA communications controller node support. However, earlier products do not support the latest versions of software and, therefore, may not support all of the latest features for communications controller nodes.

The software that provides the SNA communications controller functionality on the 37xx platforms is IBM's NCP. The NCP software manages all of the data links attached to the communications controller. It is also configured with fixed routing tables that are used to forward messages across the network. The PU, which is always a part of the communications controller node, is implemented by software within the NCP.

SNA communications controller hardware and software products are also available from vendors other than IBM. Amdahl, for example, markets a line of communications controller hardware platforms that are plug compatible with the IBM 3745 product line. These processors run IBM's NCP software. Another approach is taken by NCR Comten which provides a hardware platform that is not plug compatible with the IBM 37XX product line and, therefore, requires the use of NCR's software that provides the functionality of IBM's NCP.

4.6.3 Subarea nodes

Host nodes and communications controllers are the two types of *subarea* nodes. Subarea nodes are those nodes in a subarea network that are capable of performing the intermediate message-forwarding function to route messages across a subarea network.

Subarea nodes contain routing tables which are generated at the time that the VTAM or NCP software is configured. Subarea nodes also define subnetworks, called subareas, which are used for network addressing and routing.

4.6.4 Peripheral nodes

Peripheral nodes are the systems through which end users gain access to the network, usually to interact with host-based application programs. As the name implies, peripheral nodes exist only at the end point of a subarea network. Unlike hosts and communications controllers, peripheral nodes do not provide an intermediate message-forwarding function.

There are two very different types of peripheral nodes—type 2.0 or type 2.1 nodes. Type 2.0 nodes support only communications with host-based applications. Users on type 2.1 nodes, however, can also communicate directly with users on other type 2.1 nodes. This peer-to-peer communication between type 2.1 nodes can take place without the intervention of a type 5 host node. Type 2.1 nodes were developed and added to SNA in the mid-1980s—peer networking is not new to SNA.

Peripheral nodes contain a PU through which network management data is exchanged with an SSCP. Peripheral nodes also support LUs which are used for end-user communications. A peripheral node may contain from 1 to 255 LUs.

A wide variety of products from IBM and other vendors can function as peripheral nodes in subarea networks. IBM products such as the 3174 Establishment Controller, the AS/400, and the OS/2 Communications Server can all be configured as peripheral nodes. Most vendors of application platforms ranging from PCs to multi-user computers also supply SNA peripheral node software for their products.

4.7 Activation of subarea networks

Resources in SNA subarea networks are activated by the host nodes. The SSCP activates all data links, PUs, and LUs in subarea networks. In networks with more than one host—multidomain networks—the SSCPs also establish connections with one another in order to support communications between users in different domains.

Resource activation is initiated by a combination of definitions created during the VTAM and NCP *system generation* (sysgen) procedures and by commands entered by network operators. Like most subarea network operations, network activation is largely predefined and always driven by the VTAM host.

The network activation process begins with the activation of the resources nearest to the SSCP and then cascades through the network until all resources are activated.

4.7.1 The activation process

Figure 4.5 shows a simple subarea network whose resources are being activated. The PUs and LUs will be activated along with the data links between the host and the

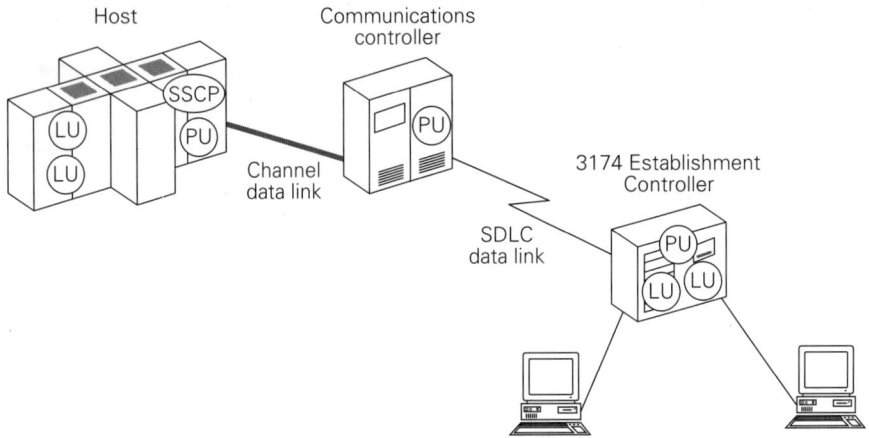

Figure 4.5　Simple subarea SNA network with resources being activated

communications controller and between the communications controller and the peripheral node. The activation of all resources is initiated by the SSCP in the host on the left side of the diagram.

The SSCP first activates the PU on the host by sending it an activation request. Note that the SSCP and the PU are both elements of VTAM. After the PU on the host is activated, it can be used to activate the local resources of the host, such as the LUs that represent the applications.

Next, the data link between the host and the communications controller must be activated. The data link is a local channel interface. Since the channel interface is a host resource, the SSCP sends the activation request to the PU that has just been activated on the host.

Next to be activated is the PU in the communications controller. When an SSCP activates an NAU, such as a PU, it enters into a session with that resource.

The SSCP sends an activation request, called an *activate physical unit* (ACTPU), to the PU in the communications controller. The ACTPU request starts an SSCP–PU session that will subsequently be used to send network management messages between the SSCP and the PU.

The data link between the communications controller and the peripheral node is the next resource to be activated. This data link is a resource that is controlled by the PU in the communications controller. The SSCP, therefore, sends a data-link activation request to the PU using the SSCP–PU session that was previously activated.

After the data link between the communications controller and the peripheral node is activated, the NAUs on the peripheral node can be activated. The peripheral node in figure 4.5 contains a PU and two LUs. PUs must always be activated before any of the LUs on a node can be activated.

The SSCP activates the PU by sending an ACTPU request. This request flows through the previously activated communications controller and data links, and activates an SSCP–PU session.

After the PU is activated, the SSCP can activate the LUs on the peripheral node. LUs are activated by *activate logical unit* (ACTLU) requests sent from the SSCP to each of the LUs. Note that the ACTLU requests do not go through the PU on the peripheral node—their destination addresses are those of the LUs that are being activated.

4.7.2 Logon procedure

After this activation procedure is completed, the LUs on the peripheral node can request sessions with mainframe-based applications. Dependent LUs send a logon request to the SSCP on the SSCP–LU session. The SSCP validates the logon request and notifies the host-based application of the logon request. The LU that represents the host-based application sends the BIND command to the LU that originated the logon request. The BIND command specifies the end-to-end protocols that will be used by the communicating LUs and it starts the LU–LU session. End-user data can then flow on the LU–LU session. The logon process can also be initiated by the host via a VTAM command or LOGAPPL initialization parameter.

4.8 The subarea transport network

The transport network is responsible for delivering messages over a subarea network. The transport network is made up of the LAN and WAN data links which interconnect the nodes and the routing functions which reside in each of the nodes. The routing performed by the transport network is defined within the SNA path control layer.

Most of the routing function is concentrated in the hosts and communications controllers, which make up the backbone of a subarea network. Hosts and communications controllers are called subarea nodes because they define areas within a network which are called subareas.

Figure 4.6 shows how subareas are defined within a network. Each host or communications controller defines a subarea. Each subarea is made up of the host or communications controller and all of the NAUs that reside on the subarea node plus all of the NAUs that reside on any peripheral nodes that are directly connected to the subarea node.

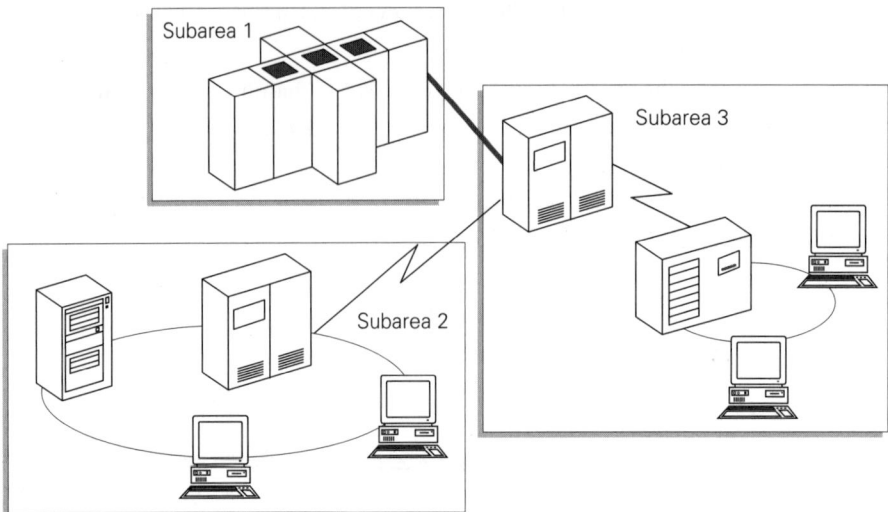

Figure 4.6   Hosts and communications controllers define an SNA subarea

Subareas are an essential element of the addressing and message routing scheme used in subarea networks. Messages are first routed to the subarea area node that supports the destination NAU. The destination subarea node then routes the message to the destination NAU within the subarea.

4.8.1 Network addressing

In subarea networks each NAU is assigned a unique address. This address is used to forward messaging between the subarea nodes which form the backbone of a subarea network. The format of these network addresses has evolved over time. Figure 4.7 shows the three network address formats that have been used in subarea networks.

The original network address format, today called nonextended network addressing, defines a 16-bit address which is partitioned into two subfields. The subarea address identifies the subarea where an NAU resides. The element address identifies the specific NAU within the subarea. Nonextended addressing allowed the network designer to set the partition between subarea and element addresses to allow from 1 to 8 bits of the address field to be used as the subarea address.

The 16-bit address space of nonextended network addressing became inadequate as SNA networks expanded. This led to the introduction of extended network addressing which expanded the address space to 23 bits. Extended network addressing reserves a fixed 8-bit subarea address field and a 15-bit element address subfield.

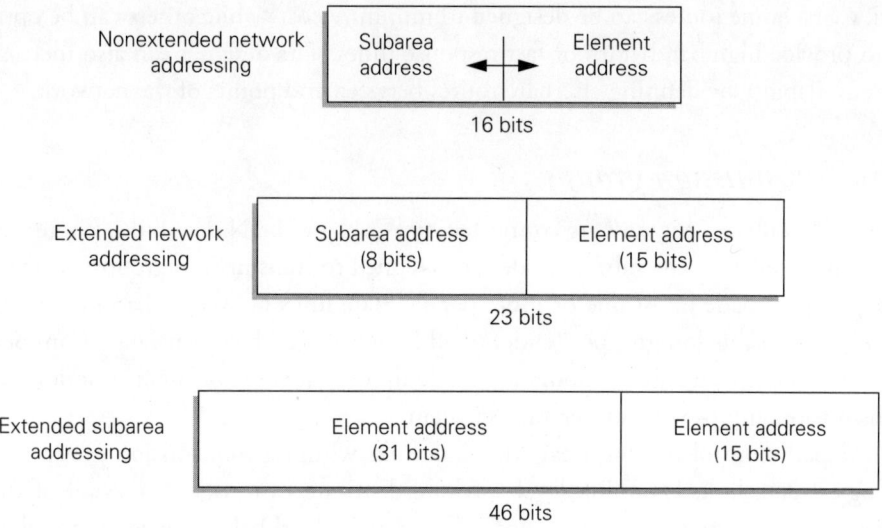

Figure 4.7 SNA addressing and extensions

The latest format for subarea network addresses is the 46-bit extended subarea addressing format. This format allocates a fixed 31-bit subarea address field and a 15-bit element address field. Only 16 bits of the subarea address field are currently used, but it can be expanded to use the full 31-bit format in the future.

Peripheral nodes employ a different addressing scheme than subarea nodes. While subarea nodes use the previously described network addresses to route messages, peripheral nodes use a local addressing scheme to identify NAUs.

These local addresses used by peripheral nodes are 8-bit identifiers that have only local significance. Unlike network addresses, they are not unique across the network.

The transformation between network and local addresses is performed by *boundary function* software which resides in the subarea nodes that support directly attached peripheral nodes.

4.8.2 Routing in subarea networks

The routes used to transport messages in subarea networks are statically defined during the system generation process for hosts in VTAM and for communications controllers in NCP. These routes are explicitly created by the system programmers during the sysgen procedure.

The designer of a subarea network must define routes between subarea nodes to support all required end user and network management sessions. The routes must provide not only connectivity, but also the levels of service and performance required by network users. Some routes can be designed to minimize costs while others can be optimized to provide high bandwidth or fast response times. The designer can also increase network availability by defining alternate routes between end points of the network.

4.8.3 *Transmission groups*

The nodes of a subarea network are connected by WAN and LAN data links. Groups of data links between adjacent subarea nodes are assigned to transmission groups. A transmission group is made up of one or more parallel data links between adjacent subarea nodes. These transmission groups are identified by numbers which can range from one to 255. Routes between subarea nodes are made up of sequences of subarea nodes and the transmission groups which interconnect them.

SNA's path control routing treats the data links within a transmission group as a single logical data link. Data-link level software distributes messages across all of the data links within the transmission groups. This provides load balancing across the data links. More importantly, multilink transmission groups can be used to improve the availability of a subarea network. In the event of a data-link failure, messages can be dynamically rerouted across the remaining data links in the transmission group. The recovery provided by multilink transmission groups is the only case where dynamic message-by-message rerouting is performed within subarea networks. In all other cases, sessions must be restarted on alternate routes after the failure of a network resource such as a data link or an intermediate subarea node. (As will be discussed later, APPN with high-performance routing supports dynamic rerouting without session interruption.)

4.8.4 *Explicit routes*

Each predefined route across a subarea network is an ordered list of the subarea nodes and *transmission groups* (TGs) that make up the route. A maximum of 16 explicit routes can be defined between any pair of subarea nodes.

Figure 4.8 shows three explicit routes defined between node 1 and node 5. The nodes in this diagram could be hosts or communications controllers:

- The definition of explicit route 1 is:
  Node 1, TG 1, node 2, TG 3, node 3, TG 5, node 5

- The definition of explicit route 2 is:
  Node 1, TG 7, node 5

- The definition of explicit route 3 is:
  Node 1, TG 8, node 4, TG 10, node 5

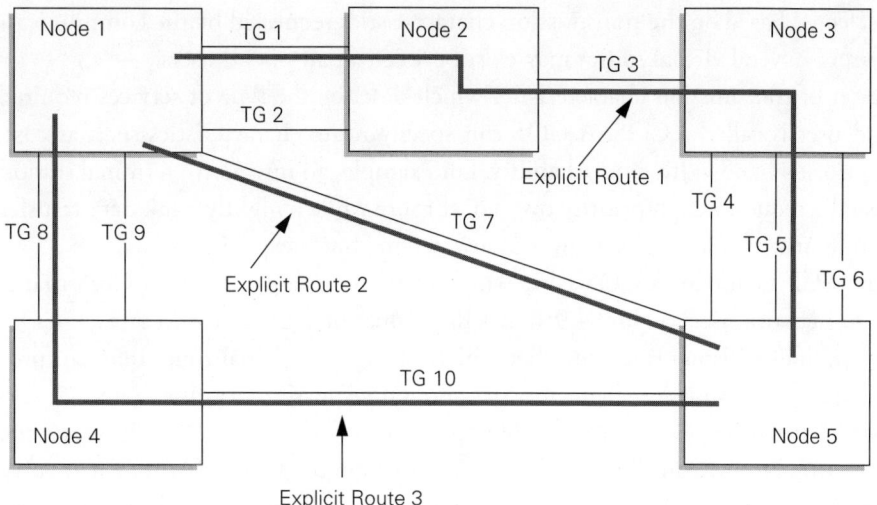

Figure 4.8 Explicit routes and transmission groups

4.8.5 Virtual routes

Virtual routes are logical connections between pairs of subarea nodes which are mapped on top of explicit routes. Each virtual route is assigned one of three transmission priorities which is used by the path-control layer to prioritize session traffic. When sessions are activated in subarea networks, they are mapped to virtual routes which, in turn, are mapped to explicit routes which describe the underlying physical path. Several virtual routes, each having different transmission priorities, may map to a single explicit route.

In addition to prioritizing session traffic, virtual routes also provide a flow control protocol which is used to prevent congestion in the network. The flow control protocol, called virtual route pacing, uses a dynamic windowing scheme to control the number of messages sent along a virtual route. An initial window size is set at the time that the virtual route is activated. The window size can be increased or decreased dynamically depending on the amount of traffic flowing on the network. Virtual route pacing is not aware of individual sessions—it controls the flow of all sessions using a given virtual route.

4.8.6 Route selection

A session is mapped to a virtual route at the time that a session is started and it is bound to that virtual route for the duration of the session. When a session is started, a virtual route is selected based on the transmission characteristics requested by the communicating end users. Several virtual routes may exist between a pair of end users.

The set of transmission characteristics which describe the type of services required by an end user is called a COS. A COS can specify route characteristics such as cost, security, priority, bandwidth, and reliability. For example, an interactive terminal session would usually request a high priority over a fast route while a nightly bank data transfer may be content with a low priority over a slow, secure, but inexpensive route.

Each SSCP maintains a COS table which contains an entry for each COS that is available to network users. Figure 4.9 shows the format of a COS table. For each COS, the table specifies a virtual route number which identifies a virtual route that can provide the required transmission characteristics and a transmission priority. Note that several possible virtual routes may be suitable for a class of service. The SSCP selects the first active virtual route from the list of possible choices in the COS table. The first entry for each COS is considered to be the optimum virtual route and each subsequent entry is less desirable.

COS name 1	Virtual route number	Transmission priority
	Virtual route number	Transmission priority
COS name 1	Virtual route number	Transmission priority
	Virtual route number	Transmission priority
	Virtual route number	Transmission priority
COS name 1	Virtual route number	Transmission priority
	Virtual route number	Transmission priority

Figure 4.9   Class of service table format

Peripheral nodes generally support only a single data-link connection to a subarea node. Therefore, the virtual route that is used to move data across the backbone of the subarea network simply maps to the data link that provides the connection to the destination peripheral node. The link between the subarea node and the peripheral node is called a peripheral link. Figure 4.10 shows the relationships between transmission groups, explicit routes, virtual routes, and route extensions.

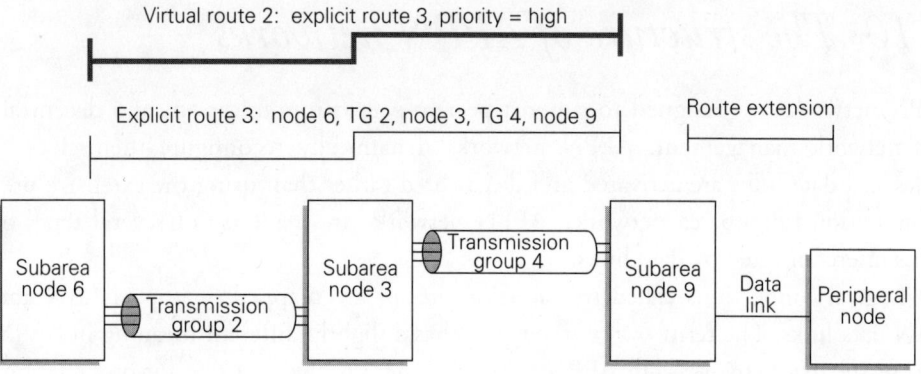

A transmission group is a group of one or more links between two subarea nodes.
Explicit routes describe the underlying physical path between two subarea nodes
as a list of nodes and transmission groups that comprise the route.
Virtual routes, each assigned a transmission priority level, are mapped to explicit routes.
A route extension describes the path between a subarea node and a peripheral node.

Figure 4.10   Transmission groups, explicit routes, virtual routes, and route extensions

4.9 Starting sessions in SNA

Using a simple example, when an SNA end user wants to start a session, assuming it is attached to a peripheral node, its LU sends a logon request to its SSCP. If the requested partner is on the host (such as an application) or elsewhere but owned by the host, the host sends to the partner LU a BIND image containing enough information about the requesting LU for it to start the session, including the routing information. The partner LU then sends a BIND message across the specified route and the session is started.

If the requested resource is owned by another host, the two hosts exchange, across their SSCP-SSCP session, the necessary information for a BIND to be generated. If the requesting LU's host does not know the location of the partner LU, a search is performed among all the hosts on the network.

Again, this was a simple and simplified example. Subarea SNA uses extensive means to ensure that sessions are correctly started and terminated, to allow for as much ease and automation for the end user as possible, such as providing logon menus, and to coordinate the use of shared resources, such as queuing for printers.

4.10 The structure of APPN networks

APPN networks are designed to support peer-to-peer communications and decentralized network management. APPN networks dynamically reconfigure themselves as nodes and data links are activated and deactivated rather than using the extensive preconfiguration for subarea networks. APPN networks are made up of several types of nodes interconnected by data links.

Logical connections called transmission groups are mapped on top of LAN and WAN data links. The term *transmission group* has a slightly different meaning in APPN than in subarea networks—in APPN networks, there is always a one-for-one relationship between data links and transmission groups.

All of the nodes in APPN networks are type 2.1 nodes which are capable of peer-to-peer communications, but the nodes can differ in capability. That is, levels of capability in type 2.1 nodes can be considered as concentric circles—they all share certain basic functionality but some nodes have more functionality. The following three categories of type 2.1 nodes can be used in APPN networks:

- Network nodes
- End nodes
- Low-entry networking (LEN) nodes

Network nodes provide the highest level of functionality and LEN nodes the lowest level. Figure 4.11 shows the structure of a simple APPN network.

4.10.1 Network nodes

The backbones of APPN networks are made up of network nodes interconnected by transmission groups. Network nodes provide a wide variety of functions in APPN networks. First, like the other node types, network nodes can support LUs that represent local end users. These end users can establish LU–LU sessions with any other LU in the network.

In addition to supporting its local users, network nodes can act as communications servers for directly attached end nodes and LEN nodes. As a server, the network node provides directory and route selection services to its LEN nodes and end nodes, as well as to its local LUs. The network nodes interact to provide a distributed directory service and to monitor network topology in order to select optimum routes for end user communications.

Each network node contains a topology database that describes all of the network nodes in the network and the characteristics of the transmission groups that connect the

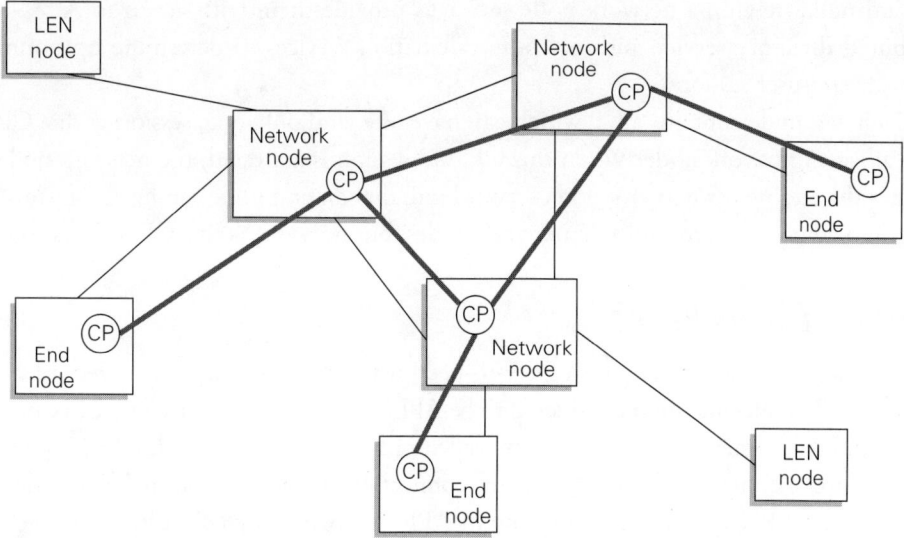

Figure 4.11   Simple APPN network

network nodes. This information is dynamically updated as resources are activated and deactivated and it is used to calculate the optimum routes between end users of the network.

Network nodes also contain directories that have entries for each local LU. The directories can also contain entries for LUs residing on the adjacent end nodes and LEN nodes for which the network node is acting as a server. A network node and the end and LEN nodes, for which it is acting as a server, are called a domain. Entries for LUs located in other parts of the network can be cached as a result of directory search operations.

Each network node contains a CP that provides services such as directory searches and topology database updates. The CPs in adjacent network nodes can establish sessions with one another to share topology updates and directory information.

4.10.2 End nodes

End nodes exist at the end points of an APPN network. They do not perform intermediate routing functions. End nodes are generally application platforms that provide network access to end users.

End nodes contain a directory of local LUs and can optionally contain entries for LUs that reside in adjacent nodes. End nodes also contain descriptions of the local transmission groups that connect it to the APPN network.

End nodes rely on a network node server to provide them with access to APPN's distributed directory service and for route calculation services to determine optimum routes for end-user sessions.

Each end node contains a CP which can have one, and only one, session with a CP on an adjacent network node. When this CP–CP session is activated, the network node becomes the end node's network node server. Note that an end node can have transmission group connections to multiple network nodes, but only one active CP–CP session.

4.10.3 LEN nodes

LEN nodes are based on an SNA peer-to-peer networking technology called LEN. Although LEN nodes are often considered to be APPN nodes, in another sense, LEN predates APPN and sometimes LEN nodes are called pre-APPN type 2.1 nodes. LEN nodes generally support only simple point-to-point connections between adjacent LEN nodes, although these LEN nodes can participate in APPN networks by connecting to a network node server. When attached to a network node, users on LEN nodes gain indirect access to APPN services such as directory searches and route calculation and users on LEN nodes can communicate with other users across the APPN network.

LEN nodes contain some simple control point software, but it is not capable of entering into a session with a CP on a network node server. The users on LEN nodes are therefore limited to indirect access to APPN services. LEN nodes also contain LUs which support local end users.

4.10.4 Activation of APPN networks

In contrast with subarea SNA networks, the activation of APPN networks is not orchestrated from any single node or category of nodes. Each node in an APPN network activates its own resources and interacts with adjacent nodes to activate data links and CP–CP sessions and to dynamically update routing tables to reflect newly activated data links and nodes.

When a node is activated in an APPN network, it activates its data links to adjacent nodes. Pairs of adjacent nodes then exchange the data-link level XID commands called XID3 commands. The XID3 commands are used to exchange basic configuration information such as the category of nodes which are establishing a connection. Each node indicates whether it is a network node, an end node, or an LEN node by putting an appropriate identifier in the XID3 command that it sends. In this way each node learns the capabilities of its neighbors.

4.10.5 CP–CP session activation

The next step in the activation process is the activation of CP–CP sessions between adjacent pairs of nodes. CP–CP sessions are not necessarily activated between every pair of adjacent nodes. End nodes, for example, can only have one CP–CP active with a network node server even though data-link connections can be established with multiple network nodes. Further, an organization with many network nodes can reduce the amount of overhead traffic between network nodes. It can do this by examining its topology and specifying that CP–CP sessions be brought up only by a minimum spanning tree. That is, CP–CP sessions would exist between the minimum number of network nodes that will ensure that each node receives all updates and requests.

The data links over which CP–CP sessions are started are determined by local configuration information in each node. Data can flow over data links between nodes even if there is no CP–CP session between them.

4.10.6 Topology database updates

The activation or deactivation of network nodes or data links between network nodes results in changes in topology which must be reflected in the topology databases that reside in each network node in the network. Figure 4.12 shows an example of a topology database update. In this example, network node A has just been activated. It has

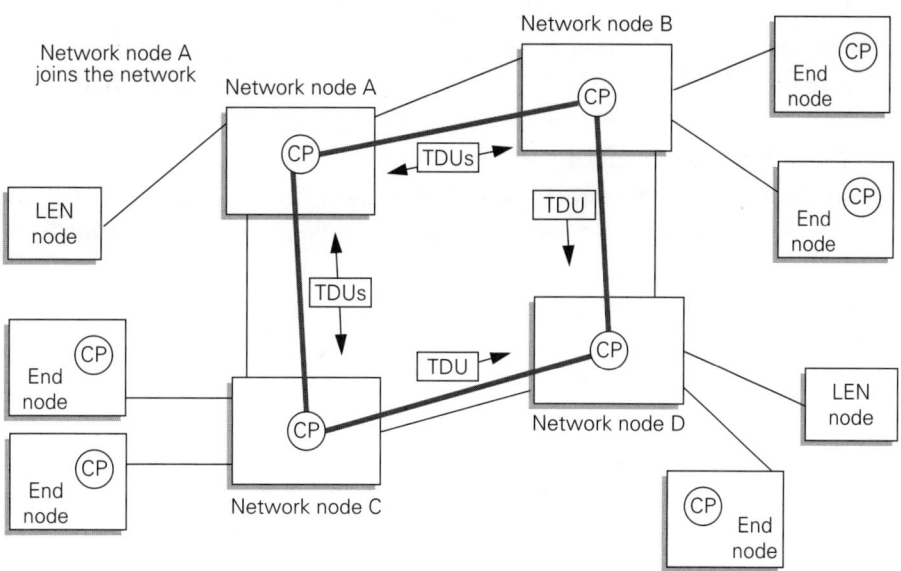

Figure 4.12 APPN topology database update

activated data links with network nodes B and C and CP–CP sessions have been activated over these data links.

When CP–CP sessions are activated between pairs of network nodes, the network nodes exchange *topology database updates* (TDUs). TDUs are exchanged between network node A and network node B. Updates are also exchanged between network node A and network node C. Then, since they have a change to report, network nodes C and B each send an update to network node D. After these updates are processed, the topology databases in network nodes A, B, C, and D will contain identical information about the topology of all network nodes and the transmission groups that interconnect them.

In order to reduce the amount of traffic generated when topology databases are updated, TDUs are assigned sequence numbers called *flow reduction sequence numbers* (FRSNs). When a transmission group between a pair of network nodes is activated, the CPs in these nodes exchange the number of the last TDU that they received. The CPs can then determine which, if any, TDUs need to be sent to the neighboring CP. The use of FRSNs is particularly useful when TGs are reactivated after a short outage. During short outages it is unlikely that many TDUs would be generated and, therefore, the FRSNs can eliminate many TDU exchanges.

4.10.7 Dynamic LU registration

During network activation, an end node can also optionally register its local LUs with the network node that will be acting as its server. This dynamic registration occurs over the CP–CP session between an end node and its network node server.

As the alternative to registering its local resources, the end node can inform its network node server that it prefers to be searched when a `locate` request is received.

Dynamic registration can reduce, or even eliminate, the need for system administrators on network nodes to manually configure information about the LUs residing on end nodes in their domain. Note that because LEN nodes do not support CP–CP sessions, LUs residing on LEN nodes must be manually configured in their network node servers.

4.11 APPN directory services and route calculation

Unlike subarea networks, APPN networks have no predefined routes that can be used to carry LU–LU session traffic. Routes across APPN networks are dynamically created when a request for a session is received by a CP from the origin LU. The CP first uses

APPN's directory services to locate the destination LU. Then it calculates the optimal route between these two LUs. (The acronyms OLU and DLU are sometimes used for these terms, but DLU is also used for dependent LU, so we will not abbreviate to avoid confusion.)

4.11.1 APPN directory services

Directory services responds to requests from an origin LU to find the location of a destination LU prior to the start of an LU–LU session. Directory services provides two types of information—the location of the destination LU and information about transmission groups that will be used to calculate the optimum route between the origin LU and the destination LU.

Note that APPN's directory service differs from the directory services of most other networking protocol suites by returning the *location* of a resource and topology information to reach it rather than the *address* of the target resource. This is because no fixed addresses are assigned to resources in an APPN network.

The routes between LUs in APPN networks are calculated from the information supplied by directory services and information obtained from the topology databases that reside on network nodes. Route identifiers are created dynamically when LU–LU sessions are started.

Figure 4.13 shows one way that directory services locates a destination LU and how it supplies the origin LU's CP with the information that it needs to calculate the route between origin LU and destination LU.

LUa which resides in node 1, an end node, is initiating an LU–LU session with LUb which resides in node 5, also an end node. The directory search begins with a search of the local directory on node 1. Local directories on end nodes contain information on local LUs and may contain entries for LUs in adjacent nodes.

If an entry for the destination LU is not found in the local directory of the end node, the search is continued by the end node's network node server, network node A. The CP in the end node sends a `locate` request to directory services in the network node server. This request is sent on the CP–CP session between the end node and its network node server.

The `locate` request includes the name of the destination LU. It also contains information that describes the transmission groups that connect the originating end node to the APPN network—that is, links to its network node server and perhaps links to other APPN nodes. This transmission group information is needed for the network node server to calculate the route between the origin LU and the destination LU. This is because the topology databases that reside in network nodes contain only information about the backbone of the APPN network which includes the network nodes and the

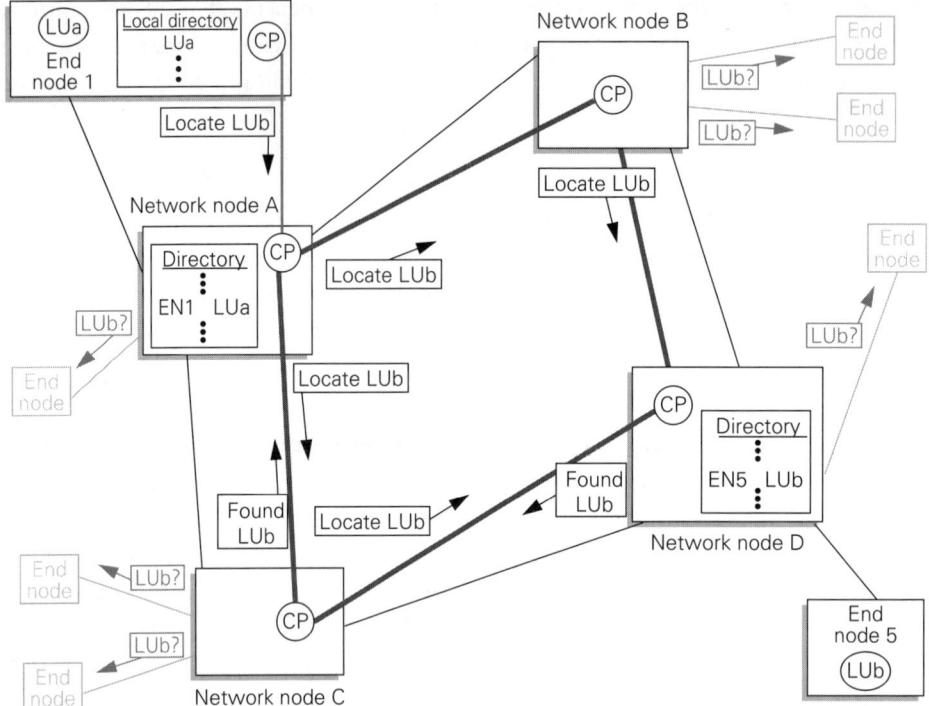

1. LUa requests a session with LUb from the end node on which it resides, end node 1.
2. End node 1 checks its local directory and does not find LUb.
3. End node 1 sends a Locate request to its network node server, network node A.
4. Network node A checks its directory and does not find LUa.
5. Network node A sends a Locate search to all its adjacent network nodes.
6. Each network node a) sends the Locate to its served end nodes that accept searches,
   b) sends the Locate on to all its adjacent network nodes, and c) checks its directory.
7. The network node that serves LUb sends back a Found message.

Figure 4.13   APPN broadcast search

transmission groups that interconnect them, but not information about links to end nodes.

Directory services supplies the information about the connections to the end node. These connections are called tail circuits and the information that describes them is contained in data structures, called tail vectors, that are carried in the `locate` request. The information contained in these tail vectors is used in the route calculation that is performed after the directory search operation is completed.

Directory services within the CP of the network node server now continues the search for the destination LU. The local directory in the network node is searched first.

This local directory contains entries for resources on the local node and, optionally, it can contain entries for resources that reside in other nodes within the network.

4.11.2 Directed searches

If an entry for the destination LU is found in the local directory, a directed search is initiated. The purpose of a directed search is to verify that the location of the resource in the local directory is still valid and, if the destination LU resides on an end node, the search operation obtains its tail circuit information that the originating network node will require to perform its route calculation.

The directed search is performed by a `locate` request sent directly from the origin LU's network node server to the destination LU's network node server. The route used for the directed search is across a series of consecutive CP–CP sessions.

If the destination LU is located on the destination network node itself, the `locate` reply, or `found` message, is simply sent back to the origin network node. If the destination LU resides on an end node that is in the domain of the destination network node server, a `locate` request is sent to that end node. The end node then sends the `locate` reply, or `found` message, that includes its tail vectors.

If the destination LU is not in the destination network node's domain, a negative `locate` reply is sent back to the originating network node.

4.11.3 Broadcast searches

When the location of a resource is not found in an origin network node server's local directory, a broadcast search operation can be initiated. A broadcast search attempts to locate resources by sending `locate` requests to every node in an APPN network.

The origin network node server initiates the broadcast search by sending `locate` requests to each of its neighboring network nodes. Each network node that receives the `locate` request will, in turn, send `locate` requests to each of its adjacent network nodes. The network nodes will also send `locate` requests to end nodes within their domain that have indicated that they support `locate` requests for resources that they have not registered with their network node server.

Network nodes attempt to minimize broadcast search traffic by discarding duplicate `locate` requests for a single destination LU and not propagating those requests across the network.

When the destination LU is found, a `locate` reply is created and sent back to the origin network node. The destination and origin network nodes can cache the location of a destination LU if they don't have an entry for the resource in their local directories.

4.11.4 Central directory servers

In order to reduce the amount of traffic produced by broadcast searches, APPN supports an optional *central directory server* (CDS) or servers. The nodes in the network that provide central directory services are identified in the topology databases that reside in each of the network nodes.

When a central directory server is available, the origin network node server can send a `locate` request directly to the server. If an entry for the requested destination LU exists in the central directory, the CDS initiates a directed search to verify the location and to collect tail vectors needed for route calculation. This information is then returned to the origin network node.

If there is no entry for the requested destination LU, the central directory server initiates a broadcast search to locate it. When the location of the destination LU is returned by the broadcast search, the destination LU location is retained in the central directory and the location and tail vectors are sent back to the origin network node that initiated the request.

Broadcast traffic is reduced with a CDS for several reasons. First, one CDS can easily be preconfigured with many LUs, while preconfiguring and updating each network node would be too much effort. Second, since the CDS sends all the broadcast messages, it has a more extensive cache of LUs than any single network node would usually have. Finally, broadcasts are only initiated by the central directory servers rather than by each of the origin network nodes attempting to locate the same resources.

4.11.5 Route calculation

After a destination LU is located by directory services, a route between the origin LU and the destination LU is calculated. Frequently, multiple potential routes are available between the origin LU and the destination LU. An element of the CP, called route selection services, is responsible for selecting the optimal route from those that are available. The route selection calculation for a session is always performed by the route selection services component in the origin network node.

The most suitable route is the one that matches, or most closely matches, a set of characteristics requested by the origin LU. The COS is a description of these characteristics. A COS describes the desired or required characteristics of the transmission groups and intermediate network nodes used to transport data for an impending LU–LU session. Some of the transmission group and node characteristics that can be factored into the route calculation include:

- Transmission groups:
  - Cost
  - Security
  - Bandwidth
  - Transit delay
  - Congestion level
  - User-defined characteristics
- Nodes:
  - Congestion level

Route selection services uses a least-weight routing algorithm to calculate the most desirable route for an LU–LU session. The COS database describes the relative desirability of various combinations of node and transmission group characteristics. More desirable combinations of characteristics are assigned a relatively low weight while less desirable node and transmission group characteristics are assigned higher relative weights.

In order to perform the least-weight calculation, route selection services must have access to a description of the characteristics of each intermediate network node and transmission group that can be considered for use in the route between the origin LU and the destination LU.

The characteristics of the nodes and transmission groups that can potentially be included in a route are obtained by route selection services from two sources that are shown in figure 4.14. Information about the characteristics of network nodes and the transmission groups which connect them is obtained from the topology databases that reside in every network node. Since route selection services runs on the origin network node, it can access this information from its local topology database.

If the origin LU and/or destination LU reside in an end node, information about the transmission groups that connect those end nodes to the APPN network is also required in order to calculate the optimum route for the LU–LU session. As we have discussed, this information is obtained during by directory services during its search for the location of the destination LU.

The TG vectors that describe the origin LU end node's transmission groups are sent to the network node server CP in the `locate` request which initiates the directory search operation. The TG vectors that describe a destination LU end node's transmission groups are returned to the origin network node in response to the search for the destination LU.

The TG descriptions obtained by directory services along with the TG and node descriptions in the origin network node's topology database provide route selection

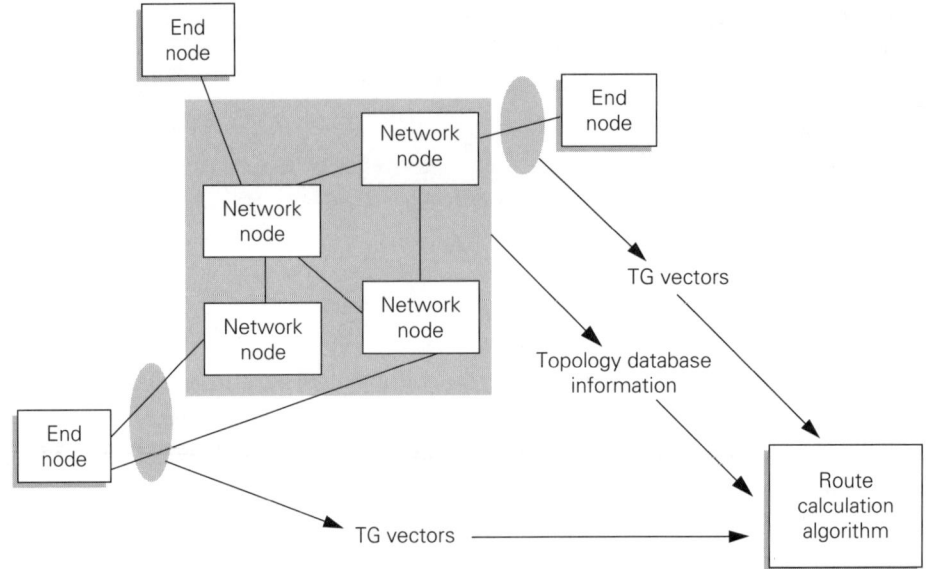

Figure 4.14 APPN route calculation input

services with a description of every node and TG that can potentially be used to build a route between the origin LU and the destination LU.

During the route calculation procedure, each of the potentially usable nodes and transmission groups must be compared to the characteristics of the requested class of service and assigned individual weights. Eligible nodes and transmission groups are then processed by the algorithms that calculate the route with the minimum total weight. In order to minimize the recurring overhead of these route selection algorithms, APPN stores the result of each route calculation in a database called a tree database.

Each route contained in the tree database will describe a route to a destination LU for a specific class of service. If an origin LU subsequently requests a route that has been stored in the tree database, the route is obtained from the tree database rather than being recalculated.

4.11.6 Connection networks

Some LAN and WAN packet-switching networks provide direct any-to-any connectivity among all systems attached to those networks. These types of networks, which include X.25 and frame relay networks, are called *shared access transport facilities* (SATF). APPN can take advantage of the connectivity provided by these SATFs through a feature called *connection networks*. The SATF and all of the end nodes defining their connection to it as a single virtual routing node are called a connection network.

Standard APPN requires defining a link between each of the APPN end nodes attached to a single SATF. In a simple example, this would involve defining a separate link for each of the ninety connections between ten nodes on a small LAN. This increases exponentially for larger or interconnected networks.

Alternatively, an end node can define a single connection to the network as a *virtual routing node*.

When two systems attached to a common connection network start a session, *route calculation services* uses the connection network definition to select a direct connection provided by the SATF. The data traffic for the session is then routed directly between those two nodes by the SATF.

4.11.7 *Route selection control vectors*

After the route calculation procedure is completed, a description of the optimum route to the destination LU is sent to the origin LU. The route description is called a *route selection control vector* (RSCV). The RSCV is an ordered list of each intermediate node and transmission group along the path to the destination LU.

The RSCV is put into the BIND command which is sent to the destination LU to activate the LU–LU session. This BIND command is forwarded along the route described by the RSCV.

The remainder of the routing process depends on which of the two APPN routing protocols is being used.

APPN with ISR   APPN's original routing protocol is called ISR. With ISR, as the BIND command is forwarded across each transmission group along the path, the path control layer in each node, including the origin node, assigns a unique identifier for the new session. This 17-bit identifier is called the *local-form session identifier* (LFSID). The LFSID is carried in the address field of the transmission header of the BIND command and subsequent messages for the session.

A different LFSID is assigned for each transmission group along the path to the destination LU. In each intermediate node, the path control layer sets up a session con-nector which is used to map the LFSID of an incoming message for the session into the identifier that will be used on the outbound transmission group. This process, called label swapping, is also used by ATM.

After the BIND message reaches the destination LU, the route is prepared to carry the session traffic for the duration of the session. At the end of the session, the session connectors and identifiers are removed from the intermediate nodes.

APPN with HPR   A more recent enhancement to APPN adds a new routing protocol, HPR. All nodes with HPR will also still have ISR and can use ISR connections to
older nodes not equipped with HPR.

Where ISR uses hop-by-hop routing with label swapping, an HPR packet carries
the entire path in its header. This eliminates the table look-up at each intermediate
node. This makes it much more efficient in high-speed networks with highly reliable
links. ISR is more reliable, however, with data links that have high error rates.

In addition to the new routing protocol, HPR also adds dynamic rerouting capability to APPN as well as a more efficient congestion control algorithm called adaptive
rate-based congestion control.

4.12 Subarea SNA and APPN interopera-
bility and integration

Although the two environments are different in many ways, IBM made extensive efforts
to ensure as seamless an integration as possible, so that customers could gradually
migrate their network. For example, VTAM can run both SNA and APPN simultaneously and can act as an interchange node between APPN and subarea components of
the network.

4.13 SNA network management

SNA's network management protocols and functionality are defined within a subarchi-
tecture called *SNA/management services* (SNA/MS), which is further described in
chapter 15.

4.14 Conclusion

In the twenty years since its introduction, SNA and its more recent incarnation, APPN,
have gone through many significant changes. It has been the single most successful protocol, dominant in several industries including banking and retail. Originally designed,
like most protocols, for an insular environment, it has nonetheless interacted with other
protocols since its early days—carrying different transports across itself or being transported across them, incorporating different data links below, and coexisting with different protocols on the same system. All of these are further discussed in subsequent
chapters.

chapter 5

Tutorial on non-SNA protocols: TCP/IP, IPX, and NetBIOS

VICTORIA C. MARNEY-PETIX
CHARLES FELTMAN

89

To complement information on the higher protocol layers of SNA, Victoria C. Marney-Petix's and Charles Feltman's tutorial is dedicated on the network and transport layers—layers 3 and 4 in the OSI model. It concentrates on TCP/IP, OSI, IPX/SPX, and NetBIOS, detailing terminology and describing the concepts of each protocol. This chapter also includes comparison of the four protocols, citing similarities and differences among the four.

5.1 Introduction and philosophy

This chapter will introduce you to the wonderful rainbow of the Internet protocol stack (TCP/IP), OSI-compliant protocols, Novell's IPX/SPX stack, and the NetBIOS protocol. We say "rainbows" though, in a sense, some of these stacks represent various hues of the same color family—for example, TCP/IP and OSI are related in many ways, as are OSI and SNA.

In order to understand SNA internetworking with these protocols, you need to understand how these stacks work, how their protocols are defined, and also the underlying philosophy that animated their creators. As you learn about these new protocols (new to you, that is), it is helpful to approach them with a mind clear of SNA design goals, requirements, and assumptions. Just as you'll never learn a new language well if you try to fit the new paradigm into the grammatical structure and assumptions of English, you will only understand and appreciate these new stacks if you can approach them with the open mind and open heart of an explorer.

TCP/IP and IPX/SPX have some important philosophical assumptions in common. Primary among these, in contrast to traditional SNA, is the assumption that the network is not composed of separate castes of devices, but instead is composed of devices with different responsibilities that interact as peers. Within this general context of egalitarian access, the two stacks have variants in specific design goals.

TCP/IP, for instance, was designed, in part, to keep the network between military research labs up and running in the event of a major North American land war. It was developed about the same time as SNA, in the early 1970s. The TCP/IP protocols in this stack focus on immediate rerouting of traffic around failed nodes and other features consistent with its original goal of robust, fail-soft operations.

Novell designed IPX/SPX (based on Xerox Network System [XNS] from Xerox) in the early 1980s as a proprietary network/transport combo underneath NetWare, its LAN networking operating-system flagship product. IPX's specific goals were simple: to make quick connections from device to server and to keep NetWare buyers firmly in the Novell camp. Therefore, interoperability with other protocols was anathema to its goals.

NetBIOS has always been a bit of a renegade, although developed by IBM (in conjunction with Sytek, now Hughes LAN Systems). It was promoted in the early 1980s by IBM's personal computer division which was intent on releasing a LAN before IBM's strategic token ring and LAN Server would be ready. It was incorporated into most early leading PC LAN architectures, including those of LAN pioneers Ungermann-Bass and 3Com. Although NetBIOS networking has been replaced by newer, less complex, and more powerful protocols, its impact on LAN internetworking continues to be felt through its large installed base of applications that write to the NetBIOS interface.

5.2 Defining networking functions

In order to understand this new networking world, we need to examine the OSI reference model, developed by the two leading international standards organizations. We must also look at how the OSI designers define the critical internetworking functions. The OSI model for network architectures includes specifications for seven layers of network functions, from the physical wiring to sophisticated applications support.

What is often spoken of as the OSI model is actually two separate elements. The OSI reference *model* describes the functions and activities of networking and the layer at which they would be implemented. The various OSI committees used this model like a building code in order to design *protocols* and *services* that fit this model. That is, the model itself defines functions; how the function is implemented is a specific protocol's job.

The exciting part of the OSI model is that a particular function can be embodied in more than one protocol. It is recognized that there is more than one right way to get a packet from here to there, to pass messages, and to create and manage sessions with a server.

5.2.1 The physical and data-link layers

The adapter cards put into network devices generally implement the first two layers—the physical and data-link layers. For LANs, the data-link layer includes the LLC and *medium access control* (MAC) sublayers. The physical and data-link layers manage local network access and include bridge operations, as described in chapter 3, the data-link layer tutorial. Above the data-link layer we have the layers most involved with internetworking.

5.2.2 The network layer

The network layer's job, as shown in figure 5.1, is to connect a network to another network. In a practical sense, it means that the packet is traveling through a router, an internetworking device that operates at the network layer. What the router is given to look at is the information carried after the data-link header, which includes the network layer header and the information that follows it. This package, inside the data-link frame, is generally known as a packet.

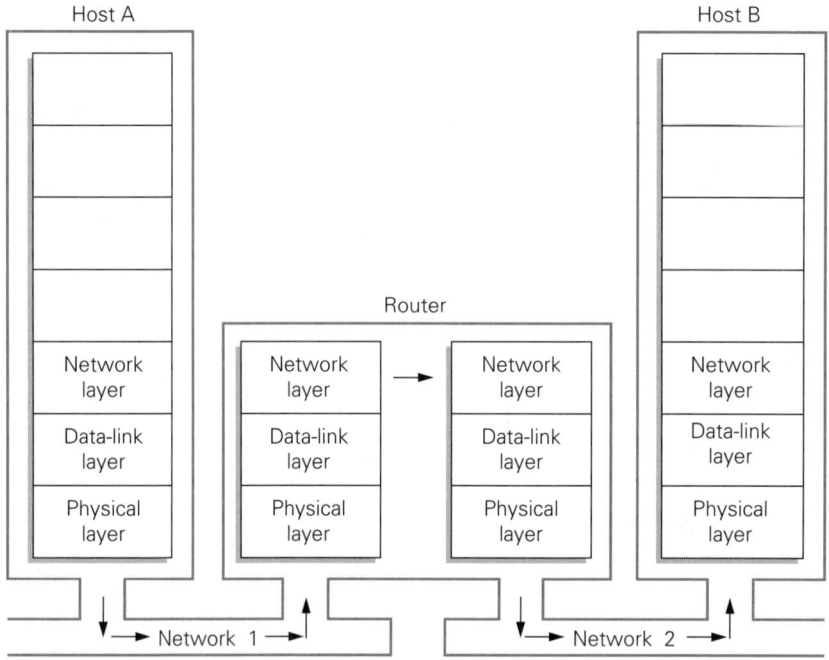

Figure 5.1   Routing at the network layer

Networks have two standard ways of routing packets between sender and receiver at the network layer:

- Virtual circuit (VC) service, also known as CONS
- Packet-switched service, also known as *datagram* or *connectionless service* (CLNS)

In packet switching, each packet is separately routed along what seems to be the fastest route available at the moment the packet arrives. This means that packets using connectionless service and taking different paths through the network could arrive out of order—although, in practice, this rarely happens.

Connectionless service is also known as best effort delivery because connectionless protocols do not have fields in the header to cope with lost packets or packets that are part of a sequence—a large data file, for instance—that may arrive out of order. The packet includes merely sender and receiver addresses and data, with an expectation that the next higher layer protocol will correct end-to-end error or misplacement problems.

The network layer in PC LANs almost always provides connectionless service because of its speed and efficiency and because connectionless packets can carry broadcast (one-to-all) and multicast (one-to-many) addresses. Protocols designed for more complex networks or networks with a high traffic volume have tended to use connection-oriented network services because they allow a higher degree of management, predictability, and reliability. The newer high-speed network protocols tend to combine some qualities of both of these models.

A common application for connectionless service at both the network and transport layer is a credit card verification network. When the store clerk runs a credit card through a machine, it creates a single packet for delivery to a distant database. A single packet returns with an answer of yes or no. If a packet gets lost, the clerk will eventually run the card through again.

5.2.3 The transport layer

Transport layer software resides on the sender and receiver devices. The transport layer provides quality control of the network's data transmission. Transport protocols are usually connection-oriented. With VC service, the device sets up the connection, transmits one or more packets, and then closes down the connection. Because it is connection-oriented, VC service cannot support broadcast or multicast addresses.

In the frames of most protocols, a transport layer header is located after the network layer header. This header usually includes fields that allow the sender and receiver to assign three types of numbers:

- VC numbers to all the packets associated with a particular message
- Acknowledgment numbers that allow the receiver to indicate that a particular packet was received
- Sequence numbers that allow the receiver to put the incoming packets that belong to a VC into proper order so that the message gets reassembled properly

Intermediate devices between end stations can operate at several different layers. Products that internetwork at layer four or above are usually called gateways. In today's LANs, most internetworking occurs at the network layer, in a router, as part of a network protocol implementing connectionless service.

5.2.4 Session, presentation, and application layers

Moving further up the OSI seven-layer reference model, the session layer, layer five, creates, manages, and terminates sessions. When LAN users log on to a server, for example, they are making a session-layer connection. Presentation layer services, at layer six, include character code translations—*American standard code for information interchange* (ASCII) and *extended binary coded decimal interchange code* (EBCDIC), for example—and screen format translations. The application layer contains the basic utilities that support the application programs like file access, remote operations, network management and electronic mail transport, not the applications themselves—the applications are considered to reside above the top of the communication stack.

In LANs, a *network operating system* (NOS) like NetWare or VINES and middleware is software at these three layers, sitting on top of a reliable transport layer. NOSs and middleware gateways can be used in an internetworking strategy in addition to or instead of routers. These upper-layer internetworking options are discussed in chapter 6 and chapters 12 through 14.

5.2.5 Routing

TCP/IP, IPX/SPX, and OSI-compliant stacks share a common design goal of assuming a primary need for immediate, dynamic rerouting around failed nodes and congested paths. The network layer protocols used in these architectures are each designed to allow the network routers to quickly see who the ultimate sender and receiver are, so they can use the dynamically updated routing tables that they build to move each packet along its best path. Figure 5.2 shows a relatively simple network that has several alternate routes between many of the networks.

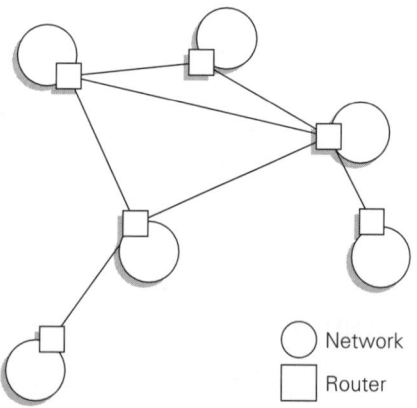

Figure 5.2   Simple internetwork with several alternate routes

Routers create dynamic routing tables by sharing routing information with each other. The rules that a router follows as it builds a routing table and decides how often to broadcast its knowledge about the network are called its routing protocol.

The TCP/IP standard specifies different dynamic routing protocols. The more prevalent protocols for interior routing are RIP and the newer OSPF. Because RIP had several performance limitations, some vendors developed proprietary routing protocols in addition to the standard. OSPF is the newer, faster way to get routers to share information on multiple available paths through the network. These protocols all follow the peer paradigm; no one is in charge or is monitoring the performance of the other devices.

Routing is a protocol-specific task. Therefore, a *multiprotocol* router is actually a box with two or more (software) routers in it. The various protocols develop routing tables independently in most cases; the existence of separate routing tables for multiple protocols is called the ships-in-the-night approach to multiprotocol networks. Some protocols can save information in a single, integrated routing table—this is called integrated routing. To date, only IP and the OSI protocols can integrate, a process we'll discuss in the OSI section. Another internetworking option is for one protocol to be enveloped inside another protocol's headers to traverse a section of the network.

Routers advertise their availability by sending out broadcasts on their LANs. The local devices—devices on each separate network segment—cache the local (media access control, or MAC) addresses of their attached routers until they need internetworking service. When they need the servers, they have a MAC address destination for their routing request. When one station wants to send data to a station on a different network, it uses the nearest router's MAC address in the data-link header, but it addresses the ultimate destination station using its network layer address in the network header, which includes information about both the individual station and the network on which it resides. The router uses the network layer address to forward the packet through the internetwork.

5.2.6 Network topologies

For internetworking purposes, the TCP/IP, IPX/SPX, and OSI-compliant stacks share a common assumption of a meshed network topology. A large network may have a topology that is an almost infinitely complex mesh.

None of these architectures *assume* a hierarchical topology. However, they can be implemented incorporating some level of distributed function or hierarchy. Having some degree of hierarchy is a good router strategy when large numbers of routers—say, over 100—or long distances are involved.

5.2.7 Addressing conventions

For most of these protocols, the network layer header specifies a network address and other parameters that routers use to get the packet to its ultimate destination. The network address specifies the ultimate sender and receiver. In contrast, a data-link address always specifies the immediate destination of a frame on the local LAN.

5.2.8 Congestion

All networks are subject to congestion. How a network architecture responds to congestion is a reflection of its design goals. IP, IPX, and the OSI-compliant protocols were all designed for networks with bursty traffic—it was more efficient for them to use connectionless protocols than to keep up a connection that was infrequently used and to allow packets to adapt to the best available path at the time it was sent. On the down side, with this process, a network packet can arrive at a router at any time, unpredictably, and the network has to be able to cope with it.

Some of the ways that a router in these networks cope with congestion include:

- Discard packets that arrive when it is too congested to process it, assuming that the transport layer VCs in the end-user devices will recover by resending
- Tell end users why their packet was thrown out
- Send a packet on a longer, more roundabout but less busy path
- Meter packets (holding them up) before they enter the network
- Buffer packets for a short while in the hope that congestion will clear

Some LANs and WANs cope with unpredictable traffic levels by overprovisioning —that is, constantly maintaining enough bandwidth for the busiest times—and so do many LANs. Throwing bandwidth at a problem is a simple but not particularly clever solution. It does produce the desired result in some cases, but it is also a more expensive solution, particularly in the wide area where monthly rates are based in part on capacity.

5.2.9 Priority

None of the protocols we are examining here have considered priority an important goal, at least until recently. Although the headers do have fields that allow you to assign priorities to traffic types, these facilities are essentially unimplemented. IP was designed for research organizations, universities, and government organizations to communicate. However, most of their traffic was intraorganizational, which was local to a single building or campus. It was enhanced for use in LANs, which again had a local geographic scope—usually one department or building.

The IP and IPX designers and users like to say they had an egalitarian mindset with regard to their initial environments. In actuality, they had the luxury of not having to face the priority issue. For IP, since the government was paying for the network, it did not need to be highly efficient—the solution to greater traffic was to add more capacity. For IPX, originally designed for one or a few geographically limited LANs, priority was also not a major issue.

Therefore, both environments were able to ignore priorities for some time because their customers didn't demand it. Users who *did* need priority management—companies with many geographically dispersed branch offices in retail, banking, insurance, and transportation—had selected SNA, which emphasized features such as prioritization and congestion control. So there hasn't been—until recently—a strong business need to overturn the original design. As TCP/IP and IPX users have expanded their networks, however, they are now demanding from their vendors what SNA users have always had. At the same time, SNA has been enhanced with several features, such as dynamic configuration and dynamic rerouting.

5.3 The OSI approach

The OSI-compliant protocols were developed through the International Organization for Standardization (ISO, from the French name). Since they were developed by an international organization, they include options for every conceivable networking need. In the internetworking area, OSI's protocols allow CLNS and CONS at most layers, with CLNS most often implemented at the network layer.

OSI uses the largest network addressing field of all—64 bits or eighteen quintillion addresses. If used most efficiently, this would allow more than three billion addresses for each person on the planet. The temptation is to claim that this is a large enough field to last forever. But this had been said of the early SNA and TCP/IP address space based on the space-supporting orders of magnitude larger than the largest imaginable network or number of networks. Given that networks will continue to develop in revolutionary steps and new categories of devices and software elements may use multiple addresses, all we can safely say is that this space is larger than can be considered necessary for the foreseeable future. (The Internet community briefly considered adopting this addressing scheme to solve some problems confronting the IP protocol, but ultimately decided against it in favor of another scheme.)

OSI does not actually use the term *address*. Instead it uses the terms *network entity title* (NET) and *network service access point* (NSAP).

OSI's transport layer gives network developers five potential classes of service for error control. Only two of these are ever implemented in the U.S.—TP0 performs no error recovery and TP4 supports a high degree of error control and corresponds to the TCP protocol in that it implements a connection-oriented service.

OSI connectionless routing uses a routing protocol called *intermediate system-to-intermediate system* (IS–IS) routing. This sounds confusing until you realize that OSI divides the world into intermediate systems (routers) and end systems (everything else, that is, the devices that use the routers).

The IS–IS protocol is for communication from router to router. The ES–IS protocol determines the format of the advertising broadcasts that routers send out to announce their availability to ESs in their attached networks. Because ESs need to know how to respond to these advertisements, the ES–IS Hellos contain an address field. Now which address is this? The data-link address! ESs send routing requests to a router at its local data-link address, not a network address.

5.4 The TCP/IP family of protocols

TCP/IP was originally developed by the designers of the U.S. Defense Department's Advanced Research Projects Agency (ARPA) network to provide internetworking over a WAN. ARPAnet was the progenitor of what is known today as the Internet, the global network of routers linking networks and host systems.[1] What is referred to collectively as the TCP/IP protocol stack comprises three layers of functionality: the routing layer, the quality layer, and a utilities layer. However, the layer-naming convention for TCP/IP has been shifting to the OSI reference model for layers, though the functions at each layer are not completely equivalent.

IP provides the routing layer services which are roughly equivalent to the OSI Model's network layer. The quality layer services, equivalent to the OSI's transport layer, are provided by TCP. The utilities layer comprises a number of protocols that provide network utilities such as *file transfer protocol* (FTP); telnet, a virtual terminal emulation protocol; and *simple mail transfer protocol* (SMTP), a network electronic mail transfer protocol.

5.4.1 Internet protocol

The IP protocol is used by routers to switch and forward packets between networks. Those networks may be physically adjacent or separated by a wide-area link. When a router receives an IP packet, it looks at the 32-bit *destination address* in the IP header to determine its ultimate recipient. The router then consults its routing tables, which contain information about the network on which the destination station resides. Based on the packet's destination, the router switches it to the appropriate output port and sends it on its way.

The router may directly link the network where the packet originated and the destination station's network, in which case it simply switches the packet between the two

---

1. The Internet—with an upper case *I*—should not be confused with an *internet*, a term often used to refer to a group of geographically remote LANs interconnected by bridges or routers and telecommunications links.

networks. However, in a large internetwork, a router may send the packet along a path that includes a series of routers linking several networks before it reaches the packet's final destination. In this case, the goal of each router is to forward the packet further along on its journey using the best path available. As is often the case in a complex internetwork, there may be more than one path on which a router can send a packet to get to its final destination. This is where the router uses RIP, OSPF, or one of the other path-selection algorithms to select the best path.

The network addresses used by IP to identify source and destination stations are different from the MAC addresses used by a network's data-link protocol—such as ethernet, token ring, or FDDI. Every LAN adapter card has a unique MAC address that is permanently embedded in the hardware and allows it to be addressed directly by the data-link layer protocol. Network layer protocols such as IP and IPX provide for a software-configurable network address for each station. The network address can be changed and is independent of the MAC address.

IP addresses are assigned to each station by a company's network administrator. Each address can be used to designate a network number, an (optional) subnetwork number, and the individual station number. Using this addressing scheme, an IP router can quickly determine where a packet is destined within a complex internetwork. IP addresses can be used to subdivide even a very large enterprise network into a manageable organization of networks and subnetworks linked by routers. The addressing scheme works equally well for routing packets among networks on a single campus or across a wide area, although a hierarchy of address servers on gateways is necessary in the largest networks to avoid the enormous overhead of constant, widespread advertising from routers.

Because the network layer IP address is independent of the data-link layer MAC addresses for each station, a way is needed to discover the MAC address for a station if only its IP address is known. A special protocol, the *address resolution protocol* (ARP), works alongside IP to handle this. To resolve addresses, an ARP server can be used, which contains tables associating MAC and network addresses for a given network.

IP also provides a way for human users to give network stations more easily remembered logical *names* to use as an alias (or aliases) for network *addresses*. The correlation of the link-station address and its one or more logical names is done by a *name service* protocol. The name service uses another table located in one or more host computers on the network. So, for example, a station with an IP address of 131.17.3.2 can also have a name such as Host1 or an even more descriptive name like AdminHost. The IP protocol uses this host names table to find the address using the logical name supplied by the user. (Note that TCP/IP uses the term *host* for all stations that are not routers, while SNA reserves the term *host* for mainframes.) One limitation of this scheme is that these tables must be manually configured and updated, although options for dynamic registration are being developed.

5.4.2 Transmission-control protocol

Where IP is connectionless and tries only to make a good effort at delivering each packet through the network from source to destination, TCP is a connection-oriented protocol. It is concerned with providing reliable end-to-end communication between two stations on the network. TCP provides four basic services:

- Provide an interface to which network applications and utilities can be written
- Ensure that packet errors are discovered and corrected, and provides flow control
- Verify that packets are correctly sequenced before they are handed over to the receiving station
- Create of a virtual-circuit connection between the two communicating stations

TCP is a network transport service for higher-layer applications and network utilities. It offers a programming interface by which those applications can directly access network services. An application on one station needing to send data to an application on another station somewhere else on the network can use the services of TCP to make sure its data arrives intact. At a programming level, this is accomplished by writing the application to utilize TCP's programming interface. Because connections to TCP from upper layers are called sockets, the most common direct programming interface to TCP is called the sockets interface, which is further discussed in chapter 6. Alternatively, many applications take advantage of several TCP/IP-related protocols, including FTP, SMTP, or the telnet interactive communication protocol.

TCP handles error detection and correction by requiring that, when the TCP layer in the receiving station receives a packet, it sends an acknowledgment back to the TCP layer in the sending station. It must do so within a specified period of time. If the sending station's TCP layer doesn't receive the acknowledgment within the specified time, it assumes the packet was lost or damaged and retransmits it. TCP also uses a checksum in each packet to provide error detection.

To further ensure the quality of transmission, TCP provides flow control. If the receiving station becomes backed up during transmission of a sequence of packets, it will cut back the flow of packets from the sending station.

Proper packet sequencing is ensured by providing a sequence number within the TCP header. If a group of packets contain sequenced data, for example portions of a data file or an electronic mail message, they must be delivered to the receiving computer system session layer in the order they were sent. However, since IP routes each packet through the internetwork separately—remember, IP is a connectionless service—the different paths they take may result in their arriving out of order. (In contrast, because subarea SNA is connection-oriented at the data-link and network layer, an out-of-sequence packet at layer four in an SNA system is clearly an indication of a significant problem, so resequencing is not used.)

In order to provide the error recovery and sequencing services, TCP must establish a VC between two nodes so that they recognize that they are communicating with one another. To do this, TCP provides procedures to request, confirm, and close a VC *connection* between two stations. Only after the VC is established can the two communicating stations take advantage of TCP's reliable transport capabilities.

As part of TCP's reliable end-to-end communication service, it also provides the ability to transmit data to a particular application on the receiving station. It recognizes that there may be multiple applications running and can address them individually, giving each application a specific port number in the TCP header.

The TCP/IP protocol stack also contains a connectionless transport mechanism at the transport layer called *user datagram protocol* (UDP). UDP is usually used for messages that are frequently repeated or updated, such as router table updates, where the loss of a single message would not have a big impact but the effort of bringing up a TCP connection each time would.

Like TCP, UDP uses IP to address and deliver its message through the network. UDP provides connectionless transport services on top of IP. Unlike TCP, it doesn't require a virtual circuit connection and doesn't provide error correction or sequencing. It does provide an application port address so that the data can be delivered to a particular application on the receiving station.

5.5 IPX and SPX: the Novell approach

Novell's NOS includes its own proprietary network and transport layer protocols. Because NetWare dominates the LAN NOS market, its networking protocol also has a large presence in the market.

The original NetWare networking protocol was quite sparse, because it was originally designed for use in an environment consisting of a few workgroups confined within a single campus LAN. It has been enhanced along the lines of the TCP/IP model. Thus, the IPX is a connectionless network layer protocol that is structured very similar to IP and supports network layer functions, as shown in figure 5.3.

IPX makes a best-effort attempt to deliver packets to the destination station using a 12-byte addressing scheme. An IPX address contains three elements: a network address

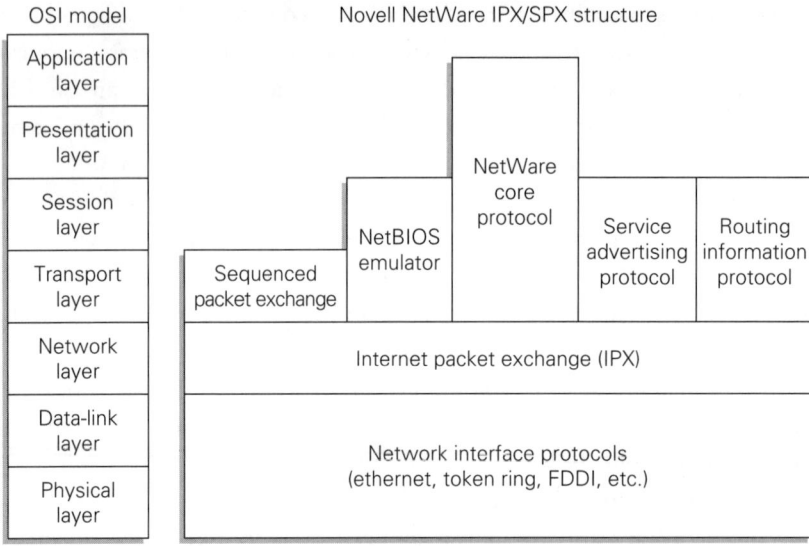

Figure 5.3 Novell NetWare IPX/SPX structure and the OSI model

used to identify individual workgroups, the node address of the individual station within the workgroup, and a socket address to identify a particular application on that station.

IPX only has one level of addressing above the node address (the workgroup address), compared to IP's network and subnetwork levels. This makes IPX less flexible and robust in large enterprise networks than its cousin, IP. Also, instead of identifying a particular application on the receiving station in the transport layer protocol, it includes the application port in the network layer address.

Other than these differences, however, IPX provides essentially the same functions as IP with regard to routing packets between networks. An IPX router reads the destination address in the IPX header, decides the best path on which to send it, and transmits it on its way through the network. Using routers and the IPX addressing scheme, network administrators can organize and manage large internetworks of workgroup LANs.

SPX provides the connection-oriented communications services of the transport layer within the Novell protocol stack. Like TCP, SPX establishes virtual circuits, provides error detection and correction, and ensures proper sequencing of packets.

Neither IPX nor SPX provides a name service that allows users to identify a station by a logical name instead of a network address. To accomplish this, NetWare uses an SAP. Every server in the network periodically broadcasts its name and address to the network, so that all other stations can record it for future reference.

Several internetworking products can carry IPX/SPX protocols over networks of different protocols such as TCP/IP and SNA. Novell is also implementing NetWare directly, or natively, on top of TCP/IP networking.

5.6 NetBIOS

NetBIOS is a programming interface and protocol originally developed by IBM for use on its early IBM PC Network product, which was itself based on Microsoft's Microsoft Networks. The PC Network was developed in the early 1980s by IBM's personal computer group which did not want to wait for the emergence of IBM's strategic token ring LAN. Because of the popularity of the IBM PC and because NetBIOS was an extension of the native BIOS of the PC, many standalone PC applications were adapted to the NetBIOS interface, though the PC Network hardware was not successful.

NetBIOS operates at the session layer and provides some of the functions of the session, transport, and network layers. The specific services provided by NetBIOS include:

- A programming interface by which higher-layer applications (usually written to run on DOS PCs) can access network services

- A name service which associates logical names with MAC addresses of network stations

- Reliable end-to-end transport service with error correction, flow control, and packet sequencing

Unlike IP and IPX, however, NetBIOS is not a *routable* protocol, that is, a packet cannot be processed for route selection by a router based exclusively on the information in packet itself. Because it was expected to be used only in small networks, it was designed to route at the data-link layer, that is, to use IBM's source route bridging scheme for sending frames between different token-passing rings.

As described in chapter 3, this source route bridging scheme requires that the sending station embed within each frame the route it will take through the network. IBM's source route bridges then use this information to forward frames from one ring to another. It uses an extension of the token ring frame format (part of the data-link layer protocol) rather than a network layer addressing and routing protocol. NetBIOS has no concept of network layer addresses, which means that it cannot be used to route packets through an internetwork in the same way that IP or IPX can.

When the NetBIOS programming interface was first published by IBM, a large number of DOS PC program developers altered their applications to bypass DOS and

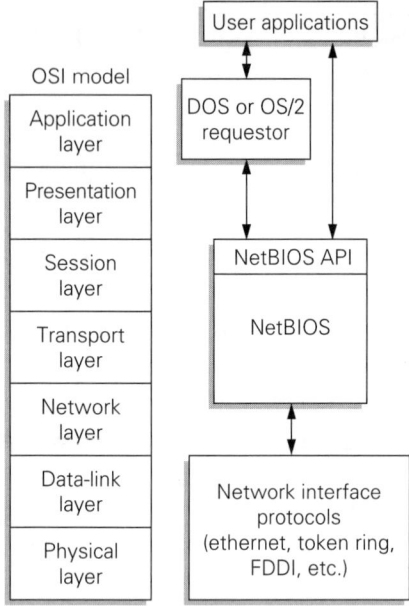

OSI model

OSI model
Application layer
Presentation layer
Session layer
Transport layer
Network layer
Data-link layer
Physical layer

User applications

DOS or OS/2 requestor

NetBIOS API

NetBIOS

Network interface protocols (ethernet, token ring, FDDI, etc.)

Figure 5.4   NetBIOS structure and the OSI model

make requests for network services directly to NetBIOS, as shown in figure 5.4. This meant that, if users wanted to run their favorite applications on a network, the NOS had to include a NetBIOS interface. Novell, Banyan, and all of the other NOS vendors quickly added what they generally called NetBIOS emulators to their products. NetBIOS has remained a part of every NOS vendor's product, including Microsoft's LAN Manager, because so many applications were written to its programming interface.

5.7 Summary

The four protocol stacks described in this chapter provide some services basic to transmission of data between stations on shared-media local area networks. Although they differ from each other and from SNA, all can roughly be represented in the blueprint shown in figure 5.5. The blueprint is further discussed in chapter 2. The OSI, TCP/IP, and IPX/SPX stacks provide more or less the same set of services, but do so in different ways. NetBIOS is less complete in that it doesn't include network layer routing.

Of the four, OSI and TCP/IP are the best for use in large, complex enterprise networks because of their flexibility in structuring multilayered network systems. IPX/SPX

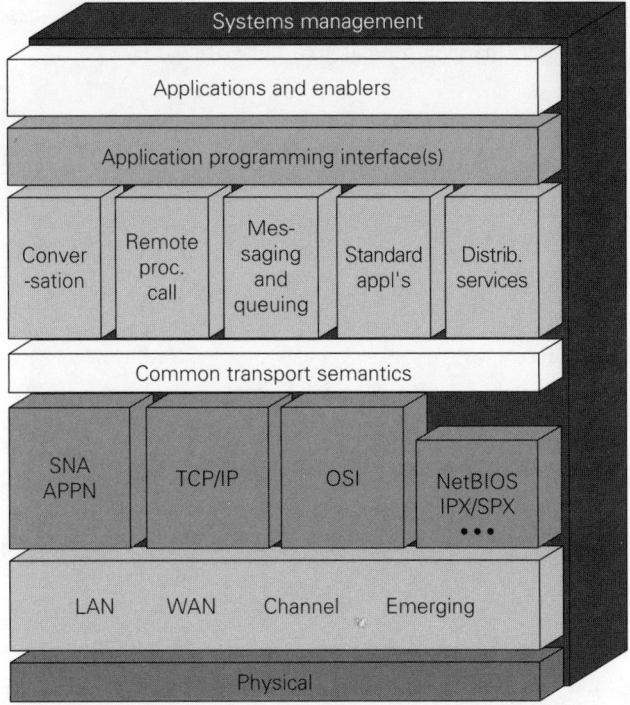

Figure 5.5 SNA, OSI, TCP/IP, IPX/SPX, and NetBIOS in the blueprint

was originally designed for use in smaller, simpler internetworks consisting of small, relatively self-contained groups of PC workstations communicating with PC servers. Where IPX/SPX has been implemented on a large scale, even though it has been enhanced, it requires a significant amount of administration.

OSI, TCP/IP, and IPX/SPX can be routed using network layer protocol routers. Each requires that the router is running the appropriate protocol. For example, to route both IP and IPX, the router must be running software for both protocols. In this case, it would be called a multiprotocol router. NetBIOS was designed to be used in a source-route bridging environment, and therefore cannot be routed using network layer protocol routers at all. A router must also be able to function as a source-routing bridge to support NetBIOS traffic.

Table 5.1 compares these four protocol stacks with regard to the key services required for communication between stations over a local area network.

Table 5.1   Protocol comparisons

	OSI	TCP/IP	IPX	NetBIOS
Network layer				
Protocol(s)	Connectionless (CLNS), connection-oriented (CONS)	Internet protocol (IP), address resolution protocol (ARP)	Internet packet exchange (IPX)	Network basic input/output system (NetBIOS)
Routable	Yes	Yes	Yes	No
Network layer address size	64 bits	32 bits	12 bytes	N/A
Network layer addressable elements	Network subnetwork station	Network subnetwork station	Workgroup station port	Port
Name-to-address resolution	Yes	Yes	Yes	Yes
Network layer-to-MAC address resolution	Yes	Yes	Yes	N/A
Transport layer				
Protocol(s)	TP0 through TP4	Transmission control protocol (TCP), user datagram protocol (UDP)	Sequenced packet exchange (SPX)	NetBIOS
Virtual circuit service	Yes	Yes	Yes	Yes
Datagram service	Yes	Yes	Yes	Yes
Application port address	Yes	Yes	No (included in IPX address)	No
Data checksum	Yes	Yes	Yes	Yes
Positive acknowledgment	Yes	Yes	Yes	Yes
Timeout and retransmit	Yes	Yes	Yes	Yes
Sequencing	Yes	Yes	Yes	No
Flow control	Yes	Yes	Yes	Yes
Programming interface	Yes	Yes	Yes	Yes

chapter 6

Tutorial on application programming interfaces

HAROLD HAUCK

This chapter tackles one of the most challenging issues in networking: application program interface. Although API was originally defined outside of the six-layer SNA model, since the purpose of any networking model is to support applications programming, the application layer was subsequently added to networking models. Harold Hauck takes us through a number of different distributed application subsystems and application programming interfaces popular in the SNA and TCP/IP worlds. Although APIs are usually associated with the underlined networking protocols, all of the primary APIs discussed in this chapter can be run across either SNA or TCP/IP networks.

6.1 Introduction to APIs

APIs provide a formally defined access and control mechanism by which application programmers may exploit the facilities and functions of specialized computing subsystems. These subsystems and their associated APIs have evolved over the past two decades, providing ever more powerful application services while masking the complexity of the underlying low-level data, system, and network services which they exploit.

APIs and specialized subsystems currently provide a broad range of application services. These have a broad range of functionality:

- Low-level access to data through support routines—such as the index sequential access method (ISAM) or the virtual storage access method (VSAM)
- Low-level networking application support facilities—such as Berkeley sockets or the System V transport layer interface (TLI)
- Very comprehensive database management systems like DB/2 or transaction monitors such as IBM's CICS.

While many applications have been written using the APIs provided by low-level subsystems, technology continues to evolve, and often using the facilities of these low-level subsystems and APIs, more powerful application support systems or *middleware* such as data base managers and transactions management systems have become prevalent. Today, application programmers are seeking ways to create network-based distributed applications which exploit the capabilities of various processor architectures and system facilities.

Distributed applications are being written using the APIs of subsystems which provide several functions:

- Minimize or remove the complexities of the underlying data networks from the application code

- Create an environment which removes or masks specific computer architecture as an application programming concern
- Provide valuable application functions such as resource security, directory and naming services, data routing and queuing capability, and error recovery services
- Ease portability of applications across operating system and network types

Using these subsystem APIs, client programs running on work stations and personal computers are providing graphical user interface and application support functions through network connections to other work stations, mini computers, main frames or super computers where server programs are executing the primary data or compute intensive application program logic.

This chapter will cover a wide range of material in the following way:

- To introduce distributed network application APIs and subsystems, we will first look at three popular models for distributed application design;
- To introduce the level of function and complexity among subsystems and APIs, we will investigate a low level subsystem—the Berkeley Software Distribution (BSD) socket interface. This subsystem and API provide the underlying support for many *remote procedure call* (RPC)-based client/server application support products;
- We will next examine the Open Software Foundation's Distributed Computing Environment (DCE) to illustrate the application facilities and the API of this RPC-based subsystem;
- We will then explore the facilities and functions of a conversation supporting subsystem such as IBM's APPC and one of its APIs, CPI-C;
- The last API and subsystem to be introduced is a message queue application support system and its *message queuing interface* (MQI) API.

6.2 Models for distributed application design

Three application models and their associated subsystem APIs have evolved to support the dispersion of function across both local and wide area networks. Figure 6.1 illustrates these application models for distributed computing.

6.2.1 RPC client/server overview

The client/server model using the RPC API is based on a running server process which is listening on a communications port for the arrival of client requests. Client processes issue RPCs asking for execution of a specific functional procedure from the remote

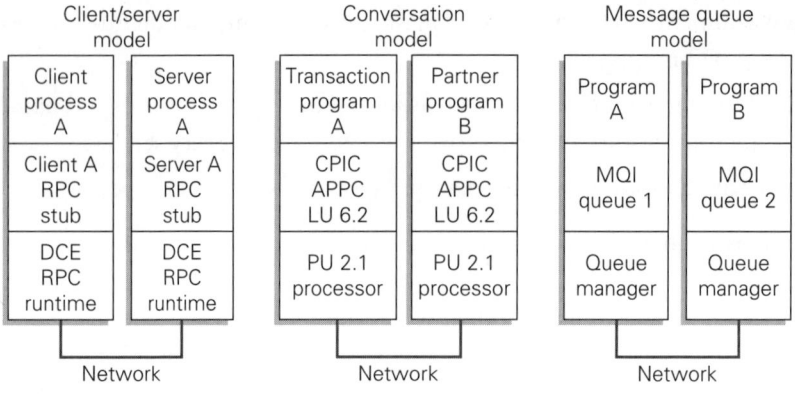

Figure 6.1   Distributed application models

server process. Upon receiving the call from a client process, the server performs the requested procedure and transmits the results to the client process.

The stub routines are located in both client and server address space. They are created by a declarative *interface definition language* (IDL) and intermediary compiler. The IDL compiler produces language-specific source code (typically C language statements) from the IDL source statements. The IDL generated stub code provides interface specifications, defines constants and data types, determines data and parameter marshaling needs, and specifies data conversion requirements for both the client and server processes.

The RPC run-time library is an interface to the stub routines for controlling the transmission and receipt of data across the network. These library routines also provide directory support so client processes can locate servers, create connections between the client and server, bind the client to the server, and maintain state conditions between the pair of processes.

On the client machine, the run-time is linked with the stub modules and the client binaries to form half of the application. Similarly on the server machine, the server binaries, stubs, and run-time are linked into a load module to complete the client/server application's executable environment.

6.2.2 Conversation model overview

Using the application programming verbs and services defined by IBM's LU 6.2 SNA specifications, applications may be designed and written to accomplish a one- or two-way dialogue across a data network. In this model, a conversation-initiating program, through the use of a set of LU 6.2 defined application verbs, requests a LU 6.2 conversation manager running on a remote system to start a specific application program and then allow a conversation in which the initiating program and the started program exchange an arbitrary number of messages.

While SNA defines a number of different LU types, only LU 6.2 is a generic, hardware-independent set of application verbs and services designed for program-to-program communication. Among the services an LU 6.2 system provides are ports for end-to-end communication across a network, management and control of the data flow between those ports through a session manager, and a resource manager for remote program initiation and termination.

APPC refers to the API and services defined by the LU 6.2 specifications. These APPC verbs and services have been accepted as an industry standard for synchronous communications. APPC verbs have been implemented by many vendors supporting a wide range of communication subsystems. In this chapter we will examine the CPI-C implementation of APPC. CPI-C provides a hardware architecture and operating system-independent API and a subsystem for the execution of conversational application programs.

Completing the functional elements of the conversational model are the SNA specifications for node type 2.1 network nodes. These lower-level nodes provide communications support between the various systems in the conversational network. At the physical level, they provide communication management services such as link activation and deactivation across any-to-any, point-to-point, and multipoint connections. Node type 2.1 nodes are also responsible for management, activation, and deactivation of LU–LU sessions.

With the advent of APPN products, the functions of node type 2.1 nodes have expanded from the initial limited capability provided by the earlier LEN nodes. LEN nodes are only capable of supporting peer-to-peer sessions across point-to-point links. The functionally rich node type 2.1 NN is capable of all LEN node functions and provides intermediate network routing support along with dynamic network configuration capability. In an APPN network, any LEN node or NN is capable of communicating and establishing LU–LU sessions with any other LEN node or NN. A network node provides distributed directory service and routing functions for the LUs running under its control. It provides these same functions for all the LUs running on other directly connected LEN node processors.

6.2.3 Message queuing overview

MQI and its associated subsystem, the *message queue manager* (MQM), provide for a very powerful distributed programming environment that supports synchronous, asynchronous, connectionless, and parallel processing application design styles.

Under this system, a message is any arbitrary string of bits or bytes which have meaning to more than one application program. Using an MQI system, programs communicate by sending and receiving messages to and from specific message queues. Application messages are inserted at the end of a named queue and removed (by default) from the front of the queue as requested by a second application process. In addition to this default first-in–first-out (FIFO) message ordering scheme, MQI also provides a priority message queue capability where messages are ordered by their individual priority. Thus high priority messages are placed in FIFO order ahead of lower priority messages residing in the same queue.

Message queues are named *objects* owned and managed by a specific message queue manager. MQMs provide message queuing facilities to their local application programs by responding to MQI program calls. MQMs may own multiple message queues and at least one MQM must be running on each system participating in the message queue network. Each MQM must have a unique name by which it is known to all other MQMs in the network. The MQMs provide all of the communication functions needed for the reliable transfer of messages between and among the various MQM queues. Because of this MQI system attribute, application programs are completely unaware of any network issues. They need only write to and read from queues managed by their local MQM.

6.3 Berkeley sockets

BSD socket protocols and API provide a low-level application service for network communication. Sockets are the basic communication structure for many of the application and system service programs in TCP/IP networks.

Through a set of library routines and C language system calls, sockets provide an interprocess communications (IPC) channel. This channel contains endpoints or ports that are described by names similar to a file system descriptor. After the endpoints used by two applications processes are connected, the processes can issue read and write systems calls to exchange data across the logical communication channel. Figure 6.2 illustrates a generalized logic flow of socket system calls using a connection-oriented TCP transport mechanism for this type of information exchange.

With reference to figure 6.2, the following describes the steps needed for an application to communicate across a socket:

1 The server process obtains a socket from the operating system kernel by issuing a `socket()` system call. A `bind()` system call is issued to assign a name to the socket in the host system's name space. This is followed by a `listen()` call which opens the port for connection. The `accept()` call either completes a connection from requests stored on a pending queue, or blocks the server process until a connection request from a client process arrives.

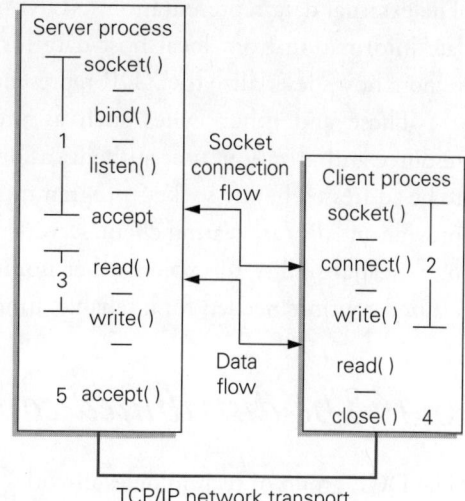

Figure 6.2 BSD socket API

2 The client process creates a socket with the `socket()` call. It connects to the named server socket with the `connect()` call. Following these initialization steps, the client issues a `write()` call which sends data to the socket port from a buffer pointed to by one of the write calls parameters. The underlying TCP protocols transport the data across the network to the server's socket port.

3 The server process receives client information through a `read()` socket call, performs the appropriate processing to satisfy the client request and, using the `write()` call, returns results to the client. The two processes may continue in this manner exchanging data by issuing alternate read and write system calls.

4 The client process, when completed with its use of the server, will issue a `close()` system call to remove the socket from the client system's name space and sever its TCP connection to the server.

5 The server will issue an `accept()` call to either obtain another client connection request or block execution pending arrival of such a request.

This primitive example of the socket API illustrates the fundamental steps required for processes to exchange information across a network. Additional programming may be required prior to socket creation and during the data transmission sections of the applications. For example, client processes may need to locate the server host address and port number. These can be found in many systems through use of the API provided by Sun's Network Information Service (NIS), formerly known as the Yellow Pages (YP).

Client and server processes are likely to be running on different processor architecture. The data they exchange must be translated into a network independent format.

The external data representation (XDR) library and API provide routines which translate information from local host data formats to an XDR representation and, on the remote host, deserialize the XDR representation back to that host's data formats.

These and other issues such as processor time synchronization, data security, resource authorization, user authentication, and error recovery processing may also need to be addressed by the sockets programmer. Thus, it can be seen that while BSD sockets provide an API for creating client/server-style distributed applications, it is the programmer's responsibility to exploit other nonintegrated support components or create specialized routines needed for a reliable, functionally complete, and secure application.

6.4 *The distributed computing environment*

The DCE group of technologies provides a rich set of application functions bound by a common API for the development of RPC-based client/server applications. The application support features of DCE remove many of the functional limitations which programmers must be concerned with when using a socket interface. As figure 6.3 illustrates, DCE implements a set of core technologies which run under many different operating systems and processor architecture.

The underlying structure of a DCE network contains an arbitrary number of heterogeneous processors. These processors may communicate and share resources across

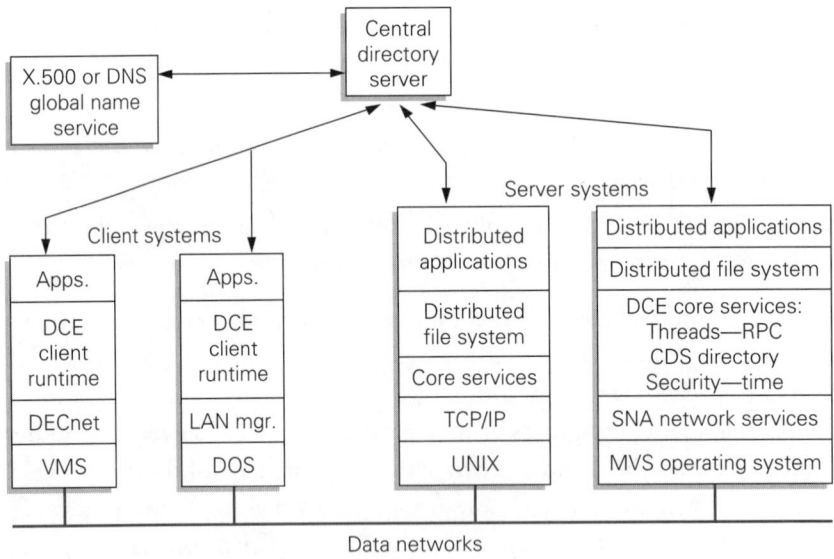

Figure 6.3 DCE cell structure

local and wide-area networks. While the DCE technology is transport protocol independent, current DCE implementations run on a TCP/IP protocol stack.

DCE core services include a process threads library, a remote procedure call API, a directory and naming service, a security service, and processor time synchronization functions. These core technologies are complemented by a distributed file system which logically combines the physical file systems from many processors into a single global hierarchical file structure. All resources in a DCE network are located and accessed through common naming semantics which, at a global level, may be implemented through either an X.500 or an internet domain name system (DNS) directory service.

6.4.1 DCE cells

For operational and administrative purposes, a collection of processors are grouped into separate domains called *cells*. A DCE cell contains the systems, resources, and users who typically share a common purpose, location, or function. A functional DCE cell must have one or more processors executing the following core server components:

- DCE threads service
- RPC library and runtime
- CDS
- DCE security service
- Distributed time service (DTS)

Additionally, the RPC library and client support for these functions must be running on all client processors in the DCE network. These components provide the underlying structure for applications and provide the base level services for the distribution of functions among the cell's processes.

In a DCE cell, client applications find their server processes through the CDS. Application servers are able to determine the resource authorization levels and authenticity of client processes from the security service. DTS provides a common notion of time for all cell processors. This, among other DTS functions, enables enforcement of user or process security lifetime values. The RPC API library provides a set of system calls which create and manage interprocess data communication channels. These system calls rely upon and are used to implement the functional services of the other DCE components. The RPC runtime provides a transport independent mechanism for the reliable exchange of data across a network of distributed processors.

DCE threads, based on the *portable operating system interface for computer environments* (POSIX) 1003.4a standard, are available to improve the performance of applications running under operating systems which do not provide a native threads capability.

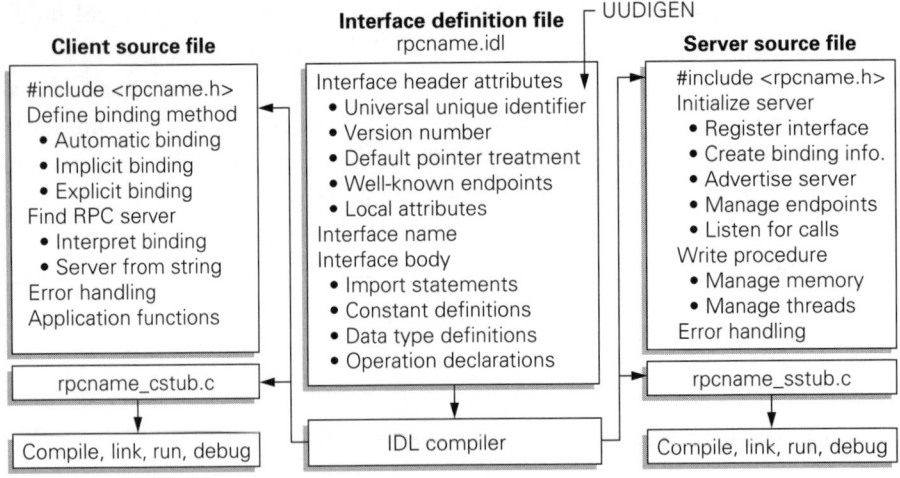

Figure 6.4 Application development components

An application may start several separate threads of execution within a single address space. Through the use of these multiple threads a server application is capable of concurrently handling multiple client requests (one for each running thread). Client processes can execute functions on alternate threads while an RPC issuing thread is blocked pending receipt of a requested service.

RPC client and server application source files contain two major components. First is the application logic code. In writing this section for servers, the programmer uses RPC system calls to initialize the server process. Then the programmer creates the actual executable procedures. On the client side the programmer, again using RPC system calls, must locate a server, bind the client to this server, and then issue the application's RPC requests to the server process. The second section of both client and server source files contain the RPC stub routines. These source statement are created by an IDL compiler.

Figure 6.4 illustrates the steps required to create a DCE RPC client/server application and identifies the major components used in the application development process.

The RPC API functions must be implemented in a prescribed sequence. First, prior to writing and compiling either the client or server components of an application, the RPC interface definition must be created. This is accomplished by the IDL compiler. IDL statements provide an interface name and version number, describe the data (arrays, pointers, constants, etc.) for the RPC, and specify the operational declarations which will be communicated between the client and server processes.

The IDL compiler creates, from these statements, C language header files and a group of C source statements. These source statements will create the client and server RPC stub routines. Next, the header file must be included and stub source statements

```
          /* FILE NAME: spell.idl */
          /* Inerface Definition to check word spelling  */
          [
IDL file  uuid(b279C356-16AF-10BB-8C52-C201AA43D6C7).      /* From UUIDGEN */
 header   version (1.0)
          ]
          interface spell     /* Interface Name Is spell */
          {                      /( Attributes, Constants, Data Type Declarations */
          Const long max_word_length  = 25;
          typedef [string] char in word[max_word-length];
          typedef [string, ptr] char out_word[max_word_length] *out_word_p;
          /* Procedure Operation Declarations  */
IDL file  long check_word_spelling
  body    (
              [in] handle_t    binding_handle,
              [in] string      in_word/max_word_length],
              [out] out_word *out_word_p
          );
          }
```

Figure 6.5 IDL file structure

merged into the client and server application C language source files. Finally, the client and server source streams can be compiled to create the executable object files.

Due to the volume and complexity of the RPC API calls, the following figures are illustrative only, they are not intended to be syntactically complete or operational code fragments. Figure 6.5 illustrates the structure of an IDL file. It shows a few of the IDL statements used to create an RPC interface definition.

The IDL file is organized into header and body sections. The syntax elements of this file enclosed in square brackets [ ] are the IDL attributes of the interface. The header text contains a *universal unique identifier* (UUID) and defines the RPC interface name. The character string following the UUID statement is obtained from a UUIDGEN utility program. Execution of this utility returns a character string based on time and network information which guarantees that the string will be unique regardless of where or when it was generated. Client programs use the UUID to identify a specific interface. The keyword *interface* followed by a word which names the interface completes the header section of the IDL file.

The body section contains data type definitions and procedure specifications. In this example, a constant max_word_length and two variables in_word and out_word are defined. The remaining portion of the body contains a procedure declaration. The parameters in and out tell the IDL compiler which direction the data is to be sent over the network.

At this point, the programmer is ready to write the application client and server source statements. With reference to figure 6.6, there are a number of steps a server process must complete prior to executing client requests. These include:

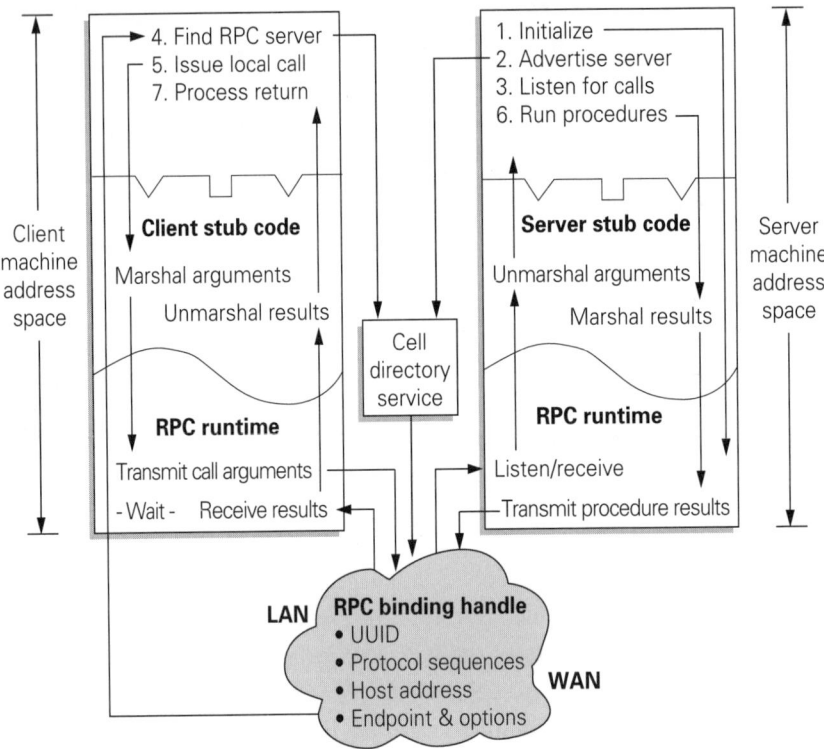

Figure 6.6 DCE RPC execution events

1 Initialize the server.

  a. The server interface must be registered with the RPC runtime.

  b. Binding information based on one or more network protocol sequences must be created.

  c. Servers which implement dynamic endpoints must register the endpoints used during the current session in the host system's endpoint map.

2 Advertise the server's host location and provide binding information. This is accomplished by storing the necessary information in a CDS name service database.

3 At this point the server is ready to process client requests and waits or listens for incoming calls.

4 Steps four through six are initialization tasks that must be executed by the client processes prior to issuing an RPC, as shown in figure 6.6. The client must define or implement a binding method and locate an RPC server process. Binding handles may be managed in one of three ways:

a. Automatic binding is the easiest in that the client stub obtains the binding information from the CDS name service database.

b. With implicit binding, client code must be written to obtain the binding information. This information is placed in a global variable from which the stub routine may pass it to the runtime.

c. Using explicit binding the client code must not only obtain the binding information, it must also pass on the binding handle to the runtime library.

5 The client must locate the server process. For clients and servers to communicate over a network they both must use the same communication protocol. During initialization, the server process registered, with the RPC runtime, the protocols it supports which, at the present time, are as follows:

a. The RPC protocols are either network computing architecture (NCA) connection-oriented protocol or NCA datagram protocol

b. The network-addressing scheme used is the IP

c. The transport protocol is either TCP or UDP.

Since a server may support multiple communication protocols, the client process must locate a server which supports its specific protocol. One method for doing this is to search the CDS name service database of registered server protocols. A client may repeatedly issue an RPC request for a new binding handle. After each call the returned binding handle is compared until the desired communication protocol is found, for example, `ncan_ip_tcp`.

6 Upon receipt of a satisfactory binding, the client is ready to issue a remote procedure call to the server process.

As can be seen from these examples, managing client and server initialization routines are significant concerns for the application programmer. Only a small subset of the available RPC routines have been discussed in this introduction to the DCE RPC API.

In addition to RPC routines, the DCE API libraries provide a rich set of tools for many other functional application requirements. There are routines to manage threads, work with the global directory service, determine and use network time, provide application security features, and obtain data from and manage the distributed file service. For a much more detailed exploration of the DCE APIs, the reader is referred to the list of reference texts at the conclusion of this chapter.

6.5 Common programming interface for communications

In the previous discussion of distributed application models, we introduced the components of a conversational API, namely the SNA LU 6.2 communication protocols and the APPC programming interface.

As designed, APPC did not impose any syntax programming rules on the application interface. As a result, LU 6.2-conforming applications have been designed and implemented across a wide range of different application support environments. For example, distributed application programs have been created through APPC extensions to the APIs of systems such as CICS, OS/400, MVS/VTAM, PC-DOS, OS/2, etc. Thus APPC has proven to be a very versatile and powerful API for distributed application development in these heterogeneous networks.

However, because there were no syntax rules defined for APPC, applications written to its specifications are generally not portable across the various LU 6.2-supported runtime environments. Multiple virtual storage (MVS) VTAM-to-PC-DOS applications cannot be easily converted to an OS/400, OS/2, or UNIX workstation network even though the underlying LU 6.2 protocols for both environments are identical.

The CPI-C API was developed to solve this incompatibility problem. This API has rapidly evolved to become a de facto standard API for the creation of distributed conversational applications in many multivendor heterogeneous network environments. CPI-C implements a proper subset of the APPC distributed functions through a strict syntax that is identical regardless of the programming language, operating system, or computer architecture upon which the underlying LU 6.2 protocols are running.

Even though the CPI-C API enforces a strict verb syntax, its programs are compatible to and may engage in conversations with programs written to the APPC API. Thus new applications using CPI-C can be written to converse with older established APPC programs with only minimal disruption to the older application environment. Also, CPI-C applications can be written using a variety of programming languages. Some of the more popular languages which support the CPI-C API are C, Common Business Oriented Language (COBOL), Formula Translator (FORTRAN), and Restructured Extended Executor (REXX). A CPI-C program written in any one of these languages may converse with a companion CPI-C or APPC program written in any of the other supported programming languages, as illustrated in figure 6.7.

Through the APPC or CPI-C APIs, the LU 6.2 protocol defines and implements either a half-duplex or full-duplex data exchange protocol. Figure 6.7 shows this send/receive structure and illustrates the logical steps that occur during a CPI-C conversation. When a CPI-C program (TP-1), issues an `Initialize_Conversation` (CMINIT) and

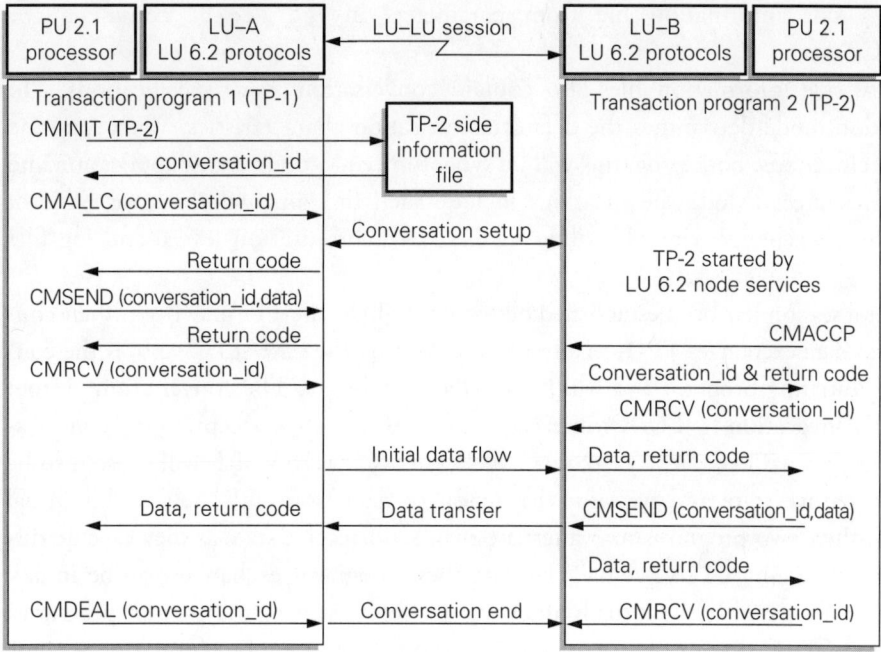

Figure 6.7 CPI-C conversation

`Allocate` (CMALLC) CPI-C verbs, it is requesting its local LU, (LU-A), to establish a session with the remote LU (LU-B) that supports the desired conversation partner program (TP-2).

In an APPN network, if LU-A is executing on a node type 2.1 LEN processor, it would need to request a connected node type 2.1 NN processor in order to use the APPN distributed directory service and locate LU-B and the conversation partner program TP-2. After locating LU-B, the NN would next establish a route through the network and then create an LU-A-to-LU-B session. It is across this session that the actual TP-1 to TP-2 conversation will occur. If the local LU was running on a NN processor, these activities would occur automatically.

Unlike APPC, where application programmers must provide parameters to describe the application's network environment, CPI-C programs obtain operational network parameters at initialization time from a side information file. A conversation-initiating program obtains a specific side information file through the `sym_dest_name` parameter of the `Initialize_Conversation` verb. This side information file contains the `partner_LU_name` and `remote_TP_name` of a partner program. It is with this information that the local LU is able to contact the remote LU, establish a session, and give the remote LU a program name to invoke for the pending conversation. The remote program selects its side information file from parameters in the `Accept_Conversation` (CMACCP) verb.

These side information files also contain conversation *mode* specifications. The conversation mode determines the default conversation characteristics. With common mode specifications, both programs will be synchronized in their use of application and network resources. Mode specifications include such fundamental things as basic or mapped data exchange, error handling methods, synchronization levels, and log files used.

After a session has been established between two LUs, the TPs may begin their conversational data exchange. TP-1, as a result of executing the CMALLC verb, is the conversation initiating program and will be in a data send state. The conversation partner TP-2, after invocation by LU-B will execute a CMACCP verb, accepting the conversation request from TP-1. Next TP-2 will issue a CMRCV verb which will cause it to be placed in receive state and wait for the arrival of data from TP-1. After this initial exchange, these two programs may alternate their send/receive state as they execute different state-changing CPI-C verbs. The data these programs exchange may be in any structure or format that is mutually understandable by each of the partner programs. LU 6.2 and CPI-C do not place any restrictions on the structure or format of application data. There are, however, two LU 6.2 data-type conventions to be considered when writing conversation programs. These are the *basic* and *mapped* conversation programming styles.

Mapped conversations are the easiest programs for high-level language programmers to write. Using mapped conversation verbs, programmers need only place data into and remove it from an LU 6.2 accessible buffer. The underlying LU 6.2 routines take care of record blocking and the transformation of the application data into a network *message unit* (MU). For mapped conversations, these MUs are sequential bit streams called *general data stream* (GDS) variables.

Basic conversations impose the complexity of dealing with variable-length data on the programmer. A 2-byte logical length (LL) indicator must be attached to and removed from application data when working in this mode. Logical records (LRs) are built by the application. Multiple LRs, each with an LL and data field may be placed in an application's send buffer. The LU transfers this buffer record to its partner LU where the partner application is able to obtain one or more LRs from its receive buffer. Thus basic mode programming provides for greater application control and flexibility over data transmission structures than the alternative mapped mode programming style.

Following is a partial list and brief functional description for some common CPI-C application program verbs:

- *Initialize_Conversation (CMINIT)*   Local program issued to set default conversation characteristics. The local LU returns a unique `conversation_ID` which must be used as a conversation-identifying parameter in all following verbs.

- *Allocate (CMALLC)*   Allocates a basic or mapped conversation, as specified in the side information file. Receipt of this call will cause the local LU to establish a session with the remote LU if one does not exist.

- *Accept_Conversation (CMACCP)*   Issued by remote program to accept conversation request. Remote LU returns a unique `conversation_ID` which must be used as a conversation-identifying parameter in all subsequent CPI-C verbs issued by the remote program. The default conversation characteristics are established from a side information file.

- *Deallocate (CMDEAL)*   Ends a conversation.

- *Send_Data (CMSEND)*   Sends basic or mapped data to the remote program. The local LU may buffer multiple CMSEND verbs into one network message.

- *Receive_Data (CMRCV)*   Receives data into the program's receive buffer.

- *Confirm (CMCFM)*   Requests confirmation from the partner program. Local program execution is suspended pending confirmation receipt.

- *Flush (CMFLUS)*   Causes transmission of the local LU's send buffer.

- *Request_To_Send (CMSRTS)*   Issuing program requests permission to send data from remote partner program.

- *Prepare_To_Receive (CMPTR)*   Sends a change of direction indicator to remote program. Local LU flushes its send buffer, and releases send state to the remote program. Local program enters receive state.

- *Send_Error (CMSERR)*   Transmits an error notification to the partner program. Upon receipt, partner program is placed in receive state pending arrival of error recovery messages.

- *Set_Conversation_Type (CMSCT)*   May set or change conversation mode characteristic to basic or mapped.

- *Set_Sync_Level (CMSSL)*   Sets conversation synchronization level to NONE, CONFIRM, or SYNC_POINT.

By necessity, this short introduction has omitted mentioning many of the functional capabilities and application support features inherent in the CPI-C API and LU 6.2 architecture. The reference list at the conclusion of this chapter contains titles which will provide a much more in-depth discussion of the topics introduced here.

6.6 Message queue interface

MQI is an API and distributed application subsystem from IBM and Apertus (formerly Systems Strategies). The MQI API is currently running on all major IBM systems, that is, MVS/ESA, TSO/E, IMS/ESA, VSE/ESA, CISC/ESA, OS/400, AIX, OS/2, DOS, and Windows. The API is also available on DEC/VMS, Tandem, and Stratus computing platforms. Additionally, IBM and Apertus provide MQI capability for HP-UX, SCO, SunOS, and UnixWare environments.

The MQI API provides application programmers with a relatively simple but very powerful object-oriented structure and call semantics for creating distributed applications. Application programs which implement the MQI API may be written using either the C or COBOL languages.

In contrast to other distributed application APIs where one application is connected to and communicates synchronously with another application program, an MQI application program is only aware of a message queue manager and input and output message queues. MQI applications are totally unaware of any underlying communication network; they are connectionless and operate asynchronously since no partner or server program need be running or even exist. MQI applications may exchange messages across SNA LU 6.2 and multi-protocol TCP/IP networks. All network issues and communication protocols are handled by an MQM which must be running on each processor in a message queue network (MQN).

6.6.1 MQI messages

Messages are created when an application issues either an MQPUT or MQPUT1 MQI system call. The MQGET call is used to get messages from a message queue. Once removed from a queue, a message ceases to exist. An MQI message has two components—application data and message control information. Application data may be any information structure which is created by one program and recognized by another program. These structures may contain one or more of the following data types:

- Character strings
- Bit strings
- Binary integers
- Packed-decimal integers
- Floating-point numbers

Other then sending application data to its destination queue, the message queue service does not transform or modify application data.

6.6.2 Message control information

Message control information is created by a sending application program. This control information is contained in an MQI defined data structure called a *message descriptor*. The values for this structure are defined by a sending application through parameters of the MQPUT or MQPUT1 MQI calls. These parameters specify various properties of the application data portion of a message. The MQGET call returns this structure to a message-receiving application program. Some of the more important properties which may be defined for a message are:

- *Message type*
  - *Datagram* Used when no reply to the message is required.
  - *Request* Used when a reply is needed.
  - *Reply* Used by receiver to acknowledge a message.
  - *Report* Used to advise programs about unanticipated events.
- *Message identifier* A 24-byte string usually created by the MQM to uniquely identify each message. Applications may create their own message identifiers, and messages may be retrieved from queues by their message identifier.
- *Priority* A sender application may specify the level of importance of one message over another.
- *Persistence* Specifies how a message should be protected in the event of a system failure. Persistent messages, once stored on disk, have delivery guaranteed to the receiving program's queue.
- *Format* An 8-byte string that a sending program can code to indicate the format of the application data structure. The receiver program can use this field to identify an appropriate data structure declaration to use in mapping the message's data content.
- *Character set identifier and encoding* The sender application identifies the character set, machine format, and representation of the characters, integers and floats in a message. The receiving program would use this field to determine if there is a need to pass the application data structure through data conversion routines.
- *Message queues* Two basic types of queues are defined for MQI applications.
  - *Local queue* Owned and controlled by a local queue manager. To access a local queue an application must issue an MQI connect MQCONN system call. Local queues may be in memory, or for persistent messages, they may be in disk files. Messages

are normally placed in local queues on a FIFO ordering scheme. Applications may alter the retrieval of messages from this scheme through use of the *priority* message control indicator or other application-defined selection criteria.

– *Remote queues*   Owned by queue managers to which the application is not connected. Typically, but not necessarily, these would be queue managers running on remote network connected systems. Applications may only open remote queues for message output.

– *Transmission queues*   Special queues maintained by the queue manager for sending messages to remote systems. When an application sends a message to a remote queue, the queue manager puts the message into a transmission queue. A message transmission program will read this queue and send the message through the network to the remote system's message queue manager. Message queue managers will always place messages received from remote systems into their local queues. Thus applications read or get remote messages as if they were generated locally.

6.6.3 Queue manager and queue names

MQI applications put and get messages from named queues. Queue names consist of two 48-byte fields. The first field contains the name of a local queue as it is known to the queue manager. The second field contains the name of a queue manager. If the name specified in the second field is not the connected queue manager's name, then the name is interpreted as the name of a transmission queue. Messages placed in this queue will be transmitted to the appropriate remote system queue manager by the message transmission program. Thus to send a message, an application need only specify the queue manager name and queue name in the object description `ObjDesc` parameter of the `MQOPEN` or `MQPUT1` MQI calls.

6.6.4 Message queue triggers

Application messages sent to predefined special queues will be recognized as a trigger event by the MQM. Whenever a trigger event is detected, the MQM sends a trigger message to a special initiation queue. This queue is read by a trigger-monitor application program which upon receiving the trigger message will take whatever action the message may specify. Typically this would be to start another program whose function would be to read the queue which contains the message that caused the trigger event.

6.6.5 MQI system calls

The MQI API consists of nine system calls. As such, it is by far the most concise and simplest API of any distributed application subsystem. Following is a brief description of these calls:

- *MQCONN—connect queue manager*   Connects an application program to a message queue manager. Successful execution of this call returns a queue manager handle. This handle is used to identify the application to the queue manager on all subsequent calls.

- *MQOPEN—open object*   Provides application access to an MQI object. Objects are defined as either a queue, a queue manager, or a process definition. Successful execution returns an object handle. This handle must be provided on all subsequent calls which operate on the object. The option parameter of this call specifies the action which may be performed or requested from the object. Some common actions include:
  - Open to get message
  - Open to browse
  - Open to put message
  - Open to inquire about object attributes
  - Open to set object attributes

- *MQINQ—inquire object attributes*   Successful execution of this call returns information about an object's attributes. For a message queue some valid attributes are:
  - Create time and date
  - Queue depth, number of messages in queue
  - Maximum message length
  - Can queue be shared
  - Trigger information
  - Number of input and output open requests

- *MQSET—set object attributes*   Will change or modify one or more message queue attributes.

- *MQGET—get a message*   Returns a message from an opened local queue. Retrieved messages are deleted from the queue. A get options parameter is available to control call behavior. Options include:
  - Wait for message to arrive
  - Get message with syncpoint
  - Browse first and browse next message
  - Get message under browse cursor

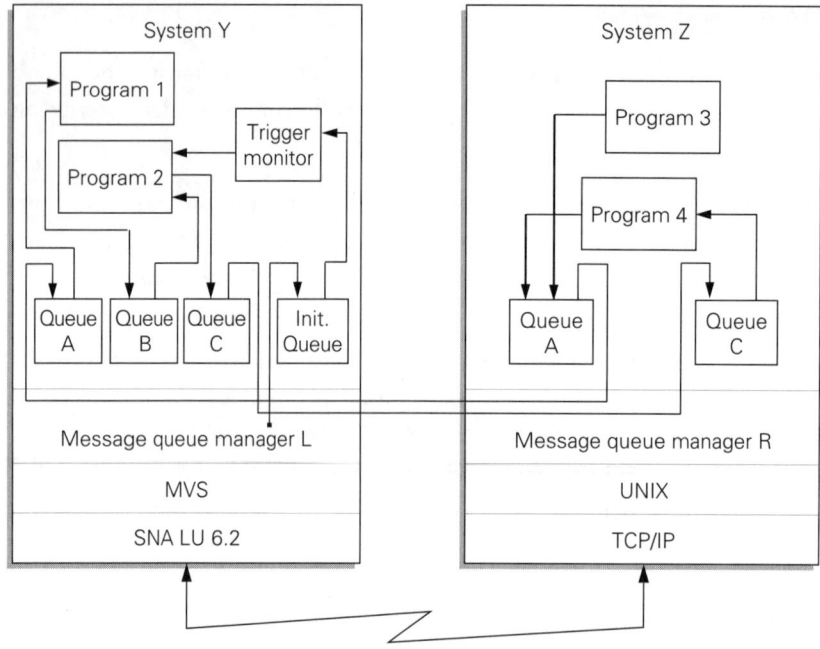

Figure 6.8   MQI network

- *MQPUT—put a message*   Puts a message from an application buffer to an opened message queue. A put options parameter is provided to control the call's behavior. Options include:
  - *Syncpoint*   Puts message inside current unit of work
  - Query and set application context information
- *MQPUT1—put one message*   Puts one message on a queue. The queue may be open or closed. This call combines the MQOPEN, MQPUT, and MQCLOSE calls into one call.
- *MQCLOSE—close object*   Removes an application's access to a previously opened object. If the object is a queue, options are available to purge messages and to delete the queue.
- *MQDISC—disconnect queue manager*   Removes the connection between an application program and a local queue manager which was established by the MQCONN call.

Figure 6.8 illustrates a hypothetical message queue network. The central components in this diagram are the MQMs labeled MQM-L and MQM-R. These queue managers are responsible for the receipt and transmission of messages into and out of their respective managed queues. The applications, Programs 1 through 4, get messages from input queues and put messages to output queues. Several different MQI capabilities are depicted in this illustration.

Sending a message across the network is demonstrated by Program 3, which is running on System Z. It puts a message to Queue A (Q-A). This queue is defined as a remote queue and managed by MQM-R as a transmission queue for messages destined for System Y's MQM-L. Upon receipt of a message from a remote system, MQM-L will place the message into each message's self designated queue, which in this example is Q-A on System Y. After placing a message in Q-A, Program 3 could terminate. Some time later, Program 1 on System Y will read its local Q-A and receive the message from Program 3.

The capability of an MQM to recognize a trigger message is illustrated next. Program 1 on System Y puts a message to Queue B (Q-B). This message is recognized as a triggering event by MQM-L and causes MQM-L to put a trigger message to a special initiation queue (I-Q). A trigger-monitor application reads this special queue and performs the task specified in the received message, for example, the trigger-manager could tell the operating system, MVS, to load and run Program 2. At this point Program 2 would read Q-B and act upon the message left by Program 1.

To continue our example, Program 2 on System Y puts a message to Queue C (Q-C), which is defined as a transmission queue for sending messages to System Z, then Program 2 ends. Upon message receipt, MQM-R puts this message on its local Q-C. Program 4 gets this message and puts a message to its local Q-A and the cycle repeats. Thus, depending upon actual application program logic, we have created the structure for a perpetual message-generating message queue network.

Obviously, this would not be desirable in a real world application; however, it does serve to illustrate the fact that applications may be connected to message queues in any number of logical or illogical configurations. As a result of this application design flexibility, various distributed processing models can be developed through a message queuing system. Some useful application design configurations follow:

- An obvious design is the synchronous-application style where one program sends a message to another application program's input queue, and then waits for a reply message from that program to appear in its input queue. The two programs continue in this manner, each sending a message and waiting for a corresponding reply until completion of the application's work.

- Asynchronous application design allows one program to send a message to another program and continue with other work or even terminate. The receiving program, which need not be running when the message was sent, will eventually read the message from a queue and do appropriate processing of the received information.

- Using connectionless application design, a program will write messages to a generalized queue. Using the MQM as an intermediary, other application programs can read messages from this queue. None of the application programs need be aware of or interact with any other application program. The mechanism these programs use to send and receive data is the MQM's generalized queue.

- Parallel processing application design is accomplished when one program sends messages to a number of different queues. Each queue could represent a specific subtask to be performed. These queues will be read by their associated programs. In a truly parallel system, each of these programs would be running concurrently on different CPUs. Each of these subtask programs would perform their specific functions and send the results back to the message-originating program's input queue.

As demonstrated in the above discussion, the MQI API is a very powerful and flexible tool for creating a variety of distributed applications. It offers a number of very powerful features:

- It provides a flexible yet powerful application design construct.

- Applications can be designed and written without any dependencies on other application programs.

- The API is very simple and straightforward; the learning curve for experienced C or COBOL programmers should be less than other more complex APIs.

- Message delivery can be guaranteed, and the API has facilities for integration with existing application systems that use syncpoint processing and the logical unit of work concept to ensure data integrity.

- MQI applications may be less consumptive of network bandwidth than comparable applications using other APIs which require dedicated communication sessions.

- Due to their asynchronous architecture, MQI applications have potentially reduced exposure to network congestion and failures.

6.7 HTTP APIs

Doug Engelbart and his team at Stanford Research Institute invented hyperlinks in the 1960s to represent the interconnections among units of information in a shared computer environment. Hyperlinks were analogous to the neural connections in the human brain, which collectively represent actionable knowledge. The goal was to augment human intellect by providing a computerized extension of memory and thought. By the 1970s, hyperlinks were imbedded in a context, most often based on collaboration. For example, hyperlinks formed an audit trail through document coauthoring, provided online access to references, or created a threaded conversation tracing the formation of ideas, proposals, and software.

The Web uses *universal resource locators* (URLs) for hyperlinks. A URL can be far more than a hyperlink. It can contain complex information-retrieval searches, arguments for programs on *hypertext transfer protocol* (HTTP) servers to interpret and execute, and SQL statements.

The original hyperlink evolved into an applet that could be interpreted and run as a filter, string search, or string manipulation program. HTTP is an application-level protocol for distributed, collaborative, hypermedia information systems. It is a generic, stateless, object-oriented protocol which can be used for many tasks, such as name servers and distributed object management systems. A major feature of HTTP is data typing and negotiation of data representation. This enables application systems to be built independently of the data being transferred.

HTTP is based on a request/response model. A client establishes a connection with a server in the form of a request method. This consists of a *universal resource identifier* (URI) which contains a protocol version number, followed by a *multipurpose Internet mail extensions* (MIME)-like message that contains request modifiers, client information, and optional body content. The server responds with a status line, which provides the message's protocol version number, a success or error code, followed by a MIME-like message containing server information, entity information, and optional body content.

HTTP has been in use by the WWW global information initiative since 1990. HTTP is also used as a generic protocol for communication between user agents and proxies/gateways to other Internet systems, including those supported by the SMTP, *network news transfer protocol* (NNTP), FTP, Gopher, and *wide area information servers* (WAIS) protocols. In this way, HTTP allows basic hypermedia access to resources available from diverse applications to determine each other's true capabilities. Chapter 18 addresses integration of Web technology and SNA systems, and chapter 19 concentrates on the promises of Java, related to SNA applications.

6.8 *Conclusion*

We have spent some time looking at a number of different distributed application subsystems and application programming interfaces. The BSD socket API might appear relatively simple when compared to the complexity of the DCE RPC API. However, when the limited function provided by sockets is compared to the rich functional menu of DCE RPC, it is apparent that the DCE structure and function actually provide a *simpler* and more robust development environment for creating client/server applications.

Similarly, the CPI-C API provides a functionally rich and robust group of services for creating conversational distributed applications. Building on the LU 6.2 architecture and APPC API, the MQI message queuing system provides a higher level, very powerful, flexible, and relatively simple-to-use distributed application API.

For those organizations with a large investment in UNIX systems and TCP/IP networks, DCE provides a very attractive development environment. Those organizations with existing SNA networks are ideally situated to take advantage of either CPI-C or MQI development environments. However, it should be emphasized, all of the primary APIs discussed in this chapter can be run across either SNA or TCP/IP networks.

6.9 References

Bloomer, J., *Power Programming with RPC*, Sebastopol, CA: O'Reilly & Associates, 1992.

Coates, P., *SAA Cooperative Processing Mainframe to PC Connectivity*, Hertfordshire: Prentice-Hall International (U.K.) Ltd., 1992.

Cypser, R.J., *Communications for Cooperating Systems: OSI, SNA, and TCP/IP*, Reading, MA: Addison-Wesley, 1991.

Edmunds, J.J., *SAA/LU6.2 Distributed Networks and Applications*, New York: McGraw-Hill Inc., 1992.

IBM Corporation, *APPC System Definitions in MVS/ESA and OS/2*, GG66-3224-00, 1992.

———, *APPC Application Examples in MVS/ESA and OS/2*, GG24-3819-00, 1992.

———, *An Introduction to Messaging and Queuing*, GC33-0805-00, 1993.

———, *Message Queue Interface Technical Reference*, SC33-0850-01, 1993.

Open Software Foundation, *OSF DCE Application Development Guide*, Englewood Cliffs, NJ: Prentice-Hall, 1993.

———, *OSF DCE Application Development Reference*, Englewood Cliffs, NJ: Prentice-Hall, 1993.

Rosenberry, W., D. Kenney, and G. Fisher, *Understanding DCE*, Sebastopol, CA: O'Reilly & Associates, 1992.

Shirley, J., *Guide to Writing DCE Applications*, Sebastopol, CA: O'Reilly & Associates, 1992.

 *chapter 7*

The networking blueprint: an introduction

RUDY J. CYPSER

This chapter covers the environments with which SNA and TCP/IP networks interact. IBM's networking blueprint, introduced by Rudy J. Cypser, provides a reliable model for understanding internetworking, promoting the common use of standards by multiple vendors for the integration of a broad range of distributed systems.

7.1 Introduction

The networking blueprint developed by IBM as an integral part of the larger open blueprint, is a clarifying view of the entire multivendor, multiprotocol, networking world. It is a flexible framework for integrating a wide range of options that are drawn primarily from international and industry standards.

Interest in the networking blueprint and similar pragmatic approaches to internetworking is strong because they facilitate use of the best modules available from multiple vendors. This pragmatism is the reason the networking blueprint is a context for several chapters related to the layers of the blueprint.

A blueprint for the future of networking must be adaptable and include options for different and changing circumstances. Such a blueprint has to be a framework to help in the orderly assessment of alternative solutions that are available today, or will be available shortly.

While a blueprint that gives new clarity to networking evolution is needed, it should be clear that this networking blueprint:

- Is not another new, competing architecture. (The industry has more than enough already.)
- Is not proprietary. (In fact, it seeks to exploit international and industry standards.)
- Is not meant as a device to reduce vendor choice. (Quite the opposite, it promotes multivendor choices.)

7.2 Breaking with tradition

In the past, the mindset has assumed a single family of tightly related communication protocols, as if the various levels of protocol were entirely dependent on each other. This is illustrated in the left side of figure 7.1. Thus, one might have an all SNA or an all TCP/IP set of protocols—in other words a full stack drawn from the same protocol family. Each application was tied to one such set and could not be used with other

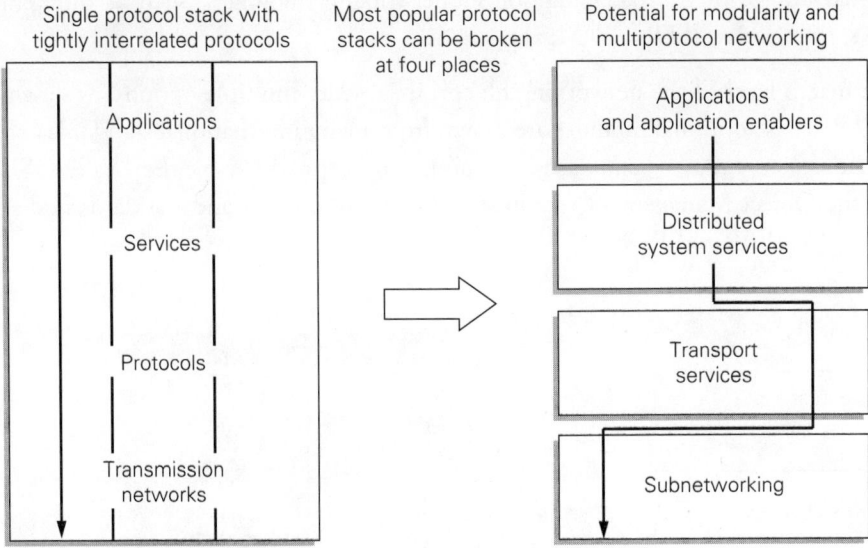

Figure 7.1 Breaking the ties

communication protocols. For many, it is a radical shift in viewpoint to consider that this need not always be the case.

Regardless of the protocol set being used, the leading protocol stacks can readily be divided into three independent macro layers:

- *Distributed systems services*   Including, for example, RPC
- *Transport services*   Including, for example, TCP/IP
- *Subnetworking*   Including, for example, LANs and WANs.

The traditional ties linking the layers of the communication stack can be broken at the horizontal breaks shown at the right side of figure 7.1. That potential for segmentation of the problem is what the networking blueprint takes advantage of. With this new-found modularity, three degrees of freedom—to choose options within each of these three macro layers—become possible. A given application and its communicating partner can then:

- Optimize communication with the most appropriate distributed systems services, such as conversational support in APPC, RPC, messaging queuing, or Web-oriented HTTP
- Use alternative transport services, such as TCP/IP, SNA, or others, to route traffic along multiple paths

- Take advantage of a broad range of subnetwork technologies, such as different LANs, frame relay, ISDN, ATM, and so on.

Each macro layer of the networking blueprint provides multiple options, as shown in figure 7.2. These optional modules are drawn from many international standards and also from de facto industry standards, including some provided by the IETF, OSF, X/Open, the Object Management Group (OMG), Java Soft and and standards bodies like ANSI, ITV, IEEE and ISO.

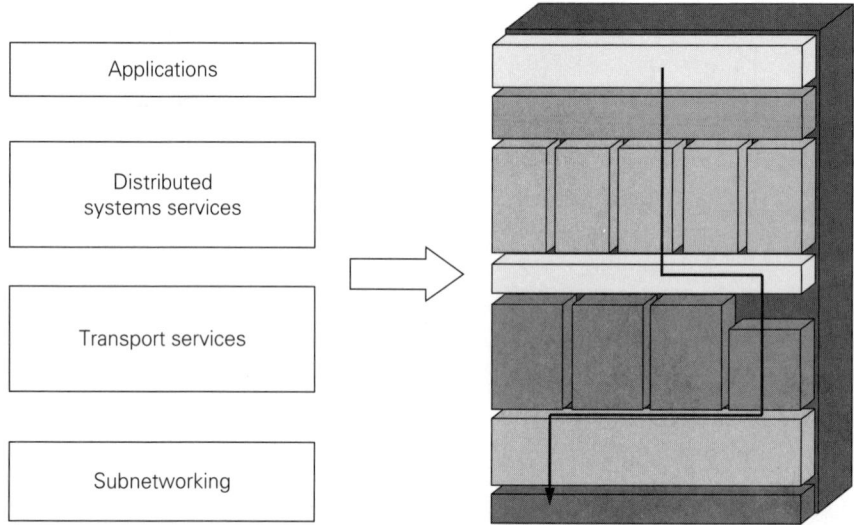

Figure 7.2   Modules within each macro layer

By using switching facilities between macro layers, the networking blueprint makes possible the splitting of protocol stacks and the forming of *mixed stacks*. By this adaptability, one can use the most appropriate complementary functions from different layers to suit the current situation. For example, applications with the best price/performance, and services like RPC, FTP, and X.400 messaging, can be used. These choices can be made independently of the underlying transport service protocols—such as SNA, TCP/IP, IPX, and NetBIOS—and also independently the subnetwork choice—including X.25, ethernet, token ring, frame relay, ISDN, SDLC, and ATM.

7.3 Switching boundaries and recommended modules

The network blueprint consists of the lower two sections of the open blueprint shown in figure 7.3:

- *Distributed systems services* Including communications services such as RPC, object management services, and distribution services such as directory and security services

- *Network services* Including transport services such as TCP/IP, subnetworking such as LANs, a signaling and control plane, and the physical network.

In the networking blueprint, three boundaries separate the macro layers of distributed systems services, transport services, and subnetworking and facilitate the selection of options in the layers above and below. The interfaces of these boundaries and the services for protocol compensation provided at these boundaries make the adaptability of the network possible. Their purpose is to provide:

- New freedom to choose many applications
- Ability to standardize on common distributed systems services
- Methods to minimize complexity with fewer transport networks
- Opportunity to use any subnetwork as technology emerges

These three boundaries are:

- *Application programming interfaces* Isolates the application from all underlying support

- *Common transport semantics (CTS)* Allows the selection of alternative transport services, such as TCP/IP or SNA

- *Subnetwork access* Allows the selection of alternative subnetwork technologies, such as LANs or frame relay

Each macro layer can contain multiple optional modules. The basic idea is that all modules and layers in the networking blueprint are independent and each module may be changed or replaced. New modules may be added as technology progresses. The networking blueprint structure, with defined boundaries between macro layers, facilitates the integration of diverse modules into a working whole.

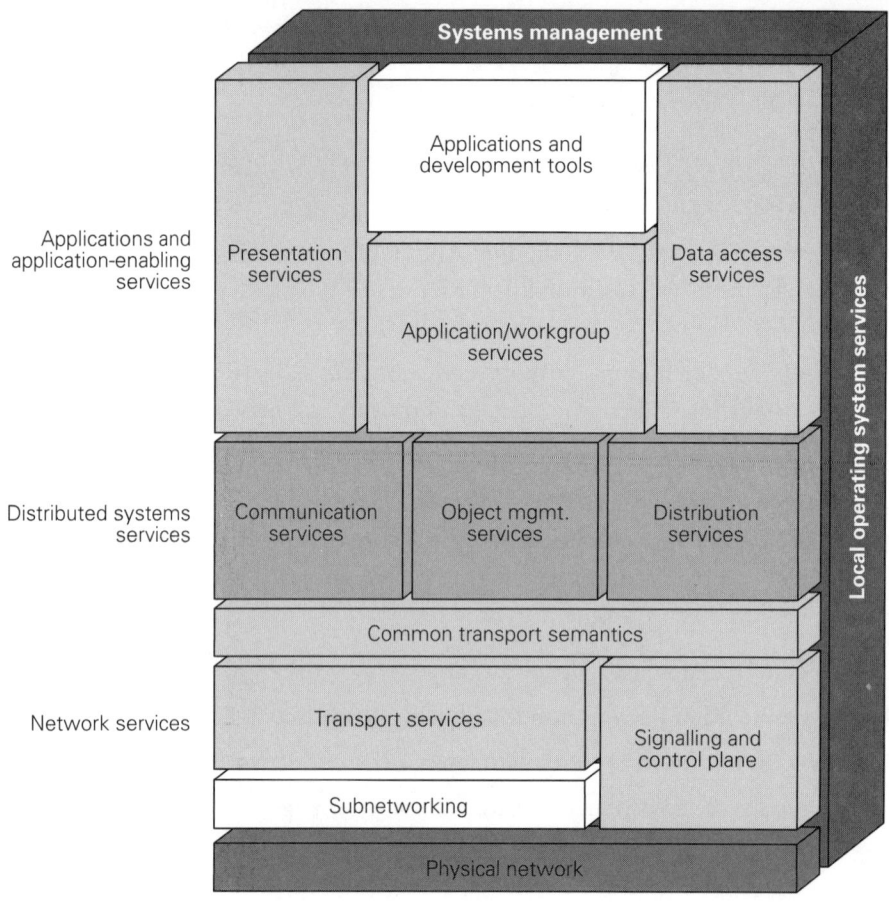

Figure 7.3   The open blueprint structure

7.4 APIs and communication services

APIs permit the selection of communication services to supply a particular type of data stream and to match the communication services of the destination. Four common communication services follow:

- *Conversational*   Handles streams of related interactions (using the CPI-C interface)
- *RPC*   Passes parameters to a remotely located subroutine (using the RPC interface)
- *Messaging and queuing*   Manages queues of messages (using the MQI)
- *HTTP*   Sends requests for service, particularly for Internet and intranet operations.

In the open blueprint, the four communications services all can use common directory and security distributions services.

Each of these APIs is discussed in more detail in chapter 6.

In addition, the networking blueprint includes a number of recommended standard applications which include their own APIs and associated communication services. TCP/IP's FTP, SMTP, and *simple network management protocol* (SNMP), are examples of such standard applications. Similar standard applications exist in OSI, such as the X.400 electronic mail standard.

Using standard APIs, together with independent modules of communication services, provides greater network flexibility:

- One can achieve greater application independence from hardware choices, operating system choices, and communication architectures
- One can more easily set up servers on mainframes, midrange computers, workstations, or a combination of these

7.5 Common transport semantics

Today's challenge is to allow users to access, integrate, and share information, regardless of technology, geography, or organizational boundaries. Toward this end, two primary multiprotocol networking approaches are reflected in the networking blueprint:

- *Server-based or network-based gateways*   Usually operating at layer four or above
- *Multiprotocol routers*   Usually operating at layer three

Multiprotocol transport network (MPTN) is an example of a gateway operating at a level above that of routers. MPTN is briefly described here and is further discussed in chapters 12 and 13. Routers are further discussed in chapter 14.

MPTN uses CTS, which is an optional boundary in the networking blueprint above the transport services layer. The purpose of this boundary is to allow communicating partners to use alternative transport services. A given application could, thus, make use of different transport protocols on different networks. Or, an enterprise could implement fewer (perhaps only one) transport services protocol, yet use applications that were designed to support different transport protocols.

In general, the goal of the networking blueprint and CTS specifically is that any stack above the CTS boundary (such as RPC or messaging and queuing) should be able to use any stack below the boundary (such as TCP/IP or SNA/APPN). This allows a major step toward the goal of any-to-any communication. It also allows taking advantage of major performance and recovery-capability differences in various network protocols.

By means of the CTS boundary, applications using any of the APIs cited above and their associated communication services are made independent of the underlying transport, and subnetwork services, as shown in figure 7.4. For example, a standard application like FTP should be able to use TCP/IP, SNA, IPX, or a number of other transport services, and any subnetwork used by those services. This is the goal even though these applications may have originated in a particular protocol environment, such as TCP/IP, or SNA. Their use is no longer to be restricted to these originating environments.

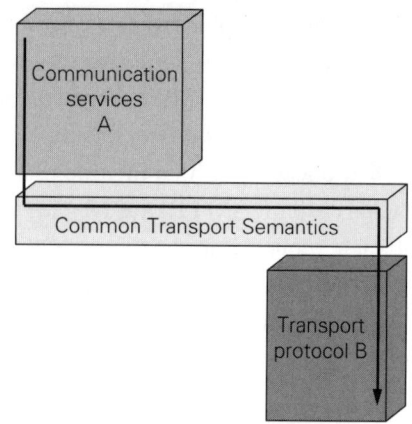

Figure 7.4   Common transport semantics

To achieve this mixed-stack goal—with little or no change to the software above the CTS—when the modules below the boundary differ in the services they provide, some compensation software to add missing function is needed. Three situations are addressed at the CTS boundary:[1]

- *Single protocol stacks*   The application may be communicating over its native stack and no support is needed at the CTS boundary.

- *Common compensation modules*   MPTN provides a common set of compensations for missing functions, which can be used by any transport protocol, which makes it a general-purpose split-stack architecture.[2] MPTN is further discussed in chapter 13.

7.6 Transport gateways

Another use of this CTS boundary is in a transport gateway that permits communication *between end systems using different transport service protocols* as shown in figure 7.5. Such a gateway, for example, might connect a TCP/IP and an SNA network.

---

1. The XTI provides access to SNA/APPN, NetBIOS, OSI, and TCP/IP, but it does not shield applications from underlying transport service differences. X/Open has adopted specifications for MPTN based upon IBM's architecture.

2. Installation is simplified and usability of products is enhanced when products focus on a narrow range of configurations. One example is the TCP 6.2 product. It implements only SNA's LU 6.2 protocols over TCP and produces the corresponding AnyNet (MPTN) protocols. Written entirely in Java, they are downloadable to any Java-enabled workstation anywhere in the world.

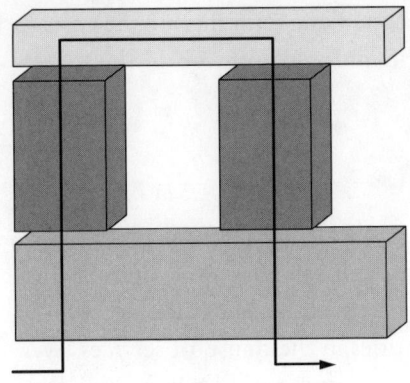

Figure 7.5   Transport gateways

If necessary, multiple transport gateways can be concatenated to interconnect more than two types of transport networks. No application changes should be required when transport gateways are implemented.

7.7 *Multiprotocol routers*

The networking blueprint also includes the use of multiprotocol router technology, in which network processors have the ability to perform transport service functions for more than one protocol. A single physical WAN is shared by *multiple logical networks, each running different transport service protocols* as shown in figure 7.6.

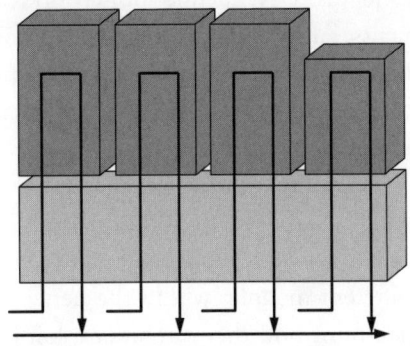

Figure 7.6   Multiprotocol routers

The multiprotocol network processors statistically multiplex all the traffic types on shared subnetwork facilities. This requires that network processors be capable of handling different protocols, such as TCP/IP, IPX, Appletalk, NetBIOS, SNA, and whatever other protocols the user requires. They transmit the multiple protocols over wide area subnetworks, such as point-to-point links, X.25 *packet switched data networks* (PSDNs), and frame relay.

Although multiprotocol routers share links, the logical transport networks associated with each protocol are independent of each other, and *there is no communication between end systems designed for different logical networks*. The use of multiprotocol routers nevertheless provides a flexible, low hardware-cost solution to the sharing of WAN lines with multiple transport service protocols. However, along with this are the costs to set up, maintain, and diagnose trouble in each of the multiple protocols in the routers throughout the network.

7.8 Subnetworking

Subnetworking is sharing a transmission resource through some form of multiplexing. The subnetwork access boundary of the networking blueprint facilitates the selection of alternative subnetwork technologies by any of the entities in the transport services layer. Subnetworks might include LANs such as ethernet, token ring, and FDDI; X.25; point-to-point lines; frame relay; broadband integrated services digital network (B-ISDN), and other cell relay (ATM) facilities. These data-link layer technologies are further discussed in chapter 3.

The networking blueprint objective is that any of these subnetworks could be used by any of the transport services protocols above the boundary. A given application, using a selected transport service could then select one or more subnetwork services.

Achieving this involves the incorporation of multiple user-network interface (UNI) standards. UNIs define subnetwork capabilities, such as address space, service commitments, fairness, and management information. Examples include the X.25 interface, the 802.2 LAN interface, the I.233 frame relay interface, and corresponding ATM interfaces. Such subnetwork UNIs are essential to the use of multivendor facilities in old and new technologies.

Coming technologies therefore fit as modules into the networking blueprint framework, using older or additional UNIs. In particular, high performance routing within the subnetwork, broadband service, and multimedia applications are widely anticipated. Different modules within the networking blueprint may incrementally be examined to determine how they can best exploit the vast capabilities of the new high speed facilities. This enables networks to evolve and to grow in a cost effective fashion.

Note that frame relay and ATM, located only in the lowest layers of the networking blueprint, will do multipath routing in these lowest layers, rather than in the higher networking layer. Since all routing can be done in the subnetwork layer, any transport services protocol and its data can then be carried simply as information. Combinations of frame relay or ATM and the various LANs thus promise a comprehensive WAN/LAN network that can readily carry multiple transport service protocols.

7.9 System management

The backplane of the networking blueprint represents the system management of the multiprotocol assemblage. In practice, this backplane includes the many connections between each of the modules in the networking blueprint and local management agents. These agents, in turn, carry out the management-oriented communications with remote (or local) management applications. Network management in multiprotocol networks with SNA is discussed in chapter 15.

The systems management services incorporate the common management facilities (XCMF) standardized by X/Open and OMG. The common object request broker architecture (COBRA) allows interoperability among independently developed, object-oriented management applications across heterogeneous computer networks.

In keeping with networking blueprint guidelines, the industry standard management protocols, SNMP, *common management information protocol* (CMIP), and SNA/MS will be accommodated. Each of these will, moreover, be disassociated from networking protocols. For example, CMIP information will be able to travel over TCP/IP, OSI, or SNA networks.

7.10 The open blueprint

To make possible seamless growth not only for communication networks but for the entire distributed information system, further standards and modularity in the upper layers are needed. The networking blueprint then becomes an integral part of the follow-on structure, the *open blueprint*, with the many application-enabling services shown in figure 7.7.

The open blueprint is structured to facilitate widely interconnected systems to function as a cohesive, *distributed operating system*. Diverse services on many connected systems manage resources cooperatively across the network, similar to the way a single operating system manages resources in one system.

The open blueprint incorporates the additonal object management services, distribution services, and specifics for the applications enabler layer.

Object management services manage discrete, self-contained components called *objects*. Objects associate information with the programming required to access or use that formation. Object management services facilitate distribution of objects across processes and across machine boundaries.

Distribution services include directory, security, time and transaction manager services.

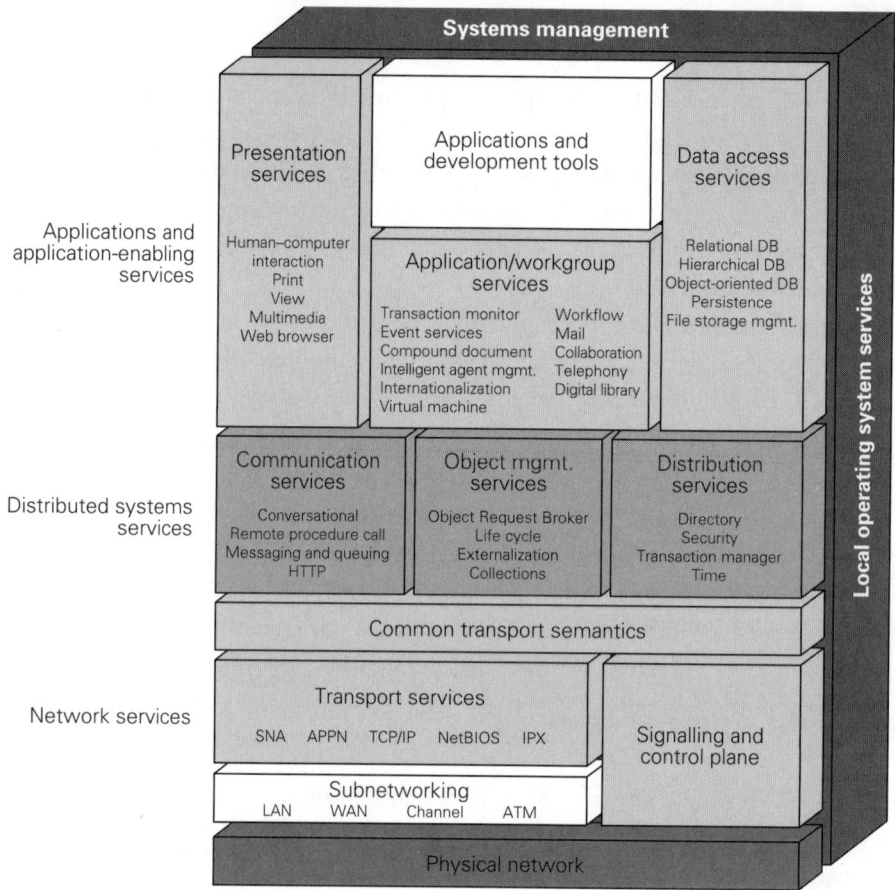

Figure 7.7 The open blueprint

A federated name space is based on X/Open Federated Naming concepts and the IETF's lightweight directory access protocol (LDAP). Directory services may be based on either ISO's X.500 or an Internet DNS and an enterprise directory service.

Application enabling services include a wide variety of functions, particularly:

- Presentation services, such as Web browser, desk-top functions, and multimedia support.

- Application/workgroup services, such as collaboration with shared workspace and shared information, and a transaction monitor that enforces data integrity.

- Data access services, that provide reliable access to databases and files.

Through the open blueprint seamless interoperability is sought so that diverse products will work together naturally and with little effort. The goal is to enable a customer to choose initially a very simple path through the blueprint, such as two separate single-stack applications environments, and then add other paths and grow easily in many directions.

The boxes in the open blueprint do not generally correspond exactly to products—these are often packaged differently on different system platforms. However, the open blueprint does call for technical attributes, desirable functional modularity, and important boundaries and interfaces. Moreover, it provides software principles and guidelines that implementers can follow to achieve interoperability and growth potential.

7.11 Conclusion

The open blueprint presents a selection of protocols, services, architectures, and standards in a clarifying, simplifying view of the multivendor, multiprotocol network world. This view should help the reader in the previous tutorial chapters.

Rather than the extremes of dogmatic adherence to a single network/application environment on the one hand or an unmanageable plethora of *laissez-faire* distributed networks on the other, the open blueprint promotes the common use of standards by multiple vendors for the integration of a broad, but specified, range of distributed system products. Its philosophy is further discussed in chapter 20.

7.12 References

Cypser, R. J., *Communications for Cooperating Systems: OSI, SNA, and TCP/IP,* Reading, MA: Addison Wesley, 1991.

———, "Evolution of an Open Communications Architecture," *IBM Systems Journal,* Vol. 31, No. 2, 1992.

Hess, M. L., J. A. Lorrain, and G.R. McGee, "Multiprotocol Networking—A Blueprint," *IBM Systems Journal,* Vol.34, No. 3, fall 1995.

IBM Corporation, *Introduction to the Open Blueprint: A Guide to Distributed Computing,* G326-0395-02 (figures 7.3 and 7.7 © IBM 1994, reproduced with permission).

———, *MPTN Architecture: Technical Overview,* GC31-7073.

———, *Networking Blueprint: Executive Overview,* GC31-7057 (figures 7.1, 7.2, and 7.4–7.6 © IBM 1992, reproduced with permission).

———, *Open Blueprint Technical Overview,* GC23-3808-02.

————, *The Open Blueprint Technical Reference Library*, SBOF-8702 (printed), SK2T-2478 (CD ROM), including papers for each Open Blueprint component.

————, *Sockets Over SNA User's Guide*, SC31-6487.

Lorrain, J. A. "The Networking Blueprint—A Progress Report," *Proceedings of SHARE Europe,* Hamburg, 1993.

chapter   8

SNA, APPN & TCP/IP:
comparisons and contrasts

Thomas J. Routt

147

To summarize the tutorials in this book, Thomas J.Routt compares today's leading enterprise networking architectures: SNA (including the recent developments of APPN/HPR) and TCP/IP. This analysis is not limited to functional comparison, but in addition focuses on similarities and differences in performance, usability, reliability, and implementation approaches for the two leading enterprise networking protocols.

The author wishes to thank Dr. John Pickens and Louise Herndon Wells for their input and review in the creation of this chapter.

8.1 Introduction

Diverse viewpoints have been presented both in the literature and in the field on the relative strengths and weaknesses of SNA with its newer middle-layer architecture (APPN) and TCP/IP—two of the most important client/server internetworking environments today.

Earlier chapters have introduced SNA in its various evolutionary states. In this chapter, we compare the world's two most popular protocols: SNA and TCP/IP. To have an apples-to-apples comparison, we focus on SNA's current middle layers—APPN—with the current middle-layer protocol family of TCP/IP.

Comparative assertions and counter-assertions have been forwarded on the relative merits of APPN and TCP/IP in resource identification (naming and addressing), routing, transport, performance throughput, and production reliability. This chapter provides a common framework for understanding both APPN and TCP/IP by:

- Comparing architectures, resource identification, routing, and transport
- Defining protocol-sensitive drivers for network design and migration
- Evaluating respective protocol engineering frameworks
- Exploring the principal application drivers of each
- Considering APPN and TCP/IP convergence
- Establishing a cross-education, common evaluation framework

8.1.1 Distributed computing trends

Several trends have presided over the migration of the information technology market to the client/server and web-based paradigms and have fueled a considerable investment stream into distributed computing. One of the most important of these is ongoing improvements in technology.

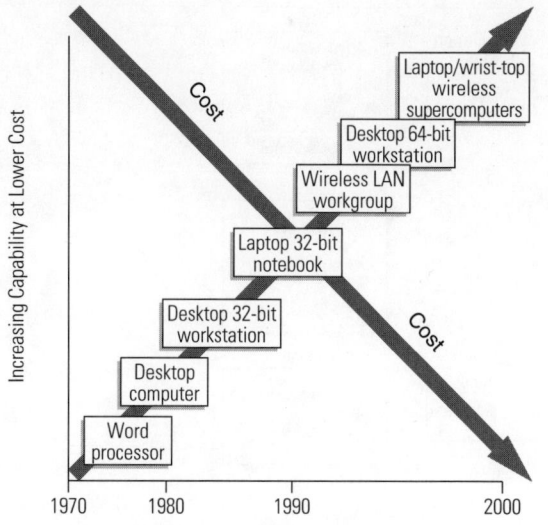

Figure 8.1 Workstation trends

Hardware and memory price-performance efficiencies continue to improve exponentially. These trends have yielded department-affordable desktop, deskside, laptop, and mobile workstation/printer solutions, and have led to desktop supercomputers, price-efficient, massively parallel, interactive multimedia servers, and perhaps even wrist-top, wireless, voice-actuated versions of all of these (therein fulfilling several of Dick Tracy's original requirements) near the turn of the century. Figure 8.1 depicts the evolution of desktop computer and workstation technology as one of increasing capability against a backdrop of rapidly diminishing cost.

8.1.2 Client/server computing paradigm

Client/server computing emerged as the information paradigm of the decade in the wake of distribution of compute- and network-intensive resources at reasonable cost. Client/server computing, as depicted in figure 8.2, enables:

- Distributed, cooperative processing
- Program-to-program connections

Applications issuing requests for services are clients, and applications responding to requests are servers. Target application locations and platform sensitivities are client-transparent services. Services include distributed database, distributed file system, distributed print/object/archival, interactive multimedia (video, text, data, image, voice, data), distributed design, and distributed manufacturing.

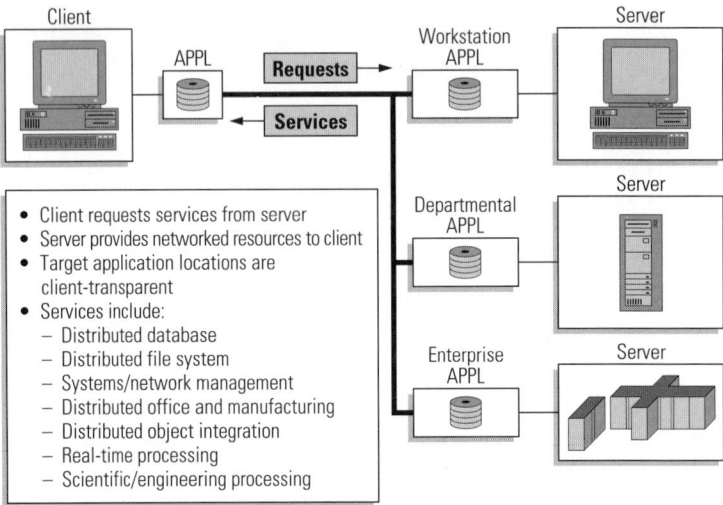

Figure 8.2   Client/server paradigm

APPN and TCP/IP each provide a foundation for networked client/server computing infrastructures. Corporate intranets have extended this paradigm through web-based applications.

8.1.3 Architecture reference models: OSI, SNA/APPN, TCP/IP

Both SNA/APPN and TCP/IP refer internally to functions described and defined in the original OSI reference model. It is therefore important to establish the relationships within and among these three significant network architectures. Figure 8.3 compares OSI, SNA/APPN, and TCP/IP.

The figure 8.3 side-by-side alignment of the OSI, SNA, and TCP/IP protocol suites suggests that their same-layer functions are identical. This is not the case. Perhaps their greatest degree of apparent similarity is that they have been drawn on the same figure. OSI and SNA, for example, are each seven-layer network architectures. However, the OSI and SNA layer functions are not exactly aligned. There are some functions found in a given OSI layer n (in OSI, layer n is the current layer under consideration) for example, that are found in SNA layer $n + 1$.

Several areas of consistency do, however, exist among the three network architectures:

• The upper layers (generally, layers 4 through 7) of the three protocol suites (OSI, SNA, TCP/IP) provide end-to-end, logical connection facilities

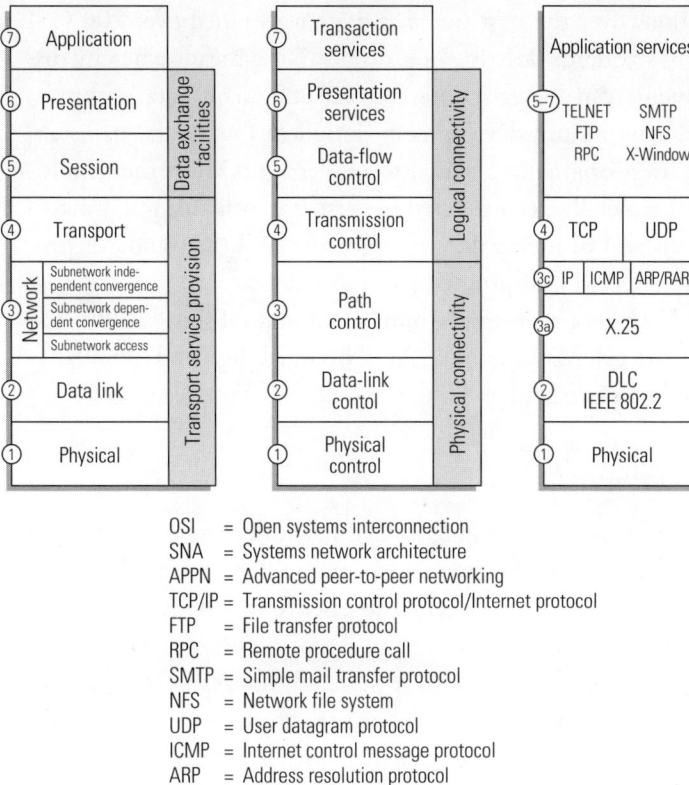

OSI	SNA/APPN	TCP/IP

OSI = Open systems interconnection
SNA = Systems network architecture
APPN = Advanced peer-to-peer networking
TCP/IP = Transmission control protocol/Internet protocol
FTP = File transfer protocol
RPC = Remote procedure call
SMTP = Simple mail transfer protocol
NFS = Network file system
UDP = User datagram protocol
ICMP = Internet control message protocol
ARP = Address resolution protocol
RARP = Reverse address resolution protocol
DLC = Data-link control
IEEE = Institute of Electrical and Electronic Engineers

Figure 8.3   OSI, SNA/APPN, TCP/IP layered models

- The lower layers (generally, layers 3 down through 1) of the three architectures provide transport facilities consisting of a variety of transmission subnetworks such as X.25, ISDN, ATM, and multihop wide-area networks using data-link controls such as SDLC, HDLC, or frame relay.

- It is also generally true (with some exceptions) that any layer n of the three protocol suites generates a layer n-specific message unit. This layer n message unit is presented to the next lower layer (layer $n-1$) as data, and layer $n-1$ adds its unique header (or header and trailer in the case of layer 2). Layer 1 in all cases does not construct message units but is concerned with placing bits over some terrestrial or celestial transmission medium (e.g., twisted pair wire, optical fiber waveguide, coaxial cable, microwave, and satellite).

Prodigious efforts by well-intentioned professionals from several countries, companies and standards organizations over the past two decades have yielded over 200 OSI international standards. These standards describe in great detail the means whereby dissimilar computing environments can logically interconnect and share data resources. Each of these standards had a minimum development period of four years, painstakingly evolved. While several users originally planned to implement OSI as their multi-vendor approach, TCP/IP has generally been selected because it is available today across a broad spectrum of platforms and products. Interestingly, the TCP/IP standards process has increasingly endorsed selected OSI protocols and services.

At the same time, IBM has been progressively more open in publishing APPN and related specifications. This process has increased APPN availability and popularity across a broadening range of developers and users.

8.1.4 Conclusions—general

Both APPN and TCP/IP are thorough, functional, layered network architectures which more than adequately serve a wide range of systems and environments within local and wide-area networks. Neither protocol suite is better in all cases for all users, nor even in most cases for most users.

Several aspects of each protocol suite offer one or more advantages to some degree in such areas as manageability, performance, or ease of use. However, some of these advantages in one area are partnered with disadvantages in another area of consideration.

Table 8.1 presents in summary form several of the points of comparison between APPN and TCP/IP to be considered herein.

We will now compare APPN and TCP/IP in the following major areas:

- Network architectures
- Nodes and links
- Resource identification: names and addresses
- Routing and topology
- Transport
- Upper layer issues and application program interfaces
- Convergence and directions

Table 8.1   Summary of general APPN and TCP/IP comparisons

		APPN	TCP/IP
Architecture	Thorough protocol stack	Yes	Yes
	Age	15 years (architecture), 10 years (products) (Subarea SNA heritage—20+ years)	20+ years
	Traditional focus	Corporate	Universities, governmental
	De facto standard	Yes	Yes
	De jure standard	No	Yes
	Development management body	IBM APPN Implementers Workshop	Internet Engineering Task Force
	Ownership	Proprietary-IBM (patent, license)	Public domain
	Specifications	Published (most)	Published (all)
Nodes and links	Vendors	40+	400+
	Number of node types	Two	Two
	End system term	End node	Host
	Intermediate system term	Network node	Router (or gateway)
	Intermediate system can have applications?	Yes	Yes
	Access from data-link interface to applications	Any application can be accessed through any adapter	Any application can be accessed through any adapter
	Able to run over any data link?	Yes—See DL requirement below. Currently implemented on most popular LANs and WANs.	Yes—Implemented on all data link types.
	Data-link requirement— connection orientation	APPN/ISR requires a connection-oriented data link	—
Resource Identification	Name	All nodes have CP name. Nodes with applications also have LU name. Except on mainframe and other nodes with multiple LUs, LU name is usually same as CP name. CP name and LU name are types of NAU name.	Only nodes with applications have names.
	Address	APPN name is also used as address; it serves most address functions. APPN name plus TG number identifies data link interface. (Session labels are sometimes called "addresses.")	Each data-link interface has an address. A node with multiple interfaces has multiple addresses. "Host ID" portion of address is interface ID.
	Name format	NetID.NAUname Each portion can be up to 8 alphanumeric characters. IBM registry for NetIDs usually allocates first two NetID characters to region (e.g., UK), up to the next four to organization (e.g., ACME), and last two to allocate NetIDs within that organization.	Example: *system.dept.company.com* Hierarchical from left (high) to right. Each portion (level) can be any number of alphanumeric characters. Highest level is organization type [e.g., com(mercial), edu(cational), or geographic (e.g., va.us)]. Next level is the autonomous domain, which is usually an organization name.

Table 8.1   Summary of general APPN and TCP/IP comparisons (continued)

		APPN	TCP/IP
Resource identification (cont.)	Address format	See name format above	32 bits. Usually represented in decimal format: four numbers represent the four octets. Example: 127.34.237.23. The bits identify the NetID and the host (interface) ID. The number of bits allocated to each ID depends on the address class. Part of the host ID bits can be used for a subnetwork ID—this part is noted in the 32-bit mask.
	Name/address relationship	APPN name is usually used as address.	Name/address pair is manually configured in domain name server. Usually, addresses in one NetID are also in same autonomous domain: e.g., addresses in NetID 127.15.0.0 are usually in domain acme.com.
	Address space capacity	Can support 1.7 million organizations in each region (e.g., UK). Should be sufficient for forseeable future.	Dramatically increased with IPing (IPv6). Transition will be annoying.
	Address groupings	APPN domain: a network node server and its served end nodes	TCP/IP subnetwork: all nodes with an interface to a single LAN or bridged LAN
	Topology groupings (to reduce topology flows)	APPN control point-to-control point minimum spanning tree. Future: APPN cluster	OSPF areas (within a NetID); OSPF designated router (within a subnetwork)
	Border between networks	APPN border node (two APPN NetIDs). Future: extended border node (multiple APPN NetIDs)	TCP/IP exterior gateway router (between autonomous domains)
	Broadcast capability (to all nodes)	No	Yes
	Multicast capability (to subset of nodes)	No general capacity. Locate flows can be used for multicast between network nodes.	Yes
Routing	Routing protocols (determining best route)	APPN/ISR APPN/HPR	IP
	Topology protocols (tracking network resources and routes)	Topology and routing services (TRS)	RIP, XNS, integrated IS-IS, OSPF…
	Topology database: fully mirrored, automatically updated, and distributed	Yes	Yes
	Distributed database tracks:	Network nodes and links	Routers and links
	Automatic route calculation	Yes	Yes
	Finding a target end system	Originating NN server uses Locate to query all NNs for NN serving destination EN. (Optional central directory server may be queried instead of all NNs.)	Originating router queries domain name server to get address of named destination host.
	Route calculation mechanism	APPN/ISR: label swapping APPN/HPR: source routing	Destination routing
	Routing connection orientation	APPN/ISR: Connection oriented—Data sent on same path for entire session. Session lost if link fails. APPN/HPR: connectionless with some connection-oriented services (e.g., resource reservation)	IP: Connectionless—Data for a single session may take different path after topology update or if link fails. Future: streams protocol for isochronous extensions will be connection-oriented.

Table 8.1   Summary of general APPN and TCP/IP comparisons (continued)

		APPN	TCP/IP
Routing (cont.)	Adaptive rerouting around congestion	Does not reroute around congestion. (See congestion control.)	Does not reroute around congestion. (See congestion control.)
	Adaptive rerouting around failure	APPN/ISR: Session dropped and restarted if any packet is lost. APPN/HPR: Nondisruptively reroutes around failure.	Nondisruptively reroutes around failure.
	Load balancing	Yes, end-to-end on a session basis. Not within a session.	OSPF: yes, end-to-end on a session basis. Not within a session.
	Topology database structure	Link state	Distance vector: RIP, XNS Link state: OSPF, integrated IS-IS
	Topology database updates	Automatic	Automatic
	Recovery from network failures	Automatic	Automatic
	Traffic characterics: class of service/type of service	Preferred COS traffic characteristics always taken into account. With COS, APPN would use links more optimally in large, complex network.	Older topology protocols do not use TOS field. OSPF can use TOS field, but most vendors do not implement.
	Priority	Priority always set by application on a session basis. (Default = normal.)	TCP/IP precedence bit used by very few implementations. Most TCP/IP implementations use BSD convention of sending interactive port traffic before batch port traffic. Many multi-protocol vendors implement vendor-specific, protocol-independent priority setting on routers.
	Resource utilization	APPN uses more resources at session startup, but headers are smaller. APPN reserves resources: response time guaranteed but resources not freed up when not used	TCP/IP packet headers are larger—each header contains entire address. TCP/IP response time depends on congestion but all resources always available to all sessions
Transport	Transport connection orientation	Connection-oriented transport	TCP—connection oriented UDP—connectionless
	Independence from upper layers (above layer 4)	No. APPN requires LU sessions (e.g., APPC)	Yes
	Sequencing and reordering	Sequencing: Yes. Reordering: No. APPN transport depends on connection-oriented data link to ensure order.	Yes
	Segmenting and reassembly	Yes. Segment size based on destination capacity and network capacity. Takes better advantage of WAN capacity.	Yes. Segment size based on destination capacity. On large internetwork, uses convention of 536-byte segments—may underutilize WAN capacity.
	Acknowledgments and retransmission	APPN requires acknowledgments. No retransmission capability. Session is dropped and restarted if any ack is not received. APPN designed to avoid packet loss by lower-layer connection orientation, so missing ack is less frequent and signifies bigger problem.	TCP requires acknowledgments. Requests retransmission if no ack received. TCP/IP designed to allow packet loss and use retransmission to compensate. Consumes fewer resources than APPN if few acks lost (e.g., low congestion or high line quality), but more if many acks lost. Connectionless UDP does not use acknowledgments.
	Flow control mechanism	Adaptive session-level pacing (a sliding windows protocol)	Sliding windows with slow-start

Table 8.1   Summary of general APPN and TCP/IP comparisons (continued)

		APPN	TCP/IP
Transport (cont.)	Congestion control mechanism	APPN/ISR: adaptive pacing hop by hop. Future: APPN/HPR with adaptive rate-based end to end. APPN/HPR congestion control expected to be more efficient than APPN/ISR or TCP/IP— fewer recalculations and less oscillation.	Allows flow control mechanism to act as congestion control also. Some vendors also implement ICMP source quench or proprietary source quench for congestion control.
	Congestion control philosophy	Proactive	Reactive
	Half or full duplex transport	FDX/HDX	Only full duplex

8.2   Network architectures

APPN and TCP/IP are thorough protocol stacks which have been implemented on a range of systems over a variety of data links to serve many classes of applications. Both TCP/IP and APPN are driven today by the same technical and business requirements. However, this was not always so.

TCP/IP and subarea SNA, APPN's predecessor, emerged at about the same time— in the early 1970s—but in very different environments and with very different goals. Even though they increasingly exist in similar environments and the goals have changed, the legacy of each network architecture remains and affects their users' points of view.

"Where you stand depends on where you sit" is a phrase that reflects the differing points of view today on the relative advantages of APPN and TCP/IP.

8.2.1   SNA/APPN

SNA was introduced by IBM in September 1974 as their strategic network architecture from which to define, design, and implement networked applications and devices. SNA is not a hardware, software, or firmware product. It is, however, implemented as a set of architectural specifications of logical structures, procedures, formats, and protocols in various hardware, software, and firmware products.

SNA superimposes a logical network interface between end users (application programs, devices) and the underlying physical network. In so doing, SNA provides end user transparency from the physical network interconnection and routing details. It defines a set of layered logical networks, where the outermost network provides the end-user interface, and each successive inner network provides a distinct set of functions to the next higher layer in a clearly defined fashion.

SNA technical design objectives are to:

- Provide a logical interface between end user programs and devices, and the network that presents a single-system image, regardless of targeted application processing environment and geographic location
- Permit resource sharing through dynamic allocation and deallocation of resources among end users
- Provide reliable data transfer and exchange
- Define and standardize data formats within the network to enable easy interpretation and processing
- Provide the ability for dynamic network reconfiguration
- Support distributed processing

SNA networks were traditionally host-centric and hierarchical in nature, providing devices with access into host applications. These host-based networks are called subarea networks. As technology improvements ushered in client/server, hostless networking, IBM enhanced SNA by introducing LEN as a precursor to APPN. LEN networks provide a basic set of peer networking functions where a host need not be present. In a LEN environment, a pair of applications can interconnect between processors (nodes) connected adjacently over a single link.

APPN enhanced LEN peer networking in several ways. APPN supports connections between applications located in nonadjacent nodes through use of a network node server. APPN was developed in response to continuing cost-performance technology improvements and to resultant user trends to increasingly distribute applications.

APPN provides a peer-to-peer networking foundation for distributed computing within client/server workgroups, distributed file systems, distributed databases, LAN file servers and groupware. APPN has been implemented on all of IBM's strategic enterprise host, departmental midrange, UNIX processors, and PC platforms. Several nonIBM vendors have also developed, announced, or marketed APPN products and directions as well.

APPN is further distinguished into APPN/ISR APPN/HPR. IBM has developed networking broadband services (NBBS) as a separate architectural direction to integrate SNA/APPN and several other (non-SNA) network protocol suites within a single, logical control point-based approach over high-speed subnetworks (i.e., ATM, frame relay).

Figure 8.4 summarizes the evolution of SNA from subarea functions (1974–onward), to LEN node functionality (1985–onward), APPN/ISR (prototyped during 1986), HPR (1994–onward), to NBBS (1994–95 onward).

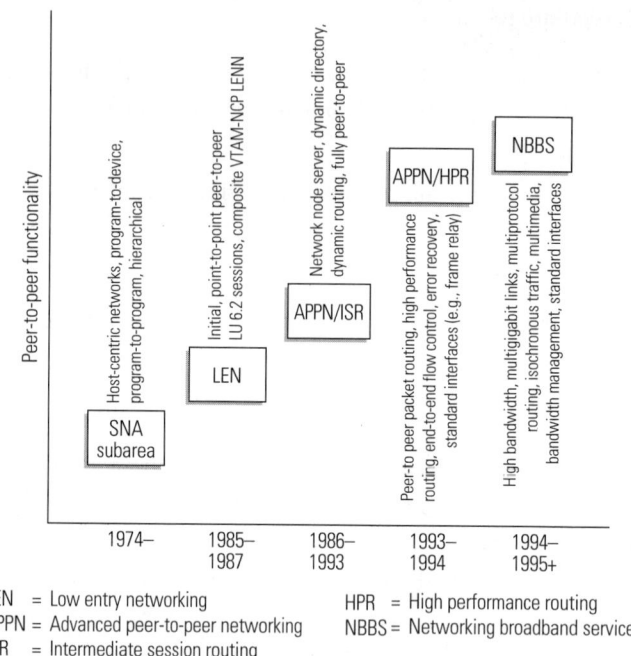

Figure 8.4   SNA/APPN evolution

LEN = Low entry networking
APPN = Advanced peer-to-peer networking
ISR = Intermediate session routing

HPR = High performance routing
NBBS = Networking broadband services

SNA/APPN architecture   SNA is organized into a seven-layer network architecture, as shown in figure 8.5. The upper four layers (layers 4 through 7) define the logical network and the lower three layers (layers 1 through 3) structure the physical configuration, or physical topology. The logical SNA network is defined by an end-user interface into network resources called an LU. The physical SNA network node is a PU.

Layer 7, transaction services (TS), provides the end user logical interface. The concern at this layer is with providing application transaction programs (ATPs) a single-system image into network services, through common command language formats. TS is responsible for several interprogram utilities including store-and-forward object distribution, distributed office services, and access to remote files and database records.

Layer 6, presentation services (PS), formats data for various presentation media (such as screens, printers, database records, file structures, storage media), and, as such, is concerned with syntactic and semantic data representations. PS is also responsible for allocation of resources to end users. These resources include machine processor cycles; real and virtual storage; disk, tape, mass storage, and related DASD I/O; terminal keyboards; displays; queues and buffers; database records; and conversations (serialized, interprogram session resources).

SNA layers		
Layer number	**Layer Name**	**Services**
7	Transaction services	Application utilities interface Single-system image
6	Presentation services	Data presentation Syntax negotiation/transforms Session profiles selection Network name/address resolution
5	Data-flow control	Session data exchange correlation Half-session data flow
4	Transmission control	End-to-end connectivity Session activation/deactivation Session-level pacing
3	Path control	Network route selection Addressing Class of service Message segmentation/blocking
2	Data-link control	Logical link initialization Data transfer Link disconnection
1	Physical control	DTE/DCE physical interface Electrical, mechanical, functional, procedural

Figure 8.5   SNA layers and services

Layer 5, *data flow control* (DFC), is concerned with data exchange correlation and flow synchronization between SNA half-sessions. SNA sessions are the means for end user applications and I/O devices to exchange data, and for every session there are two half-sessions. Each half-session, in turn, is defined by a local LU interface between the end user (program or device) and the SNA logical network.

Layer 4, *transmission control* (TC), is responsible for end-to-end connectivity, session activation/deactivation, and session send/receive pacing.

Layer 3, path control (PC), provides network route selection, class of service, and message segmentation/blocking.

Layer 2, DLC, initializes, transfers data over, and disconnects logical links between adjacent nodes.

Layer 1, physical control, provides physical connections electrically, mechanically, functionally, and procedurally between data terminal equipment (DTE) and data circuit-terminating equipment (DCE).

Peer protocols Each of the SNA layers logically communicates with its counterpart elsewhere within a network. Each SNA layer is also responsible for a specific set of network protocols. These protocols are logically conveyed between same-numbered SNA layers within message units. SNA same-layer to same-layer logical connectivity creates a peer protocol relationship. Figure 8.6 illustrates a pair of SNA end users (in this case a pair of application transaction programs) that are logically connected through a conversation running over a session. The right-side application is sending data to the left-side application. In the figure example, the right-side application presents its data locally across a layer 7 interface. Each of the figure 8.6 program end users resides in an end system. There may be one or more intermediate nodes along the path as well. If so, intermediate node protocol encapsulation and decapsulation generally proceeds to layer 3; sometimes to layer 4 (not shown in the figure).

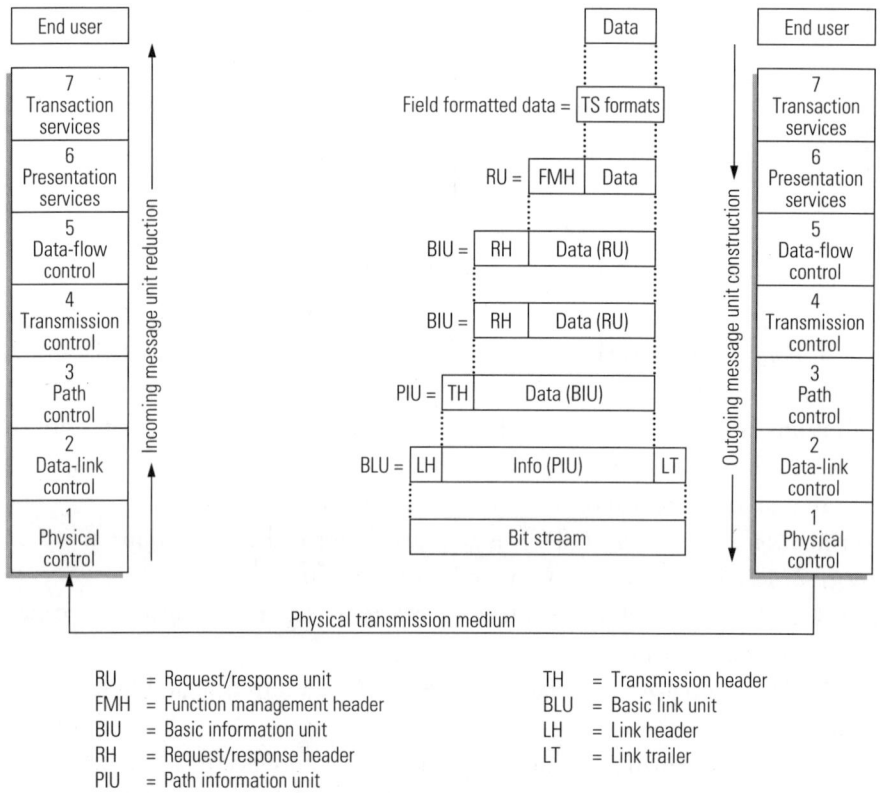

RU   = Request/response unit
FMH = Function management header
BIU = Basic information unit
RH   = Request/response header
PIU = Path information unit

TH   = Transmission header
BLU = Basic link unit
LH   = Link header
LT   = Link trailer

Figure 8.6   SNA peer protocols

Subarea versus APPN Figure 8.7 provides a comparison of SNA subarea (hierarchical, host-centric) and APPN (peer-to-peer) networks. A subarea network is shown on the left of the figure. The physical unit type 5 (PU5) host owns all other network resources, including all directly or indirectly attached PU4 communication controllers and downstream PU2.0 nodes. The PU5 host also maintains resource control over all host- and nonhost-resident LUs. The collection of one PU5 host and all of the node/PU, LU and link resources that it controls (activates, maintains, deactives) is one domain.

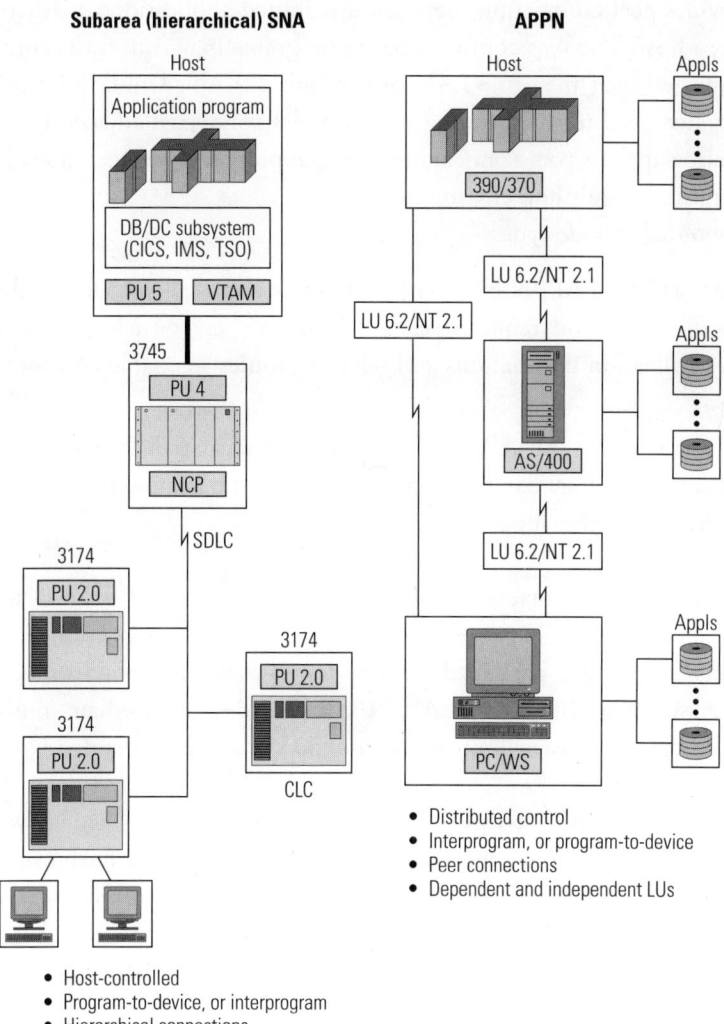

Figure 8.7 Subarea SNA versus APPN

The right-side of figure 8.7 depicts an example APPN network. Whereas subarea SNA provides multiple PU/node types with the higher-order nodes controlling lower-order nodes, APPN derives its architectural basis from only one node type, node type 2.1 (NT2.1). The right-side of the figure indicates that APPN networks are predicated upon:

- Distributed control (contrasted from subarea host centricity)
- Peer connections

APPN APPN provides peer connections between distributed applications, neither of which need reside on a host. The two communicating programs may run, for example, on workstations connected over the same LAN or through a WAN. Unlike LEN, the communicating programs need not be running within nodes connected adjacently over a single link. APPN also supports peer connections between programs between nonadjacent nodes within multilink, multihop environments.

APPN defines two major node types:

- *EN* EN includes a CP. An APPN EN registers its applications and other resources to a network node server and requests services from the server such as locating remote resource application destinations and selecting routes to enable end-to-end LU–LU sessions.
- *NN, the APPN server node* An APPN NN manages distributed directories and maintains a replicated topology database that is used for route computation, as well as EN client application server support.

APPN with ISR APPN/ISR provides connection-oriented internodal links to support end-to-end logical connections between LUs in session. The ISR connection orientation at the link level between each pair of adjacent nodes is provided through a routing technique called label swapping. In this way, APPN/ISR provides intermediate routing with separate session stages over each link, in conjunction with end-to-end, LU–LU connections.

Figure 8.8 indicates that in APPN/ISR there exists a separate session stage between each APPN node pair. These session stages are for separate active links. Each session stage is specified by an LFSID. The routing field portion of a format identification type 2 (FID2) TH, assigned by path control, has a single routing label (the LFSID) that is 17 bits in length. Each LFSID needs to be unique only over a given link between a pair of APPN nodes along a session path.

Figure 8.9 provides an architectural view of APPN/ISR routing. ISR provides LFSID label-swapping as well as session-connector-based transport functions, at each

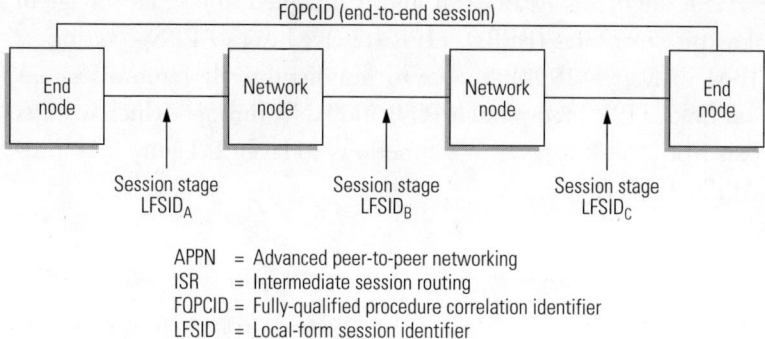

Figure 8.8 APPN/ISR session stages

intermediate node along the session path. This approach is in keeping with an APPN major design point to provide reliable support for enterprise mission-critical applications over links that may range in quality from good to poor on a node-by-node basis.

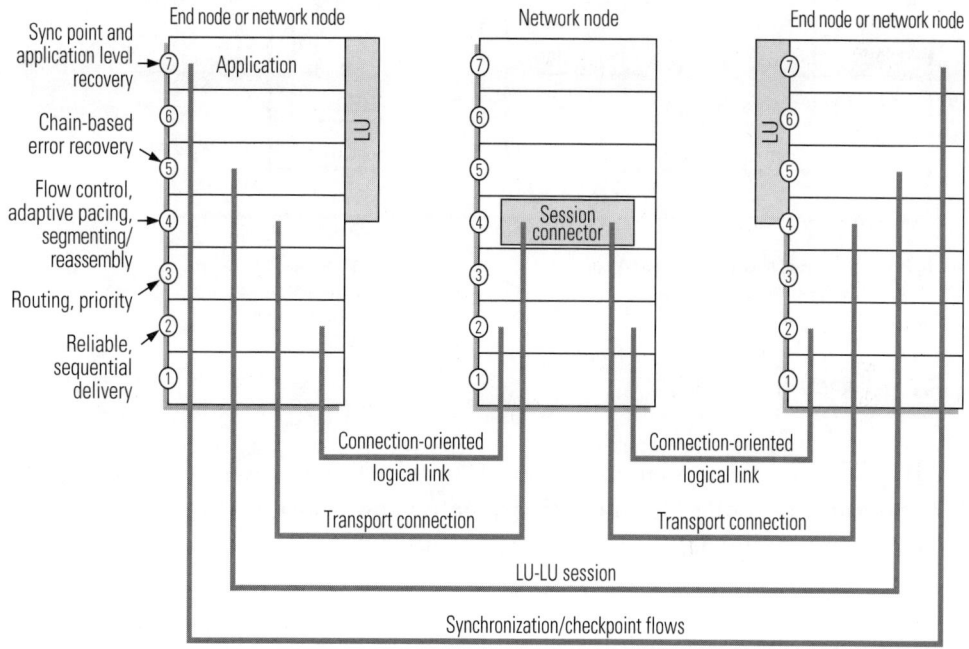

Figure 8.9 APPN/ISR routing

APPN with HPR   HPR augments APPN/ISR and is designed to take advantage of fast link speeds with low bit error rates (BERs). HPR (referred to as APPN+ during its initial disclosure by IBM in March 1992), is able to nondisruptively reroute sessions around failed nodes and links. HPR incorporates RTP and ANR through which it shifts APPN routing emphasis from the ISR layer 3–4 functions to layer 2. Figure 8.10 provides an overview of APPN/HPR routing.

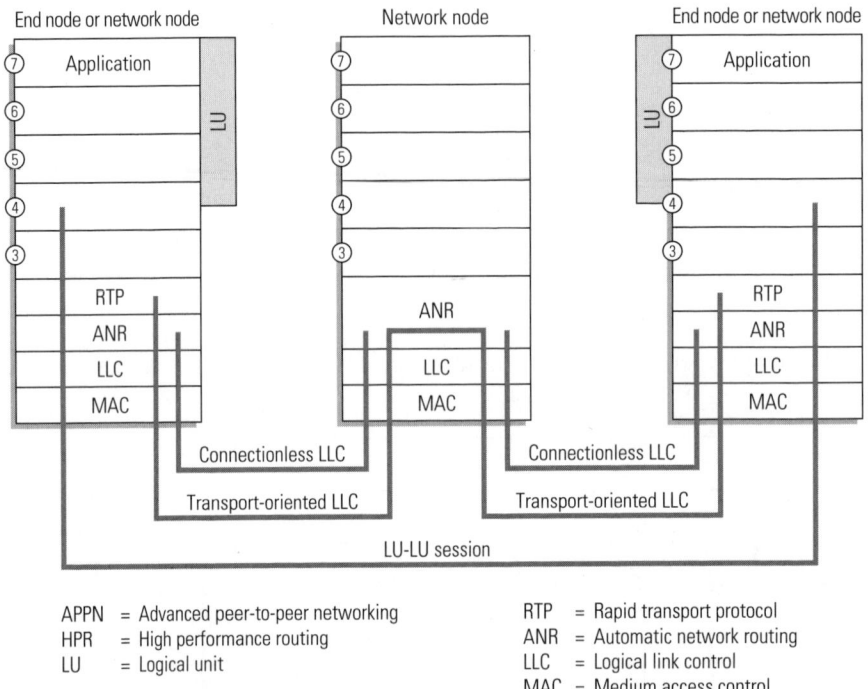

APPN	= Advanced peer-to-peer networking	RTP	= Rapid transport protocol
HPR	= High performance routing	ANR	= Automatic network routing
LU	= Logical unit	LLC	= Logical link control
		MAC	= Medium access control

Figure 8.10   APPN/HPR routing

HPR RTP is a connection-oriented, end-to-end transport protocol that runs over ANR, the latter providing deterministic connectionless source routing over minimal data-link control. In essence, RTP functions as a virtual link.

RTP functions include:

- Connection awareness of each session running over the RTP link
- Reordering, if necessary, following a path switch
- Reordering if the route contains one or more multilink TGs
- Optional reliable delivery

- Flow control and congestion control/avoidance
- Nondisruptive route switching

ANR runs logically under RTP and provides the following functions:

- Source routing with locally specified labels
- Discarding of incoming packets during congestion episodes
- Connectionless, stateless, fast routing
- Priority-based servicing of outbound transmission links

HPR uses ARB congestion control to compensate for the loss of the adaptive pacing function found in APPN/ISR intermediate routing nodes. ARB regulates the input traffic (offered load) to the RTP logical link and is preventive, not reactive. As the network approaches a congestion condition (as determined by increasing delay and diminishing throughput thresholds), ARB reduces the input-traffic rate until restoration of network capacity.

ARB employs a closed-loop feedback mechanism based upon information periodically exchanged between RTP components at the endpoints of an RTP logical link. The two feedback rates of concern are:

- The rate at which RTP accepts data arriving from the network
- The rate at which RTP conveys data to a recipient. Monitoring of these two rates provides the basis for congestion anticipation, and enables preventive throttling.

High data rate, low BER links (links with BER $\leq 10^{-7}$) are good candidates to use a connectionless DLC under RTP. These links are typically optical fiber media with digital signaling. Links with relatively high BERs would likely use a connection-oriented DLC under RTP. RTP insulates the LU upper layers and user from awareness of path switching, multipath routing, network-based congestion phenomena, retransmissions, acknowledgments, packet resequencing and multiplexing.

APPN/HPR protocols (RTP, ANR, ARB) can be considered as a set of transport-oriented LLCs. HPR integrates session class of service to priority scheduling queues by encoding priority bits into HPR headers. HPR can run over either LAN links or any transmission medium that supports connectionless (unacknowledged) service. These include IEEE 802.2 LLC, link access procedure-ISDN B channel (LAP-D; based upon LAP-balanced—LAP-B), SDLC (using unnumbered information frames), or X.25 using QLLC. Interestingly, it would be technically feasible to incorporate HPR and all of its benefits into TCP/IP (i.e., HPR/IP).

8.2.2 TCP/IP

TCP/IP was originally designed for networks of medium-sized end systems (minicomputers) to transfer files between researchers at different sites working on related projects. These early file transfers did not require fast response time because they were not designed for interactive applications. Remote, interactive terminal access to hosts was a later development that led to rapid improvements in throughput.

TCP/IP's popularity today was not the result of some grand scheme but rather the result of a series of serendipitous events. In its earliest form, it was first developed as a radio communication protocol for battlefield environments. Later, in the early 1970s, it was enchanced by DARPA and its contractors for use in a nationwide network of military installations, military contractors, and university research environments. TCP/IP thus became the network protocol for the ARPAnet, a U.S.-based packet switched network developed during the early 1970s and considered to be the granddaddy of the contemporary Internet. ARPAnet was decommissioned in June 1990.

Governmental changes in the ARPAnet led to deployment of several backbones, including the military network (MILnet) and the National Science Foundation (NSFnet), which inherited the university and research component. The result became known as the Internet, with the definite article and a capital *I*, to distinguish it from an internet, a generic term for interconnected networks. Regulations for access to and use of the Internet were relaxed and the resulting growth was exponential.

TCP/IP is a collection of application as well as network protocols interconnected by a set of routers creating a single, virtual network. Today's Internet consists of large national backbone networks (e.g., NSFnet, CREN, MILnet) and several regional and campus networks in many countries. Intranet and Internet participants have access to the Internet protocol suite, including IP connectivity, Telnet, Ping and email. Systems with exclusive email capability are not actually considered to reside on the Internet.

TCP, IP, and related Internet protocols have traditionally been developed and enhanced in the public domain though some vendors and other organizations have developed and marketed enhanced versions. Distributed users wanted the network to require minimal effort to use and maintain and were motivated to change it only when a new function was needed.

When the University of California–Berkeley was releasing its own version of the UNIX operating system in the late 1970s, it wanted to include a networking protocol. TCP/IP was chosen because it was in the public domain and because Berkeley's developers had experience with it on the ARPAnet.

TCP/IP design goals and RFCs　　The initial TCP/IP design goal was to build an interconnection of networks that provides universal communications services. The design point was to allow each physical network to maintain its own technology-unique set of communications interfaces. Internetworking within this context includes:

- Resource sharing between and among distributed processing environments
- Use of layered protocols
- Support for interprocess communication (IPC)

The TCP/IP standards are developed through an RFC process managed by the IAB and IETF. Internet RFCs are a document series begun in 1969 that describe the internet protocol suite and related studies. The RFC publication series is operated by USC-ISI, which promulgates IAB standards, formal and archival publication of individual ideas, specifications, and other items of internet community interest.

Receive RFC submission guidelines by sending email to `rfc-editor@isi.edu`. The current list of RFCs is in the file `rfc/rfc-index.txt`. To receive information on new RFCs send email to `rfc-announce@isi.edu`.

Table 8.2 provides examples of major internet RFCs.

Category		Name	RFC number
	Model and taxonomy	IAB Official Protocol Standards Assigned Numbers Host Requirements - Communications Host Requirements - Applications Gateway Requirements	1280 1060 1122 1123 1009
	Internet layer	IP - Internet Protocol IP Subnet Extension IP Broadcast Datagrams IP Broadcast Datagrams with Subnets ICMP - Internet Control Message Protocol IGMP - Internet Group Multicast Protocol	791 950 919 922 792, 1256 1112
	Transport layer	TCP - Transmission Control Protocol UDP - User Datagram Protocol	793 768
	Application layer	TELNET - Telnet Protocol and Options FTP - File Transfer Protocol SMTP - Simple Mail Transfer Protocol	854, 855 959 821
	Distributed services	DNS - Domain Name System	1034, 1035
	Network management	SNMP - Simple Network Management Protocol SNMP v2 MIB-II - Management Information Base-II RMON RMON v2	1157 1907 1213 1757 2021, 2074

Table 8.2   Major Internet RFCs

TCP/IP architecture Figure 8.11 depicts the TCP/IP architecture. TCP and IP provide transport and internet functions, respectively. However, TCP/IP application services and their underlying network infrastructure are all collectively referred to as TCP/IP. The internet function is provided through internet gateways (routers). Basic internet gateway properties include:

- Provision of a network view that the gateway is an intranetwork host
- Making the internet gateway transparent to generate a single network view
- Selection of the best route based on available routing metrics

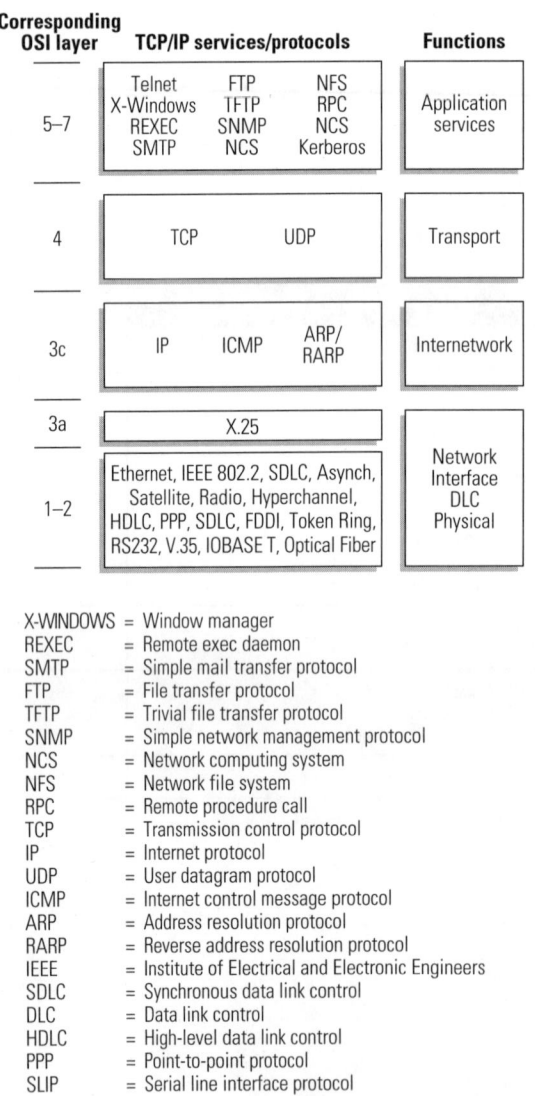

Corresponding OSI layer	TCP/IP services/protocols	Functions
5–7	Telnet FTP NFS X-Windows TFTP RPC REXEC SNMP NCS SMTP NCS Kerberos	Application services
4	TCP UDP	Transport
3c	IP ICMP ARP/RARP	Internetwork
3a	X.25	Network Interface DLC Physical
1–2	Ethernet, IEEE 802.2, SDLC, Asynch, Satellite, Radio, Hyperchannel, HDLC, PPP, SDLC, FDDI, Token Ring, RS232, V.35, IOBASE T, Optical Fiber	

X-WINDOWS = Window manager
REXEC = Remote exec daemon
SMTP = Simple mail transfer protocol
FTP = File transfer protocol
TFTP = Trivial file transfer protocol
SNMP = Simple network management protocol
NCS = Network computing system
NFS = Network file system
RPC = Remote procedure call
TCP = Transmission control protocol
IP = Internet protocol
UDP = User datagram protocol
ICMP = Internet control message protocol
ARP = Address resolution protocol
RARP = Reverse address resolution protocol
IEEE = Institute of Electrical and Electronic Engineers
SDLC = Synchronous data link control
DLC = Data link control
HDLC = High-level data link control
PPP = Point-to-point protocol
SLIP = Serial line interface protocol

Figure 8.11   TCP/IP architecture

The various internet services and protocols depicted in figure 8.11 are modeled as four functional layers: application services, transport, internetwork, and network interface and hardware. TCP/IP is a layered architecture similar to OSI. While TCP/IP and OSI architectures are quite distinct (see figure 8.3), they provide functional similarities. They support the same connectivity services and protocols at OSI layers 1 and 2 (physical and data-link layers), such as X.25, token-ring, and ethernet. IP provides functions similar to OSI layer 3 (network layer). TCP provides functions similar to OSI layer 4 (transport layer).

TCP/IP application services   TCP/IP application services are user processes that cooperate with other such processes running on the same or different hosts or workstations. TCP/IP today includes over eighty application networking functions including:

- Telnet client/server (C/S); provides terminal emulation and allows remote login to another host
- FTP C/S; provides file transfer
- NFS (trademark of SUN Microsystems, Inc.) C/S; provides file access for remote hosts
- Trivial FTP (TFTP); provides file transfer using UDP. Together with BOOTstrap protocol (BOOTP–RFC 951), or the more advanced Dynamic Host Configuration Protocol (DHCP–RFC 2131), this lets workstations boot off a server.
- SMTP C/S; provides electronic mail
- RPC; enables program execution on a remote host
- X-Window C/S; provides an API for program access to a bit mapped display
- NameServer; provides an automated address resolution system
- SNMP agent/monitor (A/M; server/client, respectively); provides network management
- Remote execution protocol (REXEC) client/daemon (C/D; client/server, respectively)
- Kerberos C/S; provides a security function to enable a client/server pair to authenticate its partner
- World Wide Web (WWW); perhaps the most popular TCP/IP applications today

These application services and protocols use either TCP or UDP as a transport mechanism. TCP provides a transport connection-orientation and UDP is a connectionless transport. Both TCP and UDP use IP to provide an underlying semi-reliable, connectionless datagram environment. Several OSI layer 7 (application layer) services are supported by TCP/IP as well. For example, OSI and TCP/IP (respectively) upper-layer functions include electronic mail (X.400 and SMTP), terminal emulation (virtual terminal and TELNET), file transfer (FTAM and FTP), and network management (common management information service (CMIS)/CMIP and SNMP).

TCP TCP provides a reliable, connection-oriented protocol. UDP is unreliable and provides no flow control. A TCP connection is defined and identified by a pair of sockets, each of which combines four parameters: originating port and IP_address, and destination port and IP_address. It is reasonable to consider a TCP socket as similar in function to an OSI transport service access point (TSAP) address. TCP is most often selected for transport and is a peer-to-peer, connection-oriented protocol that does not use master/slave relations.

Figure 8.12 illustrates a TCP header represented as encapsulated by an IP header. TCP architecturally operates above the IP layer and provides applications a flow-controlled, sequenced, reliable, end-to-end octet stream. IP, on the other hand, provides only a best-efforts datagram transmission service. Each application process connected by TCP is presumed to be running within an internet host (end system) that is identified by an IP address. Each application process (e.g., client process, server process) has avail-

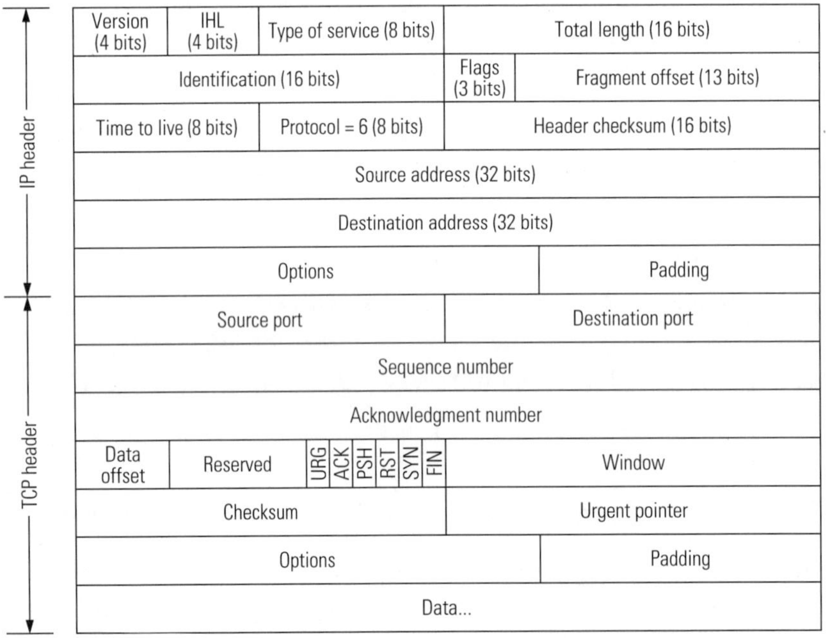

IHL = Internet header length

Figure 8.12   TCP header with IPv4

able to itself several possible logical, full duplex ports through which it can set up and make use of TCP connections.

RFC 1700, Assigned Numbers, specifies well-known ports as common TCP and UDP assignments. The list is extensive; some examples include FTP (21), TELNET (23), SMTP (25), Nameserver (42), Login (49), Domain name server (53), TFTP (69), X400 (103), RTELNET (107), SUNRPC (111), SFTP (115), SNMP (161), and BGP (179).

Hosts (end systems) that support IPv4 are identified by a 32-bit IP address, and a port is identified by a 16-bit value. Those that enable IPv6 (IPng, RFC 1752) support an IP address length of 128 bits to provide more levels of addressing hierarchy, a much greater range of addressable nodes and more straightforward address autoconfiguration.

TCP uses a flow-control window scheme in which the connection receiver reports to the sender the sequence numbers the sender can transmit at any time, and those that the receiver has received contiguously.

As shown in figure 8.12, TCP segments (shown as the TCP header) are embedded within IP datagrams (shown as the IP header) for transmission. The components of a TCP segment include:

- Source and destination port IDs (taken together with the source and destination IP addresses from the IP header, these constitute the socket pair that comprise a TCP connection ID)

- Sequence number and acknowledgment number (together, these are used to identify which data are being sent and which are being received by the TCP segment sender)

- Data offset field, indicates the number of 32-bit words within the TCP header

- Flags, signal special case conditions: URG (urgent data present), ACK (acknowledgment field is valid), PSH (push arriving data to the application level), RST (reset the connection), SYN (begin connection by synchronizing sequence numbers), and FIN (signal the finishing of transmission)

- Window field, indicates the number of octets, including the octet whose sequence number value is in the acknowledgment field that the segment sender is able to accept

- Checksum field, provided as the 16-bit 1's complement of the 1's complement sum of all 16-bit words contained within the header and text

- Urgent pointer, provided as a 16-bit value that represents an offset from the sequence number of the packet conveying the urgent pointer. The sum of urgent pointer and sequence number is the sequence number of the last octet of urgent data

- Several options, including maximum receive segment, window scale, selective ACK-permitted, SACK, TCP echo, and TCP echo reply

TCP-supporting applications generally select a client/server interaction model. Users generally invoke the client aspect of an application which then constructs a request for the named service and presents that request to the server aspect of the application. Servers are programs that receive requests, perform requested services, and propagate results back to the requesters in the form of a reply. Servers can usually accommodate multiple requests from multiple clients concurrently.

IP IP functions as the layer that makes transparent the underlying physical network by creating a virtual network view. IP is an unreliable, best-effort, connectionless packet delivery protocol. Any IP packets (datagrams) that are lost, received out of order, or accidentally duplicated are not resolved by IP. Resolution is a TCP issue.

IPv4 addresses are 32-bit fields that specify source and target hosts on the Internet, and are in the logical form `<network address>` `<host address>`. IPv6 addresses are 128-bit fields.

IP carries datagrams between source and destination hosts (end systems) that may be interconnected through one or several intermediate gateways (routers) and networks. An IP datagram is a finite-length packet of bits containing a header and payload (data). Hosts and routers are all involved in the processing of IP headers. End systems create IP headers/datagrams on sending, and process on receipt. Routers examine IP headers as input to making routing decisions and modify them as IP packets propagate from source to destination hosts. Figure 8.13 illustrates the components of an IP header.

IPv4 header field components include:

- Version number, a 4-bit field that specifies which version of the Internet packet format is in use. Most current implementations use IP version 4. There is an

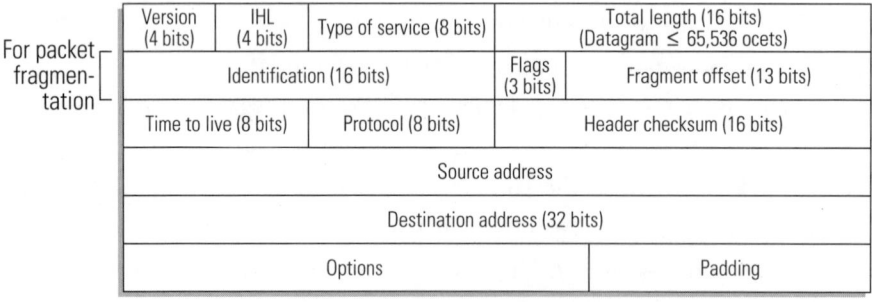

IHL = Internet header length

Figure 8.13 Internet datagram header (IPv4)

experimental Stream Protocol using IP version 5, as well as a follow-on Stream Protocol II using IP version 6.

- IHL, a 4-bit field that specifies the length of the Internet packet in 32-bit words

- Type of service (TOS) is a field that specifies the nature of the service to be provided. TOS provides a three-way tradeoff between low delay, high reliability, and high throughput. It is likely that the IAB will modify the current standard interpretations provided in RFC 791 to reflect IETF working group recommendations. For example, a new interpretation is for a 4-bit TOS field supporting up to 16 possible values. IP TOS is becoming increasingly important as networks incorporate capabilities to deliver specific classes of service and provide certain service guarantees.

- Protocol Identifier is an 8-bit field that states which upper level protocol is encapsulated by the internet packet. Several of the protocol identifier assignments are shown in table 8.3. Note that

Table 8.3 Example assigned Internet protocol numbers

Decimal	Abbreviation	Protocol Name
0	—	Reserved
1	ICMP	Internet Control Message Protocol
2	IGMP	Internet Group Management Protocol
3	GGP	Gateway-to-Gateway Protocol
4	—	Assigned
5	ST	Stream Protocol
6	TCP	Transmission Control Protocol
7	—	Assigned
8	EGP	Exterior Gateway Protocol
9	IGP	Any private interior gateway
10	—	Assigned
11	NVP-II	Network Voice Protocol
12–16	—	Assigned
17	UDP	User Datagram Protocol
18–28	—	Assigned
29	ISO-TP4	ISO Transport Protocol Class 4
30–34	—	Assigned
35-60	—	Unassigned
61	—	Any host internal protocol
62-71	—	Assigned
72-75	—	Unassigned
76-79	—	Assigned
80	CLNP	ISO Connectionless Network Protocol
81	VMTP	VMTP
82	SECURE-VMTP	SECURE-VMTP
83	VINES	VINES
84	—	Assigned
85	NSFNET-IGP	NSFNET-Internal Gateway Protocol
86-87	—	Assigned
88	IGRP	Interior Gateway Routing Protocol
89	OSPF	Open Shortest Path First Protocol
90-91	—	Assigned
92-254	—	Unassigned
255	—	Reserved

this table (showing the embedding of TCP within IP) shows that the IP header protocol identifier is set to the decimal value of 6, which is the assigned TCP value.

- Total length is a 16-bit field that defines support for internet datagram packets with length up to 65,536 octets. There is an internet requirement that all hosts (end systems) and routers support packets up to 576 octets in length without the need for packet fragmentation. This 576-octet value defines support for 512 octets of data, 20 octets of header, and 44 octets for options or lower layer protocol headers.

- Fragmentation is the breaking of packets into smaller internet packets for internet-work routing. Fragmentation is provided when the origin packet size exceeds the maximum transmission unit (MTU) size.

- Time to live (TTL). The TTL field was originally intended to indicate the number of seconds that an internet packet could exist in the Internet before being discarded (maximum value of 255 seconds). TTL has effectively functioned as a hop count of sorts, with a default value of 32.

- Checksum is a 16-bit 1's complement of the 16-bit sum of the header contents which is recalculated at each hop.

- Source and destination addresses have historically been a 32-bit field comprising the internet address space (IPv4).

- Options may or may not be present. Examples include basic security, loose source routing, internet timestamps, record route, stream ID, and strict source routing.

IP datagrams   IP datagram services are provided through an internet (interconnected set of networks) through IP gateways that exchange routing information using protocols such as border gateway protocol (BGP), EGP, HELLO protocol, and interior gateway protocol (IGP): for example, RIP, and OSPF. IP is functionally equivalent to OSI layer 3c (independent covergence sublayer) because IP routes messages across multiple networks in connectionless (best-effort) fashion.

8.2.3 SNA/APPN and TCP/IP goals and expectations

Table 8.4 provides a comparison of some of the traditional goals and expectations affecting the environments from which SNA/APPN and TCP/IP have emerged. Certainly these are generalizations if not stereotypical. For example, though SNA is the most popular protocol in the banking sector, not all banks prefer SNA. As another example, though the initial TCP and IP protocol developments were government funded, along with several other TCP/IP components, not all of TCP/IP development has been government funded.

APPN (ISR and HPR) is not as strongly affected as subarea SNA by the elements listed in table 8.4. APPN, like TCP/IP, was developed for a peer systems environment. However, even with the limitations of the goals and assumptions shown in table 8.4, the table is useful as a philosophic backdrop for this discussion of the differences between APPN and TCP/IP.

Table 8.4   Comparison of traditional goals and assumptions for SNA and TCP/IP

SNA	TCP/IP
Commercially funded	Government funded
Physical connection assumed unreliable	Physical connection assumed unreliable
Network reliable & ensures delivery	Network unreliable; end nodes ensure delivery
Origin determines route from predefined options	Network determines route
Focus on efficiency	Focus on ease of use
Management enforced	Each site responsible for management
Users: banks and insurance companies	Users: universities and research institutes
Nontechnical end users	Technical end users
Deterministic delivery, predictable response	Fastest possible delivery; delays acceptable
Proprietary development	Public domain development
Terminal-mainframe traffic	Minicomputer-to-minicomputer traffic
Hierarchical orientation	Peer orientation, avoid hierarchy
Minimize line costs	Minimize memory, storage, CPU processing
Security-conscious; restrict access	Universal access; self-monitoring (Gov't. MILnet uses tight security)
Single-company networks	Interorganizational networks
Scalable: very large network (originally, single host environment)	Scalable: many small networks
Usage accounting critical for charge-back	Flat charge for access; usage unlimited

8.3   Nodes and links

APPN (ISR and HPR) and TCP/IP differ in their representation of resources in a node. However, they both have two types of nodes: end systems and intermediate systems. These terms, which derive from OSI terminology, describe, respectively, devices that make use of the network and devices which provide network services. For example, end systems support applications but do not participate in the routing topology.

In both APPN and TCP/IP, however, an intermediate system may also be configured as an end system. For example, a PC that acts as a router may also support end-user applications.

8.3.1 End system appearance

Both architectures provide applications with network access through adapters (though some implementations may create restrictions). However, they represent these in different ways, as shown in figure 8.14.

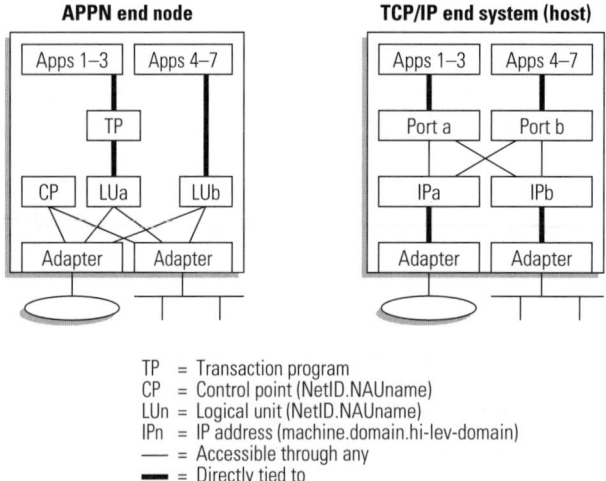

TP = Transaction program
CP = Control point (NetID.NAUname)
LUn = Logical unit (NetID.NAUname)
IPn = IP address (machine.domain.hi-lev-domain)
—— = Accessible through any
▬ = Directly tied to

Figure 8.14   Basic components of APPN end node and TCP/IP host

APPN end nodes   An APPN end node usually defines only one link to a network. However, it can have more than one name. Most APPN end node implementations, however, use the same name for both the control point and a single LU.

An end node has at least a CP name (Note: a LEN end node contains one or more LUs but does not contain a CP), which is the component that manages the resources of the node. It may also have one or more separate LU names for the LUs that provide access to the applications on the node. (An LU supports one or more applications in somewhat the same way that IP port numbers do for TCP/IP.)

If there are multiple links to the end node, traffic is directed across the network by the node's name. The network is aware that there are multiple paths to it and can select from among them. Thus, the end node can be accessed through any link. The same effect is achievable in IP, as discussed above, but is not automatic.

TCP/IP hosts   A TCP/IP end system (called a host) usually has only one link to a network. Its IP address is actually associated with the link rather than the node. On a LAN, for example, there is a one-to-one correlation between an IP address and a MAC address.

In the case where a TCP/IP host has more than one link, it is called a multihomed host. If it is multihomed, it has a separate IP address for each link. Messages sent to one IP address cannot be delivered through an interface with another address on the same device—the network perceives them as completely separate destinations.

This multihomed host limitation only presents itself as a problem during link failure. To work around this limitation, the requester's software or domain name server can be defined with the alternate address(es) associated with the same host name, to be used if the first is not available.

Any IP address can be used to access any application on that system. This is because the application is accessed through a port number that is independent of the address. The appropriate port number for access to that application or type of application is appended to the IP address (`IPaddress.PortNumber`).

8.3.2 Intermediate system appearance

The OSI reference model uses the term *intermediate system* for a node that can make routing decisions and through which data can pass from one device to another. In APPN, these are called network nodes. In TCP/IP, these intermediate systems are usually called routers.

In both environments, an intermediate node can also contain applications. For APPN, this means a network node that also has LUs. For TCP/IP, this refers to a router that has application ports as well as routing tables. For simplicity, our examples will not include these combination systems.

Figure 8.15 shows a basic overview of an APPN network node and a TCP/IP router. As with the end systems discussed above, the two environments have similar capabilities but place focus on different components.

The APPN network node has one CP name regardless of the number of links it defines to physical networks. (Each APPN link is identified by a TG number, but this is not used for locating the node.) In TCP/IP, each router has multiple addresses, one for each interface. Usually an IP router does not have a name unless it also runs applications.

Both APPN and TCP/IP intermediate nodes contain routing software. The software uses tables and caches, and coordinates with other intermediate nodes to calculate optimal routes and to route data.

Table 8.5 presents a few terms to assist in comparing APPN and TCP/IP at the node and link level.

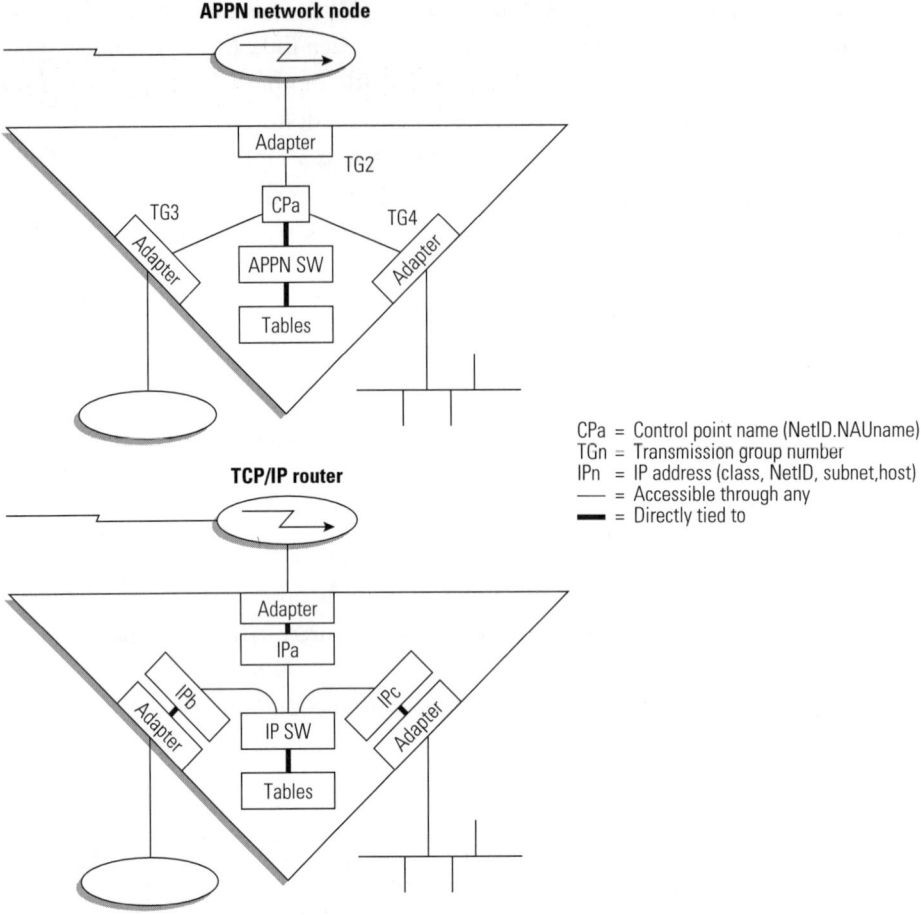

APPN network node

Adapter

TG2

CPa

TG3   TG4

Adapter   Adapter

APPN SW

Tables

TCP/IP router

Adapter

IPa

IPb   IPc

Adapter   Adapter

IP SW

Tables

CPa = Control point name (NetID.NAUname)
TGn = Transmission group number
IPn = IP address (class, NetID, subnet,host)
—— = Accessible through any
▬▬ = Directly tied to

Figure 8.15   Basic components of APPN network node and TCP/IP router

8.3.3 Implementations

APPN and TCP/IP are both capable of supporting systems ranging from small PCs and workstations to large mainframes. However, due to APPN's relatively recent arrival, TCP/IP has been installed on a wider range of processor platforms and operating environments.

TCP/IP is implemented on an extensive range of platforms using a wide variety of operating systems from more than 400 vendors, including all the major system vendors.

Table 8.5 TCP/IP and APPN node and link terminology compared

	TCP/IP	APPN	Terms used herein
Network client: node which uses the network resources	Host	End node	End system (OSI)
Node which provides network services	Router	Network node	Intermediate system (OSI)
Software/device that sends data at layer 2, disregarding network protocol	Bridge	Bridge	Bridge
Group of devices sharing one network ID	Network, autonomous domain	Network-APPN, SNI domain-subarea SNA	NetID or network
Software/device providiing connection between networks with different network IDs	Gateway	Border Node	Border gateway
Path(s) between two routers	Link, route	Link, TG, path	Link

Note: In both TCP/IP and APPN, an intermediate node might also run applications as an end system in addition to its networking function.

SNA requires connection-oriented data link Subarea SNA and APPN/ISR both require a connection-oriented data link. On LANs, this means that both subarea SNA and APPN traffic must flow across LAN adapters (and routers, if any are on the path) that are equipped with IEEE 802.2 LLC2 connection-oriented support.

One quality of connection orientation is that some of the link's resources are reserved for the application, in the way that a telephone line path is reserved for a particular call. An advantage herein is that the application can rely on a certain bandwidth and response time. Another advantage is that the connection can be used for network management and error correction. A disadvantage to connection orientation is that path resources are reserved even if the application is not currently using them and they cannot be used for other traffic.

Most token ring adapters and routers have LLC2 support, but the majority of ethernet adapters and routers do not. IBM pushed for token ring and LLC2 as a standard within the IEEE during the early 1980s because of their deterministic nature and connection-oriented support, respectively, which are compatible with SNA traffic.

Since LLC2 is supported in most token ring but not ethernet adapters, oftentimes SNA LAN traffic flows over token ring. There are, however, many SNA implementations over ethernet as well. On the other hand, ethernet has been much more popular than token ring in the TCP/IP and UNIX environments.

APPN/HPR workaround APPN/ISR experiences the same connection-oriented data-link requirement as subarea SNA. However, HPR does not, at least not in the same way. HPR replaces ISR under the path control and transmission control layers of current APPN with two protocols—RTP and ANR. RTP and ANR both reside roughly at layer 3 and upper sublayer 2 of the OSI model. ANR, which has some features of both connection-oriented and connectionless networking, treats the RTP end-to-end connection as its connection-oriented data link.

8.4 Resource identification: addressing and naming

APPN and TCP/IP approach naming and addressing quite differently. In order to understand these differences, one must first note that neither architecture uses the terms *name* and *address* the way they are used in everyday speech. In common usage the word *name* is an item's identity and the word *address* is where it is. The term *route* describes how to reach a named location. These analogies are stretched different ways in APPN and TCP/IP, and the common terms are not directly applicable to either environment.

8.4.1 TCP/IP names, addresses, and subnets

In TCP/IP, names and addresses relate primarily to IP at layer 3. Generally speaking, in TCP/IP, a name identifies a system and an address identifies an adapter on a system. (However, some exceptions are discussed below.)

IP names In IP, a name is a higher-level or more human-understandable form of identification than an address. The TCP/IP standards specify only that a name is one or more series of letters separated by periods, for example, my.very.own.system.

The Internet has developed a more specific structure. A convention was developed in which a name is constructed of several levels, such as a machine name, one or more organizational or domain names, and a top-level domain. The top-level domain partitions are shown in table 8.6. For example,

Table 8.6 Top-level Internet domains

Domain name		Meaning
	com	Commercial organizations
	edu	Educational organizations
	gov	Government institutions
	mil	Military groups
	net	Major network support centers
	org	Organizations other than those above
	int	International organizations
	county code	Each country (geographic scheme) (e.g., us, uk)

IBM uses `ibm.com` and Purdue University uses `purdue.edu`. Most TCP/IP networks conform their names to the Internet convention even if they are not connected to the Internet.

The Internet Network Information Center (InterNIC) system administers second-level names to avoid duplicates. An authority within a second level, such as a company network administrator or university network manager, administers third-level names within the organization or site. Lower-level names, if any, such as for divisions, departments, buildings, floors, or specific machines, are also managed locally.

IP addresses An IPv4 address is a 32-bit number with an optional 32-bit mask. This number consists of two fields, the NetID and the host ID. The format of this number is discussed in more detail below.

The NetID is also administered by the InterNIC. The NetID is often (but not necessarily) directly associated with the organizational name. All devices within that NetID are referred to as a network.

Each address actually identifies a network *interface* rather than an entire end system. Devices with more than one network interface, such as routers, have more than one address. Rarely, an end system can have multiple interfaces. This could lead to some inefficiencies in routing, as discussed below under multi-address end systems.

Different *classes* of addresses have been developed so that the same 32-bit IPv4 address could serve organizations with a very large number of devices as well as a large number of organizations with few devices. These IPv4 address classes are shown in figure 8.16.

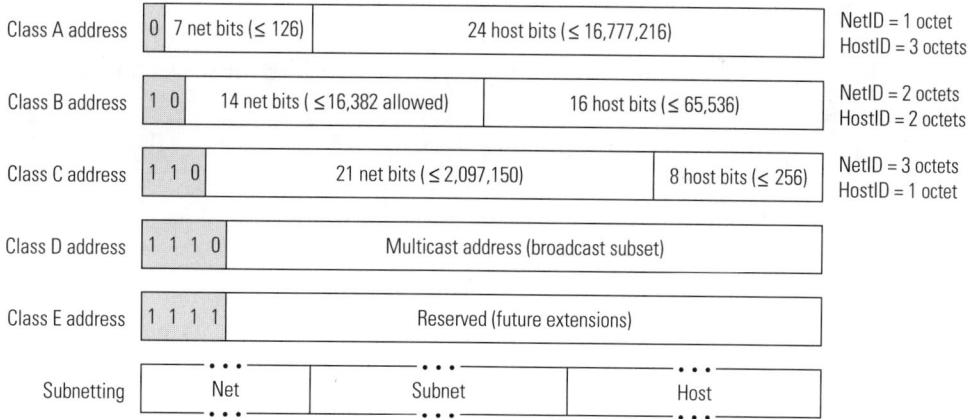

Figure 8.16 IPv4 address space

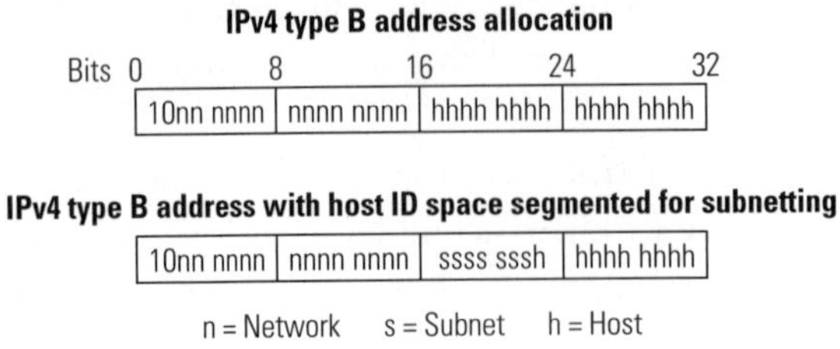

IPv4 type B address allocation

```
Bits  0        8       16      24      32
     | 10nn nnnn | nnnn nnnn | hhhh hhhh | hhhh hhhh |
```

IPv4 type B address with host ID space segmented for subnetting

```
     | 10nn nnnn | nnnn nnnn | ssss sssh | hhhh hhhh |
       n = Network   s = Subnet   h = Host
```

Figure 8.17   Splitting host ID into subnets and hosts with IPv4

Class A addresses could be assigned to up to 126 very large organizations, each with up to 16,777,216 addresses. The approximately 16,000 Class B networks can each have greater than 65,000 addresses. Class C addresses could serve about two million networks each with up to 256 addresses.

IP can also identify groups of addresses in addition to specific addresses. For example, if all the host ID bits are set to one, a packet will be broadcast to all devices on that NetID.

IPv6 addresses are 128 bit in length in three types: unicast, anycast, and multicast. Unicast addresses identify a single interface, anycast addresses support delivery to one set member, and multicast addresses enable delivery to all interfaces in a group. The IPv6 address, at 128 bits, is four times the length of the 32-bit IPv4 address and therefore generates an address space that is four billion (2^{96}) times the size of an IPv4 (2^{32}) address. The IPv6 address space can theoretically support greater than 665×10^{21} addresses per square meter on the planet; however, assignment hierarchies reduce somewhere between 8×10^{17} to 2×10^{33} nodes (still a more than adequate number for the forseeable future!).

IP subnets   Within a NetID, many companies partition their address space into three network, subnet, and host portions by splitting the bits assigned for the host ID into subnetwork and host components.

A primary benefit of subnetworking is allowing traffic destined for the same subnet to be easily recognized as local traffic. It also eases network administration and management. An example of splitting a Class B address this way is shown in figure 8.17.

TCP/IP port numbers   Below the host level, TCP/IP uses port numbers to identify the specific program or process that it wishes to reach within a host. Many port numbers are assigned to certain kinds of access, such as electronic mail and file transfer; these are referred to as well-known port numbers. Applications can use unassigned numbers for other purposes.

8.4.2 APPN names

The APPN community has no general agreement about the name/address terminology. An APPN *name* is an identifier with up to 16 bytes separated by a period into two segments each up to 8 bytes (see table 8.7). This is also often called the APPN *address*. The first 8 bytes, the NetID, are roughly equivalent to the TCP/IP NetID. The second 8 bytes, the network accessible unit name (NAUname), are similar to the host ID.

Table 8.7   APPN address space

NetID	NAUname
1 to 8 bytes	1 to 8 bytes
Alphanumeric EBCDIC characters (A-Z and 0-9, not starting with number)	Alphanumeric EBCDIC characters (A-Z and 0-9, not starting with number)
About 2×10^{12} (2 trillion) combinations*	Same
User not required to use IBM registry	No registry
IBM registry assigns the bytes as follows: 1–2 Country code (e.g., US, UK) 3–6 Organization code (e.g., IBMS) 　　　　(1.7 million per country) 7–8 Networks (up to 1296 per organization)	

* However, the number of human-readable combinations is significantly more limited.

The terms *APPN name* and *APPN address* are used here as equivalent terms. This is done for comparative purposes, since the APPN NetID.NAUname designation has some qualities like a TCP/IP name and some qualities in common with a TCP/IP address.

Some IBM literature uses the word *address* for the labels (local form session identifiers or LFSIDs) used to identify the route hops for each APPN session. However, LFSIDs are more often called *routes* or *handles*. The term *address* is not used herein in this context.

APPN NetID   The APPN address space is administered by IBM through the SNA Network Name Registry. APPN NetID names are structured so that they are unique not only within APPN but also within the OSI address space.

There is no logical limit to the number of network nodes in a single NetID. However, IBM recommends no more than 500 network nodes in a single APPN network to prevent overloading the topology database in each network node.

APPN NAUname In an APPN network, an NAUname can identify either a CP, which represents the administrative and management elements of a node, or an LU, which represents network users, applications, or other node resources. (NAUname is also the term used to identify subarea SNA resources; however in that case NAU refers to network addressable unit.) An APPN node has one CP and may have one or more LUs. Each of these may have a separate NAUname and their names may be completely unrelated.

Most APPN implementations use a single NAUname for both the CP and a single LU. Only the host APPN implementation uses multiple LUs and thus multiple LU names.

Regardless of the number of network interfaces a node has, it is assigned only one CPname, and that CPname can be accessed through any interface.

The IBM registry does not track NAUnames. Optionally, an organization may choose to manage NAUnames for uniqueness across the organization so that, if a machine or LU resource moves to another NetID, the NAUname does not need to be changed.

8.4.3 Resource identification issues

To compare naming and addressing between APPN and TCP/IP, several issues are discussed:

- Address space capacity
- Administration
- Dividing NetIDs
- Broadcast and multicast
- Multi-address nodes

8.4.4 Address space capacity

The APPN address space can accommodate about 2 trillion (2×10^{12}) NetIDs . However, as allocated by the SNA registry, the address space allows 1.7 million (1.7×10^6) NetIDs per country.

This compares to IPv4's approximately 2 million (2×10^6) NetIDs worldwide with the current class address structure: 126 Class A + 16 thousand Class B + 2 million Class C. The IPv6 128-bit address structure supports a theoretical maximum of 340×10^{36} addresses worldwide.

This top-level comparison is somewhat misleading for several reasons:

- TCP/IP can subnet, enabling a much larger number of networks than its NetID count. Even an IPv4 Class C NetID can support, for example, 4 subnets of 64 hosts, or 8 subnets of 32 hosts, or 16 subnets of 16 hosts, etc.

- Since APPN addresses are also used as symbolic names, a large number of the NetIDs yields a less astronomic number of networks. For example, since six of the eight characters of the NetID are reserved for countries and enterprises, the actual network names can only have two characters. (This still allows about 1.7 million enterprises per country and 1200 networks for each country/enterprise combination.)

- APPN names are promoted as more human-meaningful than IP addresses. However, this human-meaningfulness of the NetID is reduced by the hierarchy assignments, such as USFARM12. LU names are more likely to be human-meaningful than NetID names.

Changing IP address space   Perhaps greater than half of the IPv4 Class B networks on the Internet have fewer than 50 hosts, which could certainly be served by a Class C IPv4 address instead. (The Internet does not require NetID requesters to justify their request for a Class B address.)

An organization with fewer than 256 hosts might prefer a Class B IPv4 address over a Class C IPv4 address because it may not want the routes between its different NetIDs to be available for other organizations to use. These routes would be available to other companies given how the Internet currently operates.

Some claim that the IPv4 address space limitation is artificial since there are so many Class C addresses available and many organizations could (or should) surrender their Class B address for one or more Class C addresses. However, since the Internet allows an organization to request whatever class NetID it prefers, this switch is unlikely to occur. The TCP/IP address space limitation—that is, a limit to the type of addresses many companies prefer—is real, whether logical or not, and has been resolved with IPv6, as stated above.

As an interim solution toward IPv6, IETF endorsed CIDR (RFC 1579). CIDR extends IP addresses by changing the existing 32-bit addresses and bit mask to a hierarchical structure. This structure includes an IP address prefix for geographical regions, beginning with continents, then regional service providers, and finally the local organization. In this way, CIDR addresses would be like telephone numbers. They would also be similar to the OSI address space. IP *names* would not have to be changed to implement CIDR, only the *addresses*. Electronic mail and other applications would continue to use the same names (figure 8.18).

CIDR also allows routing tables to be much smaller since the tables need only track a small set of prefixes rather than all complete NetIDs. With CIDR, routing tables for

Classless interdomain routing (CIDR)

- 32-bit prefix bit mask + 32-bit IP address
- OSPF, RIP, BGP-4 can carry masks
- Initial deployment proposed for Class C
- Permits multiple levels of hierarchial summarization
  - Continental boundaries
  - Network service providers
  - Site level

Simple internet protocol (SIP)

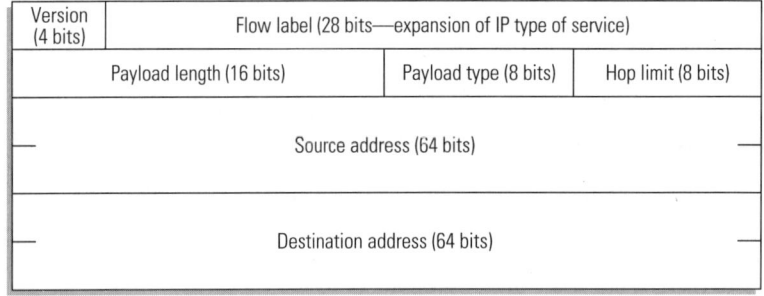

Pip

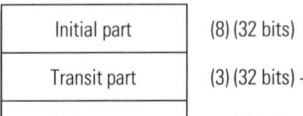

TCP and UDP with bigger addresses (TUBA)

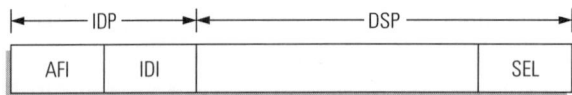

- Based on OSI NSAP addresses
- Uses OSI connectionless network protocol (CLNP)

OSPF	= Open shortest path first	DSP	= Domain specific part
RIP	= Routing information protocol	SEL	= Selection
IDP	= Initial domain part	OSI	= Open systems interconnection
AFI	= Authority and format identifier	NSAP	= Network service access point
IDI	= Initial domain identifier		

Figure 8.18   Pre-IPv6 IP address enhancement proposals

the current 10,000 networks would require fewer than 200 entries. The IP address space limitations are likely a temporary issue. SNA has twice expanded its addressing structure, to extended network architecture (ENA), and later to extended ENA (EENA).

Though the process was inconvenient, SNA users survived these transitions. TCP/IP users will similarly survive their IPv4-to-IPv6 address extension transition.

8.4.5 Administration

Administration of resource identification includes:

- Global and local assignment of names and addresses
- Maintenance of databases for name/address resolution and resource location (directory services)
- Updates of routing tables (topology services)

Names and addresses must be unique within an internet. There must be a process to guarantee and sometimes arbitrate this uniqueness. APPN and TCP/IP each have a global internetworking name and address assignment structure. At the highest level is the overall authority which assigns one or more NetIDs and/or names to an organization. Within each NetID and name space, the organization administers the unique addressing/naming of all the nodes and any subnets that participate in the network.

The address allocation and highest-level domain name registry for TCP/IP is administered by the NICs. The several NICs in the United States are coordinated through Network Solutions, Inc. (NSI) of Herndon, Virginia. NSI already managed the NIC for the NSFnet which acts as the backbone of the U.S. portion of the Internet.

IBM operates the worldwide registry for APPN. IBM assigns names and name sets—such as "all 6-character NetIDs beginning with the characters ABCD." It also guarantees uniqueness before authorizing them. The company can also assign "vanity" NetIDs for NetIDs that do not conform to the recommended structure.

TCP/IP users that are not on the Internet and APPN users with solely private networks are not required to register their NetIDs. However, they are strongly encouraged to do so to avoid problems in the future if their networks should become interconnected.

8.4.6 Dividing NetIDs

The primary issues with dividing NetIDs for both TCP/IP and APPN are:

- Structure and flexibility of NetID segmentation
- Impact of a move

TCP/IP allows users to allocate a portion of the host ID to subnetworks. Each IPv4 packet includes both a 32-bit address and a 32-bit mask, as shown in figure 8.19. The mask uses one-bits to indicate the length of the NetID and the subnet ID, with zero-bits indicating the length of the host ID.

The APPN address space does not currently implement subnetworking within a NetID. IBM has allocated APPN NetIDs so that the first two characters are geographic regions (e.g., U.S.), the next four characters are an organization code (e.g., ACME), and the final two characters can be used by that organization to indicate its multiple networks within that geographic region (e.g., 01, 02).

Distinct APPN networks can be connected through border node support. Border node—also called multi-subnet support—allows a network node to have connectivity to more than one NetID and act as a conduit between them.

8.4.7 Impact of a move

If a device on either APPN or TCP/IP is moved a short distance—within the same subnet or APPN NetID—neither needs to be renamed (nor readdressed, in the case of TCP/IP).

APPN Moves Since APPN networks can be up to 500 network nodes regardless of underlying physical topology, moving an APPN end node will *not* usually require a change in its NetID. Moving an APPN node may also require a change to the NAUname portion of its name unless the organization has enforced NAUname uniqueness among all its interconnected NetIDs.

All applications on other nodes which access that node's resources will need to be notified of its new name (NetID.NAUname), even if only the NetID part has changed. However, if a central directory server (CDS) is deployed in the customer's network, a node can ask for a resource by a non-fully-qualified name (a name in another format than NetID.NAUname) and the CDS can be configured with that name and its associated APPN name. CDS has been available since VTAM 4.1.

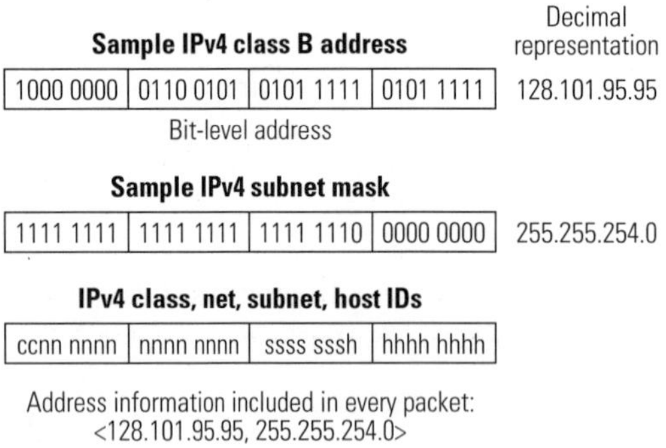

Sample IPv4 class B address   Decimal representation

| 1000 0000 | 0110 0101 | 0101 1111 | 0101 1111 | 128.101.95.95 |

Bit-level address

Sample IPv4 subnet mask

| 1111 1111 | 1111 1111 | 1111 1110 | 0000 0000 | 255.255.254.0 |

IPv4 class, net, subnet, host IDs

| ccnn nnnn | nnnn nnnn | ssss sssh | hhhh hhhh |

Address information included in every packet:
<128.101.95.95, 255.255.254.0>

Figure 8.19   Subnet identification in IPv4 address and mask

A moved end node will likely also need to be manually reconfigured to another network node as its server. This is because APPN end nodes do not have a procedure to discover a network node server, though IBM says it is developing a protocol for this purpose.

TCP/IP moves   Moving a TCP/IP node to a different subnet requires a change in its address but usually not its name. In addition, a moved TCP/IP end system will usually need to be manually configured with the IP address of at least one router on its new subnet. The domain name server, which associates TCP/IP names and addresses for its domain, must be manually updated.

Applications that communicate by name with the moved node do *not* need to be changed. Their cache for the name/address pair will be temporarily out of date, but it will be automatically updated the next time an attempt is made to communicate. Applications that communicate by address with the moved node will need to be updated.

Conclusions: APPN and TCP/IP moves   The impact of moving an APPN node to another NetID is more inconvenient than for moving a TCP/IP node. However, since APPN NetIDs are usually larger than TCP/IP subnets, moving outside of a NetID would also occur less frequently.

8.4.8 Broadcast and multicast

Broadcast   In IP, when all the host ID bits in an address field are set to one, that message is broadcast to all nodes on that network or subnet. A single message is sent and all nodes on the network or subnet read it.

There is no directly comparable provision for network broadcast in APPN to all end nodes and network nodes in a NetID.

Multicast   Multicast refers to a message sent with a single address that represents a subset of the entire network. All devices that are participating in a particular multicast group will read traffic with that multicast address.

As with broadcast, most issues usually discussed under the header of multicast relate to hardware (data link/physical) networks. This section discusses only network-level multicasting because these are most frequently used in APPN and TCP/IP for routing topology updates.

An entire class of IPv4 addresses, Class D, is set aside for multicasting. Each IP node can be configured to participate in one or more multicast groups. As stated earlier, IPv6 supports unicast, anycast, and multicast.

APPN end nodes cannot participate either in network-level multicasts or broadcasts.

There are several specific instances in APPN where messages are sent to all network nodes. Topology database updates is the most common example. In addition, when an APPN network node needs to query the network, it sends a *locate* request which is propagated to each network node. APPN implementations can use locate commands as a generic tool to multicast various types of information. For example, VTAM uses chains of locate commands to support dependent LUs across APPN.

The difference is that, in TCP/IP, a single packet is read by each device, while in APPN, there are several packets. Each network node sends a copy of the message to every other network node it has a session with, including to the node that sent it the message. Thus multicasts generate more traffic on an APPN network than on TCP/IP.

8.4.9 *Multiaddress end systems*

Most APPN and TCP/IP end systems have a single network interface. However, some end systems have multiple interfaces.

A TCP/IP end system with multiple interfaces (multihomed host) will be listed in the domain name server with multiple entries, one for each address. This could lead to inefficiencies in routing. A multihomed device might be more easily accessed via an interface on one subnet than on another, but the router will select the first entry it finds in the DNS for that name, however the DNS table is sorted. The DNS table cannot be sorted by the most efficient route.

Further, if some traffic is being sent by address rather than by name and that particular interface is down, that traffic cannot reach the end system even if the other interfaces are functional.

In contrast, APPN end nodes with either multiple interfaces or on a LAN with multiple adjacent network nodes report to their server *all* the network nodes through which they can be accessed. The network node will choose the optimal one.

Organizations that have a large network and multiple interfaces on many of their end systems will find that APPN would provide more optimal routing. Smaller networks, however, will encounter negligible impact from less-than-optimal TCP/IP routing for multihomed hosts.

8.4.10 *Resource identification process for TCP/IP and APPN*

The two sidebars, "TCP/IP sends a packet across the Internet" and "APPN sends a packet across NetIDs," present a comparison of how TCP/IP and APPN locate a target resource in a remote NetID.

TCP/IP sends a packet across the Internet

Jane Smith wants to access an application named DataApp. She is working from a workstation with TCP/IP software, the name `start.depta.school.edu`, and the IPv4 address `128.128.147.2`. We assume that Smith's school 1) has requested and received authorization from the NIC to use the domain name `school`, 2) has been assigned a network ID (NetID) of `128.128.0.0`, and 3) has selected subnets so that the address `128.128.140.0` represents the subnet where Smith's machine resides.

Her university has authority over all names with the suffix `school` and all addresses with the NetID of `128.128.0.0`. However, the names and address spaces are independent. Other nodes with the suffix `school.edu` may reside on different subnets or even in different NetIDs, such as at companies with satellite classrooms. We assume that Smith's school has a border gateway that meets the requirements of the Internet and connects to a regional network connected to the Internet.

We assume that Smith or her workstation's software know beforehand that DataApp is on a host called `goal.divb.company.com` before communication can begin. This cannot be discovered by the network. Smith enters a request to communicate with DataApp.

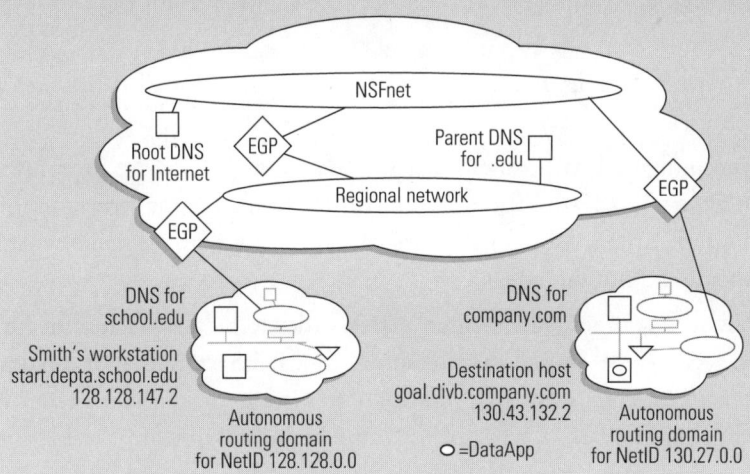

Figure 8.20   TCP/IP sends a packet across the Internet

Finding the address to match the name

Her workstation checks its table (preconfigured) or cache (discovered locations) and finds it has no IP address entry for the IP name `goal.divb.company.com`. To discover the address, her IP software sends a request to a local DNS (for `school.edu`). In this example, the DNS is on a different subnet. The request includes the address (`128.128.147.2`) of Smith's node.

- Each Internet-authorized domain must have a domain name server.
- Each IP node must be preconfigured with the address of a domain name server.
- We assume that Smith's machine has also been preconfigured with the IP address of at least one router on its subnet.
- We assume that when her system first communicated through that local router, it sent an ARP request to get the router's MAC address, which it cached.

When the request arrives at the first router (the router attached to her subnet), the subnet router checks the destination IP address of the DNS and notes that it is not on the same subnet as Smith's system. That first router then checks its regularly-updated routing table for the next appropriate router for that address and sends it to the next router toward the DNS. Each router on the path repeats this process of 1) checking whether the destination is local, 2) if not local, checking the next router on the best path, and 3) sending it to that next router. The last router will find that the DNS is local and will deliver it directly.

The DNS finds it does not have an entry cached for the name `goal.divb.company.com`, nor for `divb.company.com`, nor even for the two-level name `company.com`.

- The DNS must have preconfigured name-address table entries for all names in its own domain `school`.
- It can also be preconfigured with other entries. Today, most DNSs are preconfigured with an entry (name-address) for every one of the domain name servers in the Internet. Our example, then, assumes the rare case of a new domain name which the last DNS update did not include.
- The DNS can also cache other pairs it discovers, in order to reduce seaches for frequently used targets. Our example, then, assumes that neither Smith nor anyone else in her domain has accessed that destination system or domain recently. Although the target name (`.com`) is not in the same high-level domain (`.edu`), the DNS sends the request to its parent domain name server. The parent DNS knows about many destinations including, at least, all destinations in `.edu`. A parent DNS is also updated more frequently than a local DNS.

In the rare case that the destination is not found by the parent DNS, it sends the request to a root domain name server. A root DNS has the official table of the addresses of all the two-level names in the Internet. It forwards the request to the domain name server at `company.com` via the next router on the path to it.

The domain name server at `company.com` sends back the address, `130.43.132.2`, of the node `goal.divb.company.com` to Smith's node. (The DNS knows where to send it because the request contains Smith's address. The destination DNS cannot cache an entry for Smith, however, since the request contains only Smith's address and not her system's name.)

Requesting a connection

Smith's node then sends the initial communication, perhaps a TCP connection request, in a packet addressed to the supplied address. If the routers in Smith's autonomous routing domain have no entry for `130.43.0.0`, they forward the packet along the default route to the nearest border gateway.

- We assume this nearest border gateway, running the BGP, is connected to a regional network and not to the NSFnet backbone. The few NSFnet border gateways maintain routes to all networks in the Internet. However, regional border gateways maintain routes only to all NetIDs attached to that regional network and a default route up to the NSFnet backbone for all other destinations. The border gateway consults its table of routes for that destination. It then sends the packet to the next appropriate router. After hopping the minimum number of routers, the packet arrives at a router with the NetID `130.27.0.0`. This router recognizes the packet as being in its routing domain and forwards the packet to the router for the target subnet, `130.43.128.0`.

- IP is the common routing protocol in the three routing domains (origination, Internet, destination). However, the different domains do not need to use the same topology protocol. The two border gateways use an EGP across the Internet. The origination and destination networks can each use a different topology protocol such as RIP or OSPF. (One Internet requirement is that all border gateways attaching to the Internet must support OSPF, though they need not use it.)

- The origin and destination nodes can also be on different data-link types, such as ethernet, token ring, HDLC, and so on. Each router in the NetID checks the packet's address and subnet mask and compares them to its own. The local router realizes this packet is destined for its subnet.

Local delivery

- The subnet router checks its ARP cache to determine the data-link address corresponding to the IP address. We assume it does not have an entry with the MAC address for that IP address. (It would be rare that the cache does not have an entry, since this means that the destination node has not received packets in a long time. An ARP would have been locally broadcast to deliver packets from any IP node and all the routers would cache the pair.)

- The local router broadcasts an ARP request (which includes its own MAC address) to the entire subnet. All other nodes discard the ARP broadcast.

- The target node replies to the ARP request with its MAC address. The router appends the MAC address to the packet and delivers it to the target node.

- The node receives the packet, recognizes the request for a TCP connection and replies.

Each side of the path is now aware of the other's IP address, and the closest router to each is aware of its IP/MAC address pair for local delivery. Smith's DNS has also cached the IP name-address pair for future use. From this point, packets are delivered smoothly.

APPN sends a packet across NetIDs

Jane Smith, on a workstation called USSCHL01.DEP1STRT with APPN end node software, wants to access an application named DataApp. She or her workstation's software must know beforehand that DataApp is supported by an LU named DIVBGOAL on a NetID called UKCOMP02 before communication can begin. These cannot be discovered by the network. She requests to communicate with that application. Her end node CP checks its cache and discovers it does not know the route to that LU.

- We assume the end node CP has registered itself with its server. It must also either register its LUs or tell the network node to search it for any LU searches. Except for the mainframe, most APPN implementations have one LU per end node and use the same NAU name for both the CP and the single LU. The end node CP requests the server to find the resource UKCOMP02.DIVBGOAL for it. The end node also gives the server (1) a mode name which states the class of service and priority it wishes to use for communicating with the target and (2) its own tail vectors.

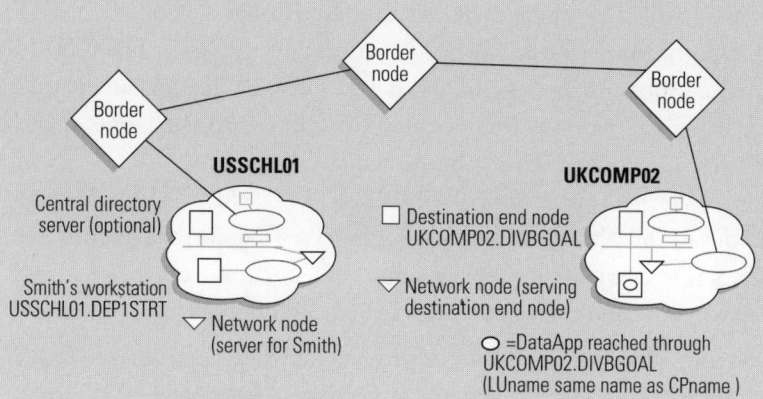

Note: APPN today does not support communications across three border nodes. IBM has stated that it will in the future.

Figure 8.21   APPN sends a packet across NetIDs

- Tail vectors are information about the links from an end node to all logically adjacent network nodes and connection networks, if any. The network node server checks its cache and does not find that LU.

- Upon entering the network, the network node server must have activated all data links to adjacent network nodes and end nodes.

- It must also have established a CP–CP session with at least one neighboring network node. A network node does not need a CP–CP session with each neighboring network node; if a data link is active between them, data can be sent on the link. The CP–CP sessions are usually minimized to a spanning tree to reduce topology data flows.

- The network node server regularly exchanges TDUs with all the network nodes in the NetID USSCHL01. The network node server notices that the requested LU is not on the same NetID. If it were, it would either send a single request to the central directory server, if one exists in this network, or broadcast a LOCATE request, as described below.

    When it realizes that the destination is on another NetID, the network node server sends a directed LOCATE to the border nodes and interchange nodes it knows about.

- Each network node server has a table of information about each other network node in the NetID. This information includes whether it supports border node. A border node will recognize the NetID UKCOMP02 as a NetID to which it has connectivity. This border node checks its cache and does not find information on that LU.

The border node will then check whether that NetID has a CDS. If NetID UKCOMP02 has a CDS, the border node will send a request directly to it. The CDS is preconfigured with a number of entries and will have a cache of all additionally discovered resources. If the LU name is found, the CDS will return the name of the network node which serves that LU to the border node.

If there is no CDS, the border node sends a LOCATE which is broadcast to all the network nodes in the NetID UKCOMP02. Each network node that receives the LOCATE propagates it to every other network node with which it has a CP–CP session. It then checks its cache and the resources its served end nodes have registered.

- An end node may either register its resources with its network node server or ask the network node server to search it whenever it needs to. If the target LU is not found in its cache, the network node server then sends a resource check to every end node it serves that has not registered its resources.

Each end node thus contacted will check its table of LU resources. The end node which has the target LU will respond to its network node server, including its tail vectors.

The network node server owning the target resource will respond to the border node with the tail vectors of the end node containing the target LU. These tail vectors are the names of all the network nodes adjacent to the LU, including its network node server, and all its connection networks.

The border node returns a LOCATED response to the originating network node, identifying itself as the owning network node. (There may be some additional messages back and forth on this locate bracket.)

The originating network node calculates the best route from the originating end node to the border node, considering (1) its topology database of all the network nodes and their links to each other (called TGs), (2) the originating node's tail vectors (all the network nodes and connection networks to which the originating end node is adjacent), and (3) the requested class of service.

This calculation results in an RSCV, which the network node passes to the originating end node. This RSCV contains a series of pairs of network node CP names and TG numbers to reach the border node.

The end node adds the RSCV to the BIND it has built. The BIND is a request to the destination LU for an LU–LU session (somewhat similar to a sockets connection) on which the applications can communicate. The BIND also includes an FQPCID, which is a unique identifier created by the end node to correlate communications for each session between APPN nodes. A session will have a single FQPCID even across border nodes and NetIDs.

- This example assumes that all the nodes along the path use APPN/ISR. The end node calculates an LFSID to identify the hop to the first network node in the path. The LFSID identifies a half-session between the two adjacent nodes. The LFSID is used for segmenting and reliable transport between the two nodes. The end node then sends the frame, including the LFSID, to that node.

  The first network node in the path will (1) keep the FQPCID for the duration of this set of exchanges, (2) keep the LFSID for communicating with the originating end node, (3) calculate an LFSID for the hop to the next network node indicated in the RSCV, and (4) send the frame to the next network node.

  The next network node will repeat the process all the way to the border node. The border node will repeat the process across the second NetID to the target end node.

8.5 Routing and topology

This section is organized into the following subsections:

- Routing protocols and topology protocols
- Basic topology configurations
- Route calculation
- Parallel paths and load balancing
- Topology database structure
- Topology database update process
- Recovery from failures
- Class/type/quality of service
- Traffic management and priority

8.5.1 Routing and topology protocols

There are two functions that are usually each termed *routing protocol*:

- The routing or network protocol defines the format of the data packet and makes routing decisions.
- The topology protocol develops and maintains the topology database from which the routing protocol can make its decisions.

Table 8.8 summarizes APPN and TCP/IP routing and topology protocols.

Table 8.8   Examples of routing and topology protocols

	TCP/IP	APPN
Routing protocol(s)	Internet protocol (IP) IPv4, IPv6	Intermediate session routing (ISR) Announced: High performance routing (HPR) with automatic network routing (ANR)
Topology protocol(s)	Routing information protocol (RIP) Interior gateway routing protocol (IGRP) and extented IGRP (EIGRP) (Cisco proprietary) Open shortest path first (OSPF)	Topology and routing services
Interdomain topology protocol(s)	Exterior gateway protocol (EGP) Border gateway protocol (BGP)	Peripheral border node Extended border node

Examples of a routing protocol or a network protocol include TCP/IP's internet protocol, APPN's ISR, and OSI's connectionless network protocol (CLNP). The term used herein is *routing protocol.*

The topology protocol is also called a routing algorithm, routing topology protocol, or (unfortunately) routing protocol. Examples include TCP/IP's RIP, APPN's topology and routing services (TRS) component, and OSI's intermediate system-to-intermediate system (IS–IS). These are referred to herein as *topology protocols.*

External topology protocols   The above topology protocols operate within a NetID. There are separate topology protocols for multiple networks. In TCP/IP, these are called exterior gateway protocols. In APPN, the gateway protocol is called border node or multisubnet support. A comparison of an APPN border node and an IP exterior gateway is shown in figure 8.22.

8.5.2 APPN routing

APPN has two routing protocols, ISR and HPR. An APPN node may support both. HPR must be supported by two adjacent links to be used on the three nodes they connect. APPN tracks whether each link is HPR-capable or supports only ISR. The total path between two APPN nodes can have some ISR links and some HPR links. But there is still a single topology database run by APPN topology and routing services.

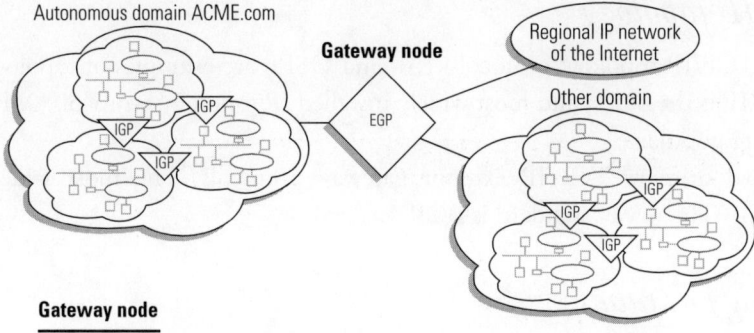

Gateway node
_____

Contains an exterior gateway protocol (EGP) or newer border gateway protocol (BGP).

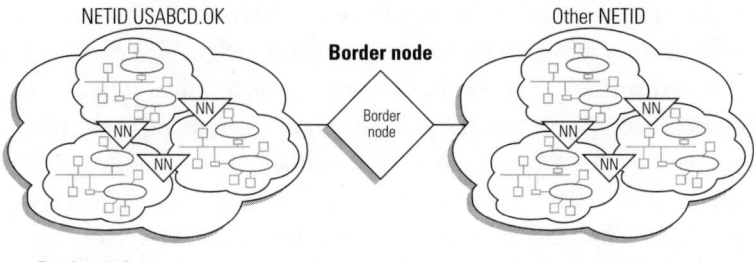

Border node
_____

Contains NN code and border node. Current peripheral border node allows access to adjacent NETID, but not through adjacent NETID to another NETID. Future extended border node will allow access through concatenated NETIDs, as well as subdividing NETIDs into clusters.

Figure 8.22   TCP/IP gateway node and APPN border node

8.5.3 *APPN topology*

In APPN, the routing topology function is provided by its TRS component. In contrast with TCP/IP, which has a single routing protocol, IP, and multiple topology protocols such as RIP and OSPF; APPN has a single topology protocol, topology and routing services, and two routing protocols, ISR and HPR.

8.5.4 *TCP/IP routing*

IP is TCP/IP's routing protocol.

8.5.5 TCP/IP topology

There are several TCP/IP topology protocols. RIP and OSPF are examples of topology protocols for IP. RIP is the oldest and most widely installed IP topology protocol. OSPF is rapidly becoming popular.

There are two primary TCP/IP exterior gateway protocols. The most widely installed one is EGP. The newer standard is BGP-4.

8.5.6 Topology databases

A topology database usually contains information about the intermediate nodes and how to reach them. End systems generally maintain local topology views of adjacent nodes. Intermediate systems track the topology of the entire network.

A topology database may be centralized, as in subarea SNA. However, in both APPN and TCP/IP, it is distributed. There are two ways to distribute a topology database. Either each intermediate system maintains a portion of the topology, which aggregates to the entire topology, or each intermediate system maintains a complete network topology. Both APPN and TCP/IP carry a full topology on each intermediate system. There are two ways to carry and update these topology data: distance vector and link state. These techniques are discussed in section 8.5.13.

A topology database may be configured manually or automatically. In both APPN and TCP/IP, each node is manually configured with its own name and links. Beyond that, the intermediate nodes automatically inform the other intermediate nodes about these, thus building the topology.

8.5.7 Topology and directory databases

A topology database is different from a directory database in that the latter tracks end systems and their resources. A directory database may be centralized or distributed or both, and may be manually configured or automatic. In both APPN and TCP/IP, directory information is partly centralized and partly distributed. For example, in both cases, intermediate nodes cache information on destinations they have reached.

8.5.8 Basic topology configurations

Figure 8.23 shows a basic network configuration with four end systems (squares) and a network of five intermediate systems (triangles). This could apply to APPN with end nodes and network nodes or to TCP/IP with hosts and routers.

In the simple system shown in figure 8.23, the ratio of end systems to intermediate systems (nearly 1:1) is excessive. This network of intermediate systems probably would support a much larger number of end systems.

Figure 8.24 shows a more detailed concept of an internetwork configuration where a backbone network provides most of the connectivity between the intermediate systems serving the separate networks. The ovals represent token-ring LANs and the straight lines represent Ethernet/IEEE 802.3 LANs. The box connecting the LANs together might be a bridge or an intermediate system.

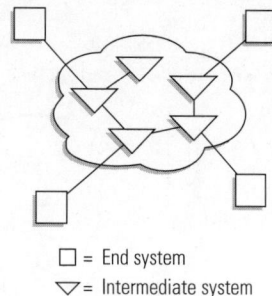

☐ = End system
▽ = Intermediate system

Figure 8.23   Basic network configuration

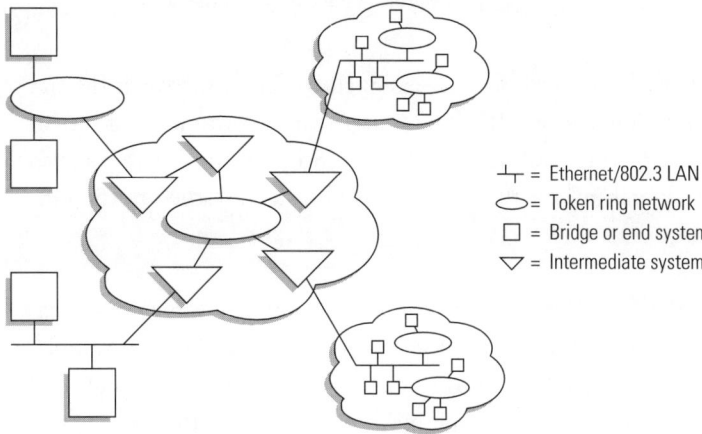

⊥⊤ = Ethernet/802.3 LAN
◯ = Token ring network
☐ = Bridge or end system
▽ = Intermediate system

Figure 8.24   Basic internetwork configuration: subnetworks and a backbone network

8.5.9 TCP/IP groupings

The IP concept of subnetwork was introduced earlier in the section on resource identification. A network (or domain) consists of all nodes having a single NetID. This network can be made up of a large number of intermediate systems and end systems.

An IP subnetwork is a set of devices that appears to the larger network as a single physical network, a single routing destination. A subnetwork can be a set of point-to-point links or can consist of a single LAN. It could be several LAN segments *bridged* together, but not divided by a router.

Figure 8.25 shows a subnetwork with the IPv4 address `<130.27.80.0,` `255.255.248.0>`. As described earlier, a subnetwork is identified by a portion of the bits assigned to the IP host ID. The final two bytes differ for each router in this example

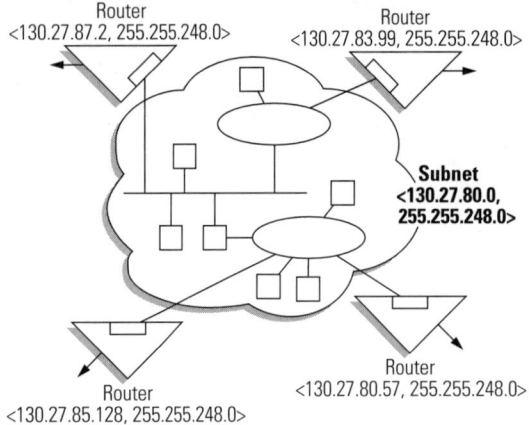

Router
<130.27.87.2, 255.255.248.0>

Router
<130.27.83.99, 255.255.248.0>

Subnet
<130.27.80.0,
255.255.248.0>

Router
<130.27.85.128, 255.255.248.0>

Router
<130.27.80.57, 255.255.248.0>

Note: Each router has multiple addresses, one for each interface.　**Figure 8.25　IPv4 subnetwork**

network because only five bits of the third byte are assigned to the subnetwork ID and the remaining bits vary with the end system ID. The routers can determine from the bit mask which bits have been used for the subnetwork ID—248 in the third byte can also be represented as 11111000, which means that the first five bits are assigned to the subnetwork ID.

Subnetwork naming is optional　There is often an association between an organization's NetID and its naming suffix in TCP/IP, though this is not required. For example, a single organization may be assigned a NetID (130.27.0.0) and a second-level domain name (acme.com). But that domain name may be associated with systems and subnetworks in other NetIDs—system3.acme.com may be in NetID 140.80.0.0. Conversely, that NetID may contain systems with names in other domains—node 130.27.16.42 may be called student.school.edu.

Direct address-name association has some administrative advantages, especially in a relatively stable network. However, these advantages are offset, if a node moves or the wiring is restructured, by having to change the name as well as the address.

Each of the four routers connected to the subnetwork represented in figure 8.25 actually has multiple network interfaces, though only the one connected to this subnetwork is shown. A router has one adapter for each subnetwork to which it connects and each interface has a separate IP address. For each router, the link connected to this subnet is assigned the same NetID and subnet address as all other nodes on that subnetwork. The host ID component is the only difference in the IP addresses of nodes on the same subnetwork.

OSPF areas   The newer topology protocols, such as OSPF, have introduced another grouping for IP called *areas*. This is a hierarchical way of organizing subnetworks which can be very helpful in large IP networks. It reduces the amount of storage required in each IP router, the flow of topology packets, and the time to converge. (OSI's IS–IS protocol also supports routing areas.)

OSPF designated router   Another benefit of OSPF is the designated router. The designated router significantly reduces topology traffic. If more than one router is attached to the same subnetwork, the routers automatically select one router to advertise the resources of and changes in that subnetwork. That same router informs the other routers on that subnetwork about all topology changes outside the subnetwork.

Interior and exterior gateway protocols   As discussed above in this section, IP supports both interior and exterior gateway protocols. Figure 8.26 shows an IP network with several interior routers and two exterior routers. The exterior routers are connected to an external network, which might be a regional backbone of the Internet.

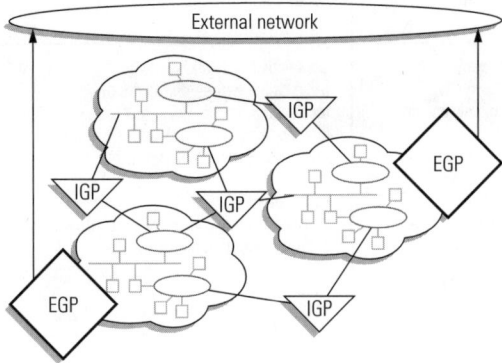

Figure 8.26   IP multisubnet domain and connection to interdomain backbone

8.5.10 APPN groupings

APPN, like TCP/IP, can subdivide networks into groupings. But APPN groupings are very different from those in TCP/IP.

Table 8.9 compares the different groupings in APPN and TCP/IP. The APPN groupings are discussed below, along with their comparison to those of TCP/IP. The TCP/IP and APPN groupings listed side by side in the table are as closely comparable as possible, but some groupings are more easily compared than others.

APPN domain   A network node and the end nodes for which it acts as a server constitute the smallest APPN grouping. This grouping is called a *domain*, derived from the subarea SNA domain. The network node's name could be considered the domain's name.

Table 8.9 APPN and TCP/IP groupings

	TCP/IP	APPN
End system	Host	End node (EN)
Intermediate system	Router	Network node (NN)
End system must be preconfigured with	Its own name, its own IP address and mask, and the IP address of at least one local router	Its own APPN name and data-link address and those of its network node server. Plus: either the APPN name and data link address of all logically adjacent NNs or its connection network name
Smallest grouping	Subnetwork (optional but very common)	Domain (required) (An EN is served by only 1 NN.) (An EN in one NetID can be served by an NN in another NetID.)
Grouping identified by	Same subnet address & mask (Host usually preconfigured with address of at least one router on subnet. Can find router.)	A network node and its served end nodes (NN server name and data link address preconfigured in end node. Can find NN.)
Geographic/physical limits	Logically adjacent (i.e., on same or bridged LAN) (Number of nodes per subnet limited by bits left in host ID)	Logically adjacent (i.e., on same or bridged LAN) (Number of end nodes per NN limited by NN memory)
Medium-size grouping (for end systems)	Named domain (optional) (Each host can be the member of only one domain.)	Connection network (Also called virtual routing node) (optional) (End nodes and network nodes can participate in many connection networks.)
Grouping identified by	Same subdomain name (preconfigured in local domain name server)	No external sign (Connection network name preconfigured in each participating node)
Geographic/physical limits	None	None (Recommended for local/campus environment)
Medium-size grouping (isolated topology domain)	Area (OSPF and IS-IS only) within a NetID, designated router within a subnetwork	Cluster (architecture discussed - not yet published/ implemented)
Grouping identified by	Area: portion of subnet address Designated router: dynamic assignment	Unknown (function of future extended border node)
Geographic/physical limits	Adjacent subnetworks	Unknown (minimally, in same NetID)
Next smallest grouping	Autonomous domain	NetID
Grouping identified by	Same domain name in address	Same NetID in name
Geographic/physical limits	None (bordered by routers with an external gateway protocol)	None (up to 500 network nodes) (bordered by network nodes with border node protocol)

The APPN network node server plays a more specific role for the end node than a router provides to a TCP/IP end system. Although a TCP/IP end system is preconfigured with the IP address of at least one router, a TCP/IP end system is not tied in any way to a specific router. Further, a router does not provide any special services to a given TCP/IP end system. In APPN, on the other hand, an end node depends on its network node server to provide a variety of functions including searches and route calculation.

An APPN network node server's domain is more a logical than physical association. Though an end node must be adjacent to its server, not all adjacent end nodes are associated with the same server. In contrast, in TCP/IP, all the nodes bounded by a single IP hop are in the same subnetwork.

APPN connection networks   APPN was developed initially for wide area networks. Connection networks were designed to adapt APPN efficiently to LAN environments. An APPN connection network is a representation of SATF such as a token ring network, that enables connection between nodes via a common virtual routing node without the need to define individual connections.

An end node has three ways to communicate with an adjacent end node:

- Requests its network node server to locate the target node by name
- Is preconfigured with the adjacent node's name and link information
- Participates in the same connection network as the target node

The simplest of the above three options is for an end node to request its network node to locate and access a target end node by name. In this case, even if the target node is adjacent—for example, on the same LAN as the originating node and the network node server—all traffic between the two end nodes will travel through the network node. The network node is unaware that they are adjacent to each other. This option makes sense if there are few adjacent end nodes and if most traffic will not be between adjacent end nodes.

The second option is to preconfigure in each end node the name and link to each adjacent end node. At least one of each pair of end nodes is preconfigured to the other. If preconfigured, the end nodes can establish communications with each other directly, without using the network node. In a point-to-point or small LAN environment, preconfiguration would involve listing only a few adjacent nodes. In this case, preconfiguring adjacent end nodes by name is convenient.

In a large LAN (logically point-to-point) environment, however, many nodes could be adjacent. Manually preconfiguring and maintaining the list of names and links in each node to every other adjacent node would be tedious at best. In this case, the

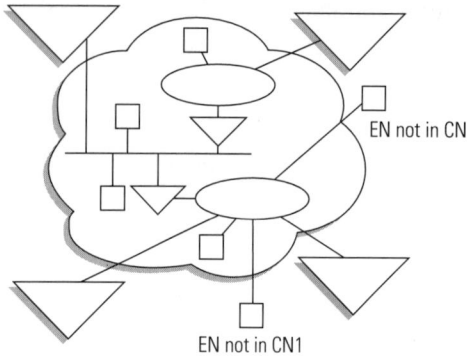

A connection network may contain any number of APPN nodes. Though designed for LANs, they can be in any configuration that can be reached by bridging, even across NNs, or across an IP network that supports a connection-oriented data link. An APPN node participates by having the CN name (e.g., CN1) added to its link database.

EN not in CN1

EN not in CN1

Figure 8.27   APPN connection network

connection networks approach is the appropriate alternative and is almost always used in LAN environments.

A connection network, as shown in figure 8.27, is a logical grouping rather than a physical one. It consists of the APPN end nodes and network nodes that are preconfigured as part of itself. Connection networks are quite flexible: on a single LAN, some devices can participate and others not. On the other hand, devices from many distinct LANs may participate in a single connection network.

To implement connection networks, an organization assigns a name—such as CN1—and allows any node to be configured as connected to CN1. A connection network can be of any size over any area on any type(s) of media which can be traversed by connection-oriented data-link connections. The organization can define any number of connection networks, and a node can participate in several connection networks.

Two end nodes configured on the same connection network appear adjacent and are directed by the network node to set up an APPN session with each other over the data-link path between them.

Connection networks over IP   A significant advantage of connection networks is that they can be defined across any facility which provides any-to-any connectivity, including X.25, frame relay, and IP networks. For example, two end nodes that have links to network nodes over an APPN backbone but also a more direct connection over an IP backbone can, by being part of the same connection network, communicate over the IP backbone.

This configuration is shown in figure 8.28. The IP routers in the figure do *not* need to have SNA or APPN, but they need to support LLC2 traffic. LLC2 support is offered today by most major IP router vendors.

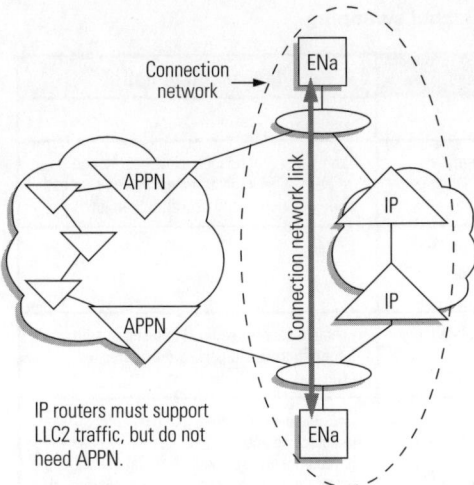

Figure 8.28   Connection network over IP

APPN clusters   APPN clusters are isolated topology domains within a NetID, similar to OSPF areas. APPN clusters have not been implemented on any product; they are only mentioned in IBM documentation. Clusters are implemented as a function of extended border node.

Automatic route calculation   Both TCP/IP and APPN are designed to perform automatic route calculation—network-layer routes are calculated from topology information. The availability of automatic route calculation in APPN is one of the leading selling points for a migration from subarea SNA, which requires thorough, preconfigured path definitions.

8.5.11 Three types of route calculation

There are three types of routing decision processes: destination routing, source routing, and label swapping (also called call mapping). Table 8.10 summarizes these three types of route calculation. Architecturally, APPN and TCP/IP can implement any of them quite effectively.

Destination routing is used at the network layer by protocols like IP and at the data-link layer by ethernet. Source routing is used at the network layer by protocols like APPN/HPR and at the data-link layer by token ring. Label swapping is used at the network layer by APPN/ISR and at the data-link layer by ATM.

In destination routing (1) the originator sends out each packet with the destination address in the header, then (2) each intermediate system reads the destination address, calculates the most efficient next hop, and forwards it. Destination routing advocates

Table 8.10   Destination routing, source routing, and label swapping

		Originating node	Intermediate node
Destination routing	At session startup	Nothing	Nothing
	For each packet	Examine packet header. Note destination address. Check table for next hop on best path to destination. Send packet to that hop.	Examine packet header. Note destination address. Check table for next link on best path to destination. Send packet to that hop.
Source routing	At session startup	Check table for best total path. Put total path information in packet header. Send packet on first hop.	Nothing
	For each packet	Add path information to each packet header.	Examine packet header. Note self in path information. Send packet to next hop listed after self.
Label swapping	At session startup	(If the source determines route:) Check table for best total path. Assign code for session. Put total path information in packet header. Assign label for first hop. Send setup packet through path.	Examine packet header. Note code for session (if source selects route) or destination address (if path not preassigned). Note label assigned for hop to self from previous node. Assign label for next hop. Enter previous-hop-label/next-hop-label pair in table. Swap labels and send to next hop.
	For each packet	Check session code. Check table for label. Put label for first hop in header. Send packet on first hop.	Examine packet header. Note label on packet. Look up label pair in table. Swap prior label with next label. Send packet to next hop.

argue that each packet can find its best path at each intermediate node and, further, end systems should not waste their resources on routing calculations.

In source routing (1) the originator discovers all routes to the destination and selects the optimal route, (2) places a list of each intermediate node and the links between them in each packet's header, and (3) each intermediate system notes the next link in the header and forwards the packet over it. Source routing proponents posit that source routing consumes fewer processing resources at intermediate nodes—the path is already calculated at the initial node. Each intermediate node need only note the next link listed in the header. Further, in some source routing implementations (such as APPN/HPR), the closest intermediate node calculates the route, rather than the end system itself, so processing overhead does not impact the end system.

In label swapping (1) the route is calculated at the beginning of a session either by the originator or at each intermediate node, (2) an initial packet is sent once over that path to allow each intermediate node to allocate its own ID for the next link for that session, and (3) each successive packet arriving on one link for that session (as identified by the label from the previous node) is forwarded over the next hop with a new label for that hop. Label swapping supporters agree with source routing proponents that the path is best predetermined. Label swapping also uses the shortest packet headers decreasing network traffic. (However, TCP/IP headers can be, and often are, compressed.)

Issues in route calculation   Most performance differences between protocols using these three techniques result from implementation rather than from architectural variations. All of the three techniques have been implemented both well and poorly.

Routing type and connection orientation   Those engaged in source- versus destination-routing polemics often sidestep into issues not directly tied to routing technique. At least two misconceptions exist regarding these techniques—the association (or lack thereof) between routing type and connection orientation and the bad reputation of label swapping. These misconceptions lead to the routing technique itself being used inappropriately for decision making.

Source routing is generally used by connection-oriented protocols, while destination routing is generally used by connectionless protocols. However, this is not always the case. APPN/HPR, for example, uses a connectionless routing protocol with a source routing process.

Label swapping is not the bad guy   APPN/ISR—which uses label swapping—performs more poorly than APPN/HPR. But this difference is not due to its use of label swapping itself.

ATM—which is a very efficient protocol—also uses label swapping. The more important differences between APPN/ISR and ATM are not related to route calculation technique—ATM can drop packets when congested and is a low state machine (few state changes).

8.5.12 Parallel paths and load balancing

Load balancing refers to how the network shares traffic between two end points with more than one optimal path between them. Load balancing can be between two adjacent nodes with multiple links or between two distant end points with multiple routes.

Both types of load balancing are shown in figure 8.29. In the first case, a pair of nodes has two links between them. Since they use load balancing, traffic for one session can be sent over either link. The second case shows load

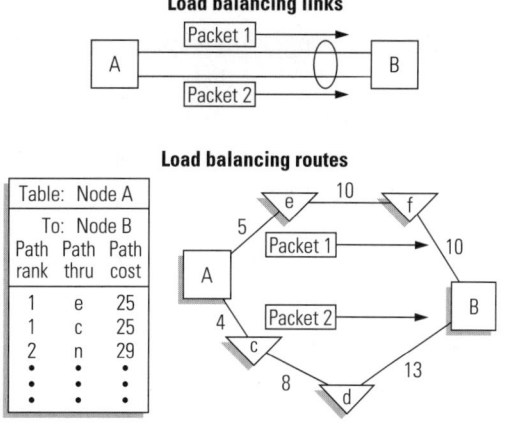

Figure 8.29   Load balancing links and routes

balancing over a pair of equidistant multihop paths. Each packet in a session may take a different path. Traffic can be sent intentionally by the source over the multiple paths in a round-robin fashion, alternating with every packet, or when load conditions shift.

There is significant debate about the value of load balancing. It optimizes use of resources, since all the available paths are used rather than only the first one. On the other hand, load balancing has several potential disadvantages if improperly designed:

- When different packets are sent across different routes, the packets are more likely to arrive out of sequence which is annoying (i.e., resource intensive) and possibly disallowed by the protocol.

- The overhead of calculating traffic balance among multiple routes might offset the advantage of efficiently using these routes.

- If several nodes reroute around congestion, the result is often that the congestion itself is rerouted, which causes oscillations in network performance.

APPN load balancing   SNA uses multilink TGs to balance traffic load across multiple links between two nodes and provide backup in case of a failed link.

- APPN route calculation places different sessions on different routes, effectively providing load balancing on a session-by-session basis.
- APPN/HPR is able to reroute around failures.
- APPN/HPR includes a congestion control/avoidance scheme (ARB).
- APPN sessions can be implemented over existing subarea SNA virtual routes/ explicit routes, if the user wants to take advantage of them, including their multilink transmission groups.

APPN uses more elements than TCP/IP to calculate optimal paths, including operational status, congestion, capacity, security, propagation delay, cost per connect time, and utilization. Each of these characteristics is preconfigured or calculated for each node and link. Since there are so many elements, it is extremely unlikely that two paths would have an equal weight. However, two paths might be nearly equal. Even so, APPN does not select these other path(s).

TCP/IP load balancing   In TCP/IP, each router is preconfigured by the user with the cost for each of its links, which it advertises to the other routers, as described below in section 8.5.14. These topology database updates are used to generate and maintain tables of all paths to each known destination and the total cost of each path.

For each incoming packet, a router checks its table for the ultimate destination and selects the next hop on the best (lowest cost) path. Because all the routers are in sync, each router sees the same best path and sends each packet along the same route to the same destination. This path changes only if some part of that path fails or the router tables are updated to show a new best route. Although IP packets can take various paths, in practice they do not.

A router table may have two or more equally good paths to the same destination. But the router selects only the path that appears first. The path that appears first is based on how the router table is sorted, such as by numeric address. Therefore, TCP/IP does not balance loads on a per-connection basis.

OSPF has the provision for load balancing, though no vendor has yet implemented this feature. Although the TCP/IP standards do not have a provision for load balancing, except for OSPF, several vendors have implemented proprietary load balancing techniques, especially for wide-area links.

Issues in load balancing   It is advantageous for a protocol to assign different equal-cost paths to different sessions. APPN does this but TCP/IP does not, which gives APPN an advantage. Some TCP/IP vendors implement proprietary load balancing; however, neither TCP/IP nor APPN/ISR performs load balancing within a session. APPN/HPR, however, supports rerouting around congested links which provides APPN an advantage.

8.5.13 *Topology database structure*

There are several similarities in the topology databases of APPN and TCP/IP:

- Distributed databases track only intermediate nodes.
- Intermediate nodes must be preconfigured with certain information.

  There are also several differences:

- TCP/IP has been implemented with several topology protocols including RIP, OSPF, and IS–IS while APPN uses one topology protocol.
- APPN uses link-state routing, while some TCP/IP topology protocols are link state and others are distance vector.

  Each of these similarities and differences is discussed below.

Intermediate nodes   Both APPN and TCP/IP maintain topology databases for intermediate nodes only and not end systems. This significantly reduces the size of a topology database. APPN topology tracks network nodes while TCP/IP topology tracks links.

In both APPN and TCP/IP, end systems and intermediate systems each maintain a database of their own links and some adjacent nodes. This could be called a *local* topology database. However, only intermediate nodes keep a topology database of the entire *network*.

Manual configuration Both APPN and TCP/IP intermediate nodes must be pre-configured with information about themselves and their links.

An APPN network node needs to be preconfigured with its own name and certain node features such as capacity and security capabilities. It also requires several characteristics of each of its links, such as data-link address, delay, throughput, and cost per connect time.

A TCP/IP router requires an IP address and a data-link address for each link as well as a cost for that link. It also requires awareness of the IP address of at least the domain name server. In addition to IP, it supports static routes, one or more routing protocols such as RIP or OSPF and may need to maintain some additional configuration for some of these protocols.

One or several protocols A single TCP/IP router may contain several topology protocols—such as RIP and OSPF. However, such a router is configured with only one topology database table and uses IP for routing. Each entry still represents one destination and includes the topology protocol(s) available for reaching that destination.

There can be several topology protocols in the TCP/IP database available to reach a particular destination. In this case, the routers must be configured with the preferred or default topology protocol for the router to choose.

In most cases, an autonomous IP domain generally uses a single topology protocol. Sometimes, however, two or more topology protocols are used in one domain; for example, when two separate departmental networks are first interconnected or during a phased migration from one topology protocol to another. They do not operate completely independently. A router with both OSPF and RIP, for example, can act as a gateway between part of a network that only supports RIP and another part that only supports OSPF.

Topology images: distance vector or link state The two major types of topology protocols are distance vector and link state. They differ both in how they update and use information. In this section, we consider how they each store and use routing information. Figure 8.30 illustrates the difference between these two topology images.

APPN uses a link-state routing topology. TCP/IP can use several topology protocols. Most, such as RIP, are distance-vector protocols while others, such as OSPF and IS–IS, are link state.

Physical topology and hop costs

Distance vector

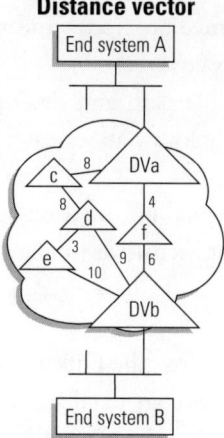

Link state

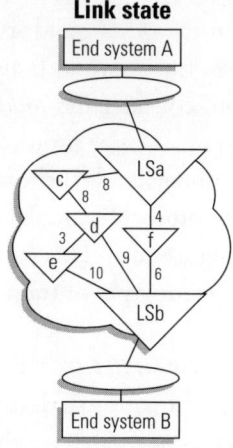

- End system A wants to talk to End system B.
- DVa finds, from directory server or search, that End System B is reachable through DVb.
- DVa then checks its table for routes to DVb.

- End system A wants to talk to End system B.
- LSa finds, from directory server or search, that End System B is reachable through LSb.
- LSa then checks its table for routes to LSb.

Portion of table: DVa*		
To: DVb		
Path rank	Path thru	Path cost
1	f	10
2	c	25
3	c	29

Portion of table: LSa		
To: LSb		
Path rank	Path thru	Path cost
1	f,b	10
2	c,d,b	25
3	c,d,e,b	29

* Note: Distance vector table only lists next hop, but tracks total path cost through each possible hop. Since all router tables are synchronized, each router on path will use same least-cost route.

DVa's view of paths to DVb

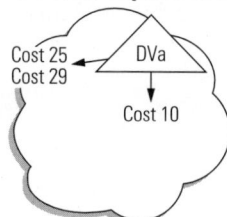

LSa's view of paths to LSb

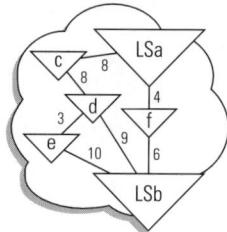

Figure 8.30 Distance-vector and link-state topology images

A distance-vector table maintains fewer pieces of information than a link-state table. A distance-vector topology node conceives of the entire network as itself and its links. Each destination, regardless of its lack of proximity, is considered as an end point on a local link with an associated cost. The same destination may be accessible through greater than one link, in which case the distance-vector table selects the link with the lower cost.

A link-state table, on the other hand, is aware of all intermediate nodes and their links and link neighbors in the network. It also tracks each link's cost.

For route calculation, consider the *total* cost of each possible path and determine the least-cost path. A distance-vector protocol may not explicitly know about each hop to the destination, but it understands the total cost to get there.

However, a link-state protocol can take into account additional information about each link when calculating a route. This can allow it to be more sensitive to changing traffic conditions and different types of traffic.

Issues in topology database structure   Both OSPF and APPN use the Dijkstra algorithm to calculate the shortest path to a destination from their topology database. However, APPN is more granular in the weights it assigns to each element before this calculation is done.

APPN will likely continue to be more discriminating than TCP/IP in route calculation. In large, complex networks, this provides APPN an advantage. In most smaller networks, however, calculating with all the variables is excessive—route optimization increases slightly while the effort required to preconfigure each node and link increases substantially.

TCP/IP routers, with fewer variables, are easier to configure. However, several default profiles exist for APPN—for example, specifying 16 Mbps token ring automatically generates the eight link characteristics most typical of this LAN. These default settings ease the APPN configuration process.

With the exception of large networks where APPN may be somewhat better at route optimization, both APPN and TCP/IP (with OSPF) will provide similar efficiency in route calculation.

8.5.14 Topology database update process

The sometimes-conflicting goals in a topology database update process are to reduce the broadcast traffic, reduce the convergence time, and yet keep the topology as current as possible.

APPN TDUs   Each APPN network node sends TDUs, which are propagated to every other network node. A TDU contains its own node and link characteristics. The information includes the network nodes accessible through each of its links.

TDUs are generated only when there is a change. The exception is a refresh broadcast every five days to remove stale database entries.

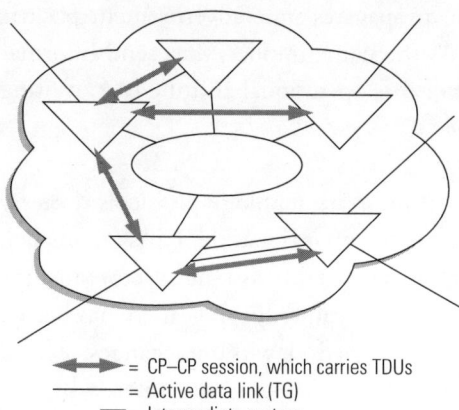

  ◄─► = CP–CP session, which carries TDUs
  ───── = Active data link (TG)
  ▽ = Intermediate system

Figure 8.31 APPN spanning tree for CP–CP sessions

There are two ways to reduce topology database flows in APPN networks—CP–CP spanning trees and clusters.

CP–CP spanning trees   TDUs are not sent across every link in the NetID. They are only sent between network nodes that have CP–CP sessions with each other. Network nodes do not need these sessions with every adjacent node. Instead, the user can configure the network nodes in a spanning tree, that is, with only sufficient CP–CP connections so that each TDU will reach all network nodes with a minimum of duplications.

As shown in figure 8.31, the five network nodes only have four CP–CP sessions. Their data links are active and available to carry traffic, but the TDUs flow only across the CP–CP sessions.

APPN clusters   APPN TDUs flow throughout a topology domain. While the APPN topology domain was orignally an entire NetID. An enhancement divides a NetID into multiple isolated topology domains called *clusters*.

Extended border node allows a NetID to be divided into two or more clusters. TDUs for nodes in the cluster will travel only within that cluster. It is conceivable, that nodes at the periphery of the cluster will advertise the cluster resources but not the cluster topology outside the cluster.

TCP/IP distance vectors and link state advertisement packets   Several topology protocols are available in IP. A RIP (distance vector) router sends messages containing each reachable destination it knows about and the total cost from itself to that destination. Every other router keeps the information and propagates the message.

In large networks, these distance vector messages become very large since they list every known destination. To artificially limit the number of routers a message can traverse, there is a so-called infinity count, equal to 15 for RIP. Despite this limit, large distance vector networks take a long time to converge after a change.

OSPF, an IP link-state topology protocol, propagates state advertisement packets (LSAs) that are equivalent to APPN's TDUs. As the name implies, they send information on the state of each link, including whether it is operational and the cost of using the link.

Link-state advantages and disadvantages   Link-state topology protocols decrease network traffic over distance-vector protocols in several ways. First, the LSAs are smaller, since they include only a node's links and neighbors, (whereas distance vectors include all reachable destinations). Second, LSAs are broadcast primarily when there has been a change, although they are also sent after a selected period without changes. Third, because of their update process, link-state protocols avoid loops encountered by distance-vector protocols.

The disadvantages of link-state protocols are that they require more router memory to maintain and often involve more elements in least-cost route calculations which increase processing overhead.

Designated routers, topology areas, and clusters   There are several ways to minimize the disadvantages of link-state protocols (LSPs). OSPF uses two techniques. First, OSPF has designated routers. Second, it can be divided into *areas*, which are similar to APPN clusters.

An OSPF designated router is selected automatically for each IP subnetwork with multiple routers. It is the only router to broadcast LSPs for all the links and routers in that subnetwork. OSI's IS–IS also uses the concept of a designated router. APPN has no concept similar to designated routers.

OSPF areas and APPN clusters, as described above, are isolated topology domains that reduce TDU traffic.

Speed of convergence   In concept, link-state protocols converge more quickly than distance-vector protocols. However, most link-state implementations are relatively new and may actually take longer to converge than some existing distance-vector products. This difference will likely decline and then reverse.

It is likely that OSPF will, in time, become the standard IP topology protocol. Therefore, the user's decision process should focus on OSPF and APPN. Both systems can scale to support very large networks. They are each link-state protocols which use the Dijkstra algorithm for route calculation.

Recovery from component failures   The most frequent type of failure is of a single component, such as a node or a link. The goal for a network protocol is to recover from such a failure as transparently as possible to the end systems. Further, the intermediate nodes should be advised as soon as possible, through a database update, that a previously-active node or link is unavailable.

Automatic, nondisruptive rerouting   APPN/ISR cannot reroute nondisruptively around failure, not without losing the sessions using that route. APPN/HPR reroutes around a failure without any session awareness or interruption. In addition, since APPN/HPR bundles multiple sessions on a single connection, rerouting requires less processing.

The ability to reroute does not mean that rerouting is always successful. If a network is in the midst of a topology update, for example, some sessions may time out before the error is detected and a new route is determined for each session. APPN learns about failed components more quickly than TCP/IP, which provides APPN with an edge here.

The ability of TCP/IP and APPN/HPR to route around failures gives them an advantage, especially in larger networks where failures are more likely to occur and where a failed component disrupts more sessions if they cannot be rerouted.

Recovery from catastrophic failures   Both APPN and TCP/IP can recover automatically from catastrophic failures. Manual intervention should not be required for the nodes to reestablish links and connections, and to regenerate and reconverge the topology database. APPN maintains its most recent topology update and caches, as do more recent TCP/IP implementations, so the restart does not begin from ground zero.

8.5.15 *Class of service/type of service/quality of service*

Traffic characteristics relate to the type of route preferred or required for a particular type of traffic. Some sessions should be carried on a series of secure hops, for example, while other sessions should be carried over high speed routes even if they are more expensive. Specifying these characteristics is the purview of COS in subarea SNA and APPN, TOS in TCP/IP, and quality of service (QOS) in OSI.

The *priority* of the packet is different from traffic characteristics. Priority relates to how quickly a packet should be attended to and is discussed in section 8.5.16.

TCP/IP users discuss TOS and priority in the same breath, while SNA/APPN users strictly differentiate between them. This reflects their relative importance in the two environments.

Subarea SNA and APPN class of service   Subarea SNA has traditionally been more concerned with traffic characteristics than TCP/IP. APPN continues this tradition.

For example, interactive traffic should be carried across low-delay routes while large file transfers should go over routes with higher bandwidth. Sessions carrying more sensitive information should be carried over more secure lines.

APPN network nodes know the characteristics of each link and node, such as security and performance. APPN uses mode names to specify a combination of requested traffic characteristics. The network node translates/interprets that mode name into route characteristics. The network node then considers, for all possible routes, whether each link and node along the path is acceptable, that is, meets the requested route characteristics. Only the acceptable paths are considered for selection as the optimal route. If there are no acceptable paths, the request is denied.

The COS request variables refer a network node to its set of COS definition tables. These tables enable network node assignment of a weight to each link and node. These weights are totaled for each potential path and the path with the lowest weight is selected.

If this COS calculation appears too onerous, it should be noted that:

- The application can set characteristics as tightly or loosely as it prefers.

- A requester can indicate that some of the requested characteristics are preferences, not requirements. For example, if a secure route is not available, another route can be selected.

- There are several default ranges that can be chosen for each characteristic rather than specific settings.

- Regardless of the mode name chosen, the network node assigns a higher (less preferable) weight to higher cost links.

- Rather than setting detailed mode parameters, SNA or APPN COS requests for SNA traffic use predefined mode names.

Most SNA and APPN requests are set to one of seven defined mode names. Three of the seven defined mode names are used for control-type traffic. The other four defined mode names are: BATCH, INTER (interactive), BATCHSC (secure batch), and INTERSC (secure interactive). The following are two examples of how these mode names are used:

- Using the mode name BATCH causes the network node (1) to set the priority to low and then use its batch table (2) to assign a higher (less preferable) weight to links with lower capacity.

- Using the mode name INTERSC causes the network node (1) to set the priority to high and then use its interactive table (2) to disallow links with a low security level, and (3) to assign a higher (less preferable) weight to links with higher delay.

TCP/IP type of service   Historically, TCP/IP has left traffic characteristic responsibility to the applications. Security, for example, is expected to be handled by encryption. In addition, the TCP/IP point of view is intended to be more democratic: each session receives the best route available at the moment and, if the network is congested, every session should suffer equally. (In practice, however, some sessions, links, or types of traffic suffer more than others.)

The TCP/IP point of view toward TOS is reflected in the following:

- TCP/IP provides a single octet for TOS.
- The TOS field is also used for priority (precedence).
- The use of the TOS field is optional and usually set to default values.
- No topology protocols except OSPF examine the TOS field.
- No OSPF vendor implements OSPF's TOS capability.
- Few router vendors actually implement TOS support (that is, implement TOS support in a proprietary way).

Over time, however, as TCP/IP has been implemented in increasingly commercial environments and used for larger networks and across wide areas, the TCP/IP community has been paying more attention to traffic characteristics.

Of the 8 bits assigned to type of service, three are assigned to precedence (priority), which is discussed below. Three others are on-off (1–0) flags which can indicate a preference for speed, high bandwidth, and high reliability. TOS cannot indicate a preference for a lower-cost line.

Many routers' software can be set to allow selected types of traffic to be sent first. This can support certain traffic characteristics, though not on a session-by-session basis.

OSI quality of service   The OSI QOS capability is similar to the TCP/IP approach. The QOS field advises the intermediate system to emphasize one characteristic over another. For example, it directs the route selection process to prefer a more reliable path rather than a less expensive path, a less expensive path rather than a faster path, or a path in which all packets are sent along the same route and arrive in order (i.e., not load balancing) rather than a faster path.

Difficult to compare points of view   The APPN and TCP/IP communities have divergent views about the role of congestion control as stated earlier. In the same way, the different points of view with regard to traffic characteristics make it difficult to directly compare the costs and benefits of COS and TOS.

Users with complex network topologies who benefit from specifying a wide range of preferred or required traffic characteristics prefer the APPN approach.

Users who believe that most route selections can be made fairly without TOS or with a few variables, and perceive the effort involved in COS (initial preconfiguration, element/table storage, and calculation overhead) as a waste of resources, prefer the TCP/IP approach.

Simpler is often sufficient   TCP/IP's type of service, where implemented, provides sufficient traffic characteristic support for most environments. Since the OSI approach is closer to the TCP/IP approach, this further demonstrates that the networking community finds the simpler approach sufficient. This is further confirmed by IBM's recommendation that APPN implementors use one of the seven defined mode names except in rare circumstances.

One big hit or many little ones   However, APPN is simpler in another way—COS is calculated only at the beginning of a connection-oriented session while TOS is included in every packet. When TOS is implemented, this could increase processing slightly at every node which has to look up not just the best path to the destination but the best path based on specified parameters.

The question is whether APPN uses significantly more resources to select paths than would be use in TCP/IP to process TOS for every packet.

We are not aware of tests that specifically measure for APPN how much more memory and CPU overhead is needed to calculate path and node weights and how much preconfiguration is required to define each element for every link and node.

Although APPN proponents agree that APPN uses more resources for a session setup than for a TCP/IP connection, they would counter that:

- APPN calculates a path once for an entire session, which serves several conversations between different pairs of applications running within a pair of end nodes, while TCP/IP must recalculate a path for each pair of destinations every time they want to communicate.

- In APPN, the route is selected once by the source which takes COS into account, while in TCP/IP, every router along the path recalculates the route after each update.

- An APPN network node that acts only as an intermediate node and not as a server at the beginning or end of a path can have smaller memories and use fewer CPU cycles.

Decision makers considering APPN and TCP/IP need to closely examine their network environment. If most end systems communicate with the same few destinations and long-duration sessions can be used extensively, the session-startup overhead is infrequent and so the significance of the difference declines. If most end systems communicate with multiple destinations and use short sessions, then the difference becomes more significant.

8.5.16 Traffic management and priority

Class/type of service and priority are often closely tied, but they are different. COS/TOS refers to the general path *characteristics* (speed, security, reliability) while priority refers to the level of *attention* given to each packet at every node.

APPN priority   APPN has four levels of priority—low, medium, high, and network. If a priority level is not set, medium is used as the default. Network priority is used primarily for network control and management information and interrupts, which should be attended to before any other queued data at each intermediate node and at the destination.

TCP/IP priority   TCP/IP records priority in three bits in the same field as TOS. These three bits allow eight levels of priority.

However, most TCP/IP topology protocols do not even consider the TOS field. OSPF *can* look at the TOS field and priority, but most OSPF implementations have not used this capability.

Configuring priority in the router   On the other hand, many router vendors have implemented the ability to set certain preferences at each router. This effectively implements priorities. For example, most routers can be set to send shorter packets ahead of longer packets, attend to one protocol type before another, or send topology packets with higher priority than data. Sending shorter packets first has the effect of assigning precedence to interactive traffic and acknowledgments. Sending encapsulated connection-oriented protocols such as SNA and NetBIOS first can avoid timeouts for their sessions.

These vendor-specific router configurations allow a user to optimize the network priority for the organization's traffic mix rather than with a single priority setting. Further, these settings can be used for all types of protocols, while TOS is limited to TCP/IP.

However, these router-based solutions are vendor specific so not all settings would be available from all vendors. Further, if different departments in a company manage their routers differently, a particular packet could receive a different level of priority at each router. In addition, specifying these features on the router has the effect of taking the choice away from the applications—an application may request higher priority from the network but this request is overridden by the router settings.

As OSPF is more widely implemented, more vendors may implement the TCP/IP priority capability and coordinate OSPF priorities with their existing router settings. When this occurs, a user can configure a router to attend to either TOS or router settings or use both while giving one higher priority. A router could be configured to send the following types with higher priority than other traffic: shorter packets, encapsulated SNA packets, TOS high-priority packets, and LSPs.

Issues in priority   Router vendors who implement OSPF will eventually implement its priority feature as well. The large installed base of existing routers will continue without this support for some time, however.

It is more difficult today to implement a priority-sensitive network with TCP/IP. Since most router vendors implement priorities in a proprietary way, users must consider whether the options provided by each vendor's model meet their needs.

Setting priorities is important within a large, busy, production network. APPN implements priority integrally. TCP/IP vendors implement it in an ad hoc fashion. Users must consider their network traffic to determine whether the TCP/IP approach to priority is sufficient for their environment.

8.6 Transport

Layer 4 of the OSI model is primarily responsible for reliable communication between two endpoints. It has two main functions: reliable delivery and flow control. Further, if the transport protocol is connection oriented, layer 4 allows connections/sessions to be set up, for example, TCP connections and LU binds.

Reliable delivery   Ensuring that each packet is delivered correctly—end-to-end reliability—is a layer 4 function. Layer 4 protocols either avoid or correct for lower-layer problems such as lost packets and duplicated packets. Most layer 4 protocols segment and reassemble packets to use the network more efficiently. Some also reorder packets that arrive out of order.

Flow control   Layer 4 tries to avoid the above errors with flow and congestion control. Flow control matches the amount of data transmitted to the capacity of the end system. Congestion control, which may be performed at layer 3, layer 4, or both, matches the amount of data transmitted to the current capacity of the network.

Flow and congestion control are complementary processes. For example, flow control techniques may respond to errors that indicate end system capacity problems, which are actually network congestion problems. Because congestion control is related to flow control, it is discussed in section 8.6.7.

8.6.1 Transport issues

There are several aspects from which APPN and TCP/IP transport can be examined. The primary topics for comparing APPN and TCP/IP transport include:

- Connection orientation
- Sequencing and reordering
- Segmenting and reassembly
- Acknowledgments and retransmission
- Flow and congestion control
- Full-duplex and half-duplex connections

Each of these topics is discussed below after a general overview of APPN and TCP/IP transport protocols.

Not all functions listed above are provided by each protocol family, often because the concept is handled in a different way. For example, APPN does not allow reordering of packets; instead, it incorporates a wide range of safeguards to avoid packets arriving out of order. On the other hand, TCP/IP makes less effort to avoid packets arriving out of order, preferring to incur the effort of reordering them if they do.

APPN and APPC   APPN's layer 4 is thin. This is due to both its relationship to APPC at the upper layers—APPC has elements in layers 4, 5, and 6—and the connection-oriented nature of the path control layer below it. However, APPN with APPC at layer 4—transmission control—provides error control, segmentation/reassembly, sequencing, acknowledgments, and reliable delivery.

Issues: APPC required for APPN   LUs provide APPN with a function similar to TCP connections. Therefore APPN, as a whole or in comparison with TCP/IP, cannot be considered apart from LU sessions.

APPN also supports dependent LU (LU 0, 1, 2, 3, 4, 7) sessions.

The APPC requirement is not a difficult problem for applications that use the native APPC API or common programming interface-communications. The APPC API and CPI-C are used almost exclusively in SNA or APPN environments. The APPC requirement is an issue, however, for any other API environment that wants to use APPN for transport.

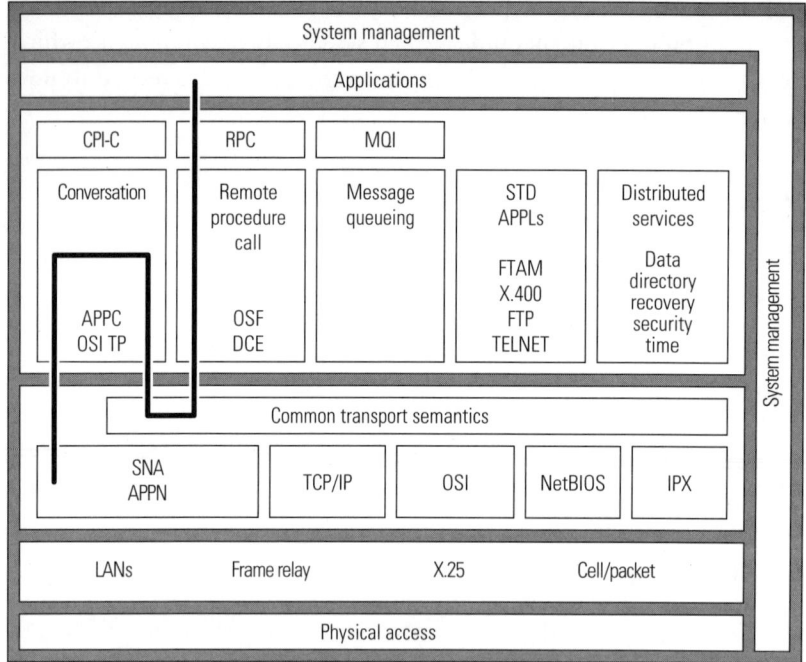

Figure 8.32 Networking blueprint and the path to APPN transport

Figure 8.32 shows an example of how the APPC requirement affects IBM's own AnyNet software for socket applications over APPN. AnyNet is based on the MPTN architecture. MPTN is IBM's transport conversion product family that allows applications expecting one transport type to run over another. For example, applications expecting APPN can run over TCP/IP or vice versa. As the figure shows, the AnyNet conversion process intercepts the procedure, diverts it from sockets, runs it through the AnyNet protocol transform at the common transport semantics level, moves up into layer 5 for LU 6.2 access, and then finally into APPN proper.

The APPC requirement presents practical problems in terms of packaging:

- IBM does not sell pieces of APPC, so a vendor or user must buy a complete APPC package or extract elements of APPC code to use a product that runs over APPN. This can involve additional training and implementation effort, as well as cost.

- The APPC documentation expects implementers to write to CPI-C or the native APPC API. It does not anticipate the need to extract just the lower-level components of APPC to use with APPN. Therefore, extracting these components is not straightforward.

To this point, we have addressed only the issues related to the transport layer. Section 8.7 compares LU 6.2, CPI-C, sockets, and TCP connections directly, as they relate to APPN and TCP/IP. Selected features for comparison of TCP/IP and APPN transport are shown in table 8.11 and are futher discussed in this chapter.

8.6.2 TCP/IP

TCP/IP offers two options for transport. The first, TCP, provides reliable, connection-oriented delivery while the second, UDP, provides a connectionless, datagram delivery transport service.

TCP transport The TCP portion of TCP/IP provides a reliable stream transport service. TCP sets up a full-duplex connection between two endpoints, using a pair of IP addresses and port numbers. It provides flow control (and some congestion control), segmentation/reassembly, sequencing/reordering, flow and congestion control, and recovers from errors such as lost or duplicated packets.

UDP transport The TCP/IP user also has the option of using connectionless UDP, which does not guarantee delivery. UDP datagrams reduce network traffic (for acknowledgments) and host processing (for sequencing). They are considered acceptable for certain kinds of traffic, and for smaller, highly-reliable physical networks like a single LAN.

Table 8.11   UDP, TCP, APPN/ISR, and APPN/HPR at the transport layer

	UDP	**TCP**	**APPN/ISR & APPC**	**APPN/HPR & APPC**
Connection (layer 4)	Connectionless	Connection-oriented	Connection oriented (APPC)	Connection oriented (APPC, RTP)
Header-address	Source & destination IP address & port # (usually compressed)	Source & destination IP address & port # (usually compressed)	LFSID, FQPCID (after bind)	Source routing labels ANR, FQPCID (after bind)
Header-sequence	No sequence # (but must request port)	Sequence number, ACK sequence number	APPC sequence number	APPC sequence number
Segmentation and reassembly	None	Yes (stream by byte)	Yes (by BIU)	Yes (by BIU)
Acknowledgments and retransmission	None	Yes	ACKs yes	Yes
Flow control and congestion control	None	Sliding windows, slow-start, (future proposals use rate-based)	Adaptive pacing (layer 3), adaptive session-level pacing (APPC) (both sliding windows)	Adaptive rate based (RTP), adaptive session-level pacing (APPC)
Full/half duplex	N/A	Full duplex	Half duplex (APPC), full duplex has been announced	Half duplex (APPC), full duplex has been announced

An example of traffic that uses UDP instead of TCP is RIP router update messages, which are frequently broadcast, so the consequences of an undelivered message are minimal. Another UDP user includes applications that provide their own error-checking and delivery guarantees and do not need these services from the network. Applications that expect single-packet responses can use UDP well.

UDP makes use of port numbers to deliver messages within a node, as does TCP. However, UDP does not use them to define a connection.

8.6.3 Connection vs. connectionless transport

Both TCP/IP and SNA/APPN have connection-oriented services between pairs of communicating end systems (end nodes). However only TCP/IP offers connectionless service within intermediate systems. Currently, SNA/APPN only provides connection-oriented service, both in the end-systems and in the hop-by-hop flows between intermediate systems.

For purposes of this analysis, a connection is defined as a data flow between communicating partners in which characteristics of flow control, reliable delivery, and guarantees of no loss of data, sequential data delivery, and no duplicate data delivery are assured. Other interesting properties of connection service are that the name or address of the partner end system (end node) is usually presented to the network only at connection establishment time, and subsequent flows use a short-hand identifier (handle) with local-only significance.

In the backbone, the core routing service differs between TCP/IP and SNA/APPN as shown in figure 8.33.

TCP/IP routing is connectionless. APPN/ISR routing is connection-oriented. APPN/HPR routing is connectionless. A discussion of each routing protocol follows.

IP backbone connection characteristic TCP connections are seen only by the end systems. The end systems inject datagrams into the network. The intermediate systems forward the datagrams. Outside of datagram forwarding, no requirement exists for the intermediate systems to guarantee order of delivery or reliability of delivery. Only the end system TCP stacks handle connection requirements.

IP architecturally defines a datagram-based type of service characteristic, which includes precedence. However, few routers implement precedence in today's IP backbone products. Few end-system implementations allow the application to supply precedence. Rather, a variety of ad hoc techniques have been defined by vendors to implement precedence based upon filters and other noted characteristics of within the TCP/IP data stream.

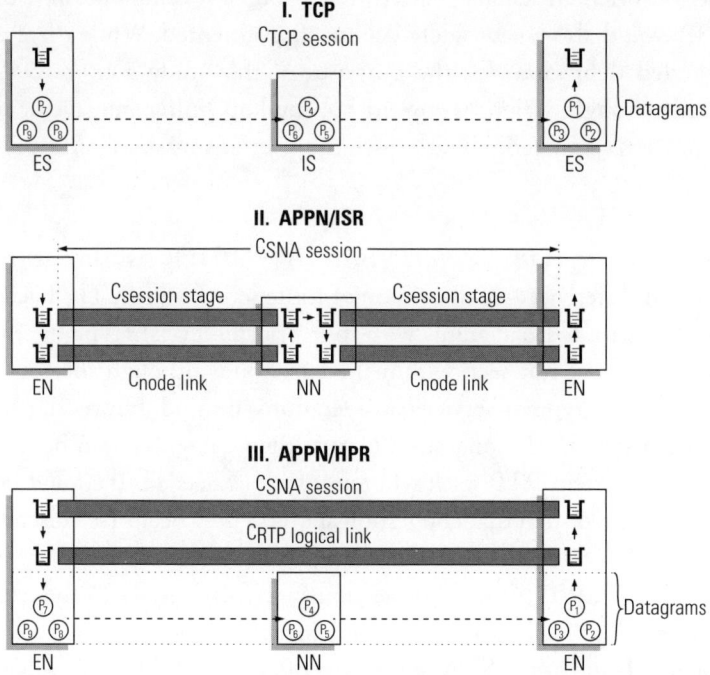

Figure 8.33 Connection/connectionless TCP/IP, APPN/ISR, APPN/HPR

APPN/ISR backbone connection characteristic APPN/ISR is not only connection-oriented, it is loaded with connection-oriented facilities:

- Point-to-point links between EN–NN and NN–NN are connection-oriented. Link layer flow control, checksums and retransmissions occur at the data-link layer.

- EN–EN sessions (e.g., LU 6.2, LU 2) are connection-oriented. No checksums or retransmission logic exists at the data-link layer. Reliability consistency checks, session flow control, segmentation, and reassembly functions do occur.

- For purposes of flow control, each EN–NN and NN–NN hop is connection oriented. (APPN calls these hop-by-hop links "session stages".)

Conflicting interpretation of "connection" A broader definition of connection might be argued. Under this broader definition, any environment that contains source routing or any reservation of resources qualifies as a connection-oriented system. APPN/HPR ANR forwarding would be considered a connection-oriented scheme. Resource reservations within NBBS would also be considered connection-oriented, even though all data is buffered and forwarded on a cell basis. However, using this broader definition, IP would become a connection-oriented scheme, since it has a source routing option. Isochronous extensions to IP would also be considered connection-oriented. While there is some merit to the expanded definition, for the purposes of this study a more constrained definition is used, strongly weighted toward hop-by-hop buffer management and flow control and an active connection state (including retransmission) on a per-packet basis.

APPN/HPR backbone connection characteristic APPN/HPR is similar to TCP/IP (with one important difference, see discussion of route setup below). The backbone is connectionless (source routed datagrams with four priority levels). Type of service (a.k.a. class of service) is really not seen within the backbone, although the route server computes ANR routes with type-of-service considerations in mind. However, priority is handled within the backbone. If congestion occurs, then datagrams can be discarded (as in IP), and the end system RTP stack will retransmit as needed. It should be noted that APPN/HPR is designed such that congestion should rarely occur (see discussion of route setup below).

APPN/HPR differs from TCP/IP in that connections are visible (only to the end systems) at two layers—at the RTP layer, where the fundamental connection characteristics are actually implemented, and at the SNA session layer (e.g., LU 2, LU 6.2), where SNA-specific connection characteristics are implemented. APPN/HPR and APPN/ISR sessions can also be concatenated (transparently). Concatenation of APPN/ISR and APPN/HPR sessions permits systems with both the old and new forms of routing to interoperate.

APPN/HPR differs from the IP layer of TCP/IP in one important respect. At the time the ANR route is established a special packet is sent to verify that sufficient resources exist in each node hop-by-hop along the route. If insufficient resources exist, the packet is discarded, and after a timeout, an alternate route will be calculated by the originating node. In this sense APPN/HPR is actually a hybrid between connection oriented and connectionless oriented—deterministic connectionless. Nevertheless, no session state or flow control feedback is required within the intermediate systems.

APPN/HPR link types in multiprotocol environments The initial APPN/HPR architecture defined link mappings for frame relay and LAN. In a homogenous APPN/HPR-only backbone, these two link mappings are sufficient. However, in a heterogenous backbone with other concurrent protocols, for example, IP and/or IPX and/or Appletalk, some method is required for concurrent link usage by multiple protocols. The most straightforward scheme is to define another PPP protocol type field and layer APPN/HPR's RTP over PPP. However, current architecture thinking within IBM leans toward the inverse approach, layer PPP atop ANR (perhaps even atop RTP). The inverse approach will be difficult to implement by router vendors. A well thought out solution is needed. Convergence of IP and APPN/HPR backbones will be the architectural driver for this requirement.

Connection/connectionless backbone analysis   The comparison of connection-oriented and connectionless backbone schemes is a complex analysis, since there are many ways of designing and implementing both of them. Sometimes the performance tradeoffs are caused by factors only peripherally related to issues of connection vs. connectionless. Issues of efficiency, cost, and performance of implementation within intermediate systems, however, are strongly affected by the choice of methodology.

The typical intermediate system today is a router (with high speed switches gaining both functionality and popularity).

Routers achieve high performance through several schemes (the list is not exhaustive):

- Minimize buffer copying in memory (goal is to move the data zero times)
- Implement as much protocol processing as possible for known addresses and paths in fast-path software logic, typically within device drivers directly serving each LAN/ WAN port
- Commit maximal amounts of processing function to hardware
- Use high-speed multiported memory for packet storage

The choice of a connection-based (as defined above) routing fabric has the following implications:

- Connections require a higher level of per-packet processing than connectionless traffic—the router must maintain state, flow control, buffering, and pacing on a per-connection basis. The higher level of per-connection processing will be more expensive to implement (and less likely to see hardware implementation) in routers than datagram forwarding processing. Routers that forward datagrams usually implement a fast path at or near the device driver layer (receive the packet from an inbound queue, perform a quick address look up, post the packet on an outgoing queue). For connection-oriented packet forwarding a given packet will see more context switches, pointer hand-offs, and perhaps buffer copies than will a comparable datagram packet.

- Connections require higher levels of memory (especially because of buffer reservation requirements). The levels of memory required are more severe if buffer pool guarantees are prereserved at connection establishment time (note: the initial release of APPN routing technology required prereservation of connection buffers for the negotiated adaptive pacing window).

The cost/performance ratio for implementing a connection-oriented router engine is higher than for connectionless backbones, i.e., connection-oriented backbones cost more and exhibit lower performance than the corresponding connectionless alternative. Furthermore, intermediate system APPN/ISR routing, which contains two layers of connection processing (link layer and session layer), will be more expensive to implement and will exhibit lower performance than either IP or APPN/HPR routing—all other factors such as memory, processor horsepower, and adapter horsepower being equal.

Some argue that high-speed networks are in fact connection-oriented, and that the above arguments do not hold. We are not using the same definition of connection. When applied to a high-speed network, the notion of a connection usually implies the determination of a route and the reservation of resources along the route. All subsequent dataflow, however, is datagram oriented. A given frame or cell can be discarded if network congestion occurs. Our definition of connection differs slightly and includes the function of reliable delivery and flow control on a hop-by-hop basis.

Because of the inherent advantages of connectionless backbone transport for APPN routers, a rapid migration away from APPN/ISR can be expected once APPN/HPR becomes available.

The ability for vendors to address connection-oriented routing with innovations, for example, cost-reduced intelligent I/O processors (all things not being equal), should never be underestimated; architecture and implementation are often on divergent tracks.

There are also disadvantages with connectionless routing. Because no connection state is maintained, the router has no per-connection method of slowing the rate of arrival of datagrams during periods of congestion. Thus a connectionless router must ultimately discard datagrams in certain cases. In connection-based routers, the routers can apply back pressure (flow control) to the upstream neighboring routers, and never be forced to discard a packet. Also, with connectionless routing, problem management and network management are more difficult on a per session hop-by-hop basis. Newer routing techniques such as broadband network services are on the horizon; they offer a blend of datagram forwarding services, route setup, and reservation services along a given route, essentially a hybrid connection/connectionless model.

8.6.4 Sequencing and reordering

Sequencing refers to numbering of segments sent by the transport of the source node, while segmenting (discussed below) refers to the source node partitioning the flow of data from the layer above it into appropriate-sized segments.

The destination node checks the sequence numbers to ensure it has received all the segments and in the proper order. Reordering is the mirror of sequencing—it involves putting segments that arrive out of sequence back in order.

APPC, APPN, and sequence numbers   Sequencing serves the same function in both APPC/APPN and in TCP/IP. But each protocol implements it very differently.

An APPC half-session acts as part of the connection-oriented component for APPN transport; it is somewhat analogous to a TCP/IP connection. APPC does this by allowing its sequence numbers to be used for transport-layer functions as well as session-layer functions. The data-flow control layer, SNA's layer 5, generates BIUs and requests layer 3, path control, to assign a sequence number to each of them. This sequence number is not carried in data flow control's RH but rather in layer 3's TH.

Reordering   TCP/IP allows reordering of packets which arrive out of sequence order while APPN does not. What this actually reflects, however, is a point of view about whether it is better to avoid out-of-sequence problems (APPN) or deal with them as they occur (TCP/IP).

Having packets arrive out of sequence is disruptive because it requires a certain amount of buffer memory to hold packets until a complete set arrives, CPU cycles to resequence them before delivering them to the upper layers, and some logic to decide whether a missing packet is lost or late.

APPN avoids reordering   APPN takes significant precautions at the lower layers so that packets do not arrive out of order. This is accomplished by APPN being connection-oriented with fixed paths at both the network layer and the data-link layer as well as pacing between every pair of hops (APPN/ISR). If packets arrive out of sequence despite these safeguards, there is most likely a more significant problem with the connection than just out-of-sequence packets. Therefore, APPN/ISR will terminate the session and restart it. APPN/HPR does not require session termination.

The APPC/APPN connections and pacing are not implemented only to avoid out-of-sequence packets. They serve several other purposes including maximum use of bandwidth and highly predictable performance.

TCP/IP allows reordering   TCP/IP designers, on the other hand, believed that packets would arrive out of sequence infrequently enough that it would be more efficient to allow for packet reordering rather than make significant efforts to avoid their occurrence.

Issues: sequencing Both APPC/APPN and TCP/IP use sequencing in a similar way for a similar purpose. The two protocols have different points of view about the appropriate place(s) to implement error recovery: TCP/IP reorders packets at the transport layer while SNA enforces sequencing at the data-link layer.

8.6.5 Segmenting and reassembly

The transport layer at the source node segments the information it receives from an application to an appropriate size for the destination node. This may involve splitting (creating multiple, smaller packets) or grouping (concatenating multiple, smaller packets into a larger, single packet). Reassembly is done by the destination's transport before it offers the information up to the application. Segmentation refers to splitting or grouping by the transport layer while fragmentation refers to splitting or grouping by the network layer.

Both APPN and TCP/IP provide segmentation and reassembly for transmission. This allows the application to be unconcerned about the packet size, while the transport sends the most efficient-sized packet for the destination.

APPN segmenting APPN's tranmission segmentation and reassembly is handled by node type 2.1 path control. Usually, BIUs from the LU are segmented into smaller BIUs to meet the limitations of the underlying data link or receiving node buffer constraints.

APPN is quite aware of the data link and therefore can efficiently segment BIUs for the network as well as the destination. APPN sends the largest-sized packet the connection and network will allow, while TCP/IP packet size is relatively fixed at connection startup. However, not all APPN nodes support BIU segmentation and reassembly.

In APPN/ISR, the BIU is segmented and reassembled on a hop-by-hop basis, which increases processing overhead at each hop to gain the increased network efficiency. It is expected that APPN/HPR will perform segmentation and reassembly on an end-to-end basis.

TCP/IP segmenting TCP uses an unstructured stream, sending an appropriate number of bytes associated with a sequence number to IP. This unit of transfer is called a segment.

At connection set-up and during the connection, each end advertises its maximum segment size. TCP uses this to calculate the maximum bytes it can offer in a segment. Over a large internet, the TCP/IP specification recommends a maximum segment size of 536 bytes to avoid IP fragmenting.

Conclusions: segmentation   APPN has an advantage in network utilization here as in other functional areas. However, we find that segmentation should not be considered a major issue in decision making for two reasons discussed here: cost/benefit and long-term trends.

Although TCP/IP *cannot* segment optimally for the network, some APPN nodes *might not* implement efficient segmenting. Further, the overhead to segment and reassemble on a hop-by-hop basis affects the network utilization benefit.

As high-speed networks continue to emerge, both APPN and TCP/IP will be able to handle larger packets. Alternatively, the lower layer protocols such as ATM will divide up the traffic themselves. Either change will render transport-level segmentation less important.

8.6.6 *Acknowledgments and retransmission*

Connection-oriented protocols ensure reliablity with acknowledgments, often called ACKs. The acknowledgment includes the sequence number of the segment it is acknowledging.

If an acknowledgment is not received within a certain timeframe, some protocols will request a retransmission and some will react by taking down and reestablishing the connection.

TCP/IP acknowledgments   Because UDP is a connectionless protocol, it does not send acknowledgments. TCP connections require an acknowledgment for every segment or group of segments.

Sliding windows   TCP does not wait for each segment to be acknowledged before sending the next. Instead, TCP uses a sliding window protocol, which is illustrated in figure 8.34. The window size is set during the connection negotiation by each end system advertising the maximum amount of data it can handle at a time.

The window size can be adjusted when a node sends a window advertisement indicating a change in capacity. In addition, the window size can be adjusted if congestion is detected. The latter adjustment is further discussed in section 8.6.8.

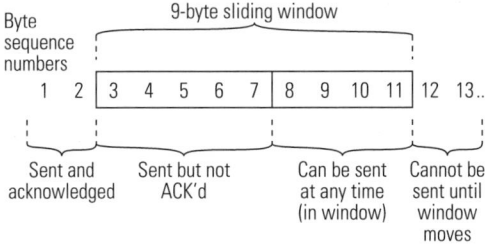

Figure 8.34   Sliding window protocol

In a sliding window protocol, the sending node tracks the window position. Whenever an acknowledgment is received for a group of segments, the window slides over that many segments. The new segments that move into the window can be sent immediately.

The window size for TCP is one byte, though a segment can be many bytes. TCP uses a cumulative scheme that allows the receiving node to acknowledge a series of bytes by responding only to the last one it has received, indicating a complete stream. That is, if a node receives 1, 2, 3, 4, 5, 6, , 8, 9, and 10, it would respond with an acknowledgment for byte 6 since it has received all the bytes up through that point.

One weakness with this scheme is that the sender cannot know that the receiver may have successfully received subsequent segments after a missing segment. Therefore, TCP will often require transmission of many segments when only one has been lost. The IETF is working to develop a selective retransmission capability to avoid this problem.

TCP/IP retransmission   TCP uses a timer for each segment. If all the bytes in a given segment have not been acknowledged in an acceptable amount of time, that is, if the timer expires, TCP retransmits the packet. It also decreases the window size, assuming that the problem is due to the volume of data it is sending.

To adapt for varying delays in an internet, the TCP timer is dynamically set using an adaptive retransmission alogrithm. TCP calculates the round-trip time (RTT) as the difference between the time it sends a segment and the time it receives an acknowledgment.

TCP constantly recalculates this value with *each* new acknowledgment. This constant recalculation is considered one of the most inefficient elements of sliding windows. Newer rate-based congestion control methods recalculate once per average RTT (or traffic rate) rather than once per packet.

APPC/APPN acknowledgments   Like TCP, APPN/ISR uses a sliding window protocol called adaptive pacing. (APPN also supports fixed pacing for subarea SNA traffic.) Adaptive pacing is done both at the network level and at the session level, where it is called session-level pacing.

APPN/ISR requires an acknowledgment for each packet rather than for a stream of segments as TCP allows. APPN detractors claim that all these acknowledgments doubled for two layers increases network traffic. But these acknowledgments are usually piggy-backed on data packets.

At both layers that support adaptive pacing, the sender must receive an explicit grant from the receiver for each window of packets it sends. The receiver adjusts the window grant for existing link conditions and traffic for each session on each link.

APPN/ISR runs over a connection-oriented data link. It depends on the data link to handle retransmissions rather than handling them at layer 4 as in TCP/IP.

Conclusions: acknowledgments and retransmissions   Although hop-by-hop pacing in subarea SNA and APPN/ISR enforces the most finely tuned network efficiency, the overhead and maintenance required for it can be an ineffective use of resources. Newer protocols, such as APPN/HPR, focus on end-to-end pacing instead and use other elements, such as adaptive-rate based congestion control, to maintain network performance.

8.6.7 Flow and congestion control

Flow and congestion control are among the most significant points of contention today between APPN and TCP/IP proponents. The debate involves design philosophy, simulation polemics, and implementation performance considerations.

Sliding windows and rate-based mechanisms   There are two primary mechanisms for flow and congestion control: sliding windows and rate based. A sliding window protocol sends information based on a rolling average of the round-trip time of each segment and its acknowledgment. Rate-based protocols also use round-trip time to adjust the sending rate; however, they test and recalculate the average round-trip time periodically rather than with every segment; this period is usually once per average round-trip time.

Most APPN and TCP/IP proponents are in general agreement that, in theory, congestion control using rate-based mechanisms should perform better at high loads than sliding windows protocols. Rate-based protocols adjust more sensitively to congestion, are less subject to oscillations, and involve less overhead for calculations.

However, there is some disagreement over how *much* better new rate-based implementations will be than existing sliding windows implementations which have been improved over time.

TCP/IP uses a sliding windows protocol for flow control. APPN/ISR uses adapting pacing at both the network and session layer. APPN/HPR uses a rate-based mechanism to replace adaptive pacing at the network layer but maintains adaptive session-level pacing.

ICMP source quench unused   TCP/IP sliding windows protocol was intended for flow control. The TCP/IP standard provides for congestion control at each router with the ICMP source quench. ICMP messages are used by hosts and gateways to report errors, problems, and operating information. Source quench allows a router to slow the rate at which one or more end systems sends traffic through it.

However, ICMP source quench is not implemented by any major router vendor. Instead, they rely on TCP/IP sliding windows flow control to also enforce congestion control. Some vendors have also implemented a proprietary source quench capability.

Adaptive versus jitter   Whether sliding windows- or rate-based, adaptive congestion control has several advantages for network efficiency. However, fluctuating flow rates introduce "jitter" problems for video or multimedia applications. These applications require a fixed allocated bandwidth.

Most or all of the proposed high-speed network replacements for TCP use a rate-based mechanism. But these proposals suggest either a fixed rate-based method or a rate-based method with adaptive or fixed selectable on a session-by-session basis.

Measuring flow control efficiency   Figure 8.35 provides a generic illustration of offered load, engineered load, and served load and how sliding windows and rate-based protocols are expected to perform.

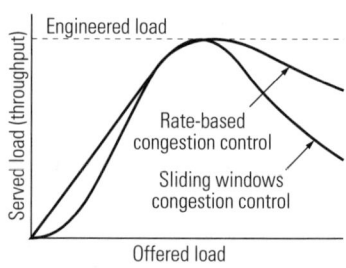

Figure 8.35   Projected impact of sliding windows and rate-based mechanisms on network throughput

Offered load is the amount of traffic all the nodes and connections present to the network at any one time. Served load, or throughput, is the actual amount of traffic the network carries. The engineered load is the point of maximum throughput the existing network can handle.

If the offered load exceeds the engineered load, that is, in the face of congestion, the network cannot deliver the entire offered load, by definition. Further, the network will not even be able to handle its engineered load. Performance drops below engineered load due to such effects as congestion, retransmissions (if any), and collisions.

The question is to what *extent* the network performance suffers, that is, how fast and how far performance drops below engineered load. The two main points of debate here are (1) how much better an adaptive rate-based protocol will be than a sliding windows protocol, and (2) how important this difference is.

Table 8.12 presents, albeit stereotypically, some points of view in this debate. These differences show why this issue is difficult to resolve. These differences are, of course, not universal—there are wide differences of opinion within IBM itself and in the SNA/APPN and TCP/IP communities on these points. However, they are valuable if considered as cultural contexts.

An APPN proponent would be impressed with a network's ability to operate at 90 percent of capacity. A TCP/IP advocate would question how much money, time, and effort are required to tune and maintain the delicate balance required for that performance level, and wonder whether those resources could have been spent to buy additional bandwidth or more routers instead.

An APPN proponent would use the example of an expensive highway that is designed to carry traffic at 75 miles per hour but requires cars to limit their speed to 45 miles per hour.

A TCP/IP proponent would use the example of a car engine: a very expensive, high-performance engine can be tuned to sustain performance at high speeds. The average car, adequate for most driving needs, is capable of speeds up to 120 miles per hour but operates most efficiently at 60–70 miles per hour.

TCP/IP congestion/flow control

In TCP/IP, if an acknowledgment is not received within a reasonable deviation from the average RTT, the packet is retransmitted. TCP uses a timeout timer initially set to about twice the average RTT.

If the lack of acknowledgment is due to congestion, retransmissions could flood the network, exacerbating the congestion. Therefore, after retransmitting a segment upon timeout, TCP also increases the timeout ratio to prevent these excess retransmissions.

Table 8.12 APPN and TCP/IP points of view regarding congestion and flow control

APPN	TCP/IP
Very important	Not as important as other areas
Congestion is a problem	Congestion is a symptom
Solve congestion	Solve problem behind congestion
Maximize use of bandwidth	Use a bigger pipe
Operating at 95% is optimal	Operating at 95% is inefficient (80/20 rule)
It's a software issue	It's a hardware issue
Bandwidth is expensive	Bandwidth will keep getting cheaper
Avoid problems	Solve problems when they occur
Control congestion tightly	Adjust when necessary
Control at every node	Control end to end, which is easier
Solve the problem "all the way"	Find the easiest solution
Maximize control	Minimize complexity
Any degradation is bad	Some degradation is acceptable
It's an architectural issue	It's an implementation issue
Provide it in the basic package	Provide it as an option

During a period of congestion, TCP adjusts the size of the sending window downward exponentially to a minimum of one segment. If congestion continues after reaching a window of one, TCP continues to throttle back by increasing timeout values before retransmitting.

TCP/IP slow start   TCP throttles back exponentially in response to congestion. After the congestion eases, TCP does not recover exponentially. Recovering exponentially after congestion causes oscillations and sometimes recreates congestion. Therefore, in the late 1980s, after a series of congestion collapses occurred on the Internet, an algorithm called slow start was developed and adopted for network recover.

Slow start sets the window to 1 and increases it in two phases:

- The window is increased exponentially up to half its previous window level. That is, after one acknowlegement, the window is set to 2; after two acknowledgments, the window is set to 4.

- When the window reaches half its previous size, the window is then increased by one for every full window of acknowledgments. For example, if the window size prior to congestion was 8, the recovery window would be set to 5 after three sets of acknowledgments (to 2 after 1 ACK, to 4 after 2 ACKs, to 5 after 3 ACKs).

APPN/ISR hop-by-hop congestion/flow control APPN/ISR uses adaptive pacing between each session stage for each session. Adaptive pacing also uses a window of packets. The window size for each session increases or decreases based on conditions at the receiver—the receiver sends an explicit window grant that takes congestion indications into account. This is different from TCP, but it is not a significant difference. In TCP/IP, the receiver window is based only on its capacity, and the sender's window is based on the receiver window or the congestion window, whichever is smaller.

Since APPN/ISR adaptive pacing is by hop, each link can adjust its capacity among the current needs of each of the sessions using that hop. Further, each receiving node can throttle back its sending partner to make sure that it never drops a packet. However, these advantages are gained at the expense of additional processing at each hop, which can decrease throughput.

In addition to this adaptive pacing in ISR, APPN uses adaptive session-level at each intermediate node for each session. This is done by the half-session at the end points and by the session connector at the intermediate nodes.

APPN/HPR congestion control In APPN/HPR, with RTP, the LU half-sessions still use adaptive session-level pacing. However, it is done end-to-end rather than at each hop.

In addition, the adaptive pacing between ISR hops is replaced by adaptive rate-based congestion control. ARB is also implemented end-to-end rather than hop-by-hop.

Comparison of TCP/IP with slow start and APPN/HPR with ARB The sidebar, "Sliding window with slow start (TCP/IP) compared to adaptive rated based (APPN/HPR)," compares the congestion control procedure used by TCP/IP with sliding windows/slow start to APPN/HPR with adapative rate-based congestion control.

One difference between sliding-window mechanisms and rate-based mechanisms is how often the parameters are recalculated. The sliding windows protocols are aware of network capacity by noting the rate (or round-trip time) experienced by each packet. Rate-based protocols note the rate by testing it once per average round-trip time. In

Sliding window with slow start (TCP/IP) compared to adaptive rate based (APPN/HPR)

TCP/IP sliding window, slow start

TCP initialization variables

Set initial timeout ratio, β, related to round trip time. ($TO = \beta \times RTT$, $\beta > 1$). Inital β set to 2 is common. During connection, timeout will be adjusted using backoff timeout ratio for congestion.

Set backoff timeout ratio, γ. Typically, $\gamma = 2$. That is, the timeout is doubled every time a retransmission is triggered. Timeout is reset to β when congestion is relieved.

Set δ to control how quickly a new round trip time sample will affect the weighted average RTT. δ must be between 0 and 1, and is usually set to 1/8.

In calculating new round trip times using variance, *difference* is the absolute value of the difference between each new sample and the existing weighted average. Deviation is the estimated mean deviation. The deviation is reset at each calculation to equal the old deviation plus the sensitivity, δ, times the difference minus the old deviation.

(Older TCP/IP used difference to recalculate RTT instead of variance. Using variance adapts better to varied network load and to higher loads.)

For each TCP connection set-up

Calculate initial round trip time (RTT) from TCP connection messages.

Use RTT to set initial timeout using set β. ($TOi = \beta \times RTT$).

Receive initial window advertisement from receiver (Wr).

Set initial window size to receiver window ($Ws = Wr$).

Set initial congestion window to advertised size ($Wc = Wr$).

APPN/HPR adaptive rate based

RTP initialization variables

Set ratio for interval value (Is). Setting Is approximately equal to RTT is good for T1/T3 networks.

Set initial burst sending rate (Rs) as maximum bits allowed per interval. Must be less than Rx, the maximum transmission rate of sender.

Set burst number (Bs) as bits allowed in one burst at rate Rs.

Note Rx, which is maximum rate at which sender can send in one interval.

Set value for sensitivity threshhold, ΔR. ΔR is most important parameter in ARB algorithm. It avoids resetting in response to probable noncongestion conditions such as change in queue length.

Set increase rate (Ri) as increment to increase Rs if network is underloaded.

Set threshold for receiver accumulation of changes of delay time, Td.

For each RTP connection set-up

Note initial RTT. Set sending interval (Is) to ratio of round trip time.

No initial receiver rate (Rr) generated during set up.

TCP/IP sliding window, slow start (continued)

APPN/HPR adaptive rate based (continued)

For each segment sent

Send all segments allowed in *Ws*.

Receive acknowlegement for first segment.

Note actual time between segment send and acknowledgment receipt.

Recalculate round trip time (*RTT*) using the new time and the formula for variance.

(*RTT* is not recalculated for segments that are retransmitted.)

Reset timeout, *TO*, to $\beta \times$ new *RTT*.

Slide window. Send next segment(s) now in window.

For each interval

Send in a burst all bits ready to send up to number allowed by *Bs*. Note number of bits actually sent as *Ra*.

After each interval in which data was sent, sender requests receipt rate (*Rr*) from receiver. *Rr* is bits received during interval, except as noted below under flow control. *Rr* acts as acknowledgment.

Interval period for receiver (*Ir*), the time between beginning to receive two sets of bursts, is very close to sending interval (*Is*).

Calculate ratio of *Rr* to *Ra*, taking into account fixed sensitivity threshold, ΔR. Use ratio below under flow control.

Timeout is fixed for duration of connection.

At beginning of next interval, send in a burst all bits ready to send, up to *Bs*.

Flow control (if *Wr* changes)

Note window advertisement (*Wr*) carried in each acknowledgment.

If *Wr* > *Ws*, increase *Ws* to equal new *Wr*.

If *Wr* < *Ws*, decrease *Ws* to equal new *Wr*.

Flow control ($Rr < Ra - \Delta R$ or $Rr > Ra$)

If *Rr* > *Ra*, increase *Rs* by increase increment, *Ri*, as long as *Rs* does not exceed maximum sending rate, *Rx*, and except as noted below.

If, during previous interval, *Rr* was *not* greater than *Ra*, keep *Rs* the same until the next interval. (This avoids oscillations.)

If $Rr < Ra - \Delta R$, reduce *Rs* by $\theta \times Rr$.

Adjust to intermediate congestion

At layer 3, intermediate nodes may use TCP/IP's ICMP source quench protocol to ask end nodes to back off, sending one source quench for each datagram they drop.

However, most routers today do not use ICMP source quench. Some use a proprietary, often more sophisticated algorithm. In either event, the effect on the source IP is to reduce its datagram sending rate.

Avoid queuing congestion

Queuing congestion may accumulate gradually enough not to trigger ΔR threshold.

To avoid this, the receiver monitors network delay and accumulates changes in delay time at each rate request.

If accumulated changes exceed a fixed threshold, *Td*, *Rr* is cut by ΔR. The accumulation of delay time is then reset to 0.

TCP/IP sliding window, slow start (continued)

For each timeout (by segment)

A timeout is reached if a segment acknowlegement is not receive within the TO value (which, as discussed above, is usually set to $2 \times RTT$).

There are three responses to a timeout:

- The segment is retransmitted.
- The sending window, Ws, is decreased by half.
- The timeout value is doubled (to four times the RTT).

If, for a different segment, another acknowledgment exceeds this new timeout, there are again three responses:

- The segment is retransmitted.
- The sending window is again decreased by half. This process can be repeated until the sending window reaches one segment.
- The timeout value is again doubled. This process can be repeated until it reaches an upper bound such as twenty times the longest delay along any path in the Internet.

APPN/HPR adaptive rate based (continued)

For each timeout (by interval)

A timeout is reached if the sender does not receive a reply to a request for Rr within the timeout fixed at beginning of connection.

There is one response to a timeout:

- The sender reduces Rs. Calculate half of Rs and compare to Rr. Set new Rs to the lower of these two.

At the next interval, the sender sends the usual measurement request.

If another Rr is not received before timeout, there is one response:

- The sender reduces Rs. Calculate half of Rs and compare to Rr. Set new Rs to the lower of these two.

Again, at the next interval, the sender sends the usual measurement request.

both cases, the protocols reset values for every measurement. This means that rate-based protocols have less frequent recalculations. If the network capacity is hundreds or thousands of packets per second and the round-trip time is one second, calculations are much less frequent.

Another difference is that sliding windows is based on the number of bytes, segments, packets, or frames that can be sent before waiting for an acknowledgment, while rate based is based on the number of bits that can be sent in a time interval.

A third difference is that sliding windows backs off if an acknowledgment is not received before a set timeout period. Rate based backs off if its rate test packet is not received before a set timeout period.

A fourth difference is that, during recovery, sliding windows with slow start increases the window first exponentially and then more gradually for each acknowledgment or set of acknowledgments successfully received. Rate based recovers by increasing the sending rate by a preset step for each test packet successfully received (i.e., within the timeout).

TCP/IP sliding window, slow start (continued)

For recovery from congestion

In a congested condition, slow start requires Ws to be set to 1.

If congestion continues after it reaches a window of one, TCP continues to throttle back by increasing timeout values before retransmitting.

For the first segment that is sent (not retransmitted) where an acknowledgment *is* received, there are four responses:

- Increase window Ws by one segment (that is, increase it to two).
- Recalculate RTT.
- Reset timeout to $\beta \times RTT$.
- Send segment.

Slow start increases Ws in two phases.

Up to half its previous window level, the window is increased exponentially.

- After one acknowledgment, double Ws, that is, set Ws to 2.
- After two more acknowledgments, again double WS, that is, set Ws to 4.

When the window reaches half its previous size:

- After each full window of acknowledgments, increase window by 1. That is, after Ws was set to 5, and 5 more acknowledgments are received, set Ws to 6.

APPN/HPR adaptive rate based (continued)

For recovery from congestion

When the timeout clears, that is, when the two consecutive Rr's are received:

- Increase Rs by Ri.

Rs is increased, at each interval, by Ri as long as $Rr < Ra - \Delta R$, or until it reaches sender's maximum rate, Rx.

8.6.8 The future of transports

TCP may go rate based   In addition to the basic transport services, all the above proposals include a rate-based flow control rather than current TCP/IP's windowing. Some proposals include adjustable, or adaptive, rate-based flow control, which is the class of mechanism used for APPN. Others proposals use fixed or allow a choice of adaptive or fixed on a session-by-session basis.

There is general (though not unanimous) agreement in the TCP/IP community that rate-based schemes are more effective. The debate involves the following issues:

- Whether the basic current TCP protocol should be adapted to require replacing all sliding windows with rate-based flow control or whether the new mechanism should be required only for the newer transport

- How the Internet will handle the new transport and flow-control mechanism to allow fair access to the network by old and new systems

It is not yet clear which new TCP/IP transport will be preferred nor how it will be integrated with existing environments. It seems clear that a rate-based mechanism will be adopted at least for the higher-speed environments.

8.6.9 Architecture and protocol taxonomy reference model

Table 8.13 summarizes several of the key TCP/IP, subarea SNA, and APPN design and reference points discussed in this section thus far and builds an architecture and protocol taxonomy reference model.

Table 8.13   Architecture and protocol taxonomy reference model

		Architecture		
	Reference points	TCP/IP	Subarea SNA	APPN
Design methodology	Historic design approach	Local/remote resource sharing with no need to modify remote program	Host-centric applications connecting terminals and applications	Peer connections of distributed applications
	Standards process	Open RFC development based on RFC 1310 Open publication, no fee Third-party aftermarket	IBM-based Reasonably open publication Third-party aftermarket for end systems (not SSCP, NCP)	IBM-based Open publication, fees Third-party aftermarket
	Management process	IAB oversees architecture IETF is major standards-making body IRTF develops/maintains net/internet studies	IBM NS Architecture Review Board	IBM NS Architecture Review Board APPN Implementer Workshop input
Design point	Network processor model	Client/server, peer-to-peer	Host-centric, hierarchical	Client/server, peer-to-peer
Naming/addressing model	Naming convention	DNS design goals in RFC 1034, 1982 RFC 1123 DNS resolver on all hosts Mechanism converts host names to/from IP addresses Full-service or stub resolver Hierarchical tree, like UNIX filesystem structure Inverted tree structure called Domain Name Space Single root at top (i.e. UNIX root directory, " ") Each name label 63 characters Domain name of node in tree Label seq.; node to inverted root Dots separate names on path Index into DNS database DNS uses either UDP or TCP TCP triple {IP Address, Port}	NAU names: SSCP, LU, PU Subarea. Element	NAU names: CP, LU NETID.NAME; Network-qualified name, ≤ 8 characters each All NAU names in a net from same name space Where NAU name not explicitly qualified, assume NETID of specified/implied parent (LU ENCP) APPN triple {NETID, LUNAME, TPNAME} session name

Table 8.13 Architecture and protocol taxonomy reference model (continued)

Reference points	Architecture		
	TCP/IP	Subarea SNA	APPN

Addressing model	IPv4 datagram protocol, 32-bit source/destination address
	Two-level hierarchy
	  High-order network number portion
	  Low-order host number portion
	Represented as dotted quads
	Limited, fixed structure:
	  Net address, Host identifier
	IP unicast address classes (A, B, C) shown as dotted quads
	Class A addr ≤ 128 (2^7) nets;
	  $\leq 16{,}777{,}216$ (2^{24}) hosts/net
	Class B addr $\leq 16{,}384$ (2^{14}) nets;
	  $\leq 65{,}536$ (2^{16}) hosts
	Class C addr $\leq 2{,}097{,}152$ (2^{21}) nets;
	  ≤ 256 (2^8) hosts
	Class D addr, multicast
	Class E addr, reserved
	Subnetting: Net.Subnet.Host
	Address range is 0.0.0.0
	  through 255.255.255.255;
	IPv6 datagram protocol, 128-bit source/destination address for unicast, anycast, multicast;
	IPv6 address space is 73^{40} x 10^{36} nodes with practical efficiency for approximately 8 x 10^{17} to 2 x 10^{33} nodes.
		EENA addressing $\leq 64K$ subareas/net
		$\leq 32K$ elements/subarea
		$\leq 16{,}777{,}216$ (2^{24}) NAUs/net
		FID0/1 THs convey historic, 16-bit addresses
		FID4 TH conveys fully-qualified net address between subareas
		FID2 TH conveys 16-bit session ID between SA-PU2.0
			T2.1 Node associates session using TG with 17-bit LFSID
			Nodes at TG endpoints use same LFSID to ID given session
			Map LFSID into FID2 TH
			Distinct LFSIDs assigned on each session stage (internode hop)
			NNCPs perform address swapping of LFSID in FID2 TH
			Each successive NNCP along session route replaces LFSID on inbound TG w/ session-assigned LFSID on outbound TG
			
			FQPCID is network-unique session identifier that:
			  Correlates internodal messages (e.g. LOCATE)
			  IDs a session for problem determination/resolution
			  IDs a session for accounting, auditing, perf. monitoring

Directory services	Domain Name System (DNS), distributed database
	
	Resolves Domain name into IP addresses, and the reverse
	
	DNS structured by domains. Each domain appears as information subtree in domain name space. Domains are hierarchical, logically inverted tree.
		Host tables (DRSCTAB, CDRSCTAB LOGMODE, COSTAB, USSTAB, INTERPRET TAB, PATHTAB)
		
		NCP distributed path tables (TRTAB)
		
		Preconfigured
			Local directory maps LU name to CP name of resident node
			LEN EN and APPN EN maintain local directories for local LUs
			APPN NN provides distributed directory services to its client ENs
			APPN NN either verifies LU location or invokes Central Directory Server
			
			Distributed Directory entries are made by either:
			  System definition via NOF
			  Resource registration from APPN EN to its NN server
			  NN caching of directory search results
			
			APPN DS returns routes

Address assignment	Internet registry ensures unique ID of each network IANA allocates/assigns network numbers	Addresses session-unique Network IDs can be user-specified or registered by IBM	Address session-unique Network IDs can be user-specified or registered by IBM

Naming/addressing model (continued)

Table 8.13 Architecture and protocol taxonomy reference model (continued)

	Reference points	Architecture TCP/IP	Subarea SNA	APPN

Naming/addressing (cont.)	Name/address resolution	Name-to-address mapping
		Address-to-name mapping
		  IP addresses are hierarchical, like domain names
		  IP addresses get more specific from left to right
		  Domain names get less specific from left to right
		  Name server responds to inverse query
		  Name server local only
			Address session-unique
			Session destination LUs pre-defined in host tables
				Address session-unique
				Session destination LUs located by NN server; routing set by RSCV

	Network/data link address resolution	**ARP:** Allows host/router to broadcast query containing an IP address and receive back associated LAN MAC address. Proxy ARP allows one device to respond on behalf of ≥ 1 others. IP ARP returns routes. **RARP:** Allows query of which IP address is bound to a given LAN MAC address	None	None
Routing model	COS/TOS	**TOS:** IDs nature of service to datagram. Tradeoffs: low delay, high reliability, high throughput Security handled as IP option	**COS:** Session COS set in host COSTAB as VRID (0–15) + TP (0–2; Low-Mid-High)	**COS:** Session COS defined as link, node, mode. Link COS characteristics include: allowed effective capacity, cost/connect time, cost/byte, RAR security level, propagation delay, user-defined variables
Datagram service characteristics	Flow control	Sliding window protocol	Adaptive pacing protocol	Adaptive pacing protocol
	Segmentation	Default IP datagram size = 576 octets Default receive segment size = 536 octets TCP max window size = 65,536 octets	RUsize ≤ 32K bytes Architecture defines ≤ 64K bytes Max window size = (64Kb) (256) = 16,777,216 bytes	RUsize ≤ 32K bytes Architecture defines ≤ 64K bytes Max window size = (64Kb) (256) = 16,777,216 bytes
	Security	Kerberos Access control filters MD-5 message-digest algorithm (symmetric) US DES (symmetric)	NBS DES/ANSI DEA Session ID/User ID Conversation-level security	NBS DES/ANSI DEA Session ID/User ID Conversation-level security
Connection service characteristics	Connection service characteristics	16-bit port value plus IP address equals socket Pair of sockets links processes Reliable, two-way data stream TCP connection distinguishes communicating process pairs	Pair of LU half-sessions comprise 1 LU session	Pair of LU half-sessions comprise 1 LU session APPN/ISR label-swaps LFSID at each NN along path FQPCID is net-unique session ID
	Congestion control	Sliding windows, slow start	Adaptive and fixed pacing	APPN/ISR, hop-by-hop adaptive pacing
	Network management	SNMP MIB	SNA MS NMVT RUs Focal/entry/service points	SNA MS NMVT RUs Nested/satellite focal points APPN MDS-MU using GDS SNMP/CMIP directions

8.7 Upper-layer issues and application program interfaces

The prevailing client/server user requirement is for openness. "Openness" to a user means the ability to access any remote application on demand with transparence, regardless of the requester or server processor architectures, runtime environments, or locations.

Unfortunately, distributed applications and their runtime platforms have been anything but open. Incompatible platforms and applications have been the primary cause of schedule and budgetary problems, both for network professionals who must build and manage the information resource, as well as for developers. Standards organizations have long pursued vendor-independent solutions but standardization-by-committee has been overtaken by selecting what is currently available. Recent history has shown that "standard standards" have not emerged or been maintained.

8.7.1 API approach

APIs provide a promising and architecture-neutral remedy to the incompatibility among end systems by enhancing application portability. An API acts as a structured protocol boundary situated between a transaction program (TP) and its underlying transport network. A TP exchanges interprogram requests, data and results across an API with its local network interface. In this way, the API logically connects the local TP to a remote TP.

Benefits to be potentially derived from APIs are quite significant and include:

- Significantly less user resistance to new solutions due to predictable similarities in end user interface across platforms

- Reliable integration of distributed, mission-critical applications

- Marked improvements in productivity of network application development

- Resistance to product obsolescence even in the midst of diminishing life cycles

- Higher development and implementation productivity due to predictable interfaces across platforms

- Enhanced likelihoods of computer manufacturer, third-party networked application developer, and end user implementation projects being completed on-time within budget

- Substantial improvements in productivity throughout all business units of an organization

- Dramatic improvements in programmer productivity, especially as APIs become increasingly object-oriented
- Closure of the chasm between host-centric and network-centric developers due to common look-and-feel throughout the distributed information resource
- Substantial improvements in organizational agility to respond to the demands of internal and external change
- High probability of meeting the fundamental user requirement: to access, create, view, and/or distribute data and information on demand in a cost-effective way
- Increased likelihood of creating applications that are kept transparent of transport network architectures

8.7.2 Which API?

Organizations tend to select SNA/APPN because their applications use IBM APIs such as high-level language application program interface (HLLAPI; provides 3270 device emulation from a PC into a host application), APPC API, and CPI-C. Similarly, TCP/IP networks have historically been selected to interconnect applications locally using the sockets interface (TCP/IP also supports nonsocket interfaces as well).

Both APPC/CPI-C and sockets APIs support conversations based upon transactions, or logical units of work between client and server program pairs. Several users have experienced that their distributed enterprise resources contain a mixture of SNA/APPN and TCP/IP networks. It is therefore important to consider major cases of API environments.

8.7.3 APPC API

IBM released APPC/LU 6.2 in 1982 to support interprogram communications within a CICS host. During the next few years APPC was enabled across all of IBM's major platforms, including System/36, System/38, AS/400, DOS, OS/2, and RS/6000. In addition, many more IBM vendors began supporting APPC. APPC began to support interprogram connections outside of host environments altogether, providing the basis for network-centric client/server computing.

APPC is equivalent to LU 6.2. LU 6.2, in turn, is IBM's mechanism to provide program-to-program connectivity within an SNA session. The APPC API provides an interface between applications and the underlying session and network resources. As such, the APPC API constructs a protocol boundary across which TPs and LU 6.2 interact. Transaction programs are not separate, standalone programs. Rather, they are generally implemented as modules within the application responsible for processing

Table 8.14   APPC API advantages and disadvantages

Advantages	Disadvantages
Partner application independent Optimized for network performance Protocol supports security Processing overhead distributed among program partners Robust reporting of errors Orderly termination of conversation TP can engage in multiple concurrent conversations Syncpoint support for protected resources	Runtime platform dependencies Code not portable among environments Incompatible base and option set functions Steep developer and implementer learning curves Loss of productivity across multiple platforms Deepens classical host-workstation rift

transactions. Transactions, in turn, are logical units of work involving data exchange between two programs. The APPC API provides these transactions as conversations.

The major advantages and disadvantages of the APPC API are summarized in table 8.14.

8.7.4 CPI-C

CPI-C was developed by IBM based upon APPC to resolve interplatform inconsistencies. CPI-C, like APPC API, provides a protocol boundary between transaction programs and LU 6.2. In so doing, CPI-C enables conversations between local/remote program pairs over LU 6.2 sessions.

The internal CPI-C call-request environment enables a local CPI-C transaction program to request a conversation with a remote CPI-C program by issuing an `Initialize_Conversation` call with a symbolic destination name `sym_dest_name`. The `sym_dest_name` is used within the node to look up side information consisting of `partner_LU_name`, `mode_name`, and `TP_name`.

This initial conversation call setup mechanism is far more straightforward in CPI-C than with the APPC API. The APPC API requires each conversation-requesting program to present and define all of the conversation and remote program/LU characteristics prior to conversation startup. CPI-C simply receives a `sym_dest_name` symbolic parameter and looks up all remote characteristics independent of the involvement of the requesting program.

The functional levels of CPI-C are summarized in table 8.15.

CPI-C, like APPC API, supports the conversational model. The conversational model provides for a logical connection between two applications where one is "speaking" and the other is "listening."

The major advantages and disadvantages of CPI-C are summarized in table 8.16.

8.7.5 Sockets

The sockets interface was developed originally to support UNIX IPC, or the sharing of data between between processes, on the same machine or across a network. From an IPC perspective, a socket is an IPC channel with its endpoints defined by descriptors. Processes connected through sockets can then read and write through the defined communications channel. (UNIX also supports other IPC APIs including Pipes and FIFOs, message queues, semaphores, shared memory, and TLI.)

The sockets API, based historically upon Berkeley sockets, and TLI have become prevalent IPC APIs, and are functionally quite similar from the perspective of an API developer. For example, the majority of RPC schemes are built atop either TLI or the sockets API.

The sockets interface is provided as both a stream interface for TCP (connection-oriented) and as a datagram interface for UDP connectionless. The sockets stream interface provides a full-duplex conversation that conveys data between a pair of interacting programs. Communicating applications can simultaneously send and receive data as a stream of bytes, rather than as one or more logical records (APPC API and CPI-C send/receive data as logical

Table 8.15   CPI-C functional levels

CPI-C level		Functions
	CPI-C 1.0	Standard base for conversational model Confirmation processing Error processing Conversation flow optimization Set and extract conversation characteristics
	CPI-C 1.1	CPI-C 1.0 base Resource recovery – Protected conversations – Distributed transactions – Syncpoint processing resource recovery Automatic parameter conversion Support for communication with non-CPI-C programs Local/remote transparency
	X/Open extensions	CPI-C 1.1 base Support for nonblocking calls Multiple conversation accept Support for data conversion (beyond parameters) Support for security parameters
	CPI-C 1.2	X/Open support for nonblocking calls X/Open support for data conversion X/Open support for security parameter specification Multiple conversations accept
	CPI-C 1.2 extensions	Server support – Name registration – Accept multiple incoming conversations – Nonblocking incoming call accepts – Context management Conversation security – Additional side information and conversation characteristics Data conversion utilities – Incoming/outgoing data EBCDIC/local encoding Extended buffer sizes

	CPI-C 2.0	Conversation send/receive FDX or HDX
		– Conversation queues; independent
		    logical channels
		Data send/receive on expedited flows
		Nonblocking enhancements
		– One outstanding conversation queue
		– Asynchronous completion notification
		Server accept conversation at specific address
		Distributed directory
		– Access via distinguished name from
		    side information
		Distributed security
		– Third-party authentication
		Automatic data conversion
		Multiprotocol support
		– CPI-C extensions for OSI TP
		– Multiprotocol transport network TCP/IP
		    interface
		Secondary return codes

Table 8.16 CPI-C advantages and disadvantages

Advantages	Disadvantages
Simpler, more powerful API than APPC API Platform-independent code portability Partner application independent Optimized for network performance Protocol supports security Processing overhead distributed among program partners Robust reporting of errors Orderly termination of conversation TP can engage in multiple concurrent conversations Syncpoint support for protected resources	Not supported in pre-ESA hosts

records). The stream interface support a basic function set of OPEN (or, LISTEN), SEND, RECEIVE, READ, WRITE, STATUS, CLOSE.

Figure 8.36 illustrates the creation of Telnet sockets with Internet ports and connection. TCP provides a reliable, serial communications path or virtual circuit, between processes (shown as client and server processes in the figure) that can send and receive in full duplex. The TCP objective is to achieve reliable, sequenced delivery of a stream of octets using an underlying, unreliable datagram service (IP). To fulfill this objective, TCP provides retransmission on timeouts and positive acknowledgments on data receipt. Due to the dual TCP artifacts of out-of-order data arrival and data duplication upon retransmission, TCP maintains an implicit 32-bit sequence number of each octet sent.

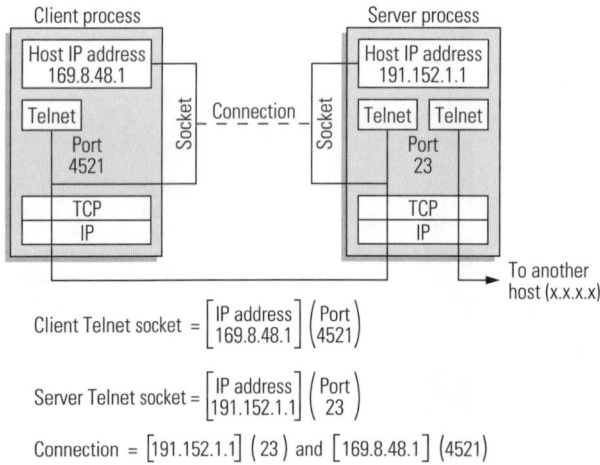

$$\text{Client Telnet socket} = \begin{bmatrix} \text{IP address} \\ 169.8.48.1 \end{bmatrix} \begin{pmatrix} \text{Port} \\ 4521 \end{pmatrix}$$

$$\text{Server Telnet socket} = \begin{bmatrix} \text{IP address} \\ 191.152.1.1 \end{bmatrix} \begin{pmatrix} \text{Port} \\ 23 \end{pmatrix}$$

$$\text{Connection} = \begin{bmatrix} 191.152.1.1 \end{bmatrix} \begin{pmatrix} 23 \end{pmatrix} \text{ and } \begin{bmatrix} 169.8.48.1 \end{bmatrix} \begin{pmatrix} 4521 \end{pmatrix}$$

Figure 8.36 Telnet sockets with Internet ports and connection

The client and server processes depicted in figure 8.36 are shown as running in internet hosts that are identified by IP addresses in the form x.x.x.x (described earlier). Each client and server process has a number of logical, full-duplex ports through which it can set up and use TCP connections. Note that port 23 is well known in the Internet as a Telnet server port.

A socket, as shown in figure 8.36, is the combination of host IP address and port. The TCP service (defined as a TCP service model in RFC 793 and RFC 1122) provides port identifiers to application processes on request, and a pair of related sockets creates a connection that links the client and server processes by a reliable, serial, two-way data stream. Note also that the server Telnet process shown in figure 8.36 is involved in more than one connection.

A major advantage of the sockets stream interface (used by TCP/IP) is that it places all received data into the correct order. The stream interface also provides congestion control. Further, if the underlying network fails or otherwise loses data, TCP provides automatic recovery.

The sockets datagram interface (used by UDP) provides simple transport of individual data packets as compared to data streams. Datagrams are connectionless and therefore do not allocate resources for each supported client program. The main advantage is that the datagram interface supports a relatively larger number of clients from a given server than does the stream interface.

The major tradeoff is that datagram applications create complexity due to the need to handle the order of received data. Individual data packets can traverse various paths through the network and may arrive out of order, requiring the receive application to buffer all data while waiting for outstanding packets, then subsequently reordering packets prior to final destination delivery.

The datagram interface also requires the application to understand network frame sizes. This is because the application must either generate packets able to fit within a single network-allowed frame or must segment data into multiple packets. Segmentation into multiple packets requires the receiving application to reassemble.

Table 8.17 summarizes the advantages and disadvantages of the sockets interface.

Table 8.17 Sockets advantages and disadvantages

Advantages	Disadvantages
Nearly universal IPC interface Client/server model HDX and FDX Stream interface congestion control Datagram interface well-suited for LANs	Often no integral error notification No protected resource synchronization (However, both available with (e.g.) transactional RPC)

8.7.6 RPC

RPC is a logical extension to local procedure call (LPC). It is based on a request-and-reply model that uses the client/server computing paradigm. In both RPC and LPC, control is passed among code segments and returns to the original segment. The major distinction however, is that whereas in LPC, all code segments reside in the same address space, in RPC, the called procedure runs in a separate address space (and generally, in a separate processor altogether) from the calling procedure. RPC arguments and return values are packed into messages and transmitted to the remote program over the network.

Importantly, the RPC mechanism appears to the programmer or user as a local procedure call. RPC provides an LPC view by hiding details of client/server networking. These details include:

- Invocation of directory services
- Use of any secured services
- Handling of various data formats (e.g., byte ordering) between possibly heterogeneous processor environments
- Fragmentation/reassembly of messages

In the RPC request-and-reply model, a client procedure sends requests to the server procedure that returns replies. Both the client and server processes interconnect and communicate through the use of stubs. Stubs are networking interfaces that specify how messages are constructed and exchanged. Stubs contain functions that map simple LPCs into a series of network RPC function calls.

Client and server processes require the ability to interconnect across a network using process architecture-independent data representation. RPC supports a single-canonical format that enables client and server stubs to translate local data to/from this form.

The major advantages and disadvantages of RPC are summarized in table 8.18.

Table 8.18 RPC advantages and disadvantages

Advantages	Disadvantages
No communication calls are required in programs Protocol and network independent Natural, intuitive extension of programmer skills Endorsed by OSF DCE for client/server	Program is blocked during call processing Complex programming may be required to build and administer subroutine stubs Program cannot change server without using complex verbs and bindings All data must be prepared prior to issuing call Multiple subroutings require calling tree

8.7.7 HLLAPI

While computing market mindshare and investment streams alike have embraced client/server computing and its web-enabled intranet extensions, 3270 applications are still playing a big role in many enterprises. Terminals have been increasingly replaced with PCs running 3270 terminal emulation software.

HLLAPI, emulator HLLAPI (EHLLAPI) and entry EHLLAPI (EEHLLAPI) provide a set of functions on a PC that simulate a user operating a 3270 terminal, including 3270 screen interaction, sending and receiving data, performing screen searches, and waiting for new screens to be delivered by the host. HLLAPI interacts with a host presentation space—an area of working memory on the workstation that is used to exchange data with the host application.

Table 8.19 provides an overview of HLLAPI advantages and disadvantages.

Table 8.19   HLLAPI advantages and disadvantages

Advantages	Disadvantages
3270 terminals increasingly replaced by workstations Extends life of host applications No additional host programming required PC/WS can interact with multiple hosts Provides GUI intuitive user interface	Host application-dependent Server must always reside on host No direct host communications Dependent upon 3270 data stream Imprecise late screen arrival error messages Unpredictable response times Password expiration coding complexity 3270 transfers restricted by screen size Cannot build next screen until previous screen returned

The major deficiency with HLLAPI in the current networked environments is that it does not enable client/server computing. The major client/server constraint is that the HLLAPI side is always governed by the host application; programs are not able to communicate as peers.

Several users have begun to convert HLLAPI applications to CPI-C/APPC interprogram environments. The advantages to conversion include:

- APPC (LU6.2) is specifically designed for distributed processing, and is an interprogram, peer-to-peer protocol. Therefore, programs interact as cooperative peers. HLLAPI, on the other hand, enforces host control over the workstation side.

- CPI-C is platform-independent.

- CPI-C/APPC provide for direct communications between client and server processes and support an extensive set of return codes and status indicators. These codes distinguish between recoverable and unrecoverable errors and provide extensive diagnostics to aid in restoration.

- APPC optimizes data transfer across platforms and intermediate nodes and links, based upon APPN node logic.

- APPC data transfers are not encumbered by 3270 screen size. Applications can send and receive up to 32Kbytes of data in a single record. Performance is therefore dramatically improved over a screen-based environment.

- APPC provides several built-in security measures to protect resources from unauthorized access, both at session and conversation levels.

- APPC is continuously aware of the status of communications with its partner program.

- 3270 applications can be converted to APPC.

However, conversion of 3270 to APPC requires significant rewrite of host as well as workstation code. While the client/server benefits are compelling, some users may conclude that their embedded base of host-terminal applications is sufficient to accomplish enterprise work processes. An interesting alternative is to migrate VTAM and 3174 controller code to supporting dependent LU server-requester. This will enable dependent SNA LU sessions (LU0, 1, 2, 3) to run over APPN connections with all of the network node topology, directory, and route selection services.

8.7.8 MQI

MQI is provided by IBM to support a messaging and queuing model. In this environment, programs do not need to be concurrently available to the underlying transport network resource. MQI provides an asynchronous, distributed message delivery service. MQI elements include applications, queue managers, and queues. The intervening transport between MQI systems can be either SNA/APPN or TCP/IP.

8.7.9 Selecting the appropriate interface

Recent solutions for application-level drivers to client/server have been to either run APPC API and CPI-C over SNA/APPN, or to interconnect sockets-supporting applications over TCP/IP or UDP/IP. Several enterprise networks have evolved separate SNA and TCP/IP infrastructures. These infrastructures have generally been developed in isolation from one another.

Whereas TCP/IP traces its history to WAN developments in the late 1960s and early 1970s, the majority of TCP/IP applications developed during the 1980s ran over LAN environments in addition to WANs.

SNA networks were historically host-centric over wide areas. APPN provides the basis for peer-to-peer, client/server SNA over local as well as wide areas. Therefore, both SNA/APPN and TCP/IP have converged to support LAN as well as WAN.

Furthermore, CPI-C and APPN have become increasingly open to non-IBM protocols and approaches. Concurrently, router providers have made great headway during the latter 1980s and early 1990s in connecting LANs running TCP/IP and a variety of additional protocols over wide areas.

One result of these trends has been that solutions within an organization are increasingly incoherent in the face of increased requirements for interoperability. Architectural, operational, and budgetary realities dictate the need for network implementers to either:

- Select SNA/APPN
- Select TCP/IP
- Select a workable, integrated, hybrid approach
- Select something else entirely

A proactive, engineered approach to network infrastructure selection is to first determine present and future user application requirements, then ensure that the networked applications use the most appropriate interface to networked resources. Selection of the appropriate interface requires consideration of at least the following possible networked applications requirements:

- Run on multiple, heterogeneous platforms, processor architectures, and operating environments
- Support full-duplex as well as half-duplex conversations for transaction processing
- Provide server support of multiple, concurrent clients
- Provide reasonable and distributed security
- Ensure adequate throughput and response time profiles for the entire range of distributed application scenarios, from simple inquiry-response to complex multimedia applications
- Include synchronization of remote and distributed databases
- Report errors

APPC API, CPI-C, sockets, and RPC each provide several advantages and disadvantages. The "bottom line," it should be emphasized, is that the most appropriate API is the natural result of the interfacing application. Application program interfaces can be converted, as described above for the HLLAPI-to-CPI-C/APPC case.

However, with the advent of MPTN, and subsequent decoupling of applications from underlying transport network infrastructures, connection of like API pairs over mixed transports is now technically feasible. This presents users who have evolved dual or multiple networks with the opportunity to consolidate infrastructures while maintaining previously existing APIs.

8.7.10 *When to select CPI-C*

In general, it is recommended that CPI-C be selected as a migration from APPC API. CPI-C and sockets are each evolving interfaces and each provide reasonable support for interoperability, half-duplex conversations, multiple concurrent clients and error reporting.

CPI-C provides full-duplex conversations at level 2.0 and onward. However, a significant percentage of client/server applications are transaction-oriented where the data are tightly coupled and correlated, lending themselves quite well to relatively noncomplex half-duplex coded environments.

Dramatic improvements in technology cost/performance ratios have spawned myriad desktop and server-based applications. Users increasingly require these programs to access remote and distributed databases. A major distributed database requirement is that of synchronization, where a local program cannot continue processing data until the data sent to the partner program have been received, processed, and acknowledged.

CPI-C provides both simple interprogram synchronization through the use of Confirm and Confirmed calls, as well as database Commit and Rollback support through the use of sync point services provided in CPI-resource recovery.

Users who have predominantly IBM SNA applications and need interprogram connectivity would best be served using APPC API over subarea networks and CPI-C over APPN networks. Users who have predominantly TCP/IP applications would do well maintaining sockets and RPC over TCP/IP or UDP/IP.

8.7.11 *When to select sockets*

Sockets support the conversational interface within client/server application environments, and are a natural interface for UNIX applications as well as any other TCP/IP or UDP/IP environment. Several TCP/IP applications make use of sockets, including RPC. As pointed out in the networking blueprint discussion, users who have developed applications using sockets but must also connect sockets and RPC through SNA/APPN transports in addition to TCP/IP or UDP/IP, can access remote sockets applications over these mixed transports. Again, like RPC, sockets are function-poor when compared with CPI-C. These deficiencies are, as with RPC, accommodated by use of other TCP/IP functions such as Kerberos and Encina to have functional richness comparable to CPI-C.

8.7.12 When to select RPC

RPC is a natural interface for applications that need to connect using a call requester model. Transactional RPC integrates two-phase commit for protected database resources. Kerberos security can also be used with RPC.

The relative absence of RPC (as well as sockets) functionality compared to CPI-C and APPC derive from some of the traditional goals and assumptions about TCP/IP as compared to SNA, described earlier in this chapter. That is, SNA was, from the beginning, designed to incorporate as much functionality as possible for commercial, mission-critical applications. A major early TCP/IP design point was relatively minimalist, to allow the distributed resource to collectively provide functions as needed. In this sense, RPC does provide all needed functions for the distributed call-request model in concert with additional TCP/IP or distributed computing environment components.

8.7.13 When to select MQI

MQI should be selected for applications that need to send data in store-forward fashion and are not response time-sensitive for that type of operation.

Messaging—and queuing—is interesting for several reasons:

- MQI is an asynchronous interface that provides store-and-forward networking and does not require participating program pairs to be concurrently available to the transport network

- MQI supports distributed database resource synchronization for commit and roll-out, through inclusion of message queues within transaction-based units of work

- MQI-participating applications need not be aware of the physical location of network queues

- MQI-participating applications can interconnect through SNA/APPN, TCP/IP, or other transport networks. This aspect of MQI makes it behave as middleware, effectively separating applications and the underlying transport infrastructure. MQI is an interface between an application program and its local queue manager.

8.7.14 Networking blueprint and MPTN

As stated earlier, distributed users and their applications need to connect and share resources transparently and coherently, yet find themselves operating within increasingly incompatible networks (the major reasons for the emergence of increasingly complex and incompatible networks are provided in the introduction to this chapter). A predominant requirement that has emerged in the wake of this issue is to enable connection of like APIs across mixed (native as well as nonnative) underlying transport networks.

IBM has forwarded a Networking Blueprint as an architectural response to the problem of increasing coexistence of multiple API/transport solutions within an organization. (See chapter 6 for additional information.) Networking blueprint objectives are:

- Integrate transaction processing, LAN and WAN solutions to allow applications running over diverse platforms to interconnect and share resources coherently. That is, to enable connection of same APIs across mixed transport networks.

- Support program-to-program communications services including conversational, remote procedure call, and messaging and queuing

- Support multiprotocol, multimedia and multivendor networking and application elements within a consistent structure

- Exploit the emergence of high speed, high bandwidth communications and carrier technologies and services such as ATM to provide effective and efficient carriage of fixed as well as variable packet lengths, diverse priority algorithms, spectrum-shaping of offered loads, bandwidth utilization metrics, optimal route assignment, and solution-independent network management

In essence, the blueprint objective is to enable connection of distributed applications calling the same APIs across any major transport network. This means, for example, that a pair of CPI-C applications could interconnect across IP as well as APPN networks. Alternatively, a pair of sockets or RPC applications could interconnect across APPN as well as IP networks. This architectural objective is being met with the emergence of MPTN. (See chapter 13 for additional details.)

8.7.15 Unified Network Model

In order to ensure end user and application transparency from the underlying application support, transport network and subnetworking functions, a Unified Network Model is proposed and presented in figure 8.37 as a fundamental extension to the networking blueprint introduced in figure 8.32. This model would enable any client/server program pair to interconnect and share data within any API-to-any-API, mixed transport networks.

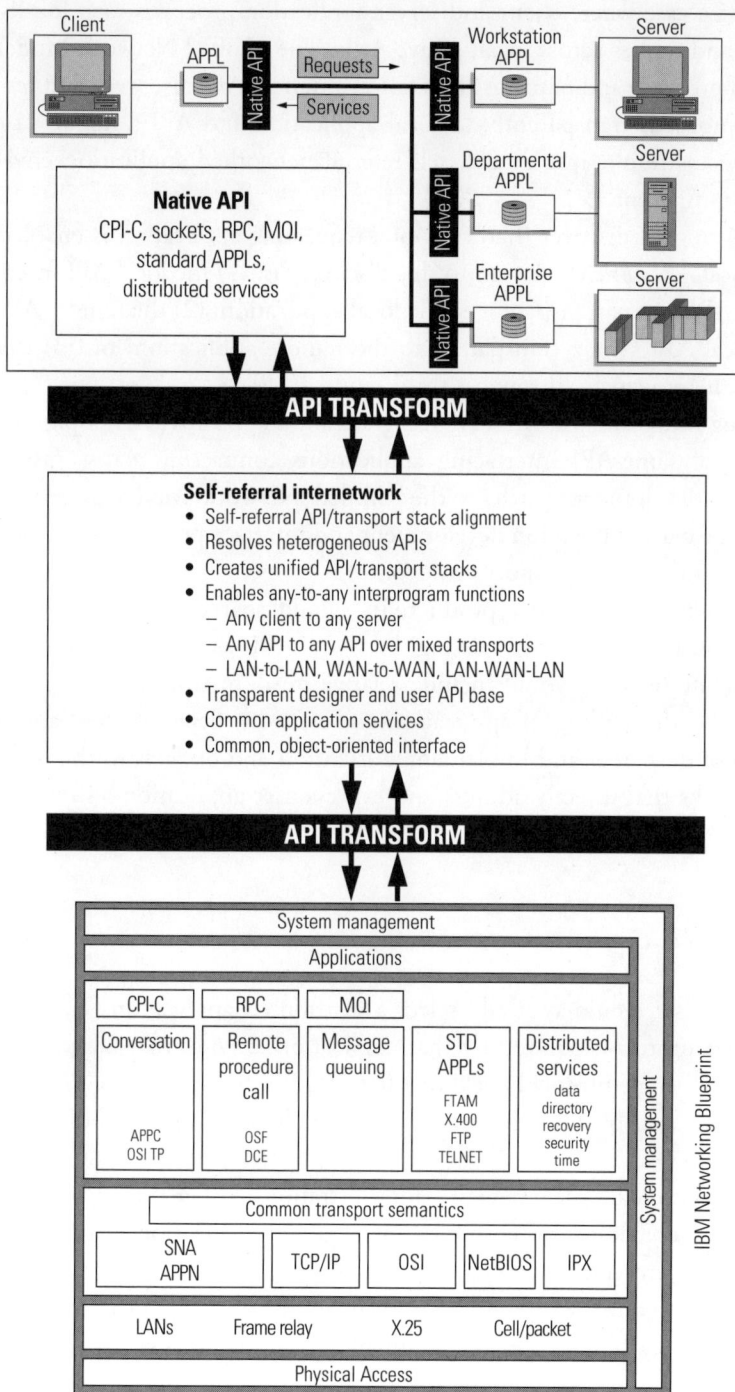

Figure 8.37 Unified Network Model

Figure 8.37 shows a case where client and server application processes each locally send/receive requests and replies across local, native APIs. The Unified Network Model provides, at each local program and native API instance, a remote API discovery and resolution process that proceeds transparently to local application and API awareness or involvement. This process results in a global, self-referral networked application environment that is API-transparent.

Local APIs in this model discover that a remote, requesting application is enabled through a different local API. The resolution to this discovery is: (1) the local API interfaces through remote API syntax transparent to the local application; (2) the remote API interfaces through local API syntax transparent to the remote application; or, (3) the two APIs resolve their heterogeneity through a third, unified API.

IBM's Networking Blueprint and MPTN are significant and positive developments to enable coexistence of same-API interfacing applications connecting across mixed transport networks. A development such as the Unified Network Model presented herein would serve to insulate application development and interface processes from one another in addition to underlying transport protocols.

Application and network developer productivity would soar due to removal of tightly coupled relationships currently existing between API as well as transport environments. Immediate benefits would include relative freedom from platform and application obsolescence, decoupling of application and network dependencies, and a significant refocusing of developer and implementer attention and budgets to the business of building networks that directly address and express user application and work-group requirements.

8.8 Convergence

In the past, a network user would typically select a distributed applications environment, install the native protocol required by that applications environment, and then install the corresponding single protocol backbone (e.g., APPN for CPI-C, TCP/IP for sockets). Often different parts of the same organization would standardize on different protocols.

As organizations consolidate their network administrations, either through a need to reduce network costs, or because of corporate mergers and acquisitions, or for any other reason, they find themselves with many protocols—SNA, TCP/IP, IPX, XNS, DECnet, AppleTalk, and so on. Users would like to converge to a single protocol, but, as the following discussion emphasizes, such a requirement is difficult to satisfy.

Like it or not, a high degree of dependency exists between application services and their underlying interfaces, transport protocol, and networking backbone. In traditional network design and deployment, it has been difficult (if not impossible) to mix and match applications, protocols, and internetworks.

Analysis of two terminal emulation architectures, 3270 from the SNA/APPN environment and telnet from the TCP/IP environment, characterizes the types of dependencies common in internetworking. First, in the SNA environment, 3270 is the dominant block mode terminal type. 3270 is heavily utilized in IBM mainframe environments and, to a lesser extent, in AS/400 environments. To fully utilize 3270:

- A 3270 device (whether cluster controller or desktop emulator) implements a data stream called the 3270 data stream, which is used for all application services. The 3270 data stream runs over an SNA LU 2 session type.

- Because the device requires logon/logoff, attention keys, response time management flows, and application interaction services, it requires both SNA SSCP–LU services and SNA LU–LU services.

- The networking backbone routes the 3270 session data, through use of both SSCP–LU (LU 0) and LU–LU (LU 2) sessions.

Second, in the TCP/IP environment, telnet (RFC 854/855) is the common method for providing character mode terminal access to hosts (usually dumb terminal emulations such as VT100/200). To implement telnet:

- Telnet requires an interface to character-streaming service, that is, the Berkeley UNIX `sockets()` interface (although some implementations use other operating system interfaces). The sockets interface maps to TCP transport, which runs over IP.

- The networking backbone routes IP.

In both the TCP/IP and SNA environments, strong dependencies exist between the layers. 3270 requires LU 2 SNA transport, which requires an SNA backbone. Telnet requires TCP transport, which, in turn, requires an IP backbone. There are mappings of 3270 data stream to other transports, for example, IETF tn3270 (3270-TCP/IP) and appc3270.

Usually some of the 3270 device functionality is lost in the mapping, such as some elements of the status line and toggle to/from the SSCP control session, all of which depend on characteristics of the type of SNA session. (This analysis does not argue that some may find the loss of function acceptable. Rather, to obtain full function today, strong application/protocol dependencies exist.)

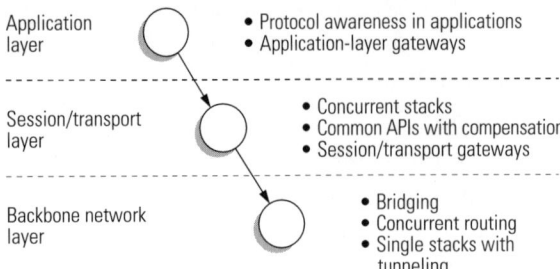

Application layer
- Protocol awareness in applications
- Application-layer gateways

Session/transport layer
- Concurrent stacks
- Common APIs with compensation
- Session/transport gateways

Backbone network layer
- Bridging
- Concurrent routing
- Single stacks with tunneling

Figure 8.38   Mixed protocol inter-networking convergence model

8.8.1 A model for mixed protocol internetworking

Most published analyses of multiprotocol internetworking tend to focus on one layer or another. To organize the thinking about multiprotocol integration, a more general model is needed as a framework for discussion. This model is used for the remainder of this analysis. Figure 8.38 shows three layers at which multiprotocol convergence can be applied:

- Backbone network layer convergence
  - bridging
  - concurrent routing
  - single stack with tunneling
- Session/transport layer convergence
  - concurrent stacks
  - session/transport gateways
- Application layer convergence
  - terminal, electronic mail, others
  - application gateways

Figure 8.39 is a pyramid that shows the relative impact of achieving convergence at each of the three figure 8.38 layers. Convergence functions achieved at the backbone layer affect all end systems. Convergence functions achieved at the session/transport layer affect all end systems with session/transport compensations installed, and a subset of end systems running native protocols. Convergence functions achieved at the applications layer affect all end systems running those applications. Nevertheless convergence at all three layers is required.

The convergence options available at each layer for TCP/IP and SNA environments are described in the following sections.

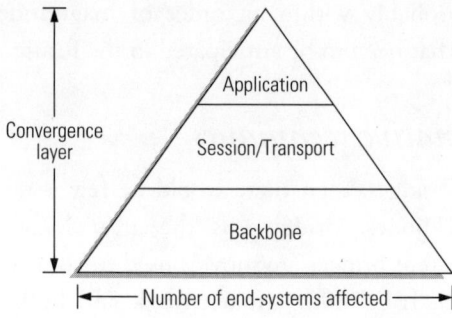

Figure 8.39   Breadth-of-coverage pyramid for convergence approach

8.8.2 Backbone network-layer convergence techniques

Figure 8.40 shows the challenge and the opportunity for creating a converged multiprotocol backbone. The alternatives are bridging backbones, concurrent routing backbones, and single stack backbones with tunneling.

Consider as a model for the future scale of backbone networks the worldwide voice/telephone network. This network is composed of over 600 million end systems (telephone instruments). The voice network makes heavy use of source routing (9 to leave the local private exchange, 1 to leave the local public exchange, etc.) but does not use multicast for address discovery functions, and does not support concurrent sessions

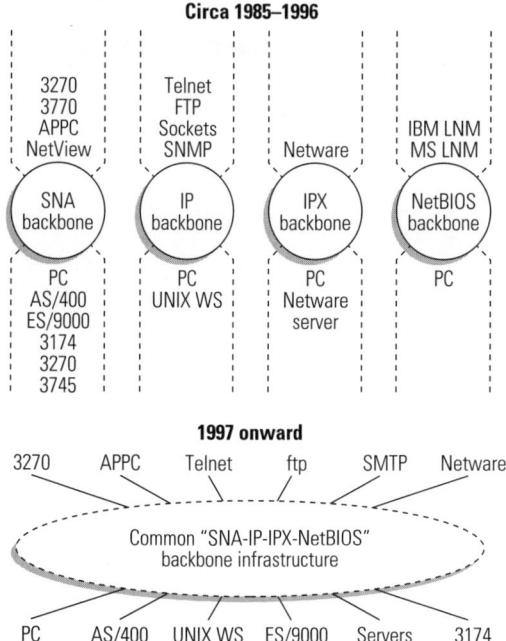

Figure 8.40   Backbone convergence challenge 1985–1994

over the same link. The voice network is probably within an order of magnitude (smaller) than the scale of backbone networks that need to be anticipated in the future.

8.8.3 Backbone convergence via native techniques

If it were feasible to build all networks with bridges, then there would be few issues about creating converged multiprotocol backbones. Bridging is the great leveler. Figure 8.41 shows bridges (source route transparent bridges are shown) used to connect multiple LAN media—IEEE 802.3 (Ethernet), IEEE 802.5 (token ring), and FDDI (X3T9/90).

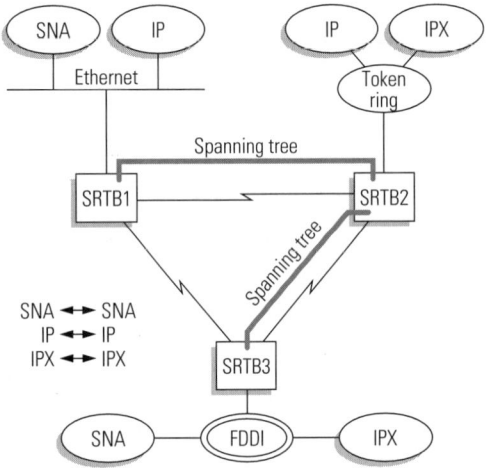

Figure 8.41 Bridges for multiprotocol environment

Bridges have the following characteristics:

- Bridges forward traffic based upon MAC layer addressing (48 bits for most IEEE 802.x LANs, 60 bits for IEEE 802.6).

- Bridges are LAN/MAN/WAN media independent; they can interconnect Ethernet, token ring, FDDI, SMDS, and so on.

- Bridging functions are independent of upper layer protocols; SNA, TCP/IP, IPX, and so on. All can be handled by bridging.

Inasmuch as higher layer protocols sometimes carry MAC layer addresses as data fields, there are exceptions to the above statements. Token ring is a particularly problematic environment, since the token ring designers chose a MAC address encoding scheme that is inverted bit-by-bit from all other IEEE 802.x media types. Thus token ring bridges must examine frames sent by certain protocols, for example, IPs ARP, and all data fields carrying MAC addresses must be bitwise-inverted when leaving/entering token ring environments.

Another issue exists with token ring's unique multicasting scheme (function addressing), which is incompatible with IEEE 802 standard methods for multicasting. These problems were overcome by the manufacturers of bridges that have developed workarounds.

Bridges, however, have not been popular as a general solution to the problem of internetworking for the following reasons:

- Bridges create a spanning tree path among connected clusters of bridges to prevent forwarding loops. Both data and path explorer frames are sent only along the spanning tree path. However, the spanning tree prevents bridges from utilizing alternate path routing to provide load leveling. In figure 8.41, for example, the spanning tree connects B1 to B2 to B3. No data can flow from B1 to B3, a more direct route (unless the topology reconfigures, e.g., a failure occurs between B1 and B2).

- Bridges have the potential to flood the network with the following types of traffic (a common problem when networks reinitialize, e.g., following a power failure):
  - The first frames from new MAC addresses (send the frame out through all active bridge ports)
  - Multicast frames
  - Broadcast frames

- Bridging does not include service enhancements such as prioritized handling of traffic.

- Source routing bridges have one additional problem: a limited number of hops.

Up to a certain level of network size and complexity, however, bridges are a viable solution to the problem of multiprotocol environments. Bridged environments as large as 32,000 nodes have been constructed.

Fast packet providers, for example, ATM vendors, have developed new core functions (switching) that make it possible to handle discovery frames and multicast/broadcast frames in more complex subnet mesh topologies. Bridging (or rather, switching)—with fast packet core assists—therefore sees a resurgence as an architecture of choice for constructing multiprotocol networks.

8.8.4 Backbone convergence via concurrent routing

Today's most realizable solution from a nuts-and-bolts perspective is to run concurrent routing within the backbone itself (figure 8.42). IP routing for IP; APPN routing for SNA; IPX routing for IPX, and so on. Each routing protocol handles its own address

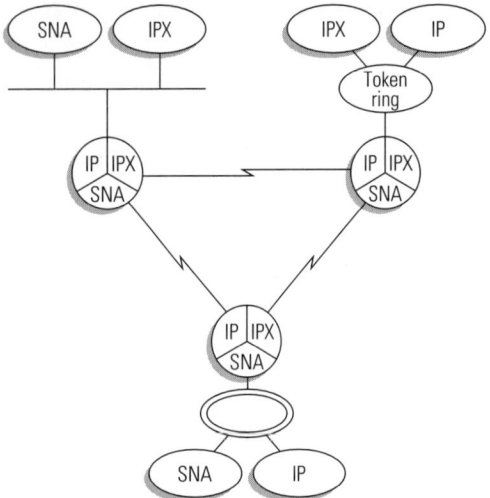

Figure 8.42   Concurrent backbone routing protocols

resolution, management, topology calculation and update as required by the individual protocols. Routing vendors today offer this solution for most protocols; the leading vendors support the most protocols. Within a single protocol more than one alternative may exist, for example, RIP or OSPF for IP routing, RIP or NLSP for IPX, and so on.

Benefits of concurrent routing include:

- Eliminates multicast and broadcast problems seen in bridged environments
- Enables the backbone to take advantage of alternate routes and load balancing on a session-by-session basis
- Enables the offering of protocol-specific services, such as class-of-service and security
- Allows the creation of protocol-specific routing topologies. (Not all routers may desire to participate in IPX routing, for example.)

Problems with concurrent routing include:

- Redundant router-to-router control traffic is needed to communicate topology changes, link outages, congestion. This control traffic consumes some (small) bandwidth.
- Administration of multiple routing domains becomes an administrative chore, especially if the same topology is desired for multiple protocols.

Because of the benefits and strong demand for router-level functionality within each protocol family (e.g., multipath routing, elimination of broadcast storms, address

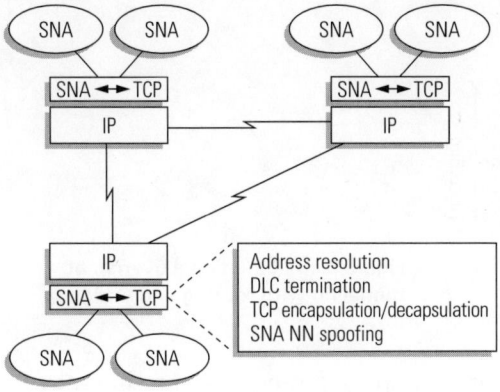

Figure 8.43 SNA tunneled over IP backbone

resolution) concurrent routing will grow in popularity for a few more years. Its decline will occur with the onset of fast packet networks with broadcast/multicast oriented core features.

8.8.5 Backbone convergence via tunneling techniques

Tunneling is one class of techniques for multiprotocol support that seems to be very popular in the multivendor backbone community today. Tunneling is a scheme for interfacing with nonnative protocols (nonnative from the perspective of the backbone network), and translating them to a protocol that can be routed over the native backbone protocol, for example, SNA over TCP/IP, IP over SNA/APPN.

Along with tunneling comes a variety of related techniques identified by buzzwords like encapsulation, termination, conversion, spoofing, passthrough, and remote polling.

Figure 8.43 shows a scenario for routing SNA over IP backbones and figure 8.44 shows the inverse scenario for routing IP over SNA backbones. Products do exist for each scenario. Unfortunately, the same cannot be said for standards (each vendor implements a proprietary tunneling scheme).

Before diving into the various flavors and copious details of tunneling, a bit more characterization is in order. Figure 8.45 summarizes typical features of tunneling schemes as compared to bridging and routing. As can

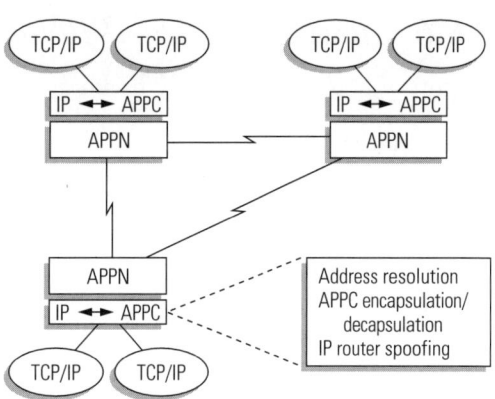

Figure 8.44 IP tunneled over SNA backbone

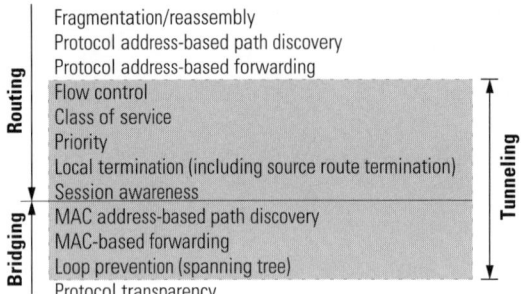

Routing

- Fragmentation/reassembly
- Protocol address-based path discovery
- Protocol address-based forwarding
- Flow control
- Class of service
- Priority
- Local termination (including source route termination)
- Session awareness

Tunneling

Bridging

- MAC address-based path discovery
- MAC-based forwarding
- Loop prevention (spanning tree)
- Protocol transparency

Figure 8.45   Functional overlap of tunneling with routing and bridging

be seen, tunneling is a hybrid technique for supporting protocols within internets. It contains elements of bridging and elements of routing. But tunneling is neither bridging nor routing. The design point for tunneling reflects a minimalist view of internetworking—do the barest minimum required to support a given protocol suite (or subset thereof), but not enough to qualify as full routing or full bridging.

Some might wonder why all the energy is being applied to tunneling schemes, when standard bridging and routing schemes are already available and accomplish the same objectives. The common thinking on this issue is that tunneling results in more memory-efficient implementations (vs. full routing), and that tunneling enables a more direct mapping to transport pipes within the single protocol backbone.

While such thinking contains an element of rationality, sometimes the solutions derived can approach the complexity of the original bridging/routing standards, but not exhibit the generality. For example, DLSw resolved the problems of loop prevention (bridging), flow control (routing), and class-of-service (routing). Using a metaphor from mythology, sometimes opening Pandora's box generates the predicted result.

8.8.6 Tunneling SNA/APPN over IP

Support of SNA/APPN over IP backbones generates the following requirements:

- SNA over LAN LLC2
- SNA over WAN SDLC
- SNA over WAN X.25
- SNA over WAN frame relay
- Dependent LU support (3270 and other pre-APPC devices)
- Independent LU support (APPC)
- PU type 4 support (3745-to-3745)

APPN plus Dependent LU Requester extensions—the standard routing architecture for SNA—addresses all but the PU type 4 requirement.

One additional set of requirements surfaces because of the unique characteristics of token ring, source routing, LLC2, and NetBIOS/LLC2 protocol:

- Extend the reachability of source routed token ring beyond the hop count limit
- Limit explorer traffic generated by source routing
- Prevent LLC2 timer expiration caused by large latency diameter WANs
- Limit multicast traffic generated by NetBIOS/LLC2
- Locally terminate LLC2 connections for NetBIOS/LLC2

A variety of mechanisms is being promoted to address the above requirements. The first few are really not tunneling per se, but are included in the discussion for completeness.

8.8.7 SDLC conversion

SDLC conversion is a technique that transforms WAN-attached SDLC devices into LAN attached LLC2 devices. The SDLC connection is terminated within the SDLC conversion device. The SDLC device is still WAN-attached; the conversion device is attached to both SDLC and a LAN. SDLC conversion can also be used in native bridging and routing backbone conversion, since some implementations skip the SDLC to LLC2 step, and convert directly from SDLC to tunneled TCP.

Figure 8.46 shows the SDLC conversion in more detail. Shown are two SDLC devices, each a 3174 establishment cluster controller. Each SDLC device is addressed by a single-byte SDLC address, 01 and 02 in this example. (They could each have the same address since they are differentiated by port number, i.e., the first device could be port 01, address 01, and the second device, port 02, address 01.)

The SDLC converter locally terminates each SDLC data link (just as an APPN router would do). The converter handles all link initialization,

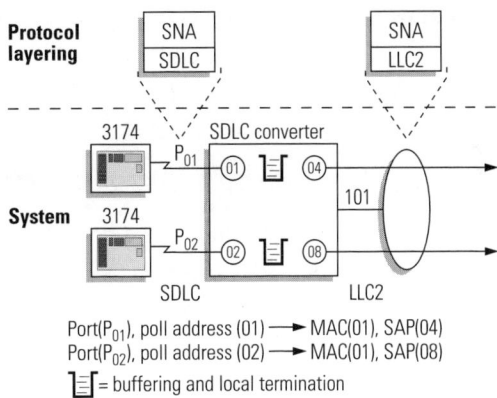

Figure 8.46   SDLC conversion with local termination

error recovery, half-duplex procedures, and inbound/outbound data buffering (sometimes this is called remote polling or proxy polling). The SDLC converter's MAC address on the token ring is 101. The basic logic of conversion, from an addressing perspective, is to map the tuple {port #, SDLC address} to the tuple {IEEE 802.5 MAC address, SAP address}.

In this case, Port(01)/Poll(01) gets mapped to MAC(101)/SAP(04), etc. Downstream devices, whether routers or bridges or front-end processors, see all data flow coming from a LAN-attached device with MAC(101) and different SAP values, one per SDLC device. On the WAN side of the SDLC conversion device, the protocol architecture is SNA over SDLC; on the LAN side it is SNA over LLC2.

From the LAN interface onward the data stream is a standard LAN-oriented SNA data stream. The data stream can be absorbed by the destination on the same LAN segment, local/remote bridged, or routed. The data stream is in native, not proprietary, format.

No easy way exists, outside of manual configuration, for identifying the target MAC/SAP address to which the SDLC device needs to be connected. Nor is there any way of performing session layer routing; only link layer. These kinds of correlations are really in the province of APPN routers. What most SDLC conversion manufacturers do is provide some type of defaults that the user can override and customize on a port-by-port basis. Usually all SDLC devices on a given SDLC conversion device will be ultimately connected to a single upstream 3745, and they will all use the same destination MAC address for link activation anyway.

Stand-alone SDLC conversion hardware will continue to grow in popularity as a migration technique for SDLC. The limitation of determining the destination address will be resolved by using a collapsed backbone architecture for SDLC (figure 8.47). In this configuration, only the address of the APPN router need be configured.

8.8.8 SDLC conversion variations

Other conversion techniques have been offered for SDLC; the SDLC conversion technique can also be used for other WAN data-link types. SDLC conversion is a fairly recent innovation. Originally, the internetworking vendors implemented alternate proprietary techniques. SDLC passthrough (depicted in figure 8.48) is a technique where every SDLC frame, whether control or data, is passed end-to-end. Matching SDLC encapsulators and deencapsulators have to be installed at each end of the link. (One vendor even maps the data stream over TCP telnet, one layer higher than TCP.)

Another technique—SDLC spoofing—recognizes that the polling traffic is nonproductive wasted bandwidth. In spoofing, the SDLC traffic is still passed end-to-end, but only a subset of the control traffic is passed end-to-end. Just enough of the polling

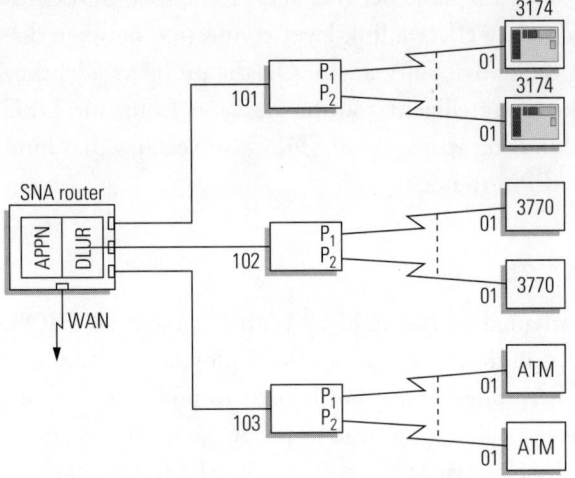

Figure 8.47   SDLC conversion in collapsed backbone configuration

ATM = Automated teller machine

traffic is allowed through to keep both ends happy enough to keep the link connection alive.

The same conversion technique can also be used for other WAN link types, for example:

- X.25 to LLC2
- Frame relay to LLC2

In fact, other combinations are possible:

- SDLC to X.25
- SDLC to frame relay
- X.25 to frame relay

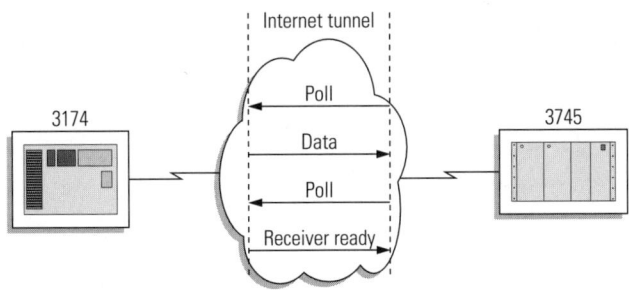

Figure 8.48   SDLC passthrough

All these conversion techniques share the same benefits and problems as SDLC-to-LLC2 conversion. On the benefit side, they effect a link-layer connection between dissimilar media types while preserving the native SNA stacks. On the problem side, they all suffer from the inability to make an intelligent routing decision from one DLC addressing space to the converted addressing space. As in SDLC conversion, that kind of mapping is in the province of the APPN router.

8.8.9 *LLC2 local termination*

IEEE 802.2 LLC2 is a connection-oriented service used by both SNA and NetBIOS. LLC2 contains two important connection timers relevant to the deployment of LLC2 in WAN topologies. The Ti timer is a keep alive timer that is used to poll a connection partner whenever the connection has been idle for a time (typically about 30 seconds). The T1 timer is a timer used to await acknowledgments (typically about 1 second). If either timer expires, resource recovery polls are sent to the connection partner. If no response is received after a period, the LLC2 connection is terminated.

LLC2 is capable of being bridged. It is also capable of being tunneled within alternate transports such as TCP/IP. However, the backbone networks supporting such alternate transports exhibit different (i.e., longer and more variable) delay characteristics than bridged backbones. Some router control points can introduce five-second delays just to reconfigure the topology of the backbone. Sometimes congestion may be the cause for the WAN delay. In any case, it is possible for WAN delays to cause LLC2 timers to expire, extra resource recovery polling traffic to be generated, and, in some cases, connections to be lost.

LLC2 local termination (figure 8.49) handles all LLC2 connection control functions in routers at the edge of the WAN: immediate acknowledgments, receiver ready, receiver not ready, and frame rejects. WAN delays therefore do not affect the integrity of LLC2 connections.

APPN routers also locally terminate LLC2 connections. Local termination is also used for SDLC conversion, for similar reasons.

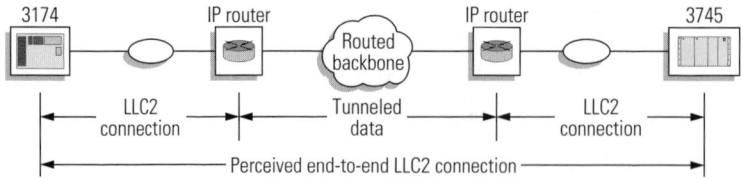

Figure 8.49   LLC2 local termination

8.8.10 Explorer propagation and NetBIOS multicast

Source routed systems use a route discovery scheme that floods the bridged network with discovery frames. NetBIOS also uses broadcast and multicast to register and search for NetBIOS names. Both discovery mechanisms can utilize a significant portion of WAN bandwidth and, in the case of explorer propagation, can utilize a significant portion of the bridge processing resources.

To address these issues, vendors have introduced schemes to minimize WAN traffic for explorer propagation and NetBIOS multicast. Three schemes have been implemented:

- Static configuration of routers/bridges to enable explorer frames to reach only selected destinations. The problem with this approach is the error-prone nature of manual configuration.

- Cache source routes and NetBIOS names within the bridge/router. Monitor explorer frames for new MACs and cache the returning source routes. Rather than forward an explorer or NetBIOS discovery frame, locally respond to the querying system. The problem with this approach is prevention of loops and other low level administration issues.

- Cache MAC addresses and provide distributed knowledge of MAC addresses via a MAC query function to other bridges and routers. The problem with this approach is that knowledge of neighboring bridges and routers still needs to be manually defined.

8.8.11 SNA over TCP tunneling standard —DLSw

SDLC (SNA), LLC2 (SNA & NetBIOS), X.25 QLLC; SNA), and frame relay (SNA & NetBIOS) are all potential candidates for TCP tunneling. The best known architecture for tunneling is DLSw. DLSw is defined by RFC 1785, and DLSw v2 by RFC 2166. DLSw addresses the following requirements:

- Support SNA and NetBIOS protocols
- Support SDLC and LLC2 data links (a subset of all possible link types)
- Minimize DLC time-outs
- Extend DLC acknowledgments to WAN
- Handle router-to-router congestion control
- Handle token ring explorer and NetBIOS broadcast control
- Reduce source routing hop count limits

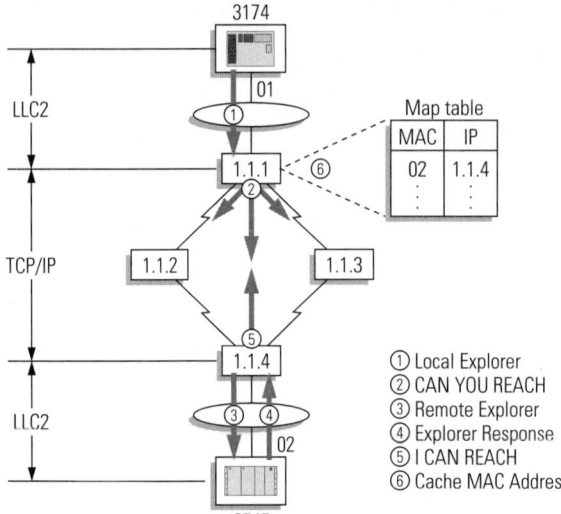

Figure 8.50   DLSw discovery architecture

Figure 8.50 illustrates the operational flows (actually a subset) of DLSw connection setup. DLSw routers participate in the explorer phase of LLC2 connection setup in order to dynamically locate MAC addresses and determine a TCP/IP route (actually IP address of the destination router).

For example, an end system issues a TEST or XID explorer frame; the local DLSw router issues a CAN YOU REACH frame to all other DLSw routers; all remote DLSw routers issue TEST/XID explorer frames. When the TEST/XID response returns, the remote router sends an I CAN REACH frame to the originating DLSw router; the IP address of the remote router is entered in the MAC-to-IP address table; and the connection setup is allowed to proceed (the example does not show additional flows—REACH ACK, CONTACT, CONTACTED—that also are part of the DLSw protocol).

Following the LLC2 connection setup, all LLC2 data flows over TCP/IP sessions.

8.8.12 Issue analysis

How well does DLSw address the SNA tunneling requirement? DLSw addresses the following requirements:

- LLC2—both NetBIOS and SNA are handled (NetBIOS name caching is not specified by the standard and is a local matter).
- SDLC is not directly addressed, but can be handled with SDLC conversion and manual configuration of port/link station mappings to MAC/SAP addresses.
- LLC2 local termination eliminates the LLC2 time-out problem.

- Explorer traffic is handled by the CAN YOU REACH–I CAN REACH protocol procedures.

- Source routing hop count limits are expanded since the DLSw router is the endpoint of every source route. Source routes are not passed across the backbone.

8.8.13 IP over SNA tunneling

IP over SNA is the inverse of SNA over IP. Figure 8.51 shows one such backbone composed of a combination of 3745 nodes running PU type 4 subarea connected to routers running APPN Network Node. An IP-to-APPC tunneling function exists at the edges of the subarea SNA network. This function might be integral to one of the subarea SNA nodal processors, or it may be an additional physical system connected to one of the LAN/WAN interfaces into the subarea SNA backbone.

IP over SNA tunneling is conceptually (architecturally) much simpler than the inverse (SNA over IP).

The IP-APPC component conceptually contains the following functions:

- *Route calculation function*   Coordinates with other IP-APPC functions. Maps the IP hierarchical address structure of incoming IP datagrams into an SNA destination accessed via APPC.

- *SNA tunnel function*   Encapsulates/deencapsulates IP datagrams to/from APPC frames

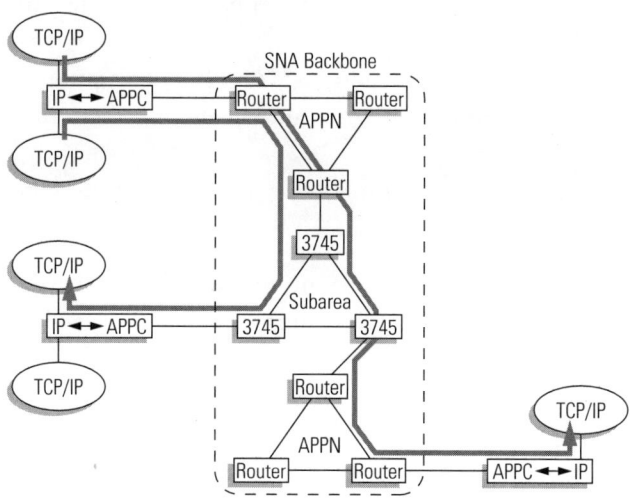

Figure 8.51   IP over SNA tunneling

- *IP node emulation function* Emulates an IP intermediate systems node from the perspective of its end systems

The simple functions of IP over SNA tunneling are to accept incoming IP datagrams addressed to the IP-to-APPC component's data-link address (MAC address for LAN), compute an SNA route to a neighbor IP-APPC component, initialize the APPC session if it is needed, encapsulate the IP frame in an APPC envelope, and send it. At the receiving IP-APPC component, the inverse set of operations is performed.

If congestion is experienced, simply discard the datagram—no requirement exists to guarantee delivery. Because the objective is to match the high forwarding rate expected by IP routers, the APPC connections will either be full-duplex or two parallel half-duplex sessions.

IP over SNA could be as complex as SNA over IP. If, for example, the end-to-end delay of SNA backbones were to exceed TCP (or other IP upper layer protocol) timers, then a similar retinue of local termination and passthrough schemes could be defined. However, TCP tends to tolerate longer delay characteristics than LLC2. SNA backbones are also not as large as the largest IP backbones (hop counts of seventeen or more are common in the Internet IP backbone; SNA backbones are smaller). (Interestingly, TCP is suffering more in the Internet backbone: because of the large number of hops in some routes, TCP sessions can fail because the IP Time To Live field expires.)

Very few IP over SNA implementations are available (or even announced). One of the earliest was done as a joint venture between IBM and Open Connect Systems, SNALINK. SNALINK uses the mainframe as the IP routing engine. The original version used LU type 0 sessions between mainframes for IP forwarding. More recent versions use APPC/LU 6.2.

A more recent product is the IP forwarding function in 3745 NCP. This product does not require a mainframe to do the forwarding, a significant benefit over the earlier SNALINK product.

IP over SNA technology is still in its infancy. The following problems remain to be addressed:

- Router-SNA-router topologies: current products seem to address mainly the requirements of end systems. A more robust solution requires that the IP-over-SNA router participate in IP router-to-router protocols. Not only should it support RIP, but OSPF, and BGP-router-to-router protocols.

- No standards exist for IP-over-SNA tunneling

While IP-over-SNA tunneling does prolong the life of existing subarea SNA backbones for a few more years, it probably will be used infrequently. At best, IP-over-SNA tunneling will satisfy the needs of a few casually connected users. IP-over-SNA will likely not take hold as long as the backbone continues to be connection-oriented, whether subarea-based or APPN/ISR based. Once the backbone migrates to APPN/HPR's more efficient ANR-based datagram model, tunneling may become a more popular offering. At that point in time, the race will be on between tunneling and the NBBS control point for multiprotocol routing.

8.8.14 Session/transport layer convergence

Since the beginning of internetworking time, users and vendors have sought the Holy Grail of multivendor networking—a networked applications environment that is free from considerations of protocol dependencies (figure 8.37). As an end to that means, over the past fifteen years multiple research projects have attempted to create a universal transport layer gateway between environments with different protocols, for example, an APPC-to-TCP gateway.

Such efforts have met with mixed success (a euphemism for failure). For example, TCP and APPC (and any other pair of protocols) have differing service models. TCP uses the tuple {IP Address (net address, subnet address, host address), Port Number} for connection establishment. APPC uses the tuple {Name (Net Name, LU Name), Transaction Program Name} for conversation establishment. Each has differing models of session bring-up/take-down, different half-duplex/full-duplex modes, and different methods of handling errors.

With proper constraints on the scope of such an effort, transport layer convergence is possible, practical, and implementable. The constraint is that convergence is to be provided for a fixed API-bound set of end-to-end transport services.

It is possible (through the compensations and architectures defined below) to enable applications written to a specific interface type, that is, sockets, to run over any protocol transport layer, such as TCP, SNA (subarea SNA or APPN), NetBIOS, or IPX. At the transport layer, it is still not possible to enable an application written to one protocol's native service interface (e.g., sockets) to communicate with an application written to a different protocol's native service interface (e.g., CPI-C).

8.8.15 Application layer convergence

Another opportunity for multiprotocol convergence occurs within the application layer. Indeed, if neither transport layer nor backbone layer convergence is available, the user is left to solve the problem at the application layer, or risk being saddled with isolated islands of networked computing.

At the applications layer two distinct convergence approaches are available: multiprotocol awareness within client/server application instances and application gateways.

The strategy of having applications support multiple transports is analogous to supporting multiple printers, or supporting multiple graphics display environments. The difference, however, is that systems have evolved universal APIs for printer and graphics support, but in this case multiple APIs have to be recognized for communications support. Nevertheless, in many cases it will be possible for application developers to create universal communications superlayers that ride atop the differing sublayers. This is possible in part because the application designers know which services and functions are required by the application.

It should also be noted that generic transport independent interfaces do exist. Both middleware APIs and remote procedure call APIs are transport independent. The issue with these APIs is that they must be made available on all systems (with middleware gateway support to span multiprotocol environments).

Common network operating systems services often use the heterogeneous application gateway approach. Electronic mail, terminal protocol converters, and database gateways are all viable examples. The advantages of the application gateway approach are:

- Homogenous applications are enabled across multiprotocol environments.
- Heterogeneous applications of the same class (e.g., email) are enabled across multiprotocol environments.

The disadvantages of the application gateway approach are:

- The breadth of applications coverage is weak; a gateway must be developed for every application, a costly and time consuming process.
- In heterogeneous environments, the respective applications are changing at different paces, and evolving in different directions; thus, the applications gateway must be burdened with the task of staying current with multiple application architectures of the same class.

Application gateways will be commonly applied to industry-wide system services like electronic mail and distributed database access; they will not be commonly seen in user-developed applications, and will be only infrequently used for other vendor-developed productivity applications.

8.8.16 Fast packet switching and control point architecture

The generic name for the alternate internetworking technologies is fast packet switching (FPS). FPS divides into two camps: frame relay and cell relay packet modes. Current examples of FPS technologies include CCITT I.122 frame relay and ATM. A further differentiation between the two types of FPS is their respective treatment of the data stream:

- The cell relay data stream is divided into fixed size cells at the source, and then it is reassembled at the destination
- The frame relay data stream is sent intact, in the original frame size sent by the origin. Of course, the frame can be segmented if the maximum frame size of the source is smaller than the maximum frame size of the FPS service

Much debate exists over which of the two packet modes is more appropriate for data communications. Both techniques exist and both may be offered in a given vendor's FPS product. FPS technology eliminates the mesh topology typically constructed beneath today's bridge and router products. Actually, FPS has the potential for pushing bridges and routers out of the picture altogether by providing direct interfaces to end systems.

Frame relay (CCITT I.122) is an interface, like X.25, to a service that routes variable length frames over WANs at layer 2. Virtually any interface speed could be offered, but the initial versions of the standard have specified 2Mbps. Routing is based upon a DLCI, which is established either at subscription time (permanent virtual circuit) or at call setup time (switched virtual circuit). However, the network simply forwards data frames—no error correction and minimal error detection.

The frame relay interface has become a de facto standard interface for the WAN technologies.

It seems that frame relay is becoming the universal connection-multiplexing interface standard, if not a backbone product in its own right.

8.8.17 ATM—the next generation

ATM represents a significant change from the conventional use of shared media LANs. At the conceptual level, ATM represents a new technology, specifically a cell-switching/relay technology for use in local and wide area networks. At the technical level, it is a series of standards developed by the CCITT and ATM forum for use in these networks.

ATM has several significant differences that separate it from conventional LAN/WAN technologies. As opposed to the variable length data packets found in Ethernet, token ring, and FDDI, ATM uses fixed-length cells. Whereas conventional shared media LANs are connectionless, ATM is a connection-oriented network, and uses dedicated media connections to provide for the connections in the network.

8.8.18 ATM network switches

Thus far, two generically different approaches have been taken in developing switches for the application of ATM interfaces to products for use in ATM networks. One approach consists of switches based on a common shared resource, typically a shared bus by which all switch interfaces intercommunicate, and the other approach consists of systems that use a single switch fabric. There are several variations for each type of switch approach.

In the first case, the most common method is to build the switch with multiple high-speed interfaces operating on a high-speed bus. Thus, most systems use a bus that operates at multi-Gbps speeds. Such systems can be considered very effective, since they use well known and established technologies, and will be adequate, as long as the aggregate speed of all connections does not exceed the speed of the bus. For example, if the switch uses fifteen connections of 100 Mbps to share a common 5.5 Gbps backplane, the switch can adequately support all traffic it is expected to serve.

However, scalability of such a system may be limited to the aggregate capacity of the bus. In the example cited above, the system could easily handle fifteen 100-Mbps connections, but if port density were increased such that the switch must now support twenty-four connections, the potential for contention for the bus would exist. This is the same situation that presently exists with shared media LANs.

For the second case, in switch-fabric-based architectures such as Bachter-Banyan based switches or the St. Louis fabric designed by Dr. John Turner, no common bus is required. All traffic is managed through a common switching fabric. Such switches can provide full ATM speeds to all connections, since there is no contention for a common communication bus. However, such networks must have additional capabilities designed for the handling of multicast and broadcast transmissions, as well as requiring a means for managing and avoiding contention for output.

8.8.19 IBM networking broadband services (NBBS) architecture

An interesting approach to fast packet switching, which combines many of the elements of fixed-cell and variable-cell technology, is IBM's NBBS architecture. NBBS (see figure 8.52) is a very flexible architecture with fast packet switching at its core. The key elements of NBBS are network control, transport services, and access services.

The following key elements exist in the network control portion of NBBS:

- Distributed control point: a control point architecture with one element in each access module and another element in every physical node. No centralized control

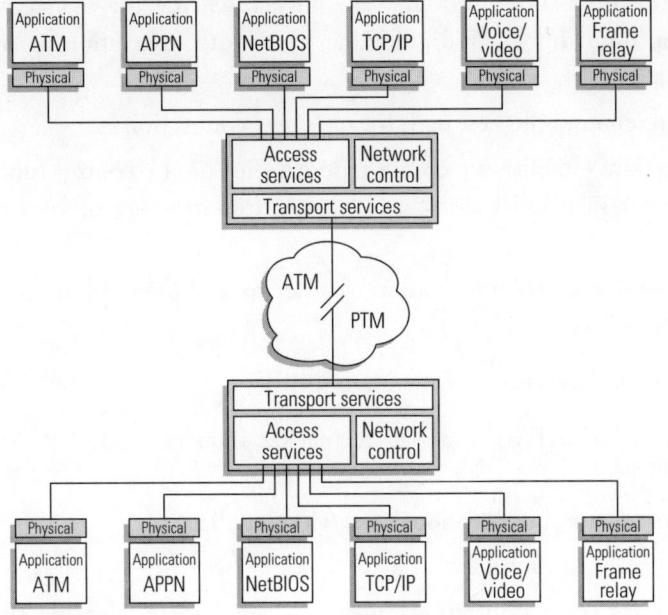

Figure 8.52 NBBS

point is required (unlike most current generation ATM products from other vendors).

- Initialization function: exchanges capabilities and other control information with other control points

- Directory services function: retrieves, distributes, and maintains information about users and resources, including resources attached to access services (such as IP and SNA addresses)

- Multicast set management function: implements multicast groups and dynamic multicast trees (used for structuring virtual bridge/router environments and other services requiring multicast)

- Bandwidth management function: handles bandwidth reservation and maintenance messages; monitors link reservation levels

- Congestion control function: an improved leaky-bucket scheme for managing bandwidth, smoothing input bursts, and enforcing bandwidth reservation agreement between network and users
- Path selection function: chooses the best path for each new connection
- CP spanning tree function: establishes a connectivity tree for use by control functions. Updates can occur in parallel along a branching tree structure of control points
- Topology data function: distributes information to other control points about network topology and link utilization

The following elements exist in the transport function of NBBS:

- Options for both cell relay (ATM) and packet (packet transfer mode—PTM) modes
- Options for both data traffic and isochronous voice/video traffic
- Support for both datagram and multicast
- Reliable delivery and error correction/retransmission are implemented within the end systems (or access systems), not within the FPS network
- Five routing modes: HPR/ANR, ANR with reverse path accumulation (the frame contains a return path), label swap routing (real time traffic), ATM routing, and tree routing (parallel distribution of data along a branching tree structure).
- The access services portion of NBBS makes integral use of NBBS control functions for transport, multicast management, and directory services support and contains interfaces defined for bridging, TCP/IP, SNA, NetBios, Voice/Video, Frame Relay, and ATM UNI/NNI.

The distributed control point architecture is perhaps the strongest element of NBBS, as is the ability to operate in both cell relay (ATM) and frame relay modes. As a product, the real question is the ability of NBBS-based products to deliver attractively priced interfaces for existing services, such as LAN-based IP and APPN end systems.

Another issue exists which is analogous to the issue raised earlier regarding IP over APPN—will the access functions be able to offer service to downstream routers (e.g. will an APPN access node implement APPN NN to NN protocols)?

8.8.20 ATM and routers

Figure 8.53 shows ATM-based internetworking product architecture. The architecture has native interfaces to ATM desktops (the first threat to routers). But for the preponderance of existing LAN-attached devices, additional functions can be incorporated into

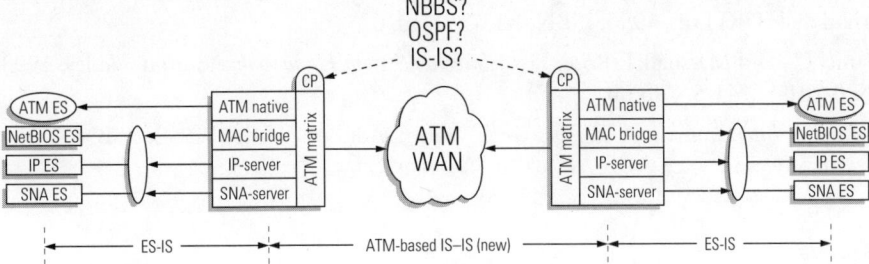

Figure 8.53   ATM's potential future

the switch, on a per-port and/or per-card basis—a MAC bridge server, an IP-routing server, and an SNA-routing server (APPN/HPR datagram routing). Upstream from the LAN-attached end systems, the switch has to support the ES-to-IS protocol, that is, present a router boundary.

Within each ATM switch node is a CP. The CP function provides topology, route selection, and directory services functions on an integrated basis for all protocols that are being serviced. Is this doable? Probably. Is this a threat to traditional routing? Most certainly.

Projection: Fast packet switching technology, e.g. ATM, poses a viable new paradigm for internetworking. In this new approach, the ES–IS interface will be provided within the nearest access node to the upstream LAN-attached end systems. The integrated control point will provide a common topology and route selection and directory service for all ES protocols. Traditional router boxes will be relegated to a more limited function, and may become the gateways into low-performance routing domains.

8.9 References

Texts

Bradner, Scott O., and Allison Mankin, Eds., *IPng—Internet Protocol Next Generation*, Addison-Wesley, 1996, ISBN 02-201-63395-7.

Comer, Douglas E., *Internetworking with TCP/IP Volume I: Principles, Protocols, and Architecture*, Second Edition, Prentice-Hall, 1991, ISBN 0-13-468505-9, 547 pp.

Comer, Douglas E., and David L. Stevens, *Internetworking with TCP/IP Volume II: Design, Implementation, and Internals*, Prentice-Hall, 1991, ISBN 0-13-472242-6, 532 pp.

———, *Internetworking with TCP/IP: Client-Server Programming and Applications, BSD Socket Version*, Prentice-Hall, 1993, ISBN 0-13-474222-2, 498 pp.

Cypser, R. J., *Communications for Cooperating Systems: OSI, SNA, and TCP/IP*, Addison-Wesley, 1991, ISBN 0-201-50775-7, 743 pp.

de Prycker, Martin, *Asynchronous Transfer Mode—Solution for Broadband ISDN*, Prentice Hall International (UK) Ltd., 1995, ISBN 0-13-342171-6.

Lynch, Daniel C., and Marshall T. Rose, Eds., *Internet System Handbook*, Addison-Wesley, 1993, ISBN 0-201-56741-5, 790 pp.

Perlman, Radia, *Interconnections: Bridges and Routers*, Addison-Wesley, 1992, ISBN 0-201-56332-0, 389 pp.

Periodicals

Business Communications Review
> "Flexibility is Key to Backbone Evolution," Thomas J. Routt, February 1997, pp. 28–35.
> "Why Hanford Nuclear Site May Switch to ATM," Dr. Jeffrey R. Phillips and Thomas J. Routt, October 1996, pp. 27–31.
> "Integration Strategies for APPN and TCP/IP," Thomas J. Routt, March 1995, pp. 43–49.
> "TCP/IP vs. APPN Performance Analysis" Thomas J. Routt and Dr. John R. Pickens, January 1994, pp. 33–38.

Computer Communications Review, "Comments on Congestion Control in TCP/IP Internetworks," Marshall T. Rose, Vol. 15, No. 5, October/November 1985.

Datamation, "Adequate Addressing with TCP/IP," Pedro Carlos, date unknown—after January 1993, (rebuts "limits" of IP addressing).

Data Communications
> "APPN and TCP/IP: Plotting a Backbone Strategy," Thomas J. Routt, March 1994, pp. 107–114.
> "APPN Rises to the Enterprise Architectural Challenge," Norman Friedman—Systems Strategies Inc., February 1993.
> "The Internet Opens Up to Commercial Use," Johna Till Johnson, March 1993.
> "Multiprotocol Gateways: Beyond Internet Connectivity," Nick Lippis, June 1991.
> "The Internetwork Decade: Supplement to Data Communications," Nick Lippis and James Herman, Northeast Consulting Resources, Inc., January 1991.
> "Toppling the SNA Internetworking Language Barrier," Benson Rosen and Brett Fromme, June 1993, 8 pp.

IBM Internet Journal, "TCP/IP and SNA Interoperability: A Focus on Useability," Ed Taylor, February 1993.

Network World
> "Survey says few sites with large local nets use routers," Eric Smalley, 10 June 1991, (IDC survey of 100 network managers).
> "IETF Leader Assesses Health of Internet," Phillip Gross—IETF Chairman, 19 April 1993.
> "Novell to go Native with TCP/IP support," Caryn Gillooly, 29 March 1993.

SNA Perspective
> "APPN: Key in IBM's Networking Blueprint," April 1992, pp. 1–14.
> "APPN Insights and Design Clues," April 1992, pp. 14–20.
> "Blueprint to Integrate the Architectures," August 1992, pp. 1–9.
> "Points of Contention: APPN vs. TCP/IP," May 1993, 15 pp.

IBM publications

"Systems Network Architecture APPN Architecture Reference," March 1993, IBM document, SC30-3422-3.

"Classic Client-Server Transactions using APPC," Lance Bader and John Q. Walker II, January 1992, 17 pp.

"APPN Architecture and Product Implementations Tutorial," June 1992, IBM document, GG24-3669-01, 190 pp.

Presentations

APPN and TCP/IP: Comparisons, Contrasts, Integration, Decision Drivers, Thomas J. Routt, VEDACOM Corporation, NetWorld & Interop April 1996 Tutorial, Las Vegas.

APPN & TCP/IP: A Comparative Analysis, Jim Lucas, SHARE March 1993 presentation—20 slides.

IBM SNA Advanced Peer-to-Peer Networking Dependent LU Support Overview, David Bryant, 1993 March SHARE presentation—20 slides.

IBM SNA Advanced Peer-to-Peer Networking Overview, David Bryant, SHARE, March 1993 presentation—26 slides.

Introduction to Fast Packet Technologies, Jim Scott, SHARE March 1993 presentation—47 slides.

APPN & TCP/IP: Comparisons, Contrasts, Integration and Decision Drivers, Thomas J. Routt, VEDACOM Corporation, SHARE Session C919, Summer 1993, Washington D.C.—40 slides.

RFCs

RFC 1190: Experimental Internet Stream Protocol, Version 2 (ST-II), October 1990, status: limited use experimental protocol.

RFC 1470 (obsoletes RFC 1147): FYI on a Network Management Tool Catalog: Tools for Monitoring and Debugging TCP/IP Internets and Interconnected Devices, R. Enger and J. Reynolds, June 1993.

APPNIP RFC AI (HAV191: Interconnection of APPN Instances via TCP/IP, David Kushi and Dennis Wind of IBM, March 1993, status: draft, 15 pp.

Criteria for Choosing IP Version 7, IPV7REQ TXT A1 (EGB191) Craig Partridge-BBN & Frank Kastenholz-FTP, 14 December 1992.

RFC 1370—Applicability Statement for OSPF, Lyman Chapin—IAB, October 1992, 2 pp.

PART II

SNA interoperability today

chapter 9

SNA across the data link

Kevin Tolly

The second part of this book describes the popular SNA interoperability solutions available today. In the first chapter of this part, Kevin Tolly presents some of the most popular strategies for SNA internetworking at the data-link layer, the breadth of which expands every day. This chapter also includes comparison of different technologies with specific recommendations on pros and cons for each alternative.

9.1 Introduction

The heart and soul of SNA internetworking rests with the fundamental issue of how SNA sessions are transported over the WAN. Whenever SNA data becomes part of a heterogeneous network, network managers must understand and consider the various physical and logical components that create connectivity between SNA and the internetwork world.

Despite the industry-wide cry for interoperability and vendor pledges to develop open products, most vendors market only the technology that sells, which often involves proprietary protocols or strategies. Because of this reality, the responsibility for understanding the costs and benefits of each of the technologies, protocols, and strategies that affect communication across complex WANs, falls squarely on the shoulders of network managers and buyers. Network decision-makers who pursue anything less than full understanding invite network congestion, breaches in reliability and security, and potential failure.

What is so difficult to understand about SNA internetworking? The choices in internetworking options have grown immeasurably. Decision makers who backed their own opinions primarily with IBM's now stand in a world of diverse technical possibilities. Issues that were once black or white appear now in innumerable shades of gray.

Yet the educated network manager can successfully select technical products and strategies by considering a broad view of the network architecture, goals, and futures. With that understanding and a knowledge of the realities of each strategy, the challenge of internetworking SNA can be relatively straightforward.

This chapter aims to help network managers better understand these realities as they relate to internetworking technologies, strategies used for SNA data transport and protocols at the data-link level. The next chapter will address these issues at the network and transport level. This chapter also describes the benefits and pitfalls of some of the most popular strategies for SNA internetworking today. This chapter concludes with a discussion of technologies worth watching as well as some final considerations on strategies for internetworking success.

9.2 Understanding data-link structures

As the armies of stand-alone PCs grew more powerful, network managers realized that connecting small workgroups of individuals through LAN technology rather than integrating them with the SNA network was often a sensible, cost-effective decision. As individual networks developed and grew, the requirement to link widely dispersed LANs emerged.

But interconnecting LANs across the wide area in addition to maintaining the existing SNA WAN infrastructures meant designing, deploying, and supporting two separate networks—an impracticable option during even the best of economic times. A single WAN infrastructure that could support traditional terminal-to-mainframe host traffic while simultaneously providing a transport for the myriad other protocols (such as IP, IPX, and NetBIOS) used in popular LAN programs would appear the ideal solution. Several options present themselves. Chapter 11 discusses carrying alternate protocols across an SNA backbone. Chapter 10 describes encapsulation of SNA in other protocols, particularly TCP/IP. Chapters 12 and 13 discuss higher layer translation protocols such as MPTN. This chapter focuses on the issues of transporting SNA across various data-link technologies and migrating between technologies, particularly from SDLC to a LAN in the local area and across the WAN.

To achieve such consolidation requires more planning than just upgrading FEPs and controllers or replacing them with bridges and routers. To migrate a traditional SNA network to a LAN/WAN internetwork—even at the data-link level—requires an understanding of protocols and session characteristics, the capabilities of devices such as bridges, routers and gateways, and the common implementation strategies for SNA internetworking.

9.2.1 Who's in charge? An overview of protocols and session characteristics

To develop an effective strategy for deploying SNA over internetworks, network managers must first understand how network architecture affects the flow of network communications. All leading LAN topologies, including Ethernet, token ring and FDDI, consist of two data-link layer sublayers that specifically address network operations: the LLC layer and the MAC layer. These are discussed in chapter 3.

SNA uses type 2 operation of LLC, which is responsible for connection-oriented service. This is because SNA's reliable architecture expects a connection-oriented data link. (The newer SNA APPN technology with high performance routing eliminates this LLC2 requirement.) (LLC type 1 deals with connectionless service, such as that used by

IPX, IP, and some NetBIOS traffic.) Before any operation can begin, LLC2 requires the establishment of a connection between the sending and receiving end stations; the connection is typically maintained until a station powers-off or unloads its networking software.

Programs written to use LLC2 typically assume that network transit delays are short, as they generally are with local LANs. Therefore, most application programs developed for LLC2 use a short, fixed timer to detect lost frames. In contrast, SNA WAN links across SDLC have variable timers to account for WAN delays.

When SNA sessions (which invariably use LLC2) must be bridged from LAN to LAN across a wide area "cloud" (see figure 9.1), they commonly experience travel delays caused by traversing a low-bandwidth link. The problem is exacerbated when an overload of LAN traffic (e.g., client/server file transfer) causes congestion on the WAN link between bridge or router pairs. Link congestion causes bridge buffers to overflow; when this happens, the bridge discards any additional frames it receives. Because frames have been discarded or captured in the bridge's buffer, the application timers can expire, which in turn can activate error-recovery mechanisms. This is particularly problematic with SNA traffic which, expecting a well-managed data link, responds with concern to such problems, such as by dropping sessions.

LLC2 also provides flow control through acknowledgments between the end stations. LLC2 allows the receiving station to confirm that it has received a frame or group of frames before those frames are flushed from the buffer of the sending station. Thus, if any frame is not received, the sending end station can retransmit it until the receiving end station acknowledges that the frame has been received. This technique serves to provide very reliable transport. It is important to note, however, that LLC flows between the two end stations only, not any bridge that the frame may traverse in the journey between the LANs. As a result, congestion somewhere on the data path between the two end stations can slow or stop the data frames and the flow control frames from successfully

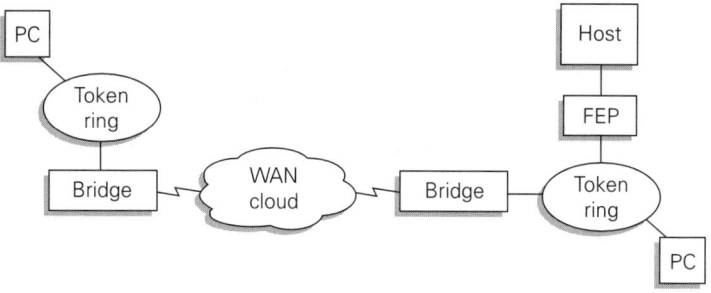

Figure 9.1 SNA sessions are bridged across the WAN cloud

reaching their destination. Because LLC recognizes only the end stations, such congestion can cause the end station to unnecessarily activate the aforementioned error-recovery mechanisms.

9.2.2 Physical connectivity mechanisms: gateways

The physical mechanism required to link SNA hosts and LANs is gateway technology. With SNA internetworking, there are two basic options for LAN-to-mainframe connectivity: full-stack and split-stack gateways. Figure 9.2 illustrates the possible gateway options. With the full-stack approach, each PC—called a *downstream physical unit* (DSPU)—implements the entire SNA protocol stack and uses the services of a PU passthrough gateway to reach the host. PU passthrough gateways can be a FEP, a 3174, 3172, and other multivendor products: that is, routers, FRADs, and PC gateways.

The DSPU approach runs native SNA data over LLC2. Each DSPU client PC has its own PU definition in the SNA host and maintains a separate LLC2 session with the host's FEP or cluster controller. DSPU clients maintain contact with the host's network management using its PU–SSCP session.

IBM is not the only vendor to offer DSPU implementations. Most third-party vendors supply IBM-compatible, full-stack DSPU implementations that communicate with the host directly, via intermediate PU passthrough gateways.

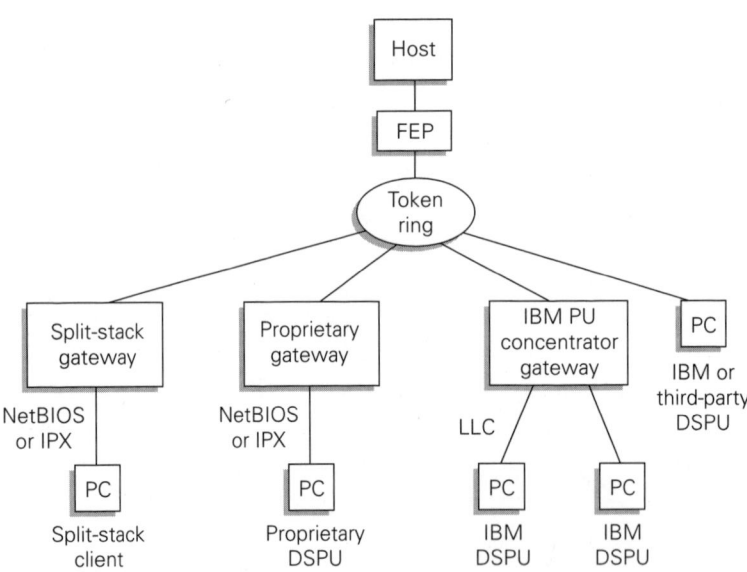

Figure 9.2 Possible gateway configurations for SNA interconnectivity

In contrast to the full-stack approach, many of the industry's third-party vendors have developed a split-stack alternative. Split-stack gateways divide the SNA stack so that the gateway (which in this context is a PC and not a FEP, 3174 or 3172) handles the PU chores, such as establishing sessions with the host, and the client PC handles the display functions, such as communicating with the end-user. In essence, split-stack software separates the SNA packets coming down from the host, replacing them with proprietary control blocks and sending only screen and proprietary protocol information—pure SNA data—to the client. Unlike full-stack gateways, in which every user appears as a separate PU to the host, split-stack gateways allow multiple LAN client stations to share a single PU. (Note: There are some split-stack alternatives that take the entire SNA data frame, encapsulate it inside a NetBIOS or IPX frame, and ship it to the end station. These approaches, called proprietary DSPU, share many of the same characteristics of split-stack gateways.)

Such a layout places the burden of the processing work onto the gateway rather than the client, reducing the memory and CPU demands on the client. However, it creates difficulties for those network managers who are pursuing interoperability. Compared with full-stack DSPU PCs, which implement vendor-independent SNA over LLC and are fully functional SNA stations, the split-stack client PCs cannot communicate directly with the host. They relay all of their SNA traffic through the intermediate gateway.

Split-stack gateways use NetBIOS, IPX, or TCP/IP as a network protocol and LLC1 datagrams or LLC2 sessions further down the stack. (As a result of this strategy, the client split-stack PC really is not even speaking SNA; it speaks NetBIOS or IPX, and does not adhere to the previously described rules of SNA or LLC2. This type of strategy can thus be called *faux SNA*.)

The architectural implications of such a strategy can be troublesome, because any clients downstream of a split-stack gateway are forced to use the vendor's proprietary protocol. Since the client-to-gateway protocols are both vendor-specific and often unpublished, network managers are locked into using a single vendor's solution. More recently, however, vendors such as Novell, Microsoft, and many 3270 terminal emulator products have allowed other vendors access to the client-gateway protocols. This allows more mixing and matching of vendors within the split-stack gateway approach.

In addition, split-stack gateways are vendor-specific in their protocols and in the way in which they divide the processing load. Proprietary DSPUs encapsulate SNA headers and information fields within non-SNA protocols like NetBIOS, IPX, and TCP/IP, using the industry-standard protocol in a proprietary manner to set up sessions between gateway and client.

In other cases, vendors actually terminate SNA at their gateway. By stripping away the SNA headers and replacing them with proprietary control blocks, vendors make decoding and debugging nearly impossible. And ironically, the proprietary replacement of SNA is typically far less efficient than native SNA.

The differences between IBM and third-party gateway configurations can cause variations in network performance. Once gateways are linked to the internetwork, inefficiencies once limited to the local network can easily spread over the corporate backbone. While split stacks often reduce memory and processing overhead on the client, lab tests prove that the exchanges between the client and gateway are never as efficient as with DSPU. The only way for the user community to prevent gateways—IBM or third-party, full-stack or split-stack—from becoming bottlenecks (or worse) is to understand the architectural design of an individual gateway product and its communication protocol before it has an opportunity to impact network performance.

9.2.3 Getting from here to there: source routing

For the last decade, IBM's method of choice for sending data across token ring networks (both local and remote) has been a technique called source routing. IBM's commitment to source routing led the company to build the technique into many of its internetworking products, including countless end-user programs, 3270 emulators, network operating system drivers and popular bridge/router products.

Despite the name, source routing is not routing at all but bridging. True routing allows a router to make decisions dynamically as network conditions change. Routing also allows the end station to actively communicate with the next nearest routing device to monitor network conditions. In contrast, source routing bridges make end stations responsible for selecting the best transport path though a network at session initiation. Once chosen, the path does not vary, regardless of the conditions that develop during data transport. End stations are oblivious to information about the network, because bridges are unable to communicate with them.

Because end stations are unable to detect changes in internetwork conditions, they are unable to dynamically modify routes based on knowledge about congestion or failure. If temporary or hard failures occur during a session, source routing devices have no dynamic capacity to adjust. This can be a critical source of failure once data tries to travel across a complicated internetwork, and it is the primary reason why source routing is not recommended as a transport protocol for complex internetworks. (Note: A few vendors have added a dynamic reconnect feature to certain source routing products. However, this feature is nonstandard and thus of little import.)

Source routing has several other inherent characteristics that make it problematic as a methodology for internetworking. Source routing includes only limited dynamic load balancing. It balances the load by selecting the best session path at the instant of session setup and not again until the next session is initiated. (Barring system downtime or scheduled maintenance, this could easily be weeks or months for devices such as 3174 LAN clients or the AS/400!)

In addition, source routing uses the network's broadcast mode to determine which paths are available between two end stations during the discovery process. Furthermore, protocols such as NetBIOS issue a significant number of broadcasts for other reasons, such as resolving network names and locating server resources. When deployed across a complex internetwork, this trait can potentially endanger the performance of the entire internetwork.

IBM's implementation of source routing has one more notable characteristic: it imposes a limit on the number of hops for frames transmitted through the internetwork. Every time a frame passes through a network device, such as a gateway or router, it is considered a hop. (See figure 9.3.) Each frame can only pass through a maximum number of network devices before arriving at the receiving end station. If the trip requires more than the allowed number of hops, the session partner will never be found, because bridges do not propagate frames whose routing information field (RIF) is full. Thus, the session is never initiated. The frame is like a vehicle traveling from New York to Los Angeles that can only change highways a limited number of times. If the driver cannot arrive in Los Angeles after he exits the N-th highway (in most cases $N = 7$, although there are some implementations allowing a larger number of hops—i.e., thirteen for the IBM LAN Bridge Program) the vehicle and driver are zapped from the planet and the trip ends. This limitation inspired many network managers to build token ring networks in a multilevel hierarchical fashion that ensured frames could reach their destination within seven hops.

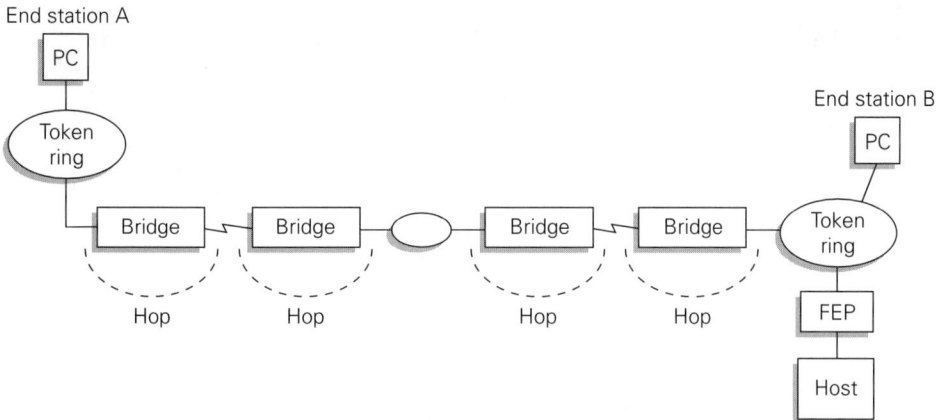

Figure 9.3   Source routing counts each device on the path as a hop

Such a limit is satisfactory, perhaps generous, in a pure SNA environment. But in complex internets, seven hops might only get a frame partially across the WAN cloud (say, to St. Louis) rather than to its final destination. (The DLSw protocol, described later in this chapter addresses this limitation.) In a complex network environment, a seven-hop or even thirteen-hop limit isn't just a problem: it can be a disaster looking for a place to happen.

9.3 Implementation strategies for SNA internetworking

The endless pressure of product vendors who hover over IS sites like a swarm of maniacal waiters can give a network manager indigestion, especially given the newspaper-sized menu of internetwork products. (The fact that the menu appears to be written in disappearing ink doesn't help, either.) However, when it comes to SNA internetworking, the solution types are thankfully straightforward.

The issues involved in SNA internetworking have admittedly become more complex. Once networking meant a single protocol WAN, SNA/SDLC, with a single set of rules, managed by a single entity, NetView. In the world of SNA internetworking, the WAN transports an arbitrary amalgam of protocols, each of which follows its own rules, with effectively no real management.

This fuzzy middle area, the WAN cloud, presents several inherent difficulties. First, WAN bandwidth is typically too low to handle the large data volumes common to SNA environments reliably. Where token ring networks offer bandwidth of 16 million bits per second, economics dictate that most companies use 56 Kbps lines (or at best a T1) for WAN traffic. This is roughly equivalent to having traffic on a hypothetical 2,000-lane superhighway merge into a seven-lane parkway. Needless to say, the backup is substantial.

In addition, the wide area links are often the least reliable portion of the internetwork. Also, the complexity of the internetwork, which can be extreme, often serves to make communication over the WAN difficult. Most network managers can successfully handle the physical and logical connectivity required within local LANs; it is in the WAN cloud, an area where connectivity solutions have only recently become important to SNA networks, where serious questions arise.

It is in traversing the WAN cloud of an internetwork that SNA data loses its hallmark reliability and robustness. The characteristics defined in the architecture that make traffic in a native SNA/SDLC network deterministic and reliable and that guarantee delivery are no longer advantageous when SNA users running over LANs compete with traffic from other protocols. LAN protocols such as IP, IPX, and NetBIOS are able to pass more frames across the bridge simply by sending more frames to the bridge. The bridge resources are allocated on a first-come, first-served basis; therefore, the least efficient protocols—usually those that generate the most frames—receive a larger allocation of the network resource.

9.3.1 Bridging solutions

Probably the simplest solution is the use of bridges to provide the mechanism for connecting end stations through the internetwork. With a bridging solution, the end station transmits the data frame, which contains appropriate source routing information in the RIF. Constantly monitoring the network for frames containing its RIF data, the bridge detects the frame sent by the end station. If the bridge is local, it transmits the frame to the appropriate LAN output port. If the bridge is remote, the frames typically are encapsulated in HDLC (or sometimes IP) and sent across the WAN cloud. Once the packet arrives at the bridge on the other side of the WAN cloud, the framing is stripped and the packet proceeds to the receiving end station.

Source routing bridges work well in pure SNA networks. But when data must pass through complex internetworks and contend for bandwidth resources against competitive LAN protocols, using bridges poses several serious problems.

First, the end stations and the bridges that serve as internetworking devices have no ability to communicate with one another in the way that routers can talk to routed end stations. This lack of communication prevents the bridges from exercising any control over the end stations. If the network becomes congested, for example, the bridges cannot ask the end stations to wait before sending more frames.

Because the only available partner for an end station is another end station, neither partner can tell when problems on the WAN cloud interfere with the passage of control frames, such as acknowledgment frames or session keep alives. When control frames fail to pass between end stations, the result is often session failure.

Because the source routing protocol charges the end stations with selecting and maintaining the path that frames take through the network, the end stations retain control no matter what. Even if network conditions change, end stations have no ability to dynamically switch paths, because source routing forces them to rely on the network path that is determined at session initiation.

The final problem posed by source routing bridges is that the limited number of hops is restrictive even in a moderately complex network. For any source routing frame to pass across a bridged network, each of the hops that comprise the frame's path through the network must be embedded in its RIF. In most cases, if the frame requires more than seven hops to travel the network, source routing drops the packet and the trip is over. Network managers have worked around this problem by building their networks as hierarchies of LANs. Unfortunately, this configuration forces a great deal of traffic over a relatively small number of regional backbone LANs, thus potentially adding to congestion and link saturation problems.

9.3.2 IP encapsulation or tunneling

For SNA sessions that must traverse an internetwork WAN cloud, encapsulation or tunneling is a valid—albeit not seamless—technique. It serves as a first step toward eliminating some of the problems posed by source routing.

When processing heterogeneous data, TCP/IP must take diverse data packets and give them uniform travel information so that they can traverse the internetwork. TCP/IP uses data encapsulation and de-encapsulation techniques to achieve this uniformity. When LLC2 traffic like SNA enters the router from a LAN, the router encapsulates the LLC2 packet with IP control information to form a frame. The packet is transmitted, traversing the internetwork along whichever paths are most efficient. As with a pure TCP/IP network, LLC2 packets that have been encapsulated can use dynamic routing as necessary to avoid trouble areas and optimize efficiencies.

The most important improvement that encapsulation offers to the source routing problems is the elimination of the hop limitation. Once the source routing frame enters the first bridge or router, the WAN cloud—no matter how complex or extensive—appears to be one hop to the source routing network. Figure 9.4 illustrates this concept.

Once the frame has passed through the cloud, the LLC2 packet is deencapsulated and transmitted to the target LAN. In that sense, the encapsulation of LLC2 data is still

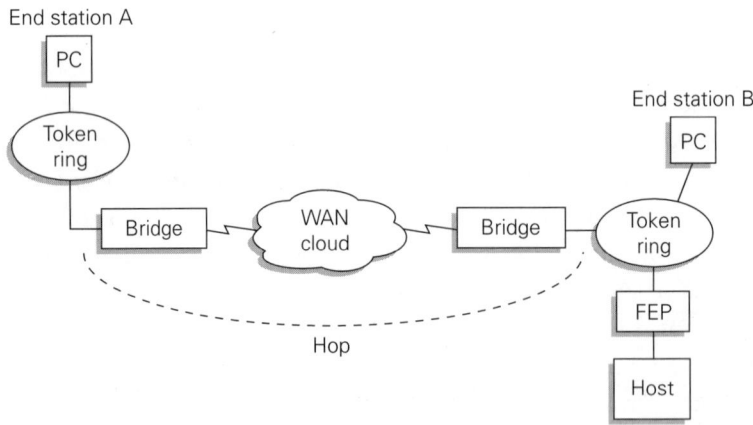

Figure 9.4 Encapsulation eliminates the hop restriction, making the WAN cloud appear as one virtual hop

CHAPTER 9 SNA ACROSS THE DATA LINK

a modified bridging solution; that is, the path is predetermined by the end station's session, which see the whole transport as a bridged solution. Only during the transport through the WAN cloud, when the encapsulation data takes control and the frame is routed along the most efficient network paths, is the transport dynamic.

Encapsulation is not a perfect solution, however. Encapsulating data in IP envelopes gives SNA frames the characteristics of TCP/IP frames: each frame is processed independently of the others, which may have traveled different routes as network conditions dictated. No sequence checking is done to ensure that frames were received in the order they were sent. Flow control and error recovery are limited. If a router becomes congested, packets may be discarded.

9.3.3 IP encapsulation with LLC local acknowledgment

One of the problems with encapsulating LLC2 data is that the constant volume of acknowledgments—often one for each data frame transmitted—and messages sent by source routing end stations can degrade performance on the internetwork. Such ineffective communications can clog the WAN links, which can in turn increase the frequency of LLC2 session time outs.

The strategy of adding local LLC acknowledgment to IP encapsulation resolves another problem created by source routing. When the router interferes at the LLC level by acknowledging data receipt to the sending end station, it is actually communicating with and at least partially controlling the data flow of the end station. The originating end station accepts the acknowledgment as if it were from the receiving end station, never realizing the communication is from the router. The router is effectively spoofing the session. (This technique has become widely used in satellite networks to reduce overhead and delay.) The routing device then sends the data on through the WAN cloud as if there had been no intervention, as shown in figure 9.5.

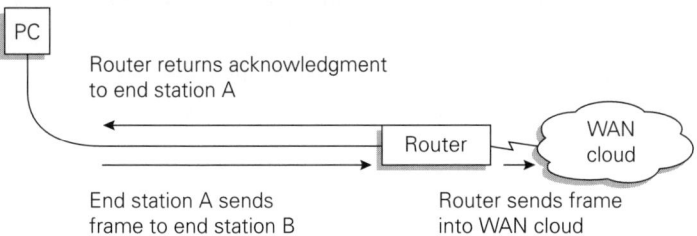

Figure 9.5   The router spoofs the sending end station by returning acknowledgment of data receipt, which is expected from the receiving end station

Although the practice of local acknowledgment can enhance performance across the internetwork and keep alive sessions that might otherwise fail, it has what can be a fatal flaw. Once the local acknowledgment is given, the connection is no longer end-to-end. Any network problems that occur after the acknowledgment is sent, either in the WAN cloud or in the receiving local LAN, can result in lost data. Since the sending end station has already flushed the data it believes was received, and the router has no capacity for re-sending the lost data, a transmission failure can be unrecoverable. So much for data integrity.

9.3.4 DLSw

What is needed to completely address the problems posed by source routing is a formalized, architected solution that provides the necessary IP encapsulation across the internetwork, but that also can guarantee delivery as LLC2 can. DLSw protocol provides one of the answers to this problem. DLSw is an open routing solution with well-defined architecture originally proposed in early 1993 by IBM. It's now known as IETF's RFC 1434, or in the more recent version RFC 1795. AIW recently approved DLSw v2 that is currently awaiting an RFC draft number assignment.

DLSw provides full SNA routing capabilities by introducing a well-defined architecture approach that formalizes the role of the router in controlling the SNA session. DLSw also includes provisions for guaranteed delivery of SNA traffic over complex internetworks by combining switching at the data-link layer, connection-oriented transport, and TCP/IP encapsulation. DLSw provides the transport information that enables SNA traffic to competitively and effectively use wide-area transports. In addition, it includes several other features that should address the problems inherent in the other solutions discussed.

Compared with traditional source routing with its end-to-end control, DLSw offers superior routing capabilities. To circumvent typical routing problems, the DLSw router's data-link switch maintains a list of all DLSw routers in the network. When an end station sends a packet, the router's DLSw terminates the LLC2 connection—and the corresponding source routing RIF—at the switch, preventing the LLC2 acknowledgments from traveling across the WAN. This feature limits the volume of slower LAN-speed LLC traffic traveling on the internetwork.

This feature also corrects source routing's seven-hop limitation problem. DLSw terminates source route bridging's RIF at the edge router, which is the router that joins the LAN segment to the internetwork. Because the connection is terminated, the sending end station receives no more information about the frame as it travels across the internetwork or throughout the receiving local LAN. Because of this limited view, the frame can still use only limited number of hops within the local LAN.

After the frame traverses the WAN cloud, it can use another seven (or even more, in some implementations) on the receiving source-routed LAN segment, because the receiving end station knows nothing of the hops through the originating LAN, or the virtual hop across the WAN cloud. This strategy extends the hop restriction to a degree that will permit the vast majority of traffic to successfully and efficiently traverse the internetwork, as illustrated in figure 9.6.

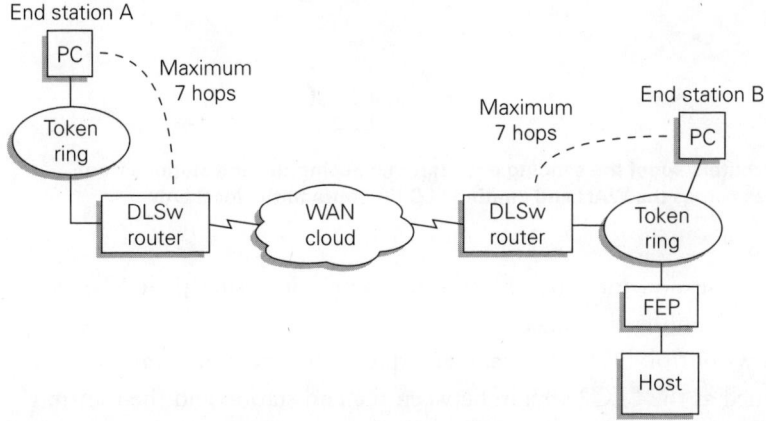

Figure 9.6   DLSw terminates the RIF at the edge router, meaning that each frame can make as many as seven hops on each of the local LANs

The DLSw router acknowledges the receipt of the frame to the sending station by masquerading as the receiving end station. This spoofing process prevents the end station from generating *receiver ready* (RR) and *receiver not ready* (RNR) messages, as well as other messages that might otherwise be sent to travel across the WAN.

Instead, DLSw multiplexes the LLC connections onto a TCP connection and sends them to another DLSw. This strategy makes the LLC connections at each end of the transmission independent, allowing routing capabilities where none were previously available. The DLSw takes responsibility for delivering frames received from one LLC connection to the other. This design limits the LLC timeouts to the local LAN, where they are far more infrequent than if they cross into the internetwork. (See figure 9.7.)

In addition, DLSw invokes the congestion and flow control mechanisms commonly found in SNA, which should help the management of both SNA and dynamic internetwork traffic. Such features are especially critical when a site has multiple data types traversing the internetwork, because they provide the reliability, dynamic recovery,

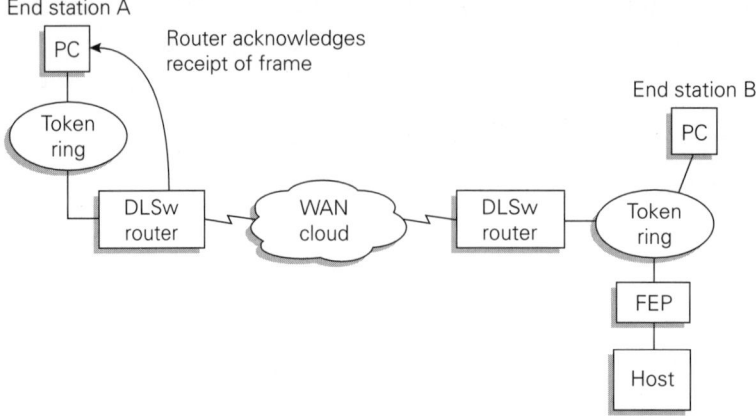

Figure 9.7   The DLSw routers spoof the sending end station, keeping the end stations from sending ready messages across the WAN and limiting LLC timeouts to the local LAN

congestion control and session integrity essential to companies using their SNA and TCP/IP networks for mission-critical data.

To assist with flow control, DLSw evaluates and queues the incoming frames by circuit. A circuit is defined as the LLC2 session between the end station and the transmitting router, the TCP/IP socket connection between the two DLSw routers, and the LLC2 connection between the receiving router and the receiving end station. Each circuit has a limited number of frames it can receive in a given period of time. As long as that limit is not exceeded, the DLSw router sends an RR frame to the sending router. If the router becomes congested or has received the maximum number of frames for the circuit, the router sends an RNR frame to the sending end station.

An additional advantage of DLSw is its support for protocol prioritization in the inbound queue, which allows it, for example, to assign a higher priority to time-sensitive protocols—i.e., SNA—over less time-dependent protocols.

DLSw achieves further congestion control by having remote routers send RNR frames to those circuits originating on their local LAN segments. Congested routers may do this to pace the data send rate of local end stations. This feature is useful for preventing the router's own buffers from becoming backlogged when they stop sending data to another congested router. When the congested router has cleared its backlog, it sends a message to the other routers; the routers then return an RR message to the sending end stations, who can resume sending frames.

Although DLSw does not yet address all of the issues or provide all of the functionality that SNA does—most notably lacking are management and security—the protocol has received broad acceptance by the majority of bridge and router vendors in the field.

In fact, to a large extent, DLSw has become a de facto standard for many sites that find the prospects of maintaining parallel SNA and TCP/IP networks too costly.

9.4 Technologies worth watching: successful SNA internetworking

The rapid development of SNA internetworking technologies and the wealth of new product solutions appearing each month may leave some IS managers with the impression that the market is in disarray. In fact, with the industry consensus favoring DLSw, successful SNA internetworking is closer to reality than ever before.

Still there are aspects of SNA internetworking that remain to be resolved. For those IS managers who object to the expense and effort required to run parallel SNA and TCP/IP networks, (that is, any network manager with a breath of life), the benefits of internetworking SNA data over the internetwork are clear. What is also obvious is that SNA users are accustomed to high levels of performance, capacity, reliability, and efficiency of the network. While many of the new technologies described in previous sections begin to address these issues, there is one function stirring up a great deal of controversy: prioritization.

Bridges and routers handle traffic on a FIFO basis. In other words, by default the bridge or router assigns no priority to data units; whatever arrives first leaves first. In a deterministic world where timing is precise and flow is rigidly controlled, FIFO works well, lending a regularity to data handling.

But when LAN protocols and SNA traffic share the typically low-bandwidth link that connects bridges or routers, contention for bandwidth is the order of the day. As noted previously, LAN protocols such as IP, IPX, and NetBIOS tend to present significantly more data for transmission than SNA and can overwhelm a WAN link, potentially displacing SNA traffic.

As a result, IS sites that attempt to run SNA data across the internetwork are often sadly disappointed with the throughput they achieve. Perhaps more importantly, the SNA session's data whose performance has plummeted is typically far more critical to the enterprise than the TCP/IP traffic of the client/server file transfer that ends up with the lion's share of the available WAN bandwidth. Not infrequently, one LAN user can saturate the WAN link. Users who are accustomed to at least predictable (if not lightning-fast) response times from the SNA network complain bitterly when their data chugs along through the internetwork.

To rectify this problem, vendors who intend to offer internetworking solutions to SNA customers have had to resort to adding a new feature: prioritization. At a minimum, prioritization can be defined as any technique that alters the FIFO scheme used by most routers. Prioritization schemes require the router to examine incoming packets to determine which protocol is present; typical prioritization techniques examine the 8-bit SAP (that is, the LLC-layer address). Then the router queues the packets for transmission according to the prioritization algorithm.

Properly implemented prioritization methodologies allow network managers to assign a priority to one or more protocols; once granted priority status, a protocol is guaranteed bandwidth and data delivery within specific time frames. More likely, successful prioritization techniques should assign high, medium, or low values to specific types of data; those with higher priority assume control of the transport as it becomes available.

Several routing vendors have already implemented some prioritization schemes. Unfortunately, most of these prioritization schemes are proprietary and generally not fully defined architecture. At best, current prioritization techniques appear to be more of a tactical patch than a thoughtful step forward. At their worst, improperly designed prioritization techniques can limit an internetwork's ability to respond to changing conditions, causing more problems than they solve.

9.5 Final considerations: planning for the new SNA and LAN interconnect

For IS planners to realize their dreams of eliminating costly, redundant SNA and internetworks, it is critical that the industry settle on an effective approach to letting native SDLC controller terminal traffic use the internetwork to communicate with the mainframe. The technology to accomplish this goal, dubbed SDLC transport by InterLAB, can be achieved using one of two methods: SDLC passthrough and SDLC conversion. Passthrough encapsulates SDLC data in TCP/IP envelopes, allowing SDLC traffic to run side-by-side with all other protocols across the WAN. SDLC conversion actually translates the SDLC frames into token ring frames and transmits them as network traffic onto the LAN. From there, the frames travel (in the same manner as any other LAN traffic) across the LAN/WAN internetwork.

While SDLC passthrough can be justified in some applications, the technology that will really push SDLC transport into the realm of efficiency is SDLC conversion. Here is how each transport strategy works:

With SDLC conversion, the converter—which can be a stand-alone device or can reside in a router—locally terminates SNA sessions and converts the traffic into LLC or LLC2 packets. The router or server then encapsulates the LLC packets and sends them

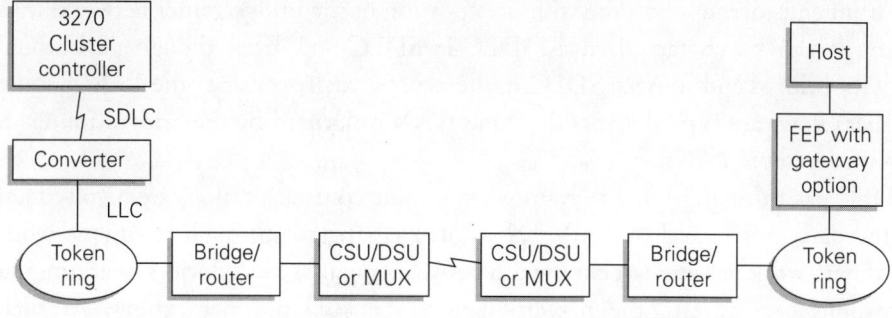

Adapted from Data Comm 7/92, p. 84, figure 1

Figure 9.8 SDLC conversion translates SDLC frames entering the controller into token ring (LLC2) frames

over the internetwork, forwarding them to the host through a gateway. (LLC packets require less overhead and can be bridged to the FEP, 3174, or 3172 gateway over the LAN with other traffic. These gateways can accept LLC2 data, so there is no need for a converter at both ends of the connection, making SDLC conversion a single-box solution.)

The SDLC converters serve as external token ring adapters for the cluster controllers; the cluster controllers are plugged into the converters, which are connected to the token ring. (See figure 9.8.) This setup eliminates the need for CSU/DSUs or modems, and significantly reduces the work for the FEP.

Because the SDLC protocol links the converter and the controller, the SDLC protocol is localized to the serial interface between two devices. The SDLC data is converted to LLC functions, making it equivalent to SNA data traveling as LLC, thereby completing the connection between the controller and the host. We can say that SDLC conversion is equivalent to SDLC-in/LLC-out. In addition, conversion lets SDLC frames take advantage of dynamic routing and high-speed links; the topology of the of networks that are crossed—including T1, T3, frame relay, ATM, and SMDS—is irrelevant.

SDLC passthrough is an encapsulation technique, which means it requires bridges or routers to be deployed in pairs—one on the controller side of the wide area link and another on the FEP side. The cluster controllers and FEPs are disconnected from the modems of the existing CSU/DSUs and connected instead to a serial port on the appropriate bridge or router.

The application data is packaged in a TCP/IP envelope and sent as session-level traffic; control frames and polling messages are encapsulated in the backbone protocol. The routers serve as multiplexers for the data. Passthrough enables the SDLC protocol to run from end-to-end across the wide area portion of the bridge/router network; thus, passthrough can be characterized as SDLC-in/SDLC-out. Even though passthrough works with bridges and routers, SDLC traffic never actually traverses the LAN, because SDLC data flows are carried across the same WAN links used by the bridges/routers to interconnect remote LANs.

SDLC passthrough is only relevant when remote communications are involved and when the data must travel over a WAN. Moreover, the passthrough technique works only if the network has enough bandwidth between any two SNA devices to ensure that transmissions can traverse the network before the session timer expires. As such, passthrough is not likely to be a beneficial strategy for large, complex internetworks, which typically take more time for data to travel.

Another disadvantage of passthrough is that it must slow the line at both ends of the connection to the maximum speed supported by the serial port of the controller and the FEP. By contrast, SDLC conversion has no such restriction, and can take full advantage of network speeds from 56K to T1.

With these facts in mind, SDLC conversion is unquestionably the method of choice for long-term planning and survival, since conversion gives network managers control over timing, retry, and similar parameters on both the SDLC and LLC sides of the link. It allows managers to fine tune performance and error recovery and to downsize the role of the FEP. (Since converters terminate the SDLC connections, there is no need to use the FEP SDLC port.) In each of the InterLAB tests performed, conversion boosted end-to-end throughput, while passthrough degraded it.

9.6 Conclusion

As the demand for SNA internetworking grows within the IS community, the breadth of data-link solutions expands, seemingly geometrically. Although the options can seem complicated, most of the market change is moving in a positive direction: more choices, lower cost, greater efficiencies. The products and strategies hitting the market are sure to help make SNA internetworking a more cost-effective, efficient solution than has ever been possible before.

Yet this good news is no replacement for involvement on the part of network management. With so much change, it is critical that those in a position to influence the vendors—that is, anyone who has corporate dollars to spend—demand the features and functionality needed to get the job done. The only way to recognize those functions is for network managers to firmly understand their sites' internetworking needs and goals, as well as how the existing base of products meets those needs. The gap between what is needed and what exists is the target; the IS community must reward vendors who strive to hit that target and financially ignore those who continue to pursue proprietary, unimaginative solutions that restrain the industry and individual IS sites from making significant internetworking progress.

With that kind of determination and a willingness to keep up with the pace of technical change, network managers will find themselves on the right path. Connecting SNA networks with internetworks will continue to require network knowledge and thoughtful selection of solutions, but for most sites, internetworking SNA is no longer an unsolvable puzzle.

chapter 10

Transporting SNA across TCP/IP

Michael Bowman

In this chapter, Michael Bowman takes us up to the higher layers of the OSI model and presents some of today's most popular interoperability solutions—encapsulation of SNA data in TCP/IP. We will see some of the reasons and rationale for encapsulating SNA data in TCP/IP. We will also examine the different issues often associated with this methodology and its positioning versus other alternatives for integration with dissimilar networking technologies.

10.1 Introduction

The concept of transporting SNA data using SDLC protocols over WANs is over twenty years old. In terms of networking technology, this makes SNA/SDLC a very mature adult—seasoned, predictable, dependable, albeit with a little gray hair. SNA/SDLC's younger sibling, SNA transport using LLC2 protocols over LANs, is now well into its adult years, perhaps already past its middle age crisis. Contrast these approaches with the concept of transporting SNA data encapsulated in TCP/IP over LAN/WAN internetworks, which is just now completing its adolescence. And, like many of our human adolescents, SNA over TCP/IP has struggled, striking out in many directions in an attempt to find itself. Multiprotocol LAN/WAN internetworks have grown rapidly to meet the new application demands of end users. Increasingly, network managers are faced with managing multiple physical and logical networks. Transporting SNA data over TCP/IP is one technique for consolidating these multiple networks.

In this chapter, we will discuss why SNA has grown into the predictable and reliable data transport that it has; explore the reasons that one might want to transport SNA data by encapsulating it within TCP/IP; examine some of the issues in transporting both native SNA and SNA encapsulated within TCP/IP; review the work that is progressing to enhance SNA-over-TCP/IP transport technology; and look at alternatives to encapsulation.

10.1.1 What's wrong with native SNA?

What's wrong with native SNA? Well, nothing. Really.

SNA's heritage from IBM has made it perhaps the most robust architecture for building large, mission-critical networks. During its twenty year history, SNA has matured into an environment that the end-user community can reliably deploy. And, up until recently, it has been the preferred architecture, despite its gray hair, for building new networks in most large end-user environments.

So, what has happened to move these end users away from deploying new SNA networks? New applications. Specifically, new applications that are being written on a computing platform other than the traditional IBM mainframe. These new applications need a networking environment tailored to support them, just as SNA supports the traditional IBM mainframe application environment. Along with the installed base of remote PC LAN and other LAN networks that now need to communicate among themselves, these new applications have driven the creation and explosive growth of the multiprotocol router marketplace.

Before multiprotocol routers became viable, users needed to deploy a new network each time a new computing platform was introduced, while maintaining the existing networks. This "parallel network syndrome" (see figure 10.1), while manageable, is generally quite costly to the organization. Multiprotocol routers have traditionally done a good job of providing the tools to collapse these parallel networks, except where one of the networks has been SNA. For both vendors and end users, the integration of SNA is where some of the greatest challenges and greatest opportunities lie.

An ongoing issue for the networking industry is that traditional SNA LAN data can only be bridged. It is not routable like layer 3 protocols such as TCP/IP. Figure 10.2 shows a simplified view of these protocol layers as referenced in IBM's open blueprint

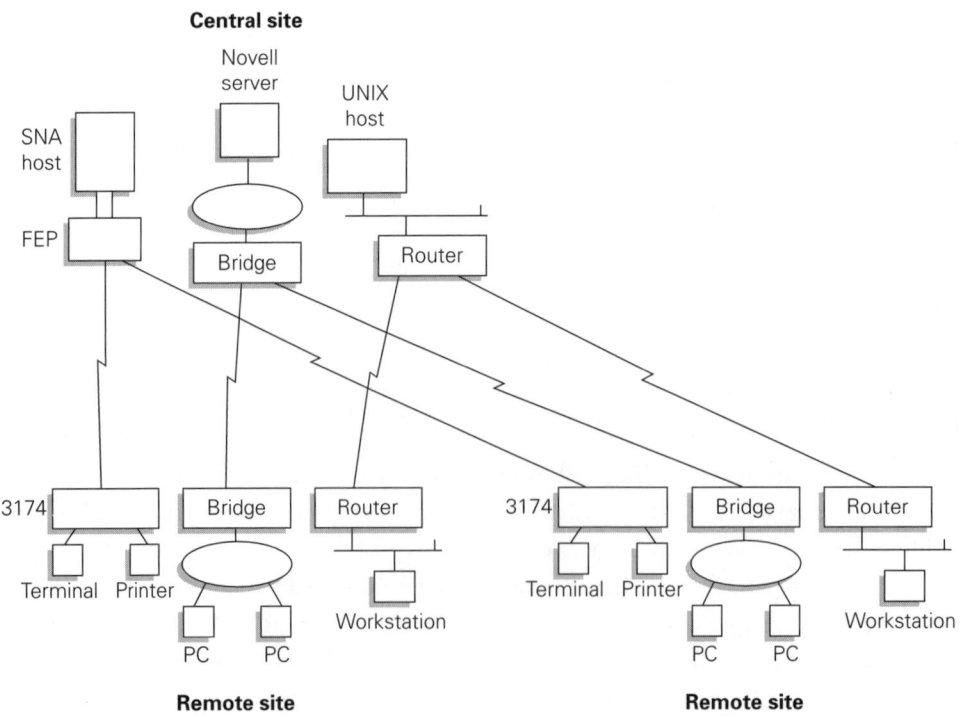

Figure 10.1   Parallel network syndrome

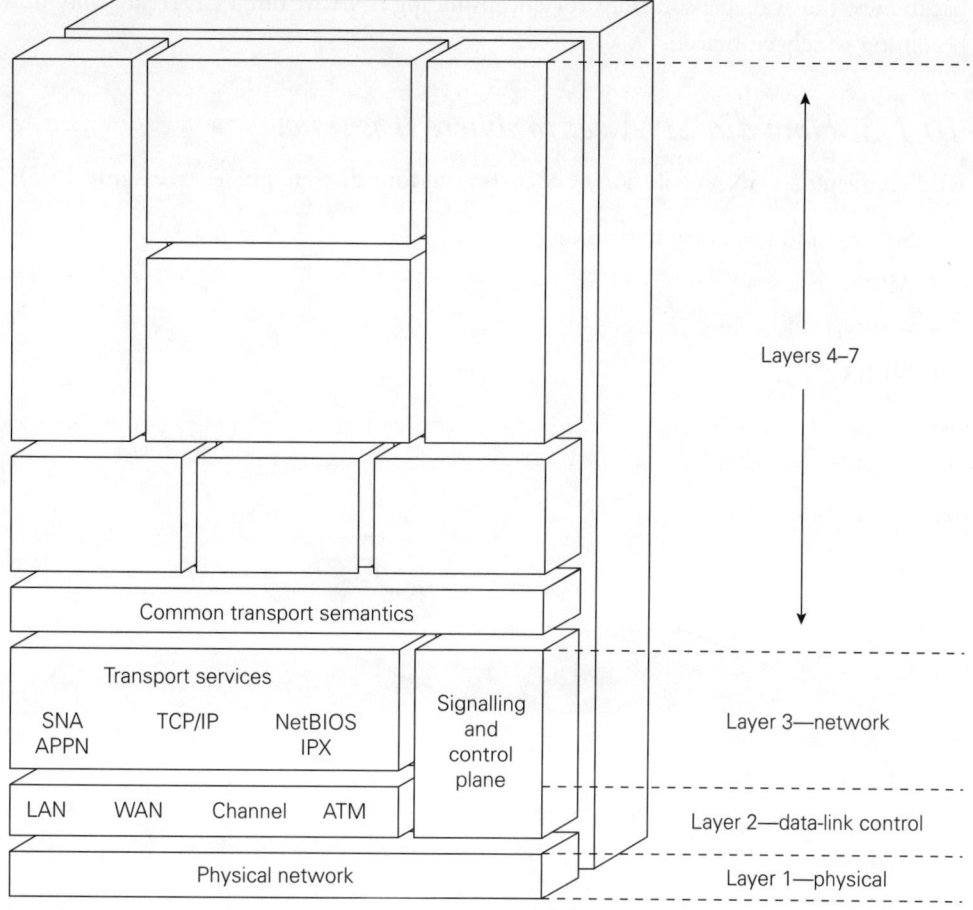

Figure 10.2 Networking layers and IBM's open blueprint structure

Within the figure:
- Layers 4–7
- Common transport semantics
- Transport services
- SNA APPN   TCP/IP   NetBIOS IPX
- Signalling and control plane
- Layer 3—network
- LAN   WAN   Channel   ATM
- Layer 2—data-link control
- Physical network
- Layer 1—physical

structure. Bridging any protocol tends to introduce additional complexity as a network becomes larger and has multiple "paths" between the bridge or router devices, particularly with regard to "broadcast" issues. Additionally, SNA has its own idiosyncrasies that must be considered when building large, bridged networks. IBM's latest methodologies, using APPN and HPR, have formed the basis of IBM's solutions to these bridging issues.

Successes achieved with open TCP/IP networking have motivated vendors to create routable SNA by encapsulating SNA data within TCP/IP frames. Today, these encapsulation mechanisms are workable, but have struggled through their adolescent stage—trying to find themselves. While there is much interest among users to build consolidated backbones, the available solutions for encapsulating SNA within TCP/IP are only now becoming widely embraced.

10.1.2 How did SNA get to where it is now?

IBM characterizes SNA evolution as occurring in four discrete phases (see figure 10.3):

- Subarea and low entry networking
- APPN
- APPN/HPR
- NBBS

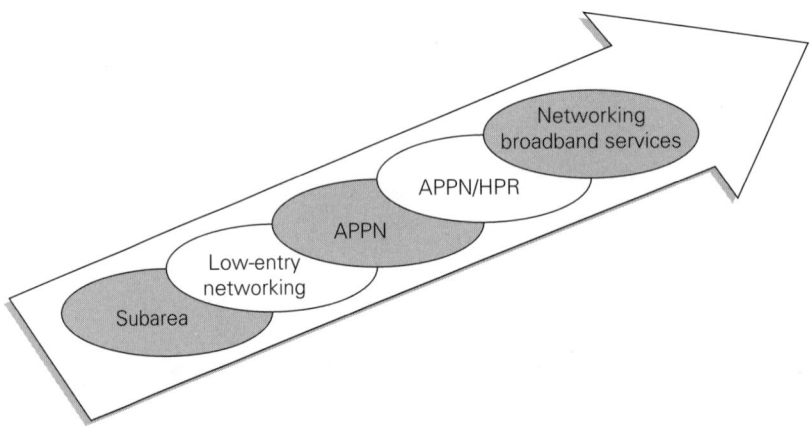

Figure 10.3   IBM's view of SNA evolution

Subarea SNA   Subarea SNA, which also encompasses LEN, takes SNA evolution from the mid 1970s through the late 1980s. The first incarnation of SNA defined hierarchical SNA PUs and LUs, primarily for use in 3270 data networks. 3270-based networks have typically been comprised of 3174-type control units (PU type 2) with attached terminal/personal computer (LU type 2) and printer (LU types 1 and 3) nodes. LEN nodes, introduced in the mid 1980s, are peer-to-peer oriented (Node type 2.1 and LU type 6.2), but are still "owned" by a hierarchical subarea network. APPC applications traditionally have utilized LEN devices. Subarea SNA is still the technology in use for most IBM mainframe networks today. WANs operating with the SDLC protocol and LANs/WANs using LLC2 protocol transport the SNA data. The SNA data (the

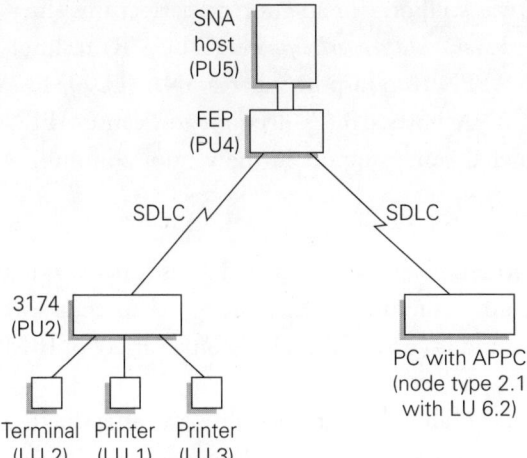

Figure 10.4 Typical SNA subarea network

RU) is identical regardless of the WAN or LAN protocol in use. Figure 10.4 illustrates a typical subarea network.

APPN IBM's introduction of APPN in conjunction with the AS/400 computing environment during the late 1980s heralded a new view toward networking IBM SNA devices. Initially, APPN was not so much an evolution of SNA but a new networking model, where true peer-to-peer capable devices could dynamically establish network connections and routes while maintaining network integrity. IBM's view is that APPN networks, together with intelligent end-user devices supporting APPC applications, would provide IBM the means to control the next generation of mission-critical applications.

Perhaps the key value that APPN technology brought to the mainframe networking environment was its facility to dynamically register each native APPN device that wished to connect to the network and then to deliver its requested network connection facilities. In fact, IBM has promoted ease of use as a primary benefit of APPN (see figure 10.3).

APPN can operate over any established SNA data-link level protocol such as SDLC and LLC2. APPN was given another boost with the introduction of the IBM 6611 multiprotocol router in 1993, which initially provided APPN functionality operating over a TCP/IP network infrastructure. A number of IBM and third party devices now support APPN, but its acceptance pales in comparison to TCP/IP.

As IBM began to promote the use of APPN for mainframe application networks, a major shortcoming surfaced—APPN could not directly accommodate the huge installed base of subarea PU2 SNA traffic. Again, another parallel network would be required, and end-user interest in APPN was stillborn. In an effort to correct this situation, IBM introduced the concept of *dependent LU server/requester* (DLUS/R) technology. DLUS/R works in conjunction with APPN to transport subarea SNA (LU 0, 1, 2, 3) traffic from existing PU 2 devices to SNA hosts. IBM's decision to license APPN technology and provide source code garnered some support in the vendor community and helped to bolster APPN.

APPN/HPR   IBM's current thrust is to establish the use of APPN as a networking model over its HPR network transport infrastructure. HPR is designed to transport both APPN and multiprotocol data traffic and is currently available on a variety of IBM devices.

HPR technology should be viewed as an alternative to building an infrastructure with TCP/IP-centric multiprotocol router technology.

NBBS   NBBS represents IBM's plans to provide fast packet and cell-based multiprotocol networks that accommodate not only conventional data traffic, but also other high-bandwidth real-time traffic required to support large scale distributed computing and multimedia applications.

NBBS is essentially IBM's ATM and switched network strategy and leverages off of their belief that frame relay networks will be feeder network connections for high bandwidth, cell-based corporate backbones. As these networks evolve, bandwidth management and deterministic delivery of real-time data will be key features.

10.2 *Transport issues*

While IBM was been busy promoting APPC, APPN, and their open blueprint structure, users were busy installing open networks. (Remember the router market explosion?) These networks generally support applications that require either TCP/IP and IPX transport. In many cases, these new application networks were installed as an alternative to writing new applications to run on the mainframe. It's significant that the mission-critical applications of the future often are not being written for the SNA mainframe environments. Even when the mainframe is still being used as part of the application solution, TCP/IP may now be the transport protocol of choice. The user has purposefully created multiple mission-critical networks—also known as the parallel network syndrome.

10.2.1 The installed base of SNA users

Remembering SNA's formative years, SDLC networks became the workhorse of corporate computing. Today, the overwhelming majority of SNA users is still utilizing PU 2 devices connected to mainframes via SDLC WANs or are connected via LAN or LAN/WAN networks that utilize LLC2 transport. Before we examine some of the more recent SNA-over-TCP/IP or SNA-over-Frame Relay advances, we must understand the needs of these users and how their native SNA networks satisfy these needs.

While the types of applications that operate on mainframes are endless, many share certain critical needs. Consider that from the 1960s through the mid 1980s, the mainframe (whether from IBM or another vendor) was the only real choice for delivering enterprise-wide applications to a large population of end users. The typical application enabled users either to create, to manipulate, or to retrieve information from the corporate data base.

These applications are by nature interactive transaction processing environments. Regardless of the specifics of any individual application, a few generalizations can be made about the nature of the environment they support. The key tenets employed as most SNA networks have been put into place follow:

1 The network is tailored for and supports SNA protocols only

2 End-user response time must be reasonable

3 End-user response time must be predictable

4 Network bandwidth is expensive

5 The network never goes down (well almost never—99.9+ percent uptime)

6 Network management tools must enable faults to be predicted or quickly detected and remedied

7 End users are generally not sophisticated and are not aware of the network that they are using

While the parameters used to value each of these items vary from enterprise to enterprise, the issues themselves are generally well understood by SNA networking professionals. The overwhelming use of 3270 applications operating over SNA/SDLC networks indicates that this environment still meets users' needs and that any replacement network must also meet these needs.

As an illustration, let's consider the following scenario:

You are responsible for network planning and management for a company that utilizes a mainframe for its accounting and customer information systems. The twenty customer service representatives at the Timbuktu site are connected to the mainframe via one 9600 bps SNA/SDLC circuit, along with forty other mainframe users at the site. Based upon the mix of typical transactions, the average response time that each customer service representative experiences is 3.5 seconds. The company needs to add ten more users and does not want the average response time to degrade more than 0.2 seconds. What changes are necessary to achieve this?

To answer this question, one could look into a crystal ball, or consult a local fortune teller. This network manager, however, would probably use both historical information about how the network has actually been operating and well-established modeling tools to empirically predict how the network should operate with the increased load. He would be able to determine not only whether the response time goal is feasible, but what network changes would make the goal achievable. Herein lies one of the primary reasons that the SNA/SDLC environment has remained successful. It is a very predictable, reliable, and stable environment.

SNA LAN and LAN/WAN environments have also met these needs of the corporate environment. *Source route bridging* (SRB), used both in local LAN and remote LAN bridging environments, has functioned well as a medium for transporting mission-critical application data. Again, it is predictable, although less so than SDLC, and large networks can be reliably deployed using SRB. Many large subarea networks have already been converted to utilize SRB LAN/WAN networks instead of SDLC networks.

While SRB is widely deployed, it does have its own shortcomings. Hop count issues and broadcast storms, especially with NetBIOS traffic, are widely documented.

10.2.2 *Today's enterprise network model*

For today's corporate network manager, the network that is being managed is likely to look like the one depicted in figure 10.5.

At first glance, this appears to be a convoluted, complex mess—and in many respects it is. As corporate networking professionals attempt to integrate the growing number of router devices into their day-to-day operation, they are now dealing with a different set of tenets for deploying these primarily non-SNA networks. The nature of these router networks is decidedly different than that of most SNA networks in existence today—not by the network manager's preference, but because of the capabilities of available multiprotocol routers. Tenets that reflect the current state of multiprotocol router networks follow:

1 The network supports multiple open, routable protocols

2 End user response time must be reasonable and generally can be made that way by adding network bandwidth

3 End-user response time must be predictable and generally can be made that way by adding network bandwidth or using router prioritization techniques

4 Network bandwidth is expensive, but necessary

5 The network should never go down

6 Network management tools must enable faults to be predicted or quickly detected and remedied

7 End users are generally not sophisticated and are not aware of the network that they are using

As you compare these tenets to the earlier set for SNA networks, you will find that there are several fundamental differences:

- Response time predictability and how it is guaranteed
- The availability and cost of network bandwidth

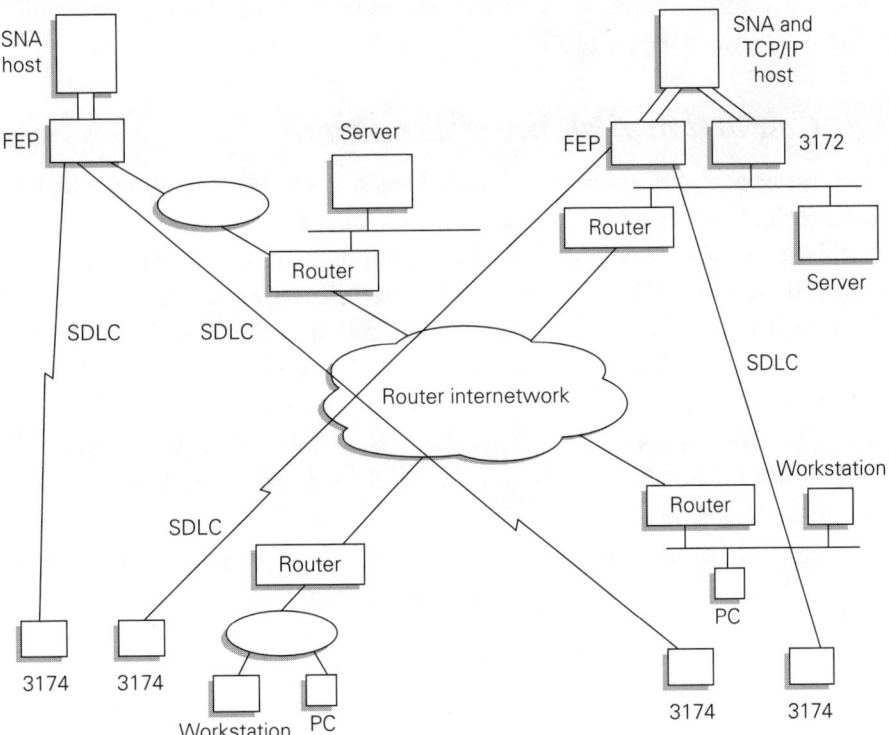

Figure 10.5 Parallel enterprise networks for SNA and multiprotocol applications

- The types of applications and protocols supported
- Network reliability

These differences create a dilemma for the network manager in trying to consolidate SNA and TCP/IP-based multiprotocol networks. Given a choice, the network manager would like to instill the determinism and network reliability aspects of SNA networks into the flexible, open multiprotocol environment. Remember that the reason these enterprises have chosen the multiprotocol environment is to support new applications operating on new platforms, not because they necessarily like the new networking environment better than the one that currently supports SNA applications.

10.3 The key differences

SNA and TCP/IP were designed to address different networking issues: SNA aimed at high bandwidth utilization and optimal response time for the users, whereas TCP/IP aimed at easier connectivity for the end users. Therefore both architectures have a different approach to networking problems.

10.3.1 Cost and availability of bandwidth

SNA networks have traditionally been designed based upon the assumption that bandwidth is scarce and expensive. WAN expense is still a large part of the network expense budget, and the cost to deploy a network to reach hundreds of remote branch office sites can be staggering. SNA/SDLC networking characteristics have enabled these networks to be engineered and tuned to squeeze as much utilization out of them as possible while minimizing WAN costs. Recent improvements in SNA-over-frame-relay product solutions accompanied by aggressive frame relay service provider pricing are now driving the move from SDLC-based networks to frame-relay-based SNA networks. In many cases, frame relay is being used to build physically consolidated, but logically separate, SNA and multiprotocol networks.

The cost and availability of bandwidth generally has not been considered as large an issue in multiprotocol router development and deployment. Consequently, a typical router network will tend to have much higher speed WAN links to smaller remote sites than typical SNA networks would. This is partly due to the nature of the router networks themselves and partly due to the variety of applications being supported, along with the multiple protocols required to support the applications.

10.3.2 Reasonable and predictable end-user response time

SNA network managers have learned how to engineer SDLC WAN and LLC2 LAN/WAN networks to ensure that end users get acceptable response time, despite having to deal with expensive bandwidth. Remember our earlier example of the network manager who needed to expand the network? He used historical data and available tools to reengineer the network to meet the criteria desired.

Managers of multiprotocol router networks are still learning how to engineer their networks and many may find that they must regularly increase the network's WAN bandwidth or invoke traffic priority features of routers to maintain acceptable response times. Until recently, the trial and error method has been the pragmatic approach to dealing with these issues. Tools are now available to test, measure, and monitor response times and their variability in these new multiprotocol router networks.

10.4 Consolidating SNA onto the multiprotocol router network

As network managers move to consolidate SNA onto their multiprotocol router networks, they find that just adding bandwidth will not solve all of the problems that arise. They find that they must learn how to engineer this new environment to ensure that both SNA and non-SNA end users continue to function normally. They must also decide how to physically and logically accomplish this consolidation:

- Whether to bridge or route the SNA data
- How to physically attach existing SNA devices to the consolidated network

SNA/LLC2 data traffic can only be bridged, so why ask the question? Because in order to overcome some of the problems associated with setting up and managing large, bridged networks, vendors have developed both proprietary and standards-based methods to encapsulate SNA data within TCP/IP. Much work has been done in the area of DLSw, the encapsulation technique introduced by IBM and then modified and adopted by the industry (IETF RFC 1795). A network using one of these approaches can then transport the SNA data without being forced to bridge the data using LLC2 protocols. So perhaps a better question is "should I bridge or encapsulate?"

There is no pat answer. Each enterprise is different and each router vendor's capabilities in SNA encapsulation technology, although based upon a standard, is likely to have its own enhancements. Remember that encapsulation technology is still struggling to mature out of its adolescent years and still developing rapidly. The technical motivation for moving to encapsulation really lies in the problems (or perceived problems) with bridging SNA/LLC2 data:

- LLC2 broadcasts at power-on time could create broadcast storms
- LLC2 keep-alive messages could create unproductive traffic
- SNA LU sessions could time out if excessive delays occur in the network
- Hop count limitations for SRB networks make topology design challenging at times for larger networks
- Bridging LLC2 data opens the door for other bridgeable traffic to flood the network

The last point may be the most pragmatic for network managers. In order to enable bridging of SNA traffic over a router network, a different type of administration problem arises—the need to create filters for each node in the network to ensure that unwanted traffic does not traverse the network because enabling bridging of SNA generally enables bridging of other protocols. Depending on the size of the network, this could become a daunting administration problem.

Encapsulation technology does address these problems:

- LLC2 broadcasts are eliminated—they are replaced by TCP/IP broadcasts, but the total number of broadcasts is minimized
- LLC2 keep-alive messages are eliminated
- SNA LU session timeouts can be minimized, since each end of the SNA connection appears to be locally connected to the other
- Most implementations make the encapsulated TCP/IP network appear as one SRB hop
- The need for enabling bridging is eliminated, thus preventing the network manager from having to deal with the bridging impacts of non-SNA protocols

If SDLC WAN links or devices can be connected to the router network, they can also benefit from the benefits that encapsulation brings.

As is often the case, some early users of encapsulation technology found the cure to be as bad as the disease. However, as DLSw technology has matured and as vendors have begun to interoperate, users now have a viable choice. So the correct answer as to whether one should bridge or encapsulate SNA data is truly enterprise dependent. Even as encapsulation technology becomes more mature, a bridging approach may still provide adequate network services for a large portion of the enterprise network. If the goal is to evolve to an infrastructure that transports only routed data, then the SNA traffic must either be encapsulated or go away.

10.5 How does TCP/IP encapsulation of SNA work?

Remember that SNA data, an RU, is the same whether it is being transported over an SDLC or an LLC2 network. Figure 10.6 reviews the general structure of these types of frames at the data-link level.

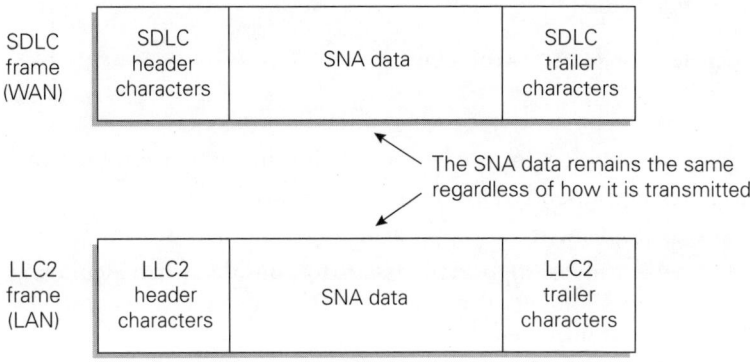

Figure 10.6 Transmitting SNA data over WANs and LANs

Unfortunately, existing router encapsulation mechanisms do not always take the same view as what they encapsulate as SNA data. There are several mechanisms for connecting SNA data links and then encapsulating the SNA data within TCP/IP for transport. They are:

- SDLC passthrough or tunneling
- SDLC and LLC2 termination
- Standalone SDLC conversion used with LLC2 termination
- DLSw

10.5.1 SDLC passthrough

The oldest and simplest method for encapsulating SNA/SDLC traffic is SDLC passthrough, also known as SDLC tunneling. This approach replaces an SDLC WAN link with a pair of routers that form a virtual wire simulating a dedicated WAN connection across the router network. Generally, the entire SDLC frame is encapsulated in TCP/IP and transported. SDLC passthrough does not attempt to address the transport of SNA/LLC2 data. Figure 10.7 illustrates the network topology and typical data flows for this approach.

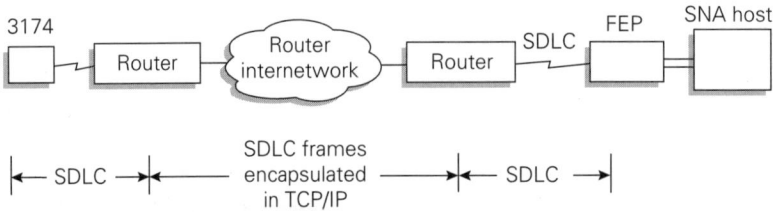

Figure 10.7   SNA encapsulation using SDLC passthrough

SDLC passthrough is the simplest form of encapsulation for users to implement, since all SDLC traffic flows end-to-end. This simplicity results in no changes being required at the FEP/host to implement this approach. Since the data stream is truly transparent, any SDLC device can be supported. Issues to consider when deploying passthrough are:

- The router network must have enough bandwidth to accommodate all of the SDLC polling traffic
- SDLC timeouts may be a problem if transit delays become significant—typical SDLC timeout values are set at three seconds
- Each router vendor's approach is proprietary

10.5.2 SDLC and LLC2 termination

SDLC and LLC2 termination are significantly different from SDLC passthrough because the SDLC or LLC2 data link is terminated at the remote router and only the SNA RU is encapsulated for transport across the router network. At the host router, the SNA RU is placed on an LLC2 connection (or, alternatively, an SDLC connection) to the FEP or LAN interconnect controller. This approach requires acknowledgment of all frames on the local data links and then timely, guaranteed delivery of the SNA RU (encapsulated in TCP/IP) across the TCP/IP network. Figure 10.8 illustrates this approach.

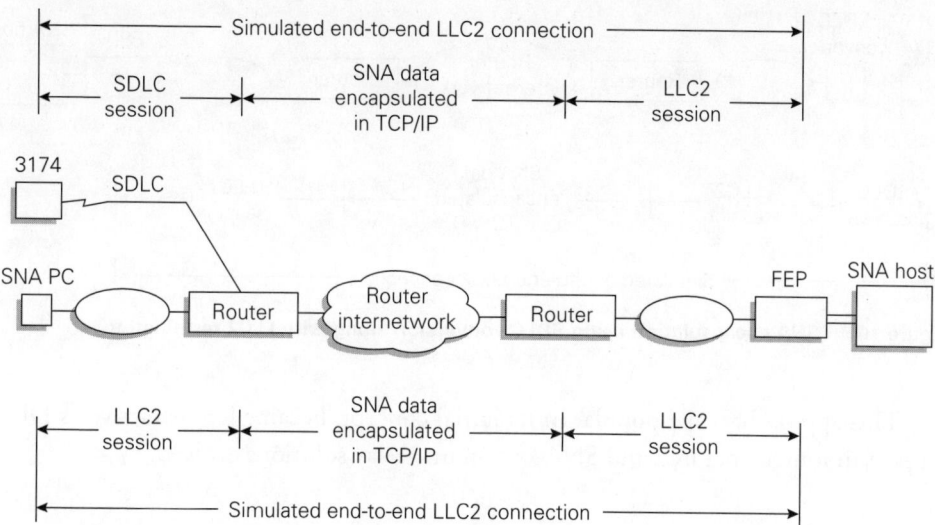

Figure 10.8 SNA encapsulation using SDLC termination and LLC2 termination

Routers implementing this approach must terminate the data-link connection on either side of the TCP/IP network and then maintain that connection as if the router were a PU4/5 device or the actual PU device.

SDLC device support for this approach has been limited to PU type 2 devices. The remote router must emulate an SNA PU type 4/5 device, with all of the polling and line handling functions required for that environment so that the SDLC device perceives it is still connected to a FEP/host. A potential concern for deploying SDLC termination is whether or not a router can adequately handle the added burden of SDLC traffic termination along with the routed multiprotocol traffic without materially affecting performance for any of the network users. The burden to support LLC2 termination is less than that required for SDLC termination and can generally be handled without creating an issue.

10.5.3 SDLC conversion used with LLC2 termination

Another approach for attaching SDLC devices and networks to TCP/IP router networks is to utilize a standalone SDLC Conversion device to terminate all of the SDLC links and present the data to the network as LLC2 data. The router network can then encapsulate the LLC2 data that needs to traverse the TCP/IP network by using LLC2 termination as described above. This approach is illustrated in figure 10.9

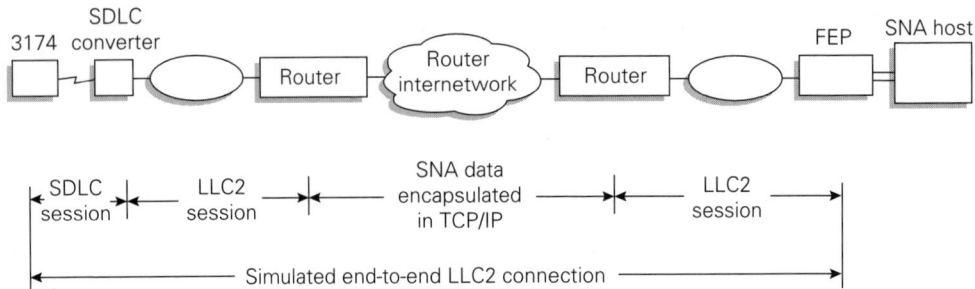

Figure 10.9   SNA encapsulation using SDLC conversion along with LLC2 termination

This approach, while popular in its initial concept, became less attractive as DLSw support in routers matured and SNA-over-frame-relay solutions evolved.

10.5.4 DLSw

IBM's introduction of its 6611 router in 1993 was significant in that it defined DLSw as a method for terminating and encapsulating SNA data from both LLC2 LAN and SDLC WAN connections, as well as NetBIOS data from LAN connections (see figure 10.10). DLSw was the first TCP/IP encapsulation method to provide functionality to:

- Locate SNA nodes in the network, and
- Control and react to network congestion.

IBM submitted its DLSw switch-to-switch protocol to the IETF and that protocol was subsequently published as RFC 1434. A collaborative effort by a number of vendors, including IBM, to enhance RFC 1434 resulted in the release of RFC 1795 in 1995. RFC 1795 forms the basis for the DLSw functionality now supported by a number of networking vendors.

Recently, the AIW created version 2 of the DLSw standard to address scaleability and connection setup timing issues. DLSw version 2 (DLSw v2), known as DLSw multicast, is defined in RFC 2166. Several vendors have endorsed this new standard, and at least one commercial implementation of the standard was available at the time of the publication, with several others to come.

As the standards for DLSw evolve, most major vendors will claim adherence to the standard and interoperability with other vendors' products. It is likely that different DLSw implementations will prove to be truly interoperable at only the most rudimentary

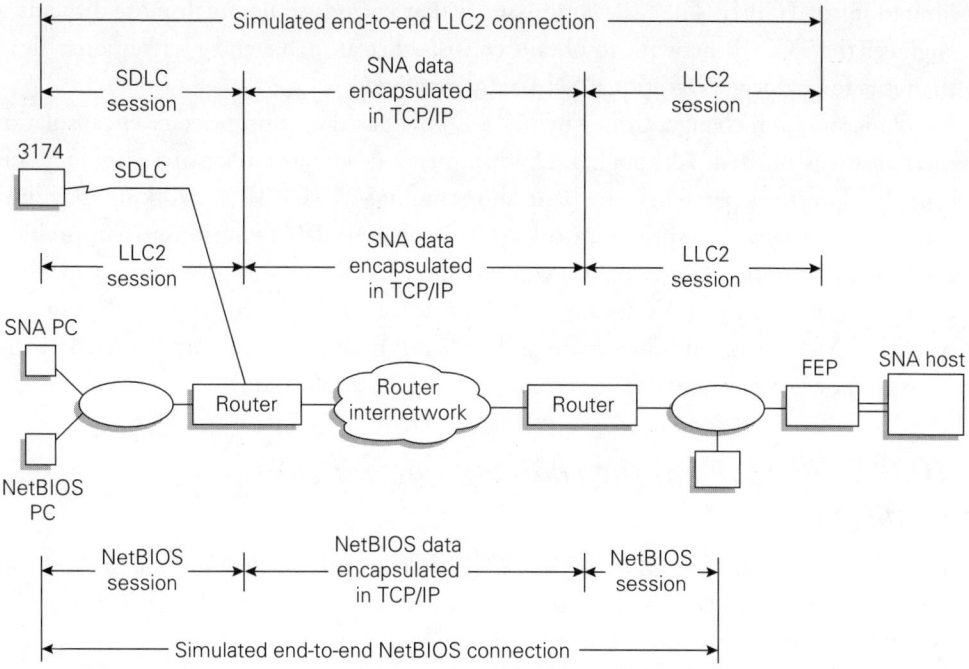

Figure 10.10   SNA and NetBIOS encapsulation by routers using DLSw

levels and that each vendor will use DLSw as the basis for adding its own differentiating features.

10.6 What problems are introduced by encapsulation?

Since current TCP/IP standards do not provide robust mechanisms for traffic prioritization or bandwidth allocation, end-user response times for TCP/IP networks are not easily predictable (remember the multiprotocol tenet on increasing WAN bandwidth to solve response time problems). SNA encapsulation traffic is certainly affected by this problem.

10.6.1 The challenge of building reliable, deterministic networks

The greatest challenges that many network managers face in building encapsulated SNA networks do not necessarily lie within the new technology, but within the present limitations of TCP/IP. The real-world issue is that it tends to be much more difficult to engineer the TCP/IP network to obtain consistent, reasonable end-user response times than it is to engineer a traditional SNA-only network.

This situation changes little whether a DLSw-based or a proprietary encapsulation mechanism is utilized. Although DLSw promises an enhanced set of technology and some level of interoperability, the basic shortcomings of TCP/IP networking may limit the benefits in some enterprise network applications. Available solutions to this problem are (1) using prioritization schemes within routers or FRADs to give priority to SNA-encapsulated traffic, or (2) building a multiprotocol packet-based (frame relay) or cell-based (ATM) network infrastructure and utilizing multiple private or switched virtual circuits to dedicate bandwidth to certain protocols or applications.

10.6.2 The continuing challenge of configuration management

The move to encapsulate SNA within TCP/IP does not address one of the network manager's biggest headaches—how to administer all of the SNA (and TCP/IP) addresses in the network. Users move. Users need access to new or different applications and hosts. Networking configurations change. The traditional subarea SNA configuration task can now be made even more complex with the introduction of encapsulation technology and the mapping of SNA destination addresses to TCP/IP addresses. A dynamic configuration and registration process, much like that promised with the APPN and DLUS/R model would certainly benefit DLSw.

A network using this approach would use DLSw-based transport of SNA/APPN data and utilize the directory service functions of APPN to help alleviate a portion of the configuration burden.

10.6.3 Other challenges—being held back by TCP/IP

The traditional IBM network user expects features and functions of SNA/SDLC and SNA/LAN networks that are not easily replicated in an encapsulated SNA network—not because vendors haven't been clever enough, but because of inherent limitations in current standards-based TCP/IP implementations. These functions include:

- Class of service
- Cost of service
- Security
- Accounting
- Flow control

Even though TCP/IP standards are evolving and will eventually add the additional functionality required to address these issues, the problem is one of timing. Users have been deploying TCP/IP-based networks at a tremendous rate to support new applications. Vendors will continue to chip away at these problems and make it more attractive to consolidate SNA onto these TCP/IP networks.

10.7 Alternatives to SNA encapsulation

Because SNA encapsulation introduces some problems, alternatives such as HPR and SNA-over-frame-relay should be considered.

10.7.1 The promise of IBM's HPR

IBM promotes its HPR technology as the ultimate approach for building high performance, deterministic, multiprotocol networks that include SNA. And HPR does appear to have the attributes necessary to back up this claim. However, choosing HPR will not be automatic for SNA or TCP/IP network managers, since deploying HPR means deploying another entirely new network infrastructure. Plus, if encapsulated SNA technology is still an adolescent, then HPR must be considered an infant. When compared to the overwhelming acceptance and growth of TCP/IP networks, HPR faces a tough, uphill battle. It may never get a chance to grow old.

10.7.2 The SNA-over-frame-relay alternative

While SNA encapsulation has certainly garnered much interest, SNA-over-frame-relay should be considered seriously. SNA-over-frame-relay experienced dramatic growth in 1996. This was due primarily to:

- Frame relay service providers becoming more aggressive on pricing, making higher capacity frame relay circuits actually cheaper than lower speed leased lines.

- Routers and FRADs evolving and becoming more cost effective

- Users beginning to trust frame relay as a dependable, shared service to transport SNA data

Utilizing frame relay, users now have a variety of options for building their networks—both with and without transporting their SNA data across TCP/IP. One of the more significant developments in the past few years is the adoption of RFC 1490, Multiprotocol Interconnect over Frame Relay. With equipment adhering to this standard, users may build physically consolidated, but still logically separate networks, with or without using SNA encapsulation. IBM's most recent releases of its NCP 6.2 and higher for its 3745/3746 FEPs have added many frame relay features for multiprotocol and SNA specific networking.

10.8 Conclusion

As we look at the merits of SNA encapsulation, we find that there are, as always, a myriad of networking issues to be considered. There are no firm and fast answers for what is right for any particular end user, but there are some items to remember:

- Encapsulation, like other techniques, serves a useful purpose in certain networking scenarios
- DLSw is the preferred encapsulation approach, because of its functionality and its industry support.
- Encapsulation has a number of deficiencies when compared to traditional SNA networks, primarily due to TCP/IP's capabilities not matching the deployed functionality in traditional SNA networks.
- Encapsulation will improve and solve more problems for users as TCP/IP is evolved.
- HPR is a valid alternative, but was not timely enough to slow the growth of, or to displace, recently installed TCP/IP infrastructure.
- SNA-over-frame-relay deserves a serious look.

SNA encapsulation is a key technology in consolidating SNA and multiprotocol networks, and will continue its maturation into adulthood, continuing to learn from its older siblings. Successful users will analyze the many available and emerging networking alternatives and formulate both short- and long- term migration plans. A prerequisite for this success is the networking vendors' commitment to ensuring their products directly meet users' business as well as technology needs.

chapter 11

Interconnecting LAN networks with SNA

JIM FLETCHER

Jim Fletcher presents a different approach for integrating SNA, TCP/IP, and other networks: utilizing the SNA infrastructure as the backbone consolidated network. Specifically, utilization of APPN/HPR, LTLW (that became a part of AnyNET offerings) are listed among other techniques. In addition to TCP/IP, encapsulation of IPX, NetBIOS, and other protocols are described in this chapter.

11.1 Introduction

In today's enterprise networks, it is very likely that there are multiple protocols in addition to a company's SNA network protocol. These non-SNA protocols often began as isolated networks with no need to intercommunicate. With the growing availability of LAN-based applications, such as email, and with the growth of TCP/IP-based products, users now have the need to interconnect these once disparate networks.

Many users facing this dilemma have an existing SNA WAN on which they have successfully operated mission-critical applications for decades. When desiring to interconnect these non-SNA networks, many network designers choose solutions such as network bridges or routers, and install parallel networks, even for casual connections between the non-SNA networks. But by installing a parallel network, the network designers may add complexities which may unnecessarily increase their network costs. Parallel networks require significantly more planning, increased line costs, and significant increases in network management complexity. Why not utilize the existing SNA network and minimize the network change? An enterprise can maintain the advantages of SNA, while supporting multiple protocols. In this chapter, we'll discuss several methods that enable the existing SNA network to be used as a transport network for non-SNA protocols. While newer options do exist, many specialized methods have appeared over the years. In this chapter, we'll take a look at some of them to help complete the internetworking puzzle.

Several networking solutions enable non-SNA network traffic to be sent across the SNA network just like any other SNA data would be sent. All implementations in this category share a common attribute. They define one or more SNA LUs as connection points for the non-SNA networks. The SNA logical units represent the edges of the SNA network. (As described in chapter 4, logical units are software representations of end points of the network, that is, the entities that would be interacting directly if the end points were local to each other and did not need the network.)

These SNA LUs are used to establish an SNA LU–LU session which traverses the SNA portion of the network. The non-SNA data is sent on these SNA sessions. Different methods are used, depending on the specific protocol and vendor's implementation, to connect the non-SNA protocol to the SNA LU, but at a conceptual level, the methods are the same. Figure 11.1 shows the basic concept used by most implementations.

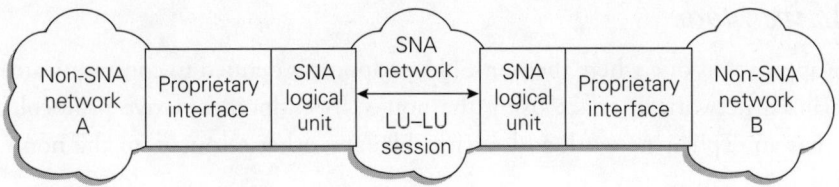

Figure 11.1 Overview of the typical configuration

In figure 11.1, two non-SNA networks are communicating using the SNA network as a logical connection between them. The SNA network could be a simple, single-domain subarea SNA network, or an extremely complex, interconnected SNA network. Further, the network could consist of a subarea-based SNA network, a pure APPN or HPR network, or combinations of these SNA protocols. The only requirement is that one be able to establish an SNA LU–LU session between the two SNA endpoints, which means the non-SNA network must be represented to SNA at each endpoint by an LU.

To support this interconnection, a specialized interface typically exists at the edges of the SNA network. This interface provides the connection between the SNA and non-SNA networks. This interface receives non-SNA data and places the data onto the SNA network by instructing its SNA logical unit to send the data across the SNA network to its session-partner LU. When the data is received by the partner SNA LU, the data is placed onto the partner non-SNA network by the specialized interface to be delivered to the partner non-SNA endpoint.

11.1.1 Passive mode

There are multiple possibilities for the implementation of the proprietary network interface processing. This interface can operate in what we will refer to as *passive mode* where the interface simply listens to the attached media, say a token ring LAN, and when it sees data destined for the partner network, it receives the data and passes it to the SNA endpoint LU. The data is then sent over the SNA network to the partner SNA endpoint LU. The partner SNA LU then passes the data to the proprietary interface which places the data onto the partner non-SNA network.

Neither non-SNA network is aware of the existence of an intermediate connection over an SNA network. No modifications are required to the non-SNA resources in order for them to communicate across the SNA network. With this approach, the SNA network access point would typically have no network address—from the non-SNA protocol's perspective. Instead the SNA network transparently connects the networks, much as though the two non-SNA networks were directly connected.

11.1.2 Active mode

An alternative approach is one where the non-SNA endpoint is defined to communicate with the specialized network interface using the non-SNA endpoint's native protocol. The interface has an explicit network address just like any other resource on the non-SNA network.

When the non-SNA network resource sends data, it directs the data to the interface network address, fully believing either that the interface is the destination resource or that it is a network routing node which will route the request to the true destination. Just as with the passive mode described previously, the endpoint non-SNA resource is unaware that an intermediate SNA network will be used to route the data to its true destination.

The proprietary interface, upon receiving the data, simply maps the data onto the SNA session associated with the partner non-SNA network. The data is then delivered using an SNA LU–LU session to the partner SNA resource at the other end of the SNA network. This SNA resource passes the data to the specialized interface. The interface processing provides the non-SNA network addressing for the data and sends the data into the non-SNA network to be delivered to the non-SNA partner resource. We will refer to this as *active mode* since the interface processing is actively involved in providing the addressing information required to interconnect the non-SNA networks.

Typically, the non-SNA data is sent intact with appropriate addressing information. The addressing information is required in order for the non-SNA network to understand the delivery of the data to its actual destination. Imagine the SNA network acting just like a network bridge, transparently interconnecting the non-SNA networks.

Technically, more complex implementations could eliminate the addressing information when entering, and reconstruct the addressing information once the data crossed the SNA network. However, typical implementations of active mode solutions do not do so, perhaps because it would be more complex to develop.

Figure 11.2 conceptually shows how SNA-encapsulated internetworking functions. In this example, the non-SNA data packet is processed by the interface processing function. That function then sends the data across the SNA LU–LU session. The non-SNA

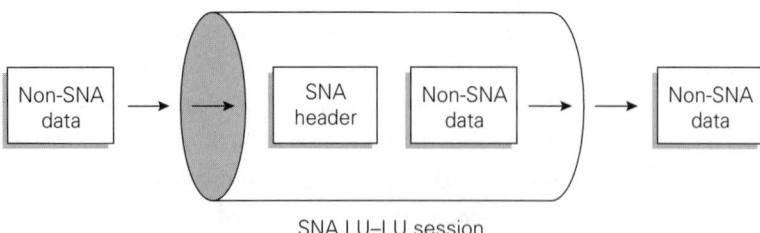

SNA LU–LU session

Figure 11.2 SNA-encapsulated internetworking

data packet is prefixed with an SNA network header and transported intact across the SNA network.

11.2 Configuration possibilities

Above we discussed the active and passive modes of accessing the SNA network. Once inside, there are numerous configuration possibilities within the SNA portion of the network.

Using a traditional subarea network, there typically are one or more VTAM nodes. As further described in chapter 4, VTAM nodes provide mainframe-based SNA networking connected to one or more communications controllers, originally called FEPs. VTAM provides the control point functions for the network such as session setup processing. The communications controllers provide the data routing for the resulting sessions to enable the network data to be routed more efficiently between the two SNA session endpoints. These communications controllers are typically strategically located within the enterprise network. The SNA network encompasses the VTAM nodes and all of their attached communications controllers.

In this environment, when using SNA-encapsulated internetworking, a typical solution would have a vendor-supplied product operating on a workstation or server attached to the non-SNA network and connected to the communications controller via either telecommunications links or directly via LAN connection. The vendor's product provides the connectivity to the non-SNA network and also has an SNA LU presence. A similar configuration exists at the partner network attachment. When non-SNA network interconnection is performed, the non-SNA data is transported across the existing SNA network, and delivered to the partner non-SNA network.

Figure 11.3 shows a simple implementation where two non-SNA LANs are interconnected using remote workstations for the interconnection. In this figure, a workstation on each of the remote LANs provides the interconnection function. The SNA LU presence is located on the workstation with the SNA session encompassing the path between the two workstations. The LAN workstation is directly connected to the communications controller perhaps using a frame relay or SDLC WAN connection. The non-SNA data is encapsulated within an SNA LU–LU session that exists between the two workstations and traverses the communication controller.

With the emergence of APPN and HPR, the SNA network no longer consists soley of mainframe-based networking. Customers can utilize the many APPN products to build peer-oriented APPN networks and can transport their non-SNA data over these networks as well. The SNA networks can consist of pure APPN/HPR networking, pure subarea-based traditional SNA networks, or combined networks combining traditional

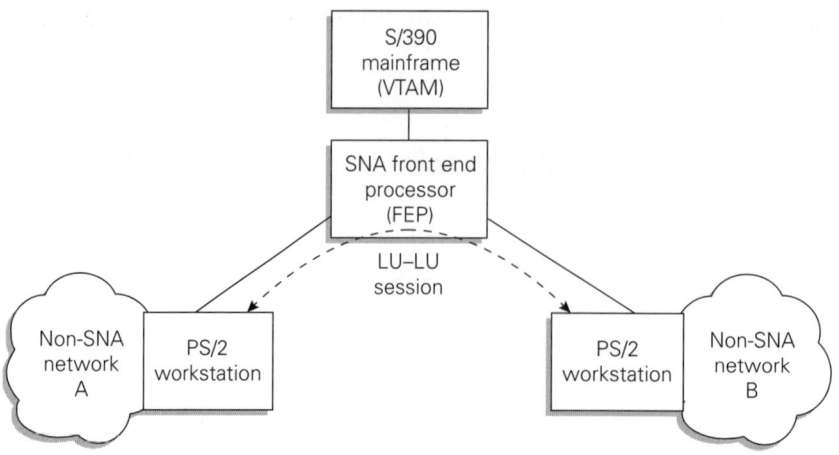

Figure 11.3　Simple implementation using remote workstation and subarea SNA

SNA with APPN/HPR networking as well. By using APPN networks or APPN connections to the traditional SNA network, the SNA network definition can be significantly reduced, or even eliminated.

Figure 11.4 represents a network where the SNA network is comprised of APPN nodes. This APPN network could perhaps be a router network, a workstation network, an AS/400 network, or even a mainframe-based network. The configuration possibilities and resulting availability are significantly improved when using an APPN/HPR network. However note that the concept is the same as that provided in figure 11.3. In either case, an LU–LU session is used to provide the communication path across the SNA portion of the network.

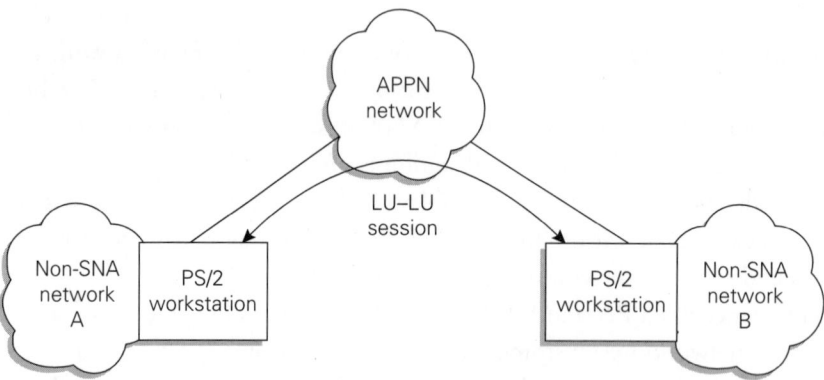

Figure 11.4　Simple implementation using remote workstation and APPN

A possible configuration not pictured, but of importance, would be an emerging APPN network resulting from a staged migration from subarea-based to APPN-based networking. In this case, the interchange node function provided by VTAM could be used to interconnect APPN/HPR networks with subarea networks and further expand the networking possibilities.

When using a solution that employs a workstation platform, the SNA LU presence can be defined to the SNA network as an SNA dependent LU. Preferably, it is defined as an independent SNA LU. The independent LU approach is preferred, when possible, since SNA support for independent LUs provides signficant reduction of the required network definition and is fully supported by all APPN-based products.

By having the SNA LU image on a remote platform, data from the connecting non-SNA network has direct access to the SNA communications controller network or APPN peer network. Therefore, the data is never required to traverse a mainframe node. This method usually provides more efficient transport of the data across the SNA network. The remote workstation approach is used by several products. We will examine, as examples, two product implementations from IBM. The LAN-to-LAN WAN (LTLW) program and the SNALINK function provided by TCP/IP for OS/2 each provide the ability to transport non-SNA protocols over the SNA networks using remote workstations as the connection point between the SNA and non-SNA networks. The LTLW program provides the ability to interconnect IPX, NetBIOS, and TCP/IP networks with an SNA network. SNALINK provides the ability to route TCP/IP data only. We'll futher discuss the details of these implementations later in this chapter.

11.2.1 Using a mainframe application

Interconnection is also possible by using mainframe SNA application programs to perform the interface function and to communicate across the SNA network. With this approach, however, the non-SNA data is required to traverse the mainframe at each SNA endpoint in order to access the SNA network which would likely result in reduced end-to-end performance over the previously discussed solution. IBM's SNALINK feature of TCP/IP for VM and MVS mainframe operating systems is implemented using the SNA mainframe applications approach. SNALINK can also be used in conjunction with a special feature of the NCP communications controller software to route TCP/IP directly through the communications controller even though the mainframe-based SNALINK is providing the TCP/IP network processing.

11.3 The SNA LU–LU session

The next element to examine is the SNA session. The SNA LU–LU session which traverses the SNA network can be a single SNA session or can consist of multiple parallel sessions. Think of a session as a logical connection between the two SNA endpoints, enabling the exchange of data. The session protocol may be any SNA session type but typically is an APPC session. APPC offers many advantages for the SNA interconnection because of its ability to establish multiple parallel sessions and its ability to multiplex within the sessions using conversations. These capabilities enable more complex interconnection possibilities between the non-SNA networks and offer better performance within the SNA network, thus improving the non-SNA user's response time.

When establishing communications across the SNA network, once again, choices must be made based on the capabilities of the SNA network endpoints. If the endpoints support parallel LU–LU sessions, then only a single SNA LU is required to be defined in the SNA network endpoints. Such multiple sessions can be established between the two endpoints. More recent SNA implementations typically support parallel sessions. APPC can exploit this advantage.

Figure 11.5 pictures an interconnection which exploits parallel sessions. In this example, only a single SNA LU is required at each endpoint in order to transport the non-SNA data across the SNA network. Multiple LU–LU sessions can be established between the two endpoints in order to provide a one-way session for sending data to the partner network and a like session for receiving data from the partner network.

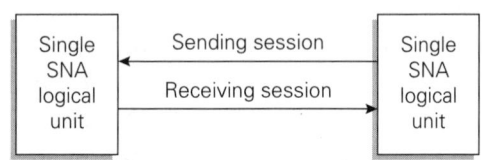

Figure 11.5   Parallel session transport

In some situations, the SNA endpoints do not support parallel sessions. In order to provide a session for sending and a separate session for receiving data between the two networks, two SNA LU instances are required at each end. With this method, one SNA LU is used for sending data to the partner SNA LU and another is used for receiving data from the partner SNA LU. Also, bidirectional communication can be established emulating a full-duplex connection.

Figure 11.6 pictures a case where multiple SNA LUs are required in order to bridge the two non-SNA networks. In this example, an SNA LU is defined for sending data to the partner non-SNA network and another SNA LU is defined for receiving data from the partner network. A single SNA LU–LU session is established from each of the LUs.

If the SNA endpoints do not support parallel sessions and multiple LU images are not desired, a single SNA LU can be defined at each endpoint and a single session established between these LUs. With this method, the SNA endpoint processing must provide a means to emulate full-duplex operation since data may only be sent or received at a given instance. Obviously this method would be the least desirable in a typical asynchronous LAN environment where data may need to be transported in each direction across the SNA network simultaneously.

Figure 11.7 shows a network where only a single LU image is provided. In this case a single SNA LU image is defined at each edge of the SNA network and a single SNA LU–LU session is established between them. An implementation-specific method is used to determine how to manage the direction in which the

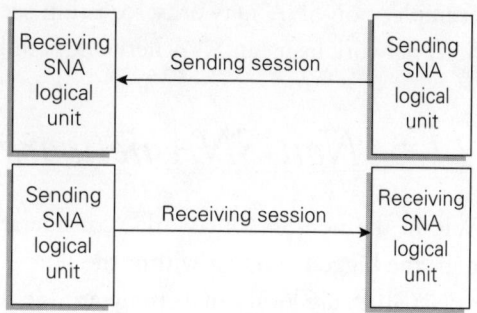

Figure 11.6   Dependent LU parallel session transport

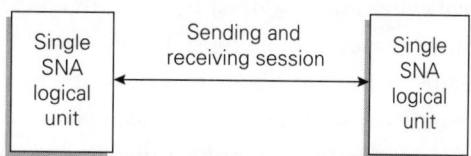

Figure 11.7   Single session transport

session is operating. Effectively, each endpoint LU must bid for the ability to send data across the session. This is typically known as a flip-flop connection since the direction for the session data would continually flip-flop from send mode to receive mode.

11.4 SNA network considerations

Within the SNA portion of the network, all of the SNA tuning parameters are applicable to the non-SNA data transport, just as they would be to other SNA sessions. The transport sessions can be assigned specific SNA COS attributes to balance the impact that these sessions have on the other data being transported by SNA with the response time requirements for the attaching non-SNA networks. For example, SNA permits the assignment of priorities to the data being transported. SNA then assures that the appropriate level of processing is given to the data based on its priority.

COS support in SNA also enables the path of a session to be determined by the network based on characteristics such as security requirements. Using this capability, for example, non-SNA networks requiring secure access can be interconnected across an SNA network using an SNA network path known to be secure.

11.5 Non-SNA network considerations

Within the non-SNA networks, considerations for network interconnection vary. Perhaps the biggest concern within the non-SNA network are local timers. Protocols such as NetBIOS use local timers to determine the duration to wait for certain events such as Name Query to complete. They issue the request and then start a timer. When the timer expires, they assume that all responses have been received and the event is complete.

Endpoint timers are generally set for operation in a single-LAN or bridged-LAN environment which operate at multimegabit media speeds. Suppose this local LAN is now interconnected to another LAN located across the SNA network. The SNA network, like most WANs, is typically connected with links operating at kilobit or low megabit speeds, but almost always at speeds below that of the LAN. When data is transported across the SNA network to the partner non-SNA network, the endpoint timers must be set with the newly added delay in mind to avoid endpoint timeouts. It is important to note that endpoint timers are of concern for any interconnection method that traverses a wide area connection, whether that connection is provided by the SNA network, a router network, or even a simple point-to-point connection between the two remote non-SNA networks.

SNA-encapsulated interconnection can aid in reducing definition conflicts. Since the intervening SNA network bridges the *data* between the networks and not the lower layer signaling information, interconnecting LANs over the SNA network can eliminate network address conflicts such as duplicate LAN addresses. With other schemes which interconnect LANs at the media layer, this isolation is not possible.

11.6 Product implementations using SNA-encapsulated internetworking

As mentioned earlier, two products which use SNA-encapsulated internetworking are IBM's SNALINK feature of its TCP/IP product, and the LTLW program.

11.6.1 SNALINK

We'll first discuss SNALINK. SNALINK provides the ability to interconnect TCP/IP networks across SNA networks. SNALINK is available for an OS/2-based workstation or for the mainframe. On the mainframe, SNALINK can be configured to use SNA LU type 0 communications protocols or SNA LU 6.2 protocols. As a result, SNALINK offers multiple configuration possibilities.

SNALINK for the mainframe can be used for two purposes. First, it provides the ability to access TCP/IP-based mainframe applications using the SNA network. Also, the customer can use the SNA network as a transport to interconnect multiple TCP/IP networks. A mainframe SNALINK implementation consists of a TCP/IP protocol stack and an SNA protocol stack. The TCP/IP and SNA protocol stacks providing the SNALINK function communicate using a specialized interface called *interuser communication vehicle* (IUCV). Figure 11.8 shows a typical SNALINK configuration.

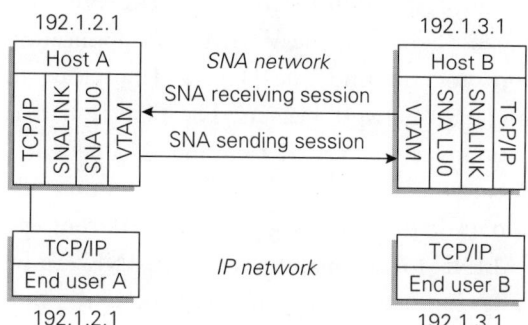

Figure 11.8   Mainframe SNALINK implementation

In this example, end user A on a TCP/IP network desires to communicate with end user B on another TCP/IP network. The interconnection is accomplished using SNALINK on the two mainframe hosts. The SNA LU is defined to represent the VTAM SNA application which will provide the interconnection. The SNALINK process is pictured to show the link between the TCP/IP and SNA network stacks. Note that, in this example, two SNA sessions are used. One session is for sending data to the partner network and the other session is used for receiving data from the partner network.

Within the TCP/IP implementation, special predefinition is performed to define the SNA network as a TCP/IP link. Definition is provided to SNALINK to indicate which TCP network address is accessible across the specified SNA network link as well as the SNA LU name representing the partner SNA LU. Note that the SNA network link is a logical link. The actual physical connection may consist of a single SNA link or multiple interconnected SNA networks.

The TCP/IP network address reachable across this SNA connection may be an explicit single-node address or, by using SNALINK's masking capabilities, may represent a group of TCP/IP resources accessible across the SNA connection. In figure 11.8, note the TCP/IP network addresses that are pictured. Each end-user station has an IP address which identifies it and each mainframe TCP/IP has an IP address to identify it as well. The SNA portion of the network simply appears as a logical connection to the IP network.

Let us suppose a TCP/IP workstation connected to a LAN wants to send data to a TCP/IP workstation connected to another LAN. These LANs are connected only by the SNA network. SNALINK provides the network interface between the TCP/IP and SNA networks at each edge of the SNA network.

Data is sent by the workstation, in native TCP/IP format, and reaches the origin-side SNALINK TCP/IP node. Based on the target network address and the predefinition to SNALINK—which identifies the resources this SNALINK services—TCP/IP on the origin-side network recognizes that the destination is across an SNALINK connection. The origin-side TCP/IP then passes the data to the VTAM SNA application program. The origin-side SNA application program sends the TCP/IP data packet to the partner SNA application program using SNA network headers. The TCP/IP data is sent intact. Once the partner SNA application receives the data from the SNA network, it strips the SNA headers and passes the data to the TCP/IP stack on the destination side SNA node. TCP/IP then delivers the data to its destination using native TCP/IP routing.

There are mutliple options with SNALINK for the mainframe. SNALINK can be configured to use a single SNA LU–LU session across the SNA network as the link between the SNA networks. Alternatively, it can be configured in *dual mode* where a pair of LU–LU sessions is established. In dual mode, each of the sessions operates as a single-direction pipeline across the SNA network. Data may be sent in each direction simultaneously. Figure 11.8 is an example of dual mode operation. A single SNA LU which supports parallel sessions is defined in each endpoint and parallel sessions are established across the SNA network.

Without dual mode, SNALINK processing must use flip-flop mode processing whereby data is only sent in a single direction at a given time. The endpoint SNA LUs must determine which end is permitted to send prior to sending any data. Obviously, this mode would not be desirable for high transaction rates because of the potential delays and additional overhead.

11.6.2 SNALINK 6.2

TCP/IP for the mainframe also offers the ability to communicate using APPC. The APPC version of SNALINK is known as SNALINK6.2. The function provided to the end user is the same as that provided by SNALINK, but the advantages of APPC communications within the subarea portion of the network are leveraged. Because not all implementations of APPC support parallel sessions, SNALINK6.2 offers the ability to operate using a send and a receive SNA LU definition, or preferably, the ability to send and receive across the SNA network using a single SNA LU definition in each endpoint of the SNA session.

With both SNALINK and SNALINK6.2, multiple TCP/IP networks can be interconnected. With each interconnected pair of networks, a logical link to cross the SNA network is defined and the name of the SNA LU which represents the destination end of the logical connection is designated. The TCP/IP network address or addresses reachable across the specified link are indicated.

11.7 SNALINK for the OS/2 environment

IBM's TCP/IP for OS/2 offers the SNALINK capability for users who want to access the SNA network from a remote workstation using IBM's OS/2 workstation operating system. With SNALINK for OS/2, the workstation provides the interface from the TCP/IP network to the SNA network. The SNA LU image is either a dependent or independent LU, depending on the capability of the SNA network to which the workstation is attaching.

When defined as an independent LU, parallel session capability is exploited to require only that a single SNA LU be defined at each endpoint for both sending and receiving data across the SNA network. Parallel sessions are established between the two SNA endpoints. The use of dependent LUs creates two requirements: first, a mainframe must exist in the network to provide services for the dependent SNA LU and, second, two SNA LUs must be defined for the SNA session endpoint. Each SNA LU image will have a single session to it. One LU session will be used for sending data across the SNA network and the other session will be used for receiving TCP/IP data from the partner TCP/IP network.

Figure 11.9 shows a typical network using SNALINK for OS/2. In this example, two end users located in separate TCP/IP networks desire to communicate. SNALINK for OS/2 provides the interconnection across the SNA network. In this example, the SNA network transport is an APPN network. The same support is possible with a traditional subarea-based SNA network or a mixed traditional subarea and APPN network. SNALINK for OS/2 obviously requires an OS/2-based workstation to provide interconnection. In addition, TCP/IP for OS/2 is required as well as Communications Manager/2, or its predecessors, to provide the SNA network connection.

SNALINK for OS/2 can be used to communicate with another SNALINK for OS/2 workstation across the SNA network, or it may be used to communicate with SNALINK on the mainframe, depending on the company's networking requirement. This is important to note in today's client/server networks where the server application

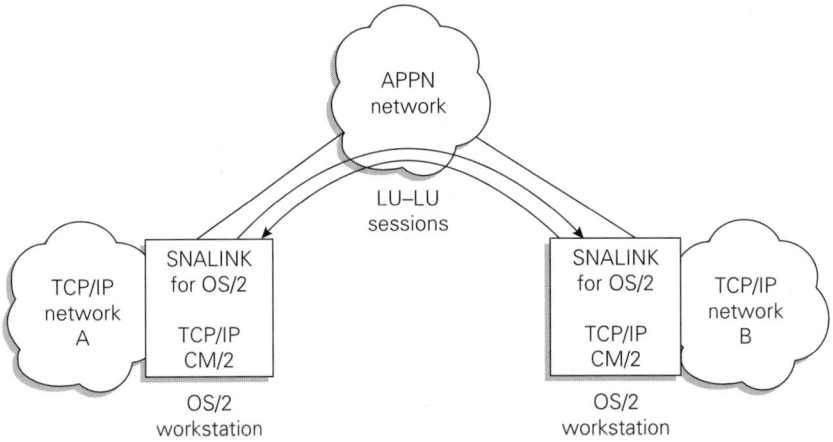

Figure 11.9 Interconnecting TCP/IP networks with SNALINK for OS/2 across an APPN network

may be mainframe-based. In this case, a remote TCP/IP-based application program could utilize SNALINK for OS/2 and communicate across the existing SNA network to a mainframe-based TCP/IP application program. The entire network could be an SNA network, with the applications being TCP-based. Figure 11.10 shows an example of an SNA network where the client workstation is on any TCP/IP-supported workstation including DOS, UNIX, or Windows. It desires to communicate with a mainframe-based TCP/IP application. The network consists of a TCP/IP-based segment and an SNA network (in this case an APPN network). The client workstation communicates using native TCP/IP protocols. The SNALINK for OS/2 workstation sees the data packets destined for the predefined target address of the mainframe TCP/IP node. It accepts the data and transports its across the SNA LU–LU session to the mainframe TCP application. Neither the mainframe application nor the end-user workstation is aware that any intermediate routing occurred across an SNA network.

11.8 NCP connectionless SNA transport LU

The SNA network communications controller NCP can act as a TCP/IP router. The TCP/IP data is routed directly between the communications controllers much like is done with SNA data. NCP connectionless SNA transport LU (NCST) functions by providing the ability to define the SNA LU presence as a special LU located on the communications controller. An SNA LU–LU session is established between the origin-side communications controller LU and the destination-side communications controller LU. The LUs communicate using the SNA LU 0 protocol. If access is required to a

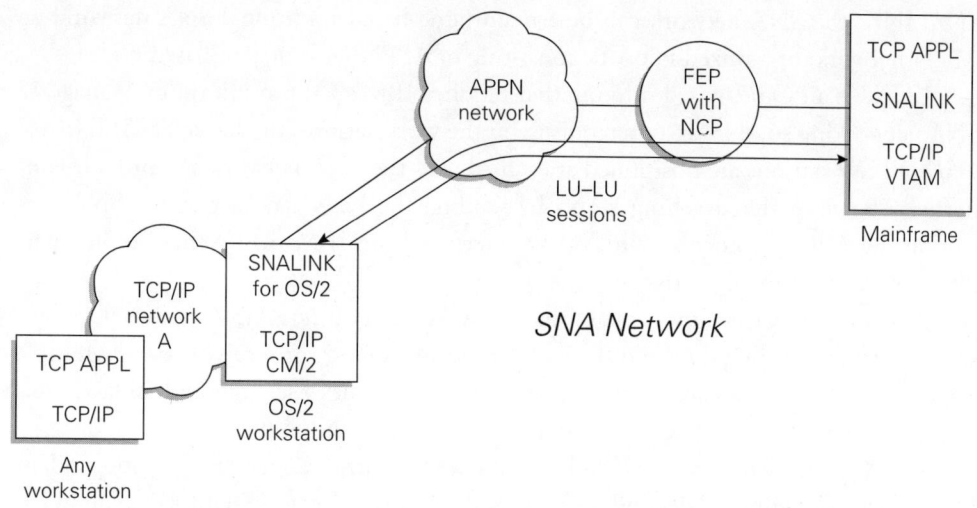

Figure 11.10 SNALINK for OS/2 communicating with mainframe TCP/IP application

mainframe TCP/IP application, then SNALINK is used to provide the access from the NCP LU to the mainframe application. With this additional functional capability, TCP/IP data can now be routed in a traditional SNA NCP-based network without the requirement that the TCP/IP data be routed through the mainframe via a VTAM application program. Even though only a single LU–LU session may be established from each of the NCP-defined dependent SNA LUs using this support, it is possible to define multiple LUs to obtain an additional capacity between the nodes. However, if access is required to the mainframe TCP/IP application, only a single session may be established to the mainframe using SNALINK.

Using this method for interconnection requires that the TCP/IP networks be directly attached to the communications controller. Since the communications controller is not capable of establishing an SNA LU–LU session without the aid of VTAM, VTAM will perform the SNA session establishment procedures. When the LU–LU session is established, the actual data routing within the SNA portion of the network will be between the two NCP-provided SNA LUs and will not be required to traverse the mainframe.

11.9 LAN-to-LAN WAN program

IBM's LTLW program is a flexible product which permits the interconnection of Novell Netware networks, IP networks, and NetBIOS networks across the SNA WAN. As with

SNALINK, the SNA network can be a mainframe-based traditional SNA network, an APPN network, or a mixed network consisting of APPN and subarea-based nodes.

LTLW is an OS/2-based offering that requires IBM's Communications Manager/2 SNA networking support as a prerequisite on the workstation. Much like SNALINK for OS/2, LTLW stations are positioned at each edge of the SNA network and provide connectivity between the attaching LANs by sending the LAN data across the SNA network using APPC protocols. With newer offerings from IBM, LTLW has become part of the Anynet family of products.

A pair of APPC sessions is established between each of the LTLW stations. One session is used for sending data and the partner session is used for receiving data. Multiple stations on the LAN can communicate across the same pair of sessions and, in fact, multiple protocols can be sent across the same pair of LTLW endpoints.

LTLW permits its SNA LUs to be configured as either dependent or independent LUs. When configured as dependent LUs, multiple LU images are required. One LU at each end is used for sending data across the SNA network and the other LU is used for receiving data. When configured using independent LUs, only a single SNA LU is required in each endpoint.

When using APPC, parallel sessions are established across the SNA network to provide the send and receive sessions. When using dependent LUs, a single session is established between each of the LUs. Since a pair of LUs is required to be defined in each endpoint, the result is that two sessions will exist, one for sending, and one for receiving.

When LAN data is to be sent across the SNA network, the data is simply sent as SNA data. The SNA data packet consists of the SNA network header, the APPC transaction information, and the non-SNA data packet. In different ways, depending on the protocol being interconnected, LTLW will provide filtering and eliminate undesired communication overhead across the SNA network.

LTLW provides the flexibility to determine when the SNA session should be established. One can indicate three options for establishing the connection across the SNA network: only when data needs to be transported across the SNA network, whenever LTLW is initialized, or when manually established by a network operator. Recovery options are provided for the automatic session establishment procedures so that one can maintain connectivity across the SNA network should an outage occur within the network. Of course, with HPR networks, the need for this option is greatly reduced.

LTLW interfaces to the LAN using the LAN standard IEEE 802.2 protocol stack. LTLW opens the LAN adapter for exclusive use. Therefore, it is not possible for other applications which may be operating on the LTLW workstation to share the adapter. A second adapter can be used to allow LAN access for these other applications.

When LTLW opens its connection with the LAN, it watches the packets which pass it. As packets, which LTLW is to route, arrive, LTLW receives the packets and determines the local SNA LU associated with this data. The data is passed to the LU instance, which determines if the needed SNA session exists. If the session exists, the data is forwarded across the SNA network. If the session does not currently exist, LTLW determines if the session should be dynamically established and, if so, uses SNA services to establish a session with the corresponding partner SNA LU. LTLW then forwards the data across the corresponding SNA session providing a logical link between the two disparate LANs.

LTLW offers a unique feature which is helpful in today's remote-access environment. One can install LTLW on an OS/2-based workstation and exploit a special feature of LTLW called a loopback driver to enable LAN-based software such as Lotus Notes to access a remote LAN across a WAN. The remote workstation need not be connected to a LAN. Instead, the loopback driver will make the application believe that it is directly communicating with a LAN when, in reality, it is communicating with a wide area connection. The result is that a remote user can access LAN-based applications without the need for specialized hardware solutions.

LTLW is aware of the specific data formats for the packets for the protocols it supports, but it does not require that additional non-SNA protocol-specific products be coresident in order to process these protocols. The interface across the SNA network is not at the media layer. Instead LTLW isolates the media protocols of the two LANs and, therefore, provides the ability to interconnect LANs which contain duplicate physical addressing. This feature of LTLW is of value for example in cases where previously isolated LANs need to intercommunicate but have duplicate addressing. LTLW can provide the needed isolation to complete the interconnection process.

When configuring LTLW, two lists may be predefined. These represent the local resources that can be accessed through that particular LTLW station. The lists are known as the IP qualifier list and the name qualifier list. The lists are defined on the local LTLW station to identify resources that a remote user can access through this LTLW station. When the LTLW station establishes its SNA session with the partner LTLW station, these lists are exchanged. This enables the partner station to determine which packets should be routed across the specific SNA connection. By using the list exchange implementation, coordinated definition within the network is eliminated. When the LTLW station receives information from the LAN, it examines the addressing information in the packet. If a corresponding entry is found in the qualifier lists, LTLW immediately knows that it should route the packet and it knows over which SNA session the packet should be routed.

When the partner LTLW station receives the data across the SNA network, it examines the sender's addressing information. It records this information so that, should it receive packets destined for that target resource, it will be able to route the packet without requiring that any predefinition for the subject resource be performed in LTLW. The concept of exchanging routing information used by LTLW is called *qualification exchange routing* (QER).

LAN applications typically operate by a requester initially contacting its server. The server then performs some operation and communicates back with the requester. With QER, only the server need be predefined to the local LTLW station if the server and requester are interconnected by LTLW. QER will learn the name and address of the requester when the initial request is sent to the server. No predefinition is required to LTLW in the server for the requester. When using IP interconnection, only the network addresses for IP networks accessible through this LTLW station need be predefined. Sending station's addresses will be learned by LTLW.

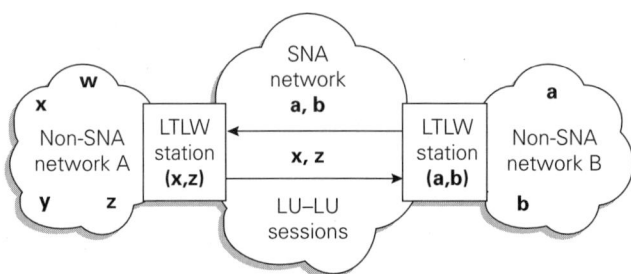

Figure 11.11   LTLW name and address qualifier list exchange initial exchange

Figure 11.11 shows two LANs interconnected using LTLW. When LTLW is configured, lists of locally accessible resources which are to be reachable from other LANs are predefined to LTLW. These resources are explicitly defined or defined using a wildcard or masking scheme. When the initial connection is established across the SNA network between the two LTLW workstations, the lists are exchanged. Now when a data packet is received by the partner workstation, that LTLW station will immediately be able to determine if the data packet should be routed across this WAN connection. In figure 11.11, the lists have been defined on to LTLW as resource *a* and *b* for one LTLW station and *x* and *z* for the partner station. This information is then exchanged.

Figure 11.12 shows the results. Each of the LTLW stations is able to determine which traffic to route without the requirement for coordinated system definition throughout the network. In addition to the initial exchange of predefined information,

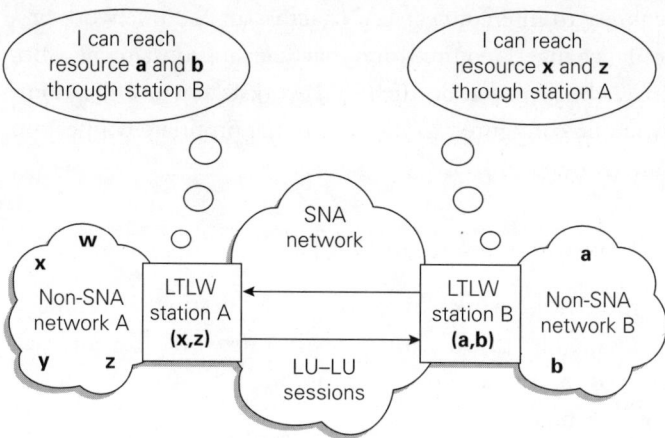

Figure 11.12   LTLW name and address qualifier list exchange after exchange

LTLW will also use its QER capability to continue to learn about network connectivity. As packets are transmitted across the LTLW connection, LTLW will remember the source address information adding it to its tables for later use in routing network traffic.

When configuring LTLW, the partner SNA LU to be accessed is predefined. Also, the COS to use for the session that traverses the SNA network may be predefined or defaulted. The COS selected will impact the SNA path selected, the interconnection to the existing SNA network, and the performance of the interconnecting session.

LTLW has a concept known as a *region*. A region is a single- or multisegment LAN which is associated with an SNA logical unit. Network broadcast traffic is permitted to flow within a region but LTLW provides isolation function to restrict the broadcast traffic from crossing region boundaries. Within a region, the MAC addresses, ring numbers, and bridge numbers must be unique, but across regions LTLW maintains isolation so the addressing information may be duplicated. The region concept is used by LTLW to the logical LAN interconnection which is to be performed. The region concept can also be used to maintain isolation between given LANs while providing others to interconnect.

Each LTLW station determines which protocols it supports. Information about the desired support is exchanged at LTLW connection time. The exchange of this information enables LTLW to only exchange network information with interconnected networks which require the specified support. For example, if, on one LAN, LTLW must support Novell Netware and NetBIOS but, on another LAN, only NetBIOS interconnection is desired, LTLW will detect this situation and not send Netware information between the two LTLW stations, reducing unnecessary network overhead.

LTLW also provides the ability to interconnect LANs across an X.25 network or a frame relay network. The only changes required are that the appropriate network adapter and its supporting drivers be provided on the OS/2 workstation and the Communications Manager/2 software be configured to indicate the appropriate connection type. No additional changes are required to LTLW.

11.9.1 Interconecting IP networks with LTLW

LTLW can be used to interconnect IP networks. Since IP is a connectionless protocol, no actual IP connection is maintained by LTLW across the SNA network. Instead, each IP packet is routed as it is received, just as would be the case in an IP network. In this environment, LTLW acts as an IP router.

The LTLW node receives the data and then uses the SNA network as a logical link for routing the IP data. LTLW uses its IP qualifier lists which contain IP network addresses and network masks to determine which packets to route and over which SNA sessions to route them. LTLW uses the IP ARP to determine the physical LAN address associated with a given IP network address. LTLW maintains statistics about the volume of data sent across the WAN for each IP address.

When a partner LTLW node receives an IP frame, it must determine if the target resource is on the local LAN or is accessed across another IP router node. LTLW determines this by examining the address. If the IP router address is the LTLW's address, then LTLW sends the data directly to the host on the local LAN. If the address is not that of this LTLW node, then the data is forwarded to the appropriate IP router.

11.10 Interconnecting NetBIOS networks with LTLW

NetBIOS is a common protocol in today's LAN environment as well. The NetBIOS protocol operates as both a connection-oriented (LLC type 2) and a connectionless (LLC type 1) protocol. NetBIOS uses resource names for communications instead of requiring a separate network addressing scheme. When a user on a LAN using NetBIOS desires to communicate with another NetBIOS user, a name query frame is sent into the NetBIOS network to determine where the partner resource is located. If the partner resource is on the same or an interconnected LAN segment, NetBIOS will obtain the address of the partner resource and establish a connection with that resource. The process of locating the partner resource is accomplished with a connectionless protocol. Once the partner resource is located, a connection is established between the two resources and communications is accomplished using a connection-oriented protocol.

When frames are from the local LAN, LTLW will respond for the partner network node. This feature enables LTLW to interconnect LANs with minimal impact to the end stations.

But suppose the LANs are not interconnected. Let us consider a case where users in different physical locations desire to communicate using Lotus Notes and NetBIOS. LTLW can be used to interconnect the two NetBIOS LANs over the SNA network. When the LANs are interconnected using LTLW, processing in LTLW will cache the name information and will intelligently provide the desired interconnection. NetBIOS names are typically 8-byte names, but the name addressing field in NetBIOS frames is 16 bytes, The name is typically located anywhere within the 16-byte field with the remaining bytes being used for application-specific data. LTLW has the ability to locate the partner name anywhere within the name addressing field, cache the name information, and then route data across the appropriate WAN connection to the partner LAN.

Since NetBIOS is a connection-oriented protocol, LTLW maintains the connection for the NetBIOS session across the WAN. This connection is known as a circuit. LTLW will maintain statistics about the amount of data routed over any given circuit.

LTLW not only offers the ability to interconnect the LANs, but it also provides the ability to filter the network traffic between the LANs and to determine which users are permitted to intercommunicate. Another advantage is that, just like with IP support, LTLW can dynamically establish the connectivity between the two LANs over the SNA network and maintain the connection for the duration of the data exchange. When one considers an environment such as electronic mail, the ability to establish connectivity only when needed could be a big cost savings when interconnecting across the SNA network.

11.11 Interconnecting Novell Netware networks with LTLW

Novell's NOS is widely installed. As further discussed in chapter 5, the Netware network protocol is IPX. With the IPX protocol, the LAN applications advertise their services to the network. These advertisements consist of the server name, its type, and its network address. Advertisements typically occur about once every minute. Routers within the network pass these advertisements between the nodes within the network. The advertisement process is known as the service advertising protocol (SAP). The process of passing these requests is known as the RIP. The network applications typically consist of servers providing print, communications, or file services. When a network user needs one of these services, it knows of its existence because of the advertisements. When a network requester needs the services of the network application, it sends out a request asking where the nearest server is located and how to access the server with which it desires to connect. Each router on the network maintains the information necessary to locate servers in other regions of the network.

When LTLW connects to a Netware network, it obtains the SAP and RIP information from the local LAN and passes the information to the LTLW partners. The remote partners pass the information to their LANs providing seamless integration of the Novell LANs across the WAN. LTLW provides the capability to filter which servers can be located across the wide area connections, thus enabling a means to intelligently interconnect Novell networks. LTLW does not rebroadcast all of its information across the WAN when a change occurs. Instead LTLW just passes the changes which occur and only at a specified interval. This reduces the impact of the interconnection on the WAN links. When a workstation on the remote LAN using Netware needs to access a network service such as a printer, it is aware of the servers within its region using native Netware function. For servers located in other regions, the LTLW station will respond that it provides the service and provide the needed interconnection. LTLW's ability to define qualifier lists combined with its wildcarding capability enables one to provide intelligent interconnection rather simply. For example, if all of the servers in the Dallas region had names beginning with DAL, and no other resources in the LTLW interconnected networks contained a name with DAL, a simple wildcard qualifier entry of DAL would cause all requests from other LTLW regions targeted for resources containing DAL to be routed across the LTLW SNA connection to the Dallas region. The user of the name qualifier lists can be of signficant value in reducing unwanted network traffic as Netware networks are interconnected across the WAN.

11.12 Multinetwork interconnection

In today's LANs, it is probable that there will not be a single non-SNA protocol. Instead, the LAN traffic may consist of Netware, NetBIOS, SNA, and TCP/IP traffic all within the same LAN. LTLW can provide an excellent means to route this multiprotocol traffic across the SNA network. In figure 11.13, multiple LAN networks are interconnected using LTLW. In this example, four LANs servicing multiple protocols are interconnected. LTLW provides the means to interconnect. Note that in this example, LTLW actually interconnects the four LANs, but LTLW provides isolation among the LANs. LTLW can be configured to only route specific protocols between specific interconnections, or even that only specific stations within the LANs may communicate.

In this example, regions B and C are interconnecting for NetBIOS workstations. Regions C and D are providing TCP/IP services, and regions A and B are interconnecting for Novell's Netware services. Regions A and D are not interconnected for non-SNA

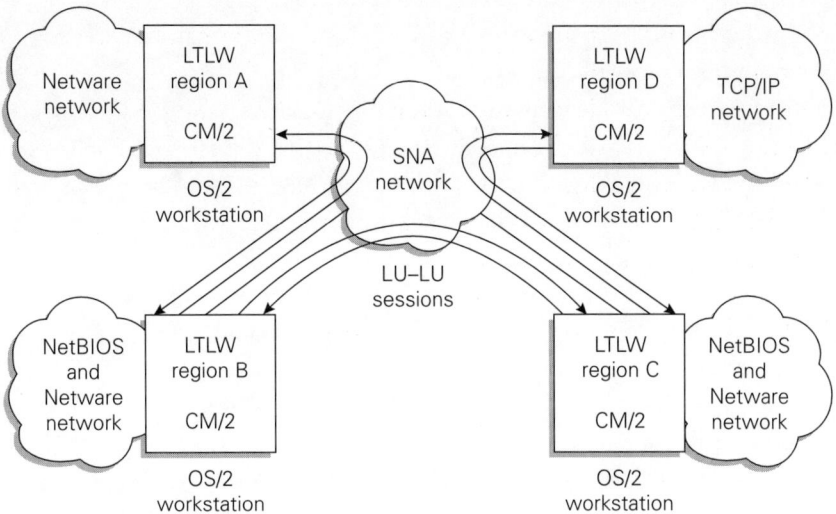

Figure 11.13 Interconnecting multiple protocols with LTLW

communications. All of these LANs are isolated from each other for all other non-SNA protocols. And within and among all of these LANs, APPN communications is possible as well. The APPN traffic will be routed natively throughout the network with the LTLW stations being able to also provide APPN network node or end node services for these SNA resources.

11.13 SNA encapsulation and multiprotocol internetworking

So, as we see, there are many possibilities for sending non-SNA data across SNA networks. All typically operate by establishing one or more SNA sessions and encapsulating the non-SNA frames within SNA frames for transport. They each provide the ability to solve some of today's multiprotocol interconnect problems without the requirement of totally reengineering the network infrastructure.

Each option offers its own strengths. Each provides the ability to exploit the traditional subarea network or APPN/HPR networks for transporting non-SNA network data without requiring that a parallel network be installed. Each provides the ability to control the networking overhead typically generated by non-SNA protocols while providing full COS support, therefore minimizing any impact on the SNA network.

The solutions are many, making the choices difficult. But whatever the choice, SNA-encapsulated internetworking is another piece in today's internetworking puzzle.

chapter 12

In the end system

DR. PETR JANECEK

In this chapter Dr. Petr Janecek takes us up the OSI model, introducing XTI—X/Open Transport Interface. He describes the functionality and usage of XTI for multiprotocol integration at the transport layer, describing the rationale of integration at the transport layer, which provides a natural boundary between users and networks for most of today's protocol suites. However, to a large extent XTI remains purely a theoretical integration option. The reader will also become familiar with some of the reasons for this phenomenon.

12.1 The multitude

I was once a member of a project team investigating how to best introduce modern computer aided design (CAD) and computer aided manufacturing (CAM) tools into a large corporation. Each member of the team was assigned a real-life problem coming from a different division of the company and, when analyzing the specific requirements, each of us became rather familiar with the ways the various divisions worked and the rules, procedures, and tools they used. The corporation was in the manufacturing business and since the CAD process starts with creating drawings, I had to become familiar with their specific format, layout, and structure. The corporation had spent considerable effort over a number of years developing its own standards for drawings and the handling of them. It had also standardized its computing environment. Since large corporations prefer buying from other large corporations, probably because of their expected longevity and stability, the computing environment was build up around a mainframe which was rented from IBM and which served an SNA network. The decision to run IBM was not entirely a political one: a major consultancy was employed to advise, and that was what they recommended.

The subsidiary whose problems I was studying, however, had been acquired only recently. It was much smaller than the corporation that bought it, but it had also spent years developing its own standards for drawings and computing. Unfortunately, their standards were different from those used by the corporation.

The question was thus: should the subsidiary's internal standards be aligned with the ones set for the other branches of the company? How long would it take for the change to become established? How much would it cost, both in direct implementation and in potential errors caused by differences between the old and the new system? And was it really worth doing after all, knowing that the subsidiary could again be sold after a few years if the merger were not profitable? Should such alignment be done for every new acquisition?

Although a believer in standardization, I realized that it is not always worthwhile and that coexistence and interoperability of various systems is an unwanted but necessary feature of life in any enterprise.

Drawings are things that everyone involved in manufacturing processes sees and has to understand, and yet it was difficult to justify the cost of standardizing them. But what about the computer environments in which they were developed, the electronic formats in which they would be stored, and the protocols by means of which they would be exchanged? One of the hopes of the project sponsors was that drawings could be linked to a database storing descriptions of the drawing's subject in different languages, thus giving a possibility of creating documentation for a particular market without the necessity of storing duplicates of drawings. Another objective was to link drawings to a different database from which one could extract production information that could be linked to financial data residing in yet another place. The production data were stored on VAXes using DECnet. The financial data resided on the mainframe running SNA. The new CAD/CAM workstations were to run UNIX and use TCP/IP.

The project would thus in its original draft have led to a distributed application ambitiously stretching over several network environments.

12.2   The application

In the project described above, the existing data and applications determined the environment, including the type of network used for communication. A few years later I was reminded that the application determines the choice of environment even when this new environment is being built from point zero.

I was hired to introduce a modern software development environment for a division of a computer vendor. The environment was to be distributed and special attention was to be paid to the possibility of introducing open systems, in clear language UNIX workstations with a central file and print server, with TCP/IP-based communications. At the heart of the entire environment for dozens of programmers was a compiler producing code for a specific microprocessor which this vendor had chosen to use in its products. The problem turned out to be that the compiler existed in a production-ready version only for a proprietary operating system. I had to advise my management that if they wanted to have a modern software development environment up and running within half a year, they had to run DECnet. Eventually, my recommendation was accepted.

I am sure that many other managers have—the hard way—reached the same conclusion that now sounds almost trivial: in the beginning there is the application… And currently, the application determines the environment, including the networking protocols.

By the way, networking protocols are necessary to make distributed applications interoperate but they cannot guarantee interoperability on their own. When two systems speak the same standardized communications language known as common protocol, they achieve something called *connectivity.* More is required for true interoperability. A simple example can be found in a LAN with DOS clients and a UNIX server. Since DOS file names can, at most, consist of eight plus three characters while UNIX files can have longer names, the clients will only be able to access UNIX files if there is an agreed on convention regarding the way to map long UNIX names onto the DOS file name format. For interoperability in this type of LAN, an extra definition is thus needed in addition to the agreement that data exchanged between the server and the client will be encoded and decoded using the same protocol. This extra convention is always specific to the potential interoperability problem. In another case, instead of a file mapping convention, an agreement on format of data being exchanged between applications might be needed. It is therefore not possible to give a well-defined recipe for what is needed to achieve interoperability. Protocols, however, provide the necessary base.

But now back to applications.

There is currently much discussion about the relative virtues of the OSI complex of communications standards developed by the United Nations' organization ISO, and TCP/IP. Actually, *discussion* is quite a polite description of a shouting match between the two groups of fanatics in the two suites, arguing about whose is the future. I think that the debate is to a large extent unnecessary since it actually misses the point, namely that customers do not primarily wish to buy a particular protocol stack but rather specific functionality associated with it. Depending on whether they are interested in transparent file access, file transfer, terminal emulation, electronic mail, transaction processing, or worldwide directory service, customers will try to get these facilities from wherever they can be obtained for a reasonable price and performance. Once again the application is king. The customer may end up with not one or the other, but with both.

Today's applications written for one suite of networking protocols mostly cannot run on top of another protocol suite. Customers expect certain services to be provided by the network, and these services differ between protocol suites.

One way of ensuring interworking within a class of applications which have the same purpose (e.g. email) but different incarnations on different protocol suites (X.400 on OSI, SMTP on Internet protocol suite, DIA and SNA/DS on SNA) is to use application gateways. This solution to the interworking problem is dealt with in other chapters of this book. Let us note here that while application gateways can be introduced without modifying the existing application code, they are by their nature specific to the type of application and the protocol suite pair in question. They are also more complex than transport gateways. This approach will probably be used for a few very important applications, like email or file transfer.

We shall instead look at the ways in which the dependence of an application program on a specific protocol suite can be reduced or, in the ideal case, removed. Should this become feasible, existing applications could run in more networks and existing networks could support more applications. That would placate the application vendors who would not have to develop and maintain separate versions of the same software package for different protocol suites, as well as customers who would get new functionality into their current environment. And if the kind of protocol loses its prominence to applications, fewer protocol suites would have to be used. Reduction in the number of protocols that must coexist and be supported in the same network would reduce demands on computer memory, network management would become easier, and the highly specialized staff could be freed for more productive tasks.

If the number of supported protocols were reduced, the formally standardized ones could be chosen, which would make governments and other standards-minded customers happy. And since standardization brings competition, it would eventually also bring down prices of networking software.

12.3   The way of merger

To have to manage a network running multiple protocols is obviously a frustrating and expensive task. Everybody would like to avoid it if possible, so over the last couple of decades, people have spent considerable effort trying to find a simplifying solution.

The simplest way of eliminating the problem of having to maintain multiple protocol suites, namely just choosing the most appropriate one and sticking to it, is not viable for reasons given above, namely the fact that users do not primarily choose networking protocols but distributed applications, and they get them with a protocol suite attached. The OSI suite was to solve the interconnection problems by providing rich functionality and thus a possibility to replace all of the current protocol suites with this one. Unfortunately, its functionality is so far least developed where it is needed most, namely in applications. It is thus not possible to easily replace whatever runs in your network with OSI. If the dream of an all-encompassing single protocol suite is still distant, what about trying to find similarities between the suites and looking for possibilities to eliminate potentially duplicated functionality?

Most protocol suites have layered architectures which means that the functions they perform can be grouped into a number of functional layers. These layers lie on top of each other creating a hierarchy of function. The lowest layer is always the physical one where the chosen voltages are applied to a specified number of pins, while the

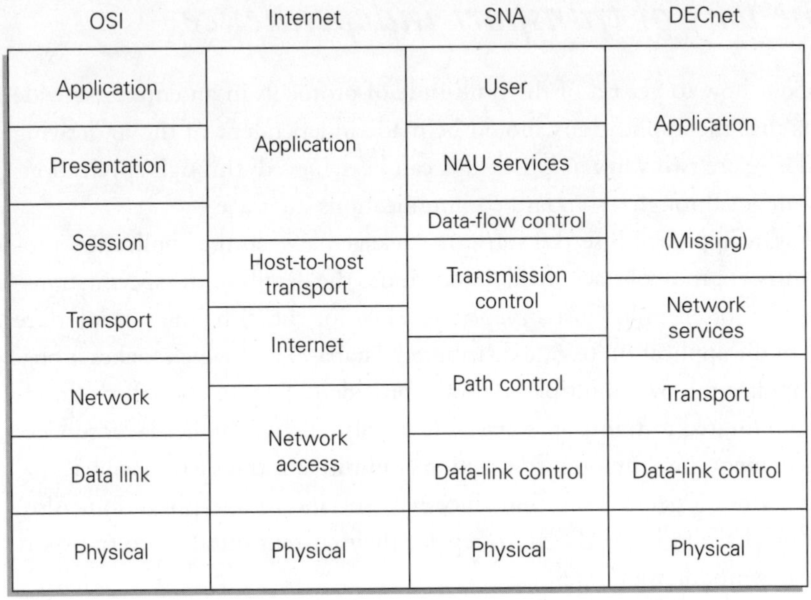

OSI	Internet	SNA	DECnet
Application	Application	User	Application
Presentation		NAU services	
Session	Host-to-host transport	Data-flow control	(Missing)
Transport		Transmission control	Network services
	Internet		
Network	Network access	Path control	Transport
Data link		Data-link control	Data-link control
Physical	Physical	Physical	Physical

Figure 12.1   Comparison of some major communication architectures

highest layer is the one where user applications reside. The layers need each other, in that a lower layer provides a service that a higher layer requires.

A comparison of how some important communications architectures are layered (see figure 12.1) unfortunately shows that they differ considerably in the purpose and use of each layer.

Only for some pairs of protocols and some of the layers, a limited merger could be achieved. Recently, for example, the Internet community started searching for a replacement to its current IP because it will soon have exhausted its limited address space, or the range of integer numbers which it uses for addresses of network nodes. One possible candidate for this replacement would seem to be the existing CLNP from the OSI suite, and such a proposal has indeed been put forward. However, political issues with roots in the history of battles between the IP and OSI proselytes cloud the issue, so the potential merger of these two protocol suites in at least one spot is far from certain. It is, however, important to realize that whichever solution the Internet community eventually adopts, it will mean a change of protocol in all of their nodes. This is neither easy nor cheap, but it will have to be done if the Internet is to grow.

12.4 The way of transport independence

Another idea about how to get rid of the multitude of protocols in an enterprise-wide network suggests that the applications should be made independent of the underlying protocol stack. There are two ways in which this can be achieved: through application-specific middleware, or through a standard communications interface.

The middleware approach inserts a software package between the application program and the transport protocol stack. Middleware hides the details of the specific transport service provider (often called just *transport provider* for short) behind an interface which is specific to the application (e.g., a distributed database) and which makes it possible to run this application over multiple transport providers. The functionality of middleware is often not limited to transport services; it can also include higher-layer services such as acknowledgment, presentation, transaction commit, and transaction rollback.

Middleware is not a general solution since it is specific to an application. Also, existing applications have to be modified, to replace their current interface to transport services with the new middleware interface.

In the other approach, a standard communications interface can be introduced into applications to achieve transport independence. Once this is done for all applications on a network node, only one of the protocol suites has to be used and maintained there.

A standard communications interface is being developed by one of the projects of the IEEE Portable Applications Standards Committee (PASC). With a programming-language-independent definition of the interface, two separate bindings to the C language are being developed. The fact that they are two rather than one reflects the politics of standardization which had to recognize that there already are two industry-wide de-facto standards in place: sockets and XTI.

Sockets has traditionally been a part of the BSD flavor of the UNIX operating system and since PASC has its roots deep in its UNIX past, there is a significant support among its members for this variant. XTI was originally developed by the global computer vendor consortium X/Open (currently including IBM along with other giant computer vendor corporations) from AT&T's TLI System V (commonly called System Five).

While sockets are so far pretty specific to the IP suite (although their implementation over OSI is reported to be in progress), the idea behind XTI has been exactly the one we are discussing here: to define an interface which application writers could use to make their products independent of the underlying transport protocols. XTI is not bound to UNIX: it has become part of the general X/Open definition of interfaces for open systems which can be, and part of it already has been, implemented on top of

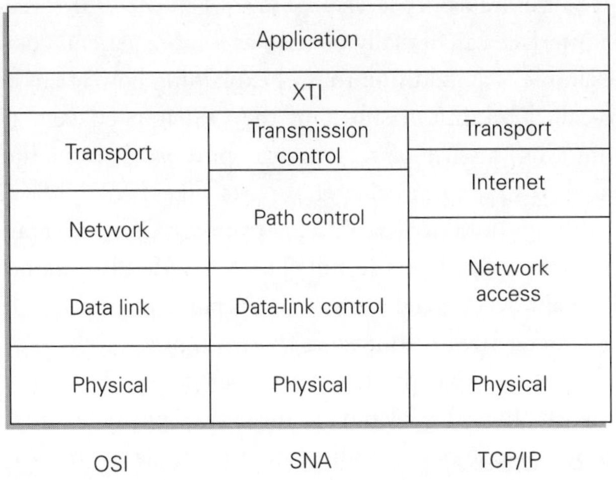

Application		
XTI		
Transport	Transmission control	Transport
		Internet
Network	Path control	Network access
Data link	Data-link control	
Physical	Physical	Physical

| OSI | SNA | TCP/IP |

Figure 12.2   Transport independence through a standard interface

other operating systems. Although the first use of XTI was envisioned to be over the OSI transport, XTI can also be run over TCP, UDP, NetBIOS and, most recently, SNA full duplex extension (see figure 12.2). Advice on how an application program can access any one of these transports using XTI is given in the X/Open specification which the upcoming IEEE standard is based on.

In principle, XTI provides an excellent means to isolate the application program from the underlying transport provider. The success of this objective is, alas, in the hands of the application programmer. Should he/she wish to use XTI in an OSI- or Internet-specific way, it can be done. In other words: XTI provides transport independence only as long as the application does not make any assumptions about the nature of the underlying transport, that is as long as it does not expect that all concepts used in one protocol exist or have the same semantics in others. If such an assumption is made, the application will not automatically run over another transport and the transport independence property will be lost.

Since XTI is meant to be used as a vehicle which can increase the number of applications running over a particular transport by way of easy porting from another transport, one would hope that the application code writers will avoid the trap of making their XTI-based software too transport specific. Advice on what concepts should be avoided to achieve full transport independence is given in the X/Open specification. These include matters like preservation of logical data boundaries across a connection, hard coding of device names, protocol-specific addressing, and semantics of expedited data. The truly transport independent applications are thus restricted to the largest common subset that is supported by all protocols over which the application is meant to run.

Although XTI's name ties it to the transport service, or layer 4 in the OSI seven-layer model (see figure 12.1), the interface can actually be used as a more general communications interface. A recent example is an addition to XTI explaining how it can be used to provide access to the so-called minimum subset of the OSI upper layers' (5 through 7) functionality, called mOSI. This use of XTI has the purpose of providing applications that are to be migrated to OSI from other transports (like TCP, UDP or NetBIOS), and easy access to what they would necessarily need from the OSI upper layers, without having to implement these upper layers in full. The XTI-OSI also extends the family of transport services available via a single protocol independent interface to all applications that require a simple octet-stream connection between processes.

Having said all that, the fact remains that the transport layer provides a natural boundary between users and networks for most of today's important protocol suites. The transport functions provided by any one of these suites are very similar to those of the other suites which makes it practical to define mappings on each other (we'll talk about this later). The transport layer boundary is also the highest point in the layered architecture where such a high degree of commonality is found and therefore it offers itself as an ideal place where a standard interface isolating everything above it from everything underneath it can be defined. The part of the protocol stack lying in the architecture below the standard transport layer interface could thus be replaced with one coming from a different protocol suite without the application or the user noticing.

There is, however, an important aspect of this solution which has an impact on its usefulness as a means of reducing the protocol multitude in a network: while XTI certainly could and should be introduced when new application programs are written or existing ones for some other reason modified, the bulk of current application software does not use XTI and probably will never be ported to it because the cost of doing so would be prohibitive and the users would have to carry it themselves.

12.5 The way of pairwise compensations

There is yet another way in which the desired result of reducing the number of transport protocols, or rather transport providers, supported in a network could be achieved. This way takes into account the possibility of introducing into the nodes on the network a mechanism that compensates for differences between the transport providers in question.

This technique has been used by those in the Internet community who wanted to run sophisticated applications defined in the OSI suite, like Directory Services or Messaging, over the TCP protocol. Therefore, they defined a mapping which provides TCP with the appearance of ISO connection-oriented transport. The mapping is documented in RFC 1006.

Similar mappings, this time for a NetBIOS service over TCP, UDP transport, are defined in RFCs 1001 and 1002 (which are two parts of a single description of the standard). The corresponding mapping for NetBIOS onto the OSI connection-oriented and connectionless transport protocols has been defined by the *manufacturing automation protocol* (MAP)/*technical and office protocol* (TOP) Users Group and is known as TOP/NetBIOS.

What I have mentioned above is of course only the standardized tip of the iceberg: under the surface dividing the standardized open world from the vast depths of proprietary systems, every major vendor has made sure that his own protocol suite implementation maps onto the important proprietary protocol suites. This is in particular true about SNA for which there are a number of proprietary gateways available on the market.

Clearly, a mapping of this kind has to be defined separately for each transport provider pair. It is in fact a many-to-many problem, so a large number of mappings are needed in order to cover all of the possible combinations that a customer can be interested in.

12.6   The way of common compensations

When one looks closer at the types of transport services offered by the important transport providers (see table 12.1), it appears that the number of mismatches between services is actually smaller than the number of possible transport provider pairs. In other words, several transport providers usually share the need to compensate for the same missing transport service. For example, both SNA and NetBIOS need compensation for expedited data supported by OSI, while SNA and OSI need compensation for multicast supported by NetBIOS. That in fact means that the many-to-many problem of pairwise compensations can be reduced to the few-to-few problem of common compensations for transport services.

Definitions of such compensation protocols form a major part of documentation of MPTN. Originally an IBM initiative, MPTN has been submitted to X/Open for review and adoption as an open-systems industry standard. MPTN is designed for interworking transport users (applications) that have the same requirements on transport services or, in other words, match each other. For example, two applications using XTI match while an XTI and a CPI-C application do not.

Table 12.1 Transport services in major transport providers

Transport service	OSI	Internet	SNA	NetBIOS
Connection/termination data	yes/no[a]	no	yes/no[a]	no
Multicast	no	yes	no	yes
Expedited data	yes	yes/no[b]	no	no
Record delivery	yes	no	yes	yes
Stream delivery	yes	yes	yes	yes

a. Yes for native connections, No for nonnative ones (native network provides the services expected by transport user and has the same addressing structure as transport user)

b. Yes via Urgent Data, No otherwise

When MPTN compensation protocols are used by applications running over the same nonnative network, for example, CPI-C applications over the Internet, the network nodes where applications reside are called MPTN access nodes (see figure 12.3).

In a nonnative network, the transport user and the transport provider, in general, use different addressing schemes. The addresses used by transport users have to be resolved and mapped onto transport provider addresses. This function is performed by the address mapper. Network nodes including the address mapper are called MPTN address mapper nodes (see figure 12.4).

The double line in figures 12.3 and 12.4 denotes the interface through which the transport user requests the transport services and receives the responses. The most valuable feature of MPTN is the fact that this interface does not have to be standardized or even changed. The interface that the application uses to interact with its native network can stay in place when the application is moved onto a nonnative network or when the native protocol suite is exchanged for a nonnative one.

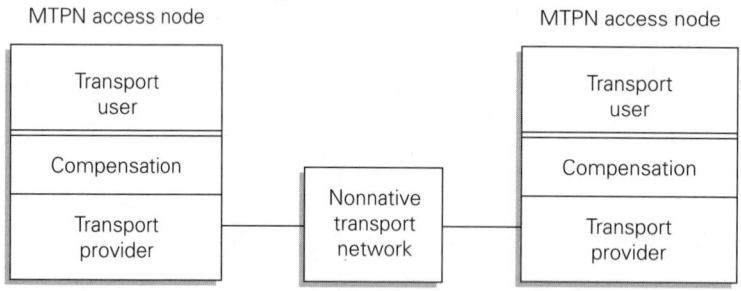

Figure 12.3 Point-to-point MPTN in a single network

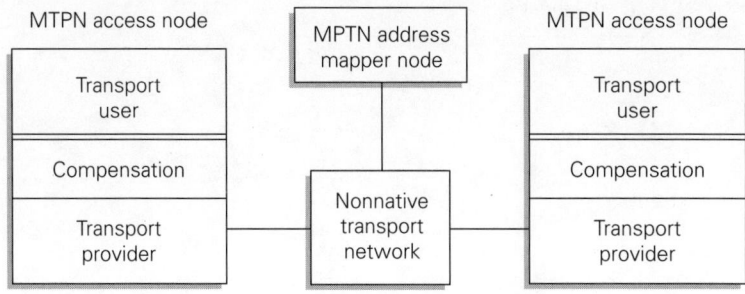

Figure 12.4　Point-to-point MPTN with address mapping

This means that the enormous investment in current applications is preserved. MPTN can be introduced only in nodes where it is needed and the applications need not be modified. The application interoperability problem can thus be addressed by MPTN at the system level where an MPTN package would provide the necessary service without affecting the applications. Since there are considerably more applications than systems, the total cost to the enterprise of this solution should be significantly lower than the cost of the approach requiring modification of existing applications.

The point-go-point use of MPTN is just one of the general scenarios where MPTN can be applied. Another one is concatenation of networks running different protocol suites, where MPTN can serve as a transport gateway. First, imagine two OSI applications, one of them running in an OSI network, the other one running in an Internet network, which makes this into a native-to-nonnative case. If these two OSI applications are to interoperate, compensation is needed at two points: where the OSI application interfaces the Internet network, and where the OSI network interfaces the Internet one. It is in this latter point that the MPTN gateway would be placed.

If the OSI network in the above example is swapped for, let's say, an SNA one, the scenario becomes a nonnative-to-nonnative case and compensation is needed in one additional point: where the OSI application which was previously running native now interfaces the SNA network.

More complicated scenarios including multiple gateways can be designed, for example, one in which one OSI application is running over Internet and another over SNA, but the two networks are connected via a third one (let's say DECnet). Such a scenario involves two gateways and four points of compensation.

In all of the above examples, the specific transport user (application)/transport provider (network) names have only been chosen to make the examples concrete and easily understandable. The names are, of course, permutable.

A more thorough discussion of issues associated with transport gateways can be found in the following chapter of this book.

chapter 13

Making SNA networks part of the Internet

DAVID OGLE
DIANE POZEFSKY

This chapter by Diane Pozefsky and David Ogle describes a practical approach of a multiprotocol gateway at the transport layer. The MPTN transport gateway is a methodology that allows, almost transparently, for the application to run it across different networks without any major development/modification effort. A combination of the transport gateway and the MPTN access node offers a variety of interoperability options, making a smoother and easier deployment and migration to many dissimilar network configurations.

13.1 Introduction

What would it be like if people with cellular phones could only talk to other people with cellular phones and people on a PBX could only talk to other people on their PBX? That has been the state of distributed computing for many years. Applications that ran on an SNA network could not have a partner in the Internet nor could Internet applications have an SNA partner: the world was divided by an impenetrable wall. Application-specific solutions, like TN3270, address this problem for a fixed set of applications and transport protocols. As we move into the electronic era, separation becomes unacceptable—the transport network should be as unimportant as the type of telephone that you are using.

There are a few indisputable facts in the communications world and one is that the world is barreling forward towards the Internet and intranet connectivity. No company can afford not to have access to the information that is available on the Internet. Even more important, no company can afford to not have access to the people who are on the Internet. The Internet is not just about web browsing and web servers: it is the means for obtaining and exchanging software and documentation and it is the connectivity tool for human communications and collaboration. The Internet is quickly becoming the basic tool of collaborative work.

At one time companies did not have multiple networks and cross-company collaboration was not common. But in recent years, this situation has changed dramatically. Cross-company projects and companies with multiple networks abound. In most companies, different sites run different networks—sometimes with the same protocol and sometimes with different protocols. The multiplicity of networks may have occurred because of company acquisitions or because it is a multisite business; the multiplicity of protocols may have occurred because of acquisitions or decentralized decision-making. However it occurred, it is now a fact of corporate life. When all networks use the same protocol, the problems are of one kind. In this paper, we address some of the issues associated with the use of different protocols.

The solution we describe in this chapter makes any SNA network a routing domain of the Internet. As such, an application running on the SNA network can be accessed from the Internet and users on the SNA network have complete access to the Internet. Two SNA networks that are attached to the Internet can use it as their means of connectivity and an SNA network can participate as an intermediate hop in any Internet connection. The intention—and reality—of this model is that the protocol being used in a routing domain is completely transparent. No one needs to know what it is! Making the SNA network an Internet routing domain provides many benefits:

- The existing SNA infrastructure can be used
- Changes to the network can be done at the rate and pace suited to the company
- Internet users have access to the SNA network's data and applications
- SNA users have full access to the power of the Internet
- The full quality of SNA is available to Internet applications

We begin by looking at the underlying technology used to provide this solution, examine some of the configurations in which the technology is used, and then look at some of the more important implementation and performance issues that are needed to provide an efficient networking solution.

13.2 The technology

In order to provide general access to applications and data across different networks, two things are needed: independence of applications from the communications network and the need to treat a confederation of diverse networks as a single logical network. MPTN was introduced as a solution to the first of these problems. In this chapter, we show how the MPTN architecture enables the development of a transport gateway to address the second of these problems. In this chapter, we prefer the term AnyNet to MPTN; while AnyNet was originally introduced as the name of a family of MPTN products, the term has been popularized as a common name for the architecture as well.

First, a brief review of AnyNet: The goal of AnyNet is the separation of communications applications from the underlying network protocols. AnyNet allows existing applications to run *unchanged* over a new networking protocol. In order to do this, AnyNet logically divides all protocol stacks at the transport level. When this division is made, it becomes clear that there is a limited number of functions provided at the transport level. In particular, AnyNet has identified and supports the following common transport functions, referred to as CTS in IBM's Open Blueprint:

- *Unicast and multicast datagram* delivery with quality of service specification

- *Connection establishment of full-duplex connections* with or without packet markers, with quality of service specification, and with the ability to negotiate connection information

- *Sending of both normal and expedited data* on a connection, with the option of identifying where in the normal stream the expedited data is sent

- *Connection termination options* that include the option of guaranteed delivery of all previously sent data, the ability to take down the full connection or only the sending half of the pipe, and the ability to send termination information

Having identified this limited set of functions, the AnyNet architecture defines a standard set of compensations to provide these functions on all transport protocols. AnyNet supports a wide range of protocols including SNA, IP, OSI, DECnet, NetBIOS, and IPX. Because of their significance in today's market, this paper focuses on SNA and IP. A computer that supports these compensations provides a consistent level of function on each network and thereby

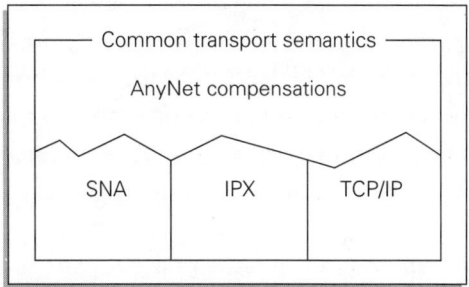

Figure 13.1   AnyNet compensations in an access node

allows applications to use a nonnative transport (see figure 13.1). Such a node is referred to as an AnyNet *access node*. For two access nodes to communicate, both must be using the same set of transport functions and the same set of application functions. For example, both partners must be using IP's socket API or both must be using SNA's CPI-C API. AnyNet does not address the problem of allowing socket applications to interoperate with CPI-C applications.

With equivalent functions on all networks, communicating across the different networks becomes a simple case of relaying between networks (see figure 13.2). With different transport providers, the compensations can be different—or, as is the case with a native partner, there can be no compensations at all. Connections across a transport gateway retain the requirement that the two endpoints must be using matching transport users (e.g., the applications at the endpoints must both be socket applications or they both must be CPI-C applications). With a transport gateway, however, the transport providers no longer need to be the same. This is the essence of the AnyNet transport gateway.

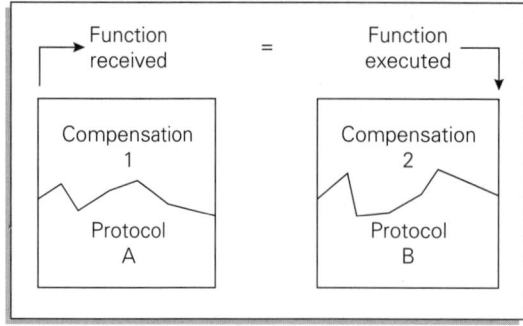

Figure 13.2   AnyNet compensations in a gateway

The key to being able to connect to a native network is that a transport gateway appears as a standard part of that network. With protocols that do not support intermediate routers, like NetBIOS, the transport gateway appears as the end system on which the resource exists. For protocols that support intermediate routers, like SNA and IP, the transport gateway appears to the native network as an intermediate router.

While the AnyNet transport gateway in its basic form is really just this simple, significant function can be added. When there are multiple gateways, it is helpful for them to communicate in order to improve performance and to learn about the rest of the network dynamically. Two important capabilities that we will discuss later are load balancing through parallel gateways and backup connections.

13.3 Configurations

To understand the potential benefits of AnyNet gateways, we will look at a fictitious company, the WhatNext Software Development Company. WhatNext is a financial software development company, whose roots began in the SNA world. They have two key development locations, in Minneapolis and Dallas. (Their motto is "A climate to suit any programmer.")

The WhatNext network configuration is shown in figure 13.3. At one time WhatNext's Dallas and Minneapolis locations worked on separate projects, and developers in one location only needed to communicate with developers in another location via the phone and fax. Joint development was not done. The most recent project that the WhatNext company is working on, however, requires collaboration between developers in both Dallas and Minneapolis. The developers at both sites need to share everything: email, files, data, Lotus Notes databases, and so on, as represented by line (1) in figure 13.3. WhatNext has contracted the publication work for this new project to a third-party vendor in Boston. The publication people have a need to share data, files,

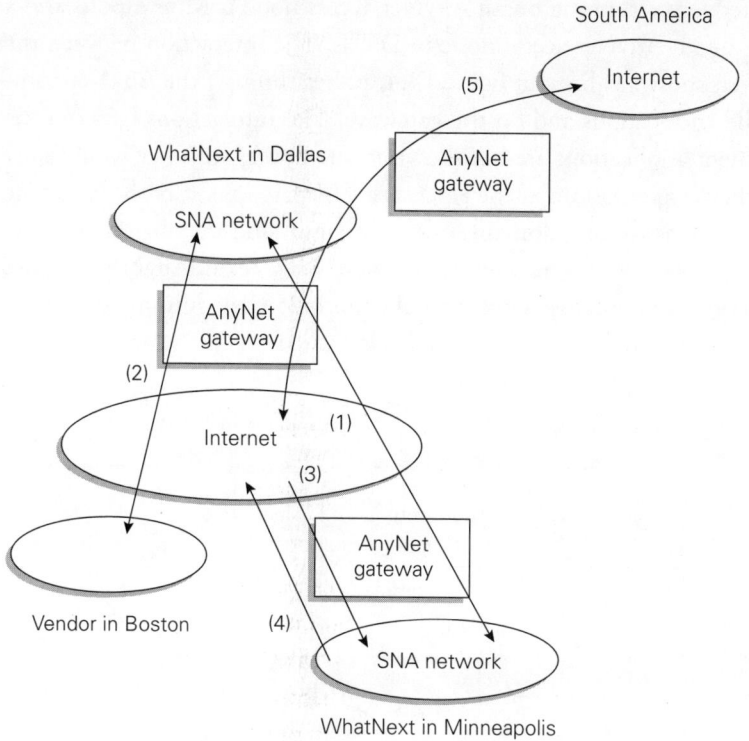

Figure 13.3   WhatNext Company network connections interactionensations in a gateway

and documentation with developers at the Dallas site as indicated by line (2). In addition, WhatNext has recognized the value of the Internet, both as a source of information and as a sales tool to reach new customers. This interaction with the Internet community is shown by lines (3) and (4). Finally, because WhatNext does business in South America, they have a good, but lightly used, connection to the Internet in South America, indicated by line (5). WhatNext is willing to make this link available for others to use.

In figure 13.3, the line labeled (1) illustrates WhatNext's usage of the Internet to connect its Dallas and Minneapolis SNA networks. This seamless integration of the SNA networks as routing domains of the Internet allows developers at WhatNext to share resources between sites. In the case of WhatNext, the developers use AnyNet access nodes to run TCP/IP-based applications, like FTP, Telnet, file servers, Notes servers and Notes clients, on the internal SNA network as well as existing SNA applications that they use to manage their development process. A more detailed example of WhatNext's usage of the Internet as a connectivity tool is shown in figure 13.4. In this figure,

WhatNext has a Notes server running on an AnyNet access node is Minneapolis and a Notes client running on an AnyNet access node in Dallas. The interaction between the Notes client and server, shown as lines in figure 13.4, passes through the AnyNet compensation layer on the end stations and on the gateways. The interactions between the native SNA management applications are not shown in the figure, and they would only need to go through the compensations at the gateways. The gateways at both sites make the SNA networks appear as routing domains of the Internet, and they handle routing the requests from the Notes client to the Notes server and back again. AnyNet provides the same level of functions to the Notes server and client applications running over SNA that these same applications would get running natively over IP.

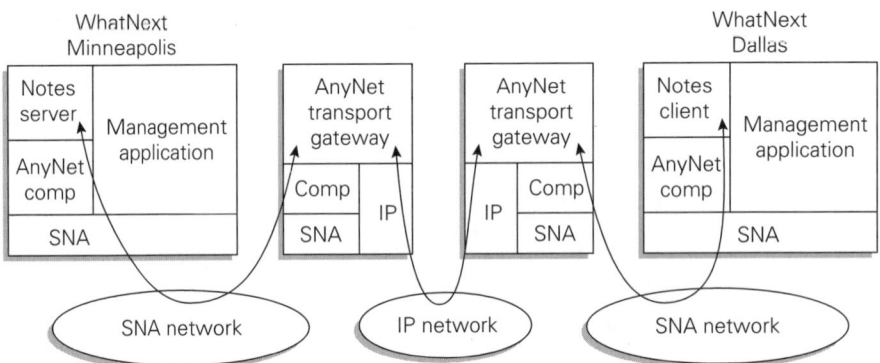

Figure 13.4 Connecting across the Internet

In figure 13.3, the line labeled (2) shows the vendor in Boston accessing WhatNext via the Internet. This example is where transparent support is the most obvious. The vendor is very secretive and no one in either the Internet community or in the What-Next company has any idea what type of network they run. The vendor has an application that interacts with an application at WhatNext, and the vendor has a connection to the Internet. The vendor may or may not have IP on their network. Because of the seamless integration of networks using AnyNet gateways no one in either the Internet community nor in WhatNext needs to know or care about the vendor's network.

Lines (3) and (4) in figure 13.3 are examples of WhatNext's usage of the Internet for obtaining and sharing information. Users in the Internet can, for example, access web servers that WhatNext has on its SNA network. This interaction is shown in more detail in figure 13.5. Developers at WhatNext can use browsers on their SNA network to find vital information from companies with web servers on the Internet. The AnyNet transport gateway deals with a native network (i.e., the Internet, where there is no AnyNet function) on one side and an AnyNet network on the other side (i.e., the

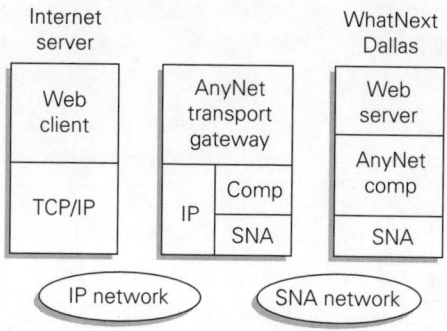

Figure 13.5   Connecting to the Internet

WhatNext SNA network running AnyNet access nodes). It is important to mention that users on the Internet do not need to change or add software to interact with sites running AnyNet. The AnyNet gateways make the SNA network appear as regular routing domains of the Internet.

Finally, line (5) in figure 13.3 shows how the WhatNext company uses AnyNet gateways to provide an alternate route for Internet traffic destined for the Internet in South America. In this example, WhatNext is allowing traffic from the Internet to flow across WhatNext's SNA link to South America. Since the AnyNet gateways make the SNA network appear as just another routing domain in the Internet, the traffic can easily flow across the SNA network from one portion of the Internet to another.

13.4 Functions in a transport gateway

Two key areas to address in an AnyNet gateway are the need to deal with a native network and performance issues to keep the transport gateway running efficiently.

What does a transport gateway need to do to support a native network? Basically, it must act as a surrogate for parts of the AnyNet network that are not on the native protocol but must be accessed from it. The key functions are:

- *Converting directory queries* into or from AnyNet protocols and responding whether the resource is found or not
- *Converting connection requests* into or from AnyNet protocols and responding whether the connection succeeds or fails
- *Forwarding datagrams* between the native connection and the AnyNet connection
- *Forwarding data packets* between the native connection and the AnyNet connection
- *Converting connection termination requests* into or from AnyNet protocols and responding when the takedown is completed

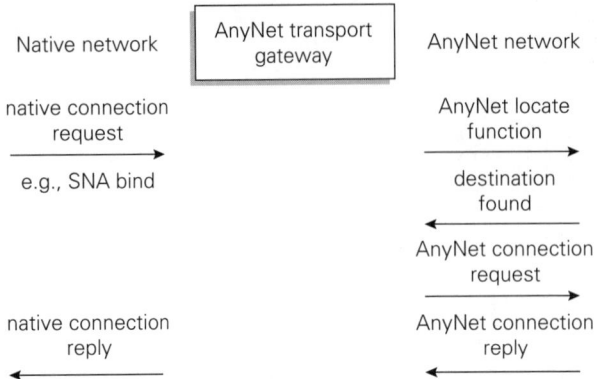

Figure 13.6 Connection establishment across an AnyNet network

Figure 13.6 illustrates the general functions required when a native connection request is received at the transport gateway.

What does it take to assure that the transport gateway can run efficiently? There are two key areas to address: how many cycles are used per packet and how much storage is required. In terms of cycles, the additional cycle utilization is only the one required to perform the compensations, and they tend to be very simple. Storage consideration is important in two cases: if data cannot be forwarded on a connection and if segments need to be reassembled.

To address the problem of forwarding data on a connection, the transport gateway uses back pressure to link the flow control in the different networks. As illustrated in figure 13.7, when the flow control in one network (protocol A) prevents the gateway from sending, it refuses to receive any more data from the other network (protocol B). When the network (protocol B) trying to send data to the gateway cannot deliver its data, it uses network protocols to reduce the traffic that it receives. In this manner, pressure is applied to the source of the data and it will stop sending data.

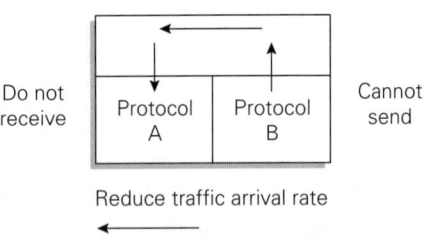

Figure 13.7 Flow control through a gateway

The other time that there is a danger of a gateway having to hold data is when the connection is being established. If the connection has not been completed when the gateway begins receiving data, it will need to queue data until the connection is established. The solution to this problem is illustrated in figure 13.8. A gateway will never respond to a connection setup request until it receives a response to its request. In this

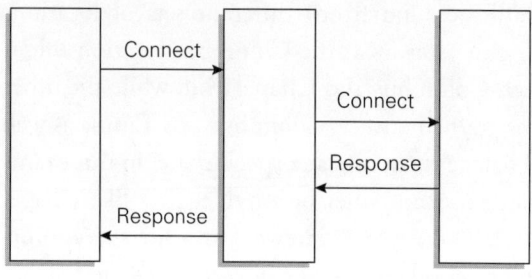

Figure 13.8 Connection completion through a gateway

way, the source node is not told that the connection is available until the path is established end-to-end. Thus, by the time that data arrives at the gateway, it can be forwarded.

The segmentation problem is addressed by never reassembling in an intermediate gateway. If a gateway cannot send a message out because it is too large, it will segment the data. When a gateway receives segments, it simply forwards them. The reassembly is performed in the end system or at a gateway that is putting data out on a native network if that network does not support segmentation.

Customers want and need the ability to place multiple gateways at a site to connect a location to the Internet or to another location. There are two main reasons for needing multiple gateways: the desire for load balancing, and the need for backup links in case a gateway crashes or goes off line. This is illustrated in figure 13.9, where the location labeled Columbus is hooked to the Internet via two AnyNet gateways, and the locations labeled Chapel Hill and Tampa are each hooked to the Internet with a single AnyNet gateway.

Load balancing is achieved when there are multiple gateways connecting a site and when the work done to connect the site is being shared among the gateways. In figure 13.9, there are two gateways connecting the network in Columbus to the Internet. In the AnyNet model, load balancing is achieved because each of these gateways

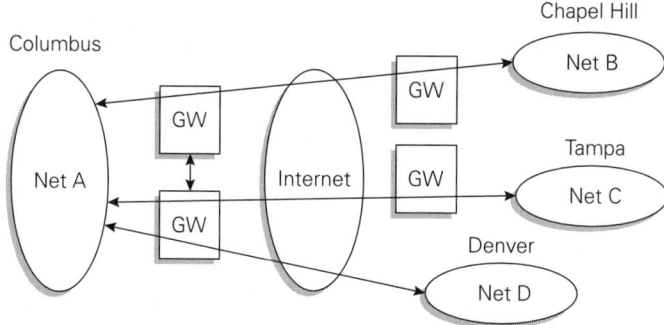

Figure 13.9 Multiple gateways for backup and load balancing

will be responsible for handling the traffic to (and from) different sets of locations (addresses) in the Internet. For example, one gateway at the Columbus location might be responsible for handling traffic between Columbus and Chapel Hill, while the other gateway might be responsible for handling traffic between Columbus and Tampa as well as between Columbus and Denver. Load balancing occurs at a specific site, in this example at the Columbus site, and the partner sites can either be AnyNet sites like Chapel Hill and Tampa or native sites like Denver. The AnyNet gateways at a site share information with each other, sending each other periodic messages allowing the load balancing algorithms to be more complex. This gives the customer some flexibility to tailor the load balancing to meet their specific requirements.

The other capability AnyNet gateways can perform is a backup function. In figure 13.9, the two gateways at the Columbus site back each other up, allowing the Columbus site to be connected to the Internet even when one of the gateways crashes or goes off line for maintenance. This backup function is achieved by having the gateways at the Columbus site exchange information periodically. A gateway can determine when one of its peers goes down because it will stop receiving the periodic message from the downed gateway. For example, in figure 13.9, assume the gateway that serves the traffic between Columbus and Tampa goes down. The other gateway at the Columbus site will notice that this gateway is down, and it will start handling the traffic between Columbus and Tampa as well as the traffic it already handled between Columbus and Chapel Hill. Once the "down" gateway comes back online, it will resume handling the traffic between Columbus and Tampa.

13.5 Summary

AnyNet access nodes and transport gateways provide the basis for making SNA networks an Internet routing domain. The AnyNet architecture allows applications to run across different networks without a significant development cost and to cross nonnative networks when that is the best or only connectivity available. Combined with the AnyNet access node, the transport gateway offers customers a range of options for deploying their network and migrating their network to many different configurations.

For companies that want to become part of the Internet and retain the benefits and investment that they already have in their SNA networks, AnyNet provides a solution. This design allows them to keep their current infrastructure and to change it at the rate and pace that they want without sacrificing immediate access to and participation in the Internet. Just as you can call your husband's cellular phone from your office, you can let your SNA user communicate with the Internet!

13.6 References

Britton, Kathryn, et. al., "Multiprotocol Transport Networking: A General Internetworking Solution," *Proceedings of the 1993 International Conference on Network Protocols*, Los Alamos, CA: IEEE Computer Society Press, October 1993, pp. 14–25.

IBM Corporation, *Multiprotocol Transport Networking: Technical Overview*, 1993, GC31-7073.

Pozefsky, Diane et al., "Multiprotocol Transport Networking: Eliminating Application Dependencies on Communications Protocols," *IBM Systems Journal*, Vol. 34, No. 3, pp. 472–500.

Robertson, Don, *Accessing Transport Networks: MPTN and AnyNet Solutions*, McGraw-Hill, 1996.

chapter   14

Multiprotocol routers bring it together: IP to APPN/HPR

Dᴀᴠɪᴅ J. Bᴇʀᴍᴀɴ

In this chapter David J. Berman recites the history of the multiprotocol router, describing how it became one of the central tools for integrating multiprotocol networks by using TCP/IP, SNA/APPN/HPR and any combination of these protocols. The future roles and possible implementations of multiprotocol routers are cited.

14.1 Internetworking and the multiprotocol router

A new phase of the data networking industry was inaugurated in the late 1980s with the introduction of the multiprotocol router. By 1995, this product category amounted to annual revenues exceeding several billion dollars, and helped change the face of networking. The router, however, was itself a response to a larger phenomenon, that of internetworking.

Initially and throughout the 1970s, the focus of data networking had been to provide a structure, a network, to allow users in one location to access resources (files, programs) in another location connected to the same network. Different types of networks evolved to meet different requirements for bandwidth, distance, cost and reliability.

During the mid-1970s university and government networking researchers began to address a different problem—how to facilitate interoperation between devices on different networks, even networks of different types (see figure 14.1). A family of protocols evolved to hide the differences between underlying networks in order to allow communication between them. The technology became known as internetworking, and the protocol family as the TCP/IP suite.

14.2 TCP/IP: the foundation of internetworking

TCP/IP is not merely a protocol, nor even a protocol stack. It is an entire family of protocols and applications intended to run on top of existing networks to allow communication between them. As such, TCP/IP is unlike other networks such as SNA or DECnet which were primarily intended for communication between terminals and host computers in relatively homogeneous environments.

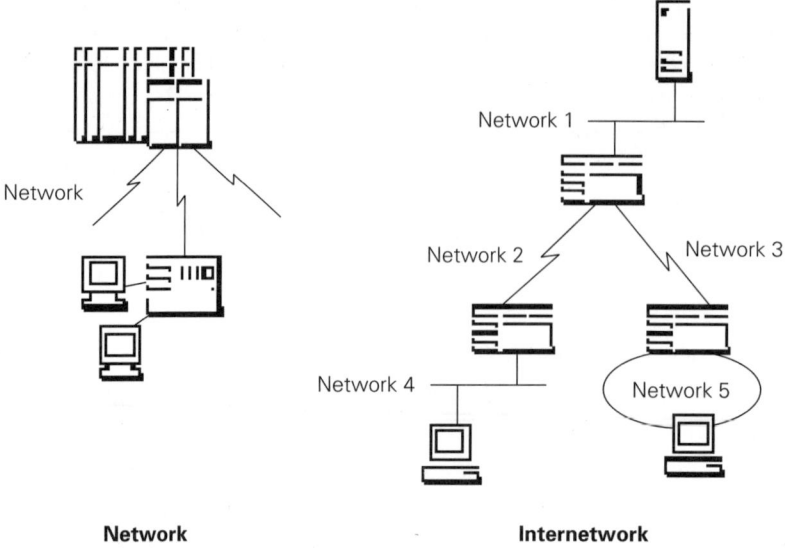

Network   **Internetwork**

Figure 14.1   Network compared with internetwork

The elements of the TCP/IP suite are shown in table 14.1. Underlying networks can include ethernet, token ring, FDDI, frame relay, X.25, SMDS, ATM, ISDN, point-to-point links, and others.

Table 14.1   Elements of the TCP/IP suite

Application protocols	File transfer protocol (FTP)	Large file transfers
	Telnet	Interactive access
	Simple message transfer protocol (SMTP)	Electronic mail
	Simple network management protocol (SNMP)	Network management
Transport protocols	Transmission control protocol (TCP)	Reliable connection-oriented service
	User datagram protocol (UDP)	Connectionless datagram service
Network protocol	Internet protocol (IP)	Connectioness routing between multiple underlying networks

14.3 Characteristics of TCP/IP

TCP/IP came into a networking world which was already beginning to be reoriented towards LANs with their broadcast-oriented protocols. TCP/IP borrowed the LAN's concept of unique addressing, where every network device is assigned a distinctive address. Unlike a LAN MAC address, however, an IP address is clearly segmented into a network portion and a host portion, to facilitate path determination by intermediate switching devices interconnecting multiple networks.

IP intermediate switching devices consider only the network portion of the address and have no knowledge of endpoints; this characteristic has enabled IP-based internetworks to support hundreds of thousands of devices. Initially, IP intermediate switching devices were called gateways, but we now know them as routers.

Compared with SNA, TCP/IP arrived into a somewhat different networking world. Primarily intended to interconnect multiple autonomous LANs using a backbone WAN, TCP/IP would have to exist in a far more dynamic environment than the relatively tightly controlled world of SNA. In addition, the internetworking focus of TCP/IP requires it to deal with a unique problem—dynamic binding of network addresses to local addresses of different forms. Both of these problems are accommodated by additional protocols in the TCP/IP suite. ARP performs address binding by building a table in the host or router (see figure 14.2). Meanwhile, a series of routing protocols perform topology acquisition and respond to changes in link status, building a table which routers consult to determine how to route an incoming packet (see figure 14.3). RIP was the first commonly used routing protocol, but RIP has now been largely superseded, at least in large networks, by the better-performing OSPF protocol.

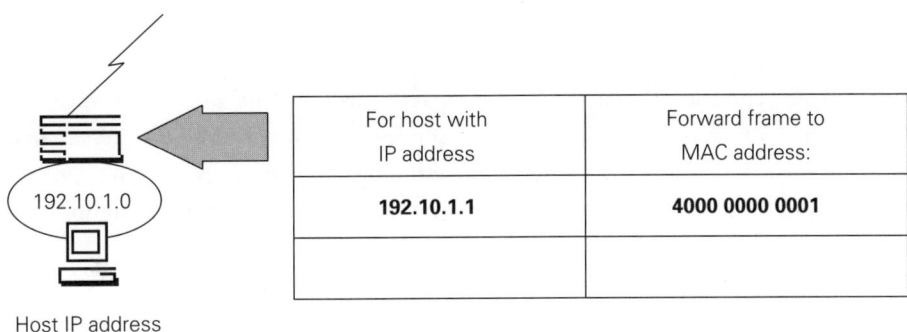

For host with IP address	Forward frame to MAC address:
192.10.1.1	**4000 0000 0001**

Host IP address
192.10.1.1
Host MAC address
4000 0000 0001

Figure 14.2   ARP table

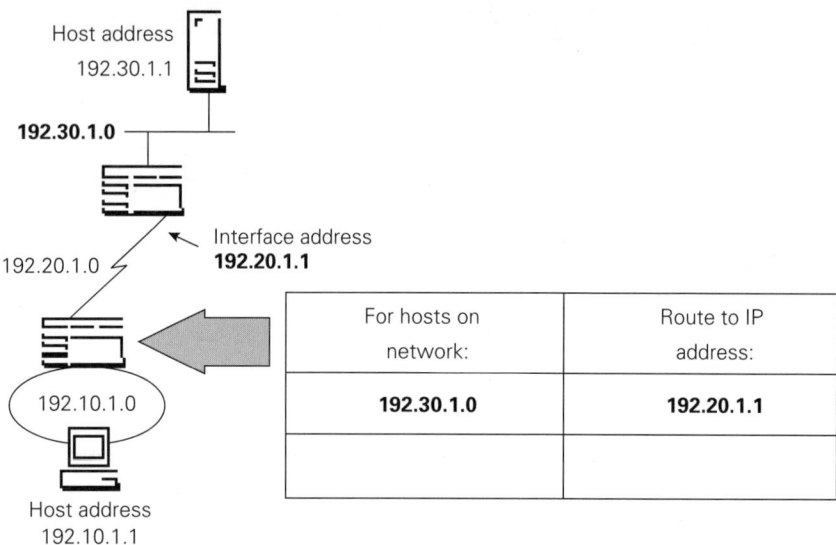

Host address
192.30.1.1

192.30.1.0

Interface address
192.20.1.1

192.20.1.0

192.10.1.0

For hosts on network:	Route to IP address:
192.30.1.0	**192.20.1.1**

Host address
192.10.1.1

Figure 14.3   Routing table

Taken together the TCP/IP protocol suite allows very large internetworks to be created, maintained and evolved without nearly the level of manual configuration required by SNA.

14.4 TCP/IP to the world, and the birth of the router

TCP/IP was originally created by the academic community in partnership with the U.S. government to extend the original ARPANET packet-switched network to an internetwork, called the Connected Internet, now just the Internet. Most university researchers were using a version of the UNIX operating system referred to as BSD. The TCP/IP suite was included in BSD version 4.0, and immediately propagated throughout the academic community. After all, not only was TCP/IP functional, it was free!

In a similar vein was the router given to the world. BSD 4.0 included a UNIX process, gate_d for gateway daemon, comprising IP, RIP and EGP—all that was necessary for an IP router to access the Connected Internet. Not only could any UNIX system be a router but gate_d made it easy for the nascent internetworking industry to create the first specialized routers.

14.5 TCP/IP and SNA: different problems, different solutions

TCP/IP represents a very different type of network architecture compared with SNA. This shouldn't be surprising; TCP/IP and SNA arrived at different points of technology evolution, and had fundamentally different problems to solve.

Mainly intended to connect terminal controllers and small distributed processors to centralized hosts, SNA was developed at a time when processing and memory resources were expensive but personnel were comparatively cheap. SNA's centralized control, static routing, and manual configuration were right for the times, minimizing costly resources for inexpensive terminal controllers, yet providing a reliable, connection-oriented communications service upon which critical applications could depend. Additionally, intended for remote communications using WAN facilities, SNA was quite efficient in its use of costly bandwidth.

TCP/IP in contrast was intended from the beginning to provide an internetwork among multiple underlying networks. Developed later than SNA when processor and memory resources were becoming relatively less costly than personnel, TCP/IP permits a large network to evolve and grow dynamically, without requiring extensive manual configuration.

Much of TCP/IP's dynamic orientation comes from its definition of network host. Unlike SNA, which assigns radically different responsibilities to VTAM hosts compared to terminal controllers, TCP/IP hosts include everything from individual workstations to supercomputers. All function equally as TCP/IP hosts. All have the same responsibilities for interacting with IP routers to select routes across the internetwork dynamically.

Also contributing to TCP/IP's dynamism is the connectionless nature of IP routing, with each packet or datagram individually transmitted to its destination without regard to sequencing or retransmission in case of errors. Connectionless datagram routing has the benefit of redirecting traffic over alternate paths in case of link failure or as new links become available. On the other hand, IP routing is considered unreliable. Packets may be dropped while rerouting is being performed or during periods of congestion. Either TCP can be used to provide a reliable connection-oriented transport service, or else the applications themselves must take responsibility for retransmission in case of packet loss.

Finally, TCP/IP's dynamic nature comes at the cost of bandwidth efficiency. Recalling that TCP/IP usually delivers its data onto a LAN where bandwidth is cheap, TCP/IP uses special ARP broadcasts to eliminate the need to manually configure host MAC addresses at the routers. Dynamic acquisition of network topology is accomplished by more broadcasts using RIP and OSPF, at the cost of WAN bandwidth. None of these protocols would have been practical in the early days of SNA when bandwidth was scarce and costly.

The divergent networking approaches represented by SNA and TCP/IP lead to a number of practical operational differences which are clearly visible to network managers. Among these is the selection of MAC addresses. On SNA LANs, MAC addresses must usually be manually configured, sometimes in thousands of locations. It is consequently common for SNA shops to use *locally administered addresses* (LAA) exclusively, to avoid the potential need to manually reconfigure many downstream device addresses in case a hardware failure requires replacing the LAN adapter in a manually configured gateway, such as a TIC in a communications controller.

This is foreign to TCP/IP shops. Dynamic resolution of IP addresses to MAC addresses means that no reconfiguration is necessary should MAC addresses change. TCP/IP LANs almost always employ hardware-based *universally administered addresses* (UAA), further reducing the amount of manual configuration required.

An even more fundamental change stems from the predictable nature of SNA compared to the variability of TCP/IP. SNA's connection orientation combined with multilevel pacing algorithms allows network response times to be tailored so precisely that network managers and users frequently contract for them. Service level agreements (SLAs) are a staple of modern MIS environments in the SNA world.

On the other hand, IP's best-effort delivery and hop-by-hop routing, combined with the often-bursty nature of LAN traffic, means that response times for TCP/IP are far too variable to permit contracted service levels. Only now, with the recent introduction of bandwidth management mechanisms in routers and with resource reservation protocols on the horizon, are TCP/IP network managers even beginning to think about introducing SLAs and the consequent support of mission-critical corporate traffic.

14.6 Bring on the PC-LAN: the focus of internetworking changes

Roughly parallel with the introduction of TCP/IP internetworking, the PC was beginning to be used by corporations for productivity applications such as spreadsheets and word processing. The PC was married to the LAN shortly afterwards to solve a very practical problem, sharing a costly laser printer among multiple PC users.

Once the LAN was installed for printing, users began to realize that its real power was in sharing files and applications. The addition of file and application sharing expanded the focus of the PC-LAN from a local printing function (contained to individual LANs) to the enterprise as a whole. Now an internetwork was needed.

PC-LAN vendors responded with sophisticated network architectures and protocols which borrowed freely from TCP/IP. Novell IPX, Banyan VINES and Apple's AppleTalk all included the concepts of network layer addressing, dynamic topology acquisition, and updating as well as MAC address binding.

PC-LANs changed the face of internetworking. While TCP/IP internetworks had been employed primarily in the university environment and technical community, PC-LANs addressed the needs of business. This was the same constituency supported by SNA.

The dramatic growth of PC-LANs, particularly Novell NetWare, between the mid-1980s to the mid-1990s meant that IPX became the dominant network protocol based on volume of traffic. Many corporate networks supported mainly SNA and IPX. Even as recently as 1995, IPX represented the dominant protocol at over fifty percent of sites, with TCP/IP second at twenty-two percent and SNA at about six percent (information from Dataquest).

14.7 The multiprotocol router

Here was a new business requirement. Large corporations, typically users of SNA for their production networks, began to set up internetworks to serve the needs of a new class of user. Typically using PCs or UNIX stations on LANs, new users might have been technical, for example, engineers using CAD/CAM applications, or managerial/professional using word processing or spreadsheet applications. Either way, their requirement for high performance for bursty traffic as well as their rapid expansion meant that an SNA network could not possibly have fulfilled the requirements of the new category of users. Dynamic routing, however, filled the bill perfectly.

So, starting in the mid-1980s, a new product category was created—the multiprotocol router. Starting with the foundation of the IP router represented by UNIX's gate_d, the industry developed specialized products which executed software-based protocol-handling functions on what were essentially special-purpose computers. The first routers accommodated only a single protocol. IP routers were available which off-loaded the routing function from UNIX hosts, thereby improving their application-handling performance. XNS routers were available for those PC-LANs which used that protocol, while Novell implemented IPX routing directly into NetWare servers.

A notable characteristic of LANs was that they permeated a corporation quickly, in a poorly coordinated way. A single building could house multiple protocols—TCP/IP for engineering, IPX for marketing, VINES for finance. When it became necessary to provide access to these networks from networks in a different location, would it be necessary to install separate routers and costly WAN links for each protocol? The router quickly evolved to make sure that didn't happen.

LAN and WAN protocols include protocol-type fields to indicate which protocol a packet represents. Using sophisticated software, a router uses this information to dispatch a packet to the correct protocol handler, to route it to its destination. Meanwhile, the router maintains separate routing tables for each different protocol, updating these routing tables by using multiple routing protocols (IP RIP, IPX RIP, OSPF) simultaneously. The result is the multiprotocol router (see figure 14.4), which quickly emerged as the solution for internetworking in the chaotic corporate environment.

In the beginning, routers were envisioned as special-purpose computers. Typically based on standard microprocessors (e.g., 680x0) and the VME bus, early routers resembled small UNIX machines. As the introduction of multiprotocol support

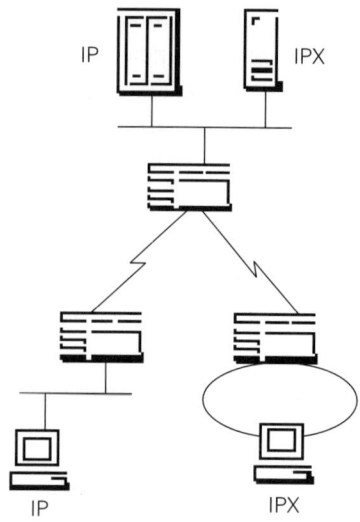

Figure 14.4 The multiprotocol router

increased the demand for performance, and as networks began to scale larger, routers evolved in a more specialized direction. Single-processor designs yielded to distributed processing and then symmetric multiprocessing architectures, while the Versa Module Europa (VME) bus yielded to proprietary buses of over 500 Mbps. throughput. Router memory grew from 2–4 MB to the point where a single router could easily support over 100 MB. Such a router could support many protocols simultaneously and could store large routing tables for an enormous worldwide network.

14.7.1 Bridging, too

The multiprotocol router became able to solve an even larger set of networking problems by subsuming the functions of the LAN bridge. Bridges initially appeared about the same time as routers, but represented an attempt to create internetworks using LAN MAC addresses only. Bridges used simple topology acquisition protocols—spanning-tree for ethernet and IBM-defined SRB for token ring.

The advantage of bridges was their insensitivity to higher-layer protocols; they worked equally well for IP, IPX, and even for SNA or NetBIOS which have no network layer protocol at all. The disadvantage, however, was that without a network layer address to work with, bridges were unable to control the level of broadcasts in the inter-network. Bridged networks were limited in their ability to grow beyond a modest scale, and by 1990 or so had been generally superseded by routers except in SNA or NetBIOS environments.

By adding transparent bridging for ethernet and SRB for token ring, multiprotocol routers could interconnect any set of LANs, regardless of network protocol involved. In addition, SRB allowed the router for the first time to support SNA networks.

14.8 Adding SNA to the mix

As we have seen, SNA represented a completely different type of network architecture compared with the dynamically routed multiprotocol LAN internetwork. The difference, however, was not merely technical. The corporate SNA network typically supported mission-critical business applications, while the LAN internetwork initially supported technical and professional users who required high bandwidth, but for whom continuous network services were considered to be less important. In addition, the wide area infrastructures were different, with SNA based on lower-speed multidrop circuits to hundreds of branch offices while LAN internetworks required high bandwidth facilities, but extended to relatively few locations.

It was, therefore, natural that corporations maintained separate networks for SNA and LANs. However, the situation in the 1990s began to change. Newer business applications began to be based on UNIX or PC-LANs, requiring LAN internetworking services rather than SNA. Furthermore, many of these new applications required access from the remote branch offices which were served only by SNA. Corporate LAN internetworks began to be extended across the enterprise, aided by a new generation of very low-cost routers. This resulted in parallel networks for SNA and LANs, yielding high expenses for routers, controllers, and most important, WAN facilities. A solution to converge the SNA networks and LAN internetworks was required.

14.8.1 Why not SNA?

Given the well-established SNA infrastructure and extensive SNA investment in place at many corporations, an early consideration was to use SNA as the backbone to carry multiprotocol LAN traffic. There were even some early products, such as IBM's LTLW feature to allow installed SNA networks to carry PC-LAN traffic.

However, the SNA backbone proved to be impractical as a mainstream solution for converged multiprotocol networks, primarily for two reasons. First, the SNA infrastructure tended to be optimized for frequent small messages requiring rapid response times but not needing high throughput. SNA was clearly an inappropriate technical solution to support typically bursty LAN traffic requiring high throughput. Second, SNA's need for extensive manual configuration was inconsistent with the need for LANs to grow and evolve quickly. Industry focus changed to providing multiprotocol LAN internetworks which could also accommodate SNA.

14.9 The first attempt: source route bridging

The first solution to converging SNA with multiprotocol LAN traffic came, indirectly, from IBM itself. The original token ring architecture reference described SRB, a solution for linking multiple token ring segments over a token ring backbone. Originally intended for campus-wide LANs, SRB could be extended over a WAN as well.

Having already introduced multiprotocol routing products, it was relatively easy for the router industry to add support for SRB. Now a multiprotocol router could offer bridging support for SNA LAN traffic at the same time as routing support for IP, IPX and others over the same set of WAN links.

SRB in a multiprotocol router initially proved to be very successful at converging a small SNA network with a lightly loaded multiprotocol internetwork. However, things didn't work as well as the network grew. The first problem was due to timing. SNA's LAN data-link layer, LLC2, uses timer values appropriate for a LAN. When carried over a WAN by a multiprotocol bridge/router, the inevitable congestion resulting from heavy LAN traffic causes the timers to be violated, breaking the SNA sessions (session timeout).

The second problem was one of scale. Unlike routed networks which can grow arbitrarily large, SRB imposes a fixed limit on the number of intermediate bridges between source and destination end stations. The hop limit severely limits the size of a network using SRB. In addition, with no routing protocol like RIP or OSPF, SRB depends on explorer broadcasts to update the network topology. Not a problem for small networks—broadcasts limit the number of end stations which an SRB network can realistically support.

Finally, unlike IP or IPX routing, SRB had no ability to reroute SNA traffic in case of failure of a link. Session disconnection was the result.

14.10 Adapting SNA to IP

The industry's response to the shortcomings of SRB was to craft hybrid solutions of SRB and IP, where IP could compensate for some of the SRB limitations. The first solution was merely to encapsulate SRB frames inside IP packets. While allowing networks to grow beyond the limits imposed by SRB and under ideal circumstances allowing rerouting to be performed on SNA traffic, IP encapsulation did little to eliminate session timeouts.

The next improvement was for the routers to terminate the LLC2 connections, not merely pass LLC2 over the internetwork. LLC2 termination changed the focus of the router entirely. No longer only an intermediate switch, a router now took on the role of a host, performing as an LLC2 end station and using TCP at the same time to guarantee reliable transport across the network. LLC2 termination was costly in terms of router processing and memory resources, but it did effectively solve the problem of session time-outs even in heavily loaded networks.

Early LLC2 termination schemes were proprietary. Users were not able to mix and match routers from different vendors in internetworks carrying SNA. IBM contributed a solution by disclosing to the industry its own comprehensive LLC2 termination mechanism, DLSw. Released initially as informational RFC 1434, DLSw included not only LLC2 termination but also sophisticated broadcast reduction, while preserving SRB's dynamic end station discovery which reduces the need for manual configuration. Taken over by a multivendor consortium, the DLSw *related interest group* (RIG), DLSw is described by RFC 1795 and has become the industry-standard technique for carrying SNA across a routed multiprotocol internetwork using TCP/IP (see figure 14.5). DLSw V2 is described by RFC 2166.

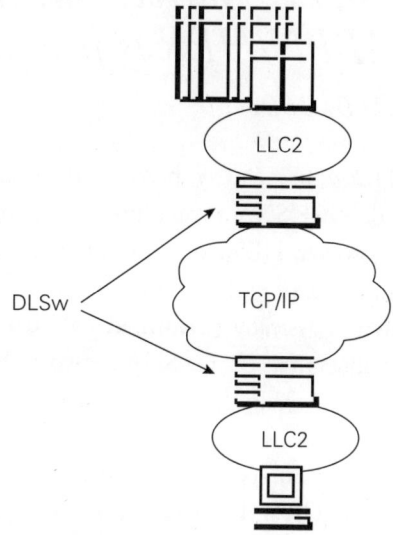

Figure 14.5 Data-link switching (DLSw)

A significant side benefit of DLSw's LLC2 termination is that other data-link protocols, including SDLC and QLLC/X.25, can be terminated as well. This means that DLSw can inherently perform link conversion such as SDLC-to-LLC2 without resorting to separate converter boxes (see figure 14.6).

With SNA session reliability issues now solved by DLSw, the industry has turned its attention to SNA response time. In order to allow SNA users to maintain their SLAs and still take advantage of the cost economies of a converged multiprotocol internetwork for SNA, router manufacturers have introduced rigorous bandwidth management features. Prioritization and bandwidth allocation features can ensure that SNA response-time objectives are satisfied, even in the presence of heavy LAN traffic on the internetwork.

The combination of DLSw, bandwidth management, and high-capacity multiprotocol routers has now given major corporations a practical way to evolve their parallel SNA and LAN internetworks to a converged internetwork based on dynamically routed IP. As a consequence, single-protocol SNA backbone networks are beginning to erode even as the volume of SNA traffic continues to increase.

14.11 Native routing: APPN/HPR is just another protocol

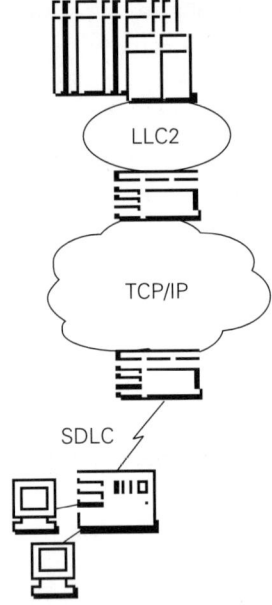

Figure 14.6 SDLC to LLC2 conversion using DLSw

DLSw has clearly become the mainstream approach to adapting SNA to a router-based multiprotocol network. However, DLSw does not actually represent SNA routing, in terms of path selection based on PU or LU names, such as is classically performed by PU4 communications controllers in a subarea SNA network. Even though IP routing is used within the internetwork, DLSw appears to the SNA end stations as an SRB.

If routers could perform true SNA routing, users would be able to offload VTAM and NCP and allow the routers to select the appropriate path to the user's desired destination directly, just as is done for IP or IPX traffic. Theoretically it should have been possible for routers to implement classical PU4 routing as performed by NCP, but the realities of the proprietary nature of NCP have prevented this, just as subarea routing's dependence on manual configuration would have made it impractical. For router manufacturers, the solution for native SNA routing is represented by APPN, supplemented by HPR (see figure 14.7).

APPN/HPR is IBM's architecture to incorporate contemporary concepts of dynamic routing into SNA. Initially developed to support small networks of midrange systems, IBM has now extended it to the S/390 mainframe world including the ability to scale to reasonably large networks. IBM licenses APPN/HPR technology to others. In fact, IBM shares the responsibility for defining APPN/HPR with a multivendor consortium, the APPN Implementers' Workshop (AIW).

APPN/HPR eliminates most of the manual configuration required by subarea SNA. Its dynamic resource registration feature allows APPN NNs, the APPN routers, to locate the user's desired application. APPN also includes dynamic topology updating

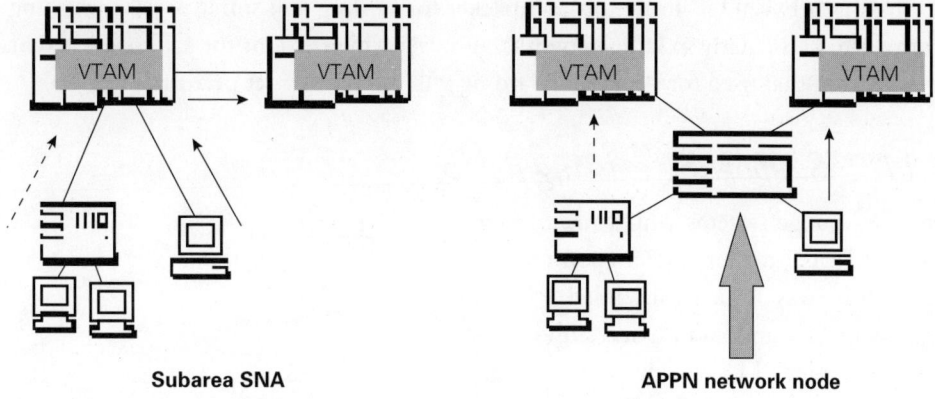

Subarea SNA   APPN network node

Figure 14.7   Native SNA routing using APPN

using a protocol very similar to IP's OSPF. Combined with the easy availability of technology via IBM license, APPN/HPR's dynamic configuration and topology acquisition make it the appropriate native SNA solution for multiprotocol routers. A multiprotocol router which supports APPN/HPR can route SNA as just another protocol, along with IP, IPX, and others.

14.11.1 Implementation considerations

APPN was initially intended to execute on midrange computers. Transplanting APPN to a router can be highly successful, but it does involve several implementation considerations. First, APPN typically occupies a significant amount of memory. The APPN NN CP is complex, and requires a lot of storage for procedure. APPN maintains a large amount of data in tables, including registered LU resources, topology information, and for the older ISR, state information for each session being routed. All of these tables require memory resources, increasing with the size of the network. Clearly, any router supporting APPN will require scaling to large memory if a large network is to be supported.

Ironically, the more sophisticated HPR places somewhat less demand on memory for routers used as intermediate nodes only, because session state information is not needed. This is not true for HPR routers used as network endpoints, however, since HPR's RTP at the endpoints does require session memory.

A second implementation consideration involves distribution of processing. Between resource registration and searches, topology updates and route calculations, the APPN CP is very CPU-intensive. The forwarding process on the other hand is much lighter in weight; this is particularly true of HPR. A router architecture which requires

CPU sharing between CP functions and packet forwarding will suffer poor forwarding performance, particularly in large networks. A router which assigns the CP to a different processor from that used for packet forwarding will offer far better performance.

14.11.2 Supporting existing devices

Born of midrange systems which make extensive use of LU6.2 for intersystem communications, APPN was initially intended to serve independent LUs and had no accommodation for the dependent LUs widely used for 3270 and other applications. IBM solved the problem technically by introducing DLUS in VTAM V4R2 and DLUR in 3174 configuration support C microcode as well as in OS/2 communications manager. The only problem was that neither 3174 nor OS/2 represent the most commonly used LUs any longer. IBM customers were at the mercy of third-party emulator vendors to provide DLUR before they could migrate to APPN.

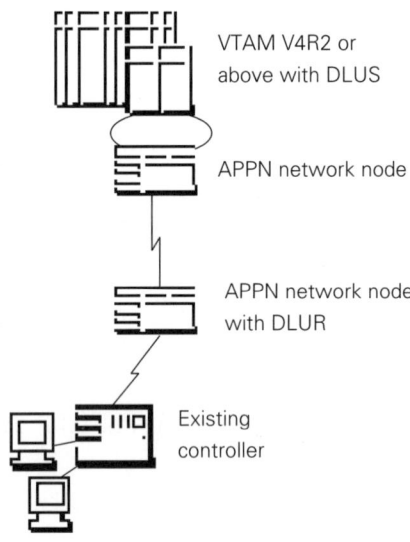

VTAM V4R2 or above with DLUS

APPN network node

APPN network node with DLUR

Existing controller

Figure 14.8 Dependent LU requester (DLUR) for existing devices

The router manufacturers recognized a clear opportunity to help solve the problem. By supplementing APPN NN with DLUR at the router, it could act as a DLUR gateway for existing dependent LU devices. In fact, coupled with the primary SDLC station feature which many routers had been supporting for some time, a router with DLUR could permit an existing fifteen-year old 3274 to access an APPN host (see figure 14.8). By preserving existing end stations, DLUR in the router is an effective aid for users to migrate to APPN gracefully and economically.

14.11.3 Benefits of APPN in the router

By adapting SNA to IP, DLSw proved the benefits of applying dynamic routing technology to SNA traffic. Unfortunately, DLSw cannot route on the basis of SNA naming, relying only on MAC addresses. As a consequence DLSw still requires that any SNA routing be performed by the host systems, absorbing valuable host *millions of instructions per second* (MIPS) which could be better applied to application processing.

APPN and HPR supported by a multiprotocol router can perform actual routing of SNA traffic, offloading this function from host systems. This is particularly beneficial

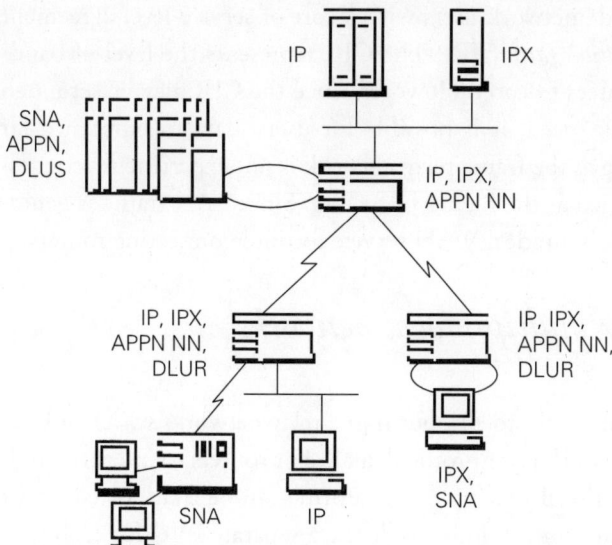

Figure 14.9 Routing of IP, IPX, and SNA using APPN

for AS/400 systems, for which APPN Network Node represents significant overhead. An AS/400 user can realize significant performance improvements (25–35%) by adding an APPN NN router in front of the AS/400, redefining the AS/400 as a less-burdensome APPN EN.

With support for APPN NN and HPR, a router can perform native routing for SNA along with IP, IPX, and others. Finally a multiprotocol router can accommodate SNA as just another protocol (figure 14.9).

14.12 Frame relay

Routers historically took advantage of high-bandwidth leased circuits to interconnect multiple geographically dispersed LANs. In the early 1990s an alternative became available—high-speed frame relay networks.

Frame relay is a type of network which provides virtual circuits to end stations, similar to X.25. Unlike X.25, frame relay uses data-link (layer 2) addresses, and currently provides only *permanent virtual circuits* (PVCs). Switching at layer 2, and performing no retransmission in case of packet loss, frame relay networks are fast. Large corporations with significant data concentration requirements may set up their own private frame relay networks, but more commonly frame relay network services are provided by the public carriers.

Frame relay networks provide network users with a sort of service level agreement referred to as *committed information rate* (CIR). The CIR represents the level of bandwidth which the network guarantees to carry. However, since the CIR may be set much lower than the actual access link speed, it is possible for users' data to burst at a far higher rate than the CIR. As long as the frame relay network is not experiencing congestion, the data frames will be carried at the higher burst rate. Since LAN traffic is generally bursty, a frame relay network is an ideal WAN service for interconnecting routers.

14.12.1 RFC 1490 for multiprotocol networks, including SNA

Routers must accommodate multiple protocols, but frame relay networks switch at layer 2 and have no visibility to the network layer protocol at all. For routers to interpret multiple protocols successfully it is critical that protocol information be transported across the frame relay network. One solution would be to define a separate PVC for each protocol, but since PVCs are generally tariffed this would not be economical. It is highly desirable to transport multiple protocols on a single PVC.

The IETF has defined a protocol intended to do just that. Originally RFC 1294, the current version of the multiprotocol-over-frame-relay protocol is RFC 1490. RFC 1490 allows multiple protocols to be encapsulated in a single frame relay PVC, along with various methods of protocol identification which allow the distant router to interpret them correctly. RFC 1490 allows simple multiprotocol networks to be built using frame relay as the only WAN service; in this case the simple routers which connect the LANs to the frame relay network are known as *frame relay access devices* (FRADs).

RFC 1490 is significant as a multiprotocol solution for SNA because IBM defined an SNA encapsulation standard for frame relay which follows the protocol identification guidelines. Not only defining the encapsulation of SNA in frame relay, IBM also implemented support in NCP V7R1 as well as in many other products, including OS/2, AS/400 and the 3174. IBM has implemented SNA encapsulation in frame relay in two formats, the simple *boundary network node* (BNN) and a more flexible format, *boundary access node* (BAN).

BAN and BNN allow SNA users to replace their existing networks of SDLC multidrop lines, substituting frame relay networks which in most cases cost less while delivering higher performance. Perhaps the most significant advantage, however, is a direct result of RFC 1490—multiprotocol LAN traffic may be combined with SNA onto a single frame relay network, without using IP as a routable backbone protocol or migrating to APPN (see figure 14.10). Of course, a complex network comprising a mix

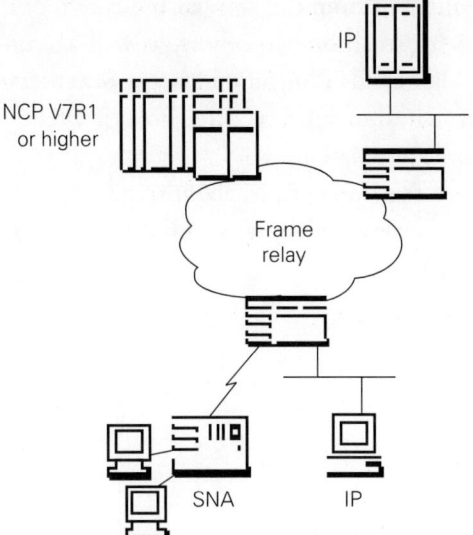

NCP V7R1
or higher

IP

Frame
relay

SNA   IP

Figure 14.10   SNA over frame relay

of frame relay and high bandwidth leased circuits will still require a routable backbone protocol like IP or APPN.

14.13 *The future of routing*

The technology which gave the world the router, the Internet, has now exploded beyond its early academic confines. Assisted by the easy-to-use WWW, the Internet has now become part of the daily routine for millions of people.

The inexpensive and functional applications for Web access, browsers, and servers, are now being widely adopted by corporations for their own information distribution and application access requirements. Such intranets will no doubt have a major impact on the network evolution plans of the corporation. Like the Internet, intranets are based on TCP/IP which means that intranets will drive IP routing deeper into the networking strategy of major corporations. Already, certain user organizations are making plans to migrate away from other PC-LAN protocols like IPX, VINES, and AppleTalk toward IP.

This kind of migration will likely encourage SNA users to explore ways of accessing their host applications using IP. For some, adapting SNA to IP using DLSw will be the best solution; others will choose to access their applications directly from TCP/IP using TN3270E or even intranet protocols (HTML) directly. Whichever solution is chosen, routers will represent the switching nodes which deliver the data to the user.

Routers in the future may exist in forms different from the familiar boxes of today. IP routing functions will be built into servers for small branch offices, as well as into high capacity frame or ATM cell switches for high bandwidth campus network centers. Routers will even be combined with ATM switches for high capacity WAN switches, supporting Internet and intranet access for a large population.

In whichever form routing takes, the rise of the Internet and the intranets derived from it will ensure that routing will remain the key technology for connecting users to their applications and data, wherever they happen to be.

chapter 15

Managing SNA networks

Robert E. Moore

395

Robert E. Moore describes the importance of network management, specifically, highlighting its role in SNA/APPN/HPR and TCP/IP networks. The importance of such network management applications as topology management and problem management is described using real-life examples. In addition to network management protocols popular both in SNA and TCP/IP, there is a discussion on future developments of Web and Java enabling techniques for network management, that are becoming popular today.

15.1 Introduction

"Just a moment" said Mary, a clerk in the athletic department ticket office. "My computer seems to be hung." Mary is about to benefit from the network management capabilities present in today's SNA networks. Figure 15.1 shows the network as it was just before a backhoe broke the underground cable[1] identified in the figure with the letter *B*. The client application program in Mary's workstation (end node [EN] 6) was in session with a host application program in the university's operations center (EN 1) that coordinates ticket sales for basketball games. Mary was about to print tickets for a fan standing in her line, but all she got on her screen was the hourglass icon. After a few seconds, the icon went away, her application started working again, and she was able to print the tickets. The remainder of this chapter tells the story of what *really* happened before, during, and after the time that Mary's application was interrupted.

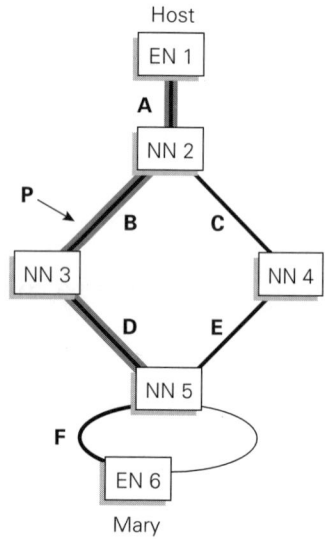

Figure 15.1 The original path of Mary's session

Figure 15.1 shows the relevant portion of the university's APPN network, including EN 1 (the host where the ticketing application program was running), NNs 2–5, EN 6 (Mary's workstation), and the links connecting them. The session between Mary's client application program and the ticketing application program was using APPN/HPR capabilities in EN 1 and NNs 2, 3, and 5. With APPN/HPR, RTP connections, informally called *RTP pipes*, are established between APPN/HPR nodes in a session's path. In figure 15.1, there is an RTP pipe *P* from EN 1 to NN 5. Mary's session is using this pipe: even though session data actually traverses the path *6–F–5–D–3–B–2–A–1* (where the numbers identify APPN nodes, and the letters identify APPN TGs, which in this case are equivalent to links), logically its path is *6–F–5–P–1*. Had Mary's workstation been capable of being the end point of an RTP pipe, the logical path could have been even simpler: 6–*P*–1.

RTP pipes introduce two major benefits into an APPN network. First, intermediate nodes in a pipe (NNs 2 and 3 for pipe *P*) can route session data much more quickly and efficiently than can APPN nodes that lack APPN/HPR capabilities, because APPN/HPR nodes route traffic at a lower layer of the functional stack and have no awareness of the sessions that pass through them.

Second, and more central to our story, an RTP pipe can be switched to a new path if its current path fails, without taking down the sessions using the RTP pipe. This is what happened during the few seconds that Mary's workstation was showing the hourglass. But we're getting ahead of ourselves; let's go back to the moment that Mary's session was interrupted.

15.2 The APPN/HPR network reacts

Within a fraction of a second after the backhoe breaks the cable, NNs 2 and 3 detect that TG *B* is down. After a few attempts to reactivate TG *B*, the two nodes decide that it really is down, and set about updating the APPN network topology database that exists at each of the NNs. The purpose of these topology updates is to remove TG *B* from consideration in any future route calculations that the NNs might perform on behalf of the LUs they serve. Later we'll see how these updates are used for topology monitoring: the network topology database is the source of information for the network topology pictures that operators view.

---

1. Before we go any further, we need to distinguish clearly three closely related items:

- The cable that was broken by the backhoe: this is a physical entity with physical properties—say, 1,000 meters long, containing 2,000 optical fibers, wrapped in red sheathing, and so forth.
- The data link connecting the APPN nodes at either end of the cable: this is an abstraction of the physical cable, with properties such as bandwidth and delay.
- The APPN TG, which is a slightly different abstraction of the physical cable: this abstraction is the one used in APPN's route-calculation algorithms.

    For a single-link TG, there's very little difference between the link and the TG: the TG's characteristics and status are just slightly repackaged versions of its underlying link's characteristics and status. With multilink TGs (which, by the way, have as a prerequisite HPR, and not just base APPN), the mappings between link characteristics and TG characteristics are more complex. A multilink TG is up if at least one of its component links is up, and down only if all of its links are down. A multilink TG's capacity is the sum of its component links' capacities, its propagation delay is a weighted average of its component links' propagation delays, and so forth.

    To simplify our example, we will assume that all of the TGs involved are single-link TGs.

15.3 The RTP pipe finds a new path

Within a few more seconds, the end points of RTP pipe P determine that communication has been interrupted over the pipe's original path. Immediately they set about finding a new path for the pipe. Depending on the timing of the topology update reporting that TG B is down, NN 5 may initially calculate the same path the pipe had before: until it knows that TG B is down, its calculation will likely yield the same path for the pipe that it did when Mary's session was originally set up—1–A–2–B–3–D–5. NN 2, however, has direct knowledge that TG B is down, so when it calculates a new path for the pipe, which it does on behalf of the RTP end point in EN 1 (since ENs do not have access to the network topology database), it will receive a new answer: 1–A–2–C–4–E–5. NN 5 will soon have this answer as well, once it has the topology update informing it that TG B is down.

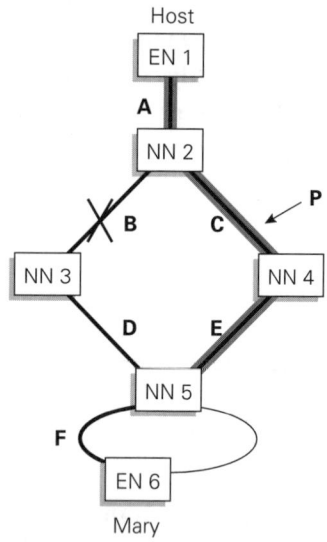

Figure 15.2 The new path of Mary's session

The RTP end points for pipe P in EN 1 and NN 5 initiate a path switch and recover any lost traffic that had been in transit when TG B went down. This traffic includes the transaction that Mary had directed to the ticketing application program at EN 1, the one whose delay caused the hour glass to appear on Mary's screen while the path switch and recovery were taking place. Had Mary not had a transaction open during this brief interval, there would have been *no* indication that the path for pipe P was being switched—the failure of TG B and the network's recovery from it would have been invisible to Mary. After the path switch has been completed, we have the situation shown in figure 15.2: Mary's session still follows the path 1–P–5–F–6, but now the RTP pipe P follows a new path through NN 4.

15.4 The shifting line between network protocols and network management

The two previous sections have talked more about APPN and HPR themselves than about their crisis management by an external monitor. This is no accident. In the early days of SNA, a network operator had two different responsibilities when reacting to a network problem: to help users affected by the problem to resume their activities as soon as possible, and actually to fix the underlying cause of the problem. Recommended actions in SNA/MS alert displays fell fairly neatly into these two categories: those that helped to restore availability immediately for end users, and those that led to identifying the exact cause of a problem and getting it fixed.[2]

As SNA has grown, the network operator has been largely relieved of the first of these activities: when TG *B* fails, existing sessions like Mary's are rerouted nondisruptively, and new sessions are automatically established over paths that do not involve TG *B*. This works, of course, only if the network has been designed with alternate paths in the first place. If TG *C* were not present in our example network, then the path switch for pipe *P* would not have been possible. In that case, sessions such as Mary's would have been unavailable until the backhoe damage to the cables underlying TG *B* had been repaired, and TG *B* had been brought back into service. The lesson here is that the time spent in careful network design, as well as the cost of the physical medium underlying TG *C* as a backup facility, will often be more than repaid by increased availability for end users such as Mary, and increased efficiency for the network operators who must react to incidents such as the one we are considering here.

15.5 Topology pictures change to show that the TG is down

As we indicated before, topology monitors for APPN take advantage of the replicated topology database that's already present in the NN's supporting route calculation. (These topology monitors are often called topology management applications. A *management application* is an application program, typically providing one or two specialized functions, that runs on top of a *management platform* (for example, the TME 10 NetView for AIX product, developed by Tivoli Systems, Inc., an IBM company) and uses generic services that the platform provides.) Since all NNs in a topology subnet[3] have exactly the same view of the network topology, a topology management application need only interrogate one NN in the subnet to get this information.

In addition to the network topology information it shares with the other NNs in its subnet, an APPN NN maintains *local* topology information, identifying the nodes

---

2. The SNA Management Services architecture is documented in two IBM publications: the *SNA Management Services Reference* (SC30-3346) and *SNA Management Services Formats* (GC31–8302).

3. An APPN *topology subnet* is defined as a set of NNs that share the same network topology awareness. In our example the topology subnet has only four NNs, but real topology subnets can have many hundreds of NNs. Thus a substantial savings is realized when a topology tracking program can monitor the topology of all of these NNs and the TGs connecting them by interrogating only one NN in the subnet.

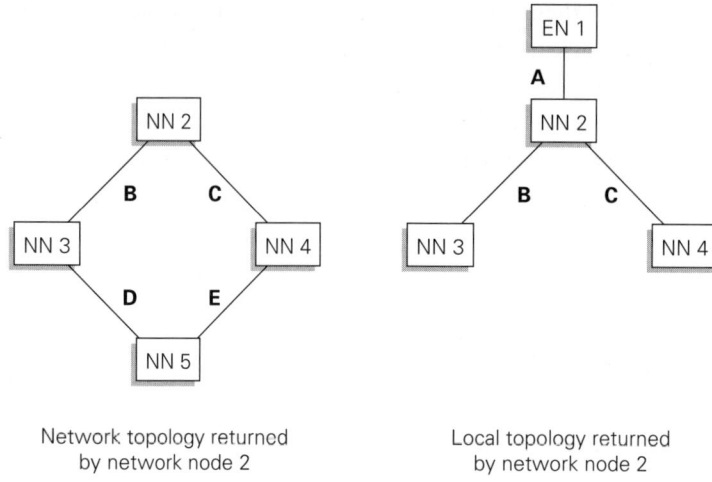

Network topology returned
by network node 2

Local topology returned
by network node 2

Figure 15.3   Topologies returned by NN 2

(both ENs and other NNs) to which it is directly attached and the TGs between itself and these nodes. APPN ENs maintain the same type of local topology information as NNs, but they maintain no network topology information. Figure 15.3 illustrates the network and local topologies that NN 2 would report in our example; NNs 3, 4, and 5 would report exactly the same network topology, but their local topologies would differ from that of NN 2.

For historical reasons, APPN products support two different technologies for returning topology information: some do it with CMIP, while others use SNMP.

15.5.1 SNMP-based APPN topology management

The SNMP MIB representing the topology of an APPN network includes tables for (1) the NNs in a topology subnet, (2) the TGs connecting them, (3) the NNs and ENs adjacent to a reporting node, and (4) the TGs connecting the reporting node to these adjacent nodes. By retrieving the first two tables from one of the NNs in a topology subnet, a topology management application can monitor the subnet's network topology. The two remaining tables provide information on a node's local topology.

A typical topology management application monitors network topology continuously, using the results to maintain an accurate map of a subnet's current topology, but requests local topology from a node only when there is some particular reason for doing so. In our example, the topology management application would maintain and display a network-topology map equivalent to the one represented on the left side of figure 15.3.

As soon as it detected that TG *B* was down, the application would signal this fact to the operator, by turning the displayed line representing TG *B* red.

Given the network's ability to recover from the loss of a TG by rerouting the RTP pipes that were using it, it might seem that a topology map provides very little value. (The process of replacing the broken cable is not triggered by TG B's turning red on the topology map. It is triggered instead by an SNA/MS alert, which we'll discuss later.) The value of the topology map lies in its ability to communicate to an operator the more remote implications of a failure. If, for example, users on the ENs attached to NN 4 call to report that their response times for interacting with applications on EN 1 have suddenly gotten longer, the operator can see at a glance what is going on: TG *C* is now having to carry all the traffic between the ENs (not generally shown in figures 15.1 and 15.2) served by NNs 3, 4, and 5 and the host EN 1, where before it had only half this load. Thus the operator will not waste time attempting to diagnose a problem with NN 4 or with the LAN to which its ENs are attached, when the real problem is on the other side of the campus, between NNs 2 and 3.

When it uses SNMP to maintain a network-topology map, an APPN topology management application is faced with the same problem that faces every SNMP-based topology management application: the SNMP management paradigm is based on polling, whereas maintaining a topology map is most naturally event-driven. For the application to turn the line representing TG *B* red immediately after TG *B* goes down, it needs the node detecting the failure to tell it that TG *B* is down as soon as the node detects it. Otherwise the application won't know that TG *B* has gone down until the next time it retrieves the table representing the TGs connecting the subnet's NNs.

Different SNMP management applications have taken different approaches to this problem of *event reaction latency.*[4] The most commonly used approach is trap-directed polling. If this approach were used by APPN, an NN would emit an unsolicited message called a *trap*—saying "Poll my network topology tables now!"—when any of the information in its network topology database changed. Upon receiving this trap, the APPN topology management application would immediately poll the node that sent the trap, and thus learn that TG *B* had gone down. There is a downside to trap-directed polling: the node that sends the trap must be preconfigured with the name or address of the node where the APPN topology management application resides.

APPN topology management does not use trap-directed polling to overcome the problem of event reaction latency. Instead, it takes advantage of two characteristics of the APPN topology protocols themselves:

---

4. The term comes from *Understanding SNMP MIBs*, by David Perkins and Evan McGinnis (Prentice-Hall, 1997). This book is an invaluable resource on techniques for defining SNMP MIBs, and on SNMP-based management in general.

- As we noted earlier, APPN has a network topology database that is fully replicated at each of the NNs in a topology subnet. Thus a management application can learn all there is to know about a subnet's topology by interacting with a single node.

- The topology database updates that flow between APPN NNs contain FRSNs, which provide a way of distinguishing between old topology information and more recent information. The SNMP network topology tables use these FRSNs as their indexes, which means that once a management application has made a first walk through a node's network topology tables, it need never walk through them again: it can simply retrieve the new rows in the tables, that is, those indexed by FRSNs larger than any it has retrieved before.

How do these two characteristics help with event reaction latency? The answer is they let an APPN topology management application poll the network topology tables much more frequently than it would otherwise be able to. An application's polling frequency is governed by two factors: how many nodes it must poll, and how long it takes to poll each node. Even if we put aside the question of network overhead, an application that is polling fifty nodes, where each poll takes thirty seconds (as it might if the application has to retrieve an entire table every time it polls a node), cannot possibly poll a given node any more frequently than once every twenty-five minutes. In this environment, trap-directed polling makes a lot of sense.

Contrast this situation with that of an APPN topology management application that is monitoring a topology subnet of fifty NNs. The application polls only one of the nodes, not all fifty. And each poll is reduced to a single operation, unless the topology has actually changed. With these advantages, it's quite reasonable for an APPN topology management application to poll for network topology changes once a minute, or even more frequently. While this solution does not provide quite the event reaction latency of trap-directed polling, it comes close, while avoiding the administrative effort of predefining a trap destination at the APPN node reporting the network topology.[5]

APPN local topology does not share these advantages of APPN network topology. Local topology is not replicated, so if a topology management application needs to monitor the local topology of fifty nodes, it must poll each one of them individually. And since there is no FRSN mechanism to guarantee that new information always appears at the bottom of a table, the entire table must be retrieved every time.

While these factors make APPN local topology a logical candidate for trap-directed polling, there is a cost to be considered as well: configuration of a trap destination at *every* node in the network. Currently the APPN MIB does not include trap-directed

---

5. For a more complete analysis of the benefits of the *FRSN-based polling* design described here, see "Advances in APPN Architecture" (Bird, et al.), in *IBM Systems Journal* vol. 34, no. 3 (1995), p. 430.

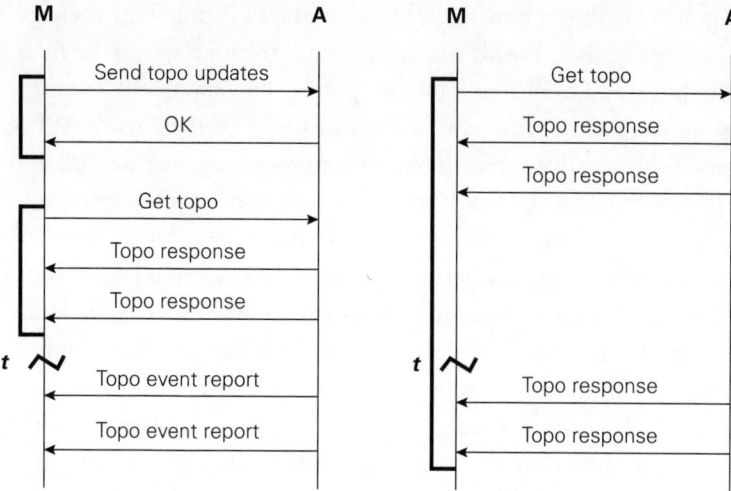

Figure 15.4   Event reports versus responses for topology updates

polling for local topology. Because of this, the normal practice is to monitor local topology at only a few nodes, either those having an especially important role in the network (such as the host EN 1), or those that are currently experiencing problems. By restricting monitoring of local topology to only a few nodes, it is possible to limit the event reaction latency associated with polling them to an acceptable value.

15.5.2 CMIP-based APPN topology management

At first glance it might seem that a CMIP-based topology management application should have no problem with event reaction latency when it's maintaining a map of a subnet's current topology, since CMIP has event reports. Once it has gotten a subnet's topology the first time, and instructed the CMIP agent it is dealing with to send it an event report whenever there's a topology change, the application should be able to simply wait to hear something from the agent. (Once again, it only takes one agent to provide network topology, because the network topology database is fully replicated at each NN.) There is, however, a weakness in this approach, illustrated in figure 15.4.

The left side of figure 15.4 shows the approach we have just discussed. Note that there are two actual transactions involving the management application *M* and the CMIP agent *A*: first, when the management application tells the agent to send it event reports detailing any future topology changes when they occur, and, second, when it retrieves the full subnet topology so it can build its initial topology map. The event reports that the agent sends later don't really qualify as transactions—they are just one-way flows from the agent to the management application.

The right side of figure 15.4 shows how the CMIP-based APPN topology management application actually works. There is only one transaction, through which the management application gets both its initial topology dump and the subsequent topology updates. These updates are triggered by the same events (changes to the agent's APPN topology database) that would have triggered the event reports in the first design, and they are just as timely. But in terms of the CMIP protocol, the updates are responses to the management application's initial request for topology, rather than event reports.

The difference between the two approaches lies in how they react to a loss of communication between the management application and the agent, illustrated in the figure by the jagged line at time t. With the event report approach, the management application has no transaction open with the agent, so it receives no indication of the communication loss. So far as it can tell, it is still capable of getting topology updates from the agent—the topology just doesn't happen to be changing. This is not good behavior for a topology management application: in addition to showing resources that are up and ones that are down, it should be able to indicate when it doesn't know the status of a resource.

This correct behavior is exactly what happens with the second approach in figure 15.4. Because the management application has a transaction open with the agent, the CMIP infrastructure knows to inform it when communication with the agent is lost. The application can then update its topology map to show that it no longer knows the status of the nodes and TGs, and give the operator the opportunity to begin monitoring the subnet via another agent.

15.5.3 The APPN topology integrator

While there were sound reasons at the time for choosing SNMP as the protocol for APPN topology management, and equally sound reasons for choosing CMIP, the fact that implementations of both can exist in the same network leads to obvious interoperability problems. Figure 15.5[6] illustrates a response to these problems, a network

---

6. The roles in figure 15.5 are currently filled by the following products:
- *CMIP manager* The SNA Topology Manager application, running on the NetView for MVS product.
- *SNMP manager* The APPN topology feature of Nways Campus Manager LAN for AIX, running on the TME 10 NetView for AIX platform.
- *Integrator* The APPN Topology Integrator, running under OS/2.
- *CMIP agents* VTAM, the APPNTAM program running in conjunction with Communications Server/2 under OS2, the 3746–950, and the 2217 SNA router.
- *SNMP agents* These are too widespread to mention them all: IBM's 6611, 2210, and 2216 network hardware devices, AS/400, Communications Server/AIX, and routers from 3COM, Bay Networks, and Cisco Systems.

management proxy or adapter called the *APPN topology integrator*. By mapping between CMIP and SNMP, the integrator provides a path for getting APPN topology data from an SNMP agent to a CMIP management application. From the management application's point of view, the integrator provides a CMIP agent appearance for an APPN node that in fact contains an SNMP agent. From an SNMP agent's point of view, the integrator is indistinguishable from a real SNMP manager.

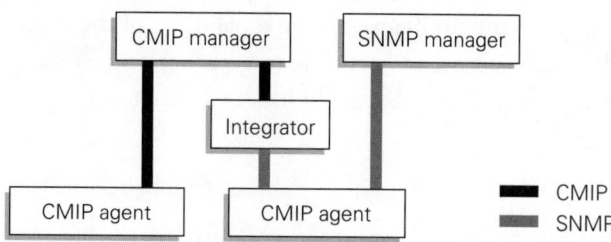

Figure 15.5   Integration of CMIP and SNMP

There is currently no reverse integrator, to provide an SNMP agent appearance for the APPN nodes that really contain CMIP agents. This is because the SNMP model for APPN topology contains slightly more information than the corresponding CMIP model, which makes it impossible for a reverse Integrator to get from a CMIP agent all of the information it needs to fully emulate an SNMP agent. While the CMIP model and the CMIP agents could be extended to remove this impediment to a reverse Integrator, it's very unlikely that this will ever happen. Any future work to integrate the different types of agents present in APPN nodes will almost certainly be based on object technologies and Java.[7]

15.6 The broken cable is repaired

There is still one remaining detail to be resolved: the broken cable itself. With HPR's nondisruptive path switch, sessions were switched from the broken cable to a good one, without impacting the users of the sessions. And with APPN's network topology database, the broken cable was automatically removed from consideration when routes for new sessions were being computed. But none of these activities causes the cable to be

---

7. For more on the use of Java for network management, see section 15.8, "The future: object technologies, Java, and the Web."

fixed. To see how this is accomplished, we must turn to SNA/MS's richest discipline, problem management.

15.6.1 First-failure data capture

A key principle underlying SNA's approach to problem management is to gather enough data at the time that a problem occurs to make it possible to diagnose and resolve the problem without having to re-create it. The name given to this principle is *first-failure data capture*. Depending on the nature of the problem and the capabilities of the detector, the first-failure data may all be packaged up and sent off to a network operator, or some of it (for example, a large storage dump) may be stored locally for later retrieval.

15.6.2 Alerts

The SNA/MS vehicle for notifying a network operator about a problem is the *alert*. Alerts are unsolicited notifications, so they fill roughly the same niche in the network management landscape as SNMP traps and CMIP event reports.

When we say that alerts are unsolicited, we are referring to the circumstances surrounding the sending of a particular alert. When a problem is detected, an alert sender doesn't wait for a poll from a manager ("Do you have any problems you'd like to tell me about?") before sending an alert; it sends the alert without being asked to. Before any alerts are sent, however, a handshake must occur to establish that a particular focal point (manager) is to be the alert receiver for a given node in the network.

SNA/MS is flexible regarding exactly what form this handshake will take. One option is for the focal point to initiate it:

FOCAL POINT: "I want to be your focal point for alerts."
NODE: "OK, I'll send my alerts to you."

Or the node that will be sending the alerts may speak first:

NODE: "I want you to be my alert focal point."
FOCAL POINT: "OK, I'll receive and process your alerts."

This flexibility reflects where the policy information that ties a particular node to a particular focal point is entered. When the focal point speaks first, it is because an operator has entered at the focal point the names of the nodes that are to send their alerts there. This is similar to the way routing of CMIP event reports is ordinarily handled: a manager is told which agent systems are to send their event reports to it, and it performs a handshake with each of these agents (by creating a CMIP event-forwarding discriminator there).

When the node speaks first, it is because an operator at the node has entered the name of the focal point to which the node is to send its alerts. This case is similar to that of SNMP traps, in which the destination(s) for an agent's traps must be configured separately at each agent. In the case of an SNMP trap, however, there is no initial handshake between trap sender and trap receiver: the first time a manager hears from an agent is when its first trap arrives.

SNA/MS does not force a network operator to choose one or the other of these options globally. A focal point may be configured with the names of some of the nodes it is to serve, and add other nodes to its sphere of control as a result of the nodes' having been configured with its name.

There is also an optimization in APPN networks that reduces the number of handshakes in which a focal point must participate. Regardless of which party initiates the handshake, an APPN NN interacts with a focal point on behalf of both itself and all of the domain ENs that it serves. So the second type of handshake we presented above should really say:

NODE: "I want you to be *our* alert focal point."
FOCAL POINT: "OK, I'll receive and process alerts from all of you."

Once an NN has completed a successful handshake with a focal point, it passes the name of the focal point down to its domain ENs, so they'll know where to send their alerts.

15.6.3 *Automation*

In a network-management context, the term automation has ordinarily been used in a fairly restrictive sense: the introduction at a manager node of a program to perform a task that was previously performed by a human operator. Initially this substitution was very straightforward: the trigger was the same display that a human operator would see, and the automation program often did no more than issue the same one-line command that, in the absence of automation, an operator would have typed in.

Over time automation programs have become much more sophisticated. Automation programs can now go through several steps to isolate the cause of a problem, and then present the results of this analysis to a human operator in an easily understood form.

One significant change that made it easier to create such programs was giving the programs access to the actual generic alerts themselves, rather than to the operator displays created from these alerts. With programs having access to this program-friendly representation of problem information, it is often possible to create in just a few minutes an automation application program that does meaningful work. For example, an automation program might scan through a list of link addresses affected by a problem, and change the color of the icons representing any addresses it found. Such a task would be easy for a program, but time-consuming and open to errors for a human operator.

There are, of course, limits to what can be automated. In our campus scenario, actually replacing the broken cable will involve a human repair crew for at least the foreseeable future. Calling this repair crew, though, and indicating to them exactly what the nature of the problem is and where it occurred are activities that can and have been automated.

It is interesting to note one important respect in which the scope of automation has actually been decreasing in the past few years. When an RTP pipe switches to a new path to bypass a broken link connection without affecting the sessions using it, this eliminates the need for reactivating the sessions manually over the new path. The term "manually" is being used here in a slightly extended sense, to embrace actions taken by a human operator and those taken by an automation program that replaces the operator in performing this task.

It could be argued that what's really going on here is just a different type of automation, embodied in the programs in the network that implement the RTP path switch. It seems more useful, though, to characterize these programs as representing the network's capability to react automatically to the loss of a link connection. With this terminology we can make the following generalization: the greater a network's capabilities for reacting to situations automatically, the less the network requires (management) automation.

15.7 Network management encodings

Over the past twenty years, network management encodings have undergone first an evolution, and then a paradigm shift. The evolution is represented by the various SNA/MS alert formats that have been introduced since the inception of SNA itself. The paradigm shift becomes clear when we examine in detail the encoding method shared by both SNMP and CMIP, and contrast it with that used for the alerts.

The first three alert formats are shown in figure 15.6.

15.7.1 RECMS

Record maintenance statistics (RECMS) comes from the very early days of SNA, when there were only a handful of SNA products. Developers from the few products that sent RECMS could work closely with developers of the one product that caught them, to ensure that both were interpreting the encoding in the same way. Another factor at that time was that since every byte was precious, developers had to choose compactness of

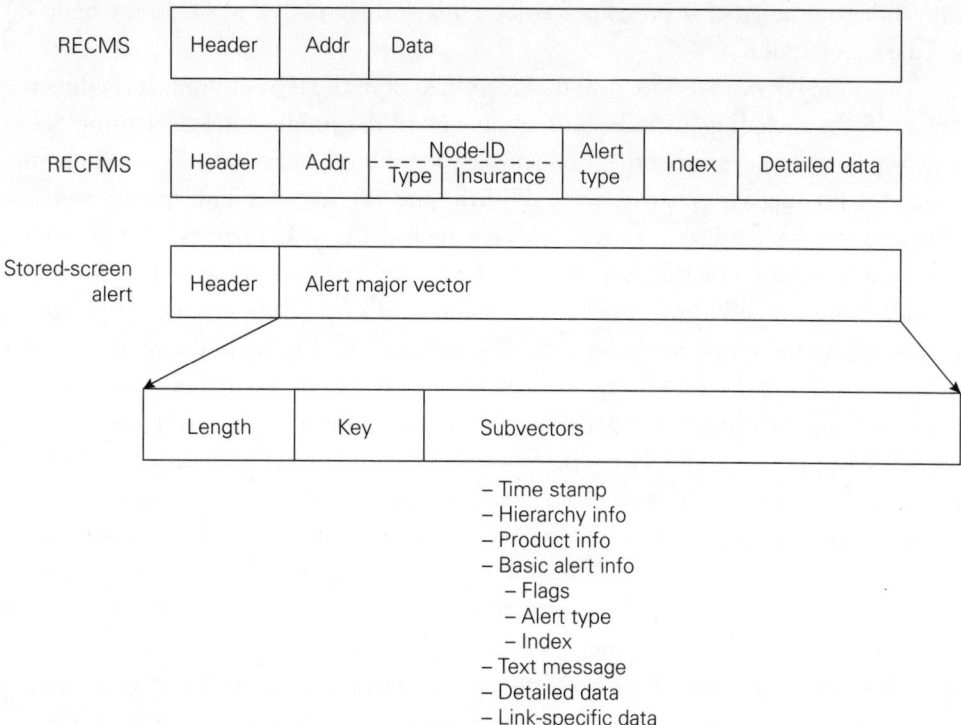

Figure 15.6   Older SNA/MS alert formats

encodings over generality, extendibility, maintainability, migratability, and the other factors that are taken as basic requirements today.

The only architectural generality in RECMS was the network address of its sender, since this was the one item that the developers could not agree upon ahead of time. Beyond that, it was a question of how much product-specific data could be packed into the available bytes.

15.7.2 RECFMS

Record formatted maintenance statistics (RECFMS) followed soon after RECMS, mostly in response to the increasing number of SNA products sending alerts. RECFMS regularized a technique begun in RECMS: economizing on bytes by sending only an index to a previously defined set of panels that the receiver of the RECFMS would display to an operator. Initially these stored screens were relatively easy to define, code, and maintain, but as more and more alert senders came along, it became necessary to impose some order on the process. RECFMS reflects this order in two of its fields: the node-ID and the screen index.

The node-ID was a 4-byte field that identified both the type of product sending the RECFMS (by including an index into a table of all the products implementing SNA) and the particular instance of the product. Neither of these items was of general use: the registry of product types was never published, and the instance information was not mappable to more familiar resource identifiers such as PU or LU names.

In conjunction with the index field, however, the type part of the node-ID was ideally suited for one task: providing an index into a set of product-specific sets of stored screens. Using these two fields, an RECFMS sender could instruct the receiver of the RECFMS to "display set #4 of my screens." These sets of screens had been defined earlier, by a team including developers from the sending product and developers from the one receiving product, the Network Problem Determination Application (NPDA).[8] The overall structure of the screens was fixed: a one-line message providing a high-level characterization of the nature of the problem and its most likely cause(s), a full screen providing more information of probable causes for the problem, as well as recommended actions for isolating, bypassing, and resolving the problem, and a full screen providing additional details on the problem that might be of use to the operator.

There were some shortcomings with this approach. First and foremost, defining a new product's set of alert screens was difficult and time-consuming, even if the screens for a previous product were taken as the starting point. Second, with each sender's screens defined separately from those of all other senders, it was inevitable that terminology differences would creep in: whether it was calling the same thing by two different names, or calling different things by the same name, such differences made it more difficult to train network operators to use the NPDA alert screens. Third, since the sender's product type was the primary index into the sets of screens, NPDA was often storing many different copies of what were essentially the same screens. Finally, the new release of NPDA containing a new sender's sets of screens *had* to be installed in a network at the same time as the new sending product (or earlier, but that rarely happened); otherwise the sender's RECFMSs provided almost no useful information to the NPDA operator.

Despite these problems, the technique of indexing alert displays stored at NPDA worked well enough to be carried over into the next generation of alerts almost unchanged. As the next section explains, it was other elements of the alert that were changing. The problems with stored-screen alerts weren't solved until the arrival of generic alerts, in 1987.

---

8. NPDA was later merged with other host-based network management products to form NetView/MVS.

15.7.3 Stored-screen alert major vector

For the core alert functions of identifying the nature of a problem, its probable causes, and a list of recommended actions for the operator to try, the stored-screen alert major vector provided almost identical function to that provided by the RECFMS. The key differences fell into two related areas. First was the move from a largely fixed format (the RECFMS RU itself), which supported only limited variability, to an almost entirely variable format, the alert major vector. Initially the contents of the alert major vector were limited by the vehicle in which it flowed, the network management vector transport (NMVT) RU. But when a better vehicle came along (APPN's multiple-domain support message unit [MDS-MU]), the alert major vector was able to take full advantage of the additional space available to it.

Even in its NMVT days, the newly found variability of the alert major vector led to a second change: better support for the ancillary alert functions, that is, those other than identification of a problem, its likely causes, and the actions an operator should take in response to it. These functions included identification of hardware and software products (both those reporting the problem and those experiencing it), reporting of link-specific information such as token ring MAC addresses and LAN routing information, and time-stamping.

There was also a third, more subtle change that came in with the major vector format: what we would now term *encapsulation*. Since product identification data, or token ring LAN data, or link-connection subsystem data, or a time stamp was encoded in a separate subvector, it became possible to write code at an alert receiver to process one of these subvectors, or code at an alert sender to build one of them, and be confident that:

- This code would be able to process its subvector in the same way every time, regardless of what other data was present in an alert[9] along with the subvector

- This code would need to be changed only if there were a subsequent change to the definition of its subvector.

This encapsulation in fact persisted right through the fundamental change to the core alert elements, when stored-screen alerts were supplanted by generic alerts. Code for processing the common subvectors discussed here did not have to be changed at all to accommodate this transition.

---

9. Or other SNA/MS major vectors. So-called common subvectors such as these appeared not only in alerts, but also in other major vectors such as problem determination statistics (link counters) and response time monitor.

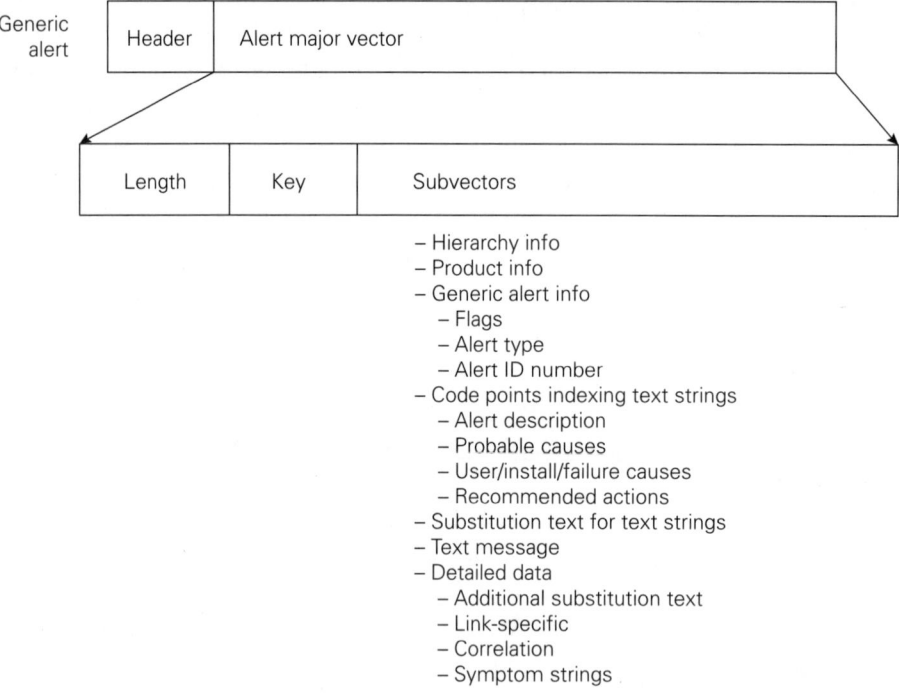

Figure 15.7   The SNA/MS generic alert

15.7.4 *Generic alert major vector*

Figure 15.7 shows the elements of a generic alert major vector. At the level of detail shown, there is very little difference between the stored-screen alert in figure 15.6 and the generic alert in figure 15.7: in both cases there is a header, an alert major vector, and the set of subvectors it contains. The differences lie in what subvectors are present, and what they accomplish.

In a generic alert, the alert sender's product type is no longer the primary index that determines the contents of alert displays (although it is still useful ancillary data). And instead of providing *an index for a set* of prebuilt displays, a generic alert sender provides *a sequence of indexes* (termed *code points*) into tables of display elements. These display elements, which include 40-character problem descriptions and 108-character recommended actions, are used by an alert receiver[10] to build a set of displays dynamically.

The generic alert solved the problems inherent in stored-screen alerts, which were discussed above in the section titled "RECFMS." Since all alert senders' code points

---

10. Now there are several: IBM offers generic alert receivers for MVS, OS/400, and AIX, and other vendors offer them as well.

were indexing a single set of tables of text elements, the opportunity for terminology differences was eliminated. Alert receivers also had much less total text to store: for example, the recommended action, check power, could be stored only once, whereas with stored-screen alerts it would have typically appeared on several sets of recommended action screens from every hardware product that sent alerts.

Code points also broke the all-or-nothing dichotomy, in which an alert receiver either supported a sender's alerts completely, or it did not support them at all. A sender could send a new recommended action such as install latest microcode level, and know that if an alert receiver's table had not been updated to include this text string, the receiver would still be able to display the default text string `Correct installation problem`.

Code points also made it practical for alert receivers to support displays in many different national languages. Alert receivers typically support tables containing text strings in various national languages, all indexed by the same code points. Of course the same sort of thing could have been done (and was done) with the stored screens indexed by the earlier types of alerts. But since each new alert sender introduced new sets of screens, and thus a new translation task, the number of languages that could be supported was extremely limited.

Given the extendible structure of the alert major vector, it is not surprising that over time, enhancements have been added to the ancillary elements of the alert as well as to its core:

- Better support for text messages
- Support for correlating alerts with other alerts, with supporting data such as storage dumps, and with problem resolution reports
- Support for additional link-specific data
- Support for extended diagnostic information for software problems (i.e., for symptom strings)

The generic alert architecture has remained remarkably durable since its introduction in 1987, primarily because of its extendibility. The core functions can be extended at very low cost, simply by defining new code points to identify new problem descriptions, probable causes, and recommended actions. An alert receiver needs no new logic to support a new code point—only a table update. It is even possible for a network operator to enter new code points and text strings into an alert receiver's tables, in case there is a delay between the time that a new alert sender comes out and the next release of the alert receiver.

Supporting new ancillary elements is a bit more costly for an alert receiver than supporting new code points, since new parsing logic is required. This cost is minimized, though, by the fact that none of the alert receiver's existing logic needs to be touched.

These cost savings for manufacturers of alert receivers directly benefit customers as well, in two ways. First, because there is a stable foundation upon which to build, alert receivers can be extended to support new functions and new environments quickly and cheaply, and so these extensions are actually delivered to customers. Second, the customer personnel responsible for resolving network problems do not have to be retrained from scratch every time a new networking technology comes along. With a stable framework of problem descriptions, causes, and recommended actions in which to work, network operators require training only in the new technology itself.

15.7.5 ASN.1/BER and modeling languages

We move now to the encoding approach used by both SNMP and CMIP, in which the task of specifying a model for a network resource is separated from specification of the formats of the data that actually flows though the network. All of the alert encodings we have discussed so far were specified in a different way: with byte-offset encodings.[11] For example, the subvector in a generic alert that carries probable cause code points is defined in table 15.1

Table 15.1

Byte 0	Length (p + 1), in binary, of the probable causes subvector
Byte 1	Key (X'93')
Bytes 2–p	One or more two-byte probable cause code points, defined in table 15.2

There is additional text describing the role of probable causes in the overall alert architecture, but really, the byte-offset description shown here is the architecture. And this architecture describes exactly the sequence of bytes that flow on the wire; a sniffer capturing this part of an alert would see:

Table 15.2 All probable cause code points and their corresponding text strings

...069305011000..., where		
X'06'	Length = 6	
X'93'	Key = X'93'	
X'0501'	Index to "Storage subsystem"	(First probable cause)
X'1000'	Index to "Software program"	(Second probable cause)

---

11. This style is in fact common to all SNA encodings. SNA encodings other than those for SNA/MS are documented in the IBM publication *SNA Formats* (GA27–3136).

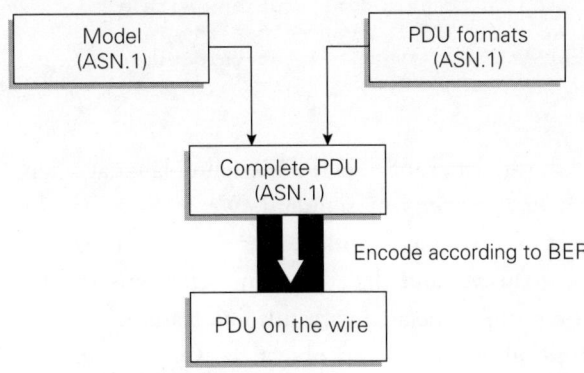

Figure 15.8 Separation of abstract syntax from encodings

Figure 15.8 shows a completely different approach, with three distinct elements:

- A model representing certain aspects of a particular set of network resources, for example, a model of APPN topology. In the figure this model is shown as being done in abstract syntax notation 1 (ASN.1). This is a slight oversimplification. SNMP uses a modeling language based on extensions to ASN.1, and CMIP uses a separate modeling language (informally referred to as GDMO because it is specified in the standard *Guidelines for the Definition of Managed Objects*[12]) containing references that resolve to ASN.1 definitions. In both cases the models themselves are focused on characteristics of the resources being modeled, and not on the formats that will actually flow between manager and agent.

- A standard, also specified in ASN.1, describing the formats of the protocol data units (PDUs) that are exchanged between a manager and an agent, for example, the format of an SNMP GET operation.

- A mapping from the ASN.1 representation of a complete management PDU to the actual sequence of bytes that flows on the wire; the rules for this mapping are specified in the basic encoding rules (BER) standard.

For example, the SNMP model for APPN topology includes the following object:

```
appnLsTgNum OBJECT-TYPE
    SYNTAX INTEGER (0..256)
    MAX-ACCESS read-only
    STATUS current
```

12. ITU-T Rec. X.722 (1992) | ISO/IEC 10165–4:1992.

```
DESCRIPTION
    "Number associated with the TG to this link station, with a
    range from 0 to 256. A value of 256 indicates that the TG
    number has not been negotiated and is unknown at this time."

::= { appnLsEntry 9 }
```

We needn't be concerned here with the details of SNMP's modeling language, represented by the *Structure of Management Information*[13] standard. We can see that this element of the model defines an object named `appnLsTgNum`, that this object takes on an integer value between 0 and 256, inclusive, and that this value represents the TG number (in APPN) of the transmission group associated with this link station.

The final line of the object definition assigns to this object the Object Identifier (OID) value { `appnLsEntry 9` }. As we'll see in a moment, `appnLsEntry` is an abbreviation for another OID value (specifically, for { `appnLsTable 1` }), which is an abbreviation for yet another OID value ({ `appnLinkStationInformation 1` }), and so forth. When everything has been expanded, the result is a sequence of nonnegative integers between curly braces, that uniquely distinguishes the object `appnLsTgNum` from all of the other information objects in the world.

Since `appnLsTgNum` is a tabular object, there will be separate instances of it for each link station in the node. These instances are distinguished from each other by having different values for the table index; in this case the link station name (in ASCII) serves as the table index. As we will see below, SNMP has a peculiar way of encoding the value of a table index, as an extension to `appnLsTgNum`'s OID.

Here are the additional definitional items needed to construct an SNMP response returning the value of this object. As is the case with many specification languages, ASN.1 requires one to follow a thread through a number of definitions in order to expand fully a high-level definition such as that for `Response-PDU`.

```
Response-PDU ::= [2] IMPLICIT PDU

PDU ::=
    SEQUENCE {request-idInteger32,
        error-status    INTEGER {
                            noError(0),
                            tooBig(1),
                            - 16 other values
                        },
        errorIndex      INTEGER(0..max-bindings),
        variable-bindings VarBindList }
VarBindList ::= SEQUENCE (SIZE (0..max-bindings)) OF VarBind
```

---

13. RFC 1902. This is one of eight standards (RFCs 1901–1908) that define the latest version of SNMP, SNMP version 2.

```
VarBind ::=
    SEQUENCE {    name        ObjectName,
            CHOICE {  value              ObjectSyntax,
                    unSpecified        NULL,
                    noSuchObject    [0]  IMPLICIT NULL,
                    noSuchInstance  [1]  IMPLICIT NULL,
                    endOfMibView    [2]  IMPLICIT NULL
                }
        }

ObjectName ::= OBJECT IDENTIFIER

ObjectSyntax ::= CHOICE {
                simple        SimpleSyntax,
                application-wide    ApplicationSyntax
        }

SimpleSyntax ::=
        CHOICE {
            integer-value  INTEGER (-2147483648..2147483647),
            string-value   OCTET STRING (SIZE(0..65535)),
            objectID-value OBJECT IDENTIFIER
            }
```

Finally, there's the mapping to BER's tag-length-value structure. For example, table 15.3 is the BER encoding for just one of the VarBinds in the response PDU. This VarBind reports that the link station named LS1 is associated with TG number 100. Notice how the table index value LS1 gets buried inside the object identifier that serves as the object name.

Table 15.3

Octet	Hex value	Meaning	
1	X'30'	Tag: SEQUENCE	
2	X'16'	Length: 22	
3	X'06'	Tag: OBJECT IDENTIFIER	begin SEQUENCE value
4	X'11'	Length: 17	
5	X'2B'	ccitt(1) + org(3)	begin OID value
6	X'06'	dod(6)	
7	X'01'	internet(1)	
8	X'02'	mgmt(2)	
9	X'01'	mib-2(1)	
10	X'22'	snanauMIB(34)	
11	X'04'	appnMIB(4)	
12	X'01'	appnObjects(1)	

Table 15.3   (continued)

Octet	Hex value	Meaning	
13	X'01'	appnNode(1)	
14	X'05'	appnLinkStationInformation(5)	
15	X'01'	appnLsTable(1)	
16	X'01'	appnLsEntry(1)	
17	X'09'	appnLsTgNum(9)	column 9 of appnLsTable
18	X'03'	length of index value	
19	X'4C'	ASCII 'L'	start of index
20	X'53'	ASCII 'S'	
21	X'31'	ASCII '1'	end of index, end OID value
22	X'02'	Tag: INTEGER	
23	X'01'	Length: 1	
24	X'64'	100	INTEGER value, end SEQUENCE value

As this example shows, there is a large gap between the SNMP model for APPN topology and the sequence of bytes that actually flows on the wire. Someone could legitimately claim to be an expert in this APPN topology model, and yet have very little idea about exactly what a sniffer would find.[14] Such a statement could not be made with respect to expertise in the generic alert architecture.

For the most part this isolation between the modeling activity and the details of the encodings is a plus, since it's possible to achieve more in the modeling sphere when all of the encoding details take care of themselves. There are, however, occasions where a modeler must think about encoding issues. For example, a perfectly legitimate model may require PDUs that are far too large for management platforms to build and process. This clean separation between modeling and encodings until the encodings raise their heads with an unexpected gotcha is among the factors that give both SNMP and CMIP modeling the feeling of an art rather than a science.

15.7.6 If the shoe fits...

Interesting issues arise when the different management technologies intersect. We've already looked at one such case, the coexistence in a single APPN network of SNMP

---

14. A trace reformatter is nice to have for viewing generic alert traces, but it's almost a necessity for viewing traces of BER-encoded data. There *are* people who are reasonably fluent in reading raw BER data, but there aren't very many of them.

topology agents and CMIP topology agents, which yielded the APPN topology integrator. A second case involves the intersection of the SNA/MS generic alert architecture with the modeling-centric CMIP and SNMP technologies.

The modeling aspects of generic alerts are fairly rudimentary. Problems have descriptions, probable causes, and recommended actions, and various sorts of resources have different types of resource-specific data: hardware products have machine types, LAN adapters have MAC addresses, switched connections have dial digits, and so forth. The strengths of the architecture lie in the breadth of the information it can represent, and in the compactness of the encodings to transfer this information. Another consideration, at least in the APPN world, is its universal deployment: *every* APPN node can send generic alerts.

The question is how to fit generic alerts into an SNMP management system. One possible approach would be to create an SNMP model with objects to represent each of the elements of a generic alert. Such a model would, for example, contain an object for a problem description, a table of probable causes, a table of recommended actions, objects for MAC addresses and dial digits, and so on. This approach was actually tried, but it turned out that while it yielded a function equivalent to that provided by generic alerts, it did very little to leverage implementations' existing investments in the generic alert architecture. Implementations of the SNMP model had to be done essentially from scratch.

Figure 15.9 illustrates a different approach to this problem. This approach assumes that implementations are already capable of building and sending SNA/MS generic alerts. Given that an implementation can already do this, it is very easy and inexpensive to insert a shunt into its code, at a point after it has built a complete alert, but before it has sent the alert to the focal point. This shunt sends the complete alert down a path where it is segmented into pieces that can be processed by existing SNMP implementations. These pieces are then placed in an SNMP trap PDU and sent off to an SNMP management station. There's a companion application at the management station that extracts the alert pieces from the trap, reassembles them into a complete alert, and then invokes the same sort of alert-processing code that a real alert focal point has.

Does this really qualify as integration of generic alerts into an SNMP management system? No. It is more accurately described as a mechanism for using the SNMP protocol to transport generic alert data to an SNMP management station that understands SNA/MS generic alerts.

The significance of this difference becomes clearer if we consider the situation where a management station doesn't have the application that reassembles a generic alert from its pieces, and then processes it according to the rules for processing SNA/MS encodings. Ordinarily there are two levels of support at a management station for a

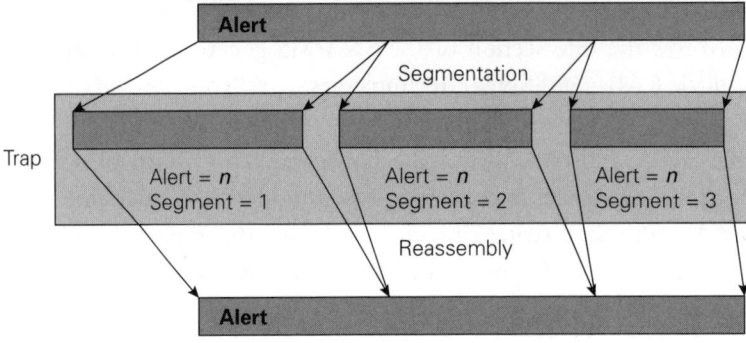

Figure 15.9 Transporting generic alert data in SNMP traps

given SNMP model. On the one hand, there might be an application specifically written for that model; an example is the APPN topology management application that uses information in the APPN MIB to draw a picture of an APPN topology subnet. Even without such an application, though, a management station always has a generic MIB browser component. Once it has been loaded with a MIB module, a MIB browser can present an operator with a list of the objects made available by that MIB, direct GET operations to any of these objects, and correctly display the results to the operator.

One of the strengths of SNMP management lies in its ability to make new types of information available to an operator in this way, without having to do anything more at the management station than simply load a new MIB module. (There's a similarity to generic alerts here, since an alert focal point can also make new types of information available to its operator, simply via additions to its code point tables.) We're focusing on a different point now, however: this easy extendibility of an SNMP management station is totally defeated by the architecture we're currently discussing. Even if it has been loaded with the SNMP MIB for sending generic alert data in traps, a MIB browser still can't provide an operator with anything intelligible: all the operator will see is an encoded generic alert. The solution, of course, is to include the alert-processing application along with the generic MIB browser, since they provide complementary extendibility.

15.8 The future: object technologies, Java, and the Web

The history of network management has seen several predictions of single unifying architectures. Most have captured some investment, only to be subsequently reclassified into the one-of-many category. So we tread carefully before making bold suggestions about the future of SNA network management.

It is reasonable to expect that solutions will continue to proliferate. But there is an important stabilizing factor: the large (customer and product) investment in current management architecture, the architecture's proven extendibility, and the need for continuous incremental improvements all point toward today's design being the base for future evolution. New methods of distributing and presenting the information will appear, but if we open the transport envelopes, we are likely to find most of today's (and yesterday's) data structures still in use.

As we write this book, Java is barely two years old. Yet it has already attracted tremendous interest across the industry as a technology that network management might be able to exploit. This exploitation might fall into any of a number of areas:

Extendibility and portability The greatest promise of Java in all areas, including network management, lies in the extendibility and portability of Java-based applications. There is, however, an important limitation to this portability. A Java application program developed for one platform won't necessarily run unchanged on another, even if the other platform supports a fully conformant Java virtual machine. There must also be uniformity in the program's environment on the two platforms; for example, if the application program makes an API call, then the called function must be supported.

For network management, this limitation affects agent implementations more than it does manager-side applications. A management application makes calls to the APIs that its management platform supports; for example, an SNMP management application might issue a call to the platform API that causes an SNMP GET operation to be sent to a specified agent. Today the different management platforms support different APIs, but this is primarily an accident of their history. One of the goals of the TME 10 management framework, an object-oriented software infrastructure developed by Tivoli Systems, is to eliminate this unnecessary diversity, and present to management applications exactly the same set of APIs on every platform. In conjunction with a Java virtual machine, such a framework would bring within reach the goal of fully portable network management applications.

The picture is quite different on the agent side. Even given a common API for passing management data, such as that being developed in the IETF by the agent extensibility working group, a management program on an agent must interact with the real resources that it instruments.[15] These latter interactions are typically platform-specific, so it's less possible to write a single Java program that implements multiple agent platforms.

Access to management data   One area that has already seen extensive prototype work is that of web client-based access to the data stored by a network management application. For customers the promise is that a network administrator will be able to interact with any network management application from any workstation. Vendors will also benefit, because they will no longer have to develop separate applications for displaying management data on each workstation platform: the vendors will simply make the data available to web browsers, and leave the workstation specifics to the browsers themselves.

New manager/agent interactions   As we've indicated above, Java looks much more promising on the manager side than for network management agents. Nevertheless, there will be cases where it makes sense to write a Java-based agent. In these cases, where a Java-based agent is interacting with a Java-based manager, there are several possible forms their interactions might take:

- Interactions between an SNMP manager and agent that happen to be implemented in Java
- Interactions between Java objects using Java's remote method invocation (RMI)
- Interactions between Java objects using an object request broker

At this point it is not clear whether one of these forms will become dominant (or, in the case of SNMP, remain dominant) if Java agents are deployed in large numbers.

15.9 Conclusion

We have touched on a number of points since we introduced the incident that affected Mary's workstation. First, we saw how APPN/HPR can often react to the loss of a network resource so quickly that users of the network are either shielded completely from the effects of losing the resource, or at worst are inconvenienced for only a few seconds. We also saw the role played by a topology management application, in helping network operators to identify the true nature and location of a problem, as well as some of its more remote consequences. We saw as well the role that problem management still plays

---

15. The purpose of this API is to allow different SNMP *subagents*, which manage different sets of resources at an agent, to be written and deployed independently of each other. In addition to the subagents, there is a *master agent* running on the agent system, whose responsibilities include passing SNMP requests to the correct subagent(s), forwarding traps issued by subagents to the appropriate destinations, and ensuring that the agent system as a whole adheres to any security and access control policies that have been specified for it.

in today's APPN/HPR networks: no matter how well the network is able to bypass problems, somebody still has to repair or replace a broken cable, which in turn means that mechanisms must be in place to signal that a cable is broken, to isolate the problem, and then to continue to track the problem until it has been resolved.

Along the way, we also looked in some detail at the evolution of network management encodings, with SNA/MS alerts serving as our primary example. We followed this evolution through to the current generation of modeling-based architectures, exemplified by SNMP. We noted as well the tendency to interject a mature, well established architecture (SNA/MS's generic alerts) into a new management system (SNMP), even if it doesn't really fit there: the existing investment in the older architecture is simply too great for it to be thrown away and a new model started once more from the beginning.

Finally, we looked briefly into the future, specifically, into the role(s) that Java might play in network management. We've indicated that from where we stand, Java appears to hold much more promise for management applications than for management agents.

Acknowledgments: Thanks to Mark Zelek, to Mary Jane Moore, and especially to Gary Schultz and Matt Hess for their reviews of early drafts of this chapter.

 *chapter 16*

Living with legacy networks: 3270 access to TCP/IP applications

RUSSELL W. TEUBNER

Russell W. Teubner takes us all the way to the application layer, describing the usage of one of the most successful and widely used SNA applications—3270 in a multiprotocol environment of SNA and TCP/IP. Solutions for providing 3270 users with access to TCP/IP applications and vice versa—solutions for providing the users of asynchronous terminals with access to SNA applications—are described in this chapter.

16.1 Introduction

Millions of IBM 3270 terminals and PCs, emulating these terminals, are still in production use across the world. However, as organizations develop and deploy applications on TCP/IP-based hosts and networks, they face a problem that can rarely be ignored: how to provide 3270 terminal users with interactive access to TCP/IP applications.

The root of this problem is that an IBM 3270 terminal is designed to access only the IBM host system to which its control unit is attached, or other IBM host systems available through SNA networking facilities. Note that the phrase *IBM 3270 terminal* also includes the millions of PCs attached to an SNA network, which emulate an IBM 3270 terminal. Although such devices are certainly not the only aspect of legacy networks that must be leveraged and/or migrated, they are arguably the most difficult.

This chapter explores the issues involved in providing IBM 3270s with the ability to access TCP/IP applications. These issues are translated into requirements for solutions. We then discuss the components of these solutions and the alternatives available.

The first question that must be answered is, "What is a TCP/IP application?" For purposes of this chapter, *TCP/IP applications* are those applications that have been designed for use on computer systems that rely upon TCP/IP as a networking protocol (along with the Telnet client/server architecture) as the primary means by which terminals gain access to such applications.

TCP/IP applications used to be practically synonymous with UNIX applications, since TCP/IP grew up and is predominant in the UNIX environment. Although many UNIX applications are installed in other environments and TCP/IP supports many other application types, the focus of the chapter is on this combination. Most of the information is relevant to the other categories as well.

16.2 So what's the problem?

Applications written for any given host or networking environment make assumptions about the characteristics of the terminals that will be used to access the application. For example, applications written to run on IBM hosts within an SNA network usually assume that the terminals used to access applications have the characteristics of an IBM 3270-type terminal.

TCP/IP applications also assume that the terminals used to access applications have certain common characteristics. The DEC VT100/200 series of terminals is one of the most common examples of such a terminal. Therefore, in this chapter, this type of terminal will be generically referred to as a VT-type terminal.

16.2.1 IBM 3270s vs. VT-type terminals

To better understand the issues involved in providing 3270s with access to TCP/IP applications, we will examine ten functional differences between 3270-type terminals and VT-type terminals:

- Code set
- Operating mode
- Keyboard management
- Processing received data
- Screen organization
- Screen management
- Visual attribution
- Input data buffering
- Input data-stream contents
- Input data validation and formatting

Code set   VT-type terminals use a code set derived from ASCII. IBM 3270 terminals use EBCDIC. If both ASCII and EBCDIC contained the same characters, then translating one to the other would be trivial. Unfortunately, they do not.

This basic difference is complicated by the fact that most countries have implemented national language extensions to ASCII and EBCDIC to accommodate their unique requirements. The differences are further complicated when the national language uses a symbolic character set, such as Japanese (kanji) and Korean (hangeul). In these cases, at least two bytes of data are used to express a single symbolic character. While both ASCII and EBCDIC support double-byte character sets, translating one to the other is far more involved.

Operating mode   VT-type terminals operate in full-duplex mode; that is, the terminal can send and receive data simultaneously. IBM 3270 terminals in an SNA network, however, operate in half-duplex mode; that is, the terminal can either send or receive data, but not both simultaneously. When an application is displaying data on the 3270 screen, the user cannot enter data at the keyboard. Conversely, when the user is entering input at the keyboard, the application cannot update the 3270 screen.

Keyboard management   The data-stream sent to a VT-type terminal rarely, if ever, indicates when the remote application has finished sending output to the terminal and is waiting for input. These types of terminals often do support a mechanism for managing the state of the keyboard. In practice, however, that feature lies dormant. As a result, the keyboard is always unlocked to the end user.

In contrast, the application must explicitly unlock the keyboard of a 3270 terminal whenever user input is to occur. As a result, IBM 3270 users rely upon the keyboard status (whether locked or unlocked) to determine when it is their turn to enter data.

Processing received data   VT-type terminals display each character on the screen as it is received. To the end user, the content of the screen visually appears as a steady stream of data. IBM 3270s within an SNA network receive data in one or more blocks. To the end user, the content of the screen visually appears as one or more bursts of data.

Screen organization   The screen of a VT-type terminal is character-oriented; that is, such terminals do not usually support any concept of grouping contiguous screen cells into fields. Although applications display screens that appear to contain multiple fields, the data-stream sent to the terminal contains no information about physical fields on the screen. Thus, a field is visual, not physical.

IBM 3270 screens are usually organized into one or more fields. Thus, every cell on the screen belongs to a field and acquires the operational and visual attributes assigned to that field. Each field attribute occupies one screen cell and visually appears as a blank on the screen. On a 3270, fields are both visual and physical.

Screen management   VT-type terminals and 3270s manage the contents of the screen much differently. For example, VT-type terminals can automatically scroll lines of data from the bottom of the screen to the top as new lines are added to the bottom; 3270 terminals do not support scrolling. A 3270 application can simulate this function by refreshing the entire contents of the 3270 screen in order to add a new line to the bottom.

Visual attribution   Most VT-type terminals support at least five types of visual attribution: normal intensity, high intensity, reverse video, blinking, and underlined. Each screen cell is independent and may have its own unique visual attribution not associated with any other cell on the screen. An individual screen cell may have multiple attributes assigned to it at the same time (e.g., reverse video and blinking).

IBM 3270 terminals depend on the control unit for their support of visual attribution. Older control units support only three types of visual attribution: normal intensity, non-display, and high-intensity. These forms of attribution are controlled through the use of field attributes. Newer control units also support extended attributes: reverse video, blinking and underlined, extended color support (seven colors), and graphics. These forms of attribution may be applied to an entire field, or to individual characters within a field, but an individual screen cell may *not* have multiple attributes assigned to it at the same time (e.g., combinations like reverse video and blinking are not supported).

Input data buffering   All terminals usually function in one of two modes: character or block. A terminal operating in character mode sends one or more characters immediately after each key is pressed. Such terminals have no buffering capability—each key the user presses sends data, control sequences, or escape sequences immediately to the host application. VT-type terminals usually operate only in this character mode.

In block mode, keyboard input is buffered until a particular control key is pressed (e.g., ENTER). Thus, keyboard input travels from the terminal to the computer system in blocks rather than keystroke by keystroke.

An IBM 3270 terminal differs from a VT-type terminal in that the 3270 relies upon a control unit for much of its intelligence. Although data transmission between the terminal and the control unit is character oriented, data transmission between the control unit and the IBM host across the SNA network is strictly block oriented. Therefore, a 3270 terminal is a character-mode device in one sense and a block-mode device in another.

When an IBM 3270 accesses an SNA application, the application interacts with the terminal as a block-mode device. The control unit sends keyboard input to the host application only when the user presses one of the keys that generates an *attention identifier* (AID). An application is unaware that anything has been entered at the terminal keyboard until one of these keys is pressed.

Input data-stream contents   VT-type terminals send information to the remote application for virtually all terminal keystrokes. For example, the input data-stream contains information regarding each cursor movement key used, as well as each time the tab key is pressed.

The IBM 3270 control unit buffers all terminal keystrokes and sends only the final buffer contents to the remote application after the user presses an AID key. As a result, the 3270 input data-stream contains information regarding only the final cursor position, rather than each cursor movement or tab key pressed.

Input data validation and formatting Character-mode devices, such as VT-type terminals, do not typically support input data validation or formatting capabilities. Instead, applications written for such terminals validate and/or format input data keystroke by keystroke, so the data-stream sent from an application to a VT-type terminal includes no information about the validation and/or formatting requirements of the input data.

The data-stream sent to an IBM 3270 terminal, however, does include rudimentary information regarding the input data validation and formatting requirements for each input field defined on the screen. For example, each input field defined on the screen has a finite length and can be defined so only certain types of data are considered as valid.

16.2.2 Summary of functional differences

Table 16.1 summarizes the ten functional differences between IBM 3270s and VT-type terminals that we have examined.

Table 16.1 Functional differences between IBM 3270s and VT-type terminals

	IBM 3270 terminals	VT-type terminals
Code set	EBCDIC	ASCII
Operating mode	Half-duplex	Full-duplex
Keyboard management	Keyboard must be explicitly unlocked whenever input is to occur.	Includes a mechanism for locking/unlocking the keyboard, but is rarely used; thus, keyboard is always unlocked.
Processing received data	Data is displayed one block at a time as received.	Data is displayed one character at a time as received.
Screen organization	Field oriented; field attributes occupy a screen cell; character attributes do not.	Character oriented; no concept of fields; character attributes do not occupy a screen cell.
Screen management	Scrolling not supported; the entire contents of the screen must be refreshed to simulate scrolling.	Scrolling is supported; data is automatically scrolled from the bottom of the screen to the top as new lines are added to the bottom.

Table 16.1 Functional differences between IBM 3270s and VT-type terminals

	IBM 3270 terminals	VT-type terminals
Visual attribution	Depends on control unit; older models support only normal, high-intensity and non-display. Newer models also support extended attributes: blink, reverse video and underline, extended colors, and graphics. Multiple extended attributes may not be applied to a single screen cell.	Normal, high-intensity, blink, reverse video, and underline. Multiple attributes may be applied to a single screen cell.
Input buffering	Yes	No
Input data-stream contents	Control unit sends only final buffer contents, not each keystroke; only the final cursor position is included in the data-stream.	Each keystroke is sent as typed by the user; all cursor movements are sent to the application as escape sequences.
Input data validation and formatting	Received data-stream contains rudimentary information regarding input data validation and formatting.	Received data-stream contains no information regarding input data validation and formatting.

16.3 Solving the problem

Having examined the differences, it should be clear that neither type of terminal was ever intended to be a plug-compatible replacement for the other. The inherent differences between these two types of terminals, however, do not imply that a meaningful level of access for non-native cannot be achieved. In fact, using IBM 3270s to access TCP/IP applications does work and can be very effective. Is it simple? No! Can it be done? Yes!

16.3.1 Solution requirements

As with any problem worth solving, certain elements characterize an ideal solution. When providing 3270 terminals with access to TCP/IP applications, the ideal solution should:

- Provide access for all 3270 terminals within the SNA network
- Leverage the existing investment in the SNA network
- Afford the widest range of TCP/IP application access possible
- Be cost effective and efficient
- Come from a solution provider with specific experience in this arena

The first four attributes are straightforward; the fifth deserves amplification. The majority of TCP/IP applications are not designed for access from a 3270 terminal. Because of all the differences between the two terminal types, designing an effective solution to allow 3270s to access TCP/IP applications can be more an art than a science.

In real life, each potential solution to a problem has advantages and disadvantages. Otherwise, there wouldn't be multiple solutions. Each organization must decide which are most relevant to its decision. Each solution presented here for providing 3270 terminals with access to TCP/IP applications is discussed in terms of these advantages and disadvantages.

16.3.2 Solution components

Any solution that allows 3270 terminals to access TCP/IP applications will have at least three components:

- Gateway (whether software or hardware) that interconnects the SNA and TCP/IP networks

- Telnet client representation (All interactive connections into a TCP/IP host use the Telnet client/server architecture.)

- Terminal emulation services (That is, at some point, the 3270 input data-stream must be transformed into a VT-type data-stream; similarly, the output from the TCP/IP application must be adapted into something that the 3270 can display.)

Some solutions offer a fourth component, layered on top of the terminal emulation component, to facilitate application access.

Application access Most TCP/IP applications assume they are interacting with a VT-type terminal. As we have seen, however, 3270s and VT-type terminals differ significantly. This creates a gap between the assumptions made by TCP/IP applications and the actual characteristics of 3270 terminals, some of which are more difficult even to adapt in terminal emulation.

The application access component seeks to compensate for these differences by going beyond terminal emulation, and focusing on the intention of the TCP/IP application. This emphasis on application access as opposed to only terminal emulation focuses on what 3270 users really care about: having the highest possible level of access to TCP/IP applications.

16.3.3 Solution alternatives

Several different approaches can provide 3270 terminals with access to TCP/IP applications. The alternatives primarily differ in where and how the SNA-to-TCP/IP transition occurs. The four basic options, which will each be discussed in this chapter, are:

- Control unit gateway
- SNA host gateway
- TCP/IP host gateway
- Network gateway

The terms SNA host gateway or TCP/IP host gateway imply that the SNA or TCP/IP host is an integral part of providing the gateway function. Typically, this involves running a TCP/IP protocol stack on the SNA host or an SNA stack on the TCP/IP host.

SNA background information   To understand the issues involved in these various solutions, a bit of SNA background might be helpful. This background information will be particularly important in understanding the differences between the alternatives discussed below.

Within an SNA network, 3270 terminals are broadly categorized as DLU or SLU. Although each of these designations has its own subtle implications, for our purposes we will consider them to be synonymous. The implication of both is that 3270s are dependent upon other components within the SNA network to establish a session with another logical unit.

Applications within an SNA network (e.g., CICS), usually function as PLUs. PLUs always exist under the control of an SSCP. Within the SNA architecture, the SSCP is classified as a PU type 5. VTAM is the most common example of an SSCP or a PU type 5.

In a traditional SNA network, PLUs can be in session with DLUs or other PLUs, but a DLU (terminal) can only establish a session with a PLU (application), not with other DLUs. Further, in order for a DLU (a terminal) to establish a session with a PLU (an application), the services of an SSCP (VTAM) are required. In order for two DLUs to exchange information, there must be a PLU (or some other component) in the middle acting as an intermediary.

Control unit gateway   This approach uses the 3270 control unit as the gateway between the 3270 terminals and the TCP/IP network, as shown in figure 16.1. The controller handles the three functional requirements outlined above. All terminals attached to such a control unit have access to the TCP/IP network. Users of the 3270 interact

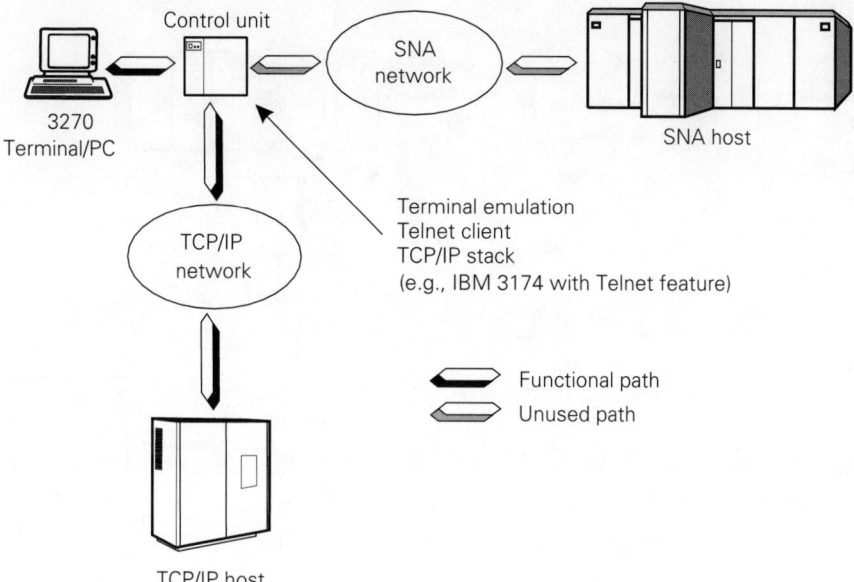

Figure 16.1   Control unit gateway

with software on the control unit to indicate whether they want to establish an SNA or TCP/IP connection.

The control unit gateway approach also requires that both the SNA and TCP/IP networks extend to each control unit. When accessing TCP/IP applications, the SNA network does not transport either the 3270 or VT-type data-streams. This solution's greatest advantage and its greatest disadvantage arise from this fact.

On the one hand, it is an advantage because only the control unit has the opportunity to handle the 3270 terminal as a true character-mode device. As a result, a control unit gateway should offer the most faithful emulation of a character-mode terminal.

On the other hand, if all 3270 terminals in the SNA network require access to TCP/IP applications, the disadvantage of this approach becomes clear: all control units must be upgraded or replaced since the majority of installed control units do not support this capability.

This approach works well in any of the following situations:

- Only a subset of the 3270 terminals/users need access to TCP/IP applications, and those who do are co-located (i.e., a limited number of control units need to be upgraded or replaced)

- The SNA network is relatively small (i.e., there are few 3270 control units in the SNA network)

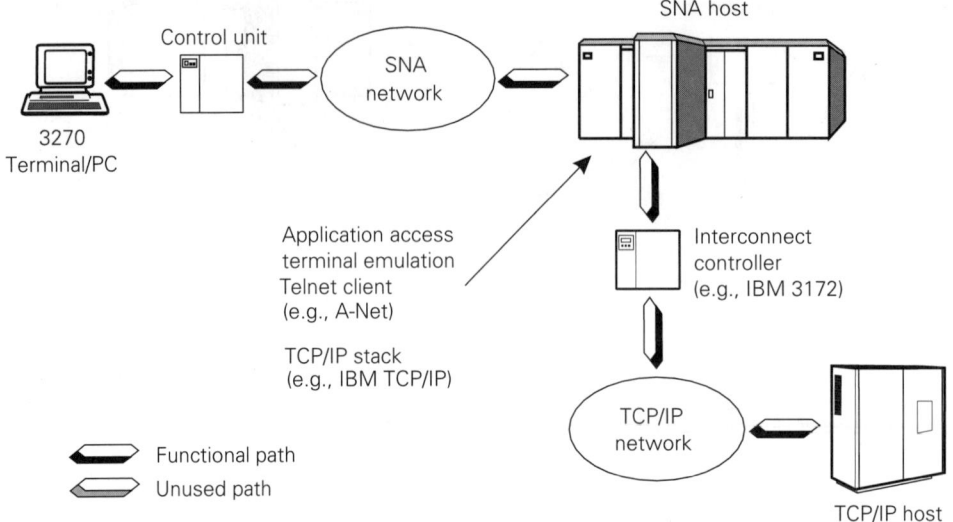

Figure 16.2   SNA host gateway

- Running parallel TCP/IP and SNA networks to each control unit is practical and not cost-prohibitive
- The targeted TCP/IP applications have very strong character-mode assumptions

SNA host gateway   The SNA host gateway approach extends the TCP/IP network into the SNA host, as shown in figure 16.2. It typically relies on two software components resident on the IBM host: (1) a TCP/IP protocol stack, and (2) a software component that provides the Telnet client, terminal emulation, and application access functions. These software components allow the 3270s to pass through the SNA network and the IBM host into the TCP/IP network. The physical connection to the TCP/IP network is usually accomplished by an external interconnect controller.

Since an SNA host-resident software component is the first point of contact, all 3270 terminals within the SNA network would have access to this capability. Thus, TCP/IP application access would extend to all users within the SNA network.

This approach leverages the investment in the existing SNA network in two ways: (1) the SNA network carries the 3270 traffic between the terminal and the SNA host, and (2) no control units need to be replaced or upgraded. As compared to the control unit gateway solution, the TCP/IP network does not have to extend to each control unit—only to the SNA host.

With this solution (and the other solutions that follow), the 3270 terminal operates as a block-mode device. Such solutions usually support character-oriented functions through the use of program function keys. Only the control unit gateway has the opportunity to handle the 3270 terminal as a character-mode device.

TCP/IP host gateway   The TCP/IP host gateway approach extends the SNA network into the TCP/IP host. Therefore, the TCP/IP network is no longer in the functional path. This approach usually relies on two software components: (1) an SNA protocol stack resident on the TCP/IP host, and (2) a software component that provides the Telnet client, terminal emulation, and application access functions.

Depending on the implementation, it may also require a software component on the SNA host. If so, then the Telnet client, terminal emulation, and application access function may exist on either the TCP/IP or SNA host. The physical connection into the SNA network is usually accomplished by a communications adapter built in to the TCP/IP host.

Instead of extending the TCP/IP network into the SNA host, we now extend the SNA network into the TCP/IP host. Instead of running a TCP/IP stack on the SNA host, we now run an SNA stack on the TCP/IP host. The philosophy of the organization (with respect to SNA and TCP/IP) will probably determine whether this difference is deemed to be an advantage or a disadvantage.

As with the SNA host gateway, this solution allows all 3270 terminals within the SNA network to access the TCP/IP host. Furthermore, the 3270 terminal is handled strictly as a block-mode device.

The type of SNA PU supported by the SNA stack determines how a session is established between a 3270 terminal and the TCP/IP host. Therefore, to accurately categorize this solution we must break it down further based upon the type of SNA PU supported by the gateway.

TCP/IP host gateway (PU 2)   A TCP/IP host gateway that supports a PU 2 cannot allow a 3270 terminal to log in directly to the TCP/IP host. This limitation is inherent in the definition of a PU 2 in the SNA architecture, that does not support direct session establishment with a DLU. Services of a PU type 5 are required for a DLU to establish a session with another LU. (Type 2.1 nodes can support both primary and secondary LUs: for example a PC running CICS/OS2, connected to a 3174 controller can act both as a PLU or SLU).

Although a 3270 terminal cannot log in directly to a TCP/IP host using a PU 2 gateway, it can log in indirectly using a software component on the SNA host, as shown in figure 16.3 This software component resolves the problem by serving as the PLU for both sides of the connection—the 3270 terminal and the LU within the TCP/IP host. In addition, this software component can provide the Telnet client, terminal emulation,

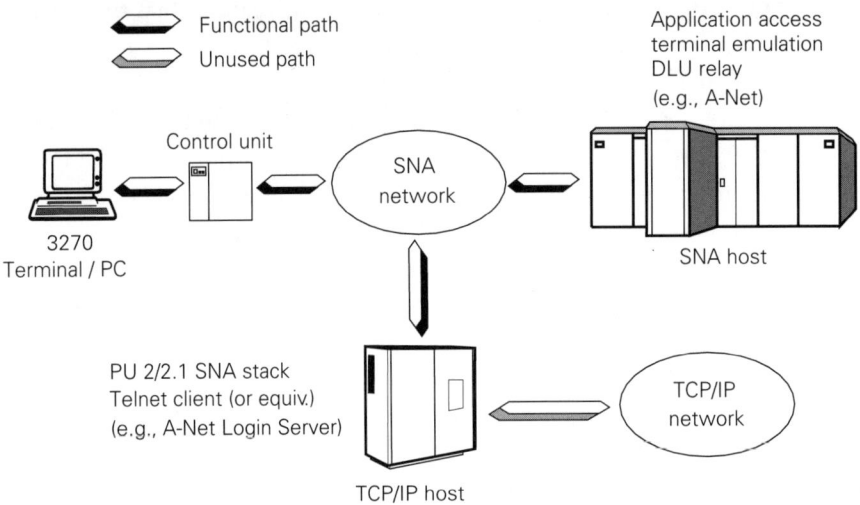

Functional path
Unused path

Control unit

SNA
network

3270
Terminal / PC

Application access
terminal emulation
DLU relay
(e.g., A-Net)

SNA host

PU 2/2.1 SNA stack
Telnet client (or equiv.)
(e.g., A-Net Login Server)

TCP/IP
network

TCP/IP host

Figure 16.3   TCP/IP host gateway (PU 2/2.1)

and application access functions. Alternatively, these functions can be distributed between the SNA and TCP/IP hosts.

Functionally, this approach resembles the SNA host gateway solution: the SNA host software allows the 3270s to pass through the SNA network/host into the TCP/IP host. The difference, however, is that the connection between the SNA host and the TCP/IP host is established across the SNA network rather than the TCP/IP network.

TCP/IP host gateway (PU type 5)   A TCP/IP host gateway that supports a PU type 5, as shown in figure 16.4, can allow a 3270 terminal to log in directly to the TCP/IP host. The TCP/IP host looks like another SNA host within the SNA network. While technically elegant, this solution does have certain implications and necessitates good planning.

Some considerations will depend on the approach taken by the solution provider to supply the SNA PU type 5 stack on the TCP/IP host. Current products on the market employ two very different approaches to implementing an SNA PU type 5 stack within the TCP/IP host: using an IBM or non-IBM SNA PU type 5 stack.

The non-IBM SNA PU type 5 stack approach uses a non-IBM SNA stack to implement the PU type 5. The SNA software runs under the TCP/IP host operating system (e.g., UNIX).

Within the SNA architecture the obligations and responsibilities of a PU type 5 are substantially greater than those of a PU type 2 or 2.1. This increase in complexity requires that three key questions be considered:

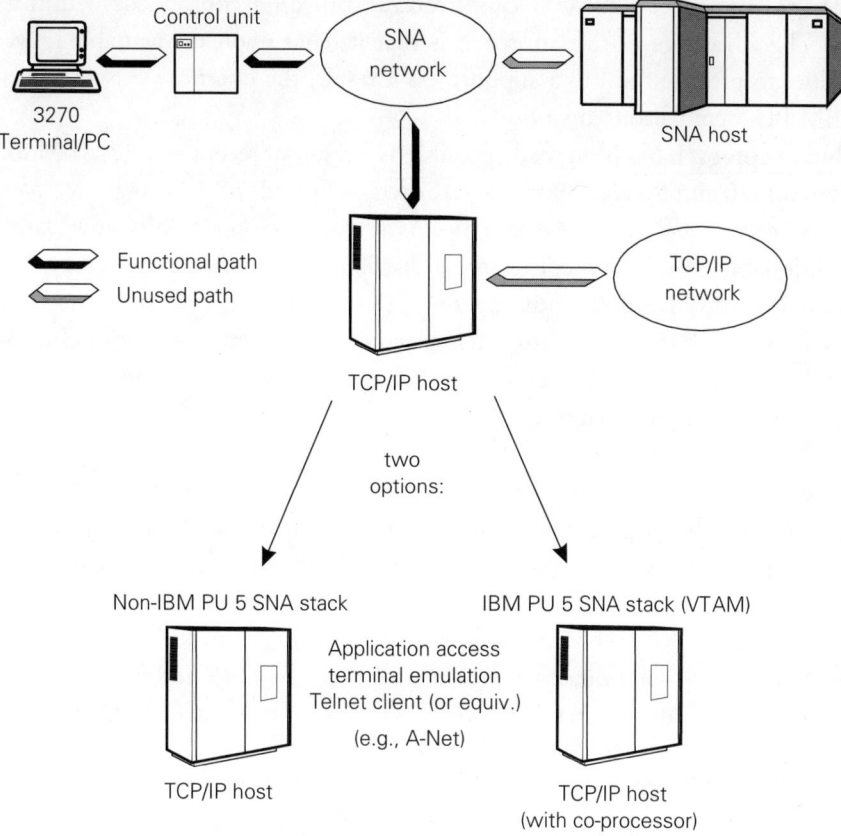

Control unit

3270
Terminal/PC

SNA
network

SNA host

Functional path
Unused path

TCP/IP host

TCP/IP
network

two
options:

Non-IBM PU 5 SNA stack

Application access
terminal emulation
Telnet client (or equiv.)

(e.g., A-Net)

TCP/IP host

IBM PU 5 SNA stack (VTAM)

TCP/IP host
(with co-processor)

Figure 16.4   TCP/IP host gateway (PU 5)

- Does the PU type 5 software implement the full PU 5 specification, or only a subset? If only a subset is supported:
  - Has the solution provider documented the subset and made it available?
  - Does the subset meet the needs of the organization?
- How committed is the solution provider to keeping its PU 5 software current with IBM standards?
- What are the resource requirements of running the PU 5 software on a particular TCP/IP host?

The answers will differ for each product and solution provider that implements this approach.

The other approach, IBM SNA PU 5 stack (VTAM), uses an IBM SNA stack to implement the PU 5; that is, IBM's VTAM program product. VTAM, of course, was never intended to run under UNIX. It can, however, run on a coprocessor within a TCP/IP host. The advantage of this approach is that it relies upon the actual VTAM program product to provide the PU 5 support. As a result, the questions raised above about non-IBM PU 5 emulations are moot.

This solution approach has been made possible as a result of recent work by IBM to reduce the System/370 and System/390 hardware architectures down to a single *complementary metal-oxide semiconductor* (CMOS) chip. As a result, the opportunity now exists to embed traditional mainframe functions into a distributed system at a fraction of the cost. Currently, the IBM RS/6000 running the AIX operating system supports this approach. An RS/6000 configured in this manner could also operate as a front end to other TCP/IP host systems. This, however, would change its role from being a TCP/IP host gateway to being a network gateway.

Network gateway Having discussed the SNA and TCP/IP host gateway solutions, we are prepared to describe the last solution to be discussed: the network gateway. As we have seen, the SNA host gateway extends the TCP/IP network (and the associated processing burden) into the SNA host. The TCP/IP host gateway, on the other hand, extends the SNA network (and the associated processing burden) into the TCP/IP host.

The network gateway solution, however, extends both the SNA and TCP/IP networks to a separate processor within the network. As a result, neither the SNA nor the TCP/IP hosts have the burden of running a foreign protocol stack. Instead, the network-based processor implements the required functions.

This approach usually relies upon two software components resident on the network-based processor: (1) a TCP/IP protocol stack and (2) an SNA protocol stack. It can also require a software component on the SNA host. If so, then the Telnet client, terminal emulation, and application access function can exist on either the SNA host or the network gateway. Communication adapters built in to the network gateway provide both the SNA and TCP/IP network connections.

As with the TCP/IP and SNA host gateways, this solution allows all 3270 terminals within the SNA network to access TCP/IP applications while operating as block-mode devices.

Like the TCP/IP host gateway, the type of SNA PU supported by the SNA stack running on the network gateway determines how a session is established between a 3270 terminal and the network gateway.

Network gateway (PU 2) As with a TCP/IP host gateway, a network gateway that implements a PU 2 cannot allow a 3270 terminal to log in directly. As we saw previously, this limitation is inherent in the definition of a PU 2 within the SNA architecture.

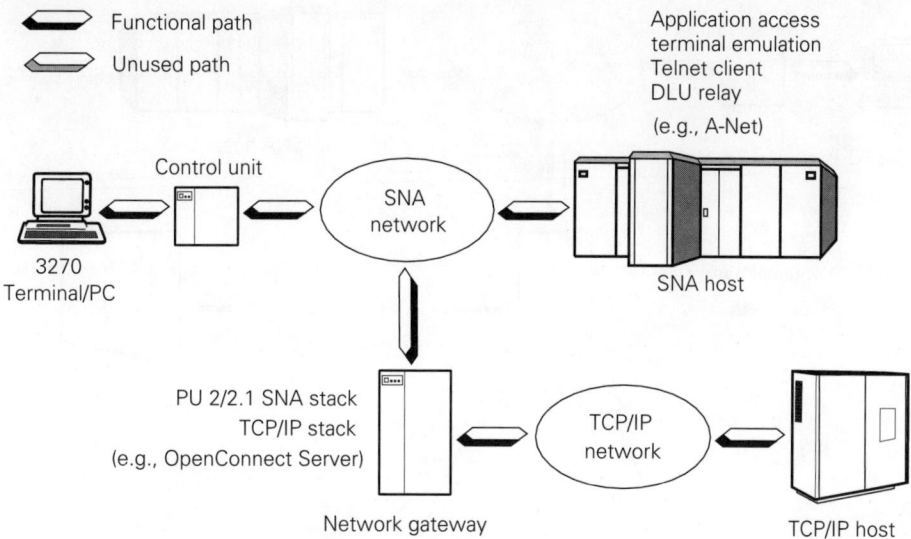

Figure 16.5 Network gateway (PU 2/2.1)

A 3270 terminal within an SNA network can, however, log in indirectly using a software component on the SNA host, as shown in figure 16.5. This software component serves as the PLU for both sides of the connection (the 3270 terminal and the LU within the network gateway). Additionally, this software component can provide the Telnet client, terminal emulation, and application access functions. Alternatively, these functions can be distributed between the SNA host and the network gateway.

Functionally, this approach is similar to the SNA host gateway solution: the SNA host software allows the 3270s to pass through the SNA network/host, into the network gateway, and then into the TCP/IP network.

Network gateway (PU type 5) A network gateway that supports a PU type 5, as shown in figure 16.6, can allow a 3270 terminal to log in directly to it. The network gateway is just like another SNA host within the SNA network. This approach has the same considerations as the TCP/IP host gateway that implemented a PU type 5.

As before, one implication is common to all PU 5 solutions: to be accessible to all 3270s within an SNA network, this new SNA host must be defined to all other SNA hosts within the network. The more SNA hosts within the network, the greater the burden this represents.

Other implications depend on the approach taken by the solution provider to provide an SNA PU 5 stack running within the network gateway. The products on the market today that implement this type of solution employ two very different approaches to

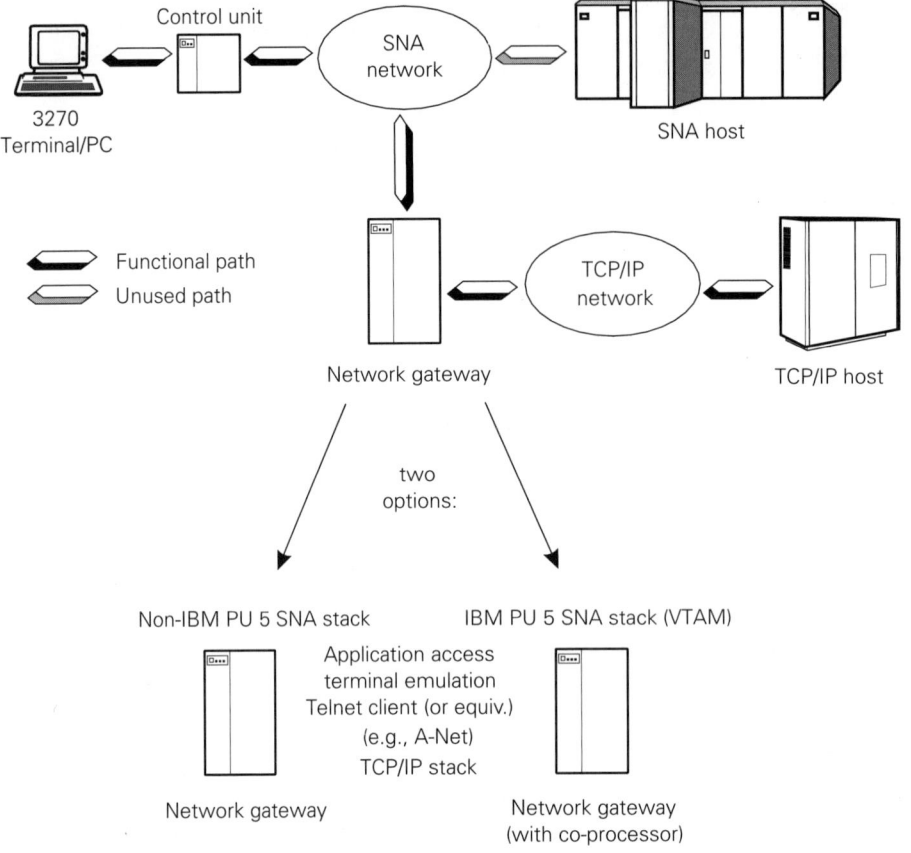

Figure 16.6   Network gateway (PU 5)

implementing an SNA PU 5 stack within the network gateway. The different approaches are the same as those with the TCP/IP host gateway.

The non-IBM SNA PU 5 stack approach uses a non-IBM SNA stack to implement the PU 5. The SNA software runs under the operating system of the network gateway. As discussed previously, within the SNA architecture the obligations and responsibilities of a PU 5 are substantially greater than those of a PU 2 or 2.1. This increase in complexity requires that several key questions be considered. Please refer back to the discussion of these questions for TCP/IP host gateways that emulate a PU 5.

As discussed previously, the IBM SNA PU 5 stack (VTAM) approach uses an IBM SNA stack to implement the PU 5: VTAM. Network gateways, however, typically run UNIX, OS/2, NetWare, or Windows NT as their operating system. And, as we observed before, VTAM was not written to run under these operating systems. It can, however, run on a coprocessor within the network gateway. As before, the advantage of this approach is that it relies upon the actual VTAM program product to provide the PU 5 support.

16.3.4 Summary

In this section, we have examined the alternatives to providing IBM 3270s with access to TCP/IP applications. Table 16.2 summarizes these various approaches.

16.4 Conclusion

Over the past two decades, organizations invested heavily in enterprise-wide SNA networks. As a result, millions of IBM 3270 terminals have been installed and are in use. Additionally, millions of personal computers which emulate a 3270 terminal and attach to the SNA network have proliferated. For such organizations, this is the network that must be leveraged and/or migrated into the world of open systems—a world where TCP/IP has been reaching a similar level of installation.

In this chapter, we have explored the issues involved in providing IBM 3270s with access to TCP/IP applications. We have examined the technical differences between 3270s and VT-type terminals, as well as the architectural issues involved, that make solving this problem very challenging. It is a problem, however, that can be solved in a number of ways.

Earlier in this chapter we posed two rhetorical questions regarding 3270 access to TCP/IP applications:

- Is it simple? No!
- Can it be done? Yes!

To these we now add a third:

- Are organizations implementing the solutions described in this chapter? Absolutely!

You won't be the first... and you probably can't afford to be the last.

Table 16.2 Solution alternatives for 3270 access to TCP/IP applications

	Accessible to all 3270s within SNA network?	Emulation mode?	Control unit upgrades required?	"Foreign" stack required on host?	Which networks transport data?	Where processing burden is focused?	SLU relay function required on SNA host?	SNA path table maintenance required?	Comments
Control unit gateway									
	no	character	yes	no	TCP/IP	control unit	no	no	Costs associated with control unit upgrades and/or replacements, and supporting parallel SNA and TCP/IP networks can be significant.
SNA host gateway									
	yes	block	no	yes, TCP/IP on SNA host	SNA and TCP/IP	SNA host	yes	no	SNA host security system can be used to validate access; depends on how SLU relay function implemented.
TCP/IP host gateway									
PU type 2	yes	block	no	yes, SNA on TCP/IP host	SNA	divided, SNA and TCP/IP hosts	yes	no	SNA host security system can be used to validate access; depends on how SLU relay function implemented.
PU type 5–IBM SNA stack (VTAM)	yes, with correct path tables	block	no	yes, SNA on TCP/IP host	SNA	TCP/IP host co-processor	no	yes	Using VTAM provides full PU type 5 functionality; ensures compatibility and stability; not available for all TCP/IP hosts.
PU type 5–non-IBM SNA stack	yes, with correct path tables	block	no	yes, SNA on TCP/IP host	SNA	TCP/IP host	no	yes	PU 5 emulators usually only support a subset of PU type 5 functionality; issues associated with compatibility and stability must be considered.
Network gateway									
PU type 2	yes	block	no	no	both	divided, SNA host and gateway	yes	no	SNA host security system can be used to validate access; depends on how SLU relay function implemented.
PU type 5–IBM SNA stack (VTAM)	yes, with correct path tables	block	no	no	both	network gateway and co-processor	no	yes	Using VTAM provides full PU type 5 functionality; ensures compatibility and stability.
PU type 5–non-IBM SNA stack	yes, with correct path tables	block	no	no	both	network gateway	no	yes	PU 5 emulators usually only support a subset of PU type 5 functionality; issues associated with compatibility and stability must be considered.

chapter   17

Connecting different worlds: PC to host using SNA gateways

Tony Wrobel

443

In this chapter Tony Wrobel continues the description of SNA gateways, providing access to SNA applications for LAN-based terminals. Different types and implementations of SNA gateways and specific vendors' products are mentioned. In addition, there is a discussion on specific questions and considerations to be addressed prior to selecting an SNA gateway.

17.1 Background

This chapter provides a brief overview of the types and implementations of SNA gateways, the network problems they are meant to address, and other considerations when choosing SNA gateways from different vendors for deployment in the enterprise. We will mention specific vendors' products only to give examples of gross types or generalized solutions, as vendors upgrade their products' capabilities too frequently to make discussion of specific functions appropriate here. We will address, however, the questions and considerations a network manager should address when selecting a SNA gateway.

17.1.1 Why SNA gateways?

SNA has long been the backbone of many large enterprises. As these enterprise networks have evolved over the years, different technologies such as small departmental LANs, have been added to them, creating integration problems. The fundamental problem being: how do PC users requiring 3270/5250 sessions and APPC sessions on these LANs get at and use data and applications residing on the SNA application servers (usually an IBM mainframe or AS/400 system)? One answer is direct connection of PCs to the application servers. This solution is often the best choice, but implementing direct connection creates problems of its own, as we'll address later. Another solution is the deployment of SNA gateways within the enterprise.

17.1.2 What types have evolved?

Let's take a brief look at how gateways have evolved in order to establish a working gateway vocabulary.

The original general purpose SNA gateway was the IBM 3174 terminal controller which functions as a PU 2 in the SNA network and serves up to 254 attached sessions. Many vendors including DCA (now Attachmate), Novell, and others developed hardware- and software-based products that emulated the *controller gateway.* These gateways served either downstream terminals or PCs running 3270/5250 emulation software.

Limitations of controller gateways include the inherent limit of 254 LUs per PU 2, an often rigid tie-in between gateway product and emulation software on the client PCs, and the lack of manageability of downstream PCs.

IBM developed more flexible variations like the front-end processor which functions as a PU 4 in the SNA network and is typified by the IBM 3745. IBM developed other gateways that supported downstream PU 2s such as the 3174 establishment controller. The industry refers to this type as a *passthrough gateway* since it functions as a multiplexing pipeline for SNA traffic from downstream PU 2s and as a LAN-to-WAN protocol converter. It, too, is represented well by third-party hardware and software products. This gateway type frees the network manager to choose any SNA PU 2 implementation for downstream PCs. It also is more easily implemented than controller gateways, but requires more overhead on the host to run since the host sees each downstream workstation as a separate PU and is therefore required to allocate and maintain resources for each one.

Yet another variation evolved called the *concentrator gateway*, which is a hybrid of the controller and the passthrough gateways in that it appears as a PU 2 to the host and a PU 4 or 5 to downstream PU 2s. In other words, it concentrated many downstream PU 2s to a single gateway PU. IBM first introduced this type with OS/2 1.2 Communication Manager. Most vendors today provide a variation on this type of gateway as it combines the advantages of the controller and passthrough gateways: since only one PU need be maintained at the host, there is less overhead. Since it talks to downstream PU 2s, any vendor's PU 2 implementation may be used for downstream PCs.

We can also classify the three basic gateway types by how the SNA stack is divided between the gateway machine or processor and the LAN client machine. By definition, the passthrough and concentrator gateways are *full-stack* gateways in that they implement a complete SNA stack on the gateway (and subsequently require a complete SNA stack on the downstream PC). In contrast, we can refer to controller gateways as a *split-stack* gateway since the SNA layers are split between the gateway box and the LAN-based PC. Indeed, the downstream layers are often razor-thin, consisting only of a portion of transaction and/or presentation services.

We'll look at the pros and cons of these types in the following sections.

17.1.3 What gateway implementations are there?

Each type has associated pros and cons. Basically, there are two implementation types: hardware-based and software-based.

We've mentioned *hardware-based* gateways already. The IBM 3174 family of communications controllers, 3270 and 3745 front-end processors, and the 3172 interconnect controller are examples. Other vendors of hardware-based gateways include the

Datastar by Apertus Technologies, the Concert Communications Processor and TCP/5250 Server by IDEA, the Integrated Enterprise Network 5000 by Hypercom Inc., and the Forest Network Resource series of turn-key gateways by Forest Computer.

The advantage of hardware gateways over the other types is the turn-key nature of their installation and the simpler nature of service and support due to the fact that fewer (or even a single) vendor is involved in providing support. The disadvantages of these gateways include accepting a possibly limited set of connectivity options and network interfaces, no integration with the underlying LAN OS (if any), and reduced scalability due to being tied to specific hardware.

Software-based gateways make up the bulk of the gateways available. Like hardware-based gateways, this group runs a spectrum from specialized to generalized solutions. They vary widely in the types of LAN/WAN connectivity supported, platforms, clients supported, and scalability.

Specialized gateways tend to offer a smaller set of connectivity or applications options, but cost less to deploy. For example, the Apertus Express gateway offers inter-connectivity for TCP/IP LANs running TN3270(E)/TN3179-G clients only. Many vendors offering specialized gateways will offer a suite of different gateway products for different needs. An example is the CQ series (CQ-3270 LAN and CQ-5250 LAN) by CQ Computer Communications, Inc., which offers IBM 390 and AS/400 connectivity respectively. Other vendors offering more specialized gateways include Attachmate, Data Interface Systems, Farabi Technology, NetSoft, and NCR Corp.

The other end of the spectrum includes the generalized gateways, which offer a rich suite of connectivity, LAN support, and client platform support. These tend to cost more than specialized solutions. CNT Corp.'s Brixton PU 2.1 SNA Server, IBM's Communications Servers, Interface System's Cleo SNA Server, Microsoft's SNA Server, NetSoft's AdaptSNA, Novell's NetWare for SAA, and OpenConnect Systems Inc.'s OC Server II are examples of the more generalized gateways.

17.2 What problems do SNA gateways address?

Let's take a look at the various problems that SNA gateways solve or mitigate. We'll focus on the base problem (LAN PC-to-SNA application server integration), but look at the various aspects of the problem.

17.2.1 Evolving network environment

Historically, many enterprises originally consisted of terminals directly attached via terminal or cluster controllers to host mainframes. These physical connections were usually made over coax or twinax cabling. Over time, enterprises introduced PCs running terminal and printer emulation software. Later, these PCs were connected together in LANs over token ring or ethernet media running 802.2 DLC protocols. As these networks evolved through upgrade, acquisition, or corporate merger, many different client platforms running different applications over different LAN protocols (some SNA, some not) were introduced. In some networks, SNA could be supported down to the client machines in the network. In other cases, it was either not desirable or not possible to deploy SNA support software on these LAN-based clients. Oftentimes the departmental LANs were tied to specific connectivity and application server interfaces at the centrally managed data center as well.

17.2.2 Increased administration burden

Directly connecting PCs to application servers incurs a significant administration burden (in terms of volume of configuration: each PC must have a corresponding VTAMLST definition on VTAM hosts for example), and in terms of sensitivity to changes (a host change could affect hundreds of client configurations). Controller or concentrator gateways can reduce dramatically the amount of configuration (by reducing the number of PUs) and the sensitivity to change (by shifting configuration to the gateway from clients). These problems have been mitigated by such features as VTAM's autoinstall.

17.2.3 Increased network downtime

Related to the problem of increased administration on hosts is the correlated necessitated downtime on those application servers when configuration changes are made there. Shifting configuration burden to the gateway limits the frequency and duration of downtime on the application server. Only users connected to affected gateways suffer impacts. By deploying clusters of gateways (a function supported by some gateways), downtime can be reduced to practically zero since multiple potential paths to a given application server are possible.

17.2.4 Degraded performance

Directly connecting PCs or sometimes even utilizing passthrough gateways can degrade overall network performance. Offloading processing from both client machines and hosts can effectively improve overall network performance and individual response times. Many PCs directly attached to a host or attached via a FEP can incur overhead due to the number of PCs the host or FEP must poll. This overhead is manifest in increased CPU or FEP cycles on the host processor and increased traffic on the lines. Removing SNA stacks from some client machines, especially DOS and Windows 3.1 platforms, can increase performance and stability by alleviating the need for real-mode DLC drivers. Clusters of gateways can improve user response time through load balancing techniques among the cluster.

17.2.5 Rigid LAN/WAN deployment

As a result of the evolution of networks, network managers are faced with a limited set of options when deciding to connect LANs directly to host systems. The use of SNA gateways allows more options: many gateways support a rich set of host and LAN connectivity options. Many can also be deployed centrally, that is, near the host systems, or in a distributed fashion, that is, nearer the supported LANs. This flexible deployment allows different connectivity to the host to be used (e.g., channel attached for close-to-host deployment). Flexible deployment allows network managers to better control what types of traffic flows in which part of the network. For example, a local or close-to-host deployment can allow a TCP/IP WAN to serve as the network backbone, while remotely deployed gateways allow an SNA backbone to be used.

17.3 What are the major deployment considerations?

As a network manager, certain characteristics of your existing enterprise will affect your choice of SNA gateway or gateways that will be deployed in the enterprise.

17.3.1 Network and organizational infrastructure

The primary driving force behind deployment decisions is the infrastructure and topology of the network itself, and the related people organizational structure. Where are application servers deployed in relation to the LANs and who manages each? If the LANs are remote from a central data center and are managed separately (a common enterprise model), LAN network managers may be restricted to gateways that operate in a distributed fashion. What is the primary existent connectivity to the hosts or is there some flexibility in this decision? For example, must SDLC over leased lines be used or is frame relay being rolled out in the enterprise? Most gateways support either SDLC or X.25 WAN connections, but not all support frame relay.

Do the departmental LANs in the organization use a specific Network OS like Novell's NetWare or Microsoft's Windows NT? Most gateways are designed to run on a specific NOS or OS and integrate with the OS, like Novell's NetWare for SAA (on NetWare and IntranetWare), and Microsoft's SNA Server (on Windows NT). Such gateways in these LANs can typically run a machine performing double or triple duty in the LAN as a file, print, and local application server.

17.3.2 What LAN protocols require conversion?

Some shops are TCP/IP-based, and the majority of gateways on the market support TCP/IP LANs in some way. Other protocols are out there, however, and you'll need to decide what protocols need to be supported. Enterprises based on Novell's NetWare depend on IPX/SPX support. Other shops have an existing base of Macintosh computers and require support for Apple's Appletalk protocol. Still others might depend on Banyan VINES support.

17.3.3 What client platforms and applications are currently deployed?

Are the end-users running PCs, UNIX, or Macintosh machines or some combination? Most multipurpose gateways will support all of these platforms, but some specialize in one, such as CNT's Brixton PU2.1 SNA Server, Data Connection's SNAP-IX, IBM's Communication Server for AIX, Interface System's Cleo SNA Server, and OpenConnects OC Server II which run on and support UNIX-based LANs.

Do the clients run a complete SNA stack, or are they split-stack in nature? For SNA-based shops, a full-stack gateway implementation like one of IBM's Communication Servers is probably in order. However, some enterprises might require a split-stack implementation if it is not possible to run SNA on each client. Microsoft, Novell, and IBM all offer a rich set of LAN and split-stack clients as well.

What applications do these clients require? Are they 3270/5250 emulation, TN3270(E), TN5250, SNA APPC/CPI-C, or some combination? What LU types need to be supported? Most support LU 2 for 3270 connections, but is LU 6.2 required? Check which clients, APIs, and LU types are supported by a gateway before deciding.

17.3.4 What network management and security requirements are there?

What existing network management infrastructure is there? Many SNA enterprises make use of NetView technology and will require gateways that support NetView RUNCMDs, alerts, and NetView RTM. This is important for concentrator gateways that see clients as complete PUs that need to be centrally managed. Most gateways that support TCP/IP also support SNMP to some degree. Some specialty UNIX-based gateways, like CNT's Brixton gateway, provide integration with multiple vendor's SNMP implementations. Find out what is the level of SNMP support in these cases.

Finally, decide what security requirements there are in the network and how a particular gateway supports security. These issues include user authentication, password validation, and password and/or data encryption.

17.3.5 What scalability requirements do you have?

If the anticipated growth of the network is high, consider gateways that scale well in terms of numbers of users and sessions. Some gateway products are designed and are tested for a small number of users. Remember that software-based gateways are usually more flexible when it comes to which platforms and CPUs they can run on, which has a direct bearing on scalability. A gateway that runs on a 386 should be flexible enough to scale up to a Pentium II P20 if need dictates.

17.3.6 Do you require a high level of fault tolerance?

Many gateways are designed to provide a high degree of network fault tolerance through two types of mechanisms: gateway clustering or pooling (some vendors, like Apertus, refer to this function as virtual gateways), and hot-standby or hot-backup capability. Clustering permits two or more gateways to work together to provide multiple data paths to hosts and session load balancing across gateways. Hot-standby or hot-backup capability provides a secondary or stand-by gateway machine that takes over support of sessions in the event of primary gateway failure. Most generalized software gateway vendors provide this capability.

17.3.7 What level of vendor support is required?

Often overlooked as a criterion, but equally as critical to the decision-making process is whether a high level of vendor support is required for the gateway environment. Are gateways deployed in a distributed fashion across a wide geographical area? It might be more cost effective to pay for extended service and support from vendors offering such support (such as IBM), than to have to train and maintain a highly skilled distributed IS force in such an enterprise.

Remember that turn-key or hardware-based solutions can significantly reduce the complexity of support by reducing the number of vendors to a few or only one.

17.4 What other aspects of SNA gateways should I consider?

Other decisions face the network manager when deploying SNA gateways, but have less bearing in terms of effects on the network or solving our fundamental underlying problem. This categorization is not to say that these considerations are less important (indeed, cost might be of utmost importance to some net managers), but their effects on building the network successfully are not as critical.

17.4.1 Cost

Cost is always an issue and functionality and support play a big part in how much a shop will pay to deploy gateways. Prices range from free (for gateways included as an option on another piece of hardware or software, like IEN's branch router gateways or IBM's Communication Server for OS/390), to several thousands of dollars in leasing expenses for high-end FEPs. Consider how a particular vendor charges for gateway licenses as well. All charge for the base gateway license in some way, but most also charge on a per-session basis. Some, however, charge based on number of user licenses required. Costs can be tailored precisely to the needs of the network using these pricing schemes.

17.4.2 Ease of gateway management and configuration

Look at the suite of tools provided by the gateway vendor to manage and administer the gateway itself. Is the product centrally manageable and configurable? These issues are important in a multigateway enterprise, or a shop where the gateway is essentially kept in a closet, and is not easily accessible. How does it integrate with its underlying OS? Some gateways exploit advanced features of an underlying OS. For example, Microsoft SNA Server takes advantage of NT's advanced GUI for management and diagnostics, and Novell's NetWare for SAA integrates with Novell Directory Services on NetWare for administration tasks. Another factor to consider is content management and software distribution. Does the gateway integrate with systems like distributed systems node executive (DSNX) for content management, like the 3174 or IBM's Communication Servers?

17.4.3 Performance, reliability and diagnostics

Look at comparative performance between gateways, all other things being equal. Take advantage of reports commissioned from such independent assessors as the Tolly Group. Remember to consider also how well a particular gateway performs as it scales.

Diagnostics are often overlooked when assessing SNA gateways (or any complex communications software, for that matter), but fill an important role in their successful deployment. If your shop creates its own applications, a robust tracing facility is a must. These include SNA protocol boundary traces and internal SNA flow traces. Some gateway vendors offer additional facilities, such as host simulation and self-test applications. Check with vendors for specifics.

17.4.4 Other value-added functions

Many gateways provide and will continue to provide additional value-added functions. Functions such as bundled applications, FTP and application servers, and Web-browser-to-SNA-application-server connectivity are some of the more interesting value-added items.

17.5 Summary

SNA gateways have become a strategic solution in most organizations that need to reliably connect PCs on LANs to IBM application server systems. The deployment of SNA gateways has increased dramatically and will continue to increase. It is important to note that the role and capabilities of the various SNA gateways on the market have evolved from simple 3270 or 5250 emulation support to become platforms that offer a wide range of application server integration services. Coupled with this increased sophistication comes the complexity of choice for network managers. We've attempted to organize the questions and thought process for deciding on an SNA gateway deployment strategy. In chapters 19 and 20, we take a closer look at these new application server integration roles for SNA gateways.

17.6 References

Baerg, Robert, "The Apertus Virtual Gateway Complex: Robust TCP/IP LAN Connectivity to SNA Hosts" (Apertus Technologies white paper), *Data Communications,* February 1995.

McLean, Michelle Rae, "CNT SNA Tools Bolster Host Linking Software," *LAN Times,* July 24, 1995.

Roberts, Erica, "Getting the Goods on SNA Gateways," *Data Communications*, May 1996, available from `http://www.data.com/Roundups/Gettingthegoods.html`.

Taylor, Ed, *Integrating TCP/IP into SNA,* Wordware Publishing, Inc., 1993.

Tolly, Kevin, "Playing to Win with IBM's LAN Gateways," *Data Communications,* Februrary 1990.

———, "Opening the Gateways to SNA Connectivity," *Data Communications*, March 1990.

"The Concepts and Practice of TCP/IP and SNA," (FTP Software white paper)

chapter 18

Integrating Web technology and enterprise systems

Russell W. Teubner
Donald H. Czubek

Russell W. Teubner and Donald H. Czubek describe how Web technology can be used to enhance, extend and leverage SNA host environments. Web-to-host solutions began to help enterprises to leverage their existing computing and communications infrastructures, while taking advantage of emerging technologies. And Web-to-host gateway products exist for this very purpose. By integrating Web technology with established host systems, enterprises can compete more efficiently, and, most important, better and more cost effectively serve the customers.

18.1 Introduction

The Internet's explosive growth has reshaped the computing and communications industry. Although the Internet has existed for many years (mainly supporting scientists and academicians), it has recently been transformed into a commercial and consumer phenomenon. The explosive growth of the Internet in these segments has been fueled by a single application—the Web.

Why has the Web enjoyed such success? The huge amount of hype surrounding the Web certainly hasn't hurt. However, there are some solid technical and business reasons for its success as well. The Web is based on a client/server computing model and it provides a platform-independent method of sharing information. One of the key benefits of the Web is that its clients, called browsers, are easy to use, inexpensive (or free), and available for most computing platforms.

Does Web technology have a role in enterprise networking? Absolutely. The design goals that are important to the research centers and universities that originally launched the Web, including ease of use and platform independence, are equally important in corporate information technology (IT) environments.

This chapter will examine some specific ways in which Web technology can be used to enhance, extend and leverage IBM host environments and their SNA networks.

18.2 Customer investments in established host systems

Most medium and large organizations have made a substantial investment in applications to support their business operations. Many of these applications are hosted on IBM hardware platforms. The two predominant IBM platforms are the System/390 family of processors, commonly called mainframes, and midrange AS/400 systems. These processors are sometimes called legacy systems, which might give the impression that they are obsolete (or close to it). However, based upon available data, nothing could be further from the truth.

Most mission-critical data is stored on mainframes and the size of these databases continues to grow. International Data Corporation (IDC) research indicates that customers continue to invest in mainframe-based applications. According to IDC, 57 percent more mainframe processing power, and over 75 percent more mainframe disk storage, were shipped in 1995 compared with 1994. Clearly, the role of the mainframe as a centralized database server continues to grow. This data is corroborated by the Gartner Group, which estimated that 85 percent of existing mainframe applications will stay right where they are to take advantage of mainframe security, performance, and reliability.

The primary networking protocol used to communicate with these mainframes is IBM's SNA. IBM estimates the number of SNA installations at approximately 50,000.

The AS/400 market is also large and growing. The IBM AS/400, used primarily by midsize enterprises, is one of the most successful multiuser application platforms in the computer industry. According to IBM, the installed base of AS/400s totaled approximately 360,000 at the end of 1995. It is estimated that IBM shipped nearly 70,000 AS/400s during 1995 alone.

Thus, despite reports of their death, IBM mainframes still run most of the mission-critical applications in large corporations. Mainframe systems, networks, and applications may be established, but they are hardly obsolete.

The Web browser: historical–but why?

From a historical perspective, the Web browser is unprecedented. Is this because the technology underlying Web browsers and servers is so revolutionary? Not really. The reason is this: For the first time, individuals on both sides of the "firewall" (both inside and outside the organization's formal boundaries) are on the same learning curve with respect to the tools and technology they use to access information. They are all using a Web browser.

Over the years, many IT organizations tried to extend access to their established host systems and applications. The use of ASCII terminal emulation software and dial-up 3270 protocol conversion products during the late 1980s and early 1990s represented one such strategy. While very well intentioned, most of these efforts achieved only limited, or short-lived, success due to one critical factor: *training*.

Training end users how to navigate and interact with a host application by using a sequence of ASCII keystrokes that simulated certain mainframe terminal keystrokes turned out to be far more difficult than expected. Thus, most organizations decided that the cost of supporting such a capability outweighed the benefits (at least for large-scale use). Note that the cost of the technology was not the problem. Instead, it was the hidden cost of a very steep learning curve. The Web solves this problem.

18.3 Host processing paradigms

To understand how Web technologies can be used to augment established IBM host environments, it is important to first consider how organizations use mainframe computer systems today. If we don't, we may fall into the trap of viewing Web-to-host as if it were monolithic, that is, a single problem to be solved. Viewing Web-to-host as a monolithic problem provides little insight into the nature of the problem, and therefore the solutions that organizations should consider implementing.

When one considers all of the processing activities that are currently based upon SNA host systems and networks, we find that the vast majority fall into three broad categories:

- Batch processing and report generation
- Online applications and transaction processing
- Database access and client/server

18.3.1 Batch processing and report generation

The batch processing model, as its name implies, was originally designed to process a group, or batch, of transactions. These transactions were usually created as part of a data entry process that occurred during an interval of time based upon the organization's business cycle (daily, weekly, monthly, etc.). The batch jobs that processed these transactions were also used to sort, select, summarize, and report on the transactions processed.

To facilitate organizations' exploiting this mode of data processing, IBM developed a line of communications devices referred to as RJE workstations. These devices allowed organizations to submit, manage, and retrieve the results of batch jobs from a remote location. To support this activity, IBM developed new communications data streams and protocols especially oriented toward efficient bulk data transfer. Support for these RJE protocols was incorporated into both the IBM operating systems, as well as the devices themselves.

Over time, most organizations found that processing mission-critical business transactions on anything but a real-time basis did not allow them to compete effectively and serve their customers efficiently. These business pressures, combined with new computing and communications technology, gave birth to the modern concept of online transaction processing (OLTP). And, as more and more organizations began to process transactions online, the role of batch processing changed.

Batch processing became the primary method used to summarize and report on the online activities. As such, batch processing became far less about processing transactions, and far more about generating operational and management reports for the organization. Reports produced in this fashion were either printed or stored in such a way that they can be viewed online.

Batch processing has come a long way over the years. However, it is still a dominant mode of operation within most organizations since the reports and business documents created in this fashion are mission-critical to the operation of the organization. Furthermore, the underlying operating system support for RJE data streams continues to be a fundamental building block within most organizations that rely upon IBM mainframes as part of their IT infrastructure.

18.3.2 Online applications and transaction processing

The modern concept of OLTP stemmed from advancements in computing and communications technology, as well as rapidly evolving business requirements. Organizations moved swiftly to exploit this new form of processing. As a result, mainframes became entrenched as the platform of choice for running mission-critical interactive applications within most large organizations.

This move from batch to online required new tools—most notably, computer terminals that would allow end users to interact with online applications. IBM introduced new communications hardware to meet this requirement and developed new data streams and protocols especially oriented toward efficient access to interactive applications. Support for these new data streams and protocols became ingrained within all the components of the computing and communications infrastructure: the communications hardware, the operating system software, as well as customer-developed application programs. To this day, the standard terminal type used to access System/390-based applications is the IBM 3270, while the IBM 5250 is the standard interactive terminal used to access AS/400s.

Some organizations continue to use these IBM fixed-function terminals. However, more often than not, the 3270 or 5250 terminal is actually a PC running a terminal emulation program. In addition to providing basic terminal emulation capabilities, these emulation programs became a new foundation on which organizations built additional front-end applications to automate (or augment) mainframe applications. The fact that the market for terminal emulation products grew to become a billion dollar industry (annually) is a testimony to the enduring nature of SNA interactive applications.

3270 *devices* may be considered by some to be antiques. However, 3270 *data streams,* and the programs that use them, are alive and well.

Limitations of traditional, two-tier client/server models

During the late 1980s and well into the 1990s, many organizations reengineered their IT infrastructure around a two-tier client/server computing model. This model was (and still is) typified by the use of complex, or thick, client software, and a back-end server that functions primarily as a database repository. Although this model succeeded in meeting the needs of many organizations, it became apparent to most of them that it also had some serious drawbacks. Specifically, that the hidden costs of implementing client/server led to a higher total cost of ownership than they expected.

Beyond its cost, another limitation of the client/server model was a lack of platform independence. Client software is usually written for a particular hardware and/or operating system platform. This factor limits the usefulness of client applications in organizations that have a variety of desktop computers and operating systems. It is a critical problem for applications, such as home banking, that are designed to be accessed directly by customers. In these environments, the application designers have no control over the type or configuration of the end users' systems.

What is needed is a thin universal client that runs on almost any end user computer. And, the Web browser fits this requirement quite nicely. Since the central design goal of the Web is to provide virtually universal access to information located on, or accessible by, a Web server, it is not surprising that organizations are beginning to rely on Web technology to augment, and in some cases replace, their current client/server computing environment.

18.3.3 Database access and client/server

With the advent of the PC, a new host processing paradigm developed. It's not that this paradigm didn't exist prior to the PC, it simply had not been exploited. Up to this point, end users interacted with data by means of host-resident application programs. There were two basic implications of this architecture.

First, the operations or analysis that could be performed on the data were determined by the functionality designed into the host-resident application program. If new information or functionality was required, the user needed to request that the host program be enhanced accordingly. In large organizations where the pace of business change was brisk, it was not uncommon for these requests, in total, to create a development backlog of hundreds (or thousands) of person-years.

Second, the physical and logical organization of the information in a file or database was understood only by the application programs that accessed it (e.g., only the payroll programs understood the organization of the payroll database). If a new field needed to be added to the file or database, each and every program that needed access to that file usually needed to be changed. This was such a burdensome process that organizations were reluctant to either (1) change the existing data structures, or (2) permit additional programs to access the existing files or database.

However, now that end users had more than just a dumb terminal sitting on their desk, such limitations were viewed as an unacceptable impediment to individual and organizational success. End users wanted access to raw data; that is, sets or subsets of data that they could download or otherwise access and manipulate without the intervention of an existing host-resident application. If they weren't afforded such access, they would often try to build their own private databases. This made matters even worse for the organization.

These factors, and others, drove organizations to begin re-structuring host-resident data into certain standard forms (e.g., SQL). By adopting these standard forms, the limitations mentioned above would be reduced, or even eliminated. And, by adopting application independent forms of data organization, businesses could allow other geographically dispersed computer systems to gain access to the data residing on the host.

As a result, the data could now be accessed by any program that understood the standard form, and the set of common verbs used to manipulate the data. The data could also be analyzed and processed by end users in ways that they felt were relevant to the organization's goals. This restructuring of host-resident data was the foundational first step toward organization's implementing a two-tier client/server architecture.

18.3.4 Summary

The purpose of this section has been to understand how organizations use mainframe computer systems today. Some organizations may have a need to integrate the Web and their IBM host in all three areas. Others may only need a solution in one or two areas. Whatever the case, organizations should ensure that they first understand the problem to be solved (at least at this level), before evaluating products or implementing particular solutions.

18.4 Business and technology drivers

The Internet has forever changed the way the world accesses information. This is as true in the world of business and commerce as it is in either the academic world (where the Internet originated) or in the consumer world (often viewed as the Internet's mainstay). Now that Internet technologies have standardized to a sufficient degree, they are being adopted by corporations as a key part of their IT infrastructure.

Moving to a new application architecture could be viewed as an expensive and overwhelming proposition by many organizations, considering that legacy applications still hold most of the critical data circulating through a corporation. Yet, most organizations can't afford to miss the opportunity to expand their established computing resources to a broader population of users (whether inside or outside their own organizational boundaries). Fortunately, by taking advantage of the Web, IT organizations can increase access to host applications with little added expense and disruption.

Before we begin to analyze specific techniques for linking Web users to established host systems, it is important to look at the business reasons that are driving this odd marriage of technologies. There are several interrelated reasons for the Web's appeal to business.

The Web's client/server architecture

Even though the Web is based on a client/server model, its approach is fundamentally different from most client/server designs. The key difference is that the Web is designed to use very simple, or thin, client: the browser.

Web browsers interpret the HTML data streams that define Web pages and then display the information on the user's screen. Web content is either stored as a collection of static pages on Web servers, or it can be dynamically generated by a program based upon user input. Such programs that run adjunct to a Web server can access virtually any type of information, contributing to the openness of the Web architecture.

The most common way that users interact with the screen content is by clicking on hyperlinks that allow them to navigate within a collection of pages on the same server, or pages that reside on a different server. Users can also fill in forms or use input mechanisms such as radio buttons or check boxes to enter information.

The design of the Web is completely decentralized. Each server operates independently, and users can connect to any server via the Internet (assuming they are suitably authorized). Users often locate information by connecting first to a server that provides

Web searching facilities. These servers systematically query other servers on the Web and build databases that describe the content of each Web server.

18.4.1 A thin and universal client

The thought of migrating or retooling their infrastructure painfully reminds many IT organizations of the costly and time-consuming venture of moving a centralized application to a client/server computing model. Unlike commonly understood client/server architectures, however, the Web relies upon a thin universal client eliminating the need for the complex, client-based software that many organizations found to be difficult to distribute, configure, and maintain. Although the use of Web browsers and servers can be viewed as an alternative to existing client/server architectures, this view is not mandatory. In fact, this universal thin client, the Web browser, along with the corresponding Web server components, can be used to augment and complement some two-tier client/server architectures, and most three-tier architectures.

18.4.2 Lower product and infrastructure costs

One of the most notable features of the Web is the low cost of the products that form its foundation. This is especially true of the browser software that runs on the client side: browsers are either free, very inexpensive, or already bundled in with the operating system. While browser vendors are obviously trying to make their money on the server side components, the pricing paradigm for server components is also modest when compared to other products that have provided similar capabilities.

Communications costs are also low because the Web relies upon the Internet for communications. Low-cost Internet access is widely available, particularly in the U.S. where competition among access providers is keeping costs very low. When you combine the inexpensive client and server-side software with the low cost and wide-spread reach of Internet service providers, it becomes clear why the Web is an attractive solution to extending access to existing host applications and data.

18.4.3 Low maintenance, support, and administration costs

One of the major hidden costs of adopting a new computing model are the maintenance, support, and administration costs that often follow. And, in these categories, the Web represents a significant step forward. Web solutions are inherently server-based thus allowing maintenance, customization ,and administration to take place in one central location. Contrast this with the client-based, or terminal emulation approach, where many maintenance and support tasks must be performed on each workstation from which the host access is needed.

18.4.4 Minimal training requirements and ease of use

Another hidden cost of adopting a new computing model is the specialized training that is usually required for end users to become proficient at accessing and navigating applications. And in this category, the Web clearly prevails. The browser's common graphical user interface is far simpler to learn than either the text-oriented user interface of host applications, or the proprietary user interface of many client/server applications. Web software is designed to allow the users to consistently navigate from site to site. It also allows them to consistently navigate between or within an application or database at the same site. Since all these actions occur using the same point and click graphical interface, new users become experienced surfers very quickly.

Web-based content and applications and are easy to use. Well designed Web-based applications often require no specific end user training. If the user knows how to use a browser and follow any on-screen directions, he or she can use the application. In fact, Web tools are becoming so accessible and easy to use that even nontechnical people can publish (not just access) their own graphical, hyperlinked Web site.

18.4.5 A broad user base

The traditional approach to extend access to host applications to individuals inside an organization is by using a PC-based terminal emulation program. Even within an organization, this thick client approach is expensive to implement, and difficult to maintain. And, when it comes to extending access to established systems to individuals who are outside the organization's formal boundaries (e.g., business partners and customers), using a terminal emulation approach is typically not even an option.

The Web's combined low cost and ease of use has resulted in explosive growth. And, the ability to reach a broad user base is a significant benefit of using the Web to provide user access to established applications. Some industry analysts predict that Web browsers will eventually become as ubiquitous as telephones. Even if this prediction doesn't come true, it is clear that the huge population of Web browsers is the key to unlocking a new generation of consumer and business applications. And, to be successful, these services will require access to applications and data residing on legacy hosts.

18.4.6 Scalability

Since the Web architecture moves much of the processing burden from the client to the server, the configuration of the workstation is of far less concern. In fact, it is far more likely that the overall performance of a Web application will be determined by the speed of the network, or the Web server, than it is by the configuration of the client workstation. Most organizations find these parts of their infrastructure more readily scalable, since nothing needs to be changed on individual workstations. By shifting the critical points of scalability away from the client and toward the server, organizations can more easily accommodate varying requirements for concurrent user access.

18.4.7 Summary

These are just a sampling of the many reasons why products and services that allow access to host-resident data and applications via the Web are becoming a standard part of the IT infrastructure within many organizations.

18.5 Web-to-host gateways: an overview

Earlier in this chapter we reviewed how organizations use mainframe computer systems today. The purpose of this analysis was to keep us from viewing Web-to-host as if it were a monolithic problem. To this end, we organized the majority of all mainframe activities as falling into one of three broad paradigms, or categories. We will now use these categories to help us see how Web technology can be used to augment established host systems. Specifically, the three categories we will examine are:

- *Host document access and delivery* Using the Web to disseminate reports and business documents generated by the host
- *Host database access* Using the Web to access data that resides in a host-resident database

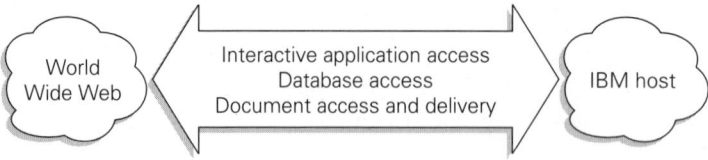

Figure 18.1 Web-to-host access usage

- *Host application access*   Using the Web to access interactive applications that reside and execute on the host

Before we examine the unique nature of each type of Web-to-host gateway, we will first explore the components that they have in common.

18.5.1 Basic architecture

Most Web-to-host gateways are built upon a server-based hardware and software platform (i.e., Microsoft Windows NT, or an implementation of UNIX), and fashioned from four major software elements:

- A TCP/IP protocol stack
- A Web server
- The Web-to-host gateway software
- An SNA protocol stack

Depending upon the specific type of gateway, additional software components may be required. However, these four are quite standard. The relationship between these elements is illustrated by figure 18.2. The Web browser and the IBM host are depicted as well.

Browsers and servers communicate using the Web-standard HTTP and TCP/IP protocols. Web severs, in turn, communicate to external programs (such as the Web-to-host gateway software) via a defined interface. The common gateway interface (CGI) is the standard interface supported by all commercial Web servers. While CGI is clearly a cross platform standard for Web servers, it does have its drawbacks—particularly in terms of performance. Thus, it is often viewed as the lowest common denominator.

In response, both Netscape and Microsoft have defined their own proprietary programming interfaces (NSAPI and ISAPI, respectively) to overcome the inadequacies of

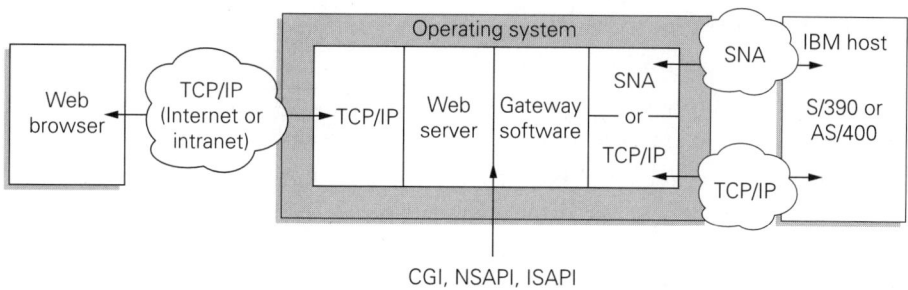

Figure 18.2   Web-to-host access usage

CGI. Gateway software that is written to support the standard CGI interface can be used with virtually any Web server that supports the same operating system environment. Gateway software that is written to support only ISAPI or NSAPI will be tied to that vendor's Web server. Some Web-to-host gateway vendors have written their software to support either CGI, NSAPI or ISAPI. This is the preferable approach, since by doing so, customers are free to select which Web server suits their total needs best.

Typically, the Web-to-host gateway communicates to the IBM host using SNA. In this case, the Web-to-host gateway software will rely upon a separate software component to provide the SNA protocol support (e.g., Microsoft SNA Server for Windows NT). Note that if the mainframe supports TCP/IP, then it is possible for the Web-to-host gateway to use that protocol instead. In this case, an SNA protocol stack would not be required on Web-to-host gateway. Instead, the same TCP/IP protocol stack used for Web communications would be used for the host communications.

The Web-to-host gateway software is responsible for mapping among the various web-centric and host-centric protocols and data streams. This protocol mapping and data stream conversion is the core of the Web-to-host gateway products.

Web protocols: HTTP and HTML

Figure 18.3 shows the protocol stack used for client/server communication on the Web. The network layer protocol is IP which enables operation over the Internet or private intranets. The upper layer protocol, HTTP, requires a reliable connection between client and server. Therefore, TCP is used to provide the client/server connection.

HTTP is the application-level protocol that browsers use to interact with Web servers. HTTP

| Hypertext markup language (HTML) |
| Hypertext transfer protocol (HTTP) |
| Transmission control protocol (TCP) |
| Internet protocol (IP) |

Figure 18.3 Web protocol stack

enables clients and servers to exchange information about their capabilities, and it is the protocol used by Web clients (browsers) to access information that resides on Web servers. Browsers access information on Web servers by sending HTTP requests. The Web servers return the requested information in HTTP responses.

The information on Web pages is formatted using the HTML. HTML is based on the industry's standard generalized markup language (SGML). HTML controls the positioning and formatting of text and graphics on Web pages. It also defines links to other pages and can be used to create data entry forms and clickable image maps that can be used to navigate through information.

18.5.2 Types of gateways

To integrate the features and services of the Web with those of an established host system, a Web-to-host gateway must perform certain functions. Furthermore, each of the three major Web-to-host categories mentioned above requires certain unique functionality. Stated differently, the functionality required to support host document access/delivery is different from the functionality required to support host database access. Similarly, the functionality required to support host database access is different from the functionality required to support host application access.

Typically, the required functionality occurs within software that runs on a computer system that serves as a gateway between the Web and the host. Such a gateway usually includes three other software components: (1) a Web server to facilitate access from Web browsers, (2) the necessary TCP/IP communications software to support the gateway's connection to the Internet/intranet, and (3) the necessary SNA communications software to support the gateway's connection to the IBM host. While it is common for all four of these components to run on a single system, it is also possible to distribute them across multiple systems. This is often desirable for purposes of scalability, redundancy, administration, or load balancing.

The next three sections discuss each type of Web-to-host gateway in more detail. The text and figures show that a separate Web-to-host gateway would be used to meet each of the three major requirements. While this is certainly possible, a single system could also be used provided that: (1) the gateway software components run under the same operating system, (2) the gateway software components can co-exist without conflict within the same system, and (3) the gateway software components do not overload the processing resources or I/O capabilities of a single system.

Host document access and delivery   Most organizations use their host systems to generate and print a tremendous volume of reports and business documents on an ongoing basis. Although we don't usually think of the mainframe as a publishing engine, in essence, it is. This content may be for internal dissemination and use (e.g., daily, weekly, or monthly financial summaries), or it may be for external dissemination and use (e.g., customer quotes, invoices, or statements). In either case, Web technology is ideally suited for facilitating dissemination of, or access to, this type of content.

A Web-to-host gateway that supports document access and delivery leverages the power of the Web to organize, publish, and/or disseminate content generated by the host. To meet this requirement, a Web-to-host gateway must do a number of things, including:

- Receiving the document from the host; ideally, this will be done in such a way that the host application will never know that its output is destined for the Web rather than a real printer.

- Transforming the content of the document from the host's content format (e.g., AFP) to that of the Web (e.g., HTML).

- Storing the document in a file system or repository that facilitates easy access and retrieval when needed; in some cases, the organization might also want to send some or all of the document as an attachment to an Internet email message.

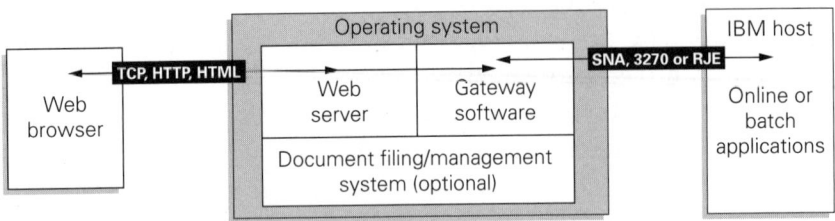

Figure 18.4 Document access and delivery

By using a Web-to-host gateway in this manner, organizations can affect immediate and significant operational cost reductions (e.g., reducing paper and transportation costs). Additionally, the use of such a Web-to-host gateway can help an organization improve its responsiveness and the level of service it provides to both internal and external customers.

Host database access   As we discussed earlier, much of the data that resides on mainframes has been restructured over time into standard relational database formats (e.g., SQL). By adopting such application-independent forms of data organization, businesses can permit geographically dispersed computer systems (and their users) to gain access to host-resident data. Access to, and management of, such relational databases is controlled by a host-resident software component called a relational database management system (RDBMS). Through the facilities and services of the RDBMS, data can be accessed by any program (or user) that is suitably authorized, and that understands the set of common verbs used to express a query and manipulate the database.

A Web-to-host gateway that supports "host database access allows Web users to access these host-resident relational databases. Such a Web-to-host gateway may support direct access, indirect access, or both. Direct access implies that the end user (using a Web browser) specifies the exact database query to be sent to the host and processed by the RDBMS. Indirect access implies that the database query is formulated on behalf of the user by another program—usually one that is running on the Web server.

Many Web-to-host gateways that support host database access work in conjunction with an RDBMS that runs on the Web server itself. Assuming that the server-resident and host-resident RDBMSs are compatible, this shifts much of the processing burden away from the actual gateway code. When configured in this manner, the Web-to-host gateway must:

- Accept the request for host database access from the Web browser.

- Translate the request into a form that is acceptable to the server-resident RDBMS and pass the request to it (at this point, the server-resident RDBMS takes responsibility for relaying the query to the host-resident RDBMS, and receiving the resulting data).

- Format the data received from the host (actually from the server-resident RDBMS) into a form suitable for presentation to the end user.

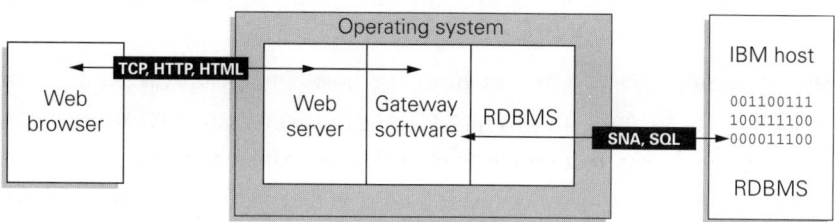

Figure 18.5   Database access

An endless array of possibilities exists for presenting the data to the end user. On the simplistic end of the spectrum, the data could be formatted as a table, using HTML, and then sent to the Web browser for viewing. On the more complex end of the spectrum, the data could be used as input to a separate application running on the Web server. Such an application might have been developed using an object-oriented Web application development tool. The middle of this spectrum might be represented by the use of a Java applet or ActiveX control that provides the user with certain options as to how the host data is displayed (or even manipulated). Regardless of the approach taken, since the host-resident data was received in a highly structured format, the amount of work that the gateway software must perform to prepare the data for presentation is significantly reduced.

Host application access A Web-to-host gateway that supports host application access supports controlled access from a Web browser to interactive applications that reside and execute on the host. For example, such an interactive application might be one or more transactions that run under the control of CICS or IMS. Interactive applications running on IBM hosts are designed to be accessed by 3270 or 5250 terminal users. Thus, a Web-to-host gateway that supports host application access must enable a user at a Web browser to look, or function, like one of these terminals.

To accomplish its purpose, such a Web-to-host gateway must do a number of things, including:

- Accepting the request for host application access from the Web browser user; maintain a session, or the functional equivalent of a session, between the Web browser and the gateway

- Initiating and maintaining an SNA LU–LU session with the host-resident application; maintain the association between the Web browser and the host session

- Maintain a context between the Web browser and the gateway whereby the various operational states of a 3270 or 5250 terminal can be detected, honored, and enforced

- Receiving the output data stream sent from the host application (i.e., a 3270 or 5250 formatted data stream); process and transform this data stream, if necessary, for presentation to the Web browser user

- Receiving input data that is entered by the user, and sent by means of the Web browser; process and transform this data stream, if necessary, and send it to the host application as input

You may have noticed that a Web-to-host gateway that facilitates application access has a much different job description than either a document access/delivery or database access gateway. Application access gateways must be designed around the need for dynamic, bidirectional transformation of host application data streams in real time.

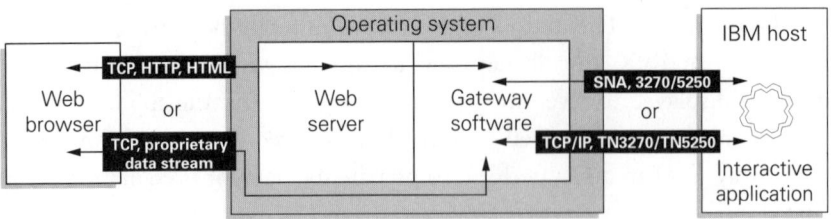

Figure 18.6 Application access

Furthermore, given the potential breadth and depth of functionality that can reside within such a gateway, one might expect the vendors of such products to take different approaches in their design and implementation. This, in fact, is the case, and we will discuss this further.

18.5.3 Summary

This section has examined the unique purpose and requirements for three different types of Web-to-host gateways.

Web-to-host products that facilitate document access or database access are somewhat simplified by the assumptions they are allowed to make. For example, Web-to-host products that facilitate document access and delivery are simplified by the assumption that data is moved (or published) in only one direction (from the host to the Web). Furthermore, Web-to-host products that facilitate host database access are simplified by the assumption that the data on the IBM host is structured in a standard form, and that a standard set of operators exist to manipulate it.

By way of contrast, there are few if any factors that simplify host application access. Web-to-host products that facilitate host application access involve moving data bidirectionally, and in real time. They also must transform interactive data streams from one content format to another (e.g., 3270-to-HTML, and vice versa). Due to these factors, and many others, host application access is usually considered to be the most complicated of the three. For this reason, the remainder of this chapter will focus on using Web technology to access IBM host applications.

18.6 Web-to-host application access gateways

To fulfill their purpose, Web-to-host gateways that provide application access must deal with a high degree of complexity. In light of this, it should come as no surprise to learn that a great deal of variation exists among the products that fall in this category. In fact, so much variation exists that it is helpful, if not necessary, to classify these products into certain subcategories.

18.6.1 Product classifications

The first classification we will consider is based upon end-user requirements. The second classification is based upon the core functionality provided by the Web-to-host application access product.

End-user requirements   One way to analyze an organization's requirement for a Web-to-host application access gateway, as well as the gateway products themselves, is to pose two questions that relate to the end users of the gateway's functionality:

- Where are they?
- What do they know?

Where are they?   This first question seeks to understand whether the end users are inside or outside the organization's formal boundaries. An alternative way of assessing this would be to ask, "Which side of the firewall are they on?"

This is important because not all products are suitable for extending access to users on both sides of the firewall. The operational, customization, and security requirements can be very different depending upon whether the user is an insider (on an intranet) or outsider (on the Internet). It is possible for Web-to-host gateway vendors to make certain trade-offs that make their product better suited for one requirement versus the other.

What do they know?   This second question seeks to assess how the end users will want to access the host application. Another way to think of this is to ask, "Which learning curve do we, or they, want to be on?"

Earlier in this chapter, we noted that the Web browser is historically significant because, for the first time, individuals both inside and outside the organization are on the same learning curve with respect to the tools and technology they use to access information. Web users are accustomed to accessing information and applications by means of a graphical, point-and-click interface. In contrast, users of 3270/5250 terminals use a combination of alphanumeric keyboard input and control keys to navigate within host-based applications.

With this in mind, a quick survey of Web-to-host product offerings reveals two basic approaches. One which extends the life of the existing 3270 learning curve; another which leverages the new Web Browser learning curve.

Extending the old learning curve   Products that fall into this first category present the host application to the end user using the traditional 3270 terminal interface: a character-oriented screen with 24 rows and 80 columns. Conceptually, these products are just like the 3270 terminal emulation products that have been around for a decade. In this case, however, the 3270 emulator is invoked by means of a Web browser and runs either inside or outside of the browser's window. (These products will be discussed further in the next section.)

These types of products are best suited for use in situations where the end user is already well versed in accessing host applications via a 3270 terminal emulator. In practical terms, this excludes everyone outside of the organization's formal boundaries (anyone on the Internet), and probably also excludes many of the organization's own employees. Thus, products that fall into this category are not well suited for extending access to users who have not already climbed the 3270 learning curve.

Provided that the organization has targeted the correct audience, deploying such a product can make very good financial sense. Such a product can help the organization lower the total cost of ownership for providing host application access (compared to the use of traditional PC-based terminal emulators). Just remember that these products are best suited for providing legacy users with access to legacy applications on an intranet.

Leveraging the new learning curve   Products that fall into this category present the host application to the end user with a true Web interface. These types of products are best suited for use in situations where the end user has no familiarity with using 3270 host applications. In practical terms, this includes everyone outside the organization's formal boundaries, and probably also includes many of the organization's own employees.

Products that fall into this category are well suited for extending host access to users who have never climbed the 3270 learning curve (and see no compelling reason to do so). They are best used to provide new users with access to host applications via the Internet or an intranet.

Summary   Figure 18.7 illustrates the matrix formed by these two questions, and the two potential answers to each questions. Using this matrix will help organizations assess their requirements, and focus their attention on the appropriate Web-to-host application access products.

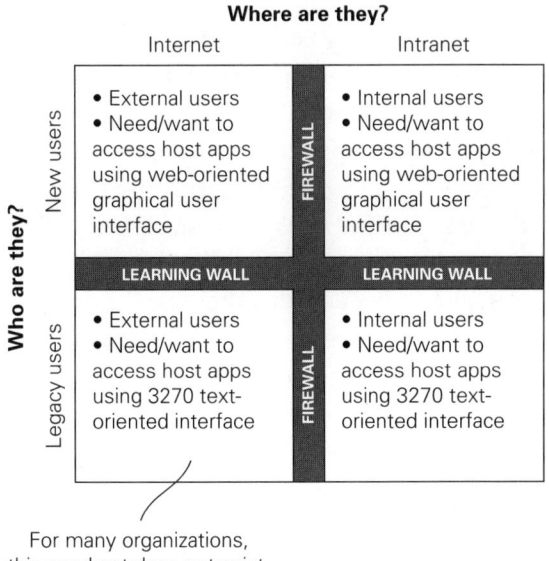

For many organizations, this quadrant does not exist.

Figure 18.7   Web-to-host users and needs

Core Functionality   Another way to classify Web-to-host application access products is based upon the core functionality provided by the product. Three broad categories exist at this time:

- Products that provide basic 3270 terminal emulation capabilities, but within a Web browser window/context
- Products that perform dynamic 3270-to-HTML data stream conversion
- Products that provide a development environment and a collection of tools to allow customers to create their own Web-to-host application

These are broad categories, and as such, should be viewed as having rather soft boundaries. Thus, an alternative way of viewing these three categories would be as points along a spectrum, as shown in figure 18.8.

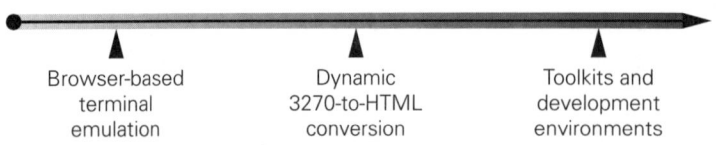

Figure 18.8   Products' positioning spectrum

Browser-based terminal emulation   Depicted on the left end of the spectrum, are those products that essentially provide 3270 terminal emulation, but within a Web browser window. The actual terminal emulation is usually performed on the client, and within the browser, by a Java applet that is downloaded from the Web server. A server-side component is used to facilitate access to the SNA host.

Once downloaded and invoked, the first thing the applet does is establish a connection back to the server-side component. However, rather than connecting back through the Web server to communicate with this component, the applet establishes a direct TCP/IP socket connection. (The security implications of this will be discussed later.) Note that the server-side component can usually be run on either the same system as the Web server or a different system.

The companies which offer these products tend to be those which also offer traditional 3270 terminal emulation products. For them, this was a natural point of entry into the Web-to-host market since they had 3270 terminal emulation code sitting on the shelf. By-and-large, these offerings provide fewer customization capabilities and somewhat buck the trend toward thinner clients. Rather than putting a true Web interface on the host application, they perpetuate the 3270 text-based interface that the application has had all along. On the positive side, these products can be of immediate value and benefit to many organizations.

Development environments and toolkits   At the right end of this spectrum are vendors who offer a toolkit or development environment. These products usually include a terminal emulator along with a collection of VBXs, OCXs, ActiveX controls and/or Java applets. The customer then uses these elements to design and develop a highly customized front end for accessing a particular host-resident application. Since these products require an up-front investment in time for code development, they offer very little immediate benefit upon installation.

Note that some of the products that are thought to fall in this category aren't really Web-to-host products at all. That is, they don't do anything to put a true Web-centric face on the host application. Instead, they put a Windows-centric face on the application, making them Windows-to-host products.

Dynamic 3270-to-HTML conversion   Depicted in the middle of the spectrum are those products that perform dynamic HTML-to-3270 translation. As previously discussed, HTML is the language used to control positioning and formatting of text and graphics on Web pages. Thus, the face of the Web is created using HTML. If the objective is to extend access to host applications using a truly Web-centric interface, then HTML will usually play an integral role. These products typically rely upon a server-side component to perform the 3270-to-HTML conversion and facilitate access to the SNA host. They are easy to administer and promote the use of a very thin client (in some cases only a rudimentary browser is required).

By-and-large, 3270-to-HTML conversion products provide much greater customization capabilities than do the browser-based terminal emulation products. However, these products fall short of the wholesale customization capabilities of those products that are fashioned as toolkits or development environments. Unlike the toolkit solutions, 3270-to-HTML products offer immediate benefit to organizations and end users after installation.

Summary   All of the Web-to-host application access products available today entered the market at a particular point along this spectrum. Whatever their point of entry may have been, vendors are enhancing their product to cover as many points along this spectrum as possible. Over time, it may become increasingly difficult to discern the true nature, or core competency, of the products available in this market. Stay tuned.

18.6.2 Design issues

The networking industry has a long history of developing gateways and protocol conversion products to interconnect different networking environments. For example, in the early days of SNA, ASCII terminals were cheap and widely used and it wasn't long before protocol converters were developed to make ASCII terminals function as 3270 display stations. This is similar to the current situation where vendors and customers are seeking to leverage the exploding population of cheap (sometimes free) Web browsers.

When it comes to designing and implementing protocol conversion gateways, vendors and customers alike must be cognizant of the features and functions that are available in one environment but not the other. Such is the case when interfacing Web browsers with IBM host applications. To successfully provide access to host applications via the Web, any number of differences must be overcome. Understanding these differences is imperative. Understanding which are truly significant issues in a given situation, or for a particular application, is equally important.

Three issues that must be addressed by any Web-to-host application access gateway are:

- Synchronizing browsers and host applications
- Keyboard mapping
- Security

We will now consider each of these issues in more detail. Note that not all products resolve these differences or issues in the same way; the best solution in one situation may not be the best solution in another.

Synchronizing browsers and host applications   While SNA 3270 and 5250 protocols ensure that strict synchronization is maintained between 3270 terminals and host-based applications, Web browsers are only loosely coupled to their servers. The diagrams below illustrate how SNA sessions are supported in a conventional SNA environment and how sessions are supported by Web-to-host gateways.

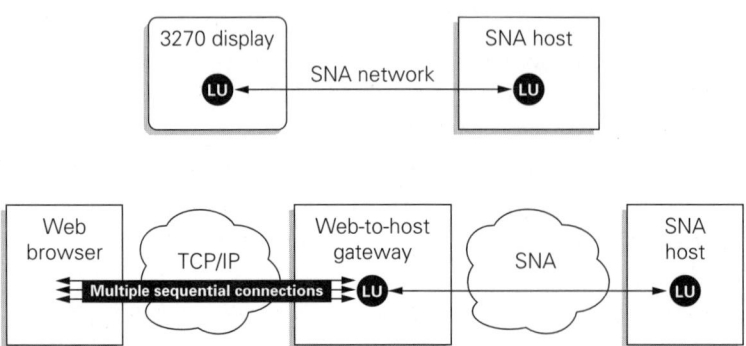

Figure 18.9   Synchronizing Web browsers with SNA terminal applications

In conventional SNA networks, 3270/5250 terminals are logically connected to host-based applications by an end-to-end LU–LU session. This is shown at the top of the diagram. When Web-to-host gateways are used, the LU–LU session extends from the host to the gateway, not the browser. This is shown at the bottom of the diagram. The gateway software is responsible for synchronizing the browser-to-server connection with the LU–LU session.

Keeping the actions of the user/browser synchronized with the host application is complicated by the fact that each request/response interaction between a Web browser and a server is usually a separate TCP connection. Furthermore, the Web server itself usually maintains no state information across TCP connections, and each interaction between the browser and the server is independent of the others. These complications stem from certain characteristics of HTTP, the underlying request/response protocol that browsers and servers use to communicate (more on this later). However, the Web-to-host gateway overcomes these complications, it must address certain key synchronization issues.

Key synchronization issues A Web-to-host gateway that facilitates application access must address two important synchronization issues: (1) unsolicited screen updates and (2) implicit session termination.

It is permissible for a host application to update the contents of the screen of it's own accord, and not in response to a specific user request. A Web-to-host gateway should be able to handle such unsolicited screen updates. To do so, the Web-to-host server component, along with any client side component, must be able to do two things. First, the server must know, or be able to determine, whether the user has begun entering data in response to the prior screen displayed by the host application. Second, the server must be able to deliver the updated information to the browser so that the display area is updated accordingly.

One common method for handling unsolicited host updates involves using a software component running on the client system (e.g., a Java applet or plug-in running under the auspices of the browser). Such a client-side software component can stand ready to receive notification from the server that the host application has generated an unsolicited screen update. Furthermore, the client software can detect whether the user has begun entering input in response to the previous screen.

Note that most host applications do not generate unsolicited screen updates. That is, they have been designed to only update the screen in response to input from the end user. When using such applications, the need for the Web-to-host gateway to handle unsolicited screen updates is minimized or negated.

Handling implicit session termination implies that the Web-to-host gateway can be made aware of two situations: (1) when the user has jumped to a different URL and

(2) when the user has terminated their browser. Both of these situations constitute an implicit termination of the host session and should be handled as such.

As with unsolicited host updates, a common method for handling implicit session termination involves the use of a client-side software component that can detect these two situations. Once the client-side software detects either of these situations, it should inform the Web-to-host gateway software running on the server. The Web-to-host gateway will then terminate the host session.

Implementation alternatives   As mentioned previously, keeping the actions of the user/browser synchronized with the host application is complicated by certain characteristics of HTTP, the underlying request/response protocol that browsers and servers use to communicate.

The initial versions of HTTP (versions 0.9 and 1.0) did not support any notion of a persistent connection between an HTTP client (browser) and server. Furthermore, the Web became so popular, so fast, that the depth of the underlying protocols did not evolve as fast as the breadth of the potential applications. To remedy this situation, various initiatives began within the Internet community to enhance HTTP. At the time of this writing, the specifications for HTTP version 1.1 have been finalized and vendors have begun implementation. HTTP 1.1 permits the client and server to maintain their connection, exchanging multiple requests and responses until one party explicitly closes the connection.

Even with support for persistent connections, HTTP 1.1 remains a stateless protocol (no information is retained by the server between requests). Thus, Web-to-host gateway vendors are still left to their own devices to keep the actions of the user/browser synchronized with the host application. Two basic approaches have surfaced, embellishing HTTP and circumventing HTTP.

One approach is to create the effect of a persistent session by adding functionality on top of HTTP. By using one or more techniques, a unique identity can be created for each Web user that is accessing a host application through the gateway. This identity is then used to tie a specific user to a specific host session. The use of a token or "cookie" passing mechanism is one such technique. Since these techniques layer on top of HTTP, they are firewall friendly (no nonstandard points of entry into or through the firewall are required). Furthermore, Web-to-host gateway products that leverage HTTP are poised to take advantage of newer versions of the protocol as it continues to evolve.

Another approach is to completely bypass HTTP by deploying a software component on the client side (e.g., a Java applet) that creates and maintains a private and persistent TCP/IP socket connection with a companion software component running on the server. While this approach can work quite nicely, it is not without certain implications. One implication of bypassing HTTP is that the industry standard security facilities built into Web browsers and servers are also bypassed. Having bypassed these powerful data-encryption and user-authentication facilities, the Web-to-host gateway must implement its own.

Circumventing HTTP by establishing a private and persistent TCP/IP socket connection between the browser environment and the Web-to-host gateway can have at least two serious side effects. First, it can create security risks and complications. Second, it can limit the population of Web users who can access the Web-to-host gateway. Each of these points will be discussed next.

Security risks and complications To establish a private and persistent TCP/IP socket connection, one or more TCP/IP ports must be assigned for this purpose. The software that runs on both the client and server must agree on which ports are to be used.

Two key functions of a firewall are to ensure that (1) the traffic that passed through it occurs on standard well-known ports, and (2) the traffic abides by standard protocols (e.g., HTTP, FTP, etc.). Note, however, that the use of a persistent TCP/IP connection uses a nonstandard port and a propriety protocol. Thus, when a Web-to-host gateway that uses a persistent connection is located behind a firewall, a hole must be created in the firewall. While organizations can do this if they wish, there is little doubt that turning your firewall into Swiss cheese should be avoided.

If all of the end users are inside the organization, then this implication of a persistent connection may not be an issue, because the Web-to-host session traffic may not have to pass through a firewall. If, however, the end users are located outside the organization, then using nonstandard points of entry, and nonstandard protocols, should be avoided. End users who are outside the firewall could include customers, distributors, agents, business partners, and even employees who are traveling or working at home.

If the end users are outsiders, then the organization must be prepared to accept the firewall implications of a persistent connection. Since the organization does have a high degree of control over the Web-to-host gateway and the host system in general, then it is plausible that they may be willing to make the necessary accommodations in their firewall. If so, the Web-to-host gateway will be accessible to two classes of end users: (1) those who are inside the firewall and (2) those who are outside the firewall, but whose traffic does not pass through another firewall at their end of connection.

Note that another possibility would be to locate the Web-to-host gateway outside the firewall. In this case, the only thing standing between the end users and the host is the Web-to-host gateway. While this may eliminate the need to punch a hole in the firewall, it obviously raises other security concerns.

Limited end user access One of the most important questions an organization can ask before implementing a Web-to-host gateway is "Where are the users?" If the end users will be outside the formal boundaries of the organization, then a Web-to-host gateway that uses a persistent connection between the client and the server can severely limit the population of end users who can access the host. To understand why, the organization must realize that their firewall is probably not the only firewall involved.

Consider the following three types of Web-to-host end users who may be outside the organization's formal boundaries:

- An end user who is accessing the Internet through their organization's intranet and firewall (e.g., an employee of a company who is a business partner).

- An end user who is accessing the Internet through a full-service ISP (e.g., a small distributor or an employee working from home).

- An end user who is accessing the Internet through an information service such as CompuServe or America Online (e.g., a customer or an international business partner).

In each of these cases, the end user exists within an environment where their traffic passes through a firewall at their end of the connection before it ever gets to the Internet. In fact, it is possible that multiple firewalls may be involved in handling the traffic before it ever reaches the Internet, your firewall and the Web-to-host gateway. As a result, if the software running adjunct to the Web-browser uses of a persistent connection between it and the Web-to-host gateway, then a hole will have to be punched in each of these firewalls.

Perhaps it should go without saying, but deciding to punch a hole in your firewall is one thing; asking another organization or service provider to punch one in theirs is quite another. The bottom line is that if the end users of the Web-to-host gateway will be outside the formal boundaries of the organization, then the use a persistent connection between the client and the server can severely limit the population of end users who can access the host. At the very least, it can create implementation nightmare.

Keyboard mapping A fundamental difference between the Web and IBM host environments is how users navigate within an application. Users of Web browsers are accustomed to navigating through hypertext pages and Web applications by means of a graphical, point-and-click interface. In contrast, users of 3270/5250 terminals use a combination of alphanumeric keyboard input and control keys to navigate within host-based applications. These control keys, which have special meaning to host applications, include such keys as ENTER, CLEAR and SYSREQ, as well as the program function (PF) keys and program attention (PA) keys.

Since Web browsers do not provide direct support for these control keys, Web-to-host application access gateways usually display icons within the browser's screen space to represent them. The icons usually appear as buttons and are labeled with the name of the key they represent (e.g., PF3 or PA1). Pointing to a button and selecting it using the mouse activates these graphical control keys. This causes the gateway to send the appropriate control key information to the host.

Some gateways also allow customers to define meaningful labels that appear on the control key icons. This can be quite helpful since control key icons can be labeled to describe their application function (e.g., END), rather than the name of the control key (e.g., PF12). Some gateways allow the customer to tailor their screens to display only the control keys that are relevant within a particular host application context. Again, this is very helpful.

It may seem odd that the F1–F12 keys on a standard PC keyboard cannot be used as though they were the PF1–PF12 keys of a 3270/5250 keyboard. The reason is quite simple: Web browsers don't support them. (At least not at the time of this writing.) Recognizing the value of mapping the keyboard in this manner, some Web-to-host vendors have overcome this problem by developing Java applets or ActiveX controls that augment the browser's normal handling of the keyboard.

Security   One of the greatest concerns about using the Internet for business applications is security. While tight security may be optional for some applications, it is essential for others, such as online banking. Fortunately, there are several ways to authenticate the identity of systems and users on the Internet and encrypt the data that flows between Web browsers and servers. The two industry-standard Internet security schemes that have emerged are:

- Secure sockets layer (SSL)
- Secure hypertext transfer protocol (S-HTTP)

SSL provides encryption and authentication services at the transport layer. This means that SSL can be used to secure HTTP messages as well as other application-level protocols, such as FTP and Telnet. One drawback of SSL is that it encrypts and decrypts all data flowing between a pair of applications. This increases processing overhead for transactions that require security for only selected fields, such as credit card numbers. Another shortcoming of SSL is that it authenticates only servers. In some applications, such as online banking, there is a requirement to authenticate the clients who are attempting to use the service.

S-HTTP is an extension to the Web's HTTP protocol and, therefore, cannot secure data used by other applications, such as FTP or Telnet. Unlike SSL, S-HTTP can selectively encrypt fields within HTTP requests and responses, thus minimizing processing overhead. S-HTTP can also authenticate both clients and servers.

Despite these differences, both SSL and S-HTTP can effectively secure communications on the Web. As a result, these security features are being widely implemented in Web browser and server products. As was alluded to above, not all Web-to-host gateway products have been designed to take advantage of these industry standard security facilities. Thus, if security is an important consideration, the burden of proof should be placed on these products to demonstrate that their user authentication and data encryption facilities are comparable. Even then, due consideration should be exercised before adopting vendor-specific or proprietary security schemes.

18.6.3 Other factors

A number of other factors should be taken into account when evaluating Web-to-host Application Access gateways. Three such factors are discussed below.

Operational recommendations   Unlike IBM 3270/5250 terminals, Web browsers were never designed to be dumb terminals. For example, most browsers have features such as local caching to improve performance. When enabled, information received from a server is cached so that subsequent requests for the same information can be handled without intervention from the server. Most Web browsers also have local navigation features that (a) remember the sequence of pages (URLs) retrieved by the user, and (b) allow the user to browse through these pages using forward and back buttons.

Use of these features can result in a loss of synchronization between the Web browser and the Web-to-host gateways. Gateway vendors often deal with these issues by providing users with a set of operational recommendations. These recommendations might include:

- Turn browser caching off when accessing a host application.
- Don't use the browser's forward and back buttons when accessing a host application; they will not allow you to navigate the host application.
- Don't use the browser's reload button to attempt to redraw a host application screen; instead, use the refresh or redraw button that the Web-to-host gateway displays on the screen.

Over time, advancements in HTML and browser implementations should minimize or eliminate such operational recommendations in the future.

Performance: intranets versus the Internet   One of the key advantages of the Web is that it relies on the Internet's low-cost and widespread communications facilities. Internet access is very inexpensive because the facilities are shared by a large population of users. This sharing also has disadvantages. Of concern to corporate users is that the performance of the Internet can fluctuate greatly. Thus, application and network designers must consider the performance characteristics of the Internet before using it as an alternative to conventional enterprise networks.

The performance of the global Internet can be summarized in two words—best efforts. Anyone who has used the Internet knows that its performance often fluctuates between excellent and unacceptable. When the Internet runs out of bandwidth it attempts to allocate the available bandwidth as fairly as possible. This is very different from corporate networks that use prioritization and bandwidth reservation to control end-user service levels.

While performance fluctuations are clearly unacceptable for certain applications, the Internet's performance is adequate for many applications. This is particularly true for new services and applications that are targeted at individuals who are already Internet users. Most of these users accept the Internet's fluctuating performance as normal. On the other hand, current users of corporate networks have higher performance and availability expectations and are likely to be much less tolerant of the Internet's performance.

These network performance issues are usually only relevant when the Web browser is communicating with the Web server over the public TCP/IP network—the Internet. Web browsers and servers can also communicate over private TCP/IP networks—referred to as intranets.

Since intranets are controlled by a single organization, they can be designed to avoid many of the network performance problems associated with the Internet. Network performance can still be an issue, but since access is usually limited to employees, the network can be more readily optimized or reengineered to deliver the required level of performance. As a result, implementing a Web-to-host gateway purely within an intranet environment mitigates many of the concerns regarding network performance.

Java—benefits and implications   The Java programming language makes it possible to significantly extend the functionality of Web browsers. The Java architecture involves downloading platform-independent application software components, called applets, from the Web server to the browser. Once downloaded, the program code contained within an applet is interpreted and executed by means of a Java virtual machine (JVM) that runs on the client computer system.

Although Java applets are restricted with respect to the kinds of operations they can perform on end users' systems, conceptually, Java applets can provide, facilitate, or enhance just about any type of functionality on the desktop. Thus, Java will enable application developers to perform virtually any type of application processing within the context of a Web browser. Obviously, this opens the door to a whole new wave of Web-centric client/server computing products and solutions.

In this chapter, we have seen how Web-to-host gateways must compensate for the differences between Web browsers and host applications. We have also observed how Web browsers, and the protocols they implement, have certain limitations that make the job of a Web-to-host gateway challenging. Thus, it should come as no surprise to see Web-to-host gateways leveraging the power of Java applets to enhanced host application access. Even simple Java applets could add important functionality such as enhanced keyboard management or input validation.

While Java applets can add useful functionality to Web browsers, there are certain implications that must also be considered. One such implication is that as more and more functionality is added to Java applets, the client-side software becomes thicker. Ironically, extensive use of Java applets can drive customers right back into a thick-client environment. Java, after all, is just a programming language. And, applications written in Java have many of the same thick-client problems as any piece of client software (e.g., increased CPU and memory requirements, and the support problems that stem from running distributed applications).

Organizations which envision widespread deployment of Java-enabled Web applications must also consider another implication: all of the Web browsers must be able to support Java. Given the facts that Java is a fairly recent innovation and that Java-capable browsers are still being developed, stabilized, and enhanced, this is a major consideration. The types and versions of Web browsers in use today are tremendously diverse. This is true within large organizations (and even those that are not so large); it is also true with respect to the Web browsers used by consumers. In the short run, a Web-to-host strategy that presumes a homogeneous base of Web browsers can be flawed from the outset.

The bottom line is that Java is a very powerful and useful extension to Web browser and server technology. However, it is not a panacea. Application designers and network managers should carefully balance its future potential with its current limitations.

18.7 Summary and conclusions

In this chapter, we have examined how Web technology can be used to enhance, extend, and leverage established IBM host environments. Two basic realities underlie our consideration of this topic. First, the Web is for real. Second, established host systems haven't gone and aren't going away. Therefore Web-to-host integration is a topic that few organizations can ignore.

Internet and Web technologies will grow to have an undeniable presence in most organizations within the next couple of years. And, it will be up to the IT professionals within these organizations to ensure that this technology is being used to its fullest potential. Merely taking advantage of Internet and Web technology for general surfing, email, or groupware ignores a critical and sustaining element within most large organizations: the host, the mainframe, the enterprise system—whatever one wishes to call it.

Even for those organizations that are continuing to move away from host systems, Web-to-host technology can play an important role. Organizations in the midst of migration often discover that retooling their application and networking infrastructure takes longer than they expected. As a result, organizations find that they must implement coexistence strategies. In this scenario, Web-to-host solutions can provide a tactical means to help organizations achieve their strategic plans and long-term goals.

In this day and age, organizations must deal with an oppressive rate of change. As a result, most organizations find themselves constantly trying to strike a balance between two, often conflicting, objectives. They want to leverage their existing computing and communications infrastructure, while at the same time take advantage of new and emerging technology. Whenever an organization is faced with such an existing–emerging dilemma, they look for innovative products, services, and solutions to help them integrate the disparate environments. Web-to-host gateway products exist for this very purpose. And by integrating Web technology with established host systems, organizations will be able to serve their customers better and to compete more effectively.

PART III

Emerging solutions

chapter 19

SNA applications and the promise of Java

James P. Gray
David L. Kaminsky
Phil Stone

According to the famous quote of the baseball legend Yogi Berra: "Prophecy is really hard... especially about the future." Substantiating this quote, in this first chapter in part III on emerging solutions James P. Gray, David L. Kaminsky, and Phil Stone describe the influence of CUA, client/server, and especially Java on presentation services within SNA applications. Smooth integration of Java into SNA networks without changes in existing applications or enterprise servers will allow enterprises that embrace Java to achieve cost savings in administering client/server systems. This chapter also presents the possible future of SNA enterprise networking as CUA-compliant client/server applications written in Java.

19.1 Introduction

In the past two decades, there have been a number of important paradigm shifts in the design, execution, and maintenance of SNA applications. While SNA introduced distributed processing in 1974, until the early 1980s the majority of applications resided on central servers and were accessed through the IBM 3270 terminal family. In the late 80s, designers of networked applications began using personal computers to take advantage of both the local processing available on PCs and of the user interface possibilities present on them. In turn, the exploitation of those devices has caused an explosion in the complexity and costs associated with some types of networked applications. Today, the use of Java-based clients promises to reduce the complexity and costs associated with the use of personal computers.

In this chapter we examine these shifts in SNA applications by discussing the impact of three computing innovations: graphical user interfaces, especially as embodied by the Common User Access (CUA) standard, client/server computing, and Java. We will establish that the future of SNA is CUA-compliant client/server applications written in Java.

19.2 The common user access revolution

Over the history of computer terminals, such as the 3270 and 5250 families, many different hardware configurations have been used to provide the same abstract model for the end user's device. The model consists of a rectangular grid of characters, usually but not always, 80 characters wide and 24 characters tall. The application makes decisions such as whether fields (strings of characters) are output-only or I/O.

Early 3270 controllers handled all cursor movement, placing keystrokes into individual input fields, and doing data-stream processing. Later designs moved keystroke and data-stream processing into the terminal. Emulators are usually built this way. At certain times, such as when the enter key or a function key is pressed, further user input is blocked while the host processes the input from that screen. As the terminals have developed, more features have been added. For example, support for color was added with the introduction of the 3279 terminal. Applications that are accessed by such terminals—the majority of existing applications as well as many new applications—use this model.

With the introduction of the Apple Macintosh in 1984, the state of the art in end-user presentation suddenly included high-level constructs that went well beyond arrays of characters. They included pop-up windows, menu bars, push buttons, scroll bars, and other components. These elements provided sophisticated cues to tell the user what to do and what not to do.

The design for these elements and their adoption across many applications helped end users transfer learning across applications. Programmers used the high-level constructs to build applications with interfaces that looked similar, even when the applications themselves differed greatly. Users who had previously used only a single application now used several.

In response, IBM and Microsoft defined a standard that embodied the ideas of the Macintosh and extended those ideas to include DOS character mode screens and 3270 terminals. Published as user interface style guides, the CUA standards cover many areas of user interface design, including windowing, window decorations, controls, error handling, help processing, and the desktop shell. CUA rules, some required, some optional, provide a yardstick for measuring CUA conformance.

19.3 CUA controls and windowing

An important feature of CUA is its replacement of 3270 fields with a set of about a dozen controls. Each control has a specific appearance and interaction technique. Text entry, text output, radio buttons, push buttons, check boxes, scroll bars, menu bars, title bars, group boxes, and various window decorations are the primitive control types. Each CUA control is designed to meet the needs of some common input scenario. The application developer selects controls that best serve the application and the user.

CUA goes beyond controls to address the use of windowing by applications. Before CUA, windows were used in limited ways in 3270 applications. For example the gas panel models of the 3270 family use tiled windows to support independent sessions, each requiring a separate logon. The CUA form of windowing goes deeper. Within a single session, or logon, CUA says multiple applications share the same screen through the use of separate windows.

CUA applications use multiple windows. CUA defines the primary window as the starting point for interaction with an application. The primary window is always active. At various times and for various reasons, the application can present additional windows. Help text, for example, is presented in help windows. If the application needs more parameters or needs to conduct a dialog with the user, one or more dialog windows can be used. The proliferation of such windows makes messy desk an apt name for this user interface metaphor.

19.4 Increasing user bandwidth

The goal of multiple sessions is to increase the amount of work the user can do through his computer. Likewise, multiple windows seek to increase the user's effectiveness. The interaction bandwidth, or ease with which useful data can pass between the computer and the end user, is a central component of effectiveness. Various rules are included in the CUA standards that have the purpose of increasing bandwidth.

When an application needs parameters for some operation, it presents a dialog window to accept them. While waiting for the user to supply the information, the application often blocks interaction with other windows. The active window is said to be modal when this happens. Because blocked windows can not be used for interaction, they decrease the overall bandwidth between the end user and the computing system. For that reason, CUA stresses the idea that modal situations are to be avoided whenever possible.

CUA suggests many subtle ways that applications can reduce and prevent errors. The time taken to correct bad input decreases the effective bandwidth of the user interface. When errors are prevented before they happen, the effective bandwidth increases. Many CUA rules, indeed many of the CUA controls, have the purpose of preventing errors instead of correcting them after they happen.

19.5 CUA application structure

While CUA compliance increases user productivity, it comes at a cost. Businesses are often running applications that do not conform to CUA, and increasing the restructuring cost is the fact that the 3270 model is at odds with the CUA standard. The 3270 hardware infrastructure suggests a synchronous model, where the user acts, the application then operates on the user's data, and the user again acts. Terminal users can identify this model by the X at the bottom of 3270 screens. When the X is present, input is blocked because the application is working. When the X is gone, the user can type, trusting that the application will not interfere with the screen.

Server support for synchronous user interaction can be supplied simply through subroutine calls. On OS/390, for example, ISPF and CICS both use subroutines, although in slightly different ways. ISPF calls subroutines that return when the X is presented. In contrast, CICS applications are called when the X is presented. In either case synchronous subroutine calls reflect the synchronous user interface.

CUA extends the synchronous model of user interaction. Except during modal dialog processing, CUA applications may have several simultaneously active windows, several of which are interactive. (Many help windows, for example, are not interactive.) If one window is busy, the others are still available to accept input. No simple synchronous structure fits this model, and existing applications that are modified to be CUA-compliant become more complex in their dispatching structure.

When multiple windows are available to the user, CUA applications must handle multiple concurrent inputs from the same user. To handle such input, CUA systems implement event handling to sequence and dispatch the work coming into the application from the end user, and application-level multitasking to allow work to be performed behind the primary event-handling layer.

The CUA standards are designed for use on both alphanumeric terminals and full GUI displays. Each control type is specified in both pixel-based GUI and alphanumeric forms. The CUA character editing rules, for example, include an overstrike model taken directly from the editing behavior of 3270 terminals. CUA rules are written so there is transfer of learning between the alphanumeric and the pixel-based renderings of each CUA construct.

PC DOS applications have adopted the CUA character-cell model extensively. Since personal computers contain full-function CPUs, it is easy for operating system suppliers to add CUA subroutine libraries to their character-based operating systems. In addition, because the applications are executed on a local CPU in close proximity to the screen, controls such as scrollbars can be implemented using instantaneous feedback from the local CPU. This allows the alphanumeric CUA model to work well on DOS machines.

The CUA standard includes 3270 constructs such as editing rules, but the 3270 data-stream does not fully support CUA. Since they have a synchronous user interaction model, 3270 terminals depend on application servers to simulate windowing. If the user selects one window and in that window starts a long running process, the user is blocked from interacting with another window, breaking the CUA rule against modality. While application level multitasking can overcome this problem, such multitasking is difficult to implement in languages and application subsystems designed for the synchronous 3270 world.

Without native support for most of the controls, 3270 terminals need simulation of pop-up windows, menu bars, list boxes and other controls. For each of these CUA elements, the application or its supporting subsystem regenerates the 3270 data-stream based on an abstract model of what the user is seeing; the 3270 does not hold the application's model for the user interface. Since the model is stored with the application rather than with the desktop, more network trips are needed to support CUA than are needed when the 3270 contains the user's model of the application.

19.6 GUI CUA: client/server

With 3270 systems unable to fully support CUA, and with applications unable to fit just on desktop systems, something more is needed. The solution is client/server applications, in which CUA processing is done on the desktop and other application processing is done in servers. The desktop is connected to the servers by a network protocol. SNA client/server applications often use APPC across the network. But when an application development team decides to build a client/server application with a CUA style of interface, they are faced with new problems. Client GUI programming libraries are large; the network, which can be largely ignored when 3270 libraries are used, has to be handled explicitly; network failures affect the application in new ways; and care has to be taken to make the application responsive to the user.

19.7 Client independence

It is desirable for applications to be independent of the details of the terminal or GUI client. This is an issue for terminals since various models have different screen sizes and different features such as color or graphics. But applications can be written to a common denominator: 80 by 24 noncolor, or, they can be written to use output formatting definitions, for example, Basic Mapping Services in CICS. When necessary they can require a certain level of support or can adapt to various features. With GUI client/server applications the story is more complicated. The different types of client-operating systems force development teams to deal with the issue of platform leveling—that is, making dissimilar platforms look the same. Since part of the application runs on the client, and uses the local operating system, it is harder to achieve GUI client independence than to achieve terminal independence.

19.8 Client/server experiences

In the past five years or so, the industry has gained considerable experience with client/server environments. The overall PC cost of ownership, including software, has turned out to be $13,000 to $18,000 per year per PC. This is much higher than the relatively low costs associated with terminal ownership, which are in the $2,000 per-year per-desk range. Thus, while users still want the productivity benefits of CUA-style interfaces, the associated costs must also be considered by the enterprise. It is important to understand what factors contribute to these high costs. Table 19.1 shows the Gartner Group's breakdown of ownership costs (as cited in *Forbes Magazine*, October 21, 1996, 280–288).

Table 19.1   Breakdown of PC ownership costs

Factor	Cost	Percentage
Hardware/software	$2,730	21%
Technical support	$3,510	27%
System administration	$1,170	9%
User time	$5,590	43%

We see that much of the cost results from administering the PCs. For a deeper understanding of cost comparison, we must examine some of the characteristics of PCs and terminals that contribute to the cost differential. One obvious difference is that PCs enable GUI presentations while terminals are primarily limited to character output. Even when a 3270 application implements the CUA standard, PC GUIs are more visually appealing, and often more intuitive for users. This difference does not increase client/server cost-of-ownership. In fact, done correctly, GUIs can increase user productivity, although that factor is typically not measured with cost-of-ownership, and is not reflected in the table.

A second distinction is that PCs have full-function processors while terminals are limited primarily to rendering. Looking back at the table, there is no indication that the full-function processor itself contributes significantly to the cost-of-ownership. Given the rapid decline in CPU prices, this is not surprising.

The distinction that does have a considerable effect is that client/server applications require client installation on each PC. In contrast, terminals use dynamic download where all the client behavior (screen displays) is downloaded from the server to the client on-the-fly, eliminating the need for client installation. Compared to on-the-fly download, client installation results in an explosion of maintenance costs. Table 19.1 shows that 9% of the cost derives from system administration and 70% from combined user administration and technical support. This includes such tasks as installing and configuring software, coping with unintended software interaction, and software-induced computer downtime. These effects are magnified by informed users customizing their work environments, further complicating administration and support. Terminals suffer none of these drawbacks. A related distinction is that PCs retain state when they are powered down while terminals lose all state. Because computers fail periodically, client state must be backed up, increasing the cost of administration.

Here is an example: a firm has five application servers, 10,000 PCs and ten key client/server applications, of which five are installed on the average PC. This firm must maintain the server piece of ten applications on its five servers for a total of fifty server-application maintenance actions. It must also maintain an average of five applications on each of its 10,000 PCs, for a total of 50,000 client maintenance actions. Contrast this with a terminal environment in which the server maintenance remains the same, but the 50,000 client maintenance actions are eliminated. Even when terminal emulation is used instead of terminals, the company must maintain one program on each client—a terminal emulator—rather than one program per application. This is a considerable savings.

While we've described some deficiencies in client/server applications, it is important to note that they are not inherent in client/server per se, but in the way it is deployed. One step forward is to eliminate client installation, which is not an inherent part of client/server. This can be done with tools that automate the transmission and installation of system files and with facilities that allow remote installation. For best results these tools must be used on highly standardized configurations, configurations that are not changed by individual users. This reduces many of the costs of client/server, but leaves application design as a major cost factor.

19.9 Design of client/server applications

Application design plays a large part in the cost of ownership. Applications have three main components: data, logic, and presentation. In a standalone application such as a personal-productivity application, data, logic, and presentation all reside on the same computer. In client/server applications, a split must occur either at the border between these components or within one of the components. In the *distributed presentation* subset of client/server, data and logic handling are performed on the server, and presentation is handled by the client. This is an application of the terminal model of network computing to client/server computing. Distributed presentation is supported by DT on ISPF and VM, by X-Windows on various platforms, and by other products including

Cytrix on Windows. It can also be achieved by design intent within other client/server frameworks. IBM's VisualAge application design tools can be used this way, for example.

The data contained in the table does not directly compare split logic client/server applications with distributed presentation applications, so we cannot determine the relative costs with precision. However, by examining the two application types, we can gain some insight. In distributed presentation, information is exchanged between client and server in a structured way. A server transmits windows to its client, along with updates to the current window. (Asynchronous events are also sent infrequently). The client simply transmits information entered by the user. The simplicity of this interaction allows distributed presentation systems to implement the networking support required to split the presentation from the data and logic below the presentation API; the programmer needn't deal explicitly with the network. This greatly simplifies creating such applications, thus reducing their initial costs. It also makes them much less costly to maintain since the manual creation of interfaces between client and server, required by the split logic model, is a difficult design task.

In addition, with the exception of asynchronous alerts, information is typically sent synchronously. The client sends information to the server only when the user indicates that interaction with a screen is complete. In response to the new information, the server typically executes a transaction and returns a new screen or an update to the prior screen. From the client, this resembles a synchronous RPC. Contrast this with client/ server applications. Since both client and server are executing logic, the range of interactions is far greater. At any point in either the client logic or the server logic, a communication event might be necessary. Structuring code to handle such asynchronous events is difficult and error prone.

While distributed presentation reduces client/server costs, Java is the real answer to the problem of client/server costs.

19.10 The promise of Java

When introduced in 1994, Java rode the Internet wave to prominence. At first, the Java language was used to program applets, small programs that could be executed within a Web browser to create animated Web pages. Suddenly the Web was transformed from a world of static content to a world of live pages. However, Java far transcends Web pages. Java allows applications to be written once and deployed across widely heterogeneous computers. Because Java is platform independent, the same Java program will run on all client computers, including network computers.

While Java's virtual machine—that is, the execution environment in which Java applications are executed—is the basis for its platform independence, Java is also a programming language. While the Java virtual machine can host any high-level programming language, the elegance of Java's language design has drawn a large number of programmers, reducing the need for the Java virtual machine to host other languages. Features of the Java language environment make Java particularly attractive as a language for programming distributed applications.

A Java programmer writes a program in the Java language and runs it through a compiler to produce Java bytecodes. The bytecodes are stored in a class file. The program runs on the Java virtual machine which dynamically converts the bytecodes to the local machine code. Since the output of the Java compiler is platform independent, the programmer has no reason to compensate for differences in platforms. All platforms are alike.

Java's class loader is an important component of the Java virtual machine. It ensures that the virtual machine has the Java classes that it needs when it needs them. It validates code correctness, caches the code, sometimes runs a just-in-time compiler, resolves symbolic links, checks the trustworthiness of the source and recursively loads any further classes. Since this is done at runtime it provides a foundation for completely installation process-free running of application code.

The Java virtual machine loads classes dynamically, when a request for a class generates a class fault. Applications begin executing before they are entirely loaded, improving responsiveness, but without explicit management of this by the application. Classes that are not accessed during a particular use of the application are not loaded, reducing application use of memory. In response to a class fault, the Java Loader loads code from either the local machine, or dynamically loads it across a network. By dynamically downloading classes, Java reduces the amount of software that must be installed on each client. Organizations save the cost of installation on each desktop and eliminate the need to upgrade each client as the code changes.

In addition to eliminating the client application installation costs of client/server computing, Java offers the opportunity to eliminate the design costs. This can be done simply by telling programming teams to write clients that only implement an application's presentation thus moving from split-logic client/server to distributed presentation, and avoiding the difficulties of synchronizing communication between clients and servers. It is important that the use of distributed presentation not come at the expense of additional network flows. But the Java interpreter can execute arbitrary code, so programmers can write clients that implement an application's presentation without relying on a server to process input. Programmers can write distributed presentation applications with few additional network flows. Of course, with the dynamic download, there will be some additional load on the network as classes are downloaded dynamically from server to client. However, these costs can be mitigated through caching and compression.

Besides enabling dynamic downloading, Java includes CUA-compliant GUI interfaces that level the various GUI platforms to which Java has been ported. This makes Java the universal CUA GUI client, just as the 3270 is the universal CUA alphanumeric client. Such a universal client promises to reduce computing costs, by lowering the technical support and administration costs. To fulfill this promise, Java must be deployed widely across network computing environments. This is happening: Java virtual machines and compilers are available everywhere and most current operating systems now include Java as a built-in component.

19.11 Networked Java

Java was bound to TCP/IP by its introduction via the World Wide Web, but is easily used in enterprise SNA networks. First, the Java class loader is changed to fetch files from SNA networks. This is not difficult since the network component of a class fault is essentially a file transfer. Second, networking APIs are added to allow Java programs to exchange data with SNA servers.

To show how Java runs with SNA, we've built a Java SNA class loader. The class loader is a replaceable part of the Java virtual machine, so this is easy. The SNA class loader uses SNA's AFTP file transfer service, which runs over APPC and is widely supported in SNA products. To improve performance, the SNA class loader caches recently requested classes, using a FIFO replacement algorithm.

Loading Java is only half the problem. Applications must also be able to access servers. In this environment Java's standard sockets APIs are available, but while sockets are available on SNA networks, SNA APIs such as the CPI-C are more widely installed and are used by many more existing applications.

For example, consider an existing CICS CPI-C application that is driven by a client written in C and is installed on a large number of computers. After several upgrades, each requiring reinstallation on every client computer, the IT director decides to deploy a Java client, eliminating the need for future installation. To avoid rewriting the server— a large development and test expense—the Java client must match the line flows of the existing client. This is most easily done by using CPI-C in the Java client.

In "Java and SNA: A Case Study" (*IBM Technical Report* 29.2168, August 1996), MacKinnon et. al describe the Java CPI-C API. By combining that work with the SNA class loader, a system that downloads Java over an LU6.2 connection and uses an LU6.2 connection to communicate with the server is created, matching Java to SNA.

While such a system will work immediately for Java applications, and hence can be used in enterprise networks, security restrictions apply to Java applets loaded into arbitrary Web browsers on the Internet. Applets are prevented from making native calls—

that is, calls to services that are not written completely in Java. The IBM Host on Demand product, a 3270 emulator written in Java and downloadable as an applet, illustrates the solution to this problem. Extensions to Host on Demand could make CPI-C and other SNA interfaces available on all Web browsers.

19.12 Conclusion

In this chapter we've discussed how SNA applications have been influenced by progress in computing, especially by CUA, client/server, and Java. Each of these technologies is important to enterprises using SNA. For many years, users have wanted more productive, CUA-conforming interfaces on enterprise applications. This desire can now be completely satisfied through the use of Java. We've shown how Java integrates into SNA networks without changes in enterprise servers or in existing applications. We've established that enterprises that embrace Java will see a reduction in the cost of administering client/server systems. The future of SNA enterprise networking is CUA-compliant client/server applications written in Java.

chapter 20

Several protocols will coexist forever

RUDY J. CYPSER

In this chapter Rudy J. Cypser asserts that multiple protocols are with us for a long time. Further, there will not be a single successful approach to support internetworking in this environment—a variety of approaches will be adopted. However, a limited number of dominant protocols is emerging, protocols which are settling into a somewhat modular structure represented by the open blueprint.

20.1 Fundamental network requirements

These days, network executives face a multitude of requirements. Two, however, are often basic:

- Economic growth of applications
- Network consolidation

Economic growth of applications pertains to the increase in the number of applications, the more widespread use of applications, and the expanded sharing of all types of multimedia information. Both current and future applications must be increasingly accessible, free from many of the constraints of the communication network. Communication is required, in principle, among clients and servers in all parts of the enterprise, in suppliers, and in other enterprises. Moreover, new types of applications that take full advantage of graphics, images, sound, and video must increasingly be accommodated.

Network consolidation emerges as a requirement since many parts of an enterprise often grow local networks independent of each other. They become isolated islands, using diverse communication protocols, unable to communicate effectively with the rest of the business world. The integration and harmonization of such islands are needed to increase the overall connectivity and to reduce training, maintenance, and management expenses. At the same time, it must be possible to take advantage of newer, often higher speed, communication facilities. Very few enterprises can afford to start networking all over again. Network consolidation therefore frequently involves moving towards a desired simplification, while incorporating multiple existing communications protocols and combining older resources with newer ones so as to use the best offerings of different vendors.

These two basic requirements, moreover, demand the appearance, to the applications and to the users, of a single integrated network, even though the components are multiprotocol and multivendor.

20.2 Different circumstances need different approaches

Not only are the circumstances in different enterprises quite diverse, but with time the networking needs of a given enterprise can change drastically. One only needs to consider the effects of new technologies, mergers, acquisitions, and shifts in product lines, manufacturing processes, or suppliers to appreciate that. To illustrate, six requirements, in particular, result from different circumstances:

1 *Connections among LANs over large distances*   When multiple network protocols are used in these LANs, the lines connecting them must carry multiple protocols. This need has led to the development of multiprotocol routers. This approach creates a very flexible network, but one that may enlarge the need for training, maintenance, and management of multiple protocols. It reduces wide area line costs, but does not address the issues of interoperability among end-systems using diverse transport service protocols.

2 *Like applications across one foreign network*   Suppose one needs to operate a pair of valuable TCP/IP applications across a foreign SNA network. Or, vice versa, to connect two SNA applications across a foreign TCP/IP network. Or, one may need to use pairs of OSI applications, or DECnet applications across either an SNA or a TCP/IP network. Such requirements leave the investments in the WAN as is, with a single protocol to manage there, but requires some type of network-protocol adapter in the end-systems or the boundary of the foreign network.

3 *Like applications across two different networks*   Consider, for example, one TCP/IP application on a TCP/IP network and its partner TCP/IP application on a foreign SNA network, with the network-protocol adapter mentioned in (2) above. This communication can leave the two different networks intact, but there is a need for a transport-gateway between the adjacent unlike networks, (that is, between the network dedicated to TCP/IP and the network dedicated to SNA).

4 *Operational cost reductions*   Training, set-up, maintenance, and management costs all increase with multiple protocols. A gradual consolidation of network protocols may be needed without affecting existing applications. This requires the ability to use existing applications over whatever transport protocol is adopted as the future standard. Again, as in (2) above, this requires some type of network-protocol adapter in the end-systems or the boundary of the target network.

5 *New subnetwork technologies*   Economic and performance needs may dictate the use of new subnetwork capabilities, such as frame relay or ATM. One would want

the option of making use of these without disrupting the existing applications or totally threatening the investments in other parts of the network. For stability and economy, for example, it may be important to continue the use of TCP/IP or SNA in the higher levels of communication protocol, while incorporating new technologies and protocols in lower levels.

6 *Internet opportunities*   Now, with the aid of a Web browser, a user can move comfortably from one document to another, and that document can be in the same or in a different location. The network must accommodate this easy access to new and old information, in a *secure* fashion, with growth pains involving greater use of graphics, audio, and video information.

In a given enterprise, any of these needs may exist or become requirements in the future. A blueprint for the future of networking therefore has to be adaptable and include options for different and changing circumstances. That blueprint has to be a framework to help in the orderly assessment of alternative solutions that are available today, or will be available shortly, for the particular circumstances of the particular network.

The networking blueprint, within the larger open blueprint, allows the formation of very simple or relatively complex network structures, using one or more sets of protocols. It is designed to facilitate the nondisruptive evolution of networks in steps affecting only one macro layer, without disturbing major prior investments in other macro layers. Of added importance is the potential for increased stability of applications during the network evolution.

20.3 *The resulting growth capabilities*

Let us summarize some of the networking purposes and methods of the open blueprint. It is a set of recommendations that follow international and industry standards. Its multiprotocol, multivendor modules fit a framework defined by key interfaces and boundaries. It allows the choice of the optimum combination of functions which are best suited to a particular application or which take advantage of available or new services. It allows a gradual and orderly evolution to emerging technologies, and new application requirements, with coexistence and migration for multiple generations of technology. An enterprise may use all the flexibility of the open blueprint or may choose to restrict options and move toward a strategic set of protocols, so as to reduce training, set-up, maintenance, and management costs. Four of its principal uses are:

1   The open blueprint creates a welcome separation between the application and application enabler worlds, on the one hand, and the complexities of the communication world on the other hand. Consistent programming interfaces across the major networking protocols simplify program development and allow the purchase or creation of applications without concern for the underlying networks. Applications originally oriented to TCP/IP, SNA, and other protocols can all be used effectively on one network. Another consequence of this application independence is that the standard applications, such as X.400 and FTP, and also the object management services and the distribution services, such as directories, security, and recovery, now can become part of a distributed network operating system, which happily can all be independent of the particular underlying communication protocols.

2   The open blueprint addresses two urgent needs: the integration of diverse networks and subnetworks which may have grown independently, and the effective management of such a consolidated structure. The goal of integration is to make possible more universal communication among all parts of the enterprise and its associates. At the same time, the open blueprint aims to facilitate taking advantage of the best features of each protocol, while, where appropriate, preserving the prior investments in applications and network facilities. As this integration takes place, the open blueprint offers the possibility of using centralized and distributed management functions in the combinations that best meet changing needs. To the degree that this is also accompanied by a reduction in the number of network protocols, costs of training, set-up, maintenance, and management can be reduced.

3   The application independence and the modularity of the structure facilitate the introduction of new technologies. This particularly includes the movement to higher and higher speeds and the associated movement to the use of multimedia such as voice, image, video, and text, as the evolution of the Internet requires. Investments made today will certainly still be valid tomorrow.

4   Seamless interoperability comes from single sign-on access to the distributed systems, network-wide security by encryption, authentication and resource control, network-wide directory services, and global transparent access independent of location.

chapter 21

Transport protocol revolution

JOHN R. PICKENS

This book concludes with a freewheeling, forward-looking chapter arguing a coming protocol revolution. "Everything that can be invented has been invented," declared Charles H. Duell, Commissioner, U.S. Office of Patents in 1899. Today, we know how far from the truth this statement was. In this last chapter John R. Pickens, describing a timeframe that probably moves into the next decade, describes some elements of the protocol revolution that can be seen in today's transports. SNA and TCP/IP are influencing and being influenced by the seeds of this revolution.

21.1 Introduction

Something strange happened on the way toward the protocol wars of the 1980s and 1990s. We forgot what protocols were meant to do, that is, provide the foundation for distributed computing. So much attention has been paid to the religious aspects of protocols, sometimes arguing technical merit based upon the source of the technology rather than the content of the technology, that sometimes the underlying needs of networked computing are being ignored. We also have come to believe, like the scientists regarding science at the turn of the century, that all knowledge regarding protocols has been discovered, and that incremental variations of the current generation of protocols will suffice for all time. Global ATM threatens to push protocol-specific routing to the edges, even to the edge of extinction.

Contrary to the desires for stability of the competing camps, protocols will change in revolutionary ways. Even the front runners of the late 1980s and early 1990s will not necessarily be the dominant protocols of the future. An extreme scenario is that there will not even be front-runners. SNA, like TCP/IP and IPX/SPX, will affect and be affected by these trends in massively fundamental ways. However, the changes will take many years to unfold.

Corresponding to the change in protocols will be a change in the ways that internetworking is performed. But first, let us look at a key driver behind the protocol revolution, the revolution in the distributed computing environment itself.

21.2 Distributed computing drivers

Distributed computing does not concern itself with protocols, per se. Rather it deals with the delivery of applications, application data, operating system services and effective utilization of computing resources within the network in support of applications and operating systems. In a distributed computing system the various resources may be (transparently) spread across a number of nodes—file servers, computer servers, database servers. Indeed, at least one systems vendor has even coined the phrase "the network is the computer" as an attempt to capture the network computing paradigm.

In the early years of network computing (1970–1980), the network was used only as method for connecting a desktop terminal to a mainframe or minicomputer. All protocols were for terminal emulation. The computational processing was performed not on the desktop, but on the centralized timesharing system accessed via terminal emulation protocols over the network. In the middle years of network computing (1980–1990) the dominant model was client/server—all systems as peers. Many peer protocols for many applications, especially mail and database, dominated this era. In the 1990s and beyond, a hybrid of the early models and middle models will be called for.

Driving the evolution of distributed computing systems in the 1990s is the rapid change within the network infrastructure itself—from a few Mbps (Arcnet, early ethernet) in the early 1980s to 10/16 Mbps (ethernet, token ring) in the late 1980s to 100-plus Mbps (FDDI, 100/1000 Mbps ethernet, ATM, and gigabit ethernet) in the 1990s. At the same time, the aggregate bandwidth is growing by orders of magnitudes as the early generation of multiuser LAN segments is giving way to switching hubs with single-user bridge-per-port and high speed aggregate switching backplanes. The net effect of this change is that a lot of bandwidth is going to be available to applications and protocol designers.

With switching hubs and gigabit ATMs it may be possible for each and every user to access up to full media speed as available application bandwidth. Figure 21.1 demonstrates this possibility. Examining the evolution from shared ethernet to switched ethernet, the number of users which can concurrently access full ethernet bandwidth varies from 1 to 100 in local environments (assuming 1-Gbps switching hub backplanes) and

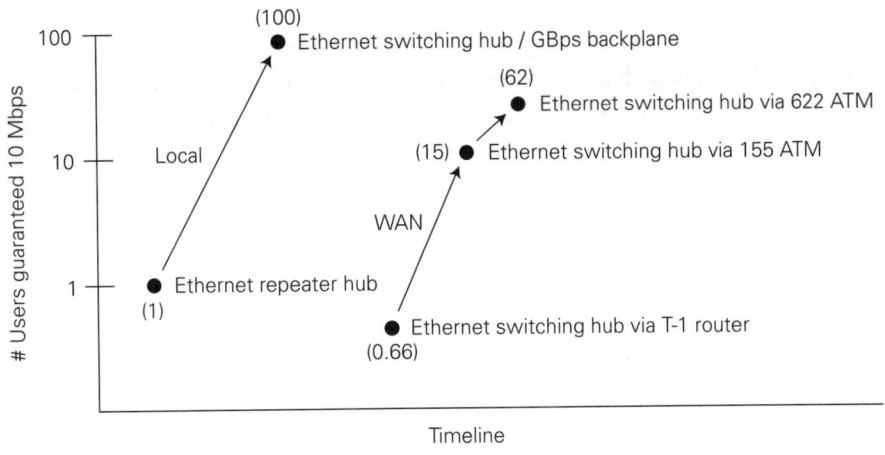

Figure 21.1 Number users with guaranteed 10 Mbps bandwith versus WAN technology timeline

DISTRIBUTED COMPUTING DRIVERS

from 0.66 to 62 across WAN environments (assuming evolution to 155 Mbps and 622 Mbps ATM). If users require less bandwidth (typical video users require 1.5 Mbps per user), then the number is much greater. Imagine millions of users running 1.5 Mbps guaranteed bandwidth video across ATM-connected LANs.

Application designers have usually tended to view networks as having infinite bandwidth and zero delay, when, in fact, the reality is very different. Table 21.1 shows the delay characteristics and unused capacity of various LAN/WAN media while sending a single-bit message and awaiting its single bit response. Despite the increasing bandwidth of modern media the relative delay as seen by applications is escalating. For example, a 15,000 kilometer 155 Mbps link experiences a round trip delay of 167,000,000 nanoseconds. One study showed that average applications executed fewer than 10^6 instructions. At a few nanoseconds per instructon cycle (for some of the faster processors on the market today), a computer system could run nearly a hundred applications in serial fashion in the time it takes to wait for a single query-response dialogue across the high bandwidth-delay characteristic of such a 155 Mbps link.

Table 21.1 Round trip time and unused capacity of transmission channel

Network type	Distance (km)	Time (ns)	Unused capacity (bits) @ 10Mbps reserved
LAN	0.1	1,000	10
	10	111,000	1,000
WAN	1,000	11,000,000	100,000
	15,000	167,000,000	1,500,000
Satellite	60,000	400,000,000	4,000,000

The types of network computing paradigms are heavily influenced by the characteristics of network bandwidth delay. A foreshadowing of this phenomenon occurred in the mid 1980s when developers attempted to migrate the PC-based electronic mail application to the remote computing environment. The hope was to make the mail application (which was developed originally for LANs) work just as well for the remote user as it did for the LAN user, but with no fundamental reengineering of the mail application. Only the data link was to be changed.

The result? It did not work. In remote configurations the application was slow. Very slow.

Most electronic mail implementations (figure 21.2) are designed with a client server model—the mail database resides on a mail server, and the client exchanges tens to hundreds of small inquiry and update transactions just to display a page of one-line

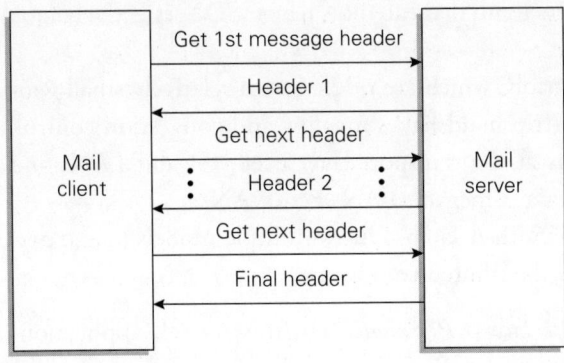

Figure 21.2 Client/server design model for email

message summaries. In a LAN with 10 Mbps throughput and a few dozen microsecond roundtrip delays, the user experiences peppy performance. But put that application into a remote environment, with under 64 Kbps throughput and dozens of millisecond roundtrip delays, and the user feels like his computer is mired in molasses. Even migrating this application to gigabit media, the user will still feel a reduction in performance in long-distance WANs compared to LANs because of the increased distance-sensitive delay.

Figure 21.3 shows the impact of both bandwidth and delay on the effective performance of client/server applications using the email example. For simplicity, the size of the request message for each header and the response message for each header is 100 bytes, and 100 message headers are retrieved. Zero application-processing delay is assumed. The speed of light is assumed to be 210,000 kilometers per second in fiber optic cable. Note that at link speeds above a megabit the impact of link distance (delay) reduces the performance to effectively submegabit speeds. In fact at 15,000 kilometers (across multiple continents) the application requires 16.7 seconds over a 64 Kbps link but only speeds up to 14.2 seconds over a gigabit link. For this application design at

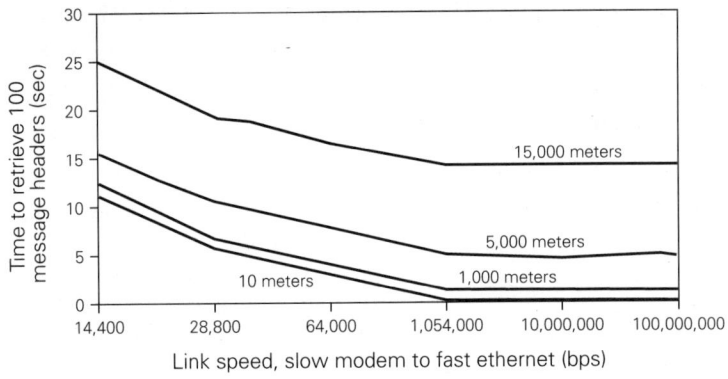

Figure 21.3 Impact of bandwidth and delay on email client/server design

long distances, dedicated gigabit ethernet and dedicated 64 Kbps ISDN effectively look the same.

Suffice it to say that current protocols, which are riddled with relatively small windows and which utilize regular round-trip handshakes for flow and congestion control, will also experience similar limitations at the transport layer itself. Gigabit LANs and WANs are not just faster versions of today's megabit LANs and WANs.

As a result of the increasing bandwidth-delay product, multiple models (a.k.a. paradigms) are taking root as the basis for distributed computing.

- *The applications programming interface (API) model*   In this model, applications utilize an explicit API such as Sockets or CPI-C. The application is responsible for formatting the data, and establishing the semantics of the data such as a function invocation, error codes, and so on (figure 21.4a). This is the most common model and also gives the most flexibility to the applications developer.

- *The RPC model*   In this model, applications utilize a procedure-call interface. No awareness of the vagaries of communications (other than delay) is required (figure 21.4b). In the ideal case the application is developed as though the library of procedure calls were locally executing. However, the application developer must be aware of latency considerations in designing both the functional characteristics of the procedures and the frequency of calling of the procedures. Also, until reply from the remote system is posted into the RPC subsystem blocks, no concurrent work gets performed. Some variants of RPC support parallel execution, that is, allow an application to execute a procedure call but not block on its outcome.

- *The remote evaluation (REV) model*   In the REV model, applications and application fragments (processes and threads) are moved to the data (figure 21.4c). For example, an application which was sorting a record-oriented file could be exported to the remote system where the file resided. No network latency would therefore be incurred as the application moved from record to record. The REV model requires efficient mechanisms whereby the remote instance (thread) of the program can execute efficient call-back functions to the local run-time environment, perhaps to collect data from the user, or read system environment variables.

- *The compute cluster model*   The compute cluster model is an extreme case of the REV model (figure 21.4d). In this model, all file, database, and compute resources are co-located on a high-speed network with small delay. Remote terminal emulation (e.g., X-Windows) is used to access applications within the cluster.

- *The memory mapped model*   In the memory mapped model the network is viewed as an extension of paged memory, and paged memory working set algorithms are used to maximize locality of data (figure 21.4e). For efficient implementation of

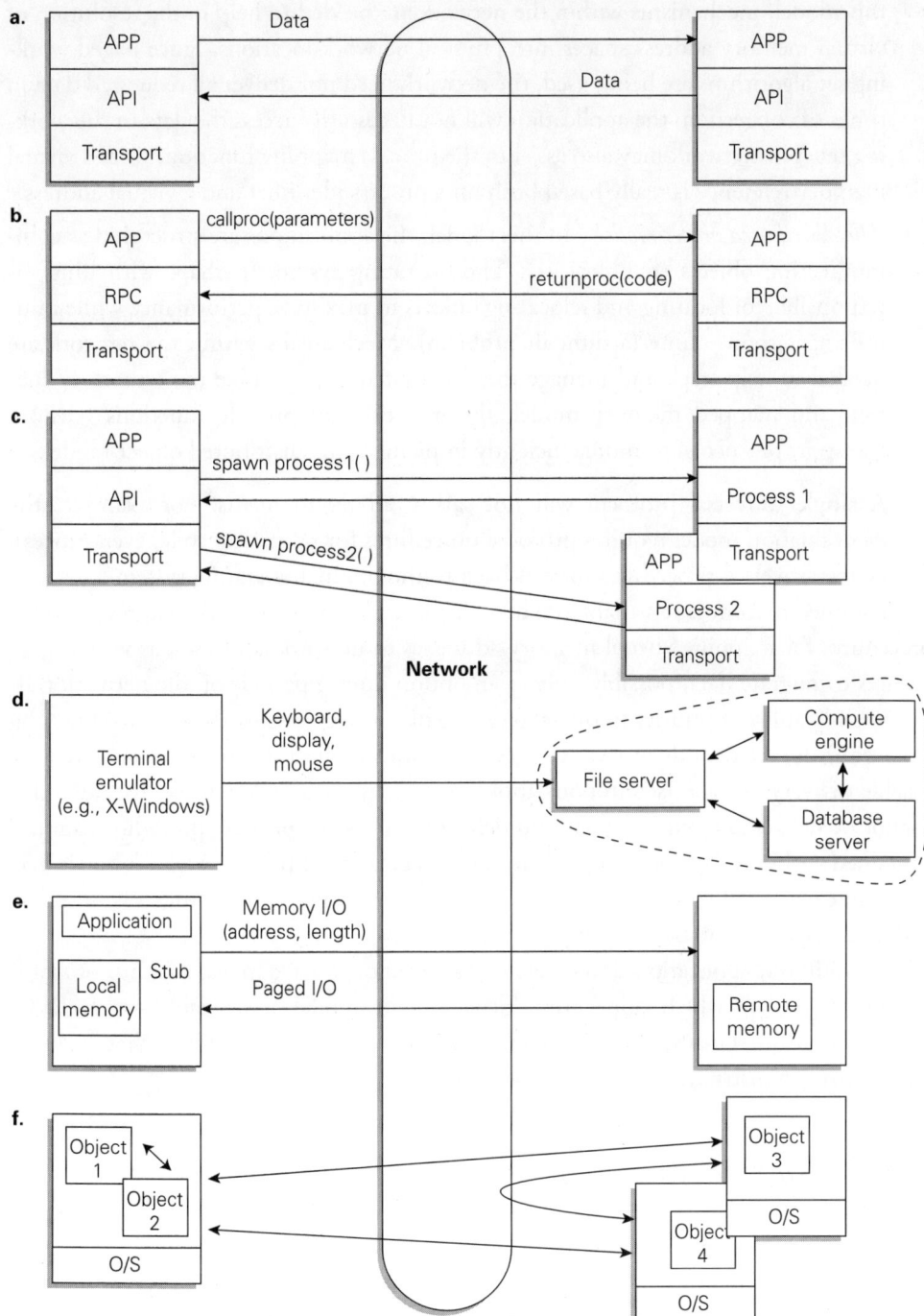

Figure 21.4   Distributed computing models

this model, mechanisms within the network are needed to help in the resolution of virtual memory address spaces into physical network locations. Since paged working set algorithms are being used, the network need not deliver all requested data in times of congestion; the application will not necessarily access the data in the working set. The network may also assist in the process mapping function, since a virtual memory reference is really based both on a process identifier and a virtual address.

- *The distributed object model* In this model, the applications are structured as communicating objects (figure 21.4f). The operating system (perhaps with hints) is responsible for locating and relocating objects to maximize performance while minimizing response time (a difficult problem). Mechanisms within the network are needed to help track and manage the distributed objects. Like the remote evaluation and mapped memory model, the network can provide functions (custom transport protocols) to more efficiently implement the distributed object model.

A single universal protocol will not satisfy all requirements. For example, the remote evaluation model requires protocol procedures for relocating code, even process, fragments, as well as procedures for call-back to the original operating system for access to run-time environment variables. The distributed memory model requires protocol procedures for mapping virtual memory addresses to network addresses, as well as procedures to migrate data, possibly only as an option during periods of idle network traffic, possibly at lower priority in order to enable discarding (essentially a cache-emptying operation) during periods of peak congestion. Some applications may not even require reliable delivery of data. Isochronous applications may require data to be discarded if it cannot be delivered within a maximum delay period. Some of these procedures are not contained within today's protocols, or are spread across multiple protocols. While it may be technically possible to layer some of these services atop existing protocols, in many cases such layering will be inefficient and unattractive.

In addition, application developers will prefer not to have to ask which protocol is supported—rather which application development model is available—API, RPC, REV, and so on. Finally, a development environment will be required that includes mechanisms to instrument, monitor, and debug distributed applications.

21.3 Sacred protocol myths exploded

Given the observations regarding distributed computing requirements (see the section on distributed computing drivers), implementation opportunities, and current research (see the section on protocol research), it is interesting to examine several of the commonly accepted myths regarding transport protocol design.

21.3.1 First myth—protocol layers are necessary

Current protocols are loaded with layers. SNA has seven layers. OSI has seven layers. TCP/IP has three to five layers, depending on which protocol family one counts.

How did protocols get layers? Nominally, layers were created as a technique for information hiding and modular design. Actually, the structure of protocols took on the structure of the institution tasked with its creation. IBM at one point in its history had its architecture organization organized into departments, one department for each layer. ISO divided itself into committees and subcommittees covering each layer that was perceived independently necessary. Fueling the fissionable layer-by-layer frenzy, the ISO OSI reference model (committee) introduced a pernicious element, the proscription of generic functions for $N-1$ users which might be redundantly made present for each N-layer, such as addressing and multiplexing (even though a single addressing and multiplexing scheme would, from a technical perspective, be perfectly adequate for the construction of many distributed computing environments). The designers of layers have often succumbed to the temptation to reinvent instances of the generic functions from the reference model, especially multiplexing services, at each layer.

Even the early protocols like SNA, in an effort to keep up with the OSI Joneses, managed to complicate a much simpler layered model (four to five layers) by inventing new layers to bring the model into architectural conformance with the seven-layer OSI model. Not to be left out, other standards committees introduced their own layering—IEEE 802 LAN/MAN standards, for example, introduced two sublayers in layer 2 (data-link layer)—the MAC layer, and the LLC layer. Whatever the historic reasons, layers have flooded into today's protocols. Other committees have subdivided even the physical layer into sublayers.

Actually, layers are useful as descriptive techniques. Unfortunately, early protocol implementations created separate procedural APIs and buffer copies for each layer, resulting in very poor implementation performance. Today's high performance implementations have become so only by eliminating the layering. In many cases a fast path model has been implemented to cover eighty percent of the common protocol cases by collapsing all layer processing into a single code fragment. Unfortunately fast path implementations, especially those with performance optimizations in response to gigabit networking requirements, make certain assumptions about the characteristics of current traffic flow which may change as the patterns of traffic flow change with new applications.

If collapsing layers is a good practice for implementation, then it is only a matter of time until layers are collapsed in the protocols themselves.

21.3.2 Second myth—a universal protocol will satisfy all

Most work in protocols to date has assumed, either implicitly or explicitly, that a universal protocol is desired by all. All applications need full congestion management and flow control. All need the same level of error control. All can be satisfied by a message stream, or by a byte stream, or by a record stream service model. All can be satisfied with the same heuristics for protocol timing. With this one-size-fits-all model in mind, it is no wonder the protocol wars have erupted with such intensity.

At the time of this writing the universal protocol of public favor is IP. However, the IP of the coming century is not the IP of its birthing years (1970s to the mid-1990s). Even IP is growing more functions—a new header, a new (huge) address space, and an evolution (some would say *revolution*, considering its roots) from the pure datagram connectionless model to a flow (some would say *connection-oriented*) model. In addition, IP is growing quality of service functions for multimedia traffic. New upper layer protocols are being developed to track this evolution of function—RSVP routing control, RTP, H.32x conferencing, and so on. One might question whether IP is a universal protocol, or an evolutionary track of protocols.

Universal protocols do have benefits—namely the benefits of ubiquity. Administrators have to learn only a minimal set of technologies. Line sniffers do not have to be continually reprogrammed. Only a small set of APIs needs be offered.

As was hinted at in the section on distributed computing paradigms, and will be further explored in the section on protocol research, the days of universal protocols may be numbered. Because of application needs such as real-time video, specialized protocols will emerge. Because of the large bandwidth-delay variation between local LANs and global WANs, protocols will emerge with different types of flow control and a richer set of configuration options for application use (like an option to mark data with colors, to denote data that must be delivered from data that can be discarded).

Universal protocols will exist into the foreseeable future. But a given universal protocol such as APPC or TCP/IP will not satisfy the needs of all applications.

21.3.3 Third myth—the paradigm of multiple concurrent routing functions

Simply stated, routing is the process of determining a path for data based upon an offered destination address. The routing decision is initially made at the point of origination of the data (i.e., outbound interface), and it is subsequently made at every intervening hop along the way to the destination point. The challenge in routing is to determine optimal paths in the face of dynamically changing topology and congestion characteristics. Historically, for internetworking, that role has been relegated to routers connected by point-to-point lines. In the new model of internetworking that model is beginning to change.

First with X.25, then with frame relay, and now with ATM, layer 2 technologies are emerging which have the potential for performing all functions that routers perform today, in a protocol-independent way. X.25 didn't catch on, however, because products (and line speeds) were too slow compared to routers. Frame relay has not caught on as an independent technology, but instead has become the preferred form for providing a packetized, versus cellularized, interface to cell-switching fabrics (e.g., ATM). ATM has every chance of becoming a dominant backbone technology, outstripping both X.25 and frame relay, primarily because of its ability to handle both isochronous multimedia and asynchronous data traffic.

X.25, frame relay, and ATM, in their most basic form, essentially introduce a new data-link layer type, with what is essentially a new layer-2 address, and routes data based upon the layer 2 address. Other devices, such as bridges and routers essentially use the new data-link layer as a logical point-to-point permanent virtual circuit between peer bridges and routers. (X.25 is defined as a layer-3 technology, but is actually used as a layer-2 technology.) Without enhancements, these layer-2 technologies have a limited functional role in the emerging multiprotocol Internet.

Routers perform protocol processing at the network layer, layer-3. For IPX, IP, or APPN, routers perform protocol-specific directory services and route-finding and route-forwarding functions on a protocol specific basis. Unfortunately, each protocol has its own competing method for handling route management—APPN for SNA, NLSP for IPX, and OSPF for IP. Certainly these competing methods cannot continue to coexist, especially in the face of new emerging protocols, and given the redundant and non-integrated routing functions being performed by ATM and other emerging high speed technologies.

Rather than parallel concurrent routing functions, an integrated routing function is needed.

IBM's NBBS architecture demonstrates one approach toward integrated routing (actually, switching). Access agents are defined that utilize the common services provided by the NBBS control point—directory, topology, set management, and so on. These access agents are performing a routing forwarding function, without requiring implementation of the protocol-specific route management functions (OSPF, APPN, or NLSP).

Work is underway to standardize protocol-independent routing over ATM, for example, *multiprotocol over ATM* (MPOA). MPOA's goal is to allow the direct and efficient transfer of unicast data between MPOA clients. MPOA utilizes other technologies —ATM Forum LAN Emulation (LANE) for layer 2 ATM-based switching, IETF Next

Hop Routing Protocol (NHRP) for cut-through switching between protocol-based subnets, and IEEE 802.1p/Q tagging for virtual LANs (VLANs), multicast, and priority.

With NBBS ATM control point or MPOA as foundations, perhaps a next step is achievable—offering protocol services for distributed operating systems—that is, the network-as-memory model or the remote evaluation model for distributed computing.

Indeed the existence of a functional, extensible, flexible common routing service, with extensibility for supporting multiple protocol and addressing types, at the layer of manageable bandwidth (e.g., ATM), may become the future alternative to the current competing standards for multiprotocol routing. Concurrent route management functions may then become obsolete.

21.4 Protocol research

In recent years research has yielded new approaches toward the definition, design, and implementation of protocols. Some of this research has been motivated by the desire to create higher throughput protocols, sacrificing the low latency characteristics of existing protocols like TCP/IP and SNA. Some has been toward higher performance implementations without requiring the hand crafted tuning that existing protocols require and some to support the unique communications needs of new distributed computing paradigms. Networks with high speed, low error links may require rate-based flow control and forward error correction versus current networks which use window-based flow control and error correction feedback.

An oft-referenced classical analysis of the negative impact of the layering between applications protocols and lower layer protocols shows that sometimes full function transport stacks can impose significant compromises on the potential performance of applications—a sort of phase-canceling effect between the competing mechanisms of lower and upper layers. This problem has generated research toward partial evaluation of protocols. In this approach a variant of a general protocol is created for use by an application. The application specifies the needed protocol facilities, either at compile time or run time, (perhaps retransmission or large windows are not required) and the system generates optimized protocol implementations on an application-by-application basis. For certain applications the achieved performance can be improved by thirty percent or more over a general purpose protocol stack.

Other research toward developing specialized protocols for optimized I/O performance or to optimized application performance is ongoing. Some of the more recent work is reported in writings by Henry Masalin, Douglas C. Schmidt, David Farber and Guru Parulkar, and Christian Tschudin (see the references listed at the end of this chapter).

Table 21.2 lists a range of protocol mechanisms which are being considered for new generation protocols. Especially notable as drivers for change are traffic shaping, rate control, and selective acknowledgments.

Table 21.2 Sampling of new protocol mechanisms

Protocol element	Description	Problem addressed
Traffic shaping	Regulate traffic flow based upon some policy, e.g., simple leaky bucket, token bucket	Prevent sessions from overrunning network resources. Multisession fairness.
Rate-based flow control	Transmit traffic at a predetermined rate	Stability of cell and packet switching backbone. Fairness.
Preemptive flow control	Monitor remote receiver and preemptively anticipate congestion	Untimeliness of reactive feedback in windowing schemes
Very large windows	Transmission windows much larger than current bounds	High bandwidth-delay networks (many bits in the pipe)
Selective acknowledgments	Acknowledge ranges of data received, rather than retransmit whole windows	Redundant retransmissions across backbone (unnecessary congestion)
Multilevel flow feedback	Sample flow rates for nodal delivery and application delivery	Coarse granularity of flow control. Inability to react to application congestions per session.
Fixed header encoding	Eliminate options. Align fields on work boundaries.	Slow processing of variable size headers.
Data coloring	Mark less important data as candidate for preferential discard during congestion, e.g., MPEG II video.	Not all data is equal. Some data can afford to be discarded.
Temporal synchronization	Assure correct ordering of datastreams with multiple object types	Synchronization of multiple object datastreams

21.5 SNA evolution: a critique

SNA has already been influenced to a significant degree toward incorporation of many (but not all) of the research mechanisms described above. However, SNA (like TCP and other existing protocols) retains certain inefficiencies and does not fully capitalize on the need and potential for protocol optimization for specific distributed computing paradigms and specific types of applications.

APPN/HPR is the most advanced variant of SNA known (at least external to IBM). More specifically within HPR is a new transport protocol type, RTP, a distant relative of XTP. RTP embodies several of the newer elements of protocol procedure from the research community.

RTP supports rate-based flow control. The RTP ARB flow- and congestion- control function regulates the input rate of traffic based upon information obtained by monitoring the receiver. Two rates are monitored in the receiver—the rate at which the receiver accepts arriving data from the network, and the rate at which the receiver delivers data to the end user. Based upon the monitored rate information, the flow control protocol state will vary from green to yellow to red. Mathematical analyis of the particular algorithm used shows favorable results with respect to prevention of buffer congestion within the network and rapid adaptation to changing conditions of network load.

RTP supports selective acknowledgment (via a special *gap detected* message) and retransmission of data. RTP selectively retransmits user data in any lost packets or packets with errors. Any user data which arrives out of order at the receiver will be buffered until the missing elements are retransmitted.

RTP does not contain other elements from recent protocol research such as fixed-location protocol headers encoding, temporal synchronization, coloring of data for congestion managment, or traffic shaping.

SNA with RTP is not yet an optimized protocol combination, however. In fact the issue is the layering itself. RTP itself has sufficient protocol mechanisms to support all session multiplexing, data blocking/deblocking, and prioritization functions of SNA. Yet these functions are redundantly present in both stacks. RTP multiplexes data via a transport identifier; higher layers of SNA multiplex data via a session identifier. RTP segments and reassembles data; higher layers of SNA segment and reassemble data too. RTP maintains four priority levels; higher layers of SNA maintain its own priority levels. RTP maintains windows; higher layers of SNA maintain its own windows. In an extremely thin stack implementation of SNA it would be possible to eliminate the redundant functions performed by the SNA stack, and map all protocol services to the RTP layer—one SNA session mapped to one RTP connection.

Further room for SNA/RTP protocol improvement remains. In fact this issue is exactly analogous to a similar issue with the convergence of protocol-specific services and ATM. A solution for the ATM environment requires a lightweight transport, which could be a role satisfied also by RTP.

21.6 *Conclusion*

Admittedly, some of these projections are far reaching in scope and long range in timeline. However, the seeds for change are sown. The evidence for change is mounting within specific protocol families—SNA, TCP/IP, Novell. New transports are emerging (XTP, RTP, MTP). Statically extensible backbones are on the horizon (NBBS, MPOA)—dynamically extensible backbones cannot be far behind. Demand for all distributed computing paradigms—API, RPC, REV, CLUSTER, MEM—is on the rise—massively parallel computing in large fat networks (LFN) will soon emerge as a networking technology driver within internets, not only within computer clusters (intranets).

While change is almost certain, certain factors will affect the rate of change. MPTN technology, for example, can play a catalytic role by enabling the intermingling of both old and new transports for applications. Both MPTN gateways (switching transports within the backbone) and MTPN access agents (switching transports in the end system) will be applicable.

A broader multiprotocol-friendly model of networking will also help accelerate the revolution. Today's generation of networking backbones works very well for a single protocol but just tolerates others (e.g. OSPF routes IP natively, but other protocols have to be less efficiently tunneled). Future ATM-based backbones have the potential (and the challenge) for supporting all protocols equally. Broad based acceptance of a general and extensible control point model, such as IBM's NBBS control point, would be key. An extreme example of change here would be to enable the ability for application-specific protocols, even compiled protocols, to be supported within the backbone.

There are impediments to change also, the two biggest being the size of the installed base and a hostile political climate. TCP/IP, and SNA all have a huge and growing installed base. All also have a sizable following in their respective protocol innovation environments. New protocols, especially application specific or operating system specific, are not desired within these communities. The resistance of the major protocol camps will act to slow the change to the new world of adaptable protocols, but will not be able to bring the wheels of change to a stop.

How rapidly the changes will come about is certainly a subject of debate. However, the reality of changes is not. Political technical communities will continue to argue the merits of their respective protocol technologies—as well they should. Customers will continue to make application/network purchasing decisions based upon the relative merits of specific protocol technologies—as well they should. The universe of protocol transports, however, is poised for expansion, not contraction. SNA, like TCP/IP and IPX/SPX, is both a driver and a victim of the tumultuous sea of protocol transports into the 21st century.

21.7 References

Abbot, M. and Larry L. Peterson, "A Language-based Approach to Protocol Implementation," *Proceedings of the 1992 SIGCOMM Symposium on Communications Architectures and Protocols,* August 1992, pp. 27–38.

ATM Forum MPOA Working Group, *Multiprotocol over ATM Version 1.0,* February 28, 1997.

Braden, B., L. Zhang, S. Berson, S. Herzog, and S. Jamin, "RSVP," Internet Draft, `draft-ietf-rsvp-spec-14.txt`.

Bradner, Scott O. and Allison Mankin, *IPng Internet Protocol Next Generation,* Reading, MA: Addison-Wesley, 1996.

Cheriton, David, "VMTP: A Transport Protocol for the Next Generation of Computer Systems," *Proceedings of the 1986 SIGCOMM Symposium on Communications Architectures and Protocols (Computer Communication Review), ACM SIGCOMM,* Vol. 16, No. 3, New York, 1986, pp. 406–415.

———, "VMTP: Versatile Message Transaction Protocol," RFC 1045, Stanford University, February 1988.

Chesson, G., et al., *XTP Protocol Definition,* Revision 3.1.G., Santa Barbara: Protocol Engines, Inc., 1988.

———, *XTP Protocol Definition,* Revision 3.4, Santa Barbara: Protocol Engines, Inc., July 1989, pp. 89–103.

Chimento, P. F., et al., "Broadband Network Services for High Speed Multimedia Networks," *IBM Network Systems Architecture,* 1993.

Clark, D., M. Lambert, and L. Zhang, "NETBLT: A Bulk Data Transfer Protocol," RFC 998, MIT, March 1987.

Clark, D.D., and D.L. Tennenhouse, "Architectural Considerations for a New Generation of Protocols," *ACM SIGCOMM,* Vol. 20, No. 4, Philadelphia, September 1990, pp. 200–208.

Doeringer, W., et al., "A Survey of Light-weight Transport Protocols for High-speed Networks," *IEEE Transactions on Communications,* Vol. 38 No. 11, November 1990, pp. 20–21.

Gray, Dr. James P. and Marsha L. Peters, "A Preview of APPN High Performance Routing," IBM Corporation, Research Triangle Park, June 24, 1993.

IEEE 802 draft standard, "P802.1p/D6 Standard for Local and Metropolitan Area Networks—Supplement to Media Access Control (MAC) Bridges: Traffic Class Expediting and Dynamic Multicast Filtering", April 28, 1997.

IEEE 802 draft standard, "P802.1Q/D6 Draft Standard for Virtual Bridged Local Area Networks", May 16, 1997.

Farber, David, and Gurudatta M. Parulkar, "Protocols for Distributed Computing over Gigabit Networks," *INET Tutorial,* June 1992.

Felten, Edward W., "Protocol Compilation: High-Performance Communication for Parallel Programs," Ph.D. Dissertation, University of Washington, 1993.

IMTC Voice over IP Forum Technical Committee, "IMTC Voice over IP Forum Service Interoperability Implementation Agreement Draft 0.91," January 13, 1997.

Katz, D. and D. Piscitello, "NBMA Next Hop Resolution Protocol (NHRP)," Internet Draft, May 1995.

Lane, Ellington, B., ed., "LAN Emulation Over ATM: Version 1.0 Specification," ATM Forum (af-lane-0021.000), January 1995.

Mars, G.J. Armitage, "Support for Multicast over UNI 3.0/3.1 based ATM Networks," RFC 2022, November 1996.

Massalin, Henry, "Synthesis: An Efficient Implementation of Fundamental Operating Systems Services," Ph.D. Thesis, Columbia University, 1992.

Minnich, Ronald G., "Mether: A Memory System for Network Multiprocessors," Ph.D. Dissertaion, University of Pennsylvania Department of Computer and Information Sciences, 1991.

Partridge, Craig, *Gigabit Networking*, Addison-Wesley, 1994.

Peters, Marshi L., "APPN and Extensions—The New Industry Standard for SNA Internetworking," TR29.1791, November 1993.

Pickens, Dr. John R. and David J. Farber, "The Overseer—A Powerful Communications Attribute for Debugging and Security in Thin-Wire Connected Control Structures," International Computer Communications Conference, August 1976.

Schmidt, Douglas C., Donald F. Bos, and Tatsuya Suda, "ADAPTIVE: A Flexible and Adaptive Transport System Architecture to Support Lightweight Protocols for Multimedia Applications on High-speed Networks," *Proceeedings of the Symposium on High Performance Distributed Computing,* Syracuse: IEEE, September 1992, pp. 174–186.

Schulzrinne, H. et al., "RTP: A Transport Protocol for Real-Time Applications," Internet Draft, March 1995.

Sterbenz, James P. G., and Gurudatta M. Parulkar, "Axon Network Virtural Storage for High Performance Distributed Applications," *10th International Conference on Distributed Computing Systems,* Washington, DC: IEEE, June 1990, pp. 484–492.

Thekkath, Chandramohan A., et al., "Implementing Network Protocols at User Level," *Proceedings of the 1993 SIGCOMM Conference,* September 1993, pp. 64–73.

"Transmission protocols for multimedia data," ITU-T Recommendation T.120, 1994.

Tschudin, Christian, "Flexible Protocol Stacks" *Proceedings of the 1991 SIGCOMM Symposium on Communications Architectures and Protocols,* September 1991, pp. 197–205.

Watson, Richard W., and Sandy A. Mamrak, "Gaining Efficiency In Transport Services by Appropriate Design and Implementation Choices," *ACM Transactions on Computer Systems,* Vol. 5, No. 2, May 1987, pp. 97–120.

acronyms

ack	acknowledgment
ACTLU	activate logical unit
ACTPU	activate physical unit
AFI	authority and format identifier
AID	attention identifier
AIW	APPN Implementer's Workshop
AIX	advanced interactive executive
A/M	agent/monitor
AMB	architecture maintenance board
ANR	automatic network routing
ANSI	American National Standards Institute
API	application program interface
APPC	advanced program-to-program communications
APPN	advanced peer-to-peer networking
ARB	adaptive rate based
ARP	address resolution protocol
ARPA	Advanced Research Projects Agency
ASCII	American Standard Code for Information Interchange
ASN	abstract syntax notation
ATM	asynchronous transfer mode
ATP	application transaction program
BAN	boundary access node
BECN	backward explicit congestion notification
BER	bit error rates
BER	basic encoding rules
BGP	border gateway protocol
B-ISDN	broadband integrated services digital network
BISYNC	binary synchronous communications, a.k.a. BSC

BIU	basic information unit
BLU	basic link unit
BNN	boundary network node
BOM	beginning of message
BOOTP	BOOTstrap protocol
BSC	binary synchronous communications, a.k.a. BISYNC
BSD	Berkeley Systems Distribution
CAD	computer aided design
CAM	computer aided manufacturing
CBA	concurrent backbone architecture
CDS	central directory server
CGI	common gateway interface
CICS	customer information control system
CIDR	classless interdomain routing
CIR	committed information rate
CLNP	connectionless network protocol
CLNS	connectionless network service
CMACCP	accept
CMALLC	allocate
CMCFM	confirm
CMDEAL	deallocate
CMFLUS	flush
CMINIT	initialize_conversation
CMIP	common management information protocol
CMIS	common management information service
CMPTR	prepare_to_receive
CMRCV	receive_data
CMSCT	set_conversation_type
CMSERR	send_error
CMSNED	send_data
CMSRTS	request_to_send
CMSSL	set_sync_level
CN	connection network
COBOL	common business-oriented language
CONS	connection-oriented network service
CORBA	Common Object Request Broker Architecture
COS	class of service
CP	control point
CPI-C	common programming interface for communications
CRC	cyclic redundancy check

CREN	Corporation for Research and Educational Networking
C/S	client/server
CSMA/CD	carrier sense multiple access/collision detection
CSU	channel service unit
CTS	common transport semantics
CUA	common user access
DARPA	Defense Advanced Research Projects Agency
DASD	direct access storage device
DCE	distributed computing environment
DCE	data circuit-terminating equipment
DDCMP	digital data communication protocol
DE	discard eligibility
DEC	Digital Equipment Corp.
DECNET	DEC network, a.k.a. DNA
DFC	data-flow control
DHCP	dynamic host configuration
DLC	data-link control
DLCI	data-link connection identifier
DLE	data-link escape
DLSw	data-link switching
DLU	dependent LU
DLUS/R	DLU server/requester
DME	distributed management environment
DNS	domain name system
DOS	disk operating system
DSAP	destination SAP
DSP	domain specific part
DSPU	downstream physical unit
DSS	decision support systems
DSU	digital service unit
DTE	data terminal equipment
DTS	distributed time service
EBCDID	extended binary coded decimal interchange code
ECN	enterprise connectivity node
EEHHLAPI	entry emulated HHLAPI
EENA	extended ENA
EGP	exterior gateway protocol
EHHLAPI	emulated HHLAPI
EN	end node

ENA	extended network addressing
EOM	end of message
ESA	enterprise systems architecture
ESCON	enterprise systems connection
ES–IS	end system-to-intermediate system routing
ETX	end of text
FAPL	formal and protocol language
FECN	forward explicit congestion notification
FEP	front-end processor
FDDI	fiber distributed data interface
FID	format identification
FIFO	first in, first out
FIN	finish
FMH	function management header
FORTRAN	formula translator
FPS	fast packet switching
FQPCID	fully qualified procedure correlation identifier
FRAD	frame relay access device
FRFH	frame relay frame handler
FRSN	flow reduction sequence numbers
FRTE	frame relay data terminal equipment
FS	future system
FSD	IBM's Federal Systems Division
FTP	file transfer protocol
GDMO	Guidelines for the Definition of Managed Objects
GDS	general data stream
GGP	gateway-to-gateway protocol
GSD	IBM's General Systems Division
GSDIA	GSD interchange architecture
HDLC	high-level data-link control
HLLAPI	high-level language application program interface
HPR	high performance routing
HTML	hypertext markup language
HTTP	hypertext transfer protocol
ICD	international code designator
ICMP	Internet control message protocol
IDC	International Data Corp.

IDI	initial domain identifier
IDL	interface definition language
IDP	initial domain part
IEEE	Institute of Electrical and Electronics Engineers
IETF	Internet Engineering Task Force
IGMP	Internet group multicast protocol
IGP	interior gateway protocol
IHL	Internet header length
IMP	interface message processor
IMS	information management system
InterNIC	Internet Network Information Center
I/O	input/output
IP	internet protocol
IPC	interprocess communications
IPng	IP version 6, a.k.a. IP next generation
IPX	internetwork packet exchange
ISAM	index sequential access method
ISAPI	Internet server application programming interface
ISDN	Integrated Services Digital Network
IS–IS	intermediate system-to-intermediate system routing
ISO	International Standards Organization (see OSI)
ISR	intermediate session routing
IT	information technology
ITU	International Telecommunications Union
JVM	Java virtual machine
LAA	locally administered addresses
LAN	local area network
LAP	link access protocol
LAPB	link access protocol-balanced
LAPD	link access procedure on D channel
LDAP	lightweight directory access protocol
LEN	low-entry networking
LFN	large fat networks
LFSID	local-form session identifier
LH	link header
LL	logical length
LLC	logical link control
LOGAPPL	logon application
LPC	local procedure call

LR	logical record
LSA	link-state advertisement
LSP	link-state protocol
LT	link trailer
LTLW	LAN-to-LAN WAN
LU	logical unit
MAC	medium access control
MAP	manufacturing automation protocol
MDS	multiple-domain support
Milnet	military network
MIB	management information base
MIME	multipurpose Internet mail extensions
MIPS	million of instructions per second
MOSI	minimum subset of OSIs (upper level)
MPEN	multiprotocol enterprise networks
MPTN	multiprotocol transport network
MpC	multiprotocol concentrator
MPC	multipath channel
MQCLOSE	close object
MQCONN	connect queue manager
MQDISC	disconnect queue manager
MQGET	get a message
MQI	message queuing interface
MQINQ	inquire objects attributes
MQM	message queue manager
MQN	message queue network
MQOPEN	open objects
MQPUT	put a message
MQPUT1	put one message
MQSET	set object attributes
MPTN	multiprotocol transport network
MPR	NetWare multiprotocol router
MTU	maximum transmission unit
MU	message unit
MVS	multiple virtual storage
nak	negative acknowledgment
NAU	network accessible unit, a.k.a. network adressable unit
NBBS	networking broadband services
NetBIOS	network basic input/output protocol

NCA	network computing architecture
NCP	network control program
NCST	NCP connectionless SNA transport LU
NET	network entry title
netID	network identifier
NFS	network file system
NSFnet	National Science Foundation network
NIC	network information center
NIS	Network Information Service
NJE	network job entry
NN	network node
NNTP	network news transfer protocol
NMS	NetWare management system
NMVT	network management vector transport
NOS	network operating system
NPDA	network problem determination application
NSAP	network service access point
NSAPI	Netscape application programming interface
NSI	Network Solutions Inc.
NVP	network voice protocol
OEM	original equipment manufacturer
OID	object identifier
OLTP	online transaction processing
OMG	Object Management Group
OPD	IBM's Office Products Division
OS/2	operating system 2
OSF	Open Software Foundation
OSI	open systems interconnection
OSPF	open shortest path first
OUI	organizationally unique identifier
PA	program attention
PASC	Portable Application Standards Committee (of IEEE)
PC	path control
PDU	protocol data unit
PF	program function
PIU	path information unit
PL/1	programming language 1
PLU	primary logical unit
POSIX	portable operation system interface for computer environments

PPP	Point-to-Point Protocol
PS	presentation service
PSDN	packet switched data networks
PSH	push
PSTN	public switched telephone network
PTM	packet transfer mode
PU	physical unit
PVC	permanent virtual circuit
QER	qualification exchange routing
QLLC	qualified logical link control
QOS	quality of service
RARP	reverse address resolution protocol
RDBMS	relational database management system
RECMS	record maintenance statistics
RECFMS	record formatted maintenance statistics
REV	remote evaluation
REXEC	remote execution
REXX	restructured extended executor
RFC	request for comments
RH	request/response header
RIF	routing information field
RIG	related interest group
RIP	routing information protocol
RJE	remote job entry
RMI	remote method invocation
RNR	receiver not ready
ROM	read only memory
RPC	remote procedure call
RR	receiver ready
RST	reset
RSCV	route selection control vector
RSVP	resource reservation protocol
RTM	response time monitor
RTP	rapid transport protocol
RTT	round-trip time
RU	request/response unit
SACK	selective ack
SAP	service access point

SAP	service advertising protocol
SATF	shared access transport facilities
SDD	IBM's Systems Development Division
SDLC	synchronous data-link control
SEL	selection
SGML	standard generalized markup language
S-HTTP	secure HTTP
SIP	simple Internet protocol
SLA	service level agreements
SLU	secondary logical unit
SNA	systems network architecture
SNA/MS	SNA management services
SMDS	switch multimegabit data service
SMTP	simple mail transfer protocol
SNAP	subnetwork access protocol
SNMP	simple network management protocol
SNI	SNA network interconnect
SOGA	SNA open gateway architecture
SPX	sequenced packet exchange
SRB	source route bridging
SSAP	source SAP
SSCP	systems service control point
SSL	secure sockets layer
ST	stream protocol
STX	start of text
SVC	switched virtual circuit
SYN	synchronize
SYSCON	system configuration
SYSGEN	system generation
TC	transmission control
TCAM	telecommunications access method
TCP/IP	transmission control protocol/internet protocol
TDU	topology database update
TFTP	trivial FTP
TG	transmission group
TH	transmission header
TLI	System V transport layer interface
TOP	technical and office protocol
TOS	type of service
TP	transaction program

TRS	topology and routing services
TS	transaction service
TSAP	transport service access point
TSO/E	time sharing option/extended
TTL	time to live
TUBA	TCP and UDP with bigger addresses
UAA	universally administered addresses
UDP	user datagram protocol
UNI	user-network interlace
URG	urgent data present
URI	universal resource identifier
URL	universal resource locator
UUID	universal unique identifier
VAN	value added network
VC	virtual circuit
VME	Versa Module Europa
VMS	virtual memory system
VSAM	virtual storage access method
VSE	virtual storage extended
VTAM	virtual telecommunications access method
WAIS	wide area information server
WAN	wide area network
WWW	World Wide Web
XCMF	common management facilities
XID	exchange ID
XDR	external data representation
XNS	Xerox Network System
XTI	X/Open transport interface
YP	Yellow Pages, now known as NIS

contributors

DAVID J. BERMAN has more than twenty years' experience in voice and data communications. He specializes in strategic planning, product definition, and market introduction, with experience in integrated voice/data switching, SNA and TCP/IP networks, and LAN/WAN integration. Berman has spoken at several industry conferences and has published articles in a number of trade publications. He is director of market development at Bay Networks, Inc.

MICHAEL BOWMAN has spent the past twenty years providing innovative networking products to corporate customers. He currently leads the sales and business development efforts for Ganymede Software, a provider of software-based network performance management products. Bowman joined Ganymede Software from Netlink, Inc., where he managed Netlink's marketing and business development efforts and led the definition and introduction of Netlink's award-winning SNA internetworking products. Prior to Netlink, Bowman held key management positions in marketing, corporate planning, and engineering with Memorex Telex, N.V., a provider of IBM-compatible networking products. He holds a B.S. degree in electrical engineering from North Carolina State University.

DR. RUDY J. CYPSER, after assignments on IBM product development and IBM corporate staff, spent several years in Europe at the headquarters of IBM laboratories there. Subsequent activities included product planning for communications-oriented hardware and software and Program Director of IBM's Systems Research Institute. Before retiring from IBM, he was Director of Technical Communications for IBM. He is the author of earlier books, *Communication Architect for Distributed Systems* and *Communications for Cooperating Systems*. Dr. Cypser is currently with Kim Pathways, a consulting and publishing firm.

DONALD H. CZUBEK is President of Gen2 Ventures, a consultancy specializing in SNA and enterprise intranets. Gen2 Ventures publishes research reports and conducts seminars on enterprise networking topics. Czubek also publishes the monthly *SNA Perspective* newsletter.

CHARLES FELTMAN has more than fifteen years' experience in information technology and data communications. He is Principal Consultant with Insight Communications, a consulting firm specializing in data network design and training. Feltman has published more than 15 articles in technical and trade publications and has been a speaker and trainer at national conferences.

JIM FLETCHER is a senior technical staff member with IBM Networking Software Products, in Research Triangle Park, N.C., primarily responsible for S/390 Communication Server (VTAM and TCP/IP) technical strategy, design, and development. Fletcher has been a featured speaker at national and international networking conferences focusing on the integration of IBM's S/390 into the network. Past accomplishments include the design and development of numerous networking technologies and the receipt of several patents in the field of networking. Fletcher is a contributing editor for *Enterprise Systems Journal*, regularly providing featured articles on networking topics.

DR. JAMES P. GRAY, Director of Network Studies in IBM's Software Solutions Division, was named to this position in June 1996 after twelve years as an IBM Fellow. Dr. Gray joined IBM in 1970, working first on microprocessor architectures and then SNA from 1972 until 1984 when he was named an IBM Fellow for his work in networking. Since 1984 he has led a variety of efforts in network technology. Dr. Gray received Ph.D. and B.E. degrees in electrical engineering from Yale.

HAROLD HAUCK has over thirty years' experience in the information processing industry. Most of this time was with IBM, where he specialized in operating system and data communication technologies. As a programmer and Consulting Systems Engineer, Hauck became an expert in VM, VSE, MVS and UNIX operating systems. He has extensive experience designing and implementing CICS transaction processing systems and TCP/IP client/server networks. For the past seven years he has owned Open Systems Computer Consulting, an independent consulting firm that provides technical support and training for organizations that are expanding their mainframe capabilities by implementing standards-based open technologies. Hauck is a Senior Manager for the computer user group SHARE, and is a frequent speaker at industry conferences. Hauck has written and published many articles on open systems topics, and he has developed and taught technical seminars on UNIX, SNA, and TCP/IP for corporate clients, industry exhibitions, and university extension courses.

DR. PETR JANECEK was born in Czechoslovakia and is a Swedish national. He holds a doctorate in mathematical physics from the University of Lund in Sweden. After several years in theoretical nuclear physics research, he was employed for a decade by the ASEA Corporation in Sweden as Project Manager responsible for computer applications using finite element methods in electromagnetic fields and dynamic simulation. Later he spent four years managing software development environments at Ericsson Information Systems and Nokia. For the past eight years, Dr. Janecek has been employed by X/Open (recently part of The Open Group), managing the development of industry standards as Director of Specification Development. He has personally started up and chaired most of the X/Open standardization programs. He serves as The Open Group's institutional representative to IEEE PASC.

DR. DAVID L. KAMINSKY is an advisory programmer in the Software Solutions Division at IBM. Kaminsky joined IBM in 1994 after receiving a Ph.D. in computer science from Yale University. After joining IBM, he worked on IBM's CommServer for OS/2, and now leads an advanced technology team that studies enterprise uses of Java.

DANIEL C. LYNCH, a mathematician by training, organized the first meetings of the Internet technical community and gradually turned them into Interop, the industry's leading technical conference and show. Lynch and Marshall Rose coedited the *Internet System Handbook*, written by the original developers of the technology. This authoritative guide was developed and produced by Manning Publications and marketed by Addison-Wesley. Lynch is currently a private venture capitalist focusing on Internet companies and is chairman of CyberCash, a public company.

VICTORIA C. MARNEY-PETIX, Chief Consultant at Marpet Technical Services, has consulted on network design and redesign for ten years. Author of eight books on networking, she has taught for local universities and serves as Dean of Instruction at Marpet University. Her latest book, *Integrating ATM with Legacy LANs*, is being published by Numidia Press. Prior to consulting, she was a network analyst, software designer and technical marketer for local network companies. She has been a speaker at international networking conferences and educational conferences, discussing networking trends and distance learning. She has launched distance-delivered certificate programs through Marpet University and the University of California, Santa Cruz Extension.

DR. ROBERT E. MOORE joined IBM in 1983 and has worked continuously in the area of network management architecture. He currently works in the Network Studies group within IBM Networking Software. Dr. Moore was involved with the definition of several functions in SNA Management Services, most notably as the architect for the generic Alert. He also participated in the development of a number of ensembles for X.700 management, both within IBM and in the ISO/IEC standards arena. More recently he has participated in the standardization of a number of SNMP MIBs for management of APPN resources. Currently he chairs both the APPN MIBs SIG in the APPN Implementers Workshop and the IETF's SNA NAU Services MIB WG. He holds a B.A. in mathematics and philosophy from Rice University, an M.A. and Ph.D. in philosophy from Duke University, and an M.S. in computer science from the University of Houston.

DR. DAVID OGLE joined IBM in 1989 as a member of the Experimental Systems Department. Dr. Ogle was the team leader for the AnyNet Sockets over SNA Release 1 on OS/2 and MVS, and worked on the Windows APPC over TCP/IP project. Dr. Ogle is currently involved in the network and application design for the 1998 and 2000 Olympics. He received his B.S., M.S., and Ph.D. degrees from Ohio State University.

DR. RADIA PERLMAN is Network Architect at Novell, Inc., designing network protocols for routing, database synchronization, and security. Prior to joining Novell, she was Routing Architect for Digital Equipment Corporation, where she designed the spanning tree algorithm which was standardized for use by bridges, and the IS-IS routing protocol. Many of her algorithms, especially robust distribution of link state information, are incorporated into other link state protocols such as OSPF. She has lectured throughout the world, including giving tutorials on routing and security at Networld+Interop. She holds a Ph.D. from MIT in computer science. Her thesis was on the design of a practical routing protocol invulnerable to denial of service attacks. She is the author of *Interconnections: Bridges and Routers*, and coauthor of *Network Security: Private Communication in a Public World*. She currently serves on the IAB.

DR. JOHN R. PICKENS, one of the early developers of the Arpanet, has over twenty years' experience in the design and development of networking technology and internetworking products. He is currently Director of Technology Development with COM21 and is specializing in the development of technology to bring high speed networking to the mass market—residential, SoHo, and corporate. Dr. Pickens has a Ph.D. from the University of California at Santa Barbara. His thesis topic was in modeling and monitoring of distributed systems interprocess communications. In addition to technology interests, he is an understudy in techniques for development of learning organizations, empowered teams, and peak performing research and development groups.

DR. DIANE POZEFSKY has worked in networking since joining IBM in 1979. She began her career in the SNA architecture organization and in 1994 was named an IBM Fellow in recognition of her work on APPN and AnyNet architectures and development. She is currently working on the network and application design for the 1998 and 2000 Olympics. Dr. Pozefsky has authored over twenty articles and holds more than a dozen patents. She received her Sc. B. from Brown University and her Ph.D. from the University of North Carolina at Chapel Hill.

EDWARD RABINOVITCH, a physicist by training, has more than twenty years' experience in information technology and data communications. He is Senior Network Design Consultant with the Global Systems Design Center at 3Com Corp. Rabinovitch has published more than 70 papers in technical and trade publications, and is a frequent speaker at national and international conferences. He is also a contributing editor with *IEEE Communications* magazine and member of the editorial review board for the *Enterprise Systems Journal* and the Computer Measurement Group (CMG).

THOMAS J. ROUTT has twenty years' experience in computer network and internetwork architecture, design, implementation, and senior management. He is President of VEDACOM Corporation in Seattle, Washington, with Fortune 1000 clients throughout fifty countries on the six continents, and has published more than one hundred papers in technical and trade publications. He has been a Networld+Interop instructor and session chair, and is a frequent speaker at key industry conferences throughout the world. Previously he was Manager of Boeing Network Architecture for Boeing, and orchestrated the architecture, integration, and network management of the Boeing Company's worldwide multivendor, multiprotocol networked applications. Routt holds an M.B.A. in information systems (Beta Gamma Sigma) from Southern Illinois University and a B.S. in environmental science (honors) from Western Washington University. VEDACOM is an Auditing Member of the ATM Forum.

PHIL STONE is a senior programmer in the Software Solutions Division at IBM. Stone joined IBM in 1982 and has worked on products related to distributed presentation since 1988. He designed and wrote the graphics subsystem used in ISPF Client/Server and the VM Distributed GUI Toolkit, and now consults with customers on strategic uses of Java in the enterprise. Stone holds a B.S. in computer science from Washington State University, and an M.B.A. from Seattle Pacific University.

RUSSELL W. TEUBNER is the founder and CEO of Teubner & Associates, Inc. Teubner's career began at the Oklahoma State University Computer Center, while pursuing graduate studies in business and computer science. During his tenure at OSU, Teubner was responsible for implementing a DEC computer system within an existing IBM SNA network. His unsuccessful efforts to find a product that would allow IBM 3270 terminals to access DEC applications led Teubner to develop one. The resulting software product, called A-Net, was first introduced in 1985 and became the most widely accepted product of its kind. Today, Teubner continues to focus his attention on the development of software products that integrate existing host-based computer systems and networking environments with emerging technologies, such as the WWW.

KEVIN TOLLY is President and CEO of The Tolly Group. He is a leading industry consultant and is responsible for guiding the technology decisions of major vendor and end-user organizations. In his consulting work, Tolly has designed enterprise-wide networks for government agencies, banks, retailers, and manufacturers for more than fifteen years. His active lecture and seminar schedule includes frequent engagements throughout the United States, Canada, Mexico, and Europe. Tolly writes regularly for *Network World*, *LAN Times*, *Computerworld*, *Communications Week*, and *Imaging* magazines on architectural and technology issues for an international audience.

TONY WROBEL is a senior software engineer with the Networking Software Pillar of IBM's Software Solutions Division. He has been with IBM for fourteen years. Twelve of those years were spent developing SNA or SNA-related software, including both full-stack and split-stack implementations, and SNA applications like software distribution and user mail/file distribution GUIs. He has a B.S. degree in mathematical sciences from the University of North Carolina at Chapel Hill.

index

Internet server application programming
interface (ISAPI) 465–466
internetwork packet exchange (IPX) 3, 7, 29,
40, 101–103, 140
sequenced packet exchange (IPX/SPX) 90
interprocess communications (IPC) 112

J

Java 420–422, 469, 474, 483–484, 489,
496–499
SNA class loader 498
virtual machine (JVM) 483, 497

K

keyboard mapping 480–481

L

label swapping 36
LAN-to-LAN WAN (LTLW) 335, 338,
343–351
layers, protocol 512–517
lightweight directory access protocol
(LDAP) 144
link access protocol-balanced (LAPB) 38, 46
link access procedure on D channel (LAPD) 38
link-state protocol (LSP) 4
load balancing 210–211
local area network (LAN) 39
local LLC acknowledgment 299–300
locally administered addresses (LAA) 382
locate reply 83
locate request 81–82
logical link control (LLC) 38, 51, 290
type 1   46, 290
type 2   39, 46, 290, 300, 304–305,
309, 387
type 2 termination 322
logical unit (LU) 14, 17–19
LU–LU session 85, 111
name 26
type 0   59
type 1   24, 59
type 2   24, 59
type 3   59

logical unit (LU) *(continued)*
type 4   59
type 6.1   23–24
type 6.2   8, 24, 59, 120
type 7   24, 59
logon request 75
low entry networking (LEN) 76–78, 111, 157

M

management information base
(MIB) 400–402, 420
manufacturing automation protocol
(MAP) 361
medium access control (MAC) 99
message queuing interface (MQI) 109,
111–112, 124–127, 129–130, 138,
254, 257
message unit (MU) 122
mixed stacks 136
multicast 51, 189
address 39
multiple-domain support message unit (MDS-
MU) 411
multipoint link 37
multiprotocol transport network
(MPTN) 290, 361, 363, 366
multipurpose Internet mail extensions
(MIME) 131

N

negative acknowledgment (nak) 35
Netscape application programming interface
(NSAPI) 465–466
NetView 296
response time monitor (RTM) 450
RUNCMD 450
NetWare 8
for SAA 8
management system (NMS) 8
multi-protocol router (MPR) 8
SNA Links 8
network 438
network accessible units (NAUs) 58
network basic input/output system
(NetBIOS) 3–5, 7, 90, 103–104

SNA management services (SNA/MS) 88,
    399, 401, 406–408, 419, 423
SNA network interconnect (SNI) 19, 26
SNA open gateway architecture (SOGA) 8
SNALINK 276, 335, 338–343
sockets 109, 112–114, 249–251, 256– 257
source SAP (SSAP) 45
spanning tree 48
spoofing 301
SSCP–LU session 69
SSCP–PU session 68
standard generalized markup language
    (SGML) 466
start of text (STX) 33
subarea nodes 66
subnetwork access protocol (SNAP) 45, 51
switch multimegabit data service (SMDS) 46
synchronous data-link control (SDLC) 8, 12,
    15, 33, 37–38, 46, 50, 55
    conversion 304
    passthrough 270, 304, 321–322
    spoofing 270
    tunneling 321
System V transport layer interface (TLI) 108
systems network architecture (SNA) 2–9,
    11–18, 21, 23, 28, 38, 43, 53–54,
    140, 150, 174, 434
    address 27
    gateways 444
systems service control point (SSCP) 14, 64
SystemView 29

T

technical and office protocol (TOP) 361
telecommunications access method
    (TCAM) 12, 17, 20, 28
Telnet 7
token ring 41, 55
topology database update (TDU) 80
transaction program (TP) 22–23
transmission control protocol (TCP) 101,
    170–172, 225–226, 233
transmission control protocol/internet protocol
    (TCP/IP) 2–7, 21, 28–29, 90, 98,
    140, 150–152, 166, 174, 377–382,435

application services 169
hosts 176
slow-start 237–238
transmission group (TG) 72
    vectors 85
transmission header (TH) 62
transport layer 93
tunneling 5
type of service (TOS) 173, 219, 221, 222

U

unicast 51
    address 39
universal resource identifier (URI) 131
universal resource locator (URL) 131
universal unique identifier (UUID) 117
universally administered addresses (UAA) 382
user datagram protocol (UDP) 101, 225–226,
    233

V

VINES 5
virtual circuit (VC) 92–93, 101
virtual routes 73
virtual storage access method (VSAM) 108
virtual telecommunications access method
    (VTAM) 12, 14, 18–22, 27

W

Web 455–485
Web browser 456
Web-to-host gateway 464–485

X

X.25 46, 86
X.400 messaging 136
X/Open 136
X/Open Transport Interface (XTI) 358–361
Xerox Network System (XNS) 90